Stalinism and the Politics of Mobilization

STALINISM AND THE POLITICS OF MOBILIZATION

Ideas, Power, and Terror
in Inter-war Russia

DAVID PRIESTLAND

OXFORD
UNIVERSITY PRESS

OXFORD
UNIVERSITY PRESS

Great Clarendon Street, Oxford OX2 6DP
United Kingdom

Oxford University Press is a department of the University of Oxford.
It furthers the University's objective of excellence in research, scholarship,
and education by publishing worldwide.
Oxford is a registered trade mark of Oxford University Press in the UK
and in certain other countries

© David Priestland 2007

The moral rights of the author have been asserted

Reprinted 2013

British Library Cataloguing in Publication Data
Data available

Library of Congress Cataloging in Publication Data
Data available

ISBN 978-0-19-924513-0

Acknowledgements

I should like to thank a number of individuals and institutions for their help with this book. I am particularly grateful to Mary McAuley, whose enthusiasm and guidance at the beginning of this project were invaluable, and to Steve Smith who made extensive and penetrating comments on the manuscript, while giving enormous encouragement. I would also like to thank Arch Getty, Rana Mitter, Michael Rosen, Erik Van Ree, Neil Robinson, and Stephen Whitefield for their incisive comments on various parts of the book, and Catriona Kelly and Andrew Kahn for their help with some of the more obscure aspects of Stalinist language. I am also grateful to the anonymous readers for Oxford University Press, whose suggestions helped me to improve the manuscript in many significant ways. Parts of chapter 1 previously appeared in the journal *Revolutionary Russia*, and I am grateful to the Study Group on the Russian Revolution for their comments on an earlier version of the article. The fellows of St Edmund Hall and Lincoln College, and the Modern History Faculty of the University of Oxford, have provided me with a stimulating and congenial working environment, and all have given me financial assistance and time to complete this project. I am also indebted to the British Academy for help with research trips to Russia. Ruth Parr at Oxford University Press has been very supportive, and Anne Gelling, Kay Rogers, and Sally McCann have helped enormously with the manuscript. I have also been greatly assisted by the staffs of the following archives and libraries: the Russian State Archive of Socio-Political History in Moscow (RGASPI); the State Archive of the Russian Federation in Moscow (GARF); the Bodleian Library, Oxford; the British Library, London; and the Russian State Library, Moscow. My greatest thanks go to Maria Misra, for reading numerous drafts and for her support during the writing of the book.

David Priestland
Oxford

Contents

Note on Transliteration and Translation

I have used the Library of Congress system, except for a few well-known names (for instance, Trotsky rather than Trotskii, and Zinoviev rather than Zinov'ev). Where letters between leaders are translated, words that were underlined once appear in italic, and those underlined twice appear in bold.

Abbreviations and Glossary

administrirovanie	administration by injunction
Agitprop	Department of Agitation and Propaganda of the Central Committee
aktiv	activists in the party and other organizations
aktivnost'	activism
byvshie	'former people': former 'class alien' or non-revolutionary groups
CCEG	Central Case Examination Group
Cheka	All-Russian Commission for the Struggle against Counter-Revolution, Sabotage, and Speculation
chinovnik	tsarist bureaucrat, bureaucrat
deliacheskii	having narrowly practical, utilitarian attitudes; neglecting principles
deliachestvo	narrowly practical, utilitarian attitudes
delovoi	business-like
demokratiia	democracy; the lower orders
edinonachalie	one-man management
glavk	chief administration of an industry
Glavpolitput'	Chief Political Administration under the People's Commissariat of the Railways
gorkom	city committee of the party
Gosbank	State Bank
Gosplan	State Planning Commission
GPU	State Political Directorate attached to the USSR Sovnarkom (secret police, successor to Cheka)
guberniia	province
Gulag	Chief Administration of Camps
intelligent	member of the intelligentsia
ispolkom	executive committee of a soviet
khozraschet	cost accounting

kombed	committee of the rural poor
Komsomol (VLKSM)	All-Union Leninist Communist League of Youth
kontrol'	supervision
korenizatsiia	'indigenization'; encouragement of indigenous national cultures and languages
KPK	Commission of Party Control attached to the Central Committee of the VKP(b)
KSK	Commission of Soviet Control
krai	territory (large administrative unit)
kraikom	territorial committee of the VKP(b)
kulak	wealthy peasant
Kul'tprop	Department of Culture and Propaganda of the Central Committee
MAPP	Moscow Association of Proletarian Writers
MECW	K. Marx and F. Engels, *Karl Marx Frederick Engels Collected Works*, 47 vols. (London, 1975–93)
MESW	K. Marx and F. Engels, *Selected Works*, 2 vols. (Moscow, 1961)
mir	peasant commune
Narkompros	People's Commissariat of Enlightenment (Education)
Narkomtiazhprom	People's Commissariat of Heavy Industry
Narkomzem	People's Commissariat of Agriculture
narod	the people
narodnyi	popular; national
NEP	New Economic Policy
nepman	beneficiary of the NEP; small trader
nizy	those at the bottom of society; the lower orders
NKPS	People's Commissariat for Transport and Communications
NKVD	People's Commissariat for Internal Affairs (political police, successor to the OGPU)
nositel'	carrier; bearer

obyvatel'skii	philistine
obkom	regional party committee
oblast'	region (large administrative unit)
OGPU	Unified State Political Directorate attached to the USSR Sovnarkom (political police, successor to the GPU)
Orgburo	Organizational Bureau of the Central Committee of the party
partiinost'	party spirit
podmena	'substitution' (one organization taking over the duties of another)
Politburo	Political Bureau of the Central Committee of the party
politika	politics, political matters (often contrasted with *tekhnika*)
politotdel	political department
PRC	People's Republic of China
PSS	V. I. Lenin, *Polnoe sobranie sochinenii*, 5th edn. (Moscow, 1958–65)
Rabkrin (NK RKI)	People's Commissariat of Workers' and Peasants' Inspection
rabochii	(industrial) worker
rabotnik	worker; official
raiispolkom	executive committee of a district soviet
raikom	district party committee
raion	district (smaller administrative unit, subdivision of *oblast'* and *krai*)
RAPP	Russian Association of Proletarian Writers
RGASPI	Russian State Archive of Social and Political History (Moscow)
RKP(b)	Russian Communist Party (Bolshevik)
semeistvennost'	nepotism; cronyism
soslovie	pre-revolutionary term for social estate or status group
soviet	elected workers' council; state body
Sovnarkom	Council of People's Commissars
tekhnika	technique; technology; technical matters (often contrasted with *politika*)

treugol'nik	factory 'triangle' (the party cell, the factory administration, and the trade-union factory committee)
troika	three-person board established to try political criminal cases
TsIK	Central Executive Committee of the Congress of Soviets
TsKK VKP(b)	Central Control Commission of the VKP(b)
VAPP	All-Union Association of Proletarian Writers
verkhi	those at the top of society; the élite
VKP(b)	All-Union Communist Party (Bolshevik)
vospitanie	(moral and ideological) education
Vesenkha (VSNKh)	Supreme Council of the National Economy
VTsIK	All-Russian Central Executive Committee of the Congress of Soviets
vydvizhenie	promotion (of workers into white-collar jobs)

Introduction
Ideas and Politics in Bolshevik Russia

Between 1936 and 1938, hundreds of thousands of citizens of the Soviet Union, many of them communist party members, were accused of a series of bizarre crimes. They were alleged to have participated in conspiracies against the Soviet state, in league with foreign intelligence agencies and oppositionist Trotskyist groups abroad. The conspirators had, it was claimed, attempted to sabotage the economy and assassinate leaders, including Stalin himself, in pursuit of their ultimate objective—the restoration of capitalism. The accused were arrested and given summary trials; many were executed and many more imprisoned.[1] These were extraordinary events but they were not entirely unprecedented. In the late 1920s and early 1930s the Stalinist leadership had also organized purges of officials and staged a series of show trials, claiming that officials were conspiring with hostile forces against it.

These repressions were all carried out in the name of socialism, and it is not surprising that the question of the Stalinist 'Great Terror' and its causes has been at the centre of political and historical debate ever since. The Terror seriously affected the standing of the Soviet model of socialism, and the admission by Khrushchev in

---

[1] According to official NKVD figures, 681,692 people were shot in 1937–8, although this includes people shot for non-political offences. 1,575,259 were arrested by the NKVD in the same period, 87 per cent of whom were accused of political offences, and 85 per cent were convicted. But this figure does not include arrests made by authorities other than the NKVD. See V. P. Popov, 'Gosudarstvennyi terror v sovetskoi Rossii, 1923–1953 gg. (istochniki i ikh interpretatsiia)', *Otechestvennye arkhivy*, 2 (1992), 20–32. The accuracy of these figures is still the subject of controversy. For the debate, see J. A. Getty and O. V. Naumov, *The Road to Terror. Stalin and the Self-Destruction of the Bolsheviks, 1932–1939* (New Haven and London, 1999), 587–94; J. A. Getty, G. T. Rittersporn, and V. N. Zemskov, 'Victims of the Soviet Penal System in the Prewar Years: A First Approach on the Basis of Archival Evidence', *AHR*, 98 (1993), 1017–49; S. Rosefielde, 'Stalinism in Post-Communist Perspective. New Evidence on Killings, Forced Labour and Economic Growth in the 1930s', *E-AS*, 46 (1996), 959–87.

1956 that thousands of innocent communists had suffered under Stalin both threatened the stability of the socialist regimes in Eastern Europe and dealt a serious blow to the communist movement in the West. Yet, despite the importance of these events and the enormous amount of attention they have attracted, the Terror still remains difficult to understand because it seems to be so irrational. Stalin's victims were of no real threat to him, and many of them were members of the industrial bureaucracies and the military high command, precisely the people whom Stalin needed to achieve some of his central objectives: the establishment of a strong state and its defence against foreign enemies. The Terror also caused enormous political and economic disruption that proved highly counterproductive on the eve of war.

For much of the post-war era the question of how far Marxist ideas contributed to Stalinist violence lay at the centre of the debate over the Terror, as was understandable at a time of ideological conflict between a liberal West and the communist world. For one group of historians, the logic of Marxist utopianism led to repression, and Stalin used terror because he was implementing a dogmatic ideological blueprint inspired by Marx and Lenin. As one recent work has argued, political violence 'stemmed from Leninist ideology and the utopian will to apply to society a doctrine totally out of step with reality'.[2] Others, however, disagreed that Marxism had any real responsibility for terror, arguing that Stalinist political practice was the consequence of Stalin's distortion of Marxism, or of Stalin's own paranoid and megalomaniacal personality.[3] But 'structuralist' historians went even further, insisting that the political violence of the 1930s was not the consequence of the peculiar

[2] S. Courtois, 'Conclusion', in S. Courtois, N. Werth, J.-L. Panne, A. Paczowski, K. Bartosek, and J.-L. Margolin (eds.), *The Black Book of Communism. Crimes, Terror, Repression* trans. by J. Murphy and M. Kramer (Cambridge, Mass., 1999), 737. Courtois is referring here to the 'Red Terror' of the civil war period, but sees Stalin's Terror as a similar phenomenon.

[3] For the argument that there were sharp differences between Stalinism and Marxism, see S. Cohen, *Rethinking the Soviet Experience* (Oxford, 1985), ch. 2. For an emphasis on Stalin's psychology, see R. Tucker, *Stalin as Revolutionary 1879–1929. A Study in History and Personality* (London, 1974); R. Tucker, *Stalin in Power. The Revolution from Above, 1928–1941* (New York, 1990). One of the most influential historians of the Terror, Robert Conquest, accepts the role of Lenin's destruction of party democracy in laying the foundations for Stalin's political violence, but he concentrates most on Stalin's 'personal and political drives', and in particular his desire to accumulate power. R. Conquest, *The Great Terror. A Reassessment* (London, 1990), 7, 53.

ideas of Stalin and the Bolsheviks at all, whether defined as ideology or psychosis.[4] Unlike 'intentionalist' historians, who stressed the centrality of Stalin's thinking and its extraordinary nature, they argued that Stalin was largely responding as a rational politician to the political and economic structures within which he operated. In particular, he was attempting to solve a fundamental problem facing the Soviet polity: the party leadership's difficulty in controlling the regions and the bureaucratic apparatus.[5]

The debate between intentionalists and structuralists has dominated the study of Stalinist high politics, but in recent years the gap between the two approaches has narrowed.[6] Historians have made greater efforts to reconcile intention and structure, and seem to be converging in their views of Stalin's motivations: he was both acting rationally, if ruthlessly, to maximize his power, and he was extremely fearful. So, while some recent intentionalist interpretations still place an analysis of Stalin's own thinking at the centre of their view of Stalinist politics in the 1930s, they do not claim, in contrast with some other intentionalist treatments, that Stalin was driven by a compulsion, inspired by Marxism-Leninism, to create a wholly unified 'totalitarian' society.[7] Rather, they argue that he was motivated partly by the desire to increase his power by replacing his top

---

[4] The terms 'intentionalist' and 'structuralist' are taken from the historiography of Nazi Germany, but they describe the debate more effectively than the terms commonly used in the historiography of Stalinism: 'totalitarian' and 'revisionist'. 'Intentionalists' stress the importance of leaders' intentions and ideas; 'structuralists' (or 'functionalists')—the 'revisionists'—emphasize the role of institutional conflict and social, economic and other forces outside the leadership. See I. Kershaw, *The Nazi Dictatorship. Problems and Perspectives of Interpretation*, 3rd edn. (London, 1997), ch. 4. For a comparison between the historiographies of Nazism and Stalinism, see G. Eley, 'History With the Politics Left Out—Again?', *RR*, 45 (1986), 387–9. For a treatment of the historiography of Stalinism that uses these concepts, see C. Ward, *Stalin's Russia*, 2nd edn. (London, 1997), ch. 4.

[5] See J. A. Getty, *The Origins of the Great Purges. The Soviet Communist Party Reconsidered, 1933–1938* (Cambridge, 1985); G. T. Rittersporn, *Stalinist Simplifications and Soviet Complications. Social Tensions and Political Conflicts in the USSR, 1933–1953* (Chur, 1991). For Getty, the Terror was in part a response to a real fear of conspiracy, but it escalated as it became intertwined with Stalin's attempts to control wayward regional party bosses and industrial managers.

[6] This process can also be observed in the historiography of Nazi Germany. See, for instance, O. Bartov (ed.), *The Holocaust. Origins, Implementation, Aftermath* (London, 2000), 4–5.

[7] For the distinction between recent and older intentionalist interpretations, see E. A. Rees, 'The Great Purges and the XVIII Party Congress of 1939', in E. A. Rees, *Centre-Local Relations in the Stalinist State, 1928–1941* (Basingstoke, 2002), 209, n. 9.

officials with more capable and loyal people, and partly by fears of foreign invasion, which led him to 'cleanse' the Soviet Union of potential 'fifth columnists'.[8] On the other side of the debate, those who emphasize 'structure' still argue that political violence was in part the outcome of tensions between various interest groups within the élite and bureaucracy. However, they also accept that Stalin was not merely a conventional, 'rational' politician intent on increasing his power within a particular institutional framework, but responded to these conflicts in an extreme, abnormal way, because he felt deeply insecure about the internal stability of the regime.[9]

Any study of the high politics of the Stalin era, and particularly of the political violence of the late 1920s and 1930s, clearly has to take account of both Bolshevik leaders' thinking and political circumstances, both domestic and international. But I shall argue that to do so convincingly, we need to reconsider the nature of the Bolsheviks' ideas and their relationship with Soviet politics, and in particular to bring Marxism-Leninism back into the picture. Stalin was a politician intent on maximizing his own power, but his behaviour makes more sense if we take account of the very specific Bolshevik ideological context within which he operated. And while Stalin and the Bolshevik leadership were extraordinarily fearful and obsessed with security, an excessive emphasis on their fear may lead us to exaggerate

---

[8] For the view that the Terror was partly designed to replace an older generation of party bosses with a rising new generation, see O. Khlevniuk, 'The Stalinist "Party Generals" ', in Rees, *Centre-Local Relations*, 59–60; Rees, 'The Great Purges', 195–6. For fears of the 'fifth column' see O. Khlevniuk, 'The Objectives of the Great Terror, 1937–38', in J. Cooper, M. Perrie and E. A. Rees (eds.), *Soviet History, 1917–1953* (Basingstoke, 1995), 158–76; O. Khlevniuk, 'The Reasons for the "Great Terror": The Foreign Political Aspect', in S. Pons and A. Romano (eds.), *Russia in the Age of Wars, 1914–1945* (Milan, 2000), 159–70; E. A. Rees, 'The Great Purges and the XVIII Party Congress of 1939', in Rees, *Centre-Local Relations*, 195–8; Silvio Pons, *Stalin and the Inevitable War, 1936–1941* (London, 2002), ch. 3. For Pons, these fears were themselves the product of a combination of factors: a rational response to a dangerous world; the experience of the foreign intervention during the civil war of 1918–20; and a deep mistrust of other powers, motivated by Marxist-Leninist preconceptions about capitalism and imperialism. For these historians, therefore, Stalin was responding to 'structural' constraints, but these were the threat of war with Nazi Germany and Japan, rather than the internal bureaucratic resistance which structuralists emphasize.

[9] For Getty and Naumov this fearfulness was, in part, an understandable response to the instability caused by the social upheavals and economic disasters of the early 1930s, but it also emerged from an ideology that assumed the existence of enemies and conspiracies, and a peculiarly fearful political culture within the party, forged during the civil war. J. A. Getty and O. V. Naumov, *The Road to Terror*, 5–24.

the extent to which the Stalinist regime reacted to events. But I shall not be returning to some traditional intentionalist interpretations, which exaggerated the coherence of Marxist and Stalinist political ideas, drew a direct and simple line between Marx and Stalin, and attributed too much power to ideology alone. This study seeks to provide a reassessment of the thinking of the Bolshevik élites which allows us to relate it more convincingly to their political behaviour. In doing so, it will attempt to provide a better understanding of the violent repressions of the pre-war Stalinist era, and of Bolshevik politics in the inter-war period more generally.

Bolshevism and its interpreters

The nature of Bolshevik ideas and their relationship with Soviet politics has given rise to an enormous, and sometimes polemical literature, and several approaches have emerged from the debate, each associated with a particular narrative of Soviet history. One of the most influential analyses of Bolshevik ideas has been put forward by proponents of what might be called a 'liberal' historiographical tradition.[10] According to these highly intentionalist interpretations, Bolshevik policy, in essence, amounted to the implementation of a blueprint for creating an illiberal, 'totalitarian' society, with its roots in Marxist-Leninist ideas. The consequence of this project was the absolute subordination of the individual and society to the state and the establishment of complete unity. As the philosopher and historian of Marxism Leszek Kolakowski explained, 'the extermination of all forms of political, economic and cultural life that are not imposed or regulated by the state' was the 'basic principle' of 'the history of the Soviet Union'.[11] The Terror was the culmination of this process, part of 'the natural logic of the system', and was designed to complete the destruction of everything that might resist the domination of Stalin and the state, including the autonomy of the family and the individual.[12]

---

[10] For the use of the term 'liberal' in this historiographical context, see E. Acton, *Rethinking the Russian Revolution* (London, 1990), 35–9.

[11] L. Kolakowski, *Main Currents of Marxism* Vol. 3: *The Breakdown* (Oxford, 1978), 7–8.

[12] On the Terror's role in 'atomizing' society, see L. Schapiro, *The Communist Party of the Soviet Union* (London, 1970), 431; L. Kolakowski, *Main Currents*, iii. 85.

Liberal writers have differed over the precise connection between the ideas of Marx and Lenin, and the 'totalitarian' outcome.[13] For some, it was Lenin, not Marx, who was largely responsible: by stressing the role of a revolutionary élite, the 'vanguard party', that could know the laws of history and intervene to create a socialist society, Lenin was guilty of transforming Marxism from an ideology of liberation to one of totalitarian repression.[14] For others, however, there are connections between Marx's own thinking and Soviet practice. Kolakowski, for instance, argued that Marx's emphasis on unity was responsible. Marx himself did not intend that repression should be used under socialism, but his utopian vision of an ideal society in which there was no conflict or competition laid the foundations for repression. Because such harmony is impossible, it was highly probable that a Marxist regime would use force or brainwashing to create it.[15] For Andrzej Walicki, similarly, Marx's rejection of liberal ideas of freedom should be seen as the main progenitor of Bolshevik authoritarianism, and ultimately of Stalinist 'totalitarianism'.[16] Martin Malia, however, implicates the socialist tradition as a whole, by blaming Marx's willingness to push the socialist commitment to equality to its logical conclusion. For Malia, Marxism's 'deep structure' was its moral commitment to full equality, and this necessarily involved the eradication of the main source of inequality: the market. Marx and the Bolsheviks argued that the market would disappear by itself, as the result of the logic of history, but when history failed to deliver, the Bolsheviks decided that they had to use the 'blunt instrument' of party rule to eliminate it.[17] Stalin and the Bolsheviks did eventually achieve this

[13] For a survey of the huge literature, see D. Lovell, *From Marx to Lenin. An Evaluation of Marx's Responsibility for Soviet Authoritarianism* (Cambridge, 1984), 10–20.

[14] See, for instance, R. Daniels, *The Nature of Communism* (New York, 1962), 20–1; M. Fainsod, *How Russia is Ruled* (Cambridge, Mass., 1953), ch. 2.

[15] L. Kolakowski, *Main Currents* Vol. 1: *The Founders* (Oxford, 1978), 420. Leszek Kolakowski, 'Marxist Roots of Stalinism', in R. Tucker (ed.), *Stalinism. Essays in Historical Interpretation* (New York, 1977), 296.

[16] Walicki argues that two elements of Marx's conception of freedom were responsible for Stalinist totalitarianism: first, the view that freedom was the 'conscious, rational control over economic and social forces'; and second, his willingness to give priority to 'species freedom' over individual freedom. He did not value 'bourgeois freedom', or the freedom from arbitrary coercion by other people. See A. Walicki, *Marxism and the Leap to the Kingdom of Freedom* (Stanford, 1995), 5, 13, 41–2.

[17] M. Malia, *The Soviet Tragedy* (New York, 1994), 494.

crude form of socialism, but they did so in a way that clearly contradicted Marx's original moral objectives. The Terror of the late 1930s, in part, emerged from this contradiction: it was designed to create ideological unity, forcing the population to ignore the regime's failure to fulfil the moral promise of socialism, and to accept that true socialism had indeed been created.[18] There was, then, a connection between the ideas of Marx and the Terror. Malia does accept that there were divisions within Bolshevism, between 'soft' Bolsheviks who advocated markets and gradualism, and Stalin's 'hard' Bolshevism. But the former was not a real alternative because it involved a pragmatic retreat from the true objectives of the regime.[19] There may have been 'advances' towards and 'retreats' from the regime's ideological goals, but this does not alter the fact that those goals were coherent, and that their essence was the creation of a non-market society welded together in a totalitarian unity.

The liberal analysis casts some helpful light on Bolshevism. The Bolsheviks were formally committed to building 'communism', as defined by Marx, which they generally saw as a unified society without the market. They also sometimes framed their disputes as conflicts over the question of 'advance' and 'retreat' towards that goal, and the Bolsheviks frequently argued over how unified the state and society were to be. But while we have to take the Bolsheviks' Marxism seriously, we need to question its coherence. Trotsky, a forthright critic of the liberal analysis and narrative, was one of the first to do so. Comparing the progress of the revolution with its French predecessor, he argued that Stalin had betrayed true Marxism and Bolshevism, and was presiding over a 'Thermidorian' order—a conservative hierarchical regime that operated in the interests of a new bureaucracy corrupted by bourgeois mores. The Terror of 1936–8 was an 'extravagant bureaucratic reaction', the culmination of an assault on revolutionary values and the result of a conflict between 'revolutionaries and Thermidorians at the very heart of the bureaucracy'.[20]

[18] Ibid., 244. Although Malia's analysis does also seek to relate ideology to political circumstances and interests.
[19] Ibid., 495.
[20] See especially L. Trotsky, *The Revolution Betrayed. What is the Soviet Union Doing and Where is it Going?* (New York, 1960), 101–4. For Trotsky's interpretation, see G. Boffa, *The Stalin Phenomenon*, trans. by N. Fersen (Ithaca, NY, 1992), 91–9. See also B. Knei-Paz, *The Social and Political Thought of Leon Trotsky* (Oxford, 1975), 380–410.

Trotsky's attempts to distance Stalin from Bolshevism, and his insistence that Stalin presided over a reactionary distortion of Bolshevism, were echoed in the work of a number of influential historians who, given their stress on divisions within Bolshevik ideology and the party, might be described as 'conflictualists'. The conflictualist interpretation, first, denied that Bolshevik Marxism was a monolithic ideology and, second, argued that Stalinism was not primarily the product of Marxism.[21] Rather, it suggested, Stalin's Bolshevism had a fundamentally statist approach to politics and was to be contrasted with a less statist Leninist tradition. The roots of this statism lay not in Marxism, but in elements of traditional Russian political culture.[22] There was, however, some disagreement over what precisely constituted the acceptable face of Bolshevism. For some, the 'left' of the Bolshevik party represented a more 'Western' and 'democratic' alternative to Stalinism.[23] For others, however, Bolsheviks on the 'right' of the party—the 'late' Lenin of 1921-4, and his ally, Nikolai Bukharin—developed the most coherent non-terroristic alternative to Stalinism.[24]

At the root of the conflictualist interpretation was a contrast between 'Bolshevism' and 'Stalinism' founded on a number of dichotomies—between a 'Western' and 'Russian' orientation, between 'modern' and 'traditional' values, and between a quasi-liberal moderate statism and extreme statism—and the history of the Soviet Union in the inter-war period was often seen as the story of the struggle between these two approaches to politics. So Moshe

[21] As Moshe Lewin put it, Stalinism was 'not a direct outgrowth of Bolshevism but rather an autonomous and parallel phenomenon...'. M. Lewin, *The Making of the Soviet System. Essays in the Social History of Inter-War Russia* (Oxford, 1985), 9.

[22] For Stalinism's debt to Russia's pre-revolutionary political culture, and particularly its peasant culture, see Lewin, *The Making of the Soviet System*, 274, 304-10. Robert Tucker also emphasized the influence of pre-revolutionary ideas, although he found it in Stalin's interest in the state-building projects of the tsars. Tucker, *Stalin in Power*, 50-8; R. Tucker, 'Stalinism as Revolution from Above', in R. Tucker, *Stalinism. Essays in Historical Interpretation* (New Brunswick, 1999), 77-108.

[23] See, for instance, R. Daniels, *The Conscience of the Revolution. Communist Opposition in Soviet Russia* (New York, 1969), 409. See also the argument that the leftist Aleksandr Bogdanov was the proponent of an acceptable, 'democratic' form of Bolshevism in Z. Sochor, *Revolution and Culture. The Bogdanov-Lenin Controversy* (Ithaca, NY, and London, 1988).

[24] M. Lewin, *Lenin's Last Struggle* (London, 1975), 136; M. Lewin, *Political Undercurrents in Soviet Economic Debates* (London, 1975), 96; S. Cohen, *Bukharin and the Bolshevik Revolution* (Oxford, 1980), ch. 5; S. Cohen, *Rethinking the Soviet Experience. Politics and History since 1917* (Oxford, 1985).

Lewin argued that Stalin led a retreat from the values of the revolution to a conservative, statist, great-power nationalist Bolshevism.[25] He also saw the roots of the Terror in this rejection of modernity: the regime, he argued, absorbed irrational beliefs in evil forces and conspiracies present within traditional peasant culture.[26] Stephen Cohen's account of the rise of Stalinism placed more emphasis on political than on social developments.[27] The history of the USSR was characterized as a series of disjunctures, marking transitions between statist orders and less statist, semi-'liberal' orders, involving the state's 'reconciliation' with, or relaxation of its pressure on, society.[28] A statist period of 'war communism' between 1918 and 1921 was succeeded by a period of Bolshevik quasi-liberalism, when a limited market was restored under the New Economic Policy (NEP). This brief Soviet 'spring' was ended by Stalin in 1928, who looked back to the war-communist experience and pursued a policy of terror in order to strengthen his own and the state's power. Bukharin and his allies in the so-called 'Right Deviation' attempted to defend the NEP settlement against Stalin, but were defeated in 1929. The conflict between the extreme statists, surrounding Stalin, and a group of quasi-liberals or 'moderates' within the leadership continued throughout the 1930s, but with the Terror Stalin restored the statism of the war-communist period, although in an even more extreme form.[29]

The conflictualist approach, in identifying tensions within Marxism-Leninism, provided a useful corrective to the liberal historians' assumption that a single, coherent ideology determined most developments in Bolshevik politics. It also pointed to the importance of cultural and ideological influences outside Marxism-Leninism. Yet

[25] M. Lewin, *The Making of the Soviet System*, 274. For comparisons between Lewin's and Trotsky's interpretations, see S. Kotkin, *Magnetic Mountain*, 5–6.

[26] M. Lewin, *The Making of the Soviet System*, 310.

[27] Although Lewin did offer a similar account to Cohen's in his *Political Undercurrents*.

[28] Cohen recognizes that Bukharin's 'moderate' alternative to Stalinism was not 'liberal' or 'democratic' in the Western liberal sense of these terms, and he provides a full and subtle analysis of Bukharin's thought, but he still describes it as a 'liberalizing' and less bureaucratic and 'statist' vision than that of Stalin. See S. Cohen, *Rethinking the Soviet Experience*, 42–50, 75–6; S. Cohen, *Bukharin*, 321. For a similar account of Bukharin's thinking, see M. Lewin, *Political Undercurrents*, 66.

[29] Cohen, *Bukharin*, 345. Tucker similarly sees the 1920s and 1930s as a period of conflict between those who favoured 'reconciliation with society' and within the party, and Stalinist hard-liners. See R. Tucker, *Stalin in Power*, 238–43.

the conflictualists' conceptual framework, while providing some insights, is of more use for analysts of the struggle between 'reformers' and 'conservatives' in the 1970s and 1980s than for historians of the inter-war period.[30] In the Brezhnev era, reverence for Stalin was indeed associated with a commitment to a hierarchical state, hostility to market reforms, and a type of Russian nationalism, while 'reformers' called for a less xenophobic communism, the dilution of centralized planning, and greater individual freedom. The ideological environment of the 1920s and 1930s, however, was rather different. First, while the Stalinist regime did make increasing use of Russian national symbols and language in the course of the 1930s, this rhetoric did not signify the end of the revolutionary project. Second, while some Bolsheviks, both on the left and the right, doubtless genuinely repelled by the regime's repressive nature, did call for a change in the relationship between the state and society and protested against centralism in the name of local autonomy, it was very difficult to build a coherent political position within Bolshevism on these issues. It was uncommon to contrast 'state' and 'society' explicitly, as this paradigm inevitably ignored the central question of class. Right and left therefore tended not to make common cause on the question of 'democracy', as they disagreed over whether proletarians or non-proletarians were to benefit from it.[31] They also risked falling into heresies that had been denounced by Marx himself. Those who argued for the protection of society against the state, as the right sometimes did, could be condemned as 'liberals'.[32] Meanwhile, those who demanded that the 'masses' fundamentally transform and 'democratize' the state, as some on the 'democratic' left did, could be accused of ignoring Marxism's commitment to modernity and the need for an integrated state and economy. In denying the need for a 'conscious' or expert elite to lead the working class to a modern communism, they could be charged with advocating the return to the egalitarianism of 'primitive' societies, in the tradition of the 'anarchists' and 'utopian' socialists.

[30] Both Cohen and Lewin were explicit in their desire to relate inter-war Bolshevism to the politics of the 1970s and 1980s. See S. Cohen, *Rethinking the Soviet Experience*; M. Lewin, *Political Undercurrents*.
[31] Although from the early 1930s Stalin did drive his leftist and rightist opponents together.
[32] For an analysis of the differences between liberal and Marxist conceptions of freedom, see A. Walicki, *Marxism*, 23 ff.

Since the failure of Gorbachev's attempts to reconcile Bolshevism with a leftist form of liberalism, historians have been less interested in the nature of Marxism-Leninism and whether or not it is compatible with liberalism. At the same time, liberal historians' assumption that we can understand Soviet history by analysing the principles of a coherent ideology has become less fashionable, as has the study of Marxism-Leninism more generally.[33] Rather, it is more common to examine Bolshevik ideas more broadly, showing how they were related to wider political cultures and political practices, providing an ideological context within which political activity took place.[34] Historians have also tended to explore ideas through the study of a wide variety of discourses, rather than through a narrow analysis of ideological principles and debates, and have redirected attention from the Soviet leadership to society as a whole.[35]

Not only have these treatments employed new approaches to the study of political ideas but they have also tended to depart from older perspectives on Bolshevism. Much of the debate about the history of the Bolshevik party during the period of the Soviet Union's existence was concerned with Bolshevism's attitude towards a set of issues that are of interest to liberals: the tension between a unity imposed by the state and the autonomy of the individual or society. In contrast, historians writing in the last decade or so, a period when Russia has been subjected to a number of programmes of liberal modernization, have tended to be more interested in the Soviet Union as a state encountering modernity, rather than as an ideological competitor to the liberal West, and they have interpreted Bolshevism as a project concerned with these

[33] Although, as will be seen below, some excellent recent studies have emphasized the role of Marxist ideas in Bolshevik politics. For contrasting interpretations, see S. Hanson, *Time and Revolution. Marxism and the Design of Soviet Institutions* (Chapel Hill, 1997); M. Sandle, *A Short History of Soviet Socialism* (London, 1999); I. Halfin, *From Darkness to Light. Class, Consciousness and Salvation in Revolutionary Russia* (Pittsburgh, 2000); E. Van Ree, *The Political Thought of Joseph Stalin. A Study in Twentieth-Century Revolutionary Patriotism* (London, 2002).

[34] Laura Engelstein has written an incisive critical survey of the impact of the 'cultural turn' on the study of modern Russian history. See L. Engelstein, 'Culture, Culture Everywhere: Interpretations of Modern Russia Across the 1991 Divide', *Kritika*, 2 (2001), 363–93.

[35] For one example of this way of treating ideology, see E. Naiman, *Sex in Public. The Incarnation of Soviet Ideology* (Princeton, 1997).

questions rather than with issues of individual rights and state repression.

So, one of the most significant recent debates has been between those who emphasize Stalinism's 'traditionalizing' features, and those who see it as an 'Enlightenment' phenomenon.[36] The former share the interest of the conflictualist school in traditional authority structures and practices, but they see them as new, 'neo-traditionalist' phenomena, rather than as straightforward survivals from the tsarist era.[37] The Bolsheviks, they argue, attempted to create a state and society based on modern universalistic principles: each citizen was to be treated equally; old tsarist distinctions between social 'estates' (*sosloviia*)—each with their own legal privileges—were to be destroyed; traditional, personal, clientelistic relationships were to be replaced with modern, impersonal, bureaucratic ones. However, in their attempts to strengthen the state, they unintentionally created hierarchical social relations similar to those of traditional status or estate societies. In severely circumscribing the market and managing the economy, the state had something in common with a traditional patrimonial regime with absolute authority over the economy and its subjects;[38] it delegated enormous powers to local bosses who now controlled resources and established patron-client networks, basing their legitimacy on a paternalistic approach to authority.[39] Also, as Sheila Fitzpatrick has argued, the Bolsheviks, in their attempts to give privileges to the loyal and to discriminate against potential enemies, inadvertently contributed to the creation of a society that shared some of the characteristics of the tsarist 'estate' (*soslovie*) order. The state divided the population into

[36] For an analysis of this debate, see S. Fitzpatrick, 'Introduction', in S. Fitzpatrick (ed.), *Stalinism. New Directions* (London, 2000), 11.

[37] See T. Martin, 'Modernization or Neo-traditionalism? Ascribed Nationality and Soviet Primordialism', in Fitzpatrick, *Stalinism. New Directions*, 348–67. See also S. Fitzpatrick, 'Ascribing Class: The Construction of Social Identity in Soviet Russia', in Fitzpatrick, *Stalinism. New Directions*, 20–46, although Fitzpatrick does not explicitly endorse the concept of 'neo-traditionalism'. See also A. Walder, *Communist Neo-Traditionalism. Work and Authority in Chinese Industry* (Berkeley and Los Angeles, 1986), 1–27; K. Jowitt, *New World Disorder: The Leninist Extinction* (Berkeley and Los Angeles, 1992), 121–58.

[38] For the application of the concept of 'patrimonialism' to communist societies, see M. Lupher, *Power Restructuring in China and Russia* (Boulder, 1996), 10–13.

[39] On paternalism, see L. Siegelbaum, ' "Dear Comrade, You Ask What we Need". Socialist Paternalism and Soviet Rural "Notables" in the mid-1930s', in S. Fitzpatrick, *Stalinism. New Directions*, 231–55; J. Brooks, *Thank You, Comrade Stalin! Soviet Public Culture from Revolution to Cold War* (Princeton, 2000), 69–70.

a number of new *soslovie*-classes, such as the 'workers', the 'collect-ivized peasants', and the 'Soviet intelligentsia', and class, sometimes seen as heritable, 'defined an individual's rights, privileges and obli-gations *vis-à-vis* the state'.[40] This approach to class, combined with popular stigmatization of the bourgeoisie, helps, she argues, to explain the continuing persecution of 'class aliens' (or people with non-proletarian backgrounds) into the 1930s. Terry Martin also suggests that this neo-traditionalist set of attitudes affected nation-ality policy, and helps us to understand the persecutions of particular ethnic groups during the Terror period.[41]

For another group of historians, however, Stalinism was a phe-nomenon that was inspired by, in Stephen Kotkin's words, the 'prevalent conception and experience of "progressive modern-ity" '.[42] The welfare state, economic planning, the surveillance of the population and the rejection of representative democracy can all be seen as elements in a political project that was ultimately founded on the European Enlightenment's ambitions to create a new harmonious society based on rational, scientific principles.[43]

Some have argued that Stalin's own political thought was firmly in the Enlightenment tradition;[44] others have suggested that an Enlightenment approach towards state-building helps to explain the political violence of the period. The Bolsheviks, they have argued, were pursuing an almost aesthetic project, inspired by an ethos of social engineering found elsewhere in European politics. They sought to 'sculpt' society, creating a pure community by 'excising' the imperfect. In practice, this involved the pursuit of violent 'cleansing' campaigns.[45]

---

[40] S. Fitzpatrick, 'Social Identities', in Fitzpatrick, *Stalinism. New Directions*, 16; Fitzpatrick, 'Ascribing Class', 36–7.

[41] Martin argues that having initially treated nationality as something that would ultimately wither away, the state unintentionally established a regime in which nationality, like *soslovie*-class, was seen as a primordial, essential characteristic. These attitudes contributed to the stigmatization of certain nationalities as 'enemy nations', culminating in the 'ethnic cleansings' of the Terror. See T. Martin, 'Mod-ernization or Neo-traditionalism?', 357–8. See also T. Martin, 'The Origins of Soviet Ethnic Cleansing', *JMH*, 70 (1998), 813–61.

[42] S. Kotkin, *Magnetic Mountain*, 20.

[43] Ibid., 6–8. David Hoffmann also argues that the Enlightenment tradition was central to Stalinist cultural norms. D. Hoffmann, *Stalinist Values. The Cultural Norms of Modernity, 1917–1941* (Ithaca, NY, 2003), esp. 7–14.

[44] E. Van Ree, *The Political Thought of Joseph Stalin*, esp. 283–7.

[45] See, in particular, P. Holquist, 'To Count, to Extract, and to Exterminate. Population Statistics and Population Politics in Late Imperial and Soviet Russia',

The 'Enlightenment' and 'neo-traditionalist' approaches both capture important aspects of Stalinist thinking, and both are valuable in relating Bolshevik ideas to broader discourses and political cultures. Yet neither convincingly accounts for the Terror of the late 1930s. Its highly disruptive, puritanical witch-hunting seems to have had little connection with a neo-traditionalist project that was primarily concerned with stability. Also the Stalinist leadership's frequent elevation of heroism over scientific rationality, and its persecution of 'wrecker' specialists who defended science against voluntaristic experiments, suggests a more Romantic view of politics than an Enlightenment one.[46]

Some historians have addressed these problems by exploring the political culture of the party, its origins as a conspiratorial secret, organization obsessed with enemies within, and the development of practices of purge, 'self-criticism', and denunciation within it.[47] Others have combined the Enlightenment approach with elements of the liberal historiographical tradition, arguing that violence was the product of a combination of the Enlightenment project with a quasi-religious, messianic ideology.[48] They see the eschatological

in R. G. Suny and T. Martin, (eds.), *A State of Nations. Empire and Nation-Making in the Age of Lenin and Stalin* (New York, 2001), 111–44. See also P. Holquist, 'What is so Revolutionary about the Russian Revolution? State Practices and New Style Politics', in D. Hoffmann and Y. Kotsonis (eds.), *Russian Modernity: Politics, Knowledge, Practices* (Basingstoke, 1999), 89–91; see also D. Hoffmann, 'European Modernity and Soviet Socialism', in Hoffmann and Kotsonis (eds.), *Russian Modernity*, 245–50.

[46] For a similar questioning of the Enlightenment interpretation, see I. Halfin and J. Hellbeck, 'Rethinking the Stalinist Subject: Stephen Kotkin's "Magnetic Mountain" and the State of Soviet Historical Studies', *JGO*, 44 (1996), 463. Kotkin has himself argued that the Enlightenment interpretation needs to be supplemented by others. As he writes, 'understanding how an enlightenment ethos of scientific social engineering and accompanying modern practices of government mixed with a theocratic party-state structure and quasi-religious systems of dogma is perhaps the principal challenge facing interpreters of revolutionary Russia'. S. Kotkin, '1991 and the Russian Revolution: Sources, Conceptual Categories, Analytical Frameworks', *JMH*, 70 (1998), 403.

[47] Getty and Naumov emphasize the peculiarly fearful political culture of the party, formed in the civil war. See J. A. Getty and O. V. Naumov, *The Road to Terror*, 16. For a stimulating study of the political culture of the party in the sphere of higher education in the 1920s, see M. David-Fox, *Revolution of the Mind*.

[48] Jacob Talmon, an important figure in developing the liberal 'totalitarianist' interpretation of modern radical anti-liberal regimes, was one of the most influential proponents of the argument that movements such as Bolshevism combined secularized religious messianism with Enlightenment rationalism. See J. Talmon, *The Origins of Totalitarian Democracy* (Harmondsworth, 1986), 6.

and utopian elements of Bolshevism as important inspirations for the persecution of 'enemies', pointing to the party's claim that mankind was living through the equivalent of the last days, and its insistence that communists had to struggle against evil elements within if they were to create a pure heaven on earth.[49]

These approaches bring us closer to a convincing explanation for the extraordinary politics of the Terror. As will be seen, much Stalinist discourse was steeped in a quasi-religious language, and the notion of political purity was a significant one. But a focus on eschatological ideas can lead us to concentrate exclusively on the issue of unity and the desire to create a conflict-free utopia, while neglecting other elements of the ideology, which explained how the unified order was to be achieved and what sort of society it was to be. So, for instance, in explaining the religious language of the Stalinist leadership, we need to explore not only its eschatological concern with establishing the perfect society, but also its almost Romantic interest in the role of non-rational forces such as 'soul' and 'faith' in creating that society.[50] During the Terror period, it was not enough that people were loyal to the leadership; they had to have commitment and enthusiasm. And this political Romanticism was combined with a powerful Manichean strain within Bolshevism, to justify a highly divisive politics of heroic 'struggle' against the 'class enemy'.[51]

I shall argue in this study that if we are to explain not only the Terror but also an important element in the thinking of Bolshevik leaders

---

[49] See, in particular, A. Weiner, *Making Sense of War. The Second World War and the Fate of the Bolshevik Revolution* (Princeton, 2001), esp. 21–39,136, 144–6. For eschatology and the religious structure of Marxist thought, see Halfin, *From Darkness to Light*, esp. ch. 1; Halfin, in his analysis of discourses within the Bolshevik party as a whole, relates this eschatology to the Terror, arguing that the achievement of socialism in 1936 radicalized attitudes towards enemies because the party believed that the Soviet Union was approaching the perfect society. He argues that the Terror can best be seen as the consequence of Bolsheviks' belief that society was approaching the apocalypse, when all would be ideologically and morally pure and heresy would be eliminated. See I. Halfin, *Terror in My Soul. Communist Autobiographies on Trial* (Cambridge, Mass., 2003), 254–5, 272–3.

[50] For explorations of Romantic elements in early Bolshevik thought, see A. Krylova, 'Beyond the Spontaneity-Consciousness Paradigm: "Class Instinct" as a Promising Category of Political Analysis', *SR*, 62 (2003), 1–23; I. Halfin, 'Between Instinct and Mind: The Bolshevik View of the Proletarian Self', *SR*, 62 (2003), 34–40.

[51] Peter Holquist, in particular, has emphasized the importance and distinctiveness of the Manichean elements within Bolshevism. P. Holquist, 'Violent Russia, Deadly Marxism? Russia in the Epoch of Violence, 1905–21', *Kritika*, 4(3) (2003), 650; P. Holquist, 'What is so Revolutionary about the Russian Revolution?', 104.

throughout the inter-war period, we need to understand a particular tendency within Bolshevism that was closely related to voluntaristic and quasi-Romantic traditions within socialism on the one hand, and to strategies of mobilization, partly designed to solve concrete economic and political problems, on the other.[52]

Yet it would be misleading to present this set of ideas as a single ideological system that constituted 'Bolshevism' or 'Stalinism', and we should not assume that one internally coherent ideology or political culture informed Bolshevik political decision-making. To understand how several diverse ideas were connected to each other within leaders' discourse, and how they were related to politics more generally, we need to revisit the question of Marxism-Leninism and its role in Soviet politics.

Ideology and politics in the Soviet Union

Marxism-Leninism may not have been a coherent blueprint guiding political action, as both Bolsheviks and liberal historians claimed; yet neither was it an infinitely malleable set of ideas. Marxism-Leninism, like other ideologies, placed real constraints on what could be said. Michael Freeden has defined ideology as 'an activity undertaken with concepts and with language...which plots the parameters of individual and group conduct'. It seeks to convert the 'inevitable variety of opinions into the monolithic certainty which is the unavoidable feature of a political *decision*, and which is the basis of the forging of a political identity'; while it is rarely successful in establishing that coherence, it still sets limits, pronouncing 'on which conceptual combinations are available to be applied to the understanding and shaping of the political world'.[53] Ideology can also be seen as a form of discourse, or act of political communication, that has particular conventions, ruling on which ideas can be included within it.[54]

---

[52] This analysis accords, therefore, with Kotkin's view of the ways in which the Terror was conducted and interpreted in Magnitogorsk. He sees the Terror as the consequence of 'the mobilization of the party for the sake of mobilizing society'. Kotkin, *Magnetic Mountain*, 286.

[53] M. Freeden, *Ideologies and Political Theory. A Conceptual Approach* (Oxford, 1996), 551.

[54] For this view of Soviet ideology as discourse, see N. Robinson, *Ideology and the Collapse of the Soviet System. A Critical History of Soviet Ideological Discourse*

Bolshevik ideology, therefore, had some autonomy, and was not ultimately controlled by those who articulated it. Although Bolsheviks could manipulate its conventions, and its inconsistencies ensured that there were many opportunities to do so, they had to make sure that they remained within limits and observed discursive rules. The ideology structured political debate and regulated what could and could not be said.

The ideology also shaped political action. Because the Bolshevik regime derived its legitimacy from its adherence to Marxism-Leninism, Bolsheviks had to act as if they were obeying its rules.[55] Marxism-Leninism was not the only discourse of importance, and it co-existed alongside and was penetrated by other discourses, but its status within the political system as the only legitimate discourse ensured that it had a special influence. Therefore Marxist-Leninist ideology can be seen as a 'structural' force within Soviet politics, which both enabled and constrained discourse and action. Yet ideology, of course, was not the only such force: it interacted with other structural factors, including the exigencies of economic development and state-building, institutional frameworks and international relations;[56] it also interacted with the political practices which political leaders employed to implement ideological objectives.[57] The traditional intentionalist approach to ideology, which assumes that some Soviet leaders implemented a set of ideological principles because they believed in them while others did not because they were cynics or pragmatists, is therefore unhelpful. The beliefs of leaders were very different, and they are difficult for

(Aldershot, 1995), 19–20; J. Schull, 'What is Ideology? Theoretical Problems and Lessons from Soviet-type Societies', *Political Studies*, 40 (1992), 728–41; R. Walker, 'Thinking about Ideology and Method', *Political Studies*, 43 (1995), 334. However, in using the term 'discourse', I shall not be adopting the approach of critical discourse theorists. For a useful discussion and critique, see M. Freeden, *Ideology, A Very Short Introduction* (Oxford, 2003), 103–9.

[55] Although Soviet leaders were often more interested in legitimizing their actions within the élite than among the population as a whole.

[56] For 'structuralist' approaches to ideology, each with different emphases, see N. Robinson, *Ideology and the Collapse of the Soviet System*; W. Sewell, 'Ideologies and Social Revolutions: Reflections on the French Case', in T. Skocpol (ed.), *Social Revolutions in the Modern World* (Cambridge, 1994), 169–98; T. Skocpol, 'Cultural Idioms and Political Ideologies in the Revolutionary Reconstruction of State Power: A Rejoinder to Sewell', in T. Skocpol, *Social Revolutions*, 199–209.

[57] For the interaction of ideology and practices, and their 'mutually constitutive and symbiotic relationship', see P. Holquist, *Making War, Forging Revolution*, esp. 6–7.

historians to recover, yet, whatever their beliefs, all Bolsheviks had to operate within the rules of the ideology.[58] At the same time, however, we need to avoid an excessively structuralist approach to ideology. Political actors, operating within the constraints of Marxism-Leninism, used elements of the ideology to justify particular courses of action taken for a variety of reasons; they could also alter it, within limits, and it changed over time.[59] Students of ideology therefore need to examine the ways in which actors intentionally deployed ideological arguments to legitimize particular actions and win specific disputes, as well as the broader ideological structures within which they were operating.[60]

What, then, were the conventions of Marxism-Leninism? Central to the ideology and its coherence was the notion that the Soviet people, led by the party, were following a particular historical path of development, progressing towards the ultimate goal—communism.[61] The legitimacy of the party, the organization declared to be the only body that knew how to reach communism, derived from this principle, as did the party's view of what was good and what was bad: all that promoted progress towards communism was approved of, and all that blocked it was not.

The fact that the regime was legitimized by this teleological ideology also had broader effects on the ways in which Bolsheviks thought about the state and how it was to be administered, as T. H. Rigby has argued, following a Weberian methodology.[62] For Weber, the ideas used to legitimize a particular 'order' were closely related to the 'mode in which the administration is carried out' and the

---

[58] As Schull has argued, 'Ideology is a set of resources, deployed by its adherents with varying intentions and a varying degree and pattern of belief, which nonetheless imposes certain commitments on them: it is an instrument with the power to influence the use that is made of it'. J. Schull, 'What is Ideology?', 729.

[59] As Sewell argues, 'Ideological structures undergo continuous reproduction and/ or transformation as a result of the combined willful actions of more or less knowledgeable actors within the constraints and the possibilities supplied by preexisting structures'. W. Sewell, 'Ideologies and Social Revolutions', 172.

[60] For an attempt to relate intention and structure in the analysis of ideologies and their role in politics, see T. Skocpol, 'Cultural Idioms', 204.

[61] This has been argued, in particular, by Robinson. See N. Robinson, *Ideology and the Collapse of the Soviet Union*, 20–4.

[62] Several authors have used Weberian theories of legitimate domination to elucidate communist politics. See K. Jowitt, *New World Disorder*, chs. 1, 4; S. Hanson, *Time and Revolution*; Walder, *Communist Neo-Traditionalism*, ch. 1; A. Janos, *Politics and Paradigms. Changing Theories of Change in Social Science* (Stanford, 1986), 106–12.

'character of the personnel'. The precise connection between the form of legitimation and the structures and methods of rule may be difficult to define, but the way in which regimes are legitimized is certainly related to a broader set of attitudes towards authority and the way it is exercised.[63] Weber himself developed three 'pure' forms of legitimation and their corresponding authority types: 'traditional' authority is justified according to the sanctity of immemorial tradition, and is commonly exercised by people who are obeyed because of their traditional status; 'charismatic' authority is founded on devotion to the 'exceptional sanctity, heroism or exemplary character' of the leader; and 'rational-legal' authority is based on a belief in the legality of impersonal rules, and the right of those elevated to authority under those rules—typically officials in a bureaucracy—to issue commands.[64] Yet as Rigby has argued, an additional type, 'goal-rationality', is needed to describe Soviet-type systems:[65] while the Soviet regime did often justify its power in rational terms, the achievement of goals was more central to it than legality and the application of rules.[66]

'Goal-rationality' certainly influenced ideas about how society was to be administered. All aspects of life, whether public or private, were supposed to be directed towards the achievement of tasks defined as steps on the way to the ultimate goal, communism—a non-market and wholly unified society. Liberal ideas were therefore marginalized, both because they assumed an autonomous private sphere, unaffected by the goal, and because they contradicted the principles of the society which the regime was committed to creating. Rigby also argued that goal-rationality affected the design of

[63] For the problems in establishing the relationship between ideas of legitimacy and the structures of domination, see T. H. Rigby, 'Introduction. Political Legitimacy, Weber and Communist Mono-organisational Systems' in T. H. Rigby and F. Feher (eds.), *Political Legitimation in Communist States* (London, 1982), 5.

[64] M. Weber, *Economy and Society*, ed. by G. Roth and C. Wittich (Berkeley and Los Angeles, 1978), i. 215.

[65] For this concept, see Rigby, 'Introduction', 1–26; T. H. Rigby, 'A Conceptual Approach to Authority, Power and Policy in the Soviet Union', in T. H. Rigby, A. H. Brown and P. Reddaway (eds.), *Authority, Power and Policy in the USSR* (London, 1983), 9–31.

[66] For Rigby, goal-rationality does not necessarily imply that the system was well-designed to achieve the goals it proclaimed, but 'the validity of its demands for compliance is *claimed* to be based on a rational relationship between the ultimate goal of communism and the specific tasks assigned to social units' and individuals' rationality 'relates to the appropriateness of the means used . . to the goals set'. T. H. Rigby, 'Introduction', 12–13.

institutions: they were organized in a hierarchical way to fulfil tasks, and unlike the 'rational-legal' bureaucracies common in Western systems, which are concerned with the application of rules and laws, Soviet bureaucracies were 'task-oriented'.

Yet while 'goal-rationality' explains some features of Bolshevik political thinking, other forms of legitimation were also important. The goal of communism was central to the architecture of Bolshevik ideology, but it was possible to argue about how the goal was to be reached, and which aspects of the new society were to be emphasized. Marxism-Leninism did pronounce on the character of communism: it was a wholly unified order in which state and society had been fused; it was a society in which men ruled themselves and worked voluntarily; and at the same time it was extraordinarily productive, without market relations but employing the latest technology. Yet there was a tension between the egalitarian, 'democratic' features of communism and its modern, economically productive aspects, and it was possible to stress one or the other. The ideology also incorporated two very different visions of the type of politics needed to achieve the goal, each of which implied a different view of legitimate authority. The first assumed that the best way to make progress was to rely on the special 'consciousness' of the collective—the working class or its representative, the party; this implied a charismatic view of authority, as power was to be exercised by people who had extraordinary qualities or access to some higher truth.[67] The second held that knowledge of science and technology would bring the regime towards communism, and assumed a Weberian 'rational' view of authority: power was to be in the hands of officials who were specifically trained for their job and had technical abilities.[68]

These tensions were not only a feature of Bolshevism. Other radical anti-liberals, such as those on the German nationalist right, similarly sought to attain a utopian goal that combined collectivism with modernity; they too tried to achieve their objectives while rejecting liberal models, and encountered difficulties in reconciling two alternative approaches to the exercise of

---

[67] M. Weber, *Economy and Society*, i. 241–45. Weber mainly saw charisma as something that belonged to individual leaders, but it is possible to see the party programme as the charismatic force within Bolshevism. See K. Jowitt, *New World Order*, 10.

[68] M. Weber, *Economy and Society*, i. 217–23.

authority—one that emphasized 'scientific' organization, and the other that stressed the role of the collective's spirit.[69]

Yet the nature of Marxism, and especially its claim that the working class was the source of charismatic, revolutionary powers, shaped this tension in particular ways, and ensured that it became closely associated with the thorny question of how to integrate workers into the new regime. To understand how these divisions operated, we need to re-examine the ideological structure established by the founding fathers, Marx and Engels, and the ways in which it interacted with other ideas about political and economic organization.

Socialisms and Marxisms

The problem of how to reconcile collectivism with modernity lay at the root of one of the central questions facing all socialists: how could the features that supposedly characterized pre-capitalist artisanal or peasant communities—egalitarianism and solidarity—be combined with industry, science, and other desirable features of modernity? And this was the question that Marx and Engels claimed to have solved. Before Marx, socialists tended to respond to this dilemma by developing schemes that embraced modernity

[69] For German radical right-wing ideologists' attempts to reconcile technology and national spirit (or 'Technik' and 'Kultur') in a 'reactionary modernist' approach to politics, see J. Herf, *Reactionary Modernism. Technology, Culture and Politics in the Third Reich* (Cambridge, 1984). German nationalist scientists were engaged in similar projects; for their efforts to create a holistic science, compatible with a world-view that recognized the power of non-mechanistic, spiritual forces, see A. Harrington, *Reenchanted Science. Holism in German Culture from Wilhelm II to Hitler* (Princeton, 1996). Once the Nazis came to power, proponents of an alternative 'Aryan' science were sidelined, and the Nazis generally favoured the rationalization of industry and the power of conventional science and expertise within the economy, in the interests of a radical foreign policy. Even so, Jeffrey Herf argues that reactionary modernism continued to be influential among the Nazis, and that it undermined the technological capabilities of the regime. J. Herf, *Reactionary Modernism*, 201–4. For challenges to technocratic approaches among inventors, see K. Gispen, *Poems in Steel. National Socialism and the Politics of Inventing from Weimar to Bonn* (New York, 2002). For hostility to technocracy in the sphere of state administration, where 'party' proponents of a dynamic 'government without administration' confronted 'state' defenders of a bureaucratic administration 'that effaced government as a political process', see J. Caplan, *Government without Administration. State and Civil Service in Weimar and Nazi Germany* (Oxford, 1988), 337.

without egalitarianism, or egalitarianism without modernity.[70] One tradition, best represented by Saint-Simon, developed a technocratic model of socialism, which envisaged a society rationally organized by an expert élite.[71] Another version of socialism, defended by socialists such as Wilhelm Weitling and Robert Owen, might be defined as 'populist socialist', and owed more to Rousseau's vision of a virtuous and unified people ruling themselves and free of the hierarchies and competitiveness of modern society.[72] Populist socialists could be accused of favouring a return to pre-capitalist society, and they also tended to have a moralistic view of politics and a voluntaristic approach to history: socialism would come about because an intrinsically virtuous people would rebel against the old order and establish a new one.

The tensions between populist and more technocratic forms of socialism were particularly sharp in Russia, where influential socialists defended the relatively egalitarian peasant communities that were being threatened by the market and the state, while at the same time accepting that poverty and 'backwardness' had to be overcome.[73] Many Russian socialists argued that the Russian state and

---

[70] There are many ways of analysing the varieties of socialism. Berki distinguishes between four components: egalitarianism, moralism, rationalism, and libertarianism. The main tension I am interested in here lies, in Berki's terms, between egalitarianism and moralism on the one side, and rationalism on the other. As Berki points out, while Marx's system included all four elements, libertarianism was the weakest; it also had little influence on Bolshevik thinking. See R. Berki, *Socialism* (Letchworth, 1975), ch. 2. For the diversity of socialist thinking, see also Freeden, *Ideologies and Political Theory*, ch. 11.

[71] Although there was also a participatory element in Saint-Simon's socialism. H. Saint-Simon, *Selected Writings on Science, Industry and Social Organization*, ed. by K. Taylor (London, 1975), 174–80; Henri Comte de Saint Simon, *Selected Writings* (Oxford, 1952), 78–80.

[72] For a definition of 'populism' as an ideology that assumed the existence of a unified, morally virtuous people set against the economically and politically powerful, and that demanded economic equality and direct democracy, see C. Calhoun, *The Question of Class Struggle. Social Foundations of Popular Radicalism during the Industrial Revolution* (Oxford, 1982), 100–1; see also D. Macrae, 'Populism as an Ideology', in G. Ionescu and E. Gellner (eds.), *Populism. Its Meanings and National Characteristics* (London, 1969), 153–65. For Weitling and Owen, see C. Wittke, *The Utopian Communist. A Biography of Wilhelm Weitling, Nineteenth-Century Reformer* (Baton Rouge, 1950), esp. ch. 7; R. Owen, *A New View of Society and Other Writings*, ed. by G. Claeys (Harmondsworth, 1991).

[73] There is a large literature on Russian socialism. See A. Walicki, *The Controversy over Capitalism. Studies in the Social Philosophy of the Russian Populists* (Oxford, 1969); F. Venturi, *Roots of Revolution. A History of the Populist and Socialist Movements in Nineteenth Century Russia* (New York, 1966); A. Mendel, *Dilemmas*

society could, in some respects at least, be reconstructed according to the model of the Russian peasant commune (*mir*);[74] the commune, they argued, was an ideal political organization because it was egalitarian, allowed peasants to live virtuous lives free from the greed and egoism that capitalism brought with it, and generated consensus, encouraging the people to rule themselves in a perfect participatory democracy without the interference of an oppressive state. It also avoided the division of labour, typical of modern capitalist societies, and therefore allowed man to be 'whole', performing a wide range of roles.[75] Yet Russian socialists were divided over the extent to which Russia would have to combine the principles of the commune with modernity and capitalism. For some at the more populist socialist end of the spectrum, they were incompatible, and it was better for Russia to be virtuous than wealthy.[76] These socialists' moralistic views accorded with a long tradition of Russian populist socialist thinking which posited a struggle between a virtuous 'people' (*narod*) or 'people at the bottom' (*nizy*), who were best suited to proper egalitarian economic and political relations, and greedy egotistical 'top people' (*verkhi*), or the 'bourgeoisie', united with arbitrary and despotic bureaucrats or 'grandees' (*vel'mozhi*).[77] Other socialists, however, tried to reconcile

of Progress in Tsarist Russia. Legal Marxism and Legal Populism (Cambridge, Mass., 1961).

[74] These socialists are often called 'Populists' (*narodniki*), although the term was a polemical one, originally used to stress differences between indigenous Russian socialists and Marxists. For the problems involved in using this term, see J. White, *Karl Marx and the Intellectual Origins of Dialectical Materialism* (Basingstoke, 1996), 364–7.

[75] For N. K. Mikhailovskii's criticisms of the modern division of labour, see Walicki, *The Controversy over Capitalism*, 47 ff.

[76] See, for instance, some of Mikhailovskii's statements. A. Vucinich, *Social Thought in Tsarist Russia. The Quest for a General Science of Society, 1861–1917* (Chicago and London, 1976), 30; Mendel, *Dilemmas of Progress*, 39. Alternatively, it could be argued that an egalitarian, virtuous economy would be more productive than a capitalist one, because the people would be more motivated to work for the good of the community than for money. See, for instance, N. G. Chernyshevskii, *Polnoe sobranie sochinenii* (Moscow, 1939–51), iv. 756; ix. 516–17; W. Woehrlin, *Chernyshevskii, Man and Journalist* (Cambridge, Mass., 1971), 223. For a discussion of such views of labour motivation within the socialist tradition, see J. Campbell, *Joy in Work, German Work* (Princeton, 1989), ch. 2.

[77] See, for instance, 'Opyt' obosnovaniia programmy narodnikov', in N. K. Karataev, *Narodnicheskaia ekonomicheskaia literatura* (Moscow, 1958), 613, 626; V. G. Bazanov, *Agitatsionnaia literatura russkikh revoliutsionnykh narodnikov: potaennye proizvedeniia 1873–1875 gg.* (Leningrad, 1970), 91.

the peasant commune with Western modernity and adopted a more scientistic and less moralistic approach to politics. They also frequently had a less optimistic view of the masses and insisted on the need for an élite to 'enlighten' them.[78]

Marx's project could also be interpreted as an attempt to combine the populist socialist and technocratic traditions of socialism, but it seemed to be more coherent and convincing than its predecessors, and it is not surprising that it was so influential in Russia. Marx tried to show how the objectives of populist socialists might be reconciled with the realities of modern societies and historical progress.[79] He started from the desire for a truly 'human' society, in which mankind would be liberated from all external, 'alien' forces.[80] By this he meant that men would be free in the social realm—from political subordination and from the market and private property—and also, crucially, free from a dependence on the forces of nature that brought with it poverty and backwardness.[81] Marx's communism, the truly 'human' society, was therefore similar in some respects to the utopias of the populist socialists. Like Rousseau's vision, it was a united egalitarian, ultra-democratic community in which the whole people ruled themselves, participating in government without the need for states or hierarchies. This freedom and equality was also extended to the economic sphere: men would work because they expressed their creativity through labour, not because they were forced to do so by fear of starvation. Yet at the same time Marx insisted that communism had to enable mankind to control the forces of nature. It therefore had to be modern, founded on the achievements of advanced capitalism and

---

[78] Nikolai Chernyshevskii was one of the foremost of these 'enlighteners' and was an important influence on Lenin. For the combination of scientism and moralism in Chernyshevskii's thought, and his ambivalent attitude towards Western modernity, see Woehrlin, *Chernyshevskii*, 225–7; Walicki, *The Controversy over Capitalism*, 16–24. Later Russian non-Marxist socialists, such as Daniel'son, also favoured some degree of Westernization. See Walicki, *The Controversy over Capitalism*, 107–31; Mendel, *Dilemmas*, 40–79; for Chernyshevskii's influence on Lenin, see C. Ingerflom, *Le citoyen impossible. Les racines russes du Leninisme* (Paris, 1988), ch. 4.

[79] Walicki similarly argues that Marx was advocating a form of 'primitive' natural economy, but at a higher level. A. Walicki, *Marxism*, 58, 84.

[80] For these ideas, see B. Yack, *The Longing for Total Revolution. Philosophic Sources of Social Discontent from Rousseau to Marx and Nietzsche* (Berkeley and Los Angeles, 1992), 256 ff.

[81] For this distinction between freedom in the relationship 'man *versus* society', and freedom in the relationship 'man *versus* nature', see A. Walicki, *Marxism*, 41.

the latest science; it could not be a reversion to the pre-capitalist past. Marx embraced science not only in his vision of the future society, but also in his explanation of historical change. He attempted to show that communism would be the product not of the will of a virtuous people, as populist socialists tended to argue, but of the largely economic forces that drove historical development—forces that, like the forces of nature, could be discovered by science. For Marx, communism was not 'an *ideal* to which reality will have to adjust itself', as 'utopian' socialists assumed, but 'the *real* movement which abolishes the present state of things'.[82]

Yet how would contemporary workers, ground down by capitalism, become creative and co-operative proletarians, with the advanced consciousness that would enable them to create a productive communism? Marx's answer was that objective and subjective forces would interact together to drive history towards communism.[83] As industry developed and conflicts between classes became sharper, workers' mentalities would change and working class associations would emerge.[84] Yet it was only the act of revolution that would be really effective in transforming the consciousness of the working class as a whole. As Marx explained, it was only in a 'practical movement, a *revolution*' that 'the alteration of men on a mass scale' and the 'production on a mass scale of this communist consciousness' would be possible.[85]

However, despite Marx's claim to have reconciled populist and technocratic socialism, and to have shown how the course of history would bring ordinary workers to become the creators of a productive communism, several ambiguities remained within his theory. First, the relationship between élites and workers remained unclear, especially in Marx's discussion of the economy after the revolution: how could a modern industrial system, based on a system of wage incentives and co-ordination by a technocratic élite, be reconciled with the desire to transform work into creative self-expression and to free workers from all subordination? And second, Marx provided different accounts of the forces that drove history forward, and in

---

[82] K. Marx and F. Engels, *Karl Marx Frederick Engels Collected Works*, [henceforth *MECW*], 47 vols. (London 1975–93), v. 49.

[83] S. Avineri, *The Social and Political Thought of Karl Marx* (Cambridge 1968), 139–44.

[84] *MECW*, iii. 313.

[85] *MECW*, v. 52–3. See also S. Hanson, *Time and Revolution*, 42.

particular the relationship between economic forces and the consciousness of the working class.[86] These two questions, and the tensions which underlay them—between élitism and non-élitism on the one hand, and scientism (the claim that all developments in human society are determined by structural, largely economic, laws) and voluntarism (or the view that revolutionaries could change society by means of will, irrespective of economic conditions) on the other—were to structure conflicts within Marxism for a long time to come. Four different solutions to these questions were possible, and each was adopted within the Marxist tradition: non-élitist and voluntaristic, élitist and scientistic, non-élitist and scientistic, and élitist and voluntaristic.[87]

Strongest support could be found within Marx's and Engels's own thought for the first two of these interpretations: the populist and voluntaristic, and the scientistic and élitist. Marx's earlier works tended to express the first. There would be little difficulty, Marx assumed, in reconciling prosperity with human 'freedom' because the proletarian already had a high level of consciousness and was on the verge of becoming a creative, co-operative, and energetic being.[88] Workers had developed a high level of proletarian

---

[86] For the tensions within Marx's views of the driving forces of historical development, see H. Fleischer, *Marxism and History* trans. by E. Mosbacher (London, 1973), ch. 1; for similar contradictions within Engels's thought, see S. Rigby, *Engels and the Formation of Marxism. History, Dialectic and Revolution* (Manchester, 1992), 144–50; S. Rigby, 'Engels after Marx: History', in M. Steger and T. Carver (eds.), *Engels after Marx* (Manchester, 1999), 124–37.

[87] Many have commented on the contradictions within Marxist thought, and this scheme seeks to build on the existing literature. Some stress the tension within Marx's ideas of the future socialist society, between a humanistic vision, in which man is free of alienation and can fulfil himself, and a scientistic and technocratic vision, in which man controls nature efficiently and abolishes poverty and exploitation. See C. Taylor, 'Socialism and Weltanschauung', in L. Kolakowski and S. Hampshire (eds.), *The Socialist Idea* (London, 1974), 45–58. See also N. Harding, 'Socialism, Society and the Organic Labour State', in N. Harding (ed.), *The State in Socialist Society* (Basingstoke, 1984), 1–50. Others present a broader picture, relating these issues to the tension between voluntarism and scientific determinism. Gouldner distinguishes between a voluntaristic 'critical' Marxism, and a deterministic 'scientific' Marxism. A. Gouldner, *The Two Marxisms. Contradictions and Anomalies in the Development of Theory* (London and Basingstoke, 1980), 32. Hanson employs a similar approach, although he uses a Weberian conceptual framework. For him, Marxists were divided over their attitudes towards time, into three groups: a charismatic 'left', a rational–legal 'right', and a neo–traditionalist 'centre'. See S. Hanson, *Time and Revolution*, 37–55. In many respects, I agree with Hanson's analysis, although my focus and use of the Weberian approach are different.

[88] See, for instance, *MECW*, iii. 313.

consciousness through their practical activity in working class organizations. As Marx noted of French workers, 'when communist artisans form associations, teaching and propaganda are their first aims. But their association itself creates a new need—the need for society—and what appeared to be a means has become an end... The brotherhood of man is no mere phrase with them, but a fact of life, and the nobility of man shines upon us from their work-hardened bodies'.[89] Workers were on the verge of becoming not only free but also extraordinarily productive: once the division of labour under the capitalist system was abolished, labour would become creative 'self-activity' and mankind would realize its potential.[90] Also, the expropriation of private owners would enable 'the development of a totality of capacities in individuals themselves'.[91]

Marx's faith in the proletariat at times also led him to emphasize the subjective consciousness of the proletariat as the driving force of history, rather than objective economic forces. In the *Communist Manifesto*, for instance, he argued that Germany in 1848 was particularly fertile ground for a proletarian revolution and communism, even though it was backward economically and unlike England and France had not undergone a bourgeois revolution. Germany, he suggested, was a special case because the proletariat there was particularly 'developed'.[92]

So, although Marx did not ground his arguments in morality, the view expressed in several of his works—that the proletariat was a

---

[89] *MECW*, iii. 313. See also K. Marx and F. Engels, *Manifesto of the Communist Party* (Beijing, 1988), 44.

[90] K. Marx, *Selected Writings*, ed. by D. McLellan (Oxford, 1977), 122.

[91] *MECW*, v. 87–8, 78. See also A. Walicki, *Marxism*, 58–9.

[92] He also argued that a bourgeois revolution in Germany would take place under 'more advanced conditions of European civilization' than had existed in England and France. He therefore urged the German proletariat to overthrow the monarchy in alliance with the bourgeoisie, and then immediately begin the struggle against capitalism which, he implied, would collapse soon thereafter. During this transitional period the proletariat would 'use its political supremacy' to centralize production under the state and 'increase the total of productive forces as rapidly as possible'. Marx was therefore implying that the political will of the proletariat would develop the economic base necessary for the emergence of communism. Marx and Engels, *Manifesto*, 77, 59. For this interpretation of the *Manifesto*, see H. Draper, *Karl Marx's Theory of Revolution*. Vol. 2: *The Politics of Social Classes* (New York, 1978), 192–3. For the argument that Marx envisaged a minority proletariat taking power in alliance with the peasantry in backward countries, see A. Gilbert, *Marx's Politics. Communists and Citizens* (Oxford, 1981), 197, 217–19; E. Van Ree, *The Political Thought of Joseph Stalin*, 37–40.

class with a special, truly 'human' consciousness that could create the new society in the near future—was not too far from the populist socialist notion that the 'people' could create socialism because they were virtuous.[93] Marx's faith in a creative, work-loving proletariat also had much in common with Romantic political thinking, and could certainly be interpreted in a Romantic way. Unlike Romantic theorists, who emphasized the power of non-rational feeling and emotion, Marx stressed the role of reason and science, interacting with economic, 'structural' forces, in history.[94] Marx saw the proletariat as a rational force, and labour as the application of reason to control nature more effectively, as well as purely physical activity.[95] Yet Marx's view of labour as a form of creative self-expression,[96] and his emphasis, at times, on the special fraternal spirit of the proletariat rather than its rationality, opened the way for a Romantic interpretation of Marxism. His ideal of a society in which economic activity should be driven, at least in part, by men's need to express themselves through work, rather than by the enslaving laws of the market, had something in common with the Romantic idea that growth and production depended not on material things but on 'the powerfully active inner or spiritual forces of man'.[97] Also, like Romantics, he argued that the market and

---

[93] Although Marx frequently used moral language, praising the collectivism of the working class and denouncing the egoism of the bourgeoisie. For moralism in Marx's thinking on the proletariat as a moral category, see D. Lovell, *Marx's Proletariat. The Making of a Myth* (London, 1988), 11–15. For a view of Marxism that stresses the importance of moral thinking, see N. Churchich, *Marxism and Morality. A Critical Examination of Marxist Ethics* (Cambridge, 1994). For the problems posed by Marx's use of moralistic language, see S. Lukes, *Marxism and Morality* (Oxford, 1985).

[94] Marx identified human creativity with the rational desire to master nature. For Marx's rationalism, even in his early thought, see A. Megill, *Karl Marx and the Burden of Reason (Why Marx Rejected Politics and the Market)* (Oxford, 2002), esp. ch. 4.

[95] For Marx's view of labour as the 'application of knowledge to the productive process', see A. Megill, *Karl Marx and the Burden of Reason*, 207–8.

[96] For Marx's debt to Romantic thought in his views of labour, see I. Halfin, *From Darkness to Light*, 43–4.

[97] This quotation is taken from the works of the German conservative Romantic nationalist thinker Adam Mueller. See Adam Mueller, 'Elements of Politics. Second Lecture', in H. Reiss, (ed.), *The Political Thought of the German Romantics, 1793–1815* (Oxford, 1955), 149–50. For the political and economic thinking of German Romantic theorists in the nineteenth century, and for comparisons with Marxism, see L. Greenfeld, *Nationalism. Five Roads to Modernity* (Cambridge, Mass., 1992), 322–95; L. Greenfeld, *The Spirit of Capitalism. Nationalism and Economic Growth* (Cambridge, Mass., 2001), 195–9. For other commentaries on the Romantic

division of labour prevented man from becoming 'whole' and from creating a society in which mankind was able to live according to his communal nature.[98] Yet, in his later works, Marx increasingly moved away from the optimistic notion that it was possible to reconcile the ideal of work as self-expression with the rational mastery of nature, and he increasingly gave the latter priority over the former, embracing a second, more élitist and scientistic socialism—an interpretation that became dominant among the leaders of the German Social Democratic Party in the 1880s and 1890s.[99] He now saw communism primarily as a society that would build on, and develop further, the rational control of the environment achieved by advanced capitalism. He therefore implied that labour could never be self-activity; man would always be subject to authority and discipline in his work, as 'all combined labour on a large scale requires ... a directing authority';[100] there could be no end to the division of labour, and true freedom, allowing the development of human capacities as an end in itself, would be possible only after the end of the labouring day, during leisure time.[101] Engels went even further, denying that labour could ever be the creative development of human capacities as an end in itself. Mankind would always be subject to centralization and the requirements of modern industry, which were the product of natural laws. He redefined 'freedom' as the 'knowledge of these laws' rather than freedom from them: once men understood objective necessities, they could subject them to rational control and

elements within Marx's thought, see A. Gouldner, For Sociology (London, 1973), 337–40; M. Abrams, Natural Supernaturalism. Tradition and Revolution in Romantic Literature (New York, 1973), 313–16.

[98] Romantic thinkers tended to defend a holistic and organicist view of the world, arguing that rationalistic and mechanistic attitudes artificially separated reason from emotion, mind from body, men from each other and from nature. See, for instance, F. Beiser, Enlightenment, Revolution and Romanticism. The Genesis of Modern German Political Thought, 1790–1800 (Cambridge, Mass., 1992), ch. 9.

[99] For Engels's views of politics in the 1880s and 1890s, see L. Wilde, 'Engels and the Contradictions of Revolutionary Strategy', in M. Steger and T. Carver (eds.), Engels after Marx (Manchester, 1999), 197–214; G. Steenson, After Marx, before Lenin. Marxism and Socialist Working-Class Parties in Europe, 1884–1914 (Pittsburgh, 1991), 24–40. For Kautsky's thought, see G. Steenson, Karl Kautsky, 1854–1938. Marxism in the Classical Years (Pittsburgh, 1978).

[100] K. Marx, Capital (New York, 1967), i. 330, 337.

[101] Marx, Capital, iii. 820. For Marx's changing attitudes towards the division of labour and the organization of industry, see A. Rattansi, Marx and the Division of Labour (London, 1982).

increase their power over nature.[102] This almost technocratic vision of the future society sometimes went together with a scientific deterministic approach to historical change: communism would be brought about by the economic forces that drove historical development, and would emerge because it was economically the most rational system;[103] workers were rational actors who would respond to underlying economic forces.[104] Such an attitude towards the forces of history implied a gradualist political strategy: socialists had to wait until economic conditions had matured and laid the foundations for socialism; revolution would only happen when productive forces had reached a certain level of development. As Marx famously declared, 'a social order never perishes before all the productive forces for which it is broadly sufficient have been developed'.[105] This approach also led Marxists to adopt relatively élitist attitudes. Populist socialist demands for working-class insurrection and the establishment of participatory democracy were declared to be premature. In the meantime, the revolutionary movement would be led by an intelligentsia which would teach the working class the truth of socialism.

Yet for some gradualist Marxists, a criticism of radical populist politics did not necessarily involve the rejection of all forms of democracy. As west European states began to democratize their institutions and incorporate the working classes into their political systems, it appeared to some Marxists that, until the revolution came, they would have to reconcile themselves with liberal democracy and participate in 'bourgeois' parliaments. A third version of Marxism therefore emerged, which was both highly scientistic, in that it took a gradualist approach to the question of progress towards socialism, and non-élitist, in the sense that it made temporary peace with many elements of the liberal order, including bourgeois democracy (although it was still élitist in the sense that it insisted that democracy be representative rather than participatory).

---

[102] MECW, xxv. 105. For this distinction between Marx's and Engels's view of freedom, see A. Walicki, Marxism, 192–6.

[103] As Marx declared, 'it is not the consciousness of men that determines their existence, but their social existence that determines their consciousness'. MECW, xxix. 263.

[104] For Marx's rationalistic interpretation of workers' motivation, see Calhoun, The Question of Class Struggle, 214–19.

[105] K. Marx, Preface and Introduction to a Contribution to the Critique of Political Economy (Beijing, 1976), 3–4.

Yet the question of how long this reconciliation with the bourgeoisie was to last was a controversial one. Engels and Kautsky themselves accepted that Marxists had to participate in liberal politics, but they also insisted that this compromise should not undermine their ultimate commitment to revolution and communism. However, they were challenged by 'revisionists' and their ideological leader, Eduard Bernstein, who were such extreme gradualists that they denied the need for revolution at all, in effect endorsing liberal democracy.[106] Revisionists, by accepting liberal values in principle, rather than as a temporary expedient, therefore effectively abandoned the Marxist tradition.

Engels may have endorsed a gradualist, scientific determinist approach to politics in Germany, but he was also influential in laying the ground for a fourth, very different version of Marxism, that was both voluntaristic and élitist.[107] Marx had always distinguished between a 'conscious' élite of communists, who understood the laws of history, and a less advanced mass of proletarians, and he was always vulnerable to the charge that he was placing his faith in the consciousness of a small group rather than the working class as a whole;[108] as the anarchist Bakunin presciently put it, Marxism would give power to 'a numerically small aristocracy of genuine or sham scientists'.[109] Yet Engels developed Marxism in particularly élitist and voluntaristic directions, because he was eager both to ground Marxism in the natural sciences and to reconcile this scientism with the promise of communist revolution.[110] Sometimes supported by Marx, he spent a great deal of time trying to show that communism would emerge because developments in all areas of life, including the natural world, followed the dialectical patterns that Hegel had discerned in history: both the natural world and human history were progressive, he argued, and the conflict of opposites

[106] Although Bernstein eventually moved away from his scientism and tried to justify his revisionism on non–scientistic, moral grounds. See D. McLellan, Marxism after Marx. An Introduction (London, 1979), 35–7.
[107] For Engels's 'dual legacy', see A. Walicki, Marxism, 196–207.
[108] MECW, vi. 497–8.
[109] For the debate between Marx and Bakunin, see D. Lovell, From Marx to Lenin, 61–4.
[110] There is disagreement over the intellectual relationship between Marx and Engels. For an approach that argues for similarities between the two, see Rigby, Engels. Others argue that Engels departed in some respects from Marx. See A. Walicki, Marxism, 111–207.

drove them forward.[111] This progress might be the result of evolutionary change but it was also, at times, revolutionary. According to Engels's first law of dialectics, the law of the 'transformation of quantity into quality', just as the gradual heating or cooling of water led to the sudden production of steam or ice at particular, 'revolutionary' points, so in history transitions could take the form of a revolutionary 'leap, a decisive change'.[112]

The argument that communism would come about as the result of the operation of revolutionary natural laws might suggest that Engels was a scientific determinist who believed that men had no role in history. But, as has been seen, he insisted that mankind could use these laws for its own ends if it understood them; as he explained in the highly influential *Anti-Dühring*: 'once we do understand them [social and natural forces], once we grasp their action, their direction, their effects, it depends only on ourselves to subject them more and more to our own will, and by means of them to reach our own ends'.[113] While Marx and Engels argued that workers themselves would eventually embody rationality and understand the laws of nature,[114] it is not surprising that Marxists could use this approach to defend a more élitist attitude towards politics. According to this view, it was not primarily workers' creativity, their ability to express themselves through labour, or their revolutionary energies, that would drive history forward towards communism. Rather, an élite, with knowledge of a special Marxist science, would harness and direct revolutionary changes in society and nature.[115] This

[111] Engels enunciated this principle in his second law of dialectics, the 'negation of the negation'. According to this 'law', everything tends to evolve progressively, in a spiral pattern, moving from one state to another which is both its opposite but also preserves its positive elements. It then moves back to a version of its original state which is at a higher level of development. So, in nature, a grain of barley produces its 'negation', the plant, and the plant in turn progresses by becoming its 'negation', producing a large number of new grains and dying. Similarly, in human history the communism of primitive societies developed into its 'negation', capitalism, and this in turn would in turn become the 'negation of the negation', an advanced, productive form of communism. See F. Engels, *Anti-Dühring*, 178–99.

[112] Ibid., 82; F. Engels, *Dialectics of Nature*, trans. by C. Dutt (London, 1940), ch. 2.

[113] F. Engels, *Anti-Dühring. Herr Eugen Dühring's Revolution in Science* (Moscow, 1959), 385–6.

[114] For Marx's belief in 1844 that workers were already displaying a commitment to science, see *MECW*, iv. 84. For this point, see A. Megill, *Karl Marx*, 341.

[115] As Walicki argues, it is possible to interpret Engels's thinking as 'profoundly voluntaristic'. A. Walicki, *Marxism*, 192–3.

interpretation of Marxism, and the 'science' of dialectical materialism, was to become very influential in the Soviet Union.

Marx's and Engels's attempts to combine technocratic and populist socialism, therefore, left their followers with four broad approaches to the forces of history and the nature of the new society.

How, then, could they be reconciled? A common solution was to follow the theory of historical development outlined sketchily by Marx, mainly in the *Communist Manifesto* and the *Critique of the Gotha Programme*. This scheme showed how both revolutionary activity and economic developments would lead humanity along a path from capitalism, *via* a technocratic socialism, to full communism, a society that was both productive and allowed labour to become self-activity.[116] Marx was accepting that his future society would not come about suddenly, all at once, but its elements would emerge over time, the less ambitious in the earlier stages and the more ambitious later on. According to this scheme, full communism would emerge only once the working class had a fully socialist mentality and the economy was sufficiently advanced. Initially, some measure of élitism would still be necessary, and during the revolutionary period Marx gave some role to 'the most advanced and resolute section of the working class parties', which would have to lead the proletariat until it had achieved the requisite level of consciousness.[117] In the early stages of communism, after the revolution, the market would give way to a rational, planned, economy, but it would be some time before workers could be trusted to administer the state themselves, and the hierarchies typical of capitalism would have to remain. Also, it would not yet be possible to rely on 'moral' incentives, trusting in workers' desire to express themselves through labour, without the carrot of a wage system and the stick of labour discipline. Immediately after the revolution, then, a new state, the Dictatorship of the Proletariat, would be established, which would exist both to suppress bourgeois opposition and to 'centralize all instruments of production', increasing 'the total of productive forces as rapidly as possible'.[118] This period

---

[116] Marx and Engels, *Manifesto*, 49–61; K. Marx, *The Critique of the Gotha Programme* (Beijing, 1976).

[117] *MECW*, vi. 497–8. See also D. Lovell, *Marx's Proletariat*, 177.

[118] Marx, *Critique of the Gotha Programme*, 27–8; Marx and Engels, *The Manifesto of the Communist Party*, 59. The question of the relationship between

would be followed by a longer phase, the 'lower' stage of communism, which the Bolsheviks called 'socialism', when workers would still be rewarded for their work. Only later, during the 'higher' stage of communism, which the Bolsheviks described as 'communism', would men work because they wanted to, without the need for 'material' wage incentives; only then would the whole of the people be able to administer the state, allowing the distinction between state and society to wither away.[119]

Marx's historical scheme, therefore, resolved some of the tensions between the four positions, by suggesting that the differences within Marxism were not about principles, but about precisely which stage humanity had reached. According to this representation of Marxist debate, then, scientistic non-élitists were suggesting that history was firmly in the capitalist stage; scientistic élitists and voluntaristic élitists that it was in the late capitalist or early socialist stages; and voluntaristic populists that it was approaching the communist stage. But the scheme did not resolve all of the conflicts, and, in particular, it did not show how voluntarism could be reconciled with scientism: Marxists did not just disagree profoundly over how far humanity had progressed along the road to communism but also over which forces would propel history forward and how revolutionary they were. Marx's and Engels's attempts to synthesize the populist and technocratic socialist traditions therefore ultimately failed, and they left an ideology riven with tensions between élitism and non-élitism, and between voluntarism and scientism. Marxists could give different answers to a number of crucial questions: was the working class ready for socialism, and what was to be the relationship between socialist élites and the workers? Could the mobilized working class push history forward, or did revolutionaries have to wait for advanced capitalism to prepare the way? Was political change to be revolutionary or evolutionary?

the Dictatorship of the Proletariat and the lower stage of communism in Marx's thought is a thorny one. For this interpretation, see A. Walicki, *Marxism*, 96. According to Engels, writing in 1891, the Dictatorship of the Proletariat would be organized as a participatory democracy, on the principles of the Paris Commune, K. Marx and F. Engels, *Selected Works* [henceforth *MESW*], 2 vols. (Moscow, 1961), i. 485.

[119] From now on I shall use Bolshevik terminology and distinguish between the 'socialist' lower phase and the 'communist' higher phase.

Marxisms and Bolshevisms

While these tensions continued to structure divisions within the Marxist movement, the nature of debate and the positions within it changed over time. In capitalist societies, Marxists mainly argued about when the revolution would take place, whether the communists should wait for economic forces or rely on the revolutionary energies of the proletariat, and how far the socialist élite should trust ordinary workers. After the revolution, however, a different set of questions faced the Bolsheviks as they thought about the type of socialist state and economy they were to establish, who was to rule and how.

Their views of how to organize socialist society were also affected by the specific circumstances of war. As Peter Holquist has argued, war gave rise to political practices—such as the use of state violence for political ends, the management of the economy, and the 'enlightenment' and surveillance of the population—which were underpinned by new, highly statist, assumptions about how best to administer Russia.[120] However, there were tensions within war-time political and economic strategies that could be seen in the context of old contradictions within Marxism. War-time mobilization involved an attempt by the state to employ all of a society's resources to achieve a common goal. It sought to unify state and society into a single, fused body, in which all existing bonds and hierarchies were superseded and each citizen was expected to show devotion to the state and its objectives. Yet states using mobilization had to resolve a tension between their attempts to create effective centralized institutions, and the desire to empower and enthuse the masses so that they might be willing to contribute fully to the state's campaigns.[121] And this tension was especially evident in

---

[120] P. Holquist, *Making War, Forging Revolution*. For the influence of the German war-time model of political and economic organization, see also T. Remington, *Building Socialism in Bolshevik Russia. Ideology and Industrial Organization, 1917–1921* (Pittsburgh, 1984), 14–17; E. Kingston–Mann, *In Search of the True West. Culture, Economics, and Problems of Economic Development* (Princeton, 1999), 160–1.

[121] See T. Remington, *Building Socialism*, 11–13; J. Horne, 'Mobilizing for Total War' in J. Horne (ed.), *State, Society and Mobilization in Europe during the First World War* (Cambridge, 1997), 1–2 . For a more abstract discussion of mobilization regimes, see D. Apter, 'The Mobilization System as a Modernization Prototype', in D. Apter, *The Politics of Modernization* (Chicago, 1967), 357–90. For comparisons between mass mobilization in Russia and western Europe, see S. Kotkin, 'Modern

Russia, where populist socialist values were particularly strong among sections of the working class and peasantry, and where the new regime pursued a policy of 'class struggle', relying on the support of previously subordinate groups rather than the whole of society.

Such contradictions were easily expressed within the framework of Marxism. Marx himself had not developed concrete plans for the post-revolutionary order, but his conception of socialism and how to reach it appeared to be relevant to contemporary problems. His attempts to reconcile participatory democracy with an integrated industrial economy seemed to address the war-time problem of combining popular participation with efficient centralization. And although he would not have thought that the mobilization regimes of the First World War resembled his 'socialism', it was not too implausible to see them as embryonic forms of the Marxist goal, which reduced the role of the market and sought to fuse state and society.[122] Pre-revolutionary debates about the relative role of economic forces and consciousness in history therefore re-emerged over the question of how quickly society could progress from a transitional order, in which many elements of liberalism and capitalism survived, to a wholly unified, non-market order. They also informed arguments about whether to use technocratic, 'scientific' methods in building the state and the economy, or whether to rely on the revolutionary energies of the working class, and influenced disputes over how best to motivate the population—whether to employ material incentives or moral incentives (that is inspiration and enthusiasm). Furthermore, divisions within Marxism over the qualities of the working class and its relationship with the revolutionary intelligentsia became conflicts over how extensive popular participation could be, and over the ideal relationship between officials and the population within the new state.

Hence different interpretations of Marxism became associated with contrasting ideas of legitimate authority and strategies of state-building and economic development. To return to the Weberian

Times. The Soviet Union and the Inter–war Conjuncture', *Kritika*, 2 (2001), 127–37; J. Horne (ed.), *State, Society and Mobilization*.

[122] As Remington puts it, in these regimes 'the reintegration of social and political authority occurred, not through the reabsorption by society of its own alienated power, as Marx had envisioned, but by the reverse process: the absorption of society by the state'. T. Remington, *Building Socialism*, 18.

framework, all action was legitimized according to a goal-oriented ideology, and everybody, at least formally, accepted the need to progress towards communism. Yet within that consensus several positions were possible, deriving from divisions between voluntarism and scientism (or 'politics' (*politika*) and 'technique' (*tekhnika*) in Bolshevik language), and élitism and non-élitism (or 'centralism' (*tsentralizm*) and 'democracy' (*demokratiia*)) on the other. The main conflict within Bolshevism lay between a voluntaristic, or 'charismatic' approach to politics and economics, which I shall call 'revivalist', and a more scientistic, Weberian 'rational' attitude, which I shall define as 'technicist'.[123] But within each approach there were further tensions: revivalists were divided between populists and élitists over the relations between élites and masses, and technicists were split between ultra-gradualist non-élitists, who were willing to tolerate the market and other features of the liberal order, and élitists, who were not.[124] In addition to these four positions, a fifth 'neo-traditionalist' position emerged within Bolshevism, which, in effect, departed from Marxism, as it involved abandoning the goal of transforming society into a fully egalitarian order. Rather, like Weber's 'traditional' form of domination, it was founded on the view that authority was to be held by members of a status group within a hierarchical estate society. In a Bolshevik context, the summit of this 'traditional' order was occupied by the 'proletarian' party élite.

[123] I have tried to use, as far as possible, terms derived from Bolshevik discourse. The term 'revival' (*ozhivlenie*) was commonly used to refer to the mobilization of the party, its ideological regeneration and purification, and its inculcation with a new revolutionary spirit. For the use of *ozhivlenie* in this context, see the Bukharin group's programme for the tenth party congress in 1921, *Desiatyi s"ezd RKP(b), mart 1921 goda. Stenograficheskii otchet* (Moscow, 1963), 826. The term also captures the vitalist language associated with this trend within Bolshevik ideology, its ambition to create activist socialist citizens, and its desire to summon up the revolutionary spirit of the past. The term is not intended to imply any comparisons with 'revivalism' in evangelical Christianity or other religions. The term 'technicist' derives from the Russian word '*tekhnika*', a term central to Bolshevik political language and used to refer to 'technology' and technical issues more broadly. Neologisms are, of course, best avoided, but the obvious alternative terms, 'left' and 'right', which were used during the period, are confusing when applied to the 1930s because they were frequently distorted in the polemics of the time. The terms 'voluntaristic' and 'scientistic', on the other hand, are too narrowly philosophical, and fail to capture the debate over the culture and behaviour of the new 'socialist man'.

[124] When using the term 'populist' to describe a variety of Bolshevism, I do not intend to suggest a comparison with the Russian 'Populists' (*narodniki*), who saw the peasantry as the class that would bring socialism.

Each of the five positions had its own analysis of the Marxist historical scheme, and could claim to provide solutions for a specific stage along the road to communism. And each had a particular view of the strategies and practices that had to be employed to reach the goal, how quickly it could be attained, the type of authority that was best able to achieve it, and what sort of people should have power. This last question was an especially important one in Bolshevik discourse, and Bolsheviks were especially concerned with the character of administrators, their 'style of leadership' (*stil' rukovodstva*), and their relationship with the 'masses'. Thus many disputes within Bolshevik politics became part of a more general conflict over political attitudes, behaviour and morality, over who the virtuous were and where the 'enemies' of socialism were to be found.

These positions are best seen as Weberian 'ideal types' that rarely existed in pure form. As will be seen, their content and influence changed over time, and there was considerable overlap between them, allowing Bolsheviks to combine them in various ways. Indeed, the 'dialectical' style of Bolshevik political thought encouraged Bolsheviks to deny the need to make choices between principles in tension with each other, and to argue instead over the balance between them. Also, while it is often possible to identify leaders' preferences for particular positions, they frequently changed their views. Even so, this framework does identify relatively coherent sets of ideas within Bolshevism, and therfore helps us to understand party debates more effectively. And while it is obviously abstract, it is not entirely artificial. Bolsheviks themselves frequently perceived political disputes in the context of tensions between these positions.

This framework also builds on other approaches, integrating their insights: it recognizes the existence of divisions over the relationship between élites and masses stressed by conflictualist historians, without exaggerating the similarities between Bolshevik and liberal conceptions of politics; it allows us to appreciate the importance of teleological ideas and disputes over whether to advance towards or retreat from the goal of communism, stressed by liberal historiography, while discussing the salience of issues other than the question of unity and disunity; and it gives due attention to the presence of Enlightenment, neo-traditionalist and quasi-religious discourses within Bolshevism.

At the core of revivalist Bolshevism was the assumption that proletarian consciousness was a vital force in history and politics, and that communism would emerge because men had the correct socialist, revolutionary attitudes. Revivalism's faith in the ability of men to alter history also gave it a more optimistic attitude towards change, and it urged rapid 'advance', away from capitalist individualistic and towards socialist, collectivist forms of organization; there was no need to wait until the economic conditions were ripe, and 'revolutionary' methods were to be applied to state-building and economic development. Its emphasis on the role played by socialist ideas, and its commitment to socialist methods of economic management, were closely connected with its assumption that economic success would best be achieved using non-material incentives. People would work most energetically if they had been psychologically transformed and mobilized, inspired by the ideas of socialism. As revivalists expressed it, *politika* and 'ideology' were to have priority over 'economics' and *tekhnika*; those who exaggerated the importance of *tekhnika* held back the advance to socialism by underestimating the power of socialist consciousness. Andrew Walder, a student of Chinese communism, has described this type of politics as 'ideological'.[125] Within the group committed to 'ideological' politics, ideological commitment is all. People are treated as 'bearers' of beliefs, and not only political opinion but every aspect of their private life and behaviour is expected to conform with them. Once in power, 'ideological' groups attempt to transform the whole of society, to create a 'virtuocracy', in which people are rewarded or punished according to politically defined criteria of virtue.[126]

As will be shown, revivalism placed an enormous emphasis on political attitudes and, sometimes, morality and virtue in all areas of life, regarding people as 'bearers' (*nositeli*) of particular values. The achievement of socialism required the indoctrination or, in Bolshevik language, ideological 'education' (*vospitanie*) of the population and the creation of a 'new man' who was self-sacrificing and enthusiastic about work, and was committed to socialism; conversely, it necessitated the expulsion or neutralization of the bearers of 'alien', dangerous ideas, who might undermine the commitment of others.

[125] A. Walder, *Communist Neo-Traditionalism*, 123–32.
[126] For the concept of 'virtuocracy', see S. Shirk, 'The Decline of Virtuocracy in China', in J. Watson (ed.), *Class and Social Stratification in Post-Revolution China* (Cambridge, 1984), 56–83.

Revivalism also often had a view of politics, and even of causation itself, that seems profoundly alien to anybody with a scientific world-view. When faced with obstacles on the path to socialism, revivalists tended to look for the causes in the influence of the bearers of hostile ideas and attitudes, rather than in objective circumstances. This view of the world could effectively be expressed using quasi-religious language, which was often employed during the period. If socialism, the collectivist heaven on earth, was to be created, men would have to be transformed into self-sacrificing, heroic, new men who 'believed' in socialism; those guilty of egotism, 'unbelief', or 'apostasy' had to be exposed, forced to confess, and recant.

Revivalist views could also be expressed using Romantic language, and underlying revivalism was an almost Romantic set of assumptions. Like most Bolsheviks after 1917, revivalists formally subscribed to Marx's rationalism. They argued that workers would become new socialist people once they had become 'conscious', using their reason to understand both the scientific laws that drove history, and their own interests in promoting revolution and building socialism. But, in insisting that men were driven by forces other than the material and rational self-interest, they often came close to a Romantic worldview, even if they did not justify it theoretically. And while revivalists never embraced irrationalism, as the Nazis did, they did use a similar Romantic language of 'will', 'energy' and 'spirit' to justify a strategy of mobilization and voluntarism. Revivalists certainly used Romantic language in their debates with their opponents. They accused them of exaggerating *tekhnika*, the material and the narrowly scientific, and condemned them for their 'philistinism' (*obyvatel'shchina*), 'narrow, unprincipled attitudes' (*deliachestvo*), and 'empiricism' (*empiritsizm*).[127] As has been seen, it was possible to find justifications for political Romanticism in Marx's own notion of the proletarian as the work-loving, creative being, but these ideas probably owed more to a broader 'Romantic anti-capitalist' tradition common among European intellectuals in the early twentieth century.[128]

---

[127] The term 'philistine' was a term commonly used in Marxist discourse to refer to insufficiently revolutionary, reformist socialists.

[128] This concept is commonly applied to right–wing German political thought. See J. Herf, *Reactionary Modernism*, 2, 230–1. For the presence of these ideas within early Soviet culture, see K. Clark, *Petersburg. Crucible of Cultural Revolution* (Cambridge, Mass., 1995), 15–23.

Revivalist ideas were not only associated with quasi-religious and Romantic discourses, but also with the political culture and practices of the party itself. The party was an organization that was supposed to lead the masses to communist consciousness. It therefore had an educational function, and a great deal of its activity involved propagating correct ideas among its own membership and the population as a whole. It was also concerned with maintaining ideological purity within its own ranks, and practices such as 'self-criticism' and the purge were designed to transform consciousness and exclude the 'alien'. At the same time, Bolsheviks often accepted that the party was to be run in a more 'comradely' and 'democratic' way than other organizations. Revivalists, and particularly populist revivalists, therefore frequently called for the 'revival' of the party and its domination of other institutions, as part of an attempt to transfer the ideal party culture and practices to other areas of society. Yet this is not to suggest that the party's culture generated a common revivalist world-view among all party members. As will be seen, there was no consensus among Bolsheviks as to what the party's role was to be and how it was to be run. The party had a managerial as well as an ideological function, and the revivalists' critics often argued that it should adopt a more technocratic style.

While all revivalists could agree on the central importance of consciousness, a crucial difficulty lay in their attempts to identify the sources of correct and dangerous attitudes. Following Marx, they associated ideas with class: socialist attitudes were proletarian; and anti-socialist ideas and habits were bourgeois.[129] Yet, like Marx, all Bolsheviks accepted that supposedly 'proletarian' virtues were not always to be found among actually existing proletarians and, even if they were, virtuous proletarians would not acquire a proper understanding of their place in history unless an élite guided them to a true proletarian consciousness. Even so, the relationship between the party and the working class remained ambiguous within Bolsheviks' thinking before and after 1917, and tensions between a more populist and a more élitist revivalism are evident throughout the inter-war period. For revivalists at the more populist end of the spectrum—most notably the Bolshevik left of the

---

[129] For this moralistic view of class within Bolshevism, see I. Halfin, *From Darkness to Light*, esp. 96–8.

revolutionary period—the working class had a high level of consciousness, even if a majority accepted that workers could not yet be
trusted to administer the state. Populist revivalists, therefore,
demanded an advance towards communism, but tended not to
demand full communism, calling only for a compromise between
élitist hierarchy and participatory democracy. The state, they argued, had to be centralized, but it had to be run in such a way that
workers were able to use their revolutionary 'energy' (*energiia*) and
'activism' (*aktivnost'*)—although only activism in the service of the
Bolshevik regime was acceptable; officials had to use a comradely
and solicitous style of leadership, which involved workers in decision-making without giving them control over it; and leaders were
not to rely on 'bourgeois' discipline, orders, and 'command
methods' (*komandovanie*). Populist revivalists were, in effect, advocating a populist form of mass mobilization, and their model of
society was perhaps closest to the small partisan military unit—a
force that had leaders but allowed rank-and-file members to take
initiative, within limits. So, while 'democracy' was central to the
message of the populist revivalists, it is important not to confuse the
term with liberal notions of democracy. Sometimes populist revivalists did, inconsistently, use liberal language, and implied that
workers had to be protected from the state. But they normally
followed Marx in refusing to defend any separation between the
individual or society and the state in principle. Their ultimate ideal
was the complete merging of state and society and the elimination
of any differences of interest.

More concretely, populist revivalists argued that such changes
could be achieved by 'proletarianizing' the bureaucracy. They
claimed that proletarians, as bearers of socialist values and ideology, were, in essence, energetic, self-sacrificing, collectivist, egalitarian, and morally pure figures, who responded well to comradely
authority relations with bosses when in a subordinate position, and
established them when in a position of responsibility. Their bourgeois counterparts, in contrast, had a selfish, utilitarian view of the
world: they had an authoritarian psychology, were predisposed to
create hierarchy, and were individualistic, corrupt, and luxury-lov-
ing; they were also sceptical of socialism, and of the abilities of the
mobilized masses to create a system fundamentally different from
capitalism—an attitude that was frequently denounced as 'rightist'.
Some populist revivalists also argued that proletarians had a special

understanding of science, and were free from conservative, bourgeois conceptions of what was scientifically possible; others denied that there was a proletarian science, but demanded that scientists take account of workers' 'practical' knowledge and 'experience'. Yet it was obviously more plausible for populist revivalists to see workers' most valuable quality as their innate love of work and revolutionary energy, rather than their mastery of science. Populist revivalists therefore tended to argue that only the proletarianization of the state would ensure success because it would allow proletarian energies to be released, while at the same time ensuring that officials would adopt socialist goals; in practice this meant that individuals defined as 'proletarian' according to a mixture of socio-economic and political criteria were to be promoted to official positions.[130] Meanwhile society, and particularly officialdom, had to be 'cleansed' of the bourgeoisie and those with bourgeois attitudes.

A more élitist revivalism, however, prevalent among some on the Bolshevik left and influential within the Stalinist leadership, was rather more sceptical of the virtues or 'maturity' of the working class.[131] Like populist revivalists, élitist revivalists maintained a voluntaristic attitude towards incentives and, more generally, to the forces of history: workers, properly enthused, would achieve extraordinary things; they could push history towards socialism through will-power; and apparently objective constraints on development as discovered by science could be overcome if the regime had the right policies and if officials and workers had the correct socialist attitudes. But they were generally hostile to attempts to 'democratize' relations between the leaders and masses or to apply concepts of class struggle to them, because they feared the divisiveness and disorder this might cause. They argued that an élite, using the state, had to organize workers and other producers; coercion would have to be used against those who would not be mobilized. They sometimes justified their élitism using the Marxist historical scheme: the time might be ripe for the end of the bourgeois order and the market, but the working class was not yet ready to rule and a rapid advance towards full communism was impractical. At other times they presented their conception of the state and economy as

---

[130] For the use of political and socio–economic criteria in definitions of class in the 1920s, see I. Halfin, *From Darkness to Light*, ch. 4.

[131] Remington similarly distinguishes between a 'technocratic left' and a 'democratic left' in the civil war period. See T. Remington, *Building Socialism*, 136–45.

close to the ideal. Their model of administration is perhaps best seen as a military one, but one closer to the well-organized, highly disciplined conventional army rather than the partisan group. An élite—a small group of intellectuals and politicians with the correct 'proletarian' attitudes, or of 'scientists' who understood a special dialectical and 'proletarian' science—would be the main driving force of progress. Élitist revivalists were often uncomfortable with the language of class and class struggle, and in the 1930s they sometimes claimed that class differences had been overcome and replaced with a unified 'nation' (although, as will be seen, it was difficult for Bolsheviks to mobilize the population on the basis of national identity). When they did use class language they sometimes did so in a different way from more populist revivalists. 'Proletarian' attitudes were associated less with an innate love of work and revolutionary energy and more with a proper understanding of 'science', by which was often meant a Marxist science that justified rapid advances towards socialism. Conversely, bourgeois attitudes were identified with scepticism of Marxist science rather than with the poor treatment of workers.

But while populist and élitist revivalists differed over their views of the working class, they still shared a common approach to politics, and there was often a significant overlap between the two positions. They both argued for the primacy of 'ideas' and for the need for ideological and cultural transformation, and they both favoured the mobilization of 'workers'. They both tended to use the language of class to identify friends and enemies, and often advocated the removal, or purging, of anybody imbued with 'bourgeois' or 'rightist' attitudes. These 'cleansings' were presented as a way of excluding those who might undermine the mobilization of the population for the struggle for communism, or as a step on the way to a wholly unified society. A variety of groups could be targeted, from peasants who refused to give up their 'petty-bourgeois' world-view, to doubting officials, and the campaigns against 'bourgeois' attitudes within officialdom, even when initiated by élitist revivalists, often had populist undertones. This was even true in the 1930s when the leadership was very cautious about promoting 'democracy' during its revivalist campaigns.

More significant, then, than the division between élitist and populist revivalism was that between revivalism and technicism, a variety of Bolshevism frequently denounced as 'rightist', and associated particularly with Bukharin and his group in the 1920s. Technicists, like élitist revivalists, were hostile to populist revivalists' belief in workers' maturity, but they were also sceptical of claims that, properly enthused, workers and officials could be motivated to perform extraordinary feats. Following a scientistic Marxism, they saw workers as self-interested, rational actors who would best be motivated by material incentives and discipline, not by enthusiasm or some special proletarian consciousness. More generally, they were unhappy with the élitist revivalists' voluntarism. They denied that political will could push society towards communism, and argued that the leadership had to base its policies on the requirements of science. According to the language of the time, *tekhnika* or 'economics' had to have priority over *politika*. They were therefore sceptical of the idea that development could be rapid and radical: a planned economy had to take account of objective constraints and allocate scarce resources in the most efficient way possible. Class and class consciousness, they insisted, were of less importance than the dictates of a class-neutral science, and they were hostile to disruptive forms of 'class struggle'. Sometimes they denied that culture and ideas were of any importance, and they were less concerned with ideological unity than revivalists. Even so, their position was often ambiguous. They may have underplayed the need for a transformation in the political consciousness of the population, but they did often have an implicit or explicit cultural agenda that diverged from the revivalist project: to imbue the population with a 'universal', class-neutral culture that would render them disciplined and productive workers, and to ensure that officials were technically able and 'business-like' ('*delovoi*');[132] they had little interest in forging a new, non-bourgeois culture. They also often had a particular view of class relations, even if they found it difficult to express it openly: they tended to favour those groups in society who had scientific expertise, such as the technical intelligentsia, and they were sceptical of measures to improve the status and influence of workers. Therefore, while all Bolsheviks accepted the view that the bourgeoisie could have a malign influence, technicists tended to stress the advantages brought by the bourgeoisie's

---

[132] The term '*delovoi*' ('business–like') was a positive version of the pejorative term '*deliacheskii*' (having 'utilitarian' or 'narrow–minded' attitudes, and without broader ideological perspectives). For this distinction, see *Slovar' sovremennogo russkogo literaturnogo iazyka* (Moscow–Leningrad, 1954), iii. 682–3, 686.

business-like spirit (*delovitost'*) rather than the ideological and psychological dangers it posed. Their 'enemy' was generally not the 'class alien' bourgeois specialist, but the poorly educated, the ill-disciplined, or the criminal.

Sometimes, technicists justified their model as close to the ultimate goal: the economy, like the state, was to be run as if it were a machine, operating like clockwork and in a state of equilibrium, governed by natural, scientific laws. Human will and consciousness could not transform them. Everybody had to act as a cog in the social and economic mechanism, obeying a set of rules defined as 'law'; there was no need to encourage workers to become heroes. At other times they followed Marx's historical scheme and accepted that their preferred model of society was only a second-best 'socialism'—the lower stage of communism—when people would still have to be paid for work and inequalities would remain. Only later, once economic and ideological conditions had changed fundamentally, would revivalist approaches be feasible. Either way, their preferred social model was closer to the large-scale modern industrial factory than the military unit.

Yet there was a tension between the technicists' insistence that the regime rely on a scientific assessment of objective reality, and their vision of an ideal order in which a unified state and society operated like a machine. Sometimes they were as committed to complete unity as the revivalists were, claiming that state and society had indeed fused, and could be run by experts from the centre. They were therefore calling for a form of economic mobilization, although their model was a much more technocratic and hierarchical one than that proposed by revivalists. But at other times they accepted that this fusion could not take place for some time to come. And a commitment to gradualism led some ultra-gradualist 'liberal' technicists to argue that a non-market form of socialism was too ambitious for Russia in its current state, and that the Bolsheviks needed to 'retreat' to a pre-socialist stage of development. Liberal technicists accepted that many elements of the liberal, bourgeois order had to survive: not only would 'bourgeois' authority relations and incentive structures have to be preserved but aspects of capitalism would also have to exist for a time. Russia was only on the threshold of socialism and the state was too weak to administer the whole economy. The market would therefore have to be permitted, particularly in the countryside, to integrate the urban and rural economies through trade, providing effective incentives for workers and peasants. The state, meanwhile, had to use law to protect productive capitalist groups, such as small-businessmen and small-holder peasants, from political interference and repression, and state officials had to learn 'trading' skills from them. Russia was not ready for any real steps towards the integration of state and society. Similarly, the regime had to allow intellectuals a degree of autonomy, because a unified socialist culture had not yet emerged. It is important, though, to recognize that liberal technicists never made a principled defence of the liberal idea that society had to be protected against the state. They all argued that liberalism and capitalism could gradually be abandoned as the state merged with society. The Bolsheviks were more hostile to liberal ideas than were most Marxists in western Europe, and liberal technicists never went as far as Bernstein did in reconciling themselves with liberal democracy. Even so, it is possible to find traces of a liberal technicism throughout the period, mainly in the thinking of Bukharin on the right, but also in the rhetoric of populist revivalist groups on the left. The left was uncomfortable using liberal ideas and could not defend them openly and consistently. But, as will be shown in Chapter 1, it sometimes found that law, as liberal technicists conceived of it, was much more effective than populist revivalist forms of 'democracy' in defending workers against a repressive 'proletarian' state.

It may have been difficult to justify liberal technicism within a Marxist framework, but it was possible. Neo-traditionalism, in contrast, contravened Marxist principles, and it should be seen as an amalgam of incoherently articulated attitudes towards authority relations, rather than as a consistent and legitimate ideological position. However, it has to be taken into account in any discussion of Soviet ideology, as elements of a neo-traditionalist worldview can be found in the discourse of some Bolsheviks, and they were also frequently identified as neo-traditionalist at the time. Neo-traditionalist attitudes were founded on the assumption that society consisted of a number of fixed status groups, or new Soviet 'estates'. One's position in this hierarchy depended on a mixture of immutable qualities—whether social background ('class origin') or nationality—and political loyalty to the regime. The loyal—the Soviet intelligentsia, the collectivized peasantry, the workers, loyal nationalities—were to live peacefully together as part of the new

Soviet order, although they had different roles in society and their legal status varied. Others, including potentially unreliable national minorities and the 'class aliens' or 'former people'—the bourgeois intelligentsia, petty-bourgeois 'traders', and kulaks—were 'hostile', or at least untrustworthy, and had to be excluded from society or policed. Membership of these groups was often seen as inherited, and for neo-traditionalists it was very difficult to overcome one's class or ethnic background. At the top of the hierarchy was the new party-state élite, an almost corporate status group which was seen as uniquely virtuous because of its proletarian class background and its past achievements in defending the revolution.[133] As in Weber's typical 'traditional' orders, loyalty to leaders was often seen as personal, and relations between bosses and their subordinates were often presented in familial, patriarchal terms.[134]

In practice, revivalist and neo-traditionalist attitudes towards class could have a great deal in common, as both were suspicious of non-proletarians. Yet neo-traditionalists had an essentialist approach to class, while revivalists, at least in principle, were most interested in class as an indicator of values. They therefore tended to reject the notion that a non-proletarian background necessarily brought with it anti-socialist attitudes, and were often critical of the pretensions of the proletarian party élite. The tension between revivalist and neo-traditionalist approaches to class became greater from the early 1930s. During the NEP period, when there were relatively free markets and when the Bolsheviks relied extensively on old-regime specialists, revivalists and neo-traditionalists could agree that people who had a 'bourgeois' economic position or social background posed a danger to the regime. But after collectivization and the promotion of proletarians to administrative positions, it was less clear that a bourgeoisie existed, and there were disagreements over whether those of bourgeois class origin were still a threat to the regime and its ambitions. Even so, revivalism could easily slip into neo-traditionalism, particularly at a time of crisis, when even revivalists accepted the need for pre-emptive persecutions of potential enemies, and agreed that it was quicker and easier to judge them

[133] See K. Jowitt, *New World Disorder*, 16–17, 140, for a discussion of the traditional status features of the party.

[134] For patriarchal attitudes towards authority, see, for instance, J. Brooks, *Thank You, Comrade Stalin!*, 83–9. See also A. Walder, *Communist Neo-traditionalism*, 130–2.

by their class or ethnic background rather than by their inner beliefs.

Bolshevik ideas and Soviet realities

Marxism-Leninism therefore inspired and justified different attitudes towards authority and legitimized a number of political and economic strategies. At the same time, however, ideology interacted with other structural factors to shape decision-making, among which were the demands of state-building and economic development in the Soviet Union, and the institutional architecture of Soviet politics. These were especially important because all leaders were committed to building a strong and wealthy state in a frequently threatening international environment, and because they sought power for themselves within a specific institutional framework. Leaders' decisions as to which position to adopt may have been affected by personal ideological preferences, but they could also be influenced by institutional interests, and by the changing perceptions and requirements of political and economic development. And each position could be useful in justifying plausible state-building strategies and particular interests. No single position gained supremacy during the period, partly because the ideology offered a number of different ways of legitimizing the Bolshevik party, and partly because no position could satisfy the objectives and interests of all within the élite.

The revivalist approach justified a strategy of popular mobilization, which could use popular enthusiasm to make up for low levels of education and poor infrastructure: just as unified armies and populations, committed to the cause of their country, could win wars, a mobilized people enthused by socialism could create a powerful state and economy. However, revivalist mobilization had serious drawbacks, because it challenged the position of the technically expert and was difficult to combine with a rationally planned economy. And populist versions of revivalism created even greater difficulties. While they promised a way of motivating potentially hostile and disaffected workers, and of putting pressure on officials through criticism from 'below', they were extraordinarily divisive and disruptive. The regime found it impossible to establish an effective, planned economy or a stable, authoritarian political system while it simultaneously challenged hierarchies throughout society. Élitist revivalist solutions provided an answer to this problem, by justifying the coercion of the disaffected, but at the risk of alienating them further.

Technicism had none of these disadvantages, as it justified a 'scientific', planned approach to economic and political development, implemented by a hierarchical bureaucracy. However, technicists did not show how a fragmented state could be integrated. Their claims that the state could be run as if it were a well-oiled machine, regulated by 'law' and without the need for aggressive interventions from the centre, failed to take account of the fact that it did not have the power or expertise to control the polity and the economy. Local bosses and managers found it easy to pursue their own interests, and technicists' insistence that objective realities be taken into account gave producers a justification for resisting the demands of the central leadership. The weak and poorly organized state apparatus did not have the information to calculate what the economy could deliver, and a purely 'scientific' approach gave the whip-hand to producers, whether factory managers or peasants, who did have the information. At the same time, the centre was unable to prevent the fragmentation of the polity into a number of bureaucratic interests and patronage networks. Indeed, the fusing of political and economic power allowed a great deal of opportunity for the 'corrupt' use of state resources for private purposes. Furthermore, the technicist strategy promised economic stability and predictability, not the rapid growth promised by revivalist mobilizers. Also, its relative lack of interest in the consciousness of the masses did not address the problem of how to create a society imbued with new socialist values.

Liberal technicists addressed some of these problems. By permitting the market to operate in some areas, they provided an effective set of incentives for producers (and in particular peasants). They also allowed the élite to integrate the fragmented Russian economy, linking town and countryside through trade: the market was a much more effective tool for co-ordinating the economy than the inefficient state. Yet liberal technicist strategies also had serious drawbacks. A reliance on agricultural development and market mechanisms was likely to generate only gradual growth. The market also exacerbated economic inequalities, and forced the regime to tolerate potentially anti-socialist, 'bourgeois' groups.

Perhaps most importantly, it was difficult to see how liberal technicist policies might promote the socialist society which was the
Bolsheviks' professed goal.

While these four strategies may all have had some advantages
for an élite whose objective was to build a modern, integrated
state, neo-traditionalist ideas justified strategies and practices that
undermined these goals. Even so, they were attractive to various
groups within the party. Unlike revivalist approaches to politics,
neo-traditionalist attitudes did not threaten existing authority, and
unlike their technicist counterparts, they offered an effective way
of legitimizing the regime and those who held power within it.
They could justify the view that party bosses were a ruling status
group, who could not be challenged, and had to be judged on the
basis of their class origin, loyalty and past service to the state, rather
than their political virtue or their technical abilities; they also
allowed regional leaders to style themselves as 'little Stalins', each
with their own hierarchy of clients below them. Furthermore, neo-
traditionalist notions of class origin and ethnicity as indicators of
political attitude could be used to justify strategies pursued by
influential officials. Party bosses could present themselves as virtuous proletarians who had to be given powers to suppress dangerous
class aliens.[135] And officials concerned with state security, such as
the secret police, could use neo-traditionalist arguments to justify
the persecution of 'enemies' on the basis of crude class and ethnic
categories, rather than making much more difficult judgements
about the ideological commitment of individuals. Yet the disadvantages for the leadership in accepting the neo-traditionalist approach
to politics are obvious. Rather than integrating the state and
society, it contributed to differentiation. And far from strengthening and centralizing the state, neo-traditionalism fragmented
it, allowing local bosses to usurp economic and political power.
The establishment of patron-client networks within the apparatus
also alienated many who were excluded from local bosses' patronage networks. More generally, these 'corrupt' practices could
undermine the legitimacy of the regime as a whole, particularly
among rank-and-file party members: neo-traditionalism clearly

---

[135] Studies of Chinese communism have noted officials' interest in defining class in
this way. See S. Shirk, 'The Decline of Virtuocracy', 64.

contradicted the Bolsheviks' claims that they were creating an egalitarian society free of all privilege.

These five positions, therefore, all had advantages and disadvantages for a Bolshevik leadership committed to building a strong state and economy. Yet Bolshevik leaders were not only motivated by the desire to enhance the power of the Soviet Union. Like all politicians, they also tried to increase their own influence and those of the institutions they led, and their institutional interests sometimes affected the position they took. So, while it would be simplistic to argue for a stable or straightforward relationship between the five positions and political and institutional interests, it is possible to identify some trends and patterns.

The power of political and economic institutions varied during this period. In the years after the revolution, the Bolsheviks had destroyed the old state structures but had not yet fully established new ones. Institutions were therefore weak, and often only gained influence when they had powerful leaders who were willing to use them to further their own personal interests. It was frequently not institutional interests that bound people together, but membership of patron-client groups; also, the role and functions of institutions, and their relations with other institutions, were not always clearly defined. So the Soviet Union was certainly not an institutionally pluralist system, in which coherent, autonomous bodies struggled for political influence. But institutions did have divergent interests, and political leaders can sometimes be found responding to the interests of particular influential institutions.[136] Given the new regime's commitment to state-led economic development, it is not surprising that some of the most powerful institutions to emerge after the revolution were the state organizations that ran industry—the trusts and the people's commissariats. They were by no means models of Weberian rational bureaucracy, but their leaders often found it useful to employ technicist arguments, which justified their control over the economy and their resistance to political intervention

---

[136] For the relationship between political leaders and institutions, stressing the weakness of institutions, see G. Gill, *The Origins of the Stalinist Political System* (Cambridge, 1990), 5–6, 324–5. For an example of political leaders adapting their political position to that of the institution they led, see S. Fitzpatrick, 'Ordzhonikidze's Takeover of Vesenkha: A Case–Study in Soviet Bureaucratic Politics', *SS*, 37 (1985), 153–72. Philip Roeder argues that political and economic institutions and the conflicts between them had become central to Soviet politics by the death of Stalin. See P. Roeder, *Red Sunset. The Failure of Soviet Politics* (Princeton, 1993).

by the party hierarchy. Technicism also helped them to defend an economic policy based on rational, fulfillable, targets, against voluntarist critics, and to protect themselves against threats from advocates of industrial 'democracy'.

One of the main rivals of these state organizations, from the early revolutionary years, was the party. The party, which had its own apparatus, parallel to the state's, sometimes competed with state economic organizations for influence, and often found populist and élitist revivalist Bolshevism useful in these struggles.[137] As has been seen, the party was a complex institution, and there were serious disagreements over its ideal character and role. However, it retained a distinct set of ideological functions, and there were good reasons for those who led party bureaucracies to justify their dominance over state officials by using the revivalist argument that ideas were central to politics, and that only a high level of ideological commitment would ensure the success of socialism.

However, another tension was probably to become more important than that between party and state: that within the party between the centre and powerful regional party bosses. By the mid-1930s the centre was putting much more pressure on regional bosses to ensure the fulfilment of plans, and they increasingly found themselves sharing interests with economic officials within their regions.[138] The central party leadership continued to use revivalist strategies to insist on high plan targets, while also occasionally using populist revivalist rhetoric to mobilize rank-and-file party members against local party bosses. At times the secret police, charged with rooting out dissent, also found revivalist ideas useful in their attempts to discipline regional officials. Regional bosses could therefore find revivalist strategies and arguments less appealing, and they sometimes preferred to legitimize their authority in neo-traditionalist terms. By presenting socialist society as a stable hierarchy with themselves near the summit, united against enemies defined by their class and ethnic origin, they could resist pressures from above and below.

The main actors in Soviet politics were Bolshevik élites, and all other groups soon lost most of the influence they had acquired

---

[137] For tensions between party and state at a local level in the 1930s, see Kotkin, *Magnetic Mountain*, ch. 7.

[138] For close relations between party and economic officials in the regions in the 1930s, see J. Harris, *The Great Urals. Regionalism and the Evolution of the Soviet System* (Ithaca, NY, 1999), 147 ff.

during the revolutionary period. However, tensions within the leadership were sometimes transmitted to broader sections of society, usually when populist revivalists attempted to appeal to groups outside the élite. There were, of course, differences between the thinking of Bolshevik élites and attitudes within the population as a whole, and the gap increased after 1917. But there had always been a certain congruence between Bolshevik populist revivalist discourses and the populist socialist discourses influential within urban popular opinion and the party rank and file.[139] And not only did some outside the élite respond to revivalist messages, but they sometimes interpreted them in ways more radical than those intended by the leadership.

Revivalism, class struggle, and terror

In explaining political behaviour, we obviously have to take account of changing circumstances, and we also need to examine the preferences and personalities of individual leaders, especially in a system in which leaders were of enormous importance. However, if we appreciate the ways in which ideology, interacting with other forces, structured and limited the strategies available to the leadership, it becomes easier to understand important aspects of Stalinist politics, and in particular the apparently irrational repressions of Soviet élites in the late 1920s and the late 1930s. Important elements of each campaign, I shall argue, can be seen as variations on the revivalist mobilization strategy, which remained remarkably appealing to some Bolshevik leaders during the period. Yet, despite its attractions, it was highly disruptive and difficult to sustain. A central objective of this book is to examine the development of revivalist ideas and strategies, and to explore leaders' responses to the problems they encountered in trying to implement them.

This is a study of the ideological context of politics. First, it attempts to provide a reassessment of the nature of debate within Bolshevism, and, in doing so, suggests that some conventional views of Marxism-Leninism are unhelpful. And second, it tries to show how

---

[139] For the power of official discourses among workers in the 1930s, see Kotkin, *Magnetic Mountain*, ch. 5; for rival discourses, see S. Davies, *Popular Opinion in Stalin's Russia. Terror, Propaganda and Dissent, 1934–1941* (Cambridge, 1997), 6–7.

an understanding of this ideological framework helps us to understand the strategies adopted by politicians and how they developed over time.[140] The main goal of the book is to understand the ideological context within which decisions were taken. In some cases it also suggests why leaders chose particular strategies at specific times, but it does so in a necessarily tentative way. It is always difficult to determine the precise role of various factors leading politicians to take individual decisions, and a broad study cannot analyse these issues in any detail.

The study addresses these issues through an examination of the statements of leaders and propagandists, using both archival and published sources, as well as the excellent secondary literature published in recent years. It has a broad scope, both in terms of its chronological coverage and its subject matter. Such an approach, I believe, helps us to contextualize Stalinist politics more effectively than would be possible in a narrower treatment, but I have inevitably had to sacrifice some depth, while focusing on particular periods and issues and discussing others in a more general and synthetic way, relying to a greater extent on the work of other scholars. At its centre is an analysis of those ideas and strategies which have been most difficult to understand: those of revivalism and revivalist mobilization. Therefore it concentrates on the campaigns of the late 1920s and second half of the 1930s, and the Terror of 1936–8 is explored in particular detail, while analysis of the period before 1928 is more general. It is primarily concerned with the thinking of the Bolshevik leadership, and while it suggests ways in which it was related to those of other groups within and outside the party, it cannot explore them in any detail. Moreover, it cannot pretend to be a comprehensive analysis of Bolshevik ideas and debate, but concentrates on a particular set of inter-related issues which were connected with the central questions of domestic politics: class, class culture, relations between leaders and 'masses' (especially the question of 'democracy' and 'bureaucratism'), the forces propelling society towards communism and the speed of the transition, incentives, economic strategy, and the role of the party. It also focuses on leaders' approaches towards those sections of the

---

[140] George Breslauer's studies of the post-Stalin leadership also examines its strategies, while taking ideas seriously. See, in particular, G. Breslauer, *Gorbachev and Yeltsin as Leaders* (Cambridge, 2002), ch. 1.

population regarded by the party as more receptive to socialist forms of politics, such as industrial and white-collar workers; it pays less attention to views of those seen as more 'backward', and so does not examine attitudes towards the peasantry or relations between Russians and non-Russian nationalities in any detail; nor does it deal with foreign relations.

This analysis of ideas and strategies suggests a rather different view of political developments in the period to some other approaches. Unlike some liberal interpretations, which present the inter-war period as one of cumulative totalitarianization, or conflictualist approaches, which posit a struggle between a true socialist or quasi-liberal Bolshevism, and a quasi-nationalist, statist Bolshevism, culminating in a fundamental ideological change at the beginning of the 1930s, this study suggests that we can discern both a zigzag pattern and more evolutionary change in the development of Bolshevik strategy over the period: the leadership launched variations on the populist revivalist strategy, and, when faced with their destabilizing effects, rejected them in favour of a more élitist politics of discipline and order, before returning to new forms of revivalism, modified in the light of experience.

The first two chapters examine the development of positions within Bolshevik politics and the debates surrounding them from the revolution to the Stalinist era. Chapter 1 shows how Lenin's uneasy synthesis of populist revivalism and a more élitist Bolshevism formulated before and during 1917 soon disintegrated as he was faced with the problem of establishing a functioning state and economy, and gave way to a combination of a much more élitist revivalism and technicism. It then examines how the left oppositions in the party responded, forging a moderate form of populist revivalism that was to lay the foundations for leftist Bolshevism in the future. As Chapter 2 argues, the division between revivalism and technicism crystallized during the NEP period in the conflict between the left and those later denounced as the 'right'. The leadership engaged in a pragmatic 'retreat' from the policies of the civil war period, adopting a combination of technicist and liberal technicist strategies, while populist and élitist revivalists forged an alliance against it in favour of 'class struggle' and an 'advance' towards socialism. During the second half of the 1920s the form of revivalism that was to have so much influence in the 1930s emerged.

Chapters 3–5 show how positions forged during the years after the revolution developed during the pre-war Stalinist era, and structured political debate and strategies. As Chapter 3 argues, at the end of the 1920s Stalin adopted an amalgam of the populist and élitist revivalist left's approaches to politics, and his revivalism was challenged from the 'right' by a group that defended a technicist approach to politics. Stalin's 'Great Break' (*velikii perelom*) led to the introduction of highly disruptive policies, all of which were part of recognizably revivalist strategies, with strong populist elements.

Chapter 4 shows how Stalin and the leadership increasingly appreciated how damaging these policies were to their authority. From the early 1930s hierarchy was restored, and populist revivalism again gave way to élitist revivalist, and increasingly technicist and liberal technicist strategies; at times, the leadership even seemed to be promoting an implicitly neo-traditionalist vision of society. Yet Stalin seems to have worried that the technicist and neo-traditionalist attitudes within the bureaucracy, which his own policies were encouraging, were inhibiting economic development and undermining his own power. As Chapter 5 argues, from 1934 to 1935 Stalin, probably responding to international pressures, intermittently adopted a more élitist version of the revivalist strategy of 1928–30, though it retained populist elements. The leadership was obsessed with security, and saw internal unity as vital if socialism were to be defended, but security campaigns were closely linked with revivalist strategies, designed to ensure that officialdom was purged of 'rightists' and 'unbelievers', and psychologically mobilized for the coming struggles against the foreign enemy. Yet what we call 'the Terror' was actually a complex series of initiatives. Predictably, revivalist campaigns escaped central control, and partly in response to fear of the resulting disorder, Stalin and the leadership directed terror against groups outside the bureaucratic apparatus. What began primarily as a violent version of a typical revivalist campaign aimed at officials became a series of mass repressions that affected all levels of society.

Victory and Fragmentation, 1917–1921

In October 1917, Lenin and the Bolsheviks came to power promising a radically new type of participatory democratic state based on the soviets, the elected workers' and soldiers' councils which had emerged in Russia since February. As Lenin wrote the following month:

Creative activity at the grass roots is the basic factor of the new public life. Let the workers set up workers' supervision [*kontrol'*] at their factories... Socialism cannot be decreed from above. Its spirit rejects the mechanical, bureaucratic approach; living, creative socialism is the product of the masses themselves.[1]

A great deal of this was rhetoric, but in the first few months after the revolution Lenin did take concrete measures to introduce a form of 'workers' control', or workers' supervision of management.[2] Yet by the April of 1918 Lenin's language and behaviour were very different. He now demanded that democracy be combined with '*iron* discipline while at work, with *unquestioning obedience* to the will of a single person, the soviet leader, while at work';[3] he also demanded 'a retreat from the principles of the [Paris] Commune'.[4]

---

[1] V. I. Lenin, *Polnoe sobranie sochinenii*, 5th edn. (Moscow, 1958–65) (henceforth *PSS*), xxxv. 57.

[2] *Dekrety sovetskoi vlasti*, Vol. 1, (Moscow, 1957), 77–85. The Russian word '*kontrol''* means supervision, rather than full 'control' over management, and Lenin was not proposing full worker self-management. He always accepted the need for central state authority over the economy and planning. For Lenin's views of workers' control, see S. Smith, *Red Petrograd. Revolution in the Factories, 1917–18* (Cambridge, 1983), ch. 9.

[3] Lenin, *PSS*, xxxvi. 203.

[4] Ibid., xxxvi. 180. Lenin was referring here to his decision to allow the bourgeois specialists to be paid more that the average worker, against the precedent of the Paris Commune.

Lenin's statements coincided with a general change in the direction of policy, towards centralization and hierarchy.[5] He now defended 'iron discipline' and the subordination of workers to their superiors; in the following period he also sanctioned the use of force against striking workers and mutinying sailors. The soviets were, by 1921, virtually powerless and a new, highly centralized party-state apparatus had taken their place. Yet this did not happen without considerable controversy within the Bolshevik party, and the years between 1917 and 1921 witnessed some of the fullest and most open discussions in the history of the Bolshevik regime. Lenin and the leadership were accused by many, particularly on the so-called 'left' of the party, of betraying the democratic ideals of Bolshevism and of creating a 'bureaucratic' regime, while the leadership, in turn, accused the left of being little more than a group of utopians. It was in these debates that the Bolsheviks, confronted with the question of how to create a socialist system, formulated positions that were to be the basis for future conflicts within the Bolshevik party.

Historians, however, have interpreted these debates in very different ways. According to the liberal view, Lenin believed that he was advancing towards communism. Despite his promises of 'democracy' in 1917, they argue, he had always intended to establish a repressive, statist system. The period should therefore be described as 'war *communist*', as the Bolsheviks believed that the authoritarian or 'totalitarian' system they were creating approached the ideological goal of full communism.[6] Others, however, have challenged this analysis from a more structuralist perspective. Lenin was not an ideological hard-liner, they have argued, but engaged in pragmatic

---

[5] For authoritarianism within party and state institutions, see, among others, R. Service, *The Bolshevik Party in Revolution, 1917–1923. A Study in Organizational Change* (London, 1979), 90–101, and *passim*; G. Gill, *The Origins of the Stalinist Political System*, 110; R. Sakwa, *Soviet Communists in Power. A Study of Moscow during the Civil War, 1918–1921* (London, 1988); for the regime's behaviour towards society, see V. Brovkin, *Behind the Front Lines in the Russian Civil War. Political Parties and Social Movements in Russia, 1918–1922* (Princeton, 1994), chs. 2, 4.

[6] For this school, see Paul C. Roberts, ' "War Communism": A Reexamination', *SR*, 29 (1970), 238–61; S. A. Pavliuchenkov, *Voennyi kommunizm v Rossii. Vlast' i massy* (Moscow, 1997); B. M. Patenaude, 'Peasants into Russians: The Utopian Essence of War Communism', *RR*, 54 (1995), 552–70; A. Walicki, *Marxism*, 376–7; M. Malia, *The Soviet Tragedy*, ch. 4. For similar interpretations in the Soviet Union during the NEP period, see Lev Kritsman, 'Geroicheskii period velikoi Russkoi revoliutsii', *VKA*, 9 (1924), 1–124.

retreat after a brief period of ideological ambition in 1917–18.[7] According to this interpretation, therefore, the left might be seen as impractical utopians, ignoring political realities during the civil war and hostile to Lenin's pragmatism.[8]

A conflictualist historiography, in contrast, identifies a conflict between different traditions of Bolshevism rather than one between ideological ambition and pragmatism. Authoritarian, statist Bolsheviks, it argues, confronted their less repressive comrades, although there is disagreement over who was on which side of the barricades. For some, the left of the party was the main opponent of authoritarian Bolshevism.[9] For others, however, leftists were the authoritarians and an embryonic right represented a form of Bolshevik liberalism.[10] Another account argues that the division between repressive 'hard-liners' and liberal moderates crossed the left-right divide, and Lenin vacillated between the two.[11]

How, then, should we analyse the debates of this period, and the positions taken by various wings of the Bolshevik party? It is perhaps understandable that observers should have found it so difficult to reach agreement, because divisions within the party were expressed in different ways and a number of debates continued concurrently. The main conflict during the period concerned the

---

[7] Lars Lih, writing largely on agrarian policy, is one of the main proponents of this view. See L. Lih, 'The Bolshevik Sowing Committees of 1920, Apotheosis of War Communism?', Carl Beck Papers in Russian and East European Studies, 803 (1990), 36–7. L. Lih, 'The Mystery of the ABC', SR, 56 (1997), 50–72. See also L. Siegelbaum, Soviet State and Society Between Revolutions, 1918–1929 (Cambridge, 1992), 63–6.

[8] Lih has not written about the debates between the left and the leadership. However, the view that the left was 'utopian' or impractical is well established. See, for instance, E. H. Carr, The Bolshevik Revolution, 1917–1923 (London, 1966), i. 203.

[9] See, for instance, R. Daniels, Conscience of the Revolution, 408–9. For a similar view of the anti-authoritarian nature of the Bolshevik left, see Sochor, Revolution and Culture, ch. 9; see also R. Service, The Bolshevik Party in Revolution, 210 for a positive evaluation of the Workers' Opposition's programme and S. Farber, Before Stalinism. The Rise and Fall of Soviet Democracy (Oxford, 1990), 176 for a similar, though more cautious, judgement.

[10] Marc Ferro argues Kamenev and Zinoviev constituted a group of 'Bolshevik democrats' in 1917. See M. Ferro, October 1917. A Social History of the Russian Revolution, trans. by Norman Stone (London, 1980), 211.

[11] For Vladimir Brovkin, a less-repressive moderate camp included the leftists N. Osinskii and V. Sapronov and the more right-leaning Kamenev and Rykov, while a more authoritarian hardline group included the leftist Mgeladze and supporters of Cheka interests. See V. Brovkin, Behind the Front Lines, ch. 1, esp. 50.

relationship between the regime and the working class. This was a critical issue at a time when the regime was fighting for its survival and was trying to maintain its legitimacy among the urban population, while also enforcing discipline. The left, which attempted to preserve some element of the populist revivalist promises of 1917, confronted Lenin and the majority of the leadership, who argued for a much more élitist order, combining élitist revivalist and technicist approaches. This division was sometimes expressed as a conflict between supporters of advance and proponents of retreat, although it was the left, not the Leninists, who were best able to present themselves as the 'advancers'. For the left, the regime could advance at least some way along the path towards full communism, when the hierarchies that were typical of bourgeois societies could be replaced by a new 'democratic' proletarian order. Lenin's and the leadership's response to this argument was contradictory: sometimes they accepted that élitism and hierarchy were elements of a bourgeois order, but they insisted that retreat had to be tolerated because the working class was not ready for 'democracy' or socialism. At other times they implied that the time would never be ripe for participatory democracy (although they never stated this explicitly); élitism and hierarchy, they suggested, had nothing to do with the bourgeoisie or with capitalism, but had to be accepted because science and objective economic realities demanded them; they were therefore inevitable whichever class was in control. Hence the debate was often less concerned with the question of advance and retreat than with the relative importance of objective economic forces and the ability of political will to change these realities, or, in the language of the time, the balance between *tekhnika* and *politika*. The related issue of class and class culture also became central. The left argued that the proletariat had a culture that was both inherently egalitarian and productive and could, if mobilized and treated in the right 'democratic' spirit, build a powerful socialist state. Meanwhile the leadership responded that only traditional methods of labour management would be effective, and workers had to absorb a class-neutral culture from those who had mastered it—the bourgeoisie.

These disputes, then, were not framed as a conflict over the relationship between state and society. It is possible to find the left using embryonically liberal arguments in its protests against Moscow's interference in the regions, yet it was very difficult for any

Bolshevik to employ them consistently. The left was therefore not a peculiar group of utopians, peripheral to Bolshevik politics; nor was it attacking Lenin from a liberal position. Rather, it was defensively trying to adapt Lenin's earlier populist revivalism and reconcile it with the recognition that the regime had to build an effective state. The difficulties in achieving this ultimately led to a split within the left, between ultra-populist fundamentalists and a more moderate group, which tried to combine populist revivalism with élitist elements.

Tensions also emerged within the leadership. All could agree that the proletariat was not ready for the transition to participatory democracy, and all accepted that hierarchy and the adoption of some form of 'bourgeois' culture of efficiency and expertise was vital. However, élitist revivalists and technicists disagreed over how rapidly the regime was to create the centralized and integrated regime characteristic of 'socialism'. Elitist revivalists sought a rapid transition to centralized political and economic structures, similar to those of a disciplined modern army. They insisted that if workers, led by an élite of knowledgeable and inspiring people, were 'militarized', mobilized, and sufficiently energetic, the regime could move rapidly towards socialism while retaining popular support—although there was to be no room for 'class struggle'. Technicists, in contrast, emphasized the need to move more cautiously, taking account of the poorly integrated, weak economic structure inherited from tsarism, and building a balanced system gradually. They also objected to revivalists' plans for labour mobilization. There was even talk of a retreat to the market in particularly 'backward' areas, such as the countryside, but here most technicist Bolsheviks drew the line, until they were forced to rethink in 1921.

The period was, then, one in which a multiplicity of splits emerged within the party—between technicists, élitist revivalists, fundamentalist and more moderate populist revivalists—and they became associated with personal and institutional conflicts, culminating in the complex dispute over the trade unions in 1920–1. Even so, by the end of the period the political spectrum had narrowed. Fundamentalist populist revivalism became less easy to defend within Bolshevism, and moderate leftists had forged a viable populist revivalism that was to have a great deal of influence in the future.

Russian Marxism and the Leninist synthesis, 1900–18

The tensions within Bolshevism can be traced back to the conflicts within Russian Marxism before 1917, and Lenin's attempts to resolve them. Commentators have been preoccupied with the question of how far Lenin's thought was faithful to the spirit of Marxism, and to what extent it constituted a peculiar 'Russianized', élitist Marxism.[12] But it becomes easier to understand Lenin if we avoid attempts to label him as either orthodox or heterodox, and rather examine his thinking both in the context of a highly ambiguous Marxist legacy, and the specific Russian conditions within which he was operating. Lenin, like Marx, Engels and their other followers, was trying to reconcile populist socialism with science and modernity, and he veered between scientism and voluntarism on the one hand, and between élitism and populism on the other. But he was doing so in a Russia which, unlike Germany, had a potentially revolutionary working class and peasantry, and where populist socialist ideas were much more prevalent. Hence, his response was likely to be very different from that of Kautsky and the 'orthodox' Marxists of the West, who were operating in very different conditions.[13] Ultimately, he found it very difficult to adhere to a fundamentally scientistic 'orthodoxy', while at the same time responding to Russian circumstances. He therefore led the Bolsheviks to power with a highly contradictory message that was to lay the foundations for many of the tensions within Bolshevism in future years.

Some of the conflicts that were to affect Russian Marxism and Bolshevism were present in Russian socialism before Marx's influence became significant. The question of the relationship between élites and masses in the revolutionary movement, or the reliability of the 'people' and the role of the revolutionary intelligentsia was central to the debates of the 1870s: 'Westernizers', such as Lavrov,

[12] For the view that Lenin is best understood in an orthodox Marxist context, see for instance, N. Harding, *Lenin's Political Thought. Theory and Practice in the Democratic and Socialist Revolutions* (London, 1983). For the view that he should be seen primarily in a specifically Russian context, see for instance, B. Wolfe, *Three Who Made a Revolution. A Biographical History* (New York, 1964), 160–2; T. Von Laue, *Why Lenin, Why Stalin?* (Philadelphia, 1964), 110.

[13] For the role of German circumstances (and particularly the absence of a revolutionary working class) in his thought, see D. Geary, *Karl Kautsky* (Manchester, 1987), ch. 7.

tended to stress the need for the peasantry to be educated by an élite before it would be ready for revolution, while their opponents, including Bakunin, had more faith in indigenous socialist traditions and the revolutionary nature of the peasantry.[14] Yet both sides agreed that the Western, capitalist form of development had to be avoided, and that Russia could travel a different path to a socialism based on the egalitarianism of the old peasant commune.[15] The claims of liberals, that the market, the break-up of older communal forms of organization, and the division of labour were all inevitable, were challenged, frequently on the grounds that society should not be based on objective, scientific economic laws but on moral principles. Mankind could create its own history.

Russian Marxism, as defended by its most influential interpreter, Georgii Plekhanov, challenged this form of socialism as excessively populist, voluntaristic, and utopian. Responding to the failure of attempts by revolutionary socialist groups to foment revolution among the peasantry, and to the stagnation of the Russian peasant economy, Plekhanov developed a Westernizing, scientistic, and élitist form of socialism. In contrast to those who insisted on the possibility of a socialist society founded on the principles of the egalitarian peasant commune—people he denounced as 'Populists' (narodniki)—he argued that Russia would have to endure a period of capitalist development before it could approach socialism; the peasant commune was backward and could not be the basis for the future industrial and proletarian socialist society. Plekhanov was importing a version of the scientistic and deterministic form of Marxism dominant in Karl Kautsky's German Social Democratic Party at the time.[16] Like Kautsky, he argued that socialism and revolution could not be forced, but would emerge as the consequence of objective laws of history that could be discovered scientifically. Yet Plekhanov's thinking still included several élitist and voluntaristic themes. He defended the role of human agency in history by arguing, like Engels, that although the 'forces of

---

[14] A. Walicki, Controversy, 36–9.

[15] For Russian socialist hostility to industrial development and capitalism, see N. K. Mikhailovskii, Polnoe sobranie sochinenii, 5th edn. (St Petersburg, 1911), i. 150; A. Vucinich, Social Thought, 30; Mendel, Dilemmas, 39. For later non-Marxist socialist views, more sympathetic to industrialization, see A. Walicki, Controversy, 107–31.

[16] For Kautsky's views, see G. Steenson, Karl Kautsky. However, as Walicki has argued, Kautsky's positivistic theory of history differed from Plekhanov's, which relied to a greater degree on Engels's Hegelianism. See A. Walicki, Marxism, 240.

production' 'in the last resort' determined the superstructure (or politics and ideas), they could also be affected by ideas.[17] And he also developed an élitist and voluntaristic interpretation of dialectical materialism.[18] History, he argued, could proceed in sudden 'leaps', and while it might be governed by objective scientific laws, mankind, by understanding these laws, could direct history.[19] Plekhanov was emphasizing the role of the proletariat's understanding of nature's laws, rather than its essential collectivist nature, in bringing about communism.[20] He was also stressing the importance of Marxist intellectuals, who understood the laws of history and would lead the proletariat towards a revolution against the autocracy (although they would only be able to establish a 'democratic' capitalist order, not socialism).[21]

Before 1914, Lenin's Marxism remained close to Plekhanov's 'orthodoxy', although he tended to take a more voluntaristic line than Plekhanov, and his position changed over time, particularly on the issue of the relationship between the intelligentsia and workers. He was closest to Plekhanov at the turn of the century, when he took his side both against non-Marxist populist socialists on the 'left', and against groups within Russian Marxism on the 'right', who, like Bernstein, were moving towards a non-élitist and scientific deterministic 'ultra-gradualist' line. Responding to setbacks and official repression, the *Rabochee Delo* and *Rabochaia Mysl'* groups, (the Economists as Lenin called them), argued that Marxists should concentrate on everyday economic struggles rather than grander political and revolutionary ambitions. It followed, they argued, that Social Democratic organizations had to be decentralized and run in a 'democratic' way, responsive to the demands of workers. Plekhanov and Lenin, predictably, criticized the Economists, first, for drifting too far towards scientific determinism, and second, for

---

[17] For an analysis of the inconsistency of Plekhanov's position, see L. Kolakowski, *Main Currents*, ii. 336–44; S. H. Baron, *Plekhanov. The Father of Russian Marxism* (Stanford, 1963), 291–3.

[18] For Plekhanov's voluntarism and his debt to Engels, see A. Walicki, *Marxism*, 238–9.

[19] G. V. Plekhanov, *Sochineniia*, ed. by D. Riazanov (Moscow, 1923–7), vii. 52; see S. H. Baron, *Plekhanov*, 291.

[20] G. V. Plekhanov, *Sochineniia*, vii. 160–2. For Plekhanov's theory of history, see J. White, *Karl Marx*, 147–8, 342–9; G. V. Plekhanov, *Selected Philosophical Works* (Moscow, 1977), 666–7.

[21] S. H. Baron, *Plekhanov*, 115–16.

adopting liberal attitudes towards 'democracy', thus ignoring the need for a high level of élitism within a party operating in a pre-revolutionary society. The Economists, they argued, underestimated the consciousness of the working class and were too pessimistic about the prospects of revolution; they were neglecting the role of the socialist intelligentsia in bringing socialist consciousness to workers who could not develop it without outside help; and in advocating 'democracy' among backward workers they would allow the emergence of non-socialist ideologies, rather than leading workers away from the bourgeoisie towards socialism.[22]

Lenin made all of these points in *What is to be Done?*, written in 1902, but he also developed an organizational solution to the problem of tsarist repression, by proposing a centralized party structure, effectively run and operating in secret. The 'democracy' within the party demanded by the Economists, he therefore argued, was impossible. Lenin's solution, in itself, did not amount to a principled voluntaristic and élitist alternative to Kautsky's and Plekhanov's orthodoxy, as many have argued.[23] Most Marxists believed that the intelligentsia had to bring consciousness to workers, and while Lenin stressed secrecy and conspiracy more than Plekhanov did, he did not, in general, challenge Kautskian orthodoxy. He justified his organizational model partly on the grounds that it was needed in the current repressive atmosphere, and partly using the language of science and modernity. The Economists, he claimed, were defending a 'handicraft' (*kustarnyi*) approach to party organization. More appropriate was the model of the centralized 'large factory', which was the 'highest form of capitalist co-operation' and would ensure proper worker discipline.[24] Party members had to be

---

[22] See, for instance, G. V. Plekhanov, *Sochineniia*, xii. 81, 101–2.

[23] The question of the 'orthodoxy' of *What is to be Done?* is a contentious one. The traditional, 'liberal' interpretation is that Lenin's theory of the vanguard party was a fundamental departure from orthodoxy towards a more voluntaristic and élitist 'Jacobin' Marxism. See, for instance, A. Walicki, *Marxism*, 294–300. For others, however, there were no significant differences between Kautsky or Plekhanov and Lenin on the question of the party. See N. Harding, *Lenin's Political Thought*, i. ch. 7; M. Donald, *Marxism and Revolution. Karl Kautsky and the Russian Marxists, 1900–1924* (New Haven, 1993), 29–31. Lars Lih goes even further and argues that Lenin had more faith in the proletariat and less in the intelligentsia than many other Marxists at the time. See L. Lih, 'How a Founding Document was Found, or One Hundred Years of Lenin's *What is to be Done?*', *Kritika*, 4 (2003), 17–19.

[24] Lenin, *PSS*, viii. 379. This quotation comes from *One Step Forward, Two Steps Back*, written in 1904.

both revolutionaries, committed to socialist ideas, and they had to be modern 'professionals'.[25] Any calls for 'democracy' within the party were a demand for a return to the 'primitive democracy' common in the early stages of the workers' movement, but inappropriate in modern societies.[26] And in entitling his work *What is to be Done?*, Lenin indicated the influence of Chernyshevskii's utopian novel of the same name, implying that he was following in the tradition of the 'enlightener' Russian socialists and demanding that a Westernizing socialist élite bring progress to Russia.[27]

As a whole, then, *What is to be Done?* was not initially controversial among the Social Democratic mainstream. Even so, Lenin's ideas did differ in some respects from those of Plekhanov and Kautsky, and his views were more voluntaristic and élitist than theirs. First, Lenin indicated his commitment to political action by describing his party vanguard as one of professional revolutionaries; Kautsky and Plekhanov, in contrast, tended to see them as a group of Marxist scientists. Second, Lenin departed from Kautsky and Plekhanov in promulgating his famous thesis, that the working class, left to itself, would generate non-socialist, and therefore 'bourgeois', consciousness; only the socialist intelligentsia could bring socialist consciousness to it.[28] While Lenin cited Kautsky in support of his formula, Kautsky's ideas were rather less élitist: he assumed that the proletariat was intrinsically socialist in a primitive way, even without the intelligentsia; the intelligentsia did bring 'socialist consciousness' to the proletariat, but by this he meant that it would offer them an awareness of scientific theory, not a socialist class consciousness.[29] So Lenin was unorthodox in proposing his famous ultra-élitist formula, and he did take a more élitist approach than Plekhanov during this period, but it is unlikely that he was expressing a fundamental loss of faith in the working class, or that he was trying to revise Marxist theory and establish a new élitist version.[30] As Robert Mayer has argued, the formula was not

---

[25] Lenin, *PSS*, vi. 171, 99–100.

[26] Ibid., v. 142–3.

[27] For Chernyshevskii's influence on Lenin, see C. Ingerflom, *Le Citoyen Impossible*, esp. 241–52.

[28] Lenin, *PSS*, vi. 39–40.

[29] For this point, see A. Walicki, *Marxism*, 298–9.

[30] 'Liberal' historians, in arguing that Lenin was developing a principled élitism, exaggerate the significance of Lenin's formula, because they fail to appreciate distinctions within Marxist thought between different forms of 'democracy'. They

repeated by Lenin subsequently, and is best seen in the context of the debates against 'Economism', as an overstatement of a commonly held view.[31]

The differences between Lenin's ideas and the Kautsky–Plekhanov view of the intelligentsia were not important when both sides were united against the Economists,[32] but they became more significant once the Economists had been defeated and renewed conflict broke out within Russian Social Democracy in 1903–4 between the Bolshevik and Menshevik factions. In many ways this dispute echoed the earlier Economist controversy, although the Mensheviks and Bolsheviks were much closer to each other than the Economists and the party majority had been.[33] While both Mensheviks and Bolsheviks accepted the need for a centralized party, and recognized the role of both historical laws and revolutionary activity in historical development, the Mensheviks defended a more moderate version of the Economists ultra-gradualism against Lenin's more voluntaristic and élitist position. Initially, the debate concerned élite-worker relations: Lenin insisted that the party remain exclusive and made up of only committed revolutionaries, while the Mensheviks, who were to be joined by Plekhanov, had a slightly more relaxed view of the membership rules, and were, in principle, happier to admit ordinary workers. But, as during the Economism debates, disputes over party organization were closely associated with differences over the proximity of revolution: Lenin was more optimistic about its chances, and demanded an ideologically committed party to take advantage of it, while the Mensheviks had a more gradualist approach and were therefore prepared to give membership to those workers who were not so 'advanced'.[34]

---

are thus unable to explain why Lenin moved towards a much more 'democratic' approach to party organization in 1905–6. In *What is to be Done?*, Lenin (supported by populist voluntarists such as Bogdanov) was largely criticizing the Economists' ultra-gradualist liberal conceptions of 'democracy', while in 1905–6 he believed that the time had come for a greater degree of populist and voluntaristic 'democracy'.

[31] See R. Mayer, 'The Status of a Classic Text: Lenin's *What is to be Done?* after 1902', *History of European Ideas*, 22 (1996), 307–20. A. A. Bogdanov, among others, believed that this was the case. See ibid., 315.

[32] L. Lih, 'How a Founding Document was Found', 12–20.

[33] For Lenin's comparison between the Mensheviks and 'Economists', see Lenin, *PSS*, viii. 243.

[34] For a similar view of the differences between Bolshevism and Menshevism, see I. Halfin, *From Darkness to Light*, 177–8.

The differences between Lenin's more voluntaristic position and the gradualism of Plekhanov and many Mensheviks became sharper during the 1905–6 revolution. But now that workers were demonstrating a revolutionary consciousness, the nature of the debate changed, as Lenin could advocate a more populist position, while accusing Plekhanov of élitism and of ignoring the demands of the proletariat. Lenin still insisted on the need for party leadership, but he now believed that the proletariat, in alliance with the peasantry, could participate in a successful revolution against the autocracy, and establish a 'democratic' capitalist order. He also defended a less hierarchical, more 'democratic', party structure.[35] At the same time, he distanced himself from élitist scientism by arguing that workers could achieve consciousness through revolutionary experience, not just through knowledge of theory.[36] In contrast, Plekhanov (unlike many other Mensheviks) continued to insist on the need for an alliance with the bourgeoisie and condemned Lenin's 'revolutionary adventurism'.[37] Even so, Lenin was careful not to go as far as some in the direction of voluntarism and, unlike the more populist and voluntaristic Trotsky, he did not accept that the revolution could set itself socialist goals in the near future.[38]

Lenin's break with the Mensheviks led him to seek new friends, and his move towards populist voluntarism led him to find an ally in Plekhanov's main ideological rival within Russian Marxism: Aleksandr Bogdanov. In contrast with Plekhanov's generally scientistic and élitist Marxism, and the Economists ultra-gradualist version, Bogdanov formulated a much more populist and voluntaristic approach. For Bogdanov, Marxists had to embark on the establishment of a new egalitarian and collectivist society. Hierarchy, modern capitalist organization, and the rigid specialization brought about by the modern division of labour were relics of bourgeois culture and had to be overcome in the near future.[39]

---

[35] Lenin, *PSS*, xi. 168–71. For Lenin's views during the 1905 revolution, see N. Harding, *Lenin's Political Thought*, 1, 213–48.

[36] For Lenin's views on this subject, see N. Harding, *Lenin's Political Thought*, 1, 242–5.

[37] S. H. Baron, *Plekhanov*, 275. For Kautsky's views, see M. Donald, *Marxism and Revolution*, 78–82.

[38] Although for the argument that Lenin's and Trotsky's views were more similar than this suggests, see M. Donald, *Marxism and Revolution*, 87–93.

[39] See A. Vucinich, *Social Thought in Tsarist Russia*, 224; Z. Sochor, *Revolution and Culture. The Bogdanov-Lenin Controversy* (Ithaca, NY, 1988), 134–40.

But how was Bogdanov's collectivism to be reconciled with the demands of modernity and science? Unlike populist socialists, Bogdanov did not use the moralistic argument that the proletariat's innate virtues would create a virtuous society. As a Marxist, he accepted that socialism had to be compatible with modernity, and indeed he placed enormous faith in science. But he insisted that science and modernity had to be radically transformed into a new 'proletarian', collectivist version. For Bogdanov, classes became dominant when their organizational abilities were superior to those of their rivals.[40] The proletariat, he argued, had a particular advantage in the struggle between classes because its experience of collaborative labour in factories had given it a collectivist and egalitarian consciousness. And in the industrial world collectivism was rational. The proletariat would therefore develop a new 'proletarian culture' and 'proletarian science' that would be much more successful than their bourgeois predecessors.[41] Workers would combine their love of work and their superior scientific abilities to master nature, creating 'new forces of labour and knowledge'.[42] Their special consciousness would enable them to create a communist society, which was both wholly egalitarian and united ('a single society with a single ideology') and extraordinarily productive and dynamic.[43] Bogdanov used Darwinist biological language to describe this unity, describing society as an 'organism', evolving and adapting to master nature in the most effective way.[44]

Bogdanov, like Lenin and Plekhanov, and all Marxists, did not believe that socialism would emerge immediately, or that all hierarchies could be dissolved forthwith. He denied that the working class was ready for socialism and insisted that a socialist intelligentsia had to guide it.[45] But he had more faith in the existing proletariat

---

[40] A. A. Bogdanov, *Empiriomonizm. Stat'i po filosofii* (Moscow, 1905), iii. 85–9.

[41] A. A. Bogdanov, 'Sotsializm v nastoiashchem', (1910), in A. A. Bogdanov, *Voprosy sotsializma* (Moscow, 1990),102; A. A. Bogdanov, 'Nauka i proletariat' (1913), in Bogdanov, *O proletarskoi kul'ture, 1904–1924* (Moscow, 1924), 222–30. For Bogdanov's views of 'proletarian ideology', see Bogdanov, *Empiriomonizm*, iii. 128–30.

[42] A. Bogdanoff, *A Short Course of Economic Science* (London, 1923), 386–7, 389.

[43] A. A. Bogdanov, *Empiriomonizm*, iii. 139.

[44] A. A. Bogdanov, 'Sobiranie cheloveka', *Pravda*, April 1904, 167–8.

[45] For an analysis of Bogdanov's thinking that stresses his élitist attitude towards relations between intellectuals and workers, see J. E. Marot, 'Alexander Bogdanov, *Vpered* and the Role of the Intellectual in the Workers' Movement', *RR*, 49 (1990), 241–64. See also R. C. Williams, *The Other Bolsheviks. Lenin and his Critics, 1904–1914* (Bloomington, 1986), 149.

than Plekhanov, Lenin, and most Russian Marxists. He also found conventional 'bourgeois' forms of organization, both within society and the party, less appealing than they did. He argued that the main task of socialist parties was the development of the socialist culture which would lay the foundations of the future society, and that this could only be achieved by promoting the non-hierarchical culture of socialism within the party itself; as he explained, 'the conscious-comradely organization of the working class in the present and the socialist organization of the whole of society in the future— these are different moments of one and the same process...'.[46] While Bogdanov accepted the need for a party and party discipline, he argued that it was to be organized in a 'democratic' way; the socialist intelligentsia was to engage in non-disciplinarian forms of 'agitation', 'propaganda', and 'education' (*vospitanie*).[47]

Bogdanov justified his emphasis on the transformative power of culture and consciousness by arguing that the superstructure—culture and ideas—did not merely reflect the material base, as the ultra-scientistic or 'mechanist' Marxists might argue, but interacted with it, organizing and creating it. He developed an epistemology that denied the difference between mind and matter and saw both as elements of one fundamental category: human 'experience'.[48] There was, for Bogdanov, no objective external reality independent of human experience, and there could be no eternal truths.[49] It is therefore not surprising that Bogdanov was accused, by more scientistic Marxists like Lenin, of 'idealism' and denying the primacy of the material.[50] Bogdanov's argument that an intelligentsia élite of organizers would create socialism by developing the workers' innate collectivism also appeared to justify a voluntaristic approach to politics.[51] For Bogdanov, the success of the transition to socialism

---

[46] A. A. Bogdanov, 'Sotsializm v nastoiashchem', 100–1.

[47] Z. Sochor, *Revolution and Culture*, 28, 34–5. For Bogdanov's views of *vospitanie*, see A. A. Bogdanov, 'Ideal vospitaniia' (1918), in A. A. Bogdanov, *O proletarskoi kul'ture*. 231–7. For differences between Lenin and Bogdanov on the issue of education and agitation, see Marot, 'Alexander Bogdanov', 257–9.

[48] For Bogdanov's philosophy, see K. M. Jensen, *Beyond Marx and Mach. Aleksandr Bogdanov's Philosophy of Living Experience* (Dordrecht, 1978), ch. 4; G. Wetter, *Der Dialektische Materializmus* (Freiburg, 1952), 102–10.

[49] A. A. Bogdanov, *Empiriomonizm*, iii. 1, 36.

[50] Bogdanov denied this, although for a defence of these charges, see D. Bakhurst, *Consciousness and Revolution in Soviet Philosophy. From the Bolsheviks to Evald Ilyenkov* (Cambridge, 1991), 102–6.

[51] For this point, see L. Kolakowski, *Main Currents*, ii. 440–1.

depended primarily on the population's adoption of a particular set of 'proletarian' attitudes and behaviour, and its rejection of the 'bourgeois' outlook.

Bogdanov was not alone in his collectivism, his belief in the ability of the proletariat to establish a new society very soon, his stress on ideas and culture, and his objection to mechanistic views of the world. Those associated with his *Vpered* (Forward) group within the Bolshevik party—most notably Anatolii Lunacharskii—shared them, as did the writer Maksim Gorky, although they were more willing than him to resort to explicitly Romantic, moralistic, and voluntaristic arguments, and they were denounced as 'God-builders' in consequence. Lunacharskii and Gorky saw Marxism as an ethical system, or even a 'religion' without God, which would inspire the working class, transforming it from the existing working class to the ideal Marxist proletariat—self-sacrificing and collectivist. Lunacharskii argued that the new socialist 'religion' would inspire workers, directing emotions and creating powerful 'energies' that would give the proletariat almost divine powers and overcome obstacles created by nature.[52] Gorky sympathized with this desire to create a new religion and set of myths that would inspire the *narod* to transform society.[53] But, as a novelist and playwright who had previously had associations with Russian populist socialism, he expressed this idealism and religiosity in the form of a more conventional literary Romanticism rather than Marxist philosophy. His writings were full of Romantic and populist socialist themes. The '*narod*', he declared, was 'the inexhaustible source of energy, alone able to transform all possibilities into the necessary, all dreams into reality... ';[54] the 'life of humanity' was 'creativity, the aspiration to victory over the resistance of dead material, the desire to master all of its secrets and compel its forces to serve the will of people for the sake of their happiness'. Ranged against the creative popular collective was 'individualism', and its embodiment, the petty-bourgeois

---

[52] A. V. Lunacharskii, *Religiia i sotsializm* (St Petersburg, 1908), 363.

[53] For Gorky's 'God-building', see T. Yedlin, *Maxim Gorky. A Political Biography* (Westport, Conn., 1999), 86–8. See also R. C. Williams, *The Other Bolsheviks*, ch. 3. For the influence of Nietzsche on Gorky, see E. W. Clowes, 'Gorky, Nietzsche and God-Building', in N. Luker (ed.), *Fifty Years On. Gorky and his Time* (Nottingham, 1987), 127–144.

[54] M. Gorky, *Sobranie sochinenii v tridtsati tomakh* (Moscow, 1953), xxiv. 5 (1908).

philistine (*meshchanin*) of the modern capitalist world.[55] Philistines, as a result of depravity, 'degeneration', and overindulgence in the good things of life, became disillusioned cynics, who did not believe in ideals, or the will to achieve them; in turn they corrupted others.[56]

As Robert Williams has argued, the *Vpered* group was influenced by the revolutionary syndicalism of Georges Sorel, the French radical thinker, who saw socialism as a new set of values that would inspire the proletariat to perform great deeds of revolutionary heroism.[57] Melding Nietzsche and Marx, Sorel believed that, with the help of a new set of socialist myths, workers would develop a quasi-military, vitalist 'proletarian spirit', characterized by 'energy' and collectivism.[58] And, as among the revolutionary syndicalists of the West, during and after 1905 this voluntarism was combined with a commitment to revolutionary activism.[59] According to the syndicalists, workers were to have nothing to do with the egotistical bourgeoisie, but were to engage in direct revolutionary action themselves. At a time of revolutionary optimism in 1905, it is understandable that these ideas were appealing to Marxists. Calls for a general strike and workers' seizures of factories were particularly common in the *Vpered* circle, and within the Bolshevik party more generally, in 1906–7.[60]

In 1905–6 Lenin sympathized with the '*Vpered*ists' faith in the revolutionary energy of the working class, but he always had a more

---

[55] On 'collectivism', see Gorky, *Sobranie sochinenii*, xxiv. 30 (1909).

[56] Gorky, *Sobranie sochinenii*, xxiv. 8, 11. See also Gorky's play, *Meshchane*, on the subject of 'philistinism'. M. Gorky, *Meshchane* (Moscow, 1950).

[57] R. C. Williams, *The Other Bolsheviks*, ch. 5; R. C. Williams, 'Collective Immortality: The Syndicalist Origins of the Proletarian Culture, 1905–1910', *SR*, 39 (1980), 389–402. See also Kharkhordin, *The Collective and the Individual*, 80 ff.

[58] For the influence of Nietzsche on the *Vpered* group, see A. L. Tait, 'Lunacharsky—A Nietzschean Marxist?', in B. Rosenthal, *Nietzsche in Russia* (Princeton, 1986), 275–96; M. Agursky, 'The Nietzschean Roots of Stalinist Culture', in B. Rosenthal (ed.), *Nietzsche in Soviet Culture. Ally and Adversary* (Cambridge 1994), 256–61, B. Rosenthal, *New Myth, New World. From Nietzsche to Stalinism* (University Park, 2002), ch. 3.

[59] For Sorel and the syndicalists, see Z. Sternhell, *Neither Left nor Right. Fascist Ideology in France* (Princeton, 1986), 66–79.

[60] See R. C. Williams, ' "Collective Immortality" ', 394–6. James C. McClelland, 'Utopianism versus Revolutionary Heroism in Bolshevik Policy. The Proletarian Culture Debate', *SR*, 30 (1971), 409. Although after 1909 Bogdanov became more pessimistic about the cultural level of workers, and he did not believe that workers were ready to take power in 1917. See J. E. Marot, 'Alexander Bogdanov', 249–56.

élitist and scientistic approach to Marxism than they did.[61] While he did call for a 'democratization' of the party, it is unlikely that he ever accepted their vision of a party organized in a 'comradely' way and run by 'democratic' educators of the working class; their views certainly contrasted with Lenin's idea of the party as a disciplined, modern organization primarily concerned with seizing political power.[62] But, more importantly, Lenin never accepted the *Vpered* group's fundamental voluntaristic and 'idealist' revision of Plekhanov's and Kautsky's scientistic Marxism. During the revolutionary wave, these tensions remained hidden, but they came out into the open when it had subsided.[63] In 1907 Lenin decided that the Bolsheviks had to accept realities and participate in parliamentary politics, while Bogdanov and others in the *Vpered* group took a much more radical line on issues of political strategy and maintained their old faith in the likelihood of a new revolutionary upsurge. Lenin therefore now found his main enemies on the *Vpere-dist* 'left' rather than the Menshevik 'right', and from this time he began to express his hostility to what he saw as the 'idealism' of the Bogdanov group. In 1908 he mounted a strong attack on Bogdanov's epistemology in his *Materialism and Empiriocriticism*, in which he condemned the Bogdanov group for denying the objective existence of the material world. But he went even further than Plekhanov did in asserting the primacy of matter. Plekhanov was a 'monist', in that he argued that the mental and the material were part of a single unity; the mental affected the material and vice

---

[61] There is disagreement over the relationship between Lenin and Bogdanov. Some argue that Bogdanov defended proletarian autonomy against Lenin's party élitism. See Z. Sochor, 'On Intellectuals and the New Class', *RR*, 49 (1990), 283–92. Others have argued that there was no fundamental difference between Lenin and Bogdanov on the issue of the relationship between the intelligentsia and workers. See J. E. Marot, 'Alexander Bogdanov', 241–64; I. Halfin, *From Darkness to Light*, 178–85. The position taken here lies between these two poles. Lenin and Bogdanov did differ over relations between élites and workers, but they were differences of degree: both denied that the working class could achieve consciousness without the intelligentsia. More serious, though, were philosophical differences on the issue of scientism and voluntarism.

[62] For tensions between Lenin and Bogdanov on the issue of 'democracy' and the relations between the socialist intelligentsia and workers after 1906, see R. C. Williams, *The Other Bolsheviks*, 156–7; Z. Sochor, 'On Intellectuals and the New Class', 285. For a different view, which stresses similarities between Lenin and Bogdanov on these issues, see J. E. Marot, 'Alexander Bogdanov', 241–64; I. Halfin, *From Darkness to Light*, 178–85.

[63] J. White, *Lenin. The Practice and Theory of Revolution*, 68–70.

versa. For Lenin, the mental was a product of the material, and the material was primary.[64]

These debates had an impact on Social Democrats throughout the Russian empire, and Iosif Stalin, then in Georgia, developed his own idiosyncratic response. Outwardly, following the split with the Mensheviks, he generally supported Lenin; he also agreed with him in essentials over philosophical issues in the debate with Bogdanov, insisting that the external world was objectively real and knowable. However, as a monist, his position was closer to Plekhanov's than Lenin's.[65] There is also evidence that he sympathized with some of Bogdanov's political views, and at times he adopted a more populist socialist view of politics than did Lenin.[66] In 1905–6 he celebrated violence against the aristocracy in bloodthirsty language, championing the power of 'the masses' and 'the street'.[67] He sympathized with Bogdanov's insistence in 1907 that Bolsheviks refuse to collaborate with liberals by boycotting the duma, though he accepted the line of Lenin and the party majority from July 1907 onwards.[68] There is also some evidence that he, at times, supported Bogdanov's view that the party leadership should be proletarianized.[69] His conception of the party was also close to the thinking of the *Vpered* group in stressing the role of ideas; it certainly differed from both Lenin's and Plekhanov's. While Lenin in *What is to be Done?* emphasized the party's modern, efficient organization, Stalin stressed the importance of ideological unity and commitment. Like Lenin, Stalin denounced pre-modern, traditional forms of organization: the days when the party had been a 'hospitable patriarchal family' willing to take on all sympathizers had to come to an end.

---

[64] Lenin, *PSS*, xviii. 53–4.

[65] For Stalin's views in this debate, and his debt to Plekhanov, see E. Van Ree, 'Stalin as a Marxist Philosopher', 265–77.

[66] R. C. Williams, *The Other Bolsheviks*, 119–23. See also R. Himmer, 'On the Origin and Significance of the Name "Stalin" ', *RR*, 45 (1986), 269–86; E. Van Ree, 'Stalin's Organic Theory of the Party', 52. Stalin's library, collected after 1917, included five copies of Bogdanov's *Kratkii kurs ekonomicheskoi nauki*, and Bogdanov's views were popular in the Caucasus in this period. See RGASPI 558/3/13, 14, 15, 16, 17.

[67] RGASPI 71/10/169, 189–90 (25 June 1905); 71/10/193, 109 (12 July 1906). For this period in Stalin's life, see E. Van Ree, 'Stalin's Bolshevism, the First Decade', *International Review of Social History*, 39 (1994), 368–70.

[68] E. Van Ree, 'Stalin's Bolshevism', 370–2.

[69] Stalin, *Sochineniia*, ii. 152–3. Though Van Ree does not see this as part of a consistent 'workerist' position. See E. Van Ree, 'Stalin's Bolshevism', 372–3.

But his alternative model of organization was not the modern factory run by 'professionals'. The party, he explained in 1905, was a 'proletarian army' defined by its intense commitment to an ideology; as he explained, 'once the unity of views collapses, the party collapses'. It was not enough for party members merely to accept the party programme superficially: to give membership to 'windbags' who formally accepted the programme but were not really committed, amounted to the 'desecration of the holy of holies of the party'. The party also had to defend itself against the ideological assault of the autocracy, which was trying to 'corrupt the consciousness of the proletariat' with a whole host of dangerous ideologies—' "trade-unionism", nationalism and clericalism'; the party therefore had to be a 'fortress', 'vigilant' against alien ideas. The gates were only to be open to those who had been 'tested'.[70] Stalin's arguments that socialism could only be achieved by a wholly united collective committed to a single ideology had something in common with the *Vpered* group's emphasis on ideas and collectivism and, as Erik Van Ree has argued, Stalin used Bogdanov's organicist language, describing the party as a 'complex organism'.[71] Many of the themes and language used in this period can be found in his later writings and speeches: the anxiety about ideological contamination by alien forces, the use of organicist metaphors, and a preference for a combination of military and religious terminology which was to become a common feature of his discourse.[72]

From mid-1907, Stalin's flirtation with the Bolshevik left was over, and by the middle of 1909 Lenin had defeated those who had called for the boycott of the duma. But, from 1912, free of enemies of the 'left', Lenin himself moved towards a more voluntaristic and populist position, responding to renewed strike activity and an increasing conviction that international capitalism was in crisis. The outbreak of war led him to reconsider his theoretical framework more fundamentally, and to move again towards voluntarism and populism. Before 1914, Lenin, despite a tendency to take a more voluntaristic view of politics, never strayed too far from Plekhanov's and Kautsky's Marxism. But during the war he finally broke with Kautsky, and by 1917 he had adopted a much more voluntaristic position than he

---

[70] Stalin, *Sochineniia*, i. 64–7.
[71] Ibid., i. 66. E. Van Ree, 'Stalin's Organic Theory of the Party', 43–57.
[72] For instance, in 1923 he compared the party with the German medieval military order of 'sword-bearers', Stalin, *Sochineniia*, v. 71.

had before, demanding an immediate advance towards socialism, not just a 'democratic' revolution leading to the bourgeois, capitalist phase, as he had during 1905. Even so, he insisted that he was remaining true to the scientistic view that only changes in the material 'base' could deliver socialism. As a result, the tensions between scientism and voluntarism within his thought became much greater than they had been before the war.

The outbreak of war was central to Lenin's radicalization. The war, for Lenin, showed the final bankruptcy of capitalism, demonstrating the end of the bourgeoisie as a progressive force. Capitalism had reached a new, militaristic and 'imperialist' stage, and it was on the verge of being destroyed by war, and by revolutionary pressure in the periphery, where it was weakest.[73] At the same time the war illustrated the 'opportunism' of Kautsky and the German party, who had supported war credits, and emboldened him in his departure from 'orthodox' Marxism. But the war, Lenin believed, also laid the foundations for socialism within Russia. As Lenin argued, the political economy of war-time mobilization both encouraged the radicalization of the population and the centralization of the economy, thus creating the preconditions for a socialist order. The longer the war lasted, the 'more governments themselves develop and must develop the *aktivnost*' of the masses, calling upon them to make extraordinary effort and self-sacrifice'.[74]

At the same time Lenin developed a more radical philosophical position as a foundation for his politics. In 1914 he worked on a new rebuttal of Bogdanov's thought, based on a Marxism that was less crudely materialistic than the philosophy of *Materialism and Empiriocriticism*.[75] He read a great deal of Hegel and began to adopt a more dialectical approach to the relationship between consciousness and matter, arguing in his unpublished *Philosophical Notebooks* that '... man's consciousness not only reflects the objective world, but creates it'.[76] He now denounced Plekhanov as a 'vulgar materialist'.[77] He also departed from *Materialism and Empiriocriticism* in applying Hegelian dialectics to nature, arguing

---

[73] For the fundamental changes in Lenin's thinking during the war, see N. Harding, *Lenin's Political Thought*, ii. 41–70.

[74] Lenin, *PSS*, xxvi. 220 (end of May to first half of June 1915).

[75] For this project, see J. White, *Lenin*, 89–90.

[76] He wrote this in his notes on Hegel's *Science of Logic*. Lenin, *PSS*, xxix. 194.

[77] Lenin, *PSS*, xxxviii. 277.

that change took the form of revolutionary leaps in both nature and politics.[78] Lenin was thus able to justify a more revolutionary politics, while at the same time rejecting Bogdanov's philosophical position.[79]

So when, in 1917, workers and peasants mounted a second revolutionary challenge to the autocracy, Lenin's theoretical reevaluations allowed him to go much further in welcoming the populist socialist demands of many workers and peasants than he had been prepared to do in 1905. As the revolution unfolded, Lenin enunciated a populist and voluntaristic faith in the consciousness of the working class and its ability to seize power and establish some form of socialism. His rhetoric owed a great deal to the Russian populist socialist tradition, and his treatment of class was often moralistic in tone, presenting the conflict between classes as one between a virtuous working 'people' and an alliance of the evil, greedy bourgeoisie and the bureaucracy. In 1917, for instance, he contrasted the masses who were 'devoted to the socialist state for ideological reasons' with bureaucrats who worked 'for the sake of a fat sum received on the 20th of each month'.[80]

Yet Lenin combined his new interest in the power of ideas with a more scientistic view of the forces driving history. He only called for an advance towards socialism once he had convinced himself that the economic forces had laid the foundations for it. Lenin was strongly influenced by Rudolf Hilferding's thesis that capitalism had reached a new phase, in which production had become highly concentrated and centralized into a few trusts and syndicates under the auspices of banks. This system of 'finance capitalism', he argued, had created the foundations for the social, collective control of the economy.[81] His observations on the German economy during the war, where planning appeared to be replacing market relations, and where the state was involved in the distribution of goods, the direction of labour, and the administration of industry, confirmed his belief in the ability of all states, including Russia, to plan the

---

[78] Ibid., xxix. 256, 317. For differences between *Materialism and Empiriocriticism* and the *Philosophical Notebooks*, see N. Harding, *Leninism* (Basingstoke, 1996), 220–39.

[79] Bogdanov was critical of the Hegelian, dialectical tradition in Marxist philosophy and placed much more emphasis on 'equilibrium' than contradiction. For his interpretation of dialectics, see Z. Sochor, *Revolution and Culture*, 48–9.

[80] Lenin, *PSS*, xxxiv. 313.

[81] For Hilferding's influence, see N. Harding, *Lenin's Political Thought*, ii. 53.

economy.[82] Lenin's assessment of Russia's level of economic development was undoubtedly over-optimistic, but implicit within his thinking were economic deterministic assumptions: socialism had to evolve from capitalism and could not be forced by will alone.

Lenin's vision of the future politics and economics of socialism was made up of a similar combination of voluntaristic and scientistic elements, although populist and voluntaristic sentiments temporarily predominated. His essay on the future society, *State and Revolution*, written in August 1917, was generally populist and voluntaristic in tone. The proletariat, he argued, was ready to smash the old bourgeois state and create a new state, the Dictatorship of the Proletariat, which would lead Russia towards socialism. The Dictatorship of the Proletariat would act to destroy the bourgeoisie, but within the Dictatorship, among proletarians, a direct, participatory democracy would operate along the lines of the Paris Commune. In contrast with liberal systems, democracy would not be limited to the election of deputies every few years. Rather, everybody in positions of responsibility in the 'commune-state', from deputies to civil servants, would be subjected to continuous control by the people; deputies could be recalled at any time and the bourgeois principle of the 'separation of powers', between elected deputies and an unelected civil service, would be abolished; a set of institutions staffed by elected delegates would deal with all aspects of government, executive and legislative.[83] In the economy, also, it would soon be possible for the 'whole of the armed population' to exercise 'supervision (*kontrol'*)' over and 'keep account' of production, distribution, and labour.[84] Managers and technical specialists would also be supervised by the workforce. Lenin was not calling for anarchism: his state would be a modern centralized polity, not the decentralized order favoured by Bakunin.[85] But he was assuming that workers would be so 'conscious' that they could run the

[82] See, for instance, Lenin, *PSS*, xxxi. 355. Shortly after the October Revolution Lenin asked Iurii Larin to investigate the German system of labour conscription, which he hoped would be a model for Russia. Lenin was also influenced by Iurii Larin's studies of the German war economy. Iu. Larin, *Gosudarstvennyi kapitalizm voennogo vremeni v Germanii (1914–1918 gg.)* (Moscow, 1928), 8. For the influence of the German example, see T. Remington, *Building Socialism in Bolshevik Russia*, 82.

[83] Lenin, *PSS*, xxxiii. 109.

[84] This would be possible, Lenin claimed, once the population was fully literate and 'trained and disciplined' by capitalism. Ibid., xxxiii. 100–1.

[85] Ibid., xxxiii. 53.

state as a unified class. During the transitional period after the revolution and before full communism, the state would become identical with the people, the separation between state and society would disappear and the state would wither away. As Lenin explained, it would be possible to

suppress the exploiters even with a very simple [state] 'machine', almost without a 'machine', without a special apparatus, by the simple organization of the armed people ... as simply and readily as any crowd of civilized people, even in modern society, interferes to put a stop to a scuffle or prevent a woman from being assaulted.[86]

Lenin, then, was expressing a high level of optimism about the proletariat's level of unity, and he also expressed the belief, evident in some of Marx's more populist and voluntaristic works, that workers would become extraordinarily productive if they were able to work for themselves, rather than for an alien power set above them:

The conscientious, bold, universal move to hand over administrative work to proletarians and semi-proletarians will, however, raise such unprecedented revolutionary enthusiasm among the people, will so multiply the people's productive forces in combatting distress, that much that seemed impossible to our narrow, old, bureaucratic forces will become possible for the millions, who will *begin to work for themselves* and not for the capitalists, the gentry, the bureaucrats, and not out of fear of punishment.[87]

At the same time, however, Lenin revealed his doubts about the ability of the working class to fulfil this role, and exposed his continuing élitism and scientism. Like Marx, he insisted that following the socialist revolution workers would only be approaching the first stage of communist society, 'socialism', and not full communism. Elements of capitalist society would still operate, including material incentives and hierarchies based on expertise. Everybody, therefore, would be paid according to the work they performed. To suggest that workers could be trusted to work without discipline imposed from above would be 'utopian'; as he explained:

We are not utopians, we do not 'dream' of dispensing *at once* with all administration, with all subordination ... No, we want the socialist

---

[86] This would be possible, Lenin claimed, once the population was fully literate and 'trained and disciplined' by capitalism. Ibid., xxxiii. 91.

[87] Ibid., xxxiv. 317 (November 1917).

revolution with people as they are now, with people who cannot dispense with subordination, supervision and 'foremen and accountants'.[88]

The state would have to exist until men were fully conscious; as Lenin put it, 'the bourgeois state, without the bourgeoisie' would have to enforce bourgeois 'right' to make sure that people were rewarded according to the work they performed.[89] The old bourgeois technical specialists would also have to be given authority over inexpert workers.[90] Only at a later stage of development, Lenin implied, would a majority of members of society 'have learned to administer the state *themselves*'.[91] Then socialism would give way to full communism and the state wither away.

Lenin was therefore simultaneously asserting that the people could be trusted to create a participatory democracy immediately after the revolution, and that they could not be trusted for some time. Yet, if they were not ready, who would run the state in the interim and how would the majority be taught how to administer the state? Lenin was evasive on this issue, and clearly did not want to address the question explicitly. Any response would have forced him to admit that the new state would be similar to the old type of state, the only difference being that it would be run by a proletarian minority rather than a bourgeois minority. Instead he obfuscated, presenting the creation of a participatory democracy as the result of an inevitable process of uncertain duration.[92]

Lenin's vagueness on the question of how far Russia could advance towards participatory democracy was matched by his failure to clarify how far the regime could go in introducing socialism in the economy. Lenin consistently advocated the abolition of market relations, but he declared that it was utopian to suggest that full socialism was feasible and that the state could immediately run the economy itself. There was to be no large-scale nationalization of the economy; rather, he implied, there was to be a mixture of nationalization and state supervision, the precise nature of which was left unclear.[93]

Lenin's writings of 1917 on the socialist future are, therefore, marked by a profound tension between populist voluntarism and élitist scientism. He was generally optimistic that socialism could be

[88] Ibid., xxxiii. 49 (*Gosudarstvoi revoliutsiia*).   [89] Ibid., xxxiii. 99.
[90] Ibid., xxxiii. 100–1.   [91] Ibid., xxxiii. 102.   [92] Ibid., xxxiii. 49.
[93] For Lenin's thinking on economic policy, see ibid., xxxi. 168; ibid., xxxii. 313; R. Service, *Lenin, A Political Life*. Vol. 2: *Worlds in Collision* (Basingstoke, 1991), 234.

achieved very soon by a responsible, revolutionary proletariat—a belief that was to become the core of the populist revivalism of the Bolshevik left. But he occasionally undermined it with a recognition that the dictates of science and expertise would have to be taken into account, and that technical experts would have to have a great deal of power in the new state—the basis of Bolshevik technicism. *State and Revolution* therefore justified two of the most influential positions within Bolshevism over the next few years. But the third, élitist revivalism, was largely absent from the text. Lenin said little about the role of the politically conscious vanguard party under socialism in *State and Revolution*. However, he did hint at its importance soon after coming to power in November 1917. In response to critics who accused him of utopianism, he admitted that the whole population was not yet ready for state administration; in the meantime 'class-conscious workers and soldiers' would train them, although this group would then begin 'at once' to 'expand' into a 'militia embracing the whole people'. Lenin also made a distinction between 'leadership', which could be entrusted to the 'class conscious workers', and more routine 'administration', which could be done by the 'vast mass' of working people.[94]

The tensions between the populist and élitist elements of Lenin's programme became evident very soon after the Bolsheviks came to power. Lenin and Bolsheviks at the centre tried to interpret 'workers' control' in a more centralist way, while workers in the localities asserted a more populist version. The outcome, the Decree on Workers' Control, was an ambiguous compromise. It established a centralized economic organization, the Supreme Council of the National Economy (Vesenkha), while at the same time granting factory committees extensive powers.[95] Even so, Lenin continued to defend the notion of 'workers' control' and insisted that it could be reconciled with centralized economic administration.[96] This view seems to have been based on the assumption, evident in his statements during this period, that workers were fundamentally responsible, collectivist, and 'conscious'.[97] So, in his work, *How to*

---

[94] Lenin, *PSS*, xxxiv. 316.

[95] Lenin, *PSS*, xxxv. 30–1; Iu. Akhapkin (ed.), *First Decrees of Soviet Power* (London, 1970), 36–8.

[96] Lenin, *PSS*, xxxiv. 320. The Factory Committees had a similar view. See S. Smith, *Red Petrograd*, 198.

[97] For Lenin's optimism, see N. Harding, *Lenin's Political Thought*, ii. 183–6.

Organize Emulation, of December 1917, he attacked the 'disgusting prejudice' that only the 'rich' could administer the state. 'Untapped talent', 'bold initiative', and 'revolutionary enthusiasm' could be found among workers and peasants, which had been stifled by capitalism; under the new order these energies could be released.[98] Lenin admitted that not all workers were perfect. There were 'parasites', or lazy and irresponsible workers, many of them from the countryside, who could not be trusted to work for themselves without external coercion;[99] there were also others who, under capitalism, had acquired the habit of trying to avoid work because they had seen labour as equivalent to slavery.[100] However, Lenin declared that 'all the class-conscious, honest and thinking peasants and working people' would fight against these old non-proletarian influences and that they would disappear of their own accord.[101]

While expressing his faith in the collectivist and selfless virtues of the working classes, Lenin condemned the vices of the bourgeois which, he argued, prevented them from running the economy effectively. The bourgeois were not only exploiters who 'robbed' and 'insulted the people', depriving them of their dignity and 'human character'; they also displayed 'slovenliness, carelessness, untidiness, lack of punctuality, nervous haste, the tendency to re-place action with discussion, work with talk ...'. Lenin, as an orthodox Marxist who rejected all concepts of morality in principle, was quick to point out that he was not making a moral judgement: these qualities did not arise from their 'bad nature, even less from their evil will'. Rather they were the product of their conditions of life in bourgeois society, including the 'abnormal separation of mental and manual labour'.[102] Yet Lenin's message was still an implicitly moral one: he was still suggesting that a productive and ultra-democratic socialism could emerge because the proletariat had a particular set of qualities or virtues, and that the bourgeoisie was unable to create this desirable system because it lacked the right psychology. So, although Lenin accepted that workers would have to rely on the 'advice' of bourgeois specialists and experts, he insisted that such groups be carefully supervised using a system of 'workers' control'; moreover, he insisted that some former bourgeois

---

[98] Lenin, *PSS*, xxxv. 195-200 ('Kak organizovat' sorevnovanie').
[99] Ibid., xxxv. 196.   [100] Ibid., xxxv. 200-1.
[101] Ibid., xxxv. 199.   [102] Ibid., xxxv. 201-2.

were 'enemies of the people' and a 'war to the death' had to be fought against them.[103]

In using a moral language, Lenin was appealing to a fundamentally moral critique of capitalism that was popular among sections of the working class. As studies of working-class attitudes have shown, much working-class radicalism displayed the moralism and egalitarianism evident in populist socialist rhetoric.[104] The discourses used by workers were multiple and overlapping. Some used one of universal citizens' rights to challenge a traditional world of status and *soslovie* that excluded and humiliated them.[105] All citizens, they argued, had the right to be treated as dignified human beings.[106] Their criticism of managers, technical specialists, and foremen was therefore based on a hostility to 'tyrants' who refused to treat workers with respect, to 'respect the humanity in each human being', who regarded them as 'machines' and 'animals'.[107] At the same time, however, a more exclusivist, class-based approach to politics is evident.[108] Many workers, and particularly skilled workers, saw themselves as a unique group and developed a particular lifestyle and morality, based on values of puritanism, self-discipline, and heroism.[109] They believed that they were ranged against the forces of reaction—the 'bourgeoisie'—a class that had no economic function but was merely parasitical, extracting resources from the real producers, the workers, and imposing an immoral, hierarchical

---

[103] Lenin, PSS, xxxv. 202, 200.

[104] This is not the place for a detailed discussion of working-class political attitudes. For useful treatments, see particularly M. Steinberg, *Voices of Revolution, 1917* (New Haven, 2001), 1–35; O. Figes and B. Kolonitskii, *Interpreting the Russian Revolution. The Language and Symbols of 1917* (New Haven, 1999), ch. 4; Tim McDaniel, *Autocracy, Capitalism and Revolution in Russia* (Berkeley, 1988). See also Mark D. Steinberg, *Moral Communities. The Culture of Class Relations in the Russian Printing Industry, 1867–1907* (Berkeley, 1992); Reginald E. Zelnik, *Labor and Society in Tsarist Russia: The Factory Workers of St Petersburg, 1855–1870* (Stanford, 1971).

[105] For this language of rights and its relation to class, see S. A. Smith, 'Workers and Civil Rights in Tsarist Russia, 1899–1917', in O. Crisp and L. Edmondson (eds.), *Civil Rights in Imperial Russia* (Oxford, 1989),145–69; O. Figes and B. Kolonitskii, *Interpreting the Russian Revolution*, 114–21.

[106] M. D. Steinberg, *Moral Communities*, 114–16.

[107] Ibid., 234–5. See also S. Smith, 'Workers and Supervisors: St Petersburg, 1905–1917 and Shanghai, 1895–1927', *Past and Present*, 39 (1993), 131–77.

[108] O. Figes and B. Kolonitskii, *Interpreting the Russian Revolution*, 107–13.

[109] T. McDaniel, *Autocracy*, 200–3.

order.[110] They saw themselves as participants in the struggle for 'democracy' (*demokratiia*), a term that was not used not only to refer to a political system, but to a particular group of the population—the 'people' (*narod*) or the 'lower classes' (*nizy*).[111] The new 'democratic' system would thus enshrine the rule of the people and would be founded on workers' egalitarian morality.[112]

During 1917, then, Lenin was able to forge a set of ideas that had a real popular resonance by emphasizing the populist and voluntaristic elements within Marxism, and using the language of Russian populist socialism. At the same time, by promising that participatory democracy and the struggle against the 'bourgeoisie' and 'bureaucracy' could be united with centralization and economic efficiency, Lenin appeared to provide a solution to Russia's problems and gave him the confidence to mobilize supporters and take the initiative. However, close reading of Lenin's statements in 1917 suggests that he himself understood the tensions within his vision, even though he did not feel compelled to explore them. In the months after the revolution, the synthesis crafted by Lenin in 1917 was to unravel.

Lenin's 'new course' of March–April 1918: the rejection of populist revivalism

Lenin's populist revivalist vision would have been difficult, if not impossible, to implement even had he not been confronted with civil war and economic collapse. He had inherited a Russia with a poorly integrated economy, a weak central state, and a population with a strong populist socialist political culture. Lenin's claim that the polity and economy had become a coherent and integrated 'machine', easily controllable by a united workforce, was evidently false, and the new regime soon found that it did not have the

---

[110] For images of the bourgeoisie, see B. Kolonitskii, 'Antibourgeois propaganda and anti-"burzhui" consciousness in 1917', *RR*, 53 (1997), 183–96; Figes and Kolonitskii, *Interpreting the Russian Revolution*, 107–13. For views of the parasitical role of the bourgeoisie in the economy, see T. McDaniel, *Autocracy*, 326.

[111] For the meaning of *demokratiia*, see O. Figes and B. Kolonitskii, *Interpreting the Russian Revolution*, 121–6.

[112] For the irrelevance of Marxist ideas of economic exploitation among Russian workers, see S. Smith, 'Workers against Foremen', in L. Siegelbaum and R. G. Suny (eds.), *Making Workers Soviet. Power, Class and Identity* (Ithaca, NY, 1994), 136–7.

organization or authority to control Russia. The notion that local and central institutions of the workers' state would easily reach consensus proved to be utopian, and factory committees, local soviets, and central institutions frequently came into conflict.[113] Relations between the regime and the population also deteriorated, and the expectation that workers and poor peasants, once they saw a workers' government in power, would automatically obey the centre, was evidently unrealistic. Many workers may have recognized the need for an integrated economy under the control of the state, but, in practice, labour discipline collapsed, and many workers continued to pursue a 'class struggle' against managers and specialists.[114] As Bolsheviks tried to impose control, often by force, workers came to see them as they had seen the old authorities: as repressive 'bureaucrats'. From the spring of 1918, the Mensheviks and Socialist Revolutionaries won majorities in increasing numbers of soviets, ousting Bolsheviks who had been victorious in the autumn of 1917.[115] Soldiers similarly resisted the regime's attempts to reduce the powers of their committees and to strengthen the authority of their hated tsarist officers.[116] The peasantry was, if anything, even more unwilling to do the regime's bidding and surrender their grain for low prices. Peasants came to regard the Bolsheviks as they had seen tsarist officials and landowners: as evil outsiders, who had no right to their grain.[117]

[113] For these conflicts, see S. Malle, *The Economic Organization of War Communism, 1918–1921* (Cambridge, 1985), 104–7; M. McAuley, *Bread and Justice. State and Society in Petrograd, 1917–1922* (Oxford, 1991), ch. 8. For the constitutional conflict over centre–local relations, see E. H. Carr, *The Bolshevik Revolution, 1917–1923* (Harmondsworth, 1973), i. 139–44.

[114] For the role of tensions between workers and specialists in undermining labour discipline, see W. J. Chase, *Workers, Society and the Soviet State. Labor and Life in Moscow, 1918–1929* (Urbana and Chicago, 1990), 35–6; K. Bailes, *Technology and Society under Lenin and Stalin: Origins of the Soviet Technical Intelligentsia, 1917–1941* (Princeton, 1978), 52–65. For the economic problems caused by 'workers' control', see A. G. Shliapnikov, 'The Conditions of the Railways under Workers' Control', in J. Bunyan and H. Fischer (eds.), *The Bolshevik Revolution, 1917–1918* (London, 1962), 654 ff., D. Mandel, *The Petrograd Workers and the Soviet Seizure of Power. From the July Days to July 1918* (London, 1984), 370. For the collapse in labour discipline, see M. McAuley, *Bread and Justice*, 195–7.

[115] V. N. Brovkin, *The Mensheviks after October. Socialist Opposition and the Rise of Dictatorship* (Cornell, 1987), 126–60.

[116] See F. Benvenuti, *The Bolsheviks and the Red Army, 1918–1922* (Cambridge, 1988), ch. 1.

[117] For peasant attitudes towards the regime, see O. Figes, *Peasant Russia, Civil War. The Volga Countryside in Revolution, 1917–1921* (Oxford, 1990), ch. 4.

By the spring of 1918 Lenin had decided that he would have to respond more decisively to this breakdown in authority. He began to distance himself from the populist elements of his rhetoric of 1917, and to adopt a mixture of élitist revivalist and technicist approaches to socialism, based on centralized organization, hierarchical command structures, and the use of coercion, material incentives, and élitist methods of mobilization. Over the next three years, these approaches were applied, albeit gradually and unevenly, to virtually all institutions. Political control was strengthened by undermining the power of the elected soviets and by creating a centralized state bureaucracy. Lenin tried to concentrate all state power in the Council of People's Commissars (Sovnarkom), a body similar to the old tsarist Council of Ministers.[118] Yet it was the Bolshevik party, and its Central Committee, which increasingly functioned as the co-ordinating centre of the administrative system. Attempts were made to transform the relatively decentralized party of the revolutionary months, with its powerful regional bosses, into a more streamlined, hierarchical organization.[119] The economic apparatus developed in similar ways in 1917–18. The factory committees were gradually undermined and subsumed into the more centralized trade unions.[120] The powers of the regional economic councils, the *sovnarkhozy*, were also reduced. The beneficiaries of this change were the Moscow-based, centralized economic organizations, such as Vesenkha and the *glavki* (branch committees) of specific industries.[121]

Within the factory also power was increasingly centralized, now vested in managers and technical specialists. In the spring of 1918, Lenin and his supporters moved away from his earlier support for significant workers' supervision over management, and began to emphasize the principle of 'one-man management'. Lenin now claimed that 'Soviet democracy' was compatible with 'unquestioning obedience to the will of a single person, the Soviet leader', and while it was possible, in theory, to reconcile supervision of

[118] See T. H. Rigby, *Lenin's Government: Sovnarkom 1917–1922* (Cambridge, 1979), ch. 3.
[119] For this process, see R. Service, *The Bolshevik Party in Revolution*; R. Service, 'From Polyarchy to Hegemony: The Party's Role in the Construction of the Central Institutions of the Soviet State, 1917–1919', *Sbornik*, 10 (1984), 77–90; R. Sakwa, 'The Commune State in Moscow, 1918', *SR*, 46 (1987), 443–8.
[120] S. Smith, *Red Petrograd*, ch. 7.
[121] T. Remington, *Building Socialism in Bolshevik Russia*, ch. 3.

management from below with discipline on the shop-floor, this model of industrial relations was rather different from that offered in 1917.[122] Workers' representation on factory management boards was also challenged by representatives of Vesenkha, and in June 1918 a compromise was reached: a 'collegial' system was established, according to which a third of members of the board (*kollegia*) was to be chosen by the workers of the factory, a third by the regional *sovnarkhoz*, and a third by Vesenkha; the board would then elect a director answerable to Vesenkha.[123] Yet even this restricted form of worker participation in management was attacked by Lenin and Trotsky, and at the ninth party congress in March–April 1920 they called for the replacement of collegiality with one-man management at all levels.[124]

Lenin justified his rejection of populist revivalist solutions ideologically in the spring of 1918, using two contradictory arguments: first, he accepted that his earlier ambitions had proved unrealistic; and second, he claimed that he had never believed that the regime was ready for revivalist 'democracy'.[125] Either way, Lenin placed his new plans in the framework of the Marxist historical scheme and used the language of 'retreat': Russia was not yet at the stage of 'socialism', but first had to build the centralized, scientifically rational, system Marx and Engels believed characterized late capitalism. Lenin exposed his analysis clearly in his tirade against the left published in May 1918, *On Left-wing Childishness and on the Petty-bourgeois Mentality*. He argued that five socio-economic structures existed side by side in Russia, each reflecting a different stage of development: 'patriarchal'—or subsistence peasant farming; 'small commodity production', which involved the 'majority of peasants who sell their grain'; 'private capitalism'; 'state capitalism'; and 'socialism'. 'Socialism', he implied, was the weakest

---

[122] Lenin, *PSS*, xxxvi. 200. There is an extensive literature on the debates over 'workers' control'. See, for instance, F. I. Kaplan, *Bolshevik Ideology and the Ethics of Soviet Labor, 1917–1920. The Formative Years* (London, 1969); Smith, *Red Petrograd*, ch. 9; C. Goodey, 'Factory Committees and the Dictatorship of the Proletariat (1918)', *Critique*, 3 (1974), 24–47; M. Brinton, *The Bolsheviks and Workers' Control* (London, 1970).

[123] *Sbornik dekretov i postanovlenii po narodnomu khoziaistvu*, 2 vols. (Moscow, 1918–21), i. 315–19.

[124] For these proposals, see R. Day, *Leon Trotsky and the Politics of Economic Isolation* (Cambridge, 1973), 28–34; S. Malle, *Economic Organization*, 128–34.

[125] Lenin, *PSS*, xxxvi. 179; ibid., xxxvi. 302–3.

element, and before it could be achieved, 'state capitalism', under the control of the proletarian state rather than the bourgeoisie, had to be built; 'socialism' and the 'socialization' of production and its administration by the working class as a whole demanded by the left was premature.[126] Lenin's 'state capitalism' required broadly technicist policies: the establishment of 'large-scale capitalist *tekhnika*, based on the last word of modern science' and 'planned state organization which keeps tens of millions of people to the strictest observance of a single norm in the production and distribution of goods'.[127] Lenin also argued that the representatives or 'bearers' of state capitalism, the big capitalists, had to be rehabilitated. They were best able to help the regime build state capitalism because they had expertise.[128] Now that they no longer posed a political threat, they were to be employed by the regime, albeit under supervision. They were to be replaced by a new enemy: the small capitalist and the small-holder capitalist peasant, who were guilty of disrupting state capitalist monopolies and of profiteering. As Lenin put it: 'It is not state capitalism that is at war with socialism, but the petty bourgeoisie plus private capitalism fighting together, jointly, against both state capitalism and against socialism.'[129] Lenin's decree on nationalization of June 1918 might suggest a new hostile attitude towards the big bourgeoisie, but he was acting largely for pragmatic reasons—to prevent foreigners gaining control over Russian industry.[130] By the end of 1920 much of industry was nationalized, and this was often justified on ideological grounds, as a step on the way to full socialism.[131] But Lenin's élitist attitude towards the working class and his insistence that the bourgeoisie be employed by the regime was not affected by these changes, and he remained committed to the 'retreat' from populist revivalism of 1918 until his death.

Lenin's new position naturally had enormous implications for his approach to labour relations. He was no longer convinced that all the Bolsheviks had to do was to unleash the energies of workers; rather, as he argued in 1918, the Russian worker was a 'bad worker' compared with Western European workers, and it was impossible for the regime to rely on propaganda and moral incentives.[132]

---

[126] Ibid., xxxvi. 296, 293.   [127] Ibid., xxxvi. 300.
[128] Ibid., xxxvi 309–10.   [129] Ibid., xxxvi. 296.
[130] S. Malle, *Economic Organization*, 59–60; I. Akhapkin, *First Decrees*, 147–53.
[131] S. Malle, *Economic Organization*, 46–68.
[132] Lenin, *PSS*, xxxvi. 189.

Hence, discipline had to be imposed from above and bourgeois 'scientific management' techniques such as Taylorism, which involved compulsion, strict labour discipline, the division of labour, and material incentives, were essential.[133] Participatory democracy, particularly in the workplace, had to be replaced with 'iron discipline . . . with unquestioning obedience to the will of a single person, the Soviet leader, while at work'.[134]

Lenin insisted that Taylorism would be stripped of the more degrading, anti-labour elements which it had acquired under capitalism, but it was left unclear what the difference between 'socialist' Taylorism and 'bourgeois' Taylorism was to be; indeed it is unlikely that Lenin seriously intended to distinguish between the two.[135] He believed that bourgeois authoritarian methods would have to be used in the medium term, and they would also have to be implemented by specialists of bourgeois class origin, people who were used to employing these management techniques. So, just as Lenin changed his view of proletarian virtue, he reassessed his negative judgement of the bourgeois specialists. He still saw them as knowledgeable and necessary for economic construction, but now no longer condemned them as impractical and lazy; rather they were 'businesslike' and effective, and therefore had to be trusted with positions of responsibility. Lenin made it clear that he was changing his assumptions at a Central Committee meeting of 31 March 1918:

It was stated that [now] the period of the conquest of power has finished, fundamental construction carries on. Knowledgeable, experienced, businesslike (*delovye*) people have to be drawn into work. The sabotage of intelligentsia circles has been broken. In the first period of conquest we did not, we could not draw in technicians. Now the situation has changed, in this sense we are following a *new course*.[136]

In response to theorists on the left of the party, such as Bogdanov, who urged that a new egalitarian and collectivist 'proletarian culture' should be developed by the Bolsheviks, Lenin argued that the bourgeoisie's qualities should be imitated by all, including the proletariat. As he explained in 1922: 'for a start, we should be satisfied with real bourgeois culture; for a start we should be satisfied with

---

[133] Lenin, *PSS*, xxxvi. 189–90.   [134] Ibid., xxxvi. 200.

[135] For the debate over Taylorism, see K. E. Bailes, 'Alexei Gastev and the Soviet Controversy over Taylorism, 1918–1924', *SS*, 29 (1977), 373–94; S. A. Smith, 'Taylorism Rules OK?', *Radical Science Journal*, 13 (1983), 3–27.

[136] *Izv TsK KPSS*, 3 (1989), 107. Emphasis added.

dispensing with the cruder types of pre-bourgeois culture, i.e., bureaucratic culture or serf culture etc.'[137]

The leadership's new conciliatory attitude towards the bourgeoisie, and its emphasis on order and discipline, was obviously incompatible with the populist revivalist class struggle rhetoric of 1917. Indeed, Lenin declared explicitly that the 'offensive against capital' be 'suspended', by which he meant that violent methods of suppression were to give way to peaceful methods of economic construction.[138] Now 'shooting on the spot' was to be replaced by trial in a court.[139] Lenin's new interest in 'law', however, should not be seen as a conversion to a liberal conception of politics. Lenin was not demanding that the rights of the individual be protected against the state; rather, the law and courts were to be used 'as an instrument *for inculcating discipline'*.[140]

Nor was Lenin rejecting the use of violence against the regime's opponents. Indeed, in the spring of 1918 he merely seemed to be trying to redirect it from the specialists and 'big bourgeoisie' towards the peasantry and petty bourgeoisie. Violence continued to be employed against groups considered to be politically unreliable, 'counter-revolutionary', or class 'alien' throughout this period.[141] The powers of the Cheka, the organization charged with rooting out these 'enemies', also increased steadily over the period.[142] However, Lenin appears to have been reluctant to return to the more populist revivalist vision of class struggle in 1918. In the few months following the 'retreat' and the restoration of the authority and status of bourgeois specialists, it appeared as if class struggle would be significantly moderated.[143]

---

[137] Lenin, *PSS*, xlv. 389.   [138] Ibid., xxxvi. 176.   [139] Ibid., xxxvi. 197.

[140] Ibid., xxxvi. 197. For an analysis of Lenin's instrumentalist conception of law in this period, see J. Burbank, 'Lenin and the Law in Revolutionary Russia', *SR*, 54 (1995), 40–4.

[141] See, for instance, Holquist's analysis of the 'de-Cossackization' campaigns of 1918–19, although the extreme policy of terror and extermination was moderated from the spring of 1919, coinciding with changes in policy towards the peasantry. P. Holquist, *Making War, Forging Revolution*, ch. 6. For the use of violence against 'enemies' throughout the period, see S. Pavliuchenkov, *Voennyi kommunizm*, ch. 6; Nicholas Werth, 'A State against its People: Violence, Repression and Terror in the Soviet Union', in S. Courtois *et al.*, *The Black Book of Communism*, 71–107.

[142] For the Central Committee's continuing willingness to grant the Cheka powers, see RGASPI, 17/2/20, 3 (11 June 1919); RGASPI, 17/2/21 1 ob. (15 June 1919).

[143] For this period, see V. Brovkin, *The Mensheviks after October*, ch. 3.

A number of events conspired to undermine this conciliatory attitude in the summer and autumn of 1918, and led to the revival of the class struggle against the bourgeoisie: foreign intervention; the deterioration in relations between the Bolsheviks and other socialist parties; and the Bolsheviks' decision to solve the increasingly critical food crisis by encouraging class struggle against alleged kulak saboteurs in the countryside. In July 1918 the Central Executive Committee of the Congress of Soviets (VTsIK) declared that the demands of war required that Soviet power protect its rear by 'putting the bourgeoisie under supervision and carrying out mass terror against it';[144] weeks later, responding to attempted assassinations of Soviet leaders, Lenin ordered the notorious 'Red Terror' against bourgeois groups.[145] In several areas individuals with 'dubious' class or political backgrounds were rounded up and kept as hostages or executed.

Yet, although this may appear to be a return to the populist revivalist class struggle of 1917–18, and despite the use of extreme rhetoric by Bolshevik leaders,[146] Lenin did not want the 'Red Terror' to become a general attack on the bourgeoisie as a class, for fear that it would destroy those on whom the regime relied for the reconstruction of the economy. A particularly controversial article was written by Martyn Latsis, deputy chairman of the Cheka, which instructed its readers in the Cheka thus:

Do not ask for incriminating evidence to prove that the prisoner opposed Soviet power by arms or word. Your first duty is to ask him what class he belongs to, what were his origins, education and occupation. These questions should decide the fate of the prisoner. This is the meaning and essence of the Red Terror.[147]

Lenin explicitly criticized this view of the class struggle on technicist grounds. The bourgeoisie, he argued, was not to be trusted politically, was to be watched carefully, and was to be suppressed if it tried to restore capitalism; but to refuse to use it for 'administration and construction' would be the height of stupidity and would damage

---

[144] E. H. Carr, *The Bolshevik Revolution*, i. 175.

[145] See Lenin to N. N. Krestinsky, 3–4 September 1918, R. Pipes (ed.), *The Unknown Lenin. From the Secret Archive* (New Haven, 1998), 56.

[146] *Severnaia kommuna*, 109 (1918), 2, quoted in G. Leggett, *The Cheka. Lenin's Political Police* (Oxford, 1986) 114; M. McAuley, *Bread and Justice*, 382–3.

[147] *Krasnyi terror*, 1 (1918) 1, quoted in G. Leggett, *The Cheka*, 113.

the regime.[148] Furthermore, he argued that their residual commitment to 'petty-bourgeois democracy' and lack of faith in Bolshevism
was not something surprising or exceptional; it was a 'necessary
product of capitalism'. Therefore, Lenin implied, if the Bolsheviks
were to use the bourgeois 'building material' left over by the capitalist social order, they would have to tolerate different attitudes and
views, as long as all were loyal to the Bolsheviks.[149] Trotsky, who
had few qualms about the use of violence against political enemies,
was particularly hostile to Latsis's views, presumably because they
threatened his policy of using old tsarist officers, or as they were
termed, the bourgeois 'military specialists', in the Red Army.[150]
Dzerzhinskii, the leader of the Cheka, himself came to object to
the populist revivalist view of the Terror, largely because it undermined the Cheka's own control over the process. So, in September
1919, following an attempt on the lives of Moscow party leaders, he
requested that the Central Committee should not announce 'official
mass red terror' but should entrust the Cheka with all operations.[151]
By 1919, therefore, while violence against 'enemy' groups continued, the leadership had become wary of presenting it as part of
a full-blown class struggle against the bourgeoisie.

The turn against 'class struggle' in the spring of 1918 did not
apply to peasants: the alliance with the big bourgeoisie was perfectly compatible with attacks on the 'petty bourgeoisie'. In the
spring and summer of 1918 as grain supplies to the towns failed,
Lenin adopted a policy of 'class struggle' in the countryside: blaming the rich peasants, the kulaks, for the shortages, he urged that a
'proletarian' alliance be created against the bourgeois saboteurs,
and 'committees of poor peasants' (*kombedy*), helped by detachments of workers, were to extract grain from the kulaks.[152] Yet, as

---

[148] Lenin, *PSS*, xxxvii. 410 (this document was written at the end of 1918 or the
beginning of 1919, but was not published until 1926). See also E. Iaroslavskii's
criticism of Latsis, *P*, 25 December 1918.

[149] Lenin, *PSS*, xxxvii. 410.

[150] Trotsky argued that Latsis's views excluded him from military work. See
RGASPI, 17/2/7 (Central Committee meeting, 19 December 1918).

[151] RGASPI, 17/2/24, 1. Although as late as May 1920 Dzerzhinskii was calling for
a terror against enemies on the basis of their 'class affiliation'. See G. Leggett, *The
Cheka*, 114.

[152] For Lenin's sympathy with the Left Communists on this issue in the spring of
1918, see Service, *Lenin. A Political Life*, iii. 8. For the *kombedy* and the Food Supply
Dictatorship, see L. Lih, *Bread and Authority in Russia, 1917–1921* (Berkeley,
1990),157 ff.; O. Figes, *Peasant Russia, Civil War*, 188–99.

these measures inevitably provoked resistance and complicated requisitioning, the leadership was forced to abandon them and make some concessions to the middle and richer peasants, who produced much of the grain. The *kombedy* were abolished in December 1918 and a relatively decentralized and unpredictable system of requisitioning was replaced by a the more stable and centralized, although still oppressive and unpopular 'food levy' (*prodrazverstka*).[153] At the eighth party congress in March 1919 the full implications of the new policy of conciliation were explained by Lenin and food supply officials. They admitted that the offensive against the kulaks, which often involved a great deal of coercion against 'middle peasants', had to be moderated.[154] Also, attempts to create a socialized, collectivized agriculture had to be postponed because they were unpopular among peasants.[155] The relatively productive peasant commune, despite its 'bourgeois' character, had to be preserved.[156] Violent methods were used in requisitioning campaigns, and they were often justified using the rhetoric of class struggle against kulaks and their influence. And ultimately this harsh requisitioning led to famine in 1920–2.[157] Even so, there was a general acceptance that the countryside had a long way to go before it could reach the threshold of socialism.[158]

Statements on the virtues of the middle peasantry might have suggested that the leadership was thinking of retreating further, at least in the agrarian sphere, from the advanced bourgeoisie's 'state capitalism' lauded by Lenin in the spring of 1918, to a version of the 'small commodity production' phase, dominated by the middle peasantry and involving the market. Yet this would have been a step too far towards an ultra-gradualist liberal technicism, and there was to be no adoption of free trade in grain. Lenin and most

---

[153] On the *razverstka* system, see Lih, *Bread and Authority*, ch. 7; O. Figes, *Peasant Russia, Civil War*, 260–1.

[154] For the moderation of the campaign against kulaks, see L. Lih, *Bread and Authority*, 175.

[155] *Vos'moi s"ezd RKP(b), mart 1919 goda. Protokoly* (Moscow, 1959), 241 (Kuraev).

[156] *Vos'moi s"ezd*, 248 (Pakhomov).

[157] Figes, *Peasant Russia, Civil War*, 267–73.

[158] This was even accepted in the influential *ABC of Communism*. See N. Bukharin and E. Preobrazhensky, *The ABC of Communism. A Popular Explanation of the Program of the Communist Party of Russia*, trans. by E. Paul and C. Paul (Ann Arbor, 1966), 316–20. See Lars Lih's analysis of the *ABC*, in L. Lih, 'The Mystery of the ABC', 65–70.

Bolsheviks ruled out such reforms on ideological and pragmatic grounds, until the announcement of the New Economic Policy in 1921.[159] In January 1919, in response to suggestions from an economist that free trade in grain might solve the food problem, he denounced it as 'equivalent to frenzied brutal speculation and the triumph of the haves over the have-nots.' 'We should not go backward through free trade', Lenin argued, 'but forward through the *improvement* of the grain monopoly'.[160] He expressed a similar view when several of those who had been the strongest advocates of compulsion in agrarian policy, such as Trotsky, began to argue that only some form of market in grain would end food shortages.[161] Lenin also rejected any liberalization of the political sphere, including representative democracy and the use of law or institutional safeguards to protect the individual against the state.[162] As will be seen, Bolsheviks generally insisted during this period that state and society were merging, and there could only be one legitimate interest, that of the united state and proletariat.

The rhetoric of 'retreat' was applied in a less ambiguous way to another group that, like the peasantry, was regarded as 'backward'—the non-Russian nationalities.[163] Lenin and Stalin, the Commissar for Nationalities, developed an approach that allowed non-Russian nationalities a degree of autonomy. In doing so, they were rejecting the views of the left of the party, and most notably

[159] Although Bukharin and Preobrazhensky, in their *ABC of Communism*, while justifying the abolition of large-scale trade, did not believe that the state was yet able to abolish 'petty private trade' and control the distribution of 'the produce of small-scale independent home industry'. Bukharin and Preobrazhensky, *The ABC of Communism*, 321–3. The abolition of trade was justified on the grounds that 'to each method of production there corresponds a special method of distribution'; with the abolition of the capitalist mode of production, the capitalist mode of distribution also had to go. Lars Lih argues that trade was largely ruled out on pragmatic rather than ideological grounds: the leadership did not believe that the requisitions apparatus could compete with private traders. L. Lih, *Bread and Authority*, 250–1.

[160] Lenin to N. A. Rozhkov, 29 January 1919, in Pipes, *The Unknown Lenin*, 62. Lenin did make it clear, however, that he was commenting on the desirability of free trade in particularly difficult circumstances, when there was an 'absolute shortage of essential produce'.

[161] L. Trotsky, *My Life. An Attempt at Autobiography* (Harmondsworth, 1975), 481–2. For this discussion, see Pavliuchenkov, *Voennyi kommunizm*, 92–3.

[162] Although Lenin's ultimate solution to the trade union controversy was a quasi-liberal one, in that it implied that the trade unions had to protect workers against the state. See below, p. 128.

[163] For this point, see Y. Slezkine, 'The USSR as a Communal Apartment, or how a Socialist State Promoted Ethnic Particularism', in Fitzpatrick, *Stalinism*, 318.

Bukharin and Piatakov, who saw nationalism as a reactionary force and predicted that separate nationalities would soon wither away as all became integrated into a single proletarian, socialist state.[164] In part, Lenin and Stalin were responding to circumstances. At a time when Soviet power was fragile they had to take account of the strength of non-Russian nationalist feeling. In part, they sympathized with nations that had been oppressed in the past by tsarist 'Great-Russian chauvinism'. They justified their policy by arguing that these areas were too 'backward' to be integrated into a centralized, unified proletarian state. Like the middle peasantry, national minorities had to be encouraged, not forced, into socialism.

In many cases, then, the leadership's policies in a whole range of areas were presented and even perceived as a 'retreat', although this was normally regarded as a carefully modulated retreat along the Marxist historical path from populist revivalism to élitist revivalism and technicism. While elements of liberal technicist approaches can be seen in policy towards 'backward' groups, such as the peasantry and some non-Russian nationalities, liberal technicism was generally rejected. Yet the leadership also, understandably, tried to avoid being labelled as pragmatists who were neglecting the ideals of the revolution, and they sometimes tried to escape the 'advance–retreat' framework, justifying their élitism on more principled grounds. Even so, they were never entirely successful, as the promise of proletarian democracy was an integral part of the Marxist project.

The leadership's discomfort in discussions of 'advance' and 'retreat' is evident in the debates with the left over the issue of 'democracy'. It gave various excuses for the failure to 'democratize'. A common argument was that poor economic conditions prevented the leadership from fulfilling its earlier pledges, and that the authoritarian methods were essential if the economy was to be

---

[164] For Piatakov's position, see *Vos'moi s"ezd*, 77–81; for Bukharin's, see *Vos'moi s"ezd*, 109–10. For differences of emphasis between Lenin and Stalin, see Martin, *The Affirmative Action Empire. Nations and Nationalism in the Soviet Union* (Ithaca, 2001), 7–8, 395–400. For nationality policies in this period, see T. Martin, 'An Affirmative Action Empire: Ethnicity and the Soviet State, 1923–1938', Ph.D. dissertation, University of Chicago, 1996, 15–32; T. Martin, *The Affirmative Action Empire*, 2–9; Y. Slezkine, *Arctic Mirrors. Russia and the Small Peoples of the North* (Ithaca, NY, 1994), 143–5; Y. Slezkine, 'The USSR as a Communal Apartment', 313–26; Jeremy Smith, *The Bolsheviks and the National Question, 1917–1923* (Basingstoke, 1999), chs. 2–3.

restored after the disruption of civil war and revolution.[165] Once the war had ended, therefore, the leadership again came under pressure to 'democratize'. Zinoviev, speaking for the Central Committee at the ninth party conference in September 1920, and Bukharin (who had abandoned his earlier fundamentalist leftism and moved closer to the leadership), speaking at the tenth party congress in March 1921, both accepted that the war had forced the leadership to create a hierarchical, bureaucratic system and now the time had come for more 'democracy'.[166] But Lenin did not agree. Even though the war had ended, Lenin argued, there could be no 'democratization': a 'war on the economic front' was beginning which would be 'more difficult and more prolonged' than the civil war;[167] hence more emphasis had to be placed on 'compulsion' than 'persuasion'.[168] While he still claimed that the regime's ultimate goal was the creation of a participatory democracy, he insisted that this would only be possible once a strong economic foundation for socialism had been created, and authoritarian, 'undemocratic' methods would be vital for this. So, at the end of 1920 he wrote:

It is the task of the Soviet government to destroy completely the old machinery of state as it was destroyed in October, and to transfer power to the soviets, but we already recognize in our programme that . . . at present no economic foundation yet exists for a genuinely socialist society.[169]

Indeed from 1920 the leadership increasingly argued that élitism would be necessary in the very long term, and that it would only be in the distant future that the fully 'democratic' 'commune state' would arrive. For Trotsky, the merging of state and society would only happen at a very late stage, and then only after the 'principle of the state' had reached its 'highest intensification'. As Trotsky explained:

Just as a lamp, before going out, shoots up in a brilliant flame, so the state, before disappearing, assumes the form of the dictatorship of the proletariat, i.e., the most ruthless form of the state, which embraces the life of the citizen authoritatively in every direction.[170]

---

[165] *Deviataia konferentsiia RKP(b) sentiabr' 1920 goda. Protokoly* (Moscow 1972),188–9 (Lenin).
[166] *Deviataia konferentsiia*, 139–56 (Zinoviev); *Desiatyi s"ezd RKP(b)*, 226 ff. (Bukharin).
[167] Lenin, *PSS*, xlii. 142 (December 1920).
[168] Ibid., xlii. 139.   [169] Ibid., xlii. 32.
[170] L. Trotsky, *Terrorism and Communism* (Ann Arbor, Mich., 1971), 170.

However, at times Lenin and some of his allies eschewed the language of 'retreat' completely, suggesting that hierarchical relations and a centralized state were not a temporary concession to the bourgeoisie but would always be necessary, and indeed were entirely compatible with socialism. Yet such statements were relatively rare and difficult to justify. Those leaders who tried to claim that hierarchies were inevitable tended to do so by implication, without theoretical justification. So, for instance, Lenin declared that the concept of 'industrial democracy' was 'theoretically false' for democracy was 'a category proper only to the political sphere', but he did not develop his argument.[171] Trotsky went even further at the ninth party congress in 1920, suggesting that compulsion and élite authority would always be required in the economic sphere because human nature made relations of domination and subordination inevitable. Man was a naturally lazy animal and only compulsion and discipline imposed from above, by some form of executive, could increase productivity. Not only was a powerful executive needed within the enterprise to organize labour but, at the level of the state, a strong executive had to 'militarize', labour so that it could be distributed according to the plan.[172] By talking of human nature, and implying that it was immutable, Trotsky seemed to be denying that popular participation in administration would ever be possible.

Trotsky was one of the more extreme élitists in the Central Committee at the time, but Lenin hinted at similar views, although in a more subtle way: by altering the meaning of political terminology. The Russian word *biurokratizm* (bureaucratism) was always used in a pejorative way, but could refer both to the concentration of power in the hands of officials and to inefficiency or 'red tape' (*volokita* or *kantseliarshchina*). The Bolsheviks in 1917 generally used the term to mean the antithesis of participatory 'democracy'. It referred to the existence of an executive 'separated' from the people, and was one of the main evils afflicting bourgeois states. The 'struggle against bureaucratism', which the party's programme declared to be one of its main objectives, thus involved the creation of a participatory 'democracy' in which a separate 'bureaucracy' no

---

[171] Lenin, *PSS*, xlii. 210–11.
[172] *Deviatyi s"ezd RKP(b), mart-aprel' 1920 g. Protokoly* (Moscow, 1960), 94 (Trotsky).

longer existed.[173] The left of the party also used the term in this sense after 1917: for Aleksandra Kollontai of the fundamentalist leftist group the Workers' Opposition, 'bureaucracy' was 'the direct negation of self-activity'.[174] At times, Lenin also used the term in this way, declaring at the eighth party congress in 1919 that 'we can fight bureaucracy to the bitter end, to a complete victory, only when the whole population participates in the work of government'.[175]

However, Lenin and the leadership increasingly used the term 'bureaucracy' to mean inefficiency and 'red-tape', rather than the absence of participatory democracy. So, in their criticisms of 'bureaucratism', they attacked the inefficiency and weakness of the executive—not its authoritarian nature or the very existence of the executive. This surreptitious change in the use of the term was noticed by Kollontai. She insisted that 'the harm of bureaucracy does not only lie in red tape as some comrades would want us to believe', but 'in the solution of all problems, not by means of an open exchange of opinions or by the immediate efforts of all concerned, but by means of formal decisions handed down from the central institutions... Some third person decides your fate: that is the essence of bureaucracy.'[176] For Kollontai, the leadership was willing to tolerate the real evil of 'bureaucratism' while limiting its concern to the inefficiency of the apparatus.

Kollontai's charges seem to have been justified. At the tenth congress Lenin criticized the Workers' Opposition for complaining about 'bureaucratism' but not making any concrete suggestions as to how to eliminate it:

We ourselves know that we have a touch of bureaucratism... We sign a paper—but how is it applied in practice? How do you check up on it, when the bureaucratic machine is enormous? If you know how to make it smaller, dear comrades, please share your knowledge with us!... you give us nothing but general statements.[177]

Lenin and the Workers' Opposition were clearly speaking at cross purposes, as they meant different things by 'bureaucratism'. Lenin

---

[173] *Kommunisticheskaia Partiia Sovetskogo Soiuza v rezoliutsiiakh i resheniiakh s"ezdov, konferentsii i plenumov TsK*, 8th edn. (Moscow, 1970), ii. 44–5.
[174] A. M. Kollontai, *The Workers' Opposition* (London, n.d.), 52.
[175] *Vos'moi s"ezd*, 62 (Lenin).
[176] A. M. Kollontai, *The Workers' Opposition*, 52 ff.
[177] *Desiatyi s"ezd*, 121 (Lenin).

now considered that it meant an excessively large, inefficient apparatus, while the Workers' Opposition defined it as the absence of participatory democracy. For Lenin in 1922, the 'bureaucrat' was no longer one of a group of 'privileged persons, cut off from the masses and standing above the masses' as he had declared in *State and Revolution*, but was 'the communist who occupies a responsible ... soviet post and has universal respect as a conscientious man ... but he has not learnt to struggle against red tape (*volokita*), he is unable to struggle against it, he covers it up'.[178] Lenin was no longer calling for the abolition of bureaucracies, but for a 'good bureaucracy'.[179] Similarly, Trotsky admitted that only the weaknesses of the 'bureaucracy' were to be eliminated, not the 'bureaucracy' as a whole. As he declared, 'we suffer, not because we adopt the bad sides of bureaucracy, but because we have failed so far to learn the good ones'.[180]

Technicism and élitist revivalism: the debate over incentives and speed

The leadership was broadly united in rejecting both liberal approaches and the populist revivalists' commitment to class struggle and their optimistic assessment of proletarian virtue. However, there was a spectrum of opinion within this élitist consensus, and serious tensions emerged within it, between revivalism and technicism. As was to be expected, one of the thorniest questions concerned incentives. Once the leadership had accepted that workers could not be trusted to work without hierarchy or external discipline, it introduced a mixture of coercion and material incentives. As Commissar for War, Trotsky introduced harsh punishments and the death sentence into the Red Army, and earlier criticisms of the 'discipline of the rod' were forgotten.[181] In industry, certain categories of workers were refused permission to leave their jobs, and the unemployed were obliged to accept any work, while trade unions established disciplinary courts with

---

[178] Lenin, *PSS*, xxxiii. 115; ibid., xlv. 15.
[179] Lenin used this phrase at the beginning of March 1921. Ibid., xliii. 373.
[180] Cited in A. Kollontai, *The Workers' Opposition*, 52 ff.
[181] F. Benvenuti, *The Bolsheviks and the Red Army, 1918–1922* (Cambridge, 1988), 16.

extensive powers.[182] These policies culminated in Trotsky's contro-versial plans to subject parts of the civilian labour force to military discipline in 1920.[183] At the same time, the authority of managers and experts over workers was strengthened and the use of material incentives became more widespread.[184] Despite some opposition, wage differentials increased over the civil war period.[185]

However, both Lenin and Trotsky hoped to combine these ma-terial incentives, and the élitist arrangements which they implied, with the continuing use of moral incentives and enthusiasm. Lenin saw the *subbotniki*, Saturdays which workers, supposedly voluntar-ily, gave up to work for the good of society, as an example of 'communist labour', when 'enthusiastic' and 'heroic' workers achieved high levels of labour productivity.[186] Yet, at the same time, he was unwilling to accept the populist revivalist argument that the regime could depend on worker enthusiasm to any signifi-cant extent. It was 'utopian', he insisted, to suggest that the *sub-botniki* were anything other than the 'feeble new shoots' of the communist order.[187]

Like Lenin, Trotsky tried to reconcile a voluntaristic approach to incentives with élitism and a hostility to class struggle. But he was willing to defend a more explicitly élitist revivalist model of organ-ization, based on a military vision of incentives and relations be-tween rulers and ruled. In Trotsky's view, workers were to be treated as if they were soldiers, subject to harsh military discipline, but they were also to be mobilized by their officers, military and political. Their 'spirit' would be cultivated, they would work 'to the sound of socialist hymns and songs';[188] 'moral influence', persuasion, educa-tion, and enthusiasm would play a central part in the organization of the workforce.[189] The initiative in developing this 'spirit' was to

[182] See J. B. Sorenson, *The Life and Death of Soviet Trade Unionism, 1917–1928* (New York, 1968), 145 ff.

[183] See, J. Bunyan (ed.), *The Origins of Forced Labor in the Soviet State, 1917–1921: Documents and Materials* (Baltimore, 1967), 95–114.

[184] For the debate over material incentives and piece-work, see M. McAuley, *Bread and Justice*, 200–3.

[185] S. Malle, *Economic Organization*, 182–3.

[186] Lenin, *PSS*, xxxix. 21 (28 June 1919). For this movement, see W. J. Chase, 'Voluntarism, Mobilization and Coercion: *Subbotniki*, 1919–1921', *SS*, 41 (1989), 111–28.

[187] Lenin, *PSS*, xxxix. 20.

[188] Quoted in I. Deutscher, *The Prophet Armed* (New York, 1965), 495.

[189] L. D. Trotsky, *Sochineniia* (Moscow, 1927), xii. 140–3.

come from the top, and there was to be no challenge to élites, whether Bolsheviks or 'bourgeois' technical experts; as Trotsky argued in his debates with the theorists of proletarian culture in the early 1920s, it was only in the distant future, once bourgeois culture had been fully utilized in economic construction, that a new egalitarian and collectivist culture would emerge.[190]

Trotsky gained the conditional backing of Lenin, at least until the end of 1920, but his plans encountered serious opposition.[191] The left was understandably the most critical, as will be seen, but he also encountered hostility from Vesenkha and the economic apparatus. Behind this conflict lay an institutional rivalry. Trotsky was pressing for the adoption of the military model in part because he hoped to maintain and expand his own influence, and that of the army, once the civil war was over. His establishment of 'labour armies', created from idle military detachments to collect food supplies or build railways naturally undermined Vesenkha.[192] According to A. I. Rykov, a Bolshevik who had taken a more gradualist and sceptical view of the question of the seizure of power in 1917, and as Vesenkha's head generally adopted a technicist view of politics, the comparison between industry and the army was an inappropriate one.[193] But Rykov was not advocating the further expansion of workers' 'democracy'; rather he advocated 'collegiality' on pragmatic grounds: workers' views were to be taken into account in order that industry would run smoothly.[194]

Closely related to this disagreement over incentives was the issue of how rapidly and by what methods Russia could 'advance' towards socialism in the economic sphere—that is towards a centralized, integrated economy. Many officials in Vesenkha and its trusts took a gradualist, technicist position that took account of economic realities; they tried to create a co-ordinated economy, but they

[190] L. D. Trotsky, *Literature and Revolution* (Ann Arbor, 1960), 198–9.

[191] For Lenin's attitude, see R. Service, *Lenin*, iii. 107.

[192] For Trotsky's ideas, see R. Day, *Trotsky*, 23–5. For the use of Trotsky's methods in the Donbass by his ally, G. I. Piatakov, see A. Graziosi, 'At the Roots of Soviet Industrial Relations and Practices. Piatakov's Donbass in 1921', *CMR*, 36 (1995), 95–138.

[193] For Rykov's opposition to an insurrectionary politics in 1917, see R. Service, *Lenin*, ii. 170; for disagreements with Lenin before then, see Service, *Lenin*, i. 187–8.

[194] *Deviatyi s"ezd RKP(b), mart-aprel' 1920 g.* (Moscow, 1934), 140 (Rykov). For Vesenkha's position on 'collegiality', see S. Malle, *Economic Organization*, 130–1. Rykov, however, did agree with Trotsky's proposals for the 'statization' of the trade unions (*Deviatyi s"ezd*, 138).

insisted that it had to be built on the foundations of existing economic institutions and structures. Vesenkha itself was founded on the *glavki*—the pre-revolutionary chief committees formed by the tsarist state during the war to control militarily important branches of industry;[195] it is therefore not surprising that its officials should have favoured the system they knew how to run, preserving the autonomy of the *glavki* and the traditional relations between them. Rykov, therefore, strongly resisted Trotsky's proposals in 1920 to centralize economic organization and draw up a single national economic plan. Trotsky's ideas, he argued, were unrealistic and overambitious given the poor state of the national economy.[196]

For Trotsky, however, '*glavkizm*', as he contemptuously described it, was a poorly co-ordinated system of economic administration, in which tens of overlapping, vertically structured organizations competed for resources and pursued autonomous policies.[197] His solution was to replace this system with a highly centralized 'single economic plan'. But Trotsky's plan was of a particular type. For Trotsky, technicist solutions were not adequate. It was not enough to discover supply and demand in the economy, to link various parts of the economy together, and to establish a mechanism operating in full equilibrium. The revolution, he argued, had destroyed all 'proportionality' between branches of the economy, and there could be no hope of establishing an equilibrium in the short term.[198] Planning therefore had to be a dynamic process, in which the state targeted lagging sectors of the economy and raised them to the level of other, more advanced areas. Trotsky proposed that this be done by 'shock methods' (*udarnost'*), which he defined as the 'concentration of strength and resources on a particular section of the economic front'.[199]

Unlike Rykov, therefore, who favoured gradual and rational economic centralization and development, Trotsky believed that the state had to use its will to transform the economy. He was applying his experience as a military commander to economic strategy, relying on determination and force to overcome obstacles.[200]

[195] S. Malle, *Economic Organization*, 218–19.
[196] E. H. Carr, *Bolshevik Revolution*, ii. 368; *Deviatyi s"ezd*, 139–40.
[197] For the problems of *glavkizm*, see S. Malle, *Economic Organization*, 218–26, 232–4.
[198] Trotsky, *Sochineniia*, xv. 216–18.
[199] Ibid., xv. 235.   [200] Trotsky, *Terrorism and Communism*, 141.

He did not explicitly try to formulate a theoretical Marxist justification for his position—the solution to Russia's problems, he
insisted, could not be found in any book.[201] Even so, his ideas
involved the application of an élitist revolutionary voluntarism to
the economy. For Trotsky, the state had replaced the working class
as the charismatic agent of change, and the state alone could use its
will to transform reality. Socialism could only be secured by an
increase in economic productivity, and the process of economic
development could, in turn, be 'hastened' by 'our energy and per-
sistence'; just as Russia had been able to 'leap' over a 'series of
stages' on its way to capitalism, so determination could push Russia
along a 'forced path' (*forsirovannyi put'*) of development.[202]

The left and the defence of 'democracy'

Trotsky's vision of socialism, however, met fierce resistance, and
throughout the period a variety of leftist groups within the party
claimed, against the élitist revivalist and technicist leadership, that a
version of the 'commune state' was still practicable.[203] Some form of
participatory democracy, they argued, could be reconciled with
planning and centralization. The left remained influential in the
party for various reasons. Ideologically, of course, leftists were in
a strong position, as they could speak the language of principle and
condemn compromise; they could claim, with some reason, to be
representing the views of many workers, who still hoped for the
creation of the Soviet workers' democracy promised in 1917; and
they could argue that truly effective mobilization required working-
class support, and that it was dangerous to alienate workers when
the regime was under attack from outside. Furthermore, the populist revivalist vision of a system in which centralization was united
with local initiative could be used by various institutions threatened
by the new hierarchical state and party organizations. Most local

---

[201] Trotsky, *Sochineniia*, xii. 143.

[202] Ibid., xii. 153.

[203] There is a large literature on the debates between the left and the Leninist
leadership. See T. Remington, *Building Socialism*, 136–45; R. Daniels, *Conscience of
the Revolution*, chs. 3–6; L. B. Schapiro, *The Origins of the Communist Autocracy:
Political Opposition in the Soviet State. First Phase, 1917–1922* (London, 1977);
R. Sakwa, *Soviet Communists in Power*, chs. 6–7.

party bosses, however much they were frustrated by the arrogance of the centre, found the leadership's élitism most appealing, particularly at a time when they were being threatened from 'below'.[204] Even so, the left did have a presence within regional party and soviet organizations under threat from the Central Committee, Vesenkha, and the commissariats. It also found support from some within the trade unions, which were being undermined by Vesenkha and Trotsky's new militarized economic organizations.[205] But the left had significant weaknesses, because the populist revivalist project was so incoherent. It was difficult to see how, in practice, participatory democracy could be reconciled with the political and economic centralization that the left realized was necessary, and many leftists increasingly accepted that if they were to be politically credible they had to compromise with Lenin and the leadership. This helps to explain why many on the left in this period developed a new 'moderate' form of populist revivalism, which incorporated, uneasily, elements of élitism.

The left first emerged in the spring of 1918 in response to Lenin's 'retreat' from populist revivalism and his decision to make peace with the Germans, which many Bolsheviks saw as a capitulation to the forces of imperialism. The Left Communists, based in the Moscow party organization and led by Nikolai Bukharin and Nikolai Osinskii, saw themselves as defenders of the promises of 1917, and their rhetoric owed a great deal to Lenin's *State and Revolution*.[206] Centralization of control over industry, they argued, could be reconciled with mass participation in administration, because the interests of 'class conscious' workers would automatically coincide with those of a proletarian executive. Discipline imposed from above was unproletarian, 'bureaucratic', and unnecessary. As Osinskii blithely stated, 'the workers in the localities will feel the growth of order,

[206] For the Left Communists, see Ronald I. Kowalski, *The Bolshevik Party in Conflict. The Left Communist Opposition of 1918* (Basingstoke, 1991). For the views of the Left Communists, see N. Osinskii, *Stroitel'stvo sotsializma—obshchie zadachi organizatsiia proizvodstva* (Moscow, 1918). See also, *Pervyi vserossiiskii s"ezd sovetov narodnogo khoziaistva, 1918 (Trudy)* (Moscow, 1918), 66 ff.; 'Tezisy o tekushchem momente', *Kommunist*, 1 (1918), 8.

organization, intelligent help from the centre. "Separatism" and "syndicalism" will immediately subside...'.[207] The Left Communists were hostile to both compulsion and material incentives, and criticized the introduction of Taylorist methods and piece-work.[208] Yet this 'democratic' order was only to apply to the proletariat. The Left Communists regarded the 'petty-bourgeois' peasantry with deep suspicion and did not plan to extend socialist forms of organization to them until they had been 'proletarianized'.[209]

A similarly fundamentalist populist revivalist outlook was defended between 1919 and 1921 by the so-called 'Workers' Opposition', led by the former commissar of labour, Aleksandr Shliapnikov, the trade union leaders S. P. Medvedev, Iu. Kh. Lutovinov, and I. I. Kutuzov, and the head of the party's women's department, Aleksandra Kollontai.[210] The Workers' Opposition, like the Left Communists, argued that full worker participatory democracy was practicable. The economy could be run by an All-Russian Congress of Producers, elected by all workers, and not just by the party, the 'vanguard' of the working class.[211] Unlike the Left Communists, however, the Workers' Opposition had little power in the upper echelons of the party, and had most influence within particular trade unions and among the party rank and file.[212]

The programmes of the Left Communists and Workers' Opposition were based on similar assumptions: that the proletariat alone had the 'culture' and virtue required to build the new state and economy. As Aleksandra Kollontai argued, the 'crucial question' in the conflict between the left and the leadership was '*who* should build the communist economy?'[213] For her, the answer was clear: the working class should construct it, as it was the class which was 'organically bound with newly-developing, painfully-born forms of production', forms of production which did not require a

---

[207] N. Osinskii, 'O stroitel'stve sotsializma', *Kommunist*, 2 (1918), 8.

[208] N. Osinskii, 'O stroitel'stve sotsializma', *Kommunist*, 1 (1918), 16.

[209] For the Left Communists' attitudes towards the peasantry, see Kowalski, *The Bolshevik Party in Conflict*, 187.

[210] For the Workers' Opposition, see L. Holmes, *For the Revolution Redeemed. The Workers' Opposition in the Bolshevik Party, 1919–1921* (The Carl Beck papers in Russian and East European Studies, 1990); Barbara Evans Clements, *Bolshevik Feminist. The Life of Aleksandra Kollontai* (Bloomington, 1979), 178–201.

[211] 'Tezisy rabochei oppozitsii', *Desiatyi s"ezd*, 689–90.

[212] See S. Pavliuchenkov, *Voennyi kommunizm*, 189–91.

[213] A. Kollontai, *The Workers' Opposition*, 29. Emphasis added.

disciplinarian executive.[214] She criticized the leadership for its 'mistrust of the working class' and alleged that it preferred to rely on non-proletarian classes 'imbued with the routine of the past'.[215]

Kollontai's views had much in common with those of Bogdanov, who promoted his ideas through the proletarian cultural organizations (Proletkul't). Bogdanov continued to argue that the proletariat would develop the 'culture' required for the victory of socialism because it was naturally collectivist and egalitarian, and insisted that the experience of workers in the factory generated a collectivist consciousness because factory work required co-operation.[216] As V. Pletnev, one of Bogdanov's followers, put it, the proletariat alone had a 'collective-class and conscious-creative psychology', and it was therefore bound to generate a more productive culture than the bourgeoisie.[217]

By 1918, however, it appeared to many on the left, as well as in the leadership, that such populist revivalist faith in the virtues of the proletariat was utopian, and could even threaten the party itself. The Left Communists split: Bukharin moved towards the leadership, while Osinskii and others in the old Left Opposition, reconstituted as the 'Democratic Centralists', tried to develop a moderate compromise position between populist and élitist revivalism. The Democratic Centralists tried to maintain their commitment to some form of participatory democracy, while recognizing the need for a strong, efficient apparatus prepared and able to use compulsion.[218] How, though, could a middle way between participatory democracy and executive efficiency be found? As is clear from their contributions to the debates in party congresses and conferences, they had enormous difficulty in answering this question. At times they seem to have experimented with an almost liberal set of solutions, attempting to draw clear distinctions between a sphere which had to be run 'undemocratically' by an executive, and another legislative sphere in which some form of 'democracy' could operate.[219] Yet

---

[214] Ibid., 32.   [215] Ibid., 129.

[216] A. A. Bogdanov, *Elementy proletarskoi kul'tury v razvitii rabochego klassa* (Moscow, 1920), 42–50.

[217] *P*, 27 September 1922.

[218] *Desiatyi s"ezd*, 243 (V.N. Maksimovskii); *Vos'moi s"ezd*, 187–97 (N. Osinskii).

[219] These proposals were generally inconsistent and poorly developed. Sapronov, for instance, argued that one-man management should be restricted to the lower levels of the factory administration while the higher levels, which were more

the Democratic Centralists were unable to pursue such schemes in any coherent way. These proposals would have amounted to a 'retreat' to liberal democracy, to the admission that there were antagonistic interests within the regime, or between the regime and society, which had to be represented.[220] Also, any suggestion that elected institutions be created and given rights to control executive bodies was unacceptably close to the bourgeois 'separation of powers' between the executive and the legislative. This arrangement had been condemned by Marx and Lenin for restricting democracy to a non-executive sphere and preventing the population from participating in administration.[221] The Democratic Centralists believed that Russia should advance towards a full participatory democracy, in which state and society had merged. They strongly objected to 'bourgeois democracy', and Osinskii explicitly condemned the separation of powers; there was no need, he claimed, to fear that 'the union of [executive and legislative] powers gives rise to arbitrariness (the common refrain of bourgeois democrats)'.[222]

Rather than pursuing liberal ideas coherently, the Democratic Centralists tended to solve their dilemma in a way that was more ideologically orthodox from a Marxist point of view, but made little sense from a liberal perspective: they demanded a watered-down 'practical' participatory democracy, a half-way house on the way to full participation. This model of 'democracy' merely demanded an alteration in leadership 'style'. It required those who administered institutions to retain 'links' (*sviazi*) with their subordinates, to 'discuss' policy with them, and 'listen to' them, to rule by inspiration

concerned with policy-making, had to be run under collegial management (*Deviatyi s"ezd*, 139, 137); Aleksandr Shliapnikov of the Workers' Opposition, speaking at the tenth congress, accepted that those organizations which were designed to 'administer' (*upravliat'*) should be run according to one-man management, while those which would 'legislate' (*zakonodatel'stvovat'*) were suitable for collegial management (*Desiatyi s"ezd*, 365). Given the mixture of legislative and executive functions in most institutions, it was difficult to see how these proposals might have been implemented. Osinskii developed another solution, arguing that extreme centralization, or 'militarization' of administration was suitable in all branches of industry at the 'front' during the civil war, while in less important branches and areas in the 'rear' there could be room for 'creative self-activity' (*Deviatyi s"ezd*, 124–5).

[220] For this point, see T. Remington, *Building Socialism*, 87.

[221] Lenin, *PSS*, xxxiii. 109. For the effects of Lenin's rejection of the separation of powers on Bolshevik theory and practice, see A. Polan, *Lenin and the End of Politics* (London, 1984).

[222] *P*, 15 January 1919.

and not by injunction; it did not *oblige* officials to take account of rank-and-file opinion, nor did it give workers or rank-and-file party members any clearly defined rights to affect decision-making. It was tantamount to calling for a new culture or spirit in existing institutions, rather than for new institutional arrangements.

Nikolai Osinskii explained this concept of democracy as 'discussion' in his contribution to the debate at the ninth party congress in 1920 between the supporters of 'collegiality' and those of 'one-man management' in industry. Osinskii accepted that some compromise was needed between the demands of efficiency and those of 'democracy' and put forward a model of management which he called 'fighting collegiality' (*boevaia kollegial'nost'*). Osinskii's 'collegiality' was to combine the 'firmness' of one-man management with the advantages of 'democracy': enterprise boards (*kollegii*) were to have only three members and each member had prescribed tasks for which he was to be held individually responsible. Osinskii was not interested in which groups would have influence over the decision-making process. The important thing was that 'discussion' and 'democratic' debate should take place:

Who will decide, the chairman personally or the *kollegiia* ... this makes absolutely no difference to the essence of collegiality. How they will debate questions also makes no difference to the essence of collegiality. The most important thing is that no question of principle is implemented ... without previous discussion in the *kollegiia*. Why is this necessary? It is so that when participating in collegial discussion people should have combined their experience and have welded themselves to each other, and not have been divided or lost in their bureaucratic work.[223]

Osinskii's model of 'democracy' lay at the centre of the Democratic Centralists' programme, and it was expressed in their demands that the regime control the masses by relying on 'persuasion', ideological 'education' (*vospitanie*), and 'agitation and propaganda' rather than 'orders' and 'commands'.[224] In many ways it was similar to Bogdanov's conception of socialist education: workers were innately socialist but were immature and had to be educated sensitively and democratically by a socialist élite. But the left also

[223] *Deviatyi s"ezd*, 184 (Osinskii).
[224] See, for instance, *Vos'moi s"ezd*, 165–6 (Osinskii). For the denunciation of 'military methods of leadership', and the contrast with 'comradely leadership', see the resolutions of the Workers' Opposition, *Desiatyi s"ezd*, 652.

justified these 'democratic' methods on more pragmatic grounds: they would, they argued, create consensus, both within the leadership, and between leaders and the masses, destroying the 'bureaucratic' 'separation' (*otryv*) between them;[225] they would also, it was commonly asserted, help to mobilize the working class to fulfil the regime's economic and political objectives.[226]

In some respects, Osinskii's position had much in common with the élitist revivalism of Trotsky. It accepted the need for one-man management and rejected full participatory democracy as impractical. It also called for a mixture of persuasion and agitation on the one side, and firm executive action on the other. Indeed, Trotsky remarked, with some amusement, that Osinskii's idea of 'collegiality' was not too different from his own concept of one-man management. It merely required that the president consult with his *kollegia* before taking a decision himself for which he, alone, was responsible.[227] Yet, while there were élitist elements in Osinskii's model of management, there were significant differences between his and Trotsky's views. First, they clearly differed on the balance between coercion and persuasion. Second, there was a tension between their respective visions of the journey to communism. While Trotsky put off the transition to 'democracy' to the distant future, Osinskii's moderate left was interested in embarking immediately on a gradual transition to 'democracy'. Third, and perhaps most importantly, they differed over the question of class and class culture. It was this issue that was to be central to the debates between the left on the one side, and Trotsky and Lenin on the other.

The left and the dilemmas of 'democratic' class struggle

At the centre of Osinskii's model, and that of the Democratic Centralists, was the insistence that the behaviour of officials and the 'culture' of the regime should change.[228] By adopting a different 'style', officials could, it was argued, use new types of incentives, based on inspiration rather than compulsion. Yet how, in practice, could new styles of behaviour be inculcated? The left based its

[225] *Vos'moi s"ezd*, 181–2 (Ignatov).
[226] *Izv TsK KPSS*, 9 (1989),165 (Smirnov).
[227] *Deviatyi s"ezd*, 196 (Trotsky).
[228] Osinskii used the word 'culture' in this sense. *Deviatyi s"ezd*, 115.

solution on notions of proletarian virtue present in Marx's thinking and dominant in 'Romantic anti-capitalist' Marxism and in Russian populist socialist discourse: proletarians were inherently 'democratic', moral, disciplined, and ideologically committed; they would therefore be able to mobilize the masses effectively, forging 'links' with them and motivating them, thus strengthening the state and the economy. Conversely, bourgeois officials had an authoritarian leadership style, were immoral, corrupt, and had no faith in socialism; they could not inspire the masses and were bound to demoralize them. It followed that one of the main obstacles to the development of socialism was the leadership's insistence on employing officials of bourgeois class origin. V. P. Antonov, a delegate from the the Saratov party organization to the eighth party congress, made this set of assumptions explicit:

the petty bourgeoisie has brought into the soviet [i.e. state] institutions those approaches, those methods, those ways of fighting for its existence, which it developed in the period of capitalism. Do not think that depravity which has shown itself in our ranks, the boorish arrogance (*khamstvo*) and authoritarian behaviour (*komissarstvo*) are brought about by one [proletarian] power. No, the [petty-bourgeois] environment, which has begun to surround our few workers, cultivates them.[229]

The analysis presented in the Workers' Opposition's resolution on party organization for the tenth party congress was very similar, although it concentrated on the danger posed to the proletarian party by the bourgeoisie in state institutions:

alien elements entering the party... cut off from the working masses, bringing a departmental[230] psychology into the party, have obstructed the education (*vospitanie*) of the masses in the spirit of self-activity, and have delayed the replacement of the system of 'administration from above' and the tutelage of the high-ups (*verkhi*) over the rank and file (*nizy*), with comradely leadership.[231]

The leftists in the Red Army, the so-called 'Military Opposition', who objected to Trotsky's decision to employ tsarist officers, also emphasized the threat posed by bourgeois officials to the proper

---

[229] *Vos'moi s"ezd*, 199. For similar views, see *Desiatyi s"ezd*, 229–30 (Kollontai).

[230] 'Departmentalism' (*vedomstvennost'*) referred to the tendency of institutions, and particularly state institutions, to pursue their own departmental interests rather than the 'proletarian' interest.

[231] *Desiatyi s"ezd*, 652.

relationship between leaders and led. For Kliment Voroshilov, for instance, one of the Opposition's leaders, the bourgeois commander was a 'dead commander'; the real commander had to be the 'soul of his unit', 'to be related to and included in the masses in order to lead them'.[232] The left's perception of the nature of the proletarian leadership style and the threat posed to it by the bourgeoisie is well described by Dmitrii Furmanov in his popular semi-autobiographical novel, *Chapaev*. He presents an account of a meeting between a group of party men in the Red Army and the Bolshevik military commander Mikhail Frunze. Frunze was surrounded by a group of 'military specialists', or former tsarist officers, who were observing strict etiquette, bending forward to catch Frunze's every word. The party visitors understood that this polite, deferential behaviour was 'discipline', and that the way they themselves behaved was not appropriate, but they could not 'strike the right note'. They could not prevent themselves from calling Frunze by the diminutive 'Misha', 'disagreeing with them as if they were at a party committee'. The bourgeois officers, meanwhile, 'listened to them in bewilderment and watched, confused', on their guard lest they break the rules of subordination under the influence of these impolite newcomers. Yet once the officers left, the atmosphere changed at once and the discussion became much more open and frank.[233] Frunze and the party men were evidently much happier in a 'democratic', 'proletarian', and 'party' atmosphere than a 'disciplined' bourgeois one.

If, according to the left, the absence of proletarians in positions of influence explained the absence of 'democracy', any programme of 'democratization' would have to involve the replacement of bourgeois officials with proletarians who had links with the masses. And indeed both the Democratic Centralists and the Workers' Opposition called for the 'workerization' (*orabochenie*) of the apparatus, to be achieved by the 'promotion' (*vydvizhenie*) of proletarians. The Democratic Centralists suggested that 'more proletarian elements, elements which are directly linked with the working masses, should be brought into party'.[234] Similarly, Kutuzov of the Workers' Opposition argued that working-class officials should replace

[232] *Izv TsK KPSS*, 11 (1989), 160.
[233] D. Furmanov, *Izbrannoe* (Moscow, 1946), 34.
[234] *Desiatyi s"ezd*, 659.

more 'bureaucratic' bourgeois officials in order to forge 'links' between the apparatus and workers:

Wherever you go, wherever you write, everywhere [you receive] a refusal from the most natural bureaucrat . . . They have put people who are alien to the working class in charge of [state] departments. In my opinion, we should put a worker in every office who would receive workers and reply to them in their own language, even if it is just for the sake of decency, as a sign. Otherwise, we find ourselves in a position in which those in factory committees say, 'when you enter an office, they laugh at you'.[235]

Yet, despite the attractiveness of the class analysis of bureaucratism, the left encountered serious difficulties in their attempts to employ it. The revivalist notion that the existing proletariat was likely to be inherently virtuous and that the bourgeoisie was the source of bureaucratism could be used to justify neo-traditionalist arguments and legitimize the power of an emerging proletarian 'caste' or 'estate'. Within a very short time after the revolution, it had become clear to many that proletarian, Bolshevik officials were using their enormous political and economic power to establish themselves as a privileged group. The Menshevik Iulii Martov, for instance, de-nounced the 'commissars' estate' in 1920–1, and the left was par-ticularly scathing about the 'bureaucratic' and morally corrupt behaviour of class-pure Bolsheviks.[236] Sapronov observed:

in many places the word 'communist' is a term of abuse, because this or that communist, at the centre or in the localities, can afford such luxury that the worker or the peasant sees his behaviour as no better than that of an old bourgeois, and he cannot relate to him in any other way.[237]

Many workers and rank-and-file party members agreed with these sentiments, and there was a real temptation to reinterpret the popu-list socialist language of 1917 to attack Bolshevik officials: the *verkhi* were now not the bourgeoisie, but the communists, the members of a 'new class'.[238] One Workers' Oppositionist set of slogans de-clared 'Down with the embourgeoisified false-communists, generals,

[235] Ibid., 374–5.
[236] Iu. O. Martov to S. D. Shchupak, 20 June 1920, in V. Brovkin (ed.), *Dear Comrades. Menshevik Reports on the Bolshevik Revolution and the Civil War* (Stanford, 1991), 210.
[237] *Deviataia konferentsiia*, 161.
[238] A local 'workers' opposition' group within the party seized power in Tula in 1920 and used this type of leftist rhetoric to justify the 'workerization' of the party committee. See S. Pavliuchenkov, *Voennyi kommunizm*, 189–91.

self-seekers, down with the privileged caste of the communist élite [*verkhushka*]!'[239]

This type of analysis was naturally very dangerous for the regime, as it seemed to justify a new revolution against the new oppressors. Understandably, very few Bolsheviks were willing to entertain the notion of a 'new class', and those who did so were condemned for their heresy.[240] It was more acceptable for Bolsheviks on the left to blame 'bureaucratism' primarily on the old bourgeoisie, and the programmes of all leftist groups called both for purges of 'clearly careerist and [class] alien elements', and for the promotion of proletarians, in order to eliminate 'bureaucratism'.[241]

But how, then, could the 'bureaucratism' that was evident among proletarians within the party be explained in a way which did not give too much ammunition to the enemies of the party? There was no satisfactory answer to this question. The left and many other Bolsheviks on all wings of the party tended to resolve it by insisting that bureaucratism had its origins in the bourgeoisie, while alleging that some proletarian communists had become 'bureaucratized' through some form of psychological corruption as a consequence of excessive contact with the bourgeoisie. So, for instance, Voroshilov alleged that bourgeois officers 'stupefy' and 'assimilate to some degree the minds of our comrades'.[242] Zinoviev,

---

[239] Cited in V. V. Zhuravlev, M. K. Gorshkov, S. V. Kuleshov, A. K. Sorokin, and V. V. Shelokhaev (eds.), *Vlast' i oppozitsiia Rossiiskii politicheskii protsess xx stoletiia* (Moscow, 1995), 98.

[240] Bogdanov did not explicitly argue that a new class had emerged in the Soviet Union, but his followers did and he was condemned for this heresy. See J. Biggart, 'Aleksandr Bogdanov and the Theory of the New Class', *RR*, 49 (1990), 215–82. Even Trotsky, the most outspoken critic of the bureaucracy in the 1930s, refused to accept that it had become a class. See Trotsky, *The Revolution Betrayed*, 248–52; L. D. Trotsky, *The Class Nature of the Soviet State* (London, 1973), 15–21. See also Knei-Paz, *The Social and Political Thought of Leon Trotsky*, 389, 418–27. The idea that the bureaucracy was a 'new class' was popularized by Milovan Djilas in *The New Class* (New York, 1957).

[241] *Desiatyi s"ezd* 657, 659, 652. Some Democratic Centralists did criticize this 'class' analysis, but it would be an exaggeration to suggest that a coherent alternative, non-class analysis of bureaucratism was developed, as Sakwa suggests in his discussion of the thinking of E. N. Ignatov, a Democratic Centralist who later aligned himself with the Workers' Opposition. While Ignatov did reject the 'class' analysis of 'bureaucratism' in 1919 and did propose institutional change rather than changes in class composition, by 1921 Ignatov was calling for a 'purge' of non-proletarian groups from the party. See R. Sakwa, *Soviet Communists in Power*, 196; *Vos'moi s"ezd RKP(b)*, 188–9 (Osinskii); *Desiatyi s"ezd*, 239 (Ignatov).

[242] *Izv TsK KPSS*, 9 (1989), 157 (Voroshilov); see also ibid., 140 (Aleksandrov).

speaking on behalf of the leadership at the ninth party conference, accepted the left's argument that the bourgeois specialists were bearers of a psychological infection which they were passing on to communists. He admitted that a process of 'psychological assimilation' of communists and bourgeois specialists had begun: 'the communist does not assimilate the specialist in the cultural sense but the specialist assimilates our brother communist', and communists had relied on the specialists 'ideologically' and imitated them in their 'form of life'. Zinoviev identified the infectious ideology with authoritarian attitudes, particularly towards workers:

We [communists] will imitate them [the specialists] in technical knowledge, if they have this knowledge, but we will remember that we must not imitate them in the sphere of their relations with the working masses.[243]

Despite a common suspicion of bourgeois groups, there were differences within the left on the question of class. As one would expect, it was the more fundamentalist left that remained most committed to class struggle. In 1918 the Left Communists strongly criticized Lenin for making concessions to the bourgeoisie, insisting that they were still engaged in 'sabotage' and therefore should not be granted positions of responsibility. Two years later the Workers' Oppositionists made similar charges against the bourgeoisie. For Shliapnikov, the bourgeois specialists, working in the economic apparatus had created a fuel shortage and, in league with counter-revolutionary organizations, were deliberately undermining the economy. The leadership had 'delivered our economy into the hands of elements which are alien to us, into the hands of enemies', and this sabotage could only be eliminated if workers were allowed to control the activities of specialists.[244] While the Workers' Opposition did not suggest that the specialists could be dispensed with completely, they did consider that they had to be kept under strict control and viewed with suspicion.[245] As Kutuzov admitted: 'Comrades, it is said that I hate the specialists. Yes, it is true, and I will die hating them ... We must rule them with a rod of iron, as they used to rule us.'[246]

[243] *Deviataia konferentsiia*, 144 (Zinoviev). See also *Desiatyi s"ezd*, 228 (Bukharin).
[244] *Desiatyi s"ezd*, 363 (Shliapnikov); ibid., 374 (Kutuzov).
[245] A. Kollontai, *Workers' Opposition*, 45.
[246] *Deviataia konferentsiia*, 187 (Kutuzov).

The Democratic Centralists, who had more support within the party apparatus, were understandably more sceptical of class struggle, fearing that it would disrupt the economy and undermine the party's authority.[247] One Democratic Centralist, for instance, accused the Workers' Opposition of 'intelligentsia-baiting' (*intelligentoedstvo*) and of behaving like the anti-semites of the past.[248] Unlike the Workers' Opposition, the Democratic Centralists did not call for a wide range of restrictions on non-proletarian party members or for compulsory manual labour for all party members.[249] However, they did not abandon the Bolshevik commitment to class discrimination, nor did they replace it with a liberal defence of 'society' against a repressive state, but remained committed to the principle of class privilege and 'democracy for the poor'.[250] They did protest against the activities of the Cheka and the repressive policies of the state. But they mainly complained about the leadership's distortion of the class struggle. The leadership and local officials, they claimed, were directing class struggle against dissatisfied workers and poor peasants rather than against those whom the left considered to be genuine class enemies, the bourgeoisie.

G. I. Miasnikov, the leader of the leftist Workers' Group, exposed the left's ambivalent attitude towards class struggle very clearly. Miasnikov wrote to the Central Committee in May 1921 demanding that all political parties, from monarchists to anarchists, should enjoy the freedom of the press.[251] Lenin replied with a traditional defence of the principle of proletarian democracy. Democracy, he insisted, should only benefit the proletariat:

Every Marxist and every worker who ponders over the four years' experience of our revolution will say: 'Let's look into this—what sort of freedom of the press? What for? For which class? We do not believe in 'absolutes'. We laugh at 'pure democracy'.[252]

---

[247] For these fears, see K. Iurenev, *Nashi nestroenia. K voprosu o preodolenii elementov upadka v RKP* (Kursk, 1920), 31. Quoted in S. Pavliuchenkov, *Voennyi kommunizm*, 190–1.

[248] *Desiatyi s"ezd*, 274 (Rafail).

[249] See *Desiatyi s"ezd*, 656–62.

[250] *P*, 15 January 1919.

[251] For this episode, see P. Avrich, 'Bolshevik Opposition to Lenin: G.I. Miasnikov and the Workers' Group', *RR*, 43 (1984), 11.   [252] Lenin, *PSS*, xliv. 78.

Miasnikov responded not by challenging Lenin's definition of democracy, but by explaining that he wished to prevent the class struggle against the bourgeoisie from being directed against the working class itself:

You say that I want freedom of the press for the bourgeoisie. On the contrary, I want freedom of the press for myself, a proletarian, a member of the party for fifteen years... The trouble is that, while you raise your hand against the capitalist, you deal a blow to the worker.[253]

The left therefore criticized repression of workers, but was unwilling to condemn class discrimination. As will be shown in later chapters, populist revivalists were to find in future years that their call for 'class struggle' against the bourgeoisie was easily converted by élitist revivalists and neo-traditionalists into aggressive campaigns against disobedient groups among the workers and poor peasantry.

Class culture, politics, and economics

The left preferred to couch the debate with the leadership in the language of class and class culture, and that of 'advance' and 'retreat', because it could criticize the leadership for its poor treatment of the proletariat and its 'retreat' towards a more 'bourgeois' order. Kollontai, for instance, argued explicitly that a choice had to be made between a 'bourgeois' strategy based on hierarchies, compulsion, and the employment of bourgeois specialists, and a 'proletarian' strategy, relying on the reliance on the energies and enthusiasm of the working class:

the root of the controversy [between the left and the leadership] and the cause of the crisis lies in the supposition [of the leadership] that 'practical men', technicians, specialists and managers of capitalist production can suddenly release themselves from the bonds of their traditional conceptions of ways and means of handling labour (which have become deeply ingrained into their very flesh through the years of their service to capital) and acquire the ability to create new forms of production, of labour organization, of incentives to work.[254]

---

[253] P. Avrich, 'Bolshevik Opposition', 11. Miasnikov subsequently stated that he wished democracy to be confined to the proletariat. See ibid., 17.
[254] A. Kollontai, *The Workers' Opposition*, 25.

At times Lenin also engaged in debate on the left's favoured ground by discussing class and culture, but he fundamentally disagreed with them over the nature of the culture the regime had to promote. As has been seen, his theory of the vanguard party had always been based on the assumption that the success of the revolution depended on the mastery of advanced capitalist culture by revolutionaries, and he continued to argue that the advantages of bourgeois culture had to be accepted now that the revolutionaries were building the new state. He admitted that the regime was employing authoritarian bourgeois personnel and practices and that he was embracing bourgeois culture, but insisted there was no alternative. Bourgeois hierarchies, he argued, were a small price to pay for the bourgeoisie's knowledge:

We can only build communism out of the material created by capitalism, out of that cultured apparatus which has been cultivated under bourgeois conditions and which—as far as concerns the human material...is therefore inevitably steeped in bourgeois psychology.[255]

Similarly, in the years after 1921 he declared that communist virtues of loyalty, honesty, and bravery were not enough now that economic tasks were primary. Communists were 'inferior to the ordinary capitalist salesmen' who had been schooled in the large firm, in their ability to manage the economy; those Bolsheviks who refused to accept their weakness were guilty of 'communist arrogance' (komchvanstvo).[256]

Generally, however, Lenin and his allies preferred to downplay the issue of class and culture, and the importance of ideas and consciousness more generally. They insisted that in endorsing hierarchy they were merely responding to objective conditions, and they refused to admit that the regime was accepting a 'bourgeois' form of authority relations. They denied that the employment of bourgeois specialists, and the authoritarian behaviour of officials, had any implications for class relations. 'Political' questions, such as authority and class relations, were no longer an issue, as they had already been solved by the revolution. The 'best politics' now would be 'less politics'; politics had already been 'learned'.[257] 'Economic tasks' and tekhnika were priorities, and if the leadership was to achieve

---

[255] Lenin, PSS, xxxvii. 409.
[256] Ibid., xlv. 82 (27 March 1922).
[257] Ibid., xlii. 156–7 (22 December 1920).

its objectives, hierarchies, with technicians, 'practical' men, and 'business-like' people at the top, were vital. As Lenin explained, the Bolsheviks were reaching the time when 'engineers and agronomists' had to be brought to the fore and party people had to learn from them.[258]

Lenin also often used the term 'culture' in a different sense from that used by the left, seeing 'culture' not as a class mentality or worldview, but as a set of accomplishments that had to be acquired by all classes, such as literacy and the sort of discipline and 'civilized' behaviour that the masses needed to master if they were to be fit for modern, hierarchical industry. At times he suggested that 'culture' was nothing more than efficient organization; as he explained in May 1919, he was hostile to the intelligentsia's dreams of 'proletarian culture'. The 'fundamental task of proletarian culture, of proletarian organization', was the organization of bread and coal distribution.[259] Lenin was particularly eager to stress this economistic approach to politics in 1919 and 1920 when he perceived a threat to the party's primacy from the Proletkul't organizations, and he returned to his earlier uncompromising materialism by publishing a second edition of *Materialism and Empiriocriticism*.[260]

The left responded to these technicist arguments by refusing to accept that 'economics' and '*tekhnika*' were the regime's priorities. So, for Kollontai, Trotsky's authoritarian position was the consequence of his tendency to 'move the central point from politics to industrial problems'.[261] Similarly, one of the Military Opposition's main criticisms of the Red Army's high command was its neglect of '*politika*' and 'ideology', and its exclusive concentration on purely 'technical' concerns.[262]

The nature of the debate between the populist revivalist left and the élitist leadership over 'political' and 'economic' tasks was described in an incisive way by Bukharin and his allies during the

---

[258] Ibid., xlii. 157.

[259] Ibid., xxxviii. 368–9.

[260] See J. Biggart, 'Bukharin and the Origins of the "Proletarian Culture" Debate', *SS*, 39 (1987), 232. See also Sochor, *Revolution and Culture*, 168–75. For Lenin's position, see C. Claudin Urondo, *Lenin and the Cultural Revolution*, trans. by Brian Dean (Sussex, 1977), 79–83. For the ambiguities in Lenin's approach to 'culture', see M. David-Fox, 'What is Cultural Revolution?', *RR*, 58 (1999), 181–201.

[261] A. Kollontai, *The Workers' Opposition*, 35.

[262] See, for instance, S. K. Minin, 'Voennoe stroitel'stvo. Tezisy', *Izv TsK KPSS*, 10 (1989), 187, 185.

debates of 1920–1 on the relationship between the trade unions, the party, and the state. They argued that there were two 'tendencies' in the discussion, 'one which assesses the situation exclusively from a political point of view, and the other which assigns primary import-ance to the economic point of view'. 'Political' tasks involved 'democratic' mobilization: they included 'the establishment of the complete unity of the proletariat' and the 'rallying of the party on the basis of the revival of party thought and of the involvement of all members of the party in its active life', presupposing 'a system of inner-party workers' democracy'. 'Economic' tasks, on the other hand, involved a more hierarchical, élitist approach to authority relations, and included the 'strengthening of a firm administrative framework' and the pursuit of 'planned work in economic life'. Bukharin and his colleagues tried to formulate a third way, in which both 'politics' and 'economics' were combined. Economic success was needed if popular discontent was to be addressed, and that success would only be possible if 'conflicts within the proletar-iat' (i.e. conflicts between the party élite and the working class) were reduced to a minimum.[263]

The struggle for the soul of the party

Bukharin's proposals were vague, and it is not immediately obvious how Bolsheviks could promote either 'political' and 'economic' approaches in practice. As has been seen, one way was to manipu-late the class composition of the apparatus: naturally 'democratic' proletarians would help the regime achieve its 'political' goals, while the bourgeoisie, or 'business-like' officials, would promote 'economic' objectives. The other solution, proposed by both left and leadership, was to alter the relationship between institutions.

Leftists' thinking on institutional reform was contradictory and ambivalent. At times their objectives were almost liberal in inspir-ation: they tried to protect organizations, particularly in the local-ities, against the increasing power of the centre, by defining the relationship between Moscow and the regions. In particular, they tried to prevent the increasingly intrusive party Central Committee from interfering in local party organizations, the soviets, and trade

---

[263] *Desiatyi s"ezd*, 826 (Bukharin *et al.*).

unions.[264] So, for instance, Osinskii called for a 'precise demarcation' of central and local powers, established 'legally'.[265] The Democratic Centralists also called for the election of party officials and for different factions to be represented within the party'.[266] Yet, as has been seen, they found it difficult consistently to pursue institutional reform along liberal lines, and most of their proposals did not have liberal, but populist revivalist goals: they were designed not to delineate the powers and roles of institutions by legal means, but to transform leadership style and, as a result, narrow the 'gap' between regime and masses.

Both the left and the leadership frequently saw institutions in the same culturalist way that they saw class: like classes, institutions were regarded as 'bearers' of particular 'cultures' and 'styles' of leadership. The party had a variety of tasks which required different forms of behaviour. It had to ensure that the whole regime was following an ideologically correct course, an objective which suggested a disciplinarian approach to politics. But it was also to create a socialist society by transforming people, educating them in socialist values, and enthusing them; therefore for both the left and the leadership it was regarded as an institution that had an intrinsically 'democratic' mobilizing culture, most suited to the performance of 'political' tasks; in contrast, the 'state' or 'soviet' institutions (by which they generally meant state economic or military organizations, or soviet executive committees, rather than the elected soviets) embodied a 'business-like' culture, appropriate for the solution of 'economic' tasks. The leadership, therefore, urged that the party be subordinated to the state and infused with the state's culture. The left, on the other hand, demanded that the party be insulated from the influence of the state's culture and communicate its 'democratic' culture to the state.[267]

---

[264] For the left's attempts to defend the local soviets and local party organizations against the centre, see R. Sakwa, *Soviet Communists in Power*, chs. 6–7.

[265] *Vos'moi s"ezd*, 196.

[266] Although they insisted that this had to be combined with party discipline and the 'unity' of the party. *Desiatyi s"ezd*, 659.

[267] By the 'left' here I mean the Left Communists and the Democratic Centralists rather than the Workers' Opposition, although the Workers' Opposition, while ambivalent about the role of the party, also championed lower party organizations. For the position of the Workers' Opposition, and the debate over party–state relations more generally, see D. Priestland, 'Bolshevik Ideology and the Debate over Party-State Relations, 1918–1921', *Revolutionary Russia*, 10 (1997), 37–61.

While the left frequently criticized authoritarian trends within the party and condemned the high-handed behaviour of the Central Committee, it still considered that the party was the quintessential 'political' organization, and it therefore argued that its influence should be increased, particularly over state organizations. As the Left Communist V. Sorin argued, state organizations suffered from 'conservatism', and their officials, often of bourgeois origin and 'inattentive to the needs of workers', were attempting to 'avoid the supervision of the party'.[268] Many on the left were, of course, party officials themselves and had their own reasons to attack the power of the state apparatus, but they were able to use a set of well-established populist revivalist arguments in the defence of their institutional interests.

The demand that the influence of the party be strengthened appears to contradict the equally strongly held view of the left that the party be separated from the state. At the eighth party congress the Democratic Centralist E. N. Ignatov argued that party committees' tendency to 'confer upon themselves the functions of the soviets' was unacceptable; instead the functions of party and soviets should be 'demarcated'.[269] Similarly, at the tenth party congress, the Workers' Opposition insisted that at least a third of the 'members of party centres' should not 'personally mix party and soviet work'.[270] The left's position, however, is only contradictory if one assumes that it was trying to delineate the functions of party and state. If we understand the Bolsheviks' idiosyncratic view of institutions, as bearers of particular cultures, the influence of which had to be extended or resisted, the left's position makes much more sense. In calling for the separation of party from state, the left was trying to insulate the party from the malign influence of the state's culture. If the party was too closely associated with the state, the state would, it was argued, infect the party with its 'bureaucratism'. As the Democratic Centralist Maksimovskii explained, 'the crisis of our party and soviet centre' was

primarily brought about by the situation in the soviets. Now it has become perfectly clear to everybody... that our soviet and party centres have become closer, that a whole range of shortcomings in our party apparatus

---

[268] *Kommunist*, 4 (1918), 7.
[269] *Vos'moi s"ezd*, 199 (Ignatov).
[270] *Desiatyi s"ezd*, 655; see also, ibid., 658.

flows from the characteristic feature that the party is a ruling party, that it is linked with state power, that it is impossible to separate the crisis of the party centres from the crisis of the soviet centres. Therefore this soviet crisis... this crisis of the bureaucratic centre, which mainly resulted from that intensive policy which was maintained by the bureaucratic centralism of our apparatus, has been discovered in and has affected the crisis in our party centre.[271]

The left's notion that institutions could transmit their values to each other is, of course, similar to its view that classes could infect each other, and the two ideas were connected: state organizations and the industrial hierarchy employed a particularly large number of bourgeois officials. The left, therefore, considered that state institutions were 'bureaucratic', partly due to their class composition and partly because of their institutional functions.[272] A close institutional relationship between party and state would help to transmit bourgeois soviet officials' attitudes and psychology to a party which in essence, if not necessarily in reality, was 'democratic' and 'proletarian'. So, according to Kollontai, 'groups standing outside the party continually exert influence on our party', and acting 'through the soviets, have a demoralizing effect on our party, forcing it to deviate in the direction of petty-bourgeois tendencies...'. She went on to describe officials in the state apparatus as 'representatives of the bourgeois world', accusing them of exerting psychological 'pressure' on the party. Kollontai's solution was to suggest that the state had to be prised away from the party in order to strengthen the party: to protect the party from alien influences, one-third of officials was to avoid participation in the activities of soviet organizations, thus creating a group of purely 'party' people who could prevent other party officials from yielding to 'class alien' and 'departmental' influences.[273]

The left's attempt to protect the party from infection by the state's 'intensive' or disciplinarian methods also lay behind its criticism of the party's excessive emphasis on 'economic' or 'state' work and its neglect of 'party' or 'political work'. Party officials, they argued, were becoming too involved in the activities of state organizations

[271] *Desiatyi s"ezd*, 246–7.
[272] For the class composition of state organizations, see D. Rowney, *The Transition to Technocracy. The Structural Origins of the Soviet Administrative State* (London, 1989), 131–59; K. Bailes, *Technology and Society*, ch. 2.
[273] *Desiatyi s"ezd*, 299–301.

and were therefore absorbing their authoritarian institutional style. As Safarov, a member of the Military Opposition, complained, party officials 'forget that they are communists above all and not military commanders'; 'isolated in a purely military sphere' they had forgotten about 'party work'.[274]

At the same time, however, both the Workers' Opposition and the Democratic Centralists insisted that the insulation of the party from the state was to be combined with the transmission of the party's culture to the state. Kollontai, having argued that party officials should not hold positions in the state apparatus in order to ensure that they performed 'party work', explained that the real objective was that 'party centres...would really serve as organs of ideological supervision over the soviet institutions and would direct their actions along clear-cut class lines'.[275] Similarly, the Democratic Centralists' programme on party organization proposed that the party's Central Committee should maintain strict supervision of party groups within soviet institutions, taking particular care to choose suitable people to lead them.[276]

Élitists within the leadership accepted the left's judgement that the party had a 'democratic' culture, while the state's was 'business-like', but their intentions were diametrically opposed to those of the left. They hoped to transform both party and state into efficient, 'business-like' organizations in which 'practical' rather than 'political' considerations were paramount. The left's subordination of the 'business-like' to the 'political' was condemned by the leadership. Zinoviev, for instance, objected to the left's complaints that Sovnarkom was too 'business-like'; rather, he argued, it was not 'business-like' enough.[277]

In their promotion of a 'business-like' culture, élitist Bolsheviks in the leadership, like the left, proposed contradictory institutional reforms. Some argued, against the left, that party cells should not be permitted to interfere in the business of managerial organizations, on the grounds that they would disrupt the fulfilment of tasks properly carried out by experts.[278] However, while arguing that

---

[274] *Izv TsK KPSS*, 9 (1989), 135. See also *Vos'moi s"ezd*, 170 (Sapronov).

[275] A. Kollontai, *The Workers' Opposition*, 58.

[276] *Desiatyi s"ezd*, 659.

[277] *Vos'moi s"ezd*, 289.

[278] *Desiatyi s"ezd*, 301 (Mashatov); for similar approaches to the role of the party cell, see ibid., 259–60 (Smilga); ibid., 294–5 (Riazanov).

soviet and economic organs should be free of party interference, élitist Bolsheviks proposed that the party should be closely associated with the state institutionally so that the state could transmit its culture to the party; the party was to be transformed into an organization similar to the state, in which 'business-like' rather than 'political' considerations were primary.[279] While Lenin and the Central Committee normally insisted that the party and state remain separate, they were moving towards support for the 'statization' of the party in particular sectors.[280] They seem to have considered that in some parts of the economy the existing party apparatus would never become elements in an efficient centralized hierarchy, and would therefore have to be replaced with a new 'statized' party organization, less 'democratic' and more suited to imposing discipline: the 'political department' (*politotdel*). The political departments first became widespread in the Red Army, and by the beginning of 1919 they had become the most powerful political bodies, removing a great deal of authority from the party committee structure at the front.[281] Their officials were appointed rather than elected, and they were similar in structure and culture to the state apparatus.[282] Championed by Trotsky, they were soon introduced into the transport sector as well.[283]

V. A. Avanesov, a member of VTsIK, explained the objectives of the leadership clearly at the eighth congress:

We [the party] are no longer an illegal organization, we have grown out of the narrow framework in which we existed before, we have become the state, but you [Osinskii and the left] want to push the state into this illegal framework and to say that we can carry out the work as we did before within this framework.[284]

Avanesov objected to Osinskii's demand for more 'party' work, arguing that 'now the broad masses expect not agitation and propaganda, but demand construction, they demand not that we should

[279] See, for instance, *Desiatyi s"ezd*, 255 (Smilga).
[280] Although Lenin did not agree with those who objected in principle to joint party–state organizations. See Lenin, *PSS*, xlv. 398.
[281] *P*, 10 January 1919.
[282] F. Benvenuti, *The Bolsheviks and the Red Army*, 52–64.
[283] W. G. Rosenberg, 'The Social Background to Tsektran', in D. P. Koenker, W. G. Rosenberg, and R. G. Suny (eds.), *Party, State and Ideology in the Russian Civil War* (Bloomington, 1989), 352–3.
[284] *Vos'moi s"ezd*, 177–8 (Avanesov).

agitate about bread but that we should provide it...'.[285] Avanesov thus provided a succinct summary of the fundamental debate between the élitist leadership and the left. For the left, the state had to adopt the 'democratic' 'political' values of the pre-revolutionary party, while, for the élitists, now the party had achieved power, it had to become similar to the more hierarchical state. The party had to give up its 'democratic', 'political work' and adopt more authoritarian 'economic work'. As one leftist complained, having planned to 'partyize' (*opartiit*') the state, the Bolsheviks had come to 'statize (*ogosudarstvit*') the party'.[286]

The trade union debate and the crisis of Bolshevik power, 1920–1

By 1920–1, therefore, the vision of socialism presented by Lenin in 1917 had disintegrated, and rivals within the party fought over its legacy. A few Bolsheviks, with some representation in the trade unions, called for a fundamentalist form of the populist revivalism advocated in *State and Revolution*. The more moderate left, particularly evident in local party and Soviet organizations, adopted a less populist revivalism, which in practice amounted to a programme of democratization of leadership style, party revival, 'democratic' class struggle and purges of the bureaucracy. Trotsky, meanwhile, with a strong base of support within the army, took a much more élitist revivalist position. He rejected class struggle and decried notions of proletarian virtue, but urged the use of harsh shock methods and mobilization to transform Russia and centralize the state. He was resisted by leaders, some of whom occupied posts in the economic bureaucracies, who used technicist arguments to defend a more gradualist approach to economic and political development. All of these groups came into conflict during the traumatic debates on the trade unions in 1920–1.[287]

---

[285] *Vos' moi s"ezd*, 177 (Avanesov).
[286] Iurenev, *Nashi nestroenia*, 6. Quoted in S. Pavliuchenkov, *Voennyi kommunizm*, 88.
[287] For accounts of this debate, see R. Daniels, *Conscience of the Revolution*, ch. 5; S. Pavliuchenkov, *Voennyi kommunizm*, 175–82; R. Sakwa, *Soviet Communists in Power*, 247 ff.

Lenin had supported Trotsky in his application of élitist revivalist solutions to the transport industry, and Trotsky proceeded to employ shock methods and tighten up labour discipline. He used Glavpolitput', the political department attached to the People's Commissariat of Railways, and Glavpolitvod, the equivalent institution in water transport, to implement his regime, and these organizations effectively absorbed the trade union apparatus, which was consolidated into a new 'statized' trade union, Tsektran. Trotsky had created a merged trade union and state body which was, in effect, controlled by new, militarized state bodies.[288] In the autumn of 1920, Trotsky proposed that this model be applied to the whole of the trade union hierarchy. He justified the merging of the state and trade union organizations as an advance towards socialism and the resulting dissolution of all divisions between state and society.[289]

Trotsky naturally encountered opposition to his plans from the Workers' Opposition and Democratic Centralists, from trade union and local party officials, and from economic institutions.[290] And in response to this hostility, Lenin and the leadership made concessions to the left at the ninth party conference, in September 1920, accepting that greater 'democracy' should be allowed in the party, and that political departments should be gradually eliminated.[291] The Central Committee also applied this 'democratization' to the industrial sphere, and ruled that the trade union bureaucracy would control Trotsky's state–union bodies. Trotsky refused to accept defeat, and fought for his militarized model of administration throughout industry, precipitating the 'trade union discussion', a debate that became a more general dispute over the question of 'democracy' within the party and the state.[292] Lenin, Rykov, and the majority of the Central Committee used highly gradualist arguments to counter the threat from Trotsky and his proposals for statized trade unions. The time was not yet ripe, Lenin argued, for the merging of workers' organizations and the state, because the state,

[288] W. Rosenberg, 'The Social Background to Tsektran', 352–3. See also L. Schapiro, *The Origins of the Communist Autocracy*, 257–62.

[289] *Desiatyi s"ezd*, 816; L. D. Trotsky, 'Rol' i zadachi professional'nykh soiuzov', in G. Zinoviev, *Partiia i soiuzy (k diskussii o roli i zadachakh profsoiuzov)* (Petrograd, 1921), 258–9, 251.

[290] Although Rykov initially supported Trotsky against the trade unions.

[291] *Deviataia konferentsiia*, 276–82.

[292] S. Pavliuchenkov, *Voennyi kommunizm*, 176–7.

while a workers' and peasants' state, suffered from a 'bureaucratic distortion', and its interests were not yet identical to those of the working class. Workers thus had to have their own organization to defend themselves against the state.[293]

The split between Trotsky and Lenin within the Central Committee also gave the left an opportunity to press its case, and the Workers' Opposition in particular found an increasingly large audience for its condemnation of the regime's 'bureaucratization' at lower levels of the party and in the trade unions.[294] The left appeared even more threatening to the leadership when, in February 1921, soldiers and workers on the Kronshtadt naval base in Petrograd rebelled, calling for a 'third revolution' against the Bolsheviks and using populist socialist slogans to challenge the new communist 'bureaucracy'.[295]

During the trade union debates, it became evident that various alliances between populist revivalists, élitist revivalists, and technicists were possible. Technicists and élitist revivalists were the most natural allies, as they were fundamentally in agreement on the central question of class and the relationship between workers and the regime. Ultimately, when the regime was challenged by the Kronshtadt rebels, they buried their differences and both supported the use of repression against the disaffected workers and the Workers' Opposition. Yet populist and élitist revivalists also had much in common, as they could agree on the question of 'advance' towards 'socialism' and integration. Unlike Lenin and Rykov, Trotsky and the Workers' Opposition both favoured the merging of the trade unions and the state, even if the Workers' Opposition hoped for a 'democratic' 'unionized' state, while Trotsky was trying to create more hierarchical 'statized' unions. Bukharin recognized the common features of the populist and élitist revivalist positions, and tried to create a compromise, 'buffer' group. He proposed that unions and state merge, and that the 'democratic' features of the unions be combined with the 'business-like' features of the state in the new merged body.[296]

[293] Lenin, *PSS*, xlii. 208.
[294] *Desiatyi s"ezd*, 845–6; Pavliuchenkov, *Voennyi kommunizm*, 189–91.
[295] P. Avrich, *Kronstadt, 1917* (Princeton, 1970), ch. 5; I. Getzler, *Kronstadt, 1917–1921. The Fate of a Soviet Democracy* (Cambridge, 1983), 233–4.
[296] *Desiatyi s"ezd*, 826–30 (Bukharin et al.).

Another, rather different but ultimately much more influential compromise between populist and élitist revivalist positions can be discerned in the speeches and writings of a relatively peripheral figure in these debates—Iosif Stalin. In this period Stalin was given a number of difficult, practical responsibilities at a time of civil war, as Commissar for Nationalities, member of the Military Revolutionary Council, and Commissar for State Control (later to become the Workers' and Peasants' Inspection head of). But his thinking was recognizably that of the Georgian party activist of the first decade of the century. He tried to transform the institutions he led—party, state, and military—into powerful unified political forces, but he insisted that in order for this to happen they had to be founded on an inspired and loyal proletariat. He also connected the question of class with that of national security, stressing the dangers from ideologically unreliable class aliens. Not only, he alleged, were they potentially disloyal at a time of war but their 'alien' ideas would also undermine effective mobilization.

He expressed these views most clearly when he allied with the leftist 'Military Opposition' against Trotsky over the role of former tsarist officers. He became involved in the military debate when, as a plenipotentiary on the southern front, he had come into conflict with Sytin, Trotsky's appointee as military commander and a former tsarist officer.[297] However, he seems to have been worried about the issue of class in the army more generally, and followed the leftist view that class aliens were likely to be both politically unreliable and less effective than proletarians. He was particularly critical of the former tsarist officers, but his mistrust also extended to kulaks among rank-and-file soldiers.[298] In his account of the reasons for the fall of Perm' in December 1918, he ascribed the army's weakness to the fact that soldiers were recruited to the army irrespective of their class or 'property status', and that the army was becoming a 'popular [narodnyi] army' rather than a proletarian 'Red Army'. Class alien soldiers and officers, he suggested, were not only potentially counter-revolutionary but also unmotivated, and in order to convert a brigade sent to him from the centre into a 'competent fighting unit', he had been forced to carry out a 'purge'

---

[297] For an account of the 'Tsaristyn group' and Stalin's role in it, see F. Benvenuti, *The Bolsheviks and the Red Army*, 42–52.
[298] *Izv TsK KPSS*, 11 (1989), 166.

and 'careful filtration'. The 'staunchness' (*stoikost'*) of the army in the early months of the civil war, he asserted, was due to the fact that only those who did not exploit labour were recruited. In future, he argued, recruits had to be strictly divided into 'propertied men (unreliable) and non-propertied men (who are alone suitable for Red Army service)'.[299] The following year, in an interview with *Pravda*, he turned his attention to the dangers presented by class 'aliens' in the 'rear'—that is in society as a whole—and outlined a scenario which was to resurface in his thinking in future years: foreign powers and white-guardist spies, he alleged, had bribed venal army officers and conspired with the 'bourgeoisie', or 'former people' (*byvshie*). They had tried to combine an offensive with a counter-revolutionary uprising in Petrograd, but fortunately their plans had been foiled.[300]

Yet, for Stalin, purges of class aliens were not the only solution to military problems. He also criticized the neglect of 'political-educational work' within the army at Perm', and he, like others in the Military Opposition, believed that 'political *vospitanie*' in the army had 'enormous significance'; soldiers had to be '*vospitany* in the revolutionary spirit'.[301] Even so, his views did not entirely coincide with others on the military left. He placed much more emphasis on the need for 'iron discipline' in the army, and he justified this view by taking a particularly pessimistic view of the peasantry. Peasants, he argued, would not fight voluntarily for socialism, and therefore had to be forced to fight.[302]

Stalin, then, saw the development of a proletarian spirit and a harsh approach to class aliens as essential if Soviet Russia was to be sufficiently unified to win the war, but interestingly he also revealed

---

[299] I. V. Stalin, *Sochineniia*, 13 vols. (Moscow, 1946–51), iv. 206–8.

[300] Ibid., iv. 267–8.

[301] Ibid., iv. 209; *Izv TsK KPSS*, 11 (1989), 164.

[302] See Stalin's objections to Smirnov's theses and his claim that they would undermine discipline, *Izv TsK KPSS*, 11 (1989), 163–4. For Smirnov's theses, see ibid., 9 (1989), 181–4. Smirnov, like Stalin, accepted that discipline had to be introduced by both political *vospitanie* and external compulsion, and that kulak elements had to be separated from the rest of the army and used only in the rear, but Stalin clearly thought that he was not sufficiently aware of the need to impose discipline on a largely peasant army. These doubts about the reliability of 'backward' classes can also be seen in Stalin's scepticism about the possibility of socialist advance in the countryside in 1917, when he opposed Lenin's call for the nationalization of land. See R. Service, 'Joseph Stalin: The Making of a Stalinist', in J. Channon (ed.), *Politics, Society and Stalinism in the USSR* (London, 1998), 18–19.

a recognition that a strong national spirit might be as valuable as a class spirit.[303] Using the organicist, vitalist language he had used in the past, he explained that if troops were to be victorious in civil war 'unity is absolutely essential, that cohesion of the living human environment, whose elements nourish and whose juices sustain these troops'. This unity could be 'national', or 'class' in nature; the Bolsheviks were succeeding partly because they had class unity, but also partly because Russia was 'nationally united and solid'. In contrast, the areas where the Whites were operating—the eastern and southern borderlands—were socially and ethnically divided, and White forces had weak roots there.[304] Stalin's view that national unity and mobilization could be as effective as class mobilization was to re-emerge in the 1930s.

During the civil war, then, Stalin occupied a position between Trotsky's élitist revivalism and the left's populist revivalism. Like Trotsky, he hoped for mobilization without a serious 'democratization' of the army, but unlike Trotsky, he believed in the need for discrimination against the bourgeoisie; only a proletarian officer corps, he insisted, could mobilize and ensure discipline. He also supported the claims of the political authorities, and the party, against those of the 'state' structures—in this case the military. Stalin's other activities and statements during the civil war suggest that this set of attitudes was reasonably consistent. As head of the Workers' and Peasants' Inspection (Rabkrin), Stalin was in charge of an institution designed by Lenin to root out 'bureaucratism' in the state machine, but he was more hostile to bourgeois experts than Lenin and Trotsky. Although 'bureaucratism' had been smashed, he argued in October 1920, 'bureaucrats' remained, people who 'started their old tricks in order to plunder state property' and 'introduced their old bourgeois customs'.[305] Trotsky clearly disapproved of this anti-'bureaucratism', and he criticized Stalin's Rabkrin for inefficiency and lack of expertise, although Lenin, at least for the time being, refused to join him.[306]

---

[303] Other leaders also shared Stalin's recognition of the power of nation and his emphasis on national unity. See J. Sanborn, *Drafting the Russian Nation. Military Conscription, Total War and Mass Politics, 1905–1925* (Dekalb, 2003), ch. 3.

[304] Stalin, *Sochineniia*, iv. 286–7. For Stalin, an advanced and unified Russia had to dominate the backward periphery. See A. Rieber, 'Stalin, Man of the Borderlands', *AHR* 106 (2001), 1651–91.

[305] Ibid., iv. 365.

[306] Trotsky, *Sochineniia*, xv. 223.

In his contribution to the trade union debates of 1920–1, Stalin's continuing interest in mobilization is clear, although he now adopted a more populist revivalist tone than he used during the military debates at the eighth congress. He defended his new approach by explaining that iron discipline had been needed in the army because it included peasants and other non-proletarian social groups; now that the party's attention had to be redirected away from military questions and the army and towards economic issues and workers, 'persuasion' was much more effective than 'force'.[307] He therefore strongly criticized Trotsky's proposal that 'military methods' be used by the regime in its dealings with the working class. Methods of 'democracy' and 'persuasion' had to be employed because the struggle against economic ruin had to become a 'vital concern of the whole working class'. If workers were not involved and enthused, 'victory on the economic front cannot be achieved'.[308]

Stalin, then, at times advocated harsh discipline, and at other times 'democratic' mobilization, depending on circumstances and the social groups involved. But throughout the period it is possible to discern his interest in class and class discrimination. This is also suggested by Andrea Graziosi's study of the conflicts between Trotsky's protégé, Piatakov, and a group of officials associated with Stalin in the Donbass.[309] Piatakov and Stalin's group were equally harsh and disciplinarian in their behaviour towards workers, and both tried to use state power to mobilize them. Where they differed was in their approach to class and the specialists. Unlike Piatakov, who followed Trotsky's line and defended the specialists, the Stalinists took a more populist, anti-bourgeois position. This combination of populist and élitist revivalism was strikingly similar to the position that he was to defend at the end of the 1920s.

---

[307] RGASPI 558/11/1101, 108–10 (speech to Moscow Party Committee, 1921). Stalin's language was different from Lenin's during this period. In his speech of December 1920, Lenin appreciated the importance of popular enthusiasm, but insisted that the turn from the military to the 'economic front' demanded 'new forms [of organization] associated with compulsion'. Lenin, *PSS*, xlii. 144.

[308] Stalin, *Sochineniia*, v. 9.

[309] A. Graziosi, 'At the Roots of Soviet Industrial Relations and Practice. Piatakov's Donbass in 1921', *CMRS*, 36 (1995), 130–2.

2

The Emergence of Left
and Right, 1921–1927

After 1918 the Bolsheviks had tried to establish control over Russia and revive its economy with a mixture of compulsion, material, and, to some extent, moral incentives. But as inflation soared and industrial production collapsed, material incentives became increasingly ineffective. Even if the requisitioning of grain left peasants with some surplus over and above their tax, there was little to exchange it for—money lost its value and there were few industrial goods.[1] Peasants therefore refused to grow or give up their grain to the state and the towns. Workers were in a similar position. The regime's attempts to introduce bonus schemes and piece-rates to stimulate productivity were undermined by the worthlessness of money and the shortage of food.[2] The Bolsheviks therefore had only one weapon left in their armoury: force. Compulsion was increasingly used to extract grain from the peasantry and to discipline workers. But by the beginning of 1921 it had become evident to many in the Bolshevik élite that this strategy was not working. The state was not strong enough to take the surplus from the peasantry, and urban strikes and rural rebellions were threatening the Bolsheviks.

In 1921 Lenin realized that the regime was on the verge of collapse, as it had been in 1918. He now understood that both technicist and élitist revivalist approaches had to be reconsidered, just as he appreciated in 1918 that populist revivalism had failed. The technicist assumption that in the absence of market relations the state and economy would operate like a well-tuned machine was

---

[1] See L. Lih, *Bread and Authority*, 259–60.
[2] E. H. Carr, *The Bolshevik Revolution, 1917–1923* (Harmondsworth, 1971), ii. 219–20.

clearly false. The élitist revivalist view that the state could mobilize the population and thus force economic development, irrespective of objective constraints, could also no longer be sustained. Lenin therefore gave in to overwhelming pressures and introduced a whole series of measures to expand the role of material incentives by restoring the market, as part of his New Economic Policy (NEP). The period also saw a number of other developments that involved less state compulsion and centralization. There was some attempt to accommodate the old intelligentsia, and some limits were placed on the Cheka.[3] Moscow also continued and deepened its policy of developing indigenous cultures and political élites in non-Russian republics, although within a centralized Soviet Union.[4] All of these changes took place within a framework of party and state control: the political monopoly of the party was maintained, as was state control over heavy industry. Despite this, however, it is understandable that all of these measures should have provoked opposition from within a party that had been so hostile to the market for so long.[5] The party was convulsed with ideological conflict throughout the period, between the Politburo majority, which included Bukharin and Stalin, and the left, now joined by Trotsky. And at the centre of debate was the question of the NEP's legitimacy.

The nature of this debate has been the subject of a great deal of controversy. For some conflictualist historians, divisions within the Bolshevik party were transformed during the NEP. The NEP came to be seen by Bukharin and those described by the Stalinists as the 'right', as a new model of socialism—a coherent, semi-liberal alternative to the statist socialism of the civil war and Stalinist periods.[6] Had Lenin lived or Bukharin been victorious in the political struggles

[3] S. Fitzpatrick, 'The "Soft" Line on Culture and its Enemies: Soviet Cultural Policy 1922–1927', *SR*, 33 (1974), 267–87. For a different emphasis, see K. Clark, 'The "Quiet Revolution" in Russian Intellectual Life', in S. Fitzpatrick, A. Rabinowitch, and Richard Stites (eds.), *Russia in the Era of NEP* (Bloomington, 1991), 210–30. For limits on the Cheka, see below.

[4] For the relationship between these developments and the NEP, see Yuri Slezkine, 'The Soviet Union as a Communal Apartment, or How a Socialist State Promoted Ethnic Particularism', in S. Fitzpatrick, *Stalinism*, 318–19. See also J. Smith, *The Bolsheviks and the National Question*, chs. 6–8.

[5] See, for instance, R. Service, *Lenin: A Political Life*. vol. 3: *The Iron Ring* (Basingstoke, 1995), 214–18.

[6] S. Cohen, *Rethinking the Soviet Experience*, 74–8; Cohen, *Bukharin*, 147; Lewin argues that the NEP model was a 'liberal dictatorship'. M. Lewin, *Political Undercurrents*, 46–7, 96.

of the 1920s, a liberal, market socialism might have continued to provide an alternative to the extremism and statist coercion of the Stalin era.[7] Liberal historians, however, have argued for continuities. The NEP was a straightforwardly pragmatic 'retreat' from the Bolsheviks' ideological goals to an incoherent and ultimately unsustainable mixture of a fundamentally illiberal Bolshevism and liberalism. The party was therefore divided between 'advancers' and 'retreaters', but, given the Bolsheviks' militant commitment to the preservation of the party's monopoly and the achievement of socialism, it was only a matter of time before the retreaters lost and the NEP was abandoned.[8] An alternative conflictualist interpretation also discerns continuities. For Robert Daniels, the left represented a vision of Bolshevism that was 'more Western-oriented' and 'more democratic than the Lenin-Stalin current'.[9] The 1920s therefore saw the continuation of the civil war conflict between a 'democratic', outward-looking left and the Russian-centred statist Bolshevism of the Politburo majority.

This chapter will suggest that political discussion during the NEP era makes most sense if we see the period as a transitional one, in which the large number of positions expressed in the civil war conflicts coalesced into the revivalist and technicist Bolshevisms that dominated the politics of the late 1920s and underlay that of the 1930s. We can therefore see both continuities and changes in the nature of debate after 1921. While the introduction of the NEP did alter the context of the divisions within the party, there was no fundamental change from the divisions of the civil war period, whether to a simple conflict between ideological advancers and pragmatic retreaters or to a dispute between semi-liberals and statists. Nor did a confrontation between Western-oriented democratic Marxists and Russocentric statists dominate Soviet politics. Although Trotsky did indeed call for greater integration into the international economy and he was critical of the autarkic and

---

[7] S. Cohen, 'Bolshevism and Stalinism', in R. Tucker (ed.), *Stalinism. Essays in Historical Interpretation* (New York, 1977), 3–30.

[8] M. Malia, *The Soviet Tragedy*, 174–5. See also V. Brovkin, *Russia after Lenin. Politics, Culture and Society, 1921–1929* (London, 1998), 14. Lih defends a slightly different view, arguing that Lenin and Bukharin had a coherent position, but never saw the NEP as anything more than a temporary stage on the way to full socialism. L. Lih, 'The Political Testament of Lenin and Bukharin and the Meaning of NEP', *SR*, 50 (1991), 241–52.

[9] R. Daniels, *Conscience of the Revolution*, 409.

nationalistic implications of Stalin's and Bukharin's call for 'socialism in one country', Trotsky's allies on the left did not always share his views on the issue, and the dispute between 'isolationists' and 'internationalists' cut across the divisions between left and right.[10] Rather, the central debates of the period should be seen in the context of continuing tensions between technicists, élitist revivalists, and populist revivalists. As before, questions of class, class culture, leadership style, incentives, the relationship between *politika* and *tekhnika*, and the pace of advance towards socialism structured the conflict. Populist and élitist revivalists both called for an improvement in the position of the proletariat and demanded rapid advance towards socialism: élitist revivalists criticized the NEP's gradualism for delaying socialism and industrialization, and hence undermining the broader interests of the working class; while populist revivalists condemned it for establishing 'bourgeois' inequalities and undermining workers' living standards. Cohen's view of the left as the representatives of a militarist, 'revolutionary heroic' tradition in Bolshevism is, therefore, valid but one-sided, as it neglects the populist 'democratic' element in some leftist thought.[11] Yet neither should the left be seen as quasi-liberal: like the left of the civil war period, the NEP left was revivalist. Lenin and the supporters of NEP, meanwhile, generally based their arguments on broadly technicist principles. They were still defending the primacy of *tekhnika* and expertise, the need to take account of objective conditions, and move forward to socialism gradually. Their attitude towards the working class was similarly technicist, and did not change much from the civil war period: in the industrial 'socialist' sector of the economy, discipline and hierarchy were to reign.

However, the NEP did bring several important changes to the debate within the party. First, most technicists within the leadership moved, albeit inconsistently, towards a liberal technicist position. Their commitment to change within the limits of 'scientifically' objective possibilities forced them to accept, even more so than in 1918–19, that the backward, 'petty-bourgeois' sectors of the economy, and in particular the agrarian economy, were firmly in

[10] The leftist economist Preobrazhenskii, for instance, disagreed with Trotsky on these questions. For the relationship between the debate over 'socialism in one country' and the conflicts between left and right, see R. Day, *Leon Trotsky and the Politics of Economic Isolation* (Cambridge, 1973), 145–8.

[11] S. Cohen, *Bukharin*, 129–32.

the capitalist stage of development and could not be treated as if they were on the threshold of the socialist stage. As conflictualist historians have argued, some liberal technicists, led by Bukharin, at times tried to present their acceptance of the market as an element in a new form of 'liberal' Bolshevism, applicable in both political and economic spheres, which was not just a pragmatic retreat but was desirable in itself. However, given Marxism–Leninism's hostility to political and economic liberalism, they could not succeed, and it would be an exaggeration to see Bukharin as the advocate of a cogent 'anti-statist' Marxism.[12] Second, the issue of advance and retreat became much more central to the debate than it had been before. While Lenin had often tried to avoid explicit discussions of this question before 1921, by legalizing the market he was admitting that he was retreating from the socialist elements of the civil war regime, and it was inevitable that disputes between revivalists and technicists would normally be framed as a conflict between supporters of rapid advance to socialism and pragmatic supporters of the NEP retreat. Third, the focus of the debates within the party had changed. The central question facing the Bolsheviks was no longer how best to deal with unreliable and frequently hostile urban workers, or how to mobilize them in a civil war against the internal enemy. Now the war was over, and it was clear that the international revolution was a long way off, the stability of the regime and its defence against external enemies depended on economic reconstruction, and attention understandably turned to the question of long-term economic development and industrialization. Old debates over class and the advance towards socialism therefore became associated with the issue of economic strategy. Populist revivalists on the left now argued that the mobilization of working-class energies would deliver rapid economic growth, while the Politburo majority defended the technicist view that industry would work best if expert managers controlled and disciplined workers. At the same time, other groups on the left within the party developed more élitist revivalist arguments, using dialectical materialist interpretations of science to argue for economic 'leaps forward', while the Politburo majority defended the technicist view that a broad

[12] For the view that Bukharin was a 'moderate anti-statist', see P. Ferdinand, 'Bukharin and the New Economic Policy', in A. Kemp-Welch (ed.), *The Ideas of Nikolai Bukharin* (Oxford, 1992), 40–68.

equilibrium between resources and output had to be maintained. Fourth, the pattern of ideological alliances changed, as one would expect. During the civil war period the main conflict had concerned the question of the regime's relationship with the working class and Lenin's alleged 'retreat' from populist revivalism in 1918. Elitist revivalists and technicists, believing that the regime had to combat excessive 'democratism', had united against various populist revivalist groups. After 1921, however, it was more likely that revivalists would unite against an alliance of technicists and liberal technicists under the slogans of 'advance' towards socialism and the defence of the proletariat against the bourgeoisie. Élitist and populist revivalists both criticized NEP on the grounds that the market was a retreat from socialism, even though their visions of that socialism were rather different.

The emergence of a powerful revivalist coalition on the left of the party was accompanied by the popularity of revivalist ideas in a whole range of institutions. Many, of course, found revivalist ideas appealing on purely ideological grounds, as they saw them as a return to the values of 1917. However, it is also probable that several groups in the party found these ideas useful in the pursuit of their own particular interests. Party intellectuals and academics, competing with old 'bourgeois' élites, echoed some of the themes in Bogdanov's thought, emphasizing the need for an educational system that inculcated a special 'proletarian culture' and demanding the development of a specifically Marxist science. Economic organizations also found that they could use revivalist voluntaristic arguments to justify more investment. Yet these groups' revivalist sympathies did not necessarily lead them to ally with the left. Indeed, some of the most influential officials, the regional party bosses, found the left's populist revivalism threatening, even though they were dissatisfied with many features of the NEP.[13] Stalin succeeded in attracting this powerful group from the middle of the 1920s, by creating a synthesis of élitist and populist revivalist approaches that, at least initially, did not appear to threaten the party apparatus.

---

[13] For the influence of these interests after the death of Lenin, when a divided leadership sought their support, see G. Gill, *The Origins of the Stalinist Political System*, 172–3.

The New Economic Policy: temporary retreat or diversion?

When Lenin legalized trade in grain in March 1921 he did not foresee its full implications; it was only in the following months that the leadership realized that a whole range of market reforms would be required if these market incentives were to work. Small-scale consumer industry had to be revived to produce goods for the peasant market, and as the state did not have the resources or ability to do so itself, they were to be leased to co-operatives or individuals, and even to former owners. The new strategy also had implications for financial policy: a stable currency was needed if peasants were to be induced to sell their grain, and a new currency backed by gold was introduced in 1924. Inevitably, this brought with it cuts in the state budget. State-owned heavy industry, in particular, suffered from reductions in subsidy, and market disciplines were introduced to ensure that they cut costs.[14]

The leadership now admitted that the state did not have the power to integrate the economy by means of administrative command alone. Only money and market incentives could link the industrial and agricultural economy together, maintain a balance between supply and demand, and ensure that goods were produced as efficiently and cheaply as possible. The old civil war system, by which enterprises fulfilled central orders and were allocated supplies by the state, gave way to market relations between state enterprises. Trade between enterprises was increasingly regulated by the syndicates, organizations which subjected them to market disciplines and forced them to fulfil the demands of their consumers.[15] Enterprises also had to operate to make a profit, according to commercial principles of 'cost accounting' (*khozraschet*).[16] In their search for efficiency, managers now had to continue to promote 'capitalist' forms of labour management, including labour discipline, wage differentials, and managerial power in the workplace.[17]

[14] See E. H. Carr, *The Bolshevik Revolution*, ii. chs. 18–19.
[15] D. Shearer, *Industry, State and Society in Stalin's Russia, 1926–1934* (Ithaca, NY, 1996), 53–66.
[16] E. H. Carr, *The Bolshevik Revolution*, ii. 302–9.
[17] For attempts to increase labour productivity in the workplace, see W. J. Chase, *Workers, Society and the Soviet State*, ch. 6. As Chase argues, from 1926 attempts were made to use production conferences to mobilize workers. See ibid., 271–82.

The regime also increasingly accepted that the private sector would be the main motor of growth in the economy. Peasants were to be given market incentives to farm profitably; an improving agricultural economy, the leadership claimed, would stimulate consumer industry, which would, in turn, create demand for heavy industrial goods and revive the state sector.[18] The élitist revivalist notion that the state could force growth by 'storming' and political campaigns was now rejected.

Naturally the NEP attracted its strongest institutional support from the Commissariat of Agriculture and the guardian of financial stability, the Commissariat of Finance, led by Sokol'nikov.[19] But it was also welcomed by many within the industrial apparatus, who were glad to see the end of disruptive mobilizations and valued the new status and power granted to managers and officials. Rykov believed that the NEP would allow the Soviet Union to rebuild industry on the basis of technology from the West; his successor as head of Vesenkha until 1926, Dzerzhinskii, was also a strong supporter of stability and gradualism.[20]

The restoration of a market economy also required a more 'liberal' approach to politics. If the bourgeoisie was to be allowed to exploit the new market then it had to be protected against those forces which might undermine its ability to create wealth. L. B. Krasin, political and trade representative in Britain, made precisely this point to Lenin in November 1921: as long as 'organizations and investigators who are incompetent and even downright ignorant in questions of the *tekhnika* of production leave technicians and engineers to rot in jail' for alleged 'technical sabotage' or 'economic espionage', the Bolsheviks would be unable to attract foreign capitalists to invest in Russia.[21] Krasin's complaints were particularly aimed at the Cheka, and during the 1920s some of its

---

[18] N. I. Bukharin, *Tekushchii moment i osnovy nashei politiki* (Moscow, 1925), 4.

[19] For the position of the Commissariat of Agriculture, see M. Wehner, *Bauernpolitik im Proletarishchen Staat* (Köln, 1998), 87–93, 230–7.

[20] For Rykov's position, see Day, *Leon Trotsky*, 48–51. For Dzerzhinskii's support for the NEP, see A. Graziosi, 'Building the First System of State Industry', *CMRS*, 32 (1991), 548–50; N. Valentinov, *Novaia ekonomicheskaia politika i krizis partii posle smerti Lenina* (Moscow, 1991), ch. 5.

[21] Krasin to Lenin, 8 November 1921, in A. V. Kvashonkin, A. Ia Livshin, and O. V. Khlevniuk (eds.), *Bol'shevistskoe rukovodstvo. Perepiska, 1912–1927. Sbornik dokumentov* (Moscow, 1996), 216. For Krasin's role in the Anglo-Russian trade agreement, see T. O'Connor, *The Engineer of Revolution. L. B. Krasin and the Bolsheviks, 1870–1926* (Boulder, 1992), ch. 11.

responsibilities were handed over to the judicial organizations. While there was no serious attack on the Cheka's position, it did become weaker.[22]

Yet how could this set of policies, introduced on pragmatic grounds, be justified theoretically? Many of them, of course, were not new. The use of material incentives in industry and agriculture was entirely compatible with Marx's lower stage of 'socialism', and operated in some areas during the civil war. But the NEP differed from 'war communism' (as the leadership now described it) in its attempts to strengthen these material incentives by accepting the market. Marx had assumed that under socialism the state would be so effective and the working class so mature and disciplined that a system of material incentives could be organized without the market. The state would be able to organize production and distribution to provide workers and peasants with the goods they wanted, at an acceptable price, in exchange for their labour; workers would therefore be motivated to work hard and create a prosperous economy. Yet the crises of 1921 had shown that the state was incapable of achieving this: it was too weak and the machinery of accounting and control was ineffective. Hence, according to the Marxist historical scheme, the Bolsheviks had to admit that Russia was not yet ready to abandon the market. It was precisely on these grounds that Lenin justified the retreat to NEP in 1921. During the civil war, he argued,

we made a mistake, we decided to make a direct transition to communist production and distribution. We decided that the peasant through the *razverstka* would give us the necessary quantity of bread, and we would apportion it among plants and factories, and we would have communist production and distribution.

I cannot say that we drew up such a plan so definitely and clearly, but we acted more or less in this spirit . . . only a little experience brought us to the conviction that this attitude was erroneous . . . In the theoretical literature from 1917 . . . it was definitely stressed that there would be a long and complex transition from capitalist society . . . a transition through socialist accounting and control is necessary . . . [23]

---

[22] For the strengthening of law in this period, see P. H. Solomon, *Soviet Criminal Justice under Stalin* (Cambridge, 1996), 26. Krylenko of the Commissariat of Justice (Narkomiust) mounted an assault on the powers of the Cheka in 1925. See Dzerzhinskii to Mekhlis, no earlier than 1 May 1925, *Bol'shevistskoe rukovodstvo*, 302–5.

[23] Lenin, *PSS*, xliv. 157–8 (17 October 1921). It is significant that Lenin was only claiming that during the civil war period the leadership had been interested in 'communist production and distribution', and not communist authority relations.

Lenin, then, saw the retreat in ideological, 'theoretical' terms, as a transition from socialism to some form of capitalism. He was calling for a retreat from the dreams of socialism to 'state capitalism';[24] indeed, it could be argued that in some sectors of the economy he was permitting a retreat to the third and fourth stages of the five-stage model he had enunciated in 1918: 'private capitalism' and 'small commodity production'.[25] Yet, having retreated, the Bolsheviks were left with the question raised by Lenin: how could a transition from the market 'through socialist accounting and control' to communism be achieved? What path of development was the regime now to take, and how was the 'road to socialism' to be rejoined? This question lay at the heart of the political conflicts of the period. For the enthusiastic supporters of the NEP, the regime could advance towards socialism by strengthening the market; the market, therefore, would last for a long time. Only in the distant future would it be overcome. For the sceptics, however, the development of the market led Russia away from socialism and had to be treated with great caution.

Both NEP enthusiasts and sceptics could appeal to Marx's and Engels's analysis of the transition from capitalism to socialism. Marx and Engels had presented late capitalism as a combination of technicist and liberal models of society. In centralizing the economy, concentrating production, and improving its efficiency, capitalism established the foundations for socialism; in some respects, therefore, capitalism would evolve into socialism. Yet capitalism also had a liberal side: the market. This aspect of capitalism produced exploitation and social inequality, was irrational, and led to social conflict; it would have to be destroyed in a revolutionary struggle. But another aspect of the liberal model, the use of material incentives, would not be destroyed by the revolution; rather, material incentives would give way to moral incentives, presumably peacefully. The NEP enthusiasts could, therefore, argue that capitalism could be a positive force in Russia, in so far as it co-ordinated the economy and established effective incentives. Now that the proletarian state owned the means of production and could discourage inequality and exploitation, they argued, a peaceful transition from capitalism to socialism was feasible. Yet the sceptics could also appeal to Marxist orthodoxy. Reasonably, from a Marxist

---

[24] Lenin, *PSS*, xliv. 206–7.   [25] Ibid., xxxvii. 296.

perspective, they denied that a market could peacefully develop into socialism and that a bourgeoisie, which profited from market relations, would willingly accept collective, socialized production. How would a bourgeoisie, motivated by the acquisition of wealth, be transformed into a group willing to abandon the market? Not even the gradualist Kautsky had imagined that the market could peacefully 'grow into' socialism without a revolution against the bourgeoisie.

Lenin recognized the difficulty of combining the market with socialism, and he explicitly addressed the question in several speeches and articles in the period, but his solutions were contradictory and ambiguous. At times he implied that the capitalist and socialist elements of the NEP were in conflict.[26] Capitalists in industry had to be allowed to operate because they would act as an example to communists and teach them to 'trade'; communists meanwhile would learn from them how to run the economy, but would be in competition with them.[27] Yet at other times Lenin was more willing to envisage some form of peaceful evolution from capitalism to socialism, through peasant co-operatives. The co-operation movement was established to help peasants to produce and sell their goods more efficiently, but co-operatives generally did not involve collective production and they normally benefited better-off rather than poor peasants.[28] In his article of 1921, *The Tax in Kind*, Lenin recognized that retail co-operatives were formally capitalist institutions and benefited the petty bourgeoisie, but he still argued that they constituted an advance towards socialism from the traditional small producer economy because they promoted co-ordination between peasants.[29] By 1923 in his article *On Co-operation*, Lenin was willing to go further. He argued that now the proletarian state was in power and the land and means of production belonged to the state, co-operatives nearly always 'coincided' with socialism.[30] Lenin was implying that a peasantry, operating within a market system could gradually and peacefully

---

[26] Ibid., xliii. 224 (21 April 1921).   [27] Ibid., xlv. 78–83, 94.

[28] For co-operatives, see M. Lewin, *Russian Peasants and Soviet Power. A Study of Collectivization* (London, 1968), 93–102; V. P. Danilov, *Rural Russia under the New Regime* trans. by O. Figes (London, 1988), 155–6.

[29] Lenin, *PSS*, xliii. 225–6.

[30] 'co-operation under our conditions nearly always entirely coincides with socialism (*splosh' da riadom sovershenno sovpadaet s sotsializmom*)', Lenin, *PSS*, xlv. 374–6.

evolve into a socialist peasantry, if it joined the co-operatives. Capitalism and socialism were therefore not in conflict.

Attempts to resolve the tension between the evolutionary and conflictual approach to the relationship between capitalism and socialism under the NEP had more than a theoretical significance. If socialism could grow out of the market, then there was no need to have any qualms about encouraging the growth of the private sector; if socialism and the market were in competition or conflict, then the regime would have to limit and 'squeeze out' the market. In the first years of the NEP the conflictual approach was dominant, and the state intervened in the market to prevent the emergence of a peasant bourgeoisie and to keep food prices low relative to the prices of industrial goods. But it was not easy to encourage the peasantry to produce by using the market and material incentives, while at the same time interfering with these incentives. The tensions within the approach emerged with the 'scissors crisis' of 1923. Peasants refused to sell their grain in exchange for expensive industrial goods, towns suffered from food shortages, and working-class unrest again unsettled the Bolsheviks.[31] The leadership was therefore faced with another choice, between an 'advance' towards the technicist model and planning, and a further 'retreat' towards the market. The majority of the leadership, now dominated by Stalin, Kamenev, Zinoviev, and Bukharin, resolved to do the latter. Industry was therefore forced to cut costs and operate closer to market principles, and the peasantry was given freer rein to produce for profit without state interference.

The move towards a more liberal technicist model in the mid-1920s was justified most coherently by Bukharin, who developed the evolutionary ideas sketched by Lenin. Under a socialist system, with the help of the proletarian state, he argued, trade and credit co-operatives would 'inevitably grow into a system of proletarian economic organizations'. Peasants would initially see the advantages of buying machinery collectively, and they would then realize the benefits of collective production. Peasants would therefore realize that the 'transition to collective forms of labour' from collective forms of trade was in their selfish economic interests.[32] Economic

---

[31] For the economic and political crises of this period, see E. H. Carr, *The Interregnum, 1923–1924* (Harmondsworth, 1969), ch. 3.
[32] N. I. Bukharin, 'Put' k sotsializmu i raboche-krest'ianskii soiuz' (1925), in Burkharin, *Izbrannye proizvedeniia* (Moscow, 1988), 171–5.

inequalities between peasants could be controlled by a redistributive state. Bukharin had no qualms about issuing the slogan to peasants 'enrich yourselves'; their enrichment would ultimately lead to socialism.[33]

There were, of course, serious problems with Bukharin's path to socialism. It was difficult to see how the state could use markets to encourage the peasantry to produce while enforcing economic equality, because markets created inequality, at least in the short to medium term. Also, in reality, markets were more likely to produce peasants who were more, not less, 'bourgeois' and wedded to the market; the market was unlikely to transform peasants who benefited from it into proponents of collective production. Bukharin's difficulty in defending his unstable combination of the liberal and technicist models was inherently flawed. He in effect admitted this, when he accepted that his appeal to the peasantry to 'enrich yourselves' was 'erroneous'.[34]

The New Economic Policy, politics, and culture

In the political and cultural sphere, also, some technicists found that their commitment to gradualism led them to adopt semi-liberal attitudes and policies, and it is possible to identify a tentative movement towards liberal approaches in the mid-1920s.[35] It became clear that if bourgeois groups, such as the peasantry, were to be allowed the economic freedoms that would ensure high productivity, they would have to be protected from those in the regime who might discriminate against them. Liberal technicists similarly argued that if bourgeois specialists and intellectuals were to make the best use of science, they had to be secure from the threat of persecution; a sphere of 'culture', separate from politics, had to be recognized, in which a plurality of opinions could exist, until the single unified socialist culture was created at some time in the future. However, as in economic policy, they found it difficult to defend these liberal ideas in principle, because they, as Bolshevik

---

[33] For this slogan, subsequently withdrawn by Bukharin, see P, 24 April 1925.

[34] P, 14 November, 1925.

[35] This accords with Cohen's analysis of Bukharin's ideas: in 1921–2 he was 'reflective' and 'tentative', and it was only in 1923 that he articulated new, more liberal themes. S. Cohen, Bukharin, 138–9.

Marxists, had to see a liberal order as a temporary phase on the way to socialism.

Liberalism was perhaps least in evidence in industrial relations policy, and throughout the NEP period the Politburo majority continued to defend technicist approaches. Lenin's attempts during the civil war to use political authority and 'law' to control workers continued, and order and discipline within the workplace were reinforced. As Stalin declared in 1926, industrial managers had to be wholeheartedly supported in building industry, not undermined and criticized.[36] Lenin did realize that the extreme élitist revivalism of the civil war period, culminating in the militarization of labour, was no longer sustainable, practically or ideologically, and he tried to fuse a technicist with a liberal approach. Trade unions were permitted to 'defend the interests' of workers against the state, and Lenin even envisaged strikes in socialized enterprises.[37] Yet there was considerable opposition to the liberal notion that workers had separate interests from the socialist state, and in practice the Politburo majority supported the technicist vision within the enterprise—of strict hierarchies and discipline.[38] From the middle of the 1920s, Taylorism and 'scientific management' were endorsed by the leadership, and managers used them to challenge more traditional, collectivist forms of labour organization and intensify labour productivity.[39]

The leadership took a similarly technicist view of the relationship between party and state. Party organizations, it was made clear, were to support the state authorities in their attempts to revive the economy. They were also to concentrate on 'economic' rather than 'political' work; as the resolutions of the twelfth party congress of April 1923 explained, the party, while 'not forgetting for a minute its permanent revolutionary-educational tasks', had to accept that

[36] Stalin, *Sochineniia*, viii. 139; see also *Trinadtsatyi s"ezd RKP(b), mai 1924 goda. Stenograficheskii otchet* (Moscow, 1963), 242 (Zinoviev).

[37] *PSS*, xliv. 343–4, 349–50.

[38] For opposition to Lenin's proposals from Andreev and others, see Rudzutak to Lenin, 10 January 1922, *Bol'shevistskoe rukovodstvo*, 234–5. For labour policy under the NEP, see W. J. Chase, *Workers, Society, and the Soviet State*, 221–4.

[39] For the 'scientific organization of labour' and Soviet Taylorism, see K. Bailes, 'Alexei Gastev', 373–94; Z. Sochor, 'Soviet Taylorism Revisited', *SS*, 33 (1981), 246–64. For *artely* and other collectivist forms of labour organization, see C. Ward, *Russia's Cotton Workers and the New Economic Policy. Shop-floor Culture and State Policy 1921–1929* (Cambridge, 1990), 93–100; L. Siegelbaum, 'Soviet Norm Determination in Theory and Practice, 1917–1941', *SS*, 36 (1984), 45–68.

in the current constructive, economic period of the revolution the basic content of the work of the party is, and must be, the leadership of the work of economic organizations in the fundamental areas of socialist construction.[40]

The party was still to 'lead' economic organizations, but it was made clear that this leadership was largely to be exercised on the state's terms: party organizations were to avoid direct interventions in the 'everyday current work' of economic organizations and were to eschew 'direct administrative methods (administrirovanie)'.[41] Party leaders were to become more expert in administrative matters and become 'closer' to their colleagues in the state apparatus: as Kaganovich argued in 1924, there was to be a 'growing together' of party and state organizations.[42] The leadership also hoped that the party's good relations with the state would bolster the authority of industrial managers. On the shop-floor, a closely knit 'triangle' (treugol'nik) of party secretary, director, and trade union secretary emerged in factories, strengthening management and protecting it from criticism from 'below'. Although the triangle was an unofficial body, it was openly defended by some leaders.[43]

Technicist approaches were also dominant in cultural policy. The leadership strongly challenged leftist, Proletkul'tist theorists on the question of proletarian culture. Lenin and Bukharin, some of the most outspoken on this issue, both argued that the working class was not able to run industry by itself, and the old bourgeois technical and cultural intelligentsia therefore had to be given authority. They rejected Bogdanov's view that workers could develop their own collectivist 'proletarian culture' and were therefore able to administer in a new, more creative way than the bourgeoisie; rather, they insisted, the regime had to adopt most elements of the science and culture of the past in the interests of production. As has been seen, Lenin's attitude towards culture was ambiguous, but he generally regarded 'culture' as a set of practical accomplishments and

---

[40] Dvenadtsatyi s"ezd, 17–25 aprelia 1923 goda. Stenograficheskii otchet (Moscow, 1968), 687.

[41] Ibid.

[42] Chetyrnadtsataia konferentsiia VKP(b). Stenograficheskii otchet (Moscow–Leningrad, 1925), 39.

[43] Piatnadtsataia konferentsiia VKP(b), 26 oktiabria—3 noiabria 1926 g. Stenograficheskii otchet (Moscow–Leningrad, 1927), 296 (Uglanov). See also Trinadtsatyi s"ezd, 280 (Kuibyshev).

subordinated cultural policy to economic requirements; there was no need to build a special proletarian culture.[44] Bukharin, in contrast, insisted that there was such a thing as a 'proletarian culture' and he was indebted in some respects to Bogdanov's thought.[45] He took culture much more seriously than Lenin, refused to confine the regime's tasks to economic development, and accepted that non-proletarians were still too influential in cultural and educational institutions.[46] But, like Lenin, he disagreed with Bogdanov's notion that the proletariat was well on the way to creating a new egalitarian culture.[47] Also Bukharin's views of the content of this proletarian culture were different from those of Bogdanov: at least in the medium term, it was not to involve the end of the traditional division of labour, but was to imply high levels of specialization and hierarchies based on technical expertise.[48] Bukharin's vision of the new proletarian culture was welcomed by one of the most enthusiastic spokesmen for a technicist interpretation of proletarian culture, Aleksei Gastev.[49] Gastev, a popularizer of Taylorist ideas of 'scientific management' and founder of the Central Labour Institute, an institution with considerable support within the leadership, sought to establish a system of 'mechanized collectivism'.[50] The 'human organism' was seen as a

---

[44] See p. 119 above.

[45] For this debt, see N. I. Bukharin, *Proletariat i voprosy khudozhestvennoi politiki. Stenogramma rechi, proiznesennoi na literaturnom soveshchanii pri TsK v fevrale 1925 g.* (Letchworth, 1979), 4; J. Biggart, 'Bukharin's Theory of Cultural Revolution', in A. Kemp-Welch (ed.), *The Ideas of Nikolai Bukharin* (Oxford, 1992), 131–48; I. Susiluoto, *The Origins and Development of Systems Thinking in the Soviet Union. Political and Philosophical Controversies from Bogdanov to Bukharin and Present-day Re-evaluations* (Helsinki, 1982), 94.

[46] See J. Biggart, 'Bukharin's Theory of Cultural Revolution', 148–52. For his complaints about non-proletarian influence, see N. I. Bukharin, *Bor'ba za kadry. Rech'i i stat'i* (Moscow–Leningrad, 1926), 140.

[47] N. I. Bukharin, *Proletarskaia revoliutsiia i kul'tura* (Petrograd, 1923), 22; Bukharin, *Proletariat i voprosy khudozhestvennoi politiki*, 4–5; Bukharin, 'Burzhuaznaia revoliutsiia i revoliutsiia proletarskaia', in S. Heitman (ed.), *Put' k sotsializmu v Rossii. Izbrannye proizvedeniia N. I. Bukharina* (New York, 1967), 173–4. See also J. Biggart, 'Bukharin and the Origins of the "Proletarian Culture" Debate', *SS*, 39 (1987), 233.

[48] N. I. Bukharin, 'Problema kul'tury v epokhu rabochei revoliutsii', *P*, 11 October 1922.

[49] For Gastev's support for Bukharin, see K. Bailes, 'Alexei Gastev', 387–8; Susiluoto, *The Origins and Development of Systems Thinking*, 109.

[50] For Gastev's ideas, see K. Johansson, *Aleksei Gastev. Proletarian Bard of the Machine Age* (Stockholm, 1983); K. Bailes, 'Alexei Gastev', 376–85. For his concept of 'mechanized collectivism', see A. Gastev, 'O tendentsiiakh proletarskoi kul'tury', *PK*, 9–10 (1919), 44–5. See also S. Smith, 'Taylorism Rules OK? Bukharin, Taylorism and

'magnificent machine' that could be trained to perform repetitive work efficiently.[51] Workers had to be motivated by material incentives and there would be little reliance on worker creativity or enthusiasm. Gastev saw the ideal 'bearer and agent of culture' as the industrial worker, or 'fitter', rather than the 'teacher', 'missionary', or 'orator'.[52] It is not surprising that Bogdanov strongly criticized him for justifying the enslavement of men by machines.[53]

By 1924–5 it became possible to find some within the leadership using more liberal arguments to bolster the position of the bourgeois cultural and technical intelligentsia. According to this discourse, the intelligentsia had to be protected politically and legally from an interfering party and working class, and a sphere of 'science' and 'culture' had to be separated from 'politics'. In 1924 Rykov, for instance, insisted that the 'specialist, the engineer, the man of science and *tekhnika* must have full autonomy and independence to express his opinion on science and *tekhnika*'; 'cringing before the public—that is the fear of spoiling relations with workers—or [cringing] before the [factory] administration, is unacceptable'.[54] Many in the leadership, including Bukharin and Trotsky, applied this approach to the literary intelligentsia during a series of debates on the attitude of the party to the literary intelligentsia in 1924–5, and opposed the attempts by leftist literary organizations, such as the All-Union Association of Proletarian Writers (VAPP), to exclude the non-proletarian, non-Bolshevik writers from the literary arena. Bukharin formulated one of the most explicitly liberal positions, arguing that a cultural 'monopoly' during the transition to socialism was unattainable. Rather, intellectuals had to be allowed to develop the new culture without too much political interference:

the Technical Intelligentsia in the Soviet Union, 1917–1941', *Radical Science Journal*, 13 (1983), 15–18.

[51] A. Gastev, *Kak nado rabotat'* (Moscow, 1972), 45.

[52] A. Gastev, *Poeziia rabochego udara* (Saratov, 1921), 229, quoted in Johansson, *Aleksei Gastev*, 114.

[53] For Bogdanov's criticisms of Gastev, see I. Susiluoto, *Origins*, 100–6.

[54] *I*, 4 December 1924. Although Rykov did say that engineers had to be connected with 'public opinion' (*obshchestvennost'*) and he criticized their bourgeois 'arrogance' (*chvanstvo*).

Let there be one thousand [literary] organizations, let there be two thousand organizations. Let there be alongside MAPP [the Moscow Association of Proletarian Writers] and VAPP as many organizations as you wish.[55]

Bukharin's and Rykov's more liberal approach to culture was associated with a more general concern that 'proletarian' institutions, such as the party, were interfering in the activities of productive bourgeois classes, whether the peasantry or the intelligentsia, and, as a consequence, undermining the economy.[56] There was, for Bukharin, a real danger that the 'communist arrogance' and 'arbitrariness' of 'privileged communist groups' would alienate the intelligentsia and the peasantry. Bukharin and the Politburo majority therefore tried to bolster the economic reforms of the NEP with liberal political reforms designed to protect productive groups against communists. In the autumn of 1924 the leadership launched a new slogan, 'face to the countryside', which attempted to transform the relationship between the regime and the peasantry by 'reviving' rural soviets.[57] New elections to the soviets were held in 1925. Non-party peasants were encouraged to participate, and the vote was restored to many of those previously excluded from the franchise for class and political reasons. The soviets were to be transformed into organizations trusted by the peasantry; they were to be 'polite, attentive, listening to the voice of the peasantry', to respect 'revolutionary legality', and were not to behave arbitrarily, unlike some communists. Kaganovich argued that if this were not done there would be no 'safety valve' for the dissatisfaction of the peasantry, and the economic policy of the regime would be imperilled.[58]

Bukharin, however, went further than Kaganovich and at times implied that the new liberal technicist policies were more than a

---

[55] N. I. Bukharin, *Proletariat i voprosy khudozhestvennoi politiki*, 12.

[56] Bukharin himself pointed out that his attitude towards the intelligentsia was consistent with his attitude towards the peasantry. The left's hostility towards the fellow-travellers in literature, he argued, was equivalent to Preobrazhenskii's leftist antagonism towards the peasantry. See N. I. Bukharin, *Proletariat i voprosy khudozhestvennoi politiki*, 10.

[57] See L. M. Kaganovich, *Ocherednye zadachi partraboty posle XIV konferentsii* (Moscow, 1925), 35. For the January 1925 conference on the revival of the soviets, see *Soveshchanie po voprosam sovetskogo stroitel'stva. Ianvar' 1925 g.* (Moscow, 1925). For the campaign, see E. H. Carr, *Socialism in One Country, 1924–1926* (London, 1990), ii. 356–62.

[58] L. M. Kaganovich, *Ocherednye zadachi partraboty*, 36–7.

temporary retreat forced on the regime by economic circumstances. In a letter to Dzerzhinskii in 1924, he called for limitations on the powers of the secret police as part of a rapid transition 'to a more "liberal" [*liberal'noe*] form of Soviet power: less repression, more legality, more discussion, self-management (under the leadership of the party, *naturaliter*) and so on'. For Bukharin, this was a matter of 'principle' (although interestingly he still interspersed a liberal language of 'legality' with a language of 'self-management' that had populist revivalist implications).[59] His most explicit defence of a liberal approach to the political sphere came in a speech in 1924, when he called for the establishment of 'a whole number of voluntary organizations, circles, associations, built according to different principles, setting themselves different tasks', encouraging 'decentralized initiative' and linking the apparatus to the masses. These would, he argued, express 'the growth of what I here conditionally call "soviet public opinion [*sovetskaia obshchestvennost'*]" '.[60]

Those who characterize Bukharin as a genuinely 'liberal' Bolshevik have rightly remarked on the significance and novelty of such statements, but they have not always noted the ideological difficulties which Bukharin encountered and the serious contradictions within his thinking.[61] His ideas were based on the assumption that just as the peasant, if allowed to trade, would become more socialist, so the intelligentsia, if granted greater political freedom and liberated from the interference of the party and secret police, would increasingly move towards socialism.[62] Bukharin's 'voluntary organizations' in the political sphere were therefore similar to his peasant co-operatives in the economic sphere: by giving the non-proletarian masses more freedom, they would gently 'draw' them

---

[59] Bukharin to Dzerzhinskii, not later than 24 December 1923, *VI KPSS*, 11 (1988), 42–3.

[60] N. I. Bukharin, 'Zadachi vypusknika sverdlovtsa', in N. I. Bukharin, *Bor'ba za kadry*, 75.

[61] Cohen, in his survey of Bukharin's thought, does accept that Bukharin's thinking on economics had its weaknesses, but he tends to present his political thinking as a coherent 'revised doctrine of Bolshevism', *Bukharin*, 208. Harding does point to incoherence, but gives a different explanation to that presented here, suggesting that his failure to take his 'incipient social and economic pluralism' to its logical conclusion owed much to his 'naive relativism . . . in regard to political institutions and procedures'. N. Harding, 'Bukharin and the State', in A. Kemp-Welch, *The Ideas of Nikolai Bukharin*, 111–12.

[62] N. I. Bukharin, 'Diktatura proletariata i rabkorskie organizatsii', in N. I. Bukharin, *O rabkore i sel'kore. Stat'i i rechi* (Moscow, 1926), 16–21.

into the socialist sector.[63] Bukharin's logic was, of course, questionable. As many feared, the 1925 elections, far from increasing the legitimacy of the regime in the countryside, reduced the representation of communists within the soviets and allowed anti-communist forces to organize.[64]

Similar problems were evident in Bolshevik policy towards the non-Russian nationalities. As has been seen, before 1921 Lenin and Stalin adopted an approach to them that had a great deal in common with the leadership's attitude towards the peasantry under the NEP. Indeed, Stalin explicitly compared the two areas of policy.[65] Just as the peasantry had to be protected from rapid proletarianization because the time was not ripe for the backward peasants to adopt socialist culture, so 'nations' had to be built outside Russia because national minorities were not ready for full integration and had to go through a bourgeois nationalist phase. Under the policy of 'indigenization' (*korenizatsiia*), preferences in certain job appointments had to be granted primarily on the basis of ethnicity, and indigenous cultures and language had to be encouraged. The ultimate objective, as with the peasantry, was that these 'backward' groups would gradually progress towards full integration and socialism and that they would, in Stalin's words, 'catch up with central—proletarian—Russia'.[66] But for critics within the party, and particularly Russians who were disadvantaged by positive discrimination programmes in favour of non-Russians, there was a real danger that the policy would produce local nationalisms and nations dominated by the local bourgeoisie.[67]

The New Economic Policy and class

The leadership's faith in the virtues of non-proletarian classes and the possibility of 'proletarianizing' them gradually and peacefully

[63] N. I. Bukharin, 'Rabsel'kory—kusochek proletarskoi demokratii', in N. I. Bukharin, *O rabkore i sel'kore*, 69.

[64] For the threat to the Bolsheviks posed by these elections, see V. Brovkin, *Russia after Lenin*, 71–80. For criticisms of the elections, see *Chetyrnadtsataia konferentsiia*, 24–5 (Pozern).

[65] *Dvenadtsatyi s"ezd*, 481–2.

[66] Stalin, *Sochineniia*, v. 44.

[67] Y. Slezkine, 'The Soviet Union as a Communal Apartment', 324–6. For criticisms of *korenizatsiia* and tensions produced by it, see T. Martin, *The Affirmative Action Empire*, 20–1, 123–4, 137–9.

was accompanied by a pessimistic view of industrial workers. The leadership's attitude towards class in this period was ambiguous. On the one hand, the 1920s saw an increasing concern with the proletarianization of the party and the 'promotion' (*vydvizhenie*) of proletarians into higher education. The purge of 1921, the partial purge of 1924–5, and the 'Lenin levy' of 1924, by which large number of workers were recruited into the party, all attest to this. In part such campaigns were justified using the language of the left: they were a response to the increased danger of contamination by bourgeois attitudes at a time when the market was operating and concessions had been made to the bourgeoisie.[68] It is likely that the leadership, like the left, was worried about the effects of bourgeois influence on society and the party, but it was also probably responding to leftist criticisms that it was doing little to encourage the narrowing of the 'gap' between élite and masses; it was also attempting to improve relations between managers and workers at a time when it was trying to raise productivity.[69]

Yet the leadership often interpreted 'proletarianization' differently from the left. One of the main targets of the purges were leftist party members: the 1921 purge was in part aimed at 'syndicalists' and 'Mensheviks' who had challenged the party leadership during the disturbances of the previous months and who were alleged to be prey to petty-bourgeois egalitarian ideologies.[70] Similarly, the purges of 1924–5 were partly targeted at supporters of Trotsky, particularly in universities.[71] The leadership also tended to have less faith in the virtues of party members of proletarian class origin than the left, even when it used leftist language. Bukharin, for instance, argued for the narrowing of the 'gap' between *verkhi* and *nizy*, for a continuing struggle against 'bureaucratism', and for the establishment of the 'commune-state'.[72] Yet his definitions of *verkhi* and *nizy*

---

[68] See, for instance, the purge instructions of 1921, *Odinadtsatyi s"ezd RKP(b), mart-aprel' 1922 goda. Stenograficheskii otchet* (Moscow 1961), 742.

[69] For explanations for the 'Lenin levy', see J. Hatch, 'The "Lenin Levy" and the Social Origins of Stalinism: Workers and the Communist Party in Moscow, 1921–1928', *SR*, 48 (1989), 558–77.

[70] *Odinadtsatyi s"ezd*, 741.

[71] For the 1924 purge in the universities, see I. Halfin, *From Darkness to Light*, 264–82; M. David-Fox, *Revolution of the Mind*, 127 ff.; P. Konecny, 'Chaos on Campus. The 1924 Student *Proverka* in Leningrad', *E–AS*, 46 (1994), 617–35.

[72] N. I. Bukharin, 'Rabsel'kory—kusochek proletarskoi demokratii', 75; see also N. I. Bukharin, 'Tekushchii moment i zadachi pechati', *P*, 2 December 1928.

were very different from those of the left. He tended to see the bureaucratic *verkhi* as groups of 'proletarian origin' with 'calloused hands';[73] the *nizy*, on the other hand, he identified with non-party groups—largely peasants—persecuted by communists and workers.[74] Bukharin was, then, implicitly attacking the populist revivalist position on the grounds that it was tantamount to a neo-traditionalism which justified the power of a new proletarian élite. Bukharin took a similar line when discussing workers. He had little interest in condemning officials' mistreatment of workers.[75] He accepted that workers' correspondents (*rabkory*), attached to newspapers, should play a role in criticizing bureaucratic officials, but he warned them against supporting unreasonable demands from workers; while they were to expose the misdemeanours of factory administrations, they were not to look on the red director as 'alien', slander managers, or indulge in 'demagogic' behaviour.[76]

Bukharin's implicit distinction between 'democracy' for non-proletarian groups and 'democracy' for the proletariat is particularly evident in his contribution to a debate in the Central Committee in January 1924. Anastas Mikoian had complained that the leadership's policy of encouraging elections to the rural soviets brought enormous dangers, because it was allowing richer peasants to use democracy to remove 'our [i.e. party] people from the soviets' and replace them with 'their own people, who are largely prosperous and hostile to the workers'. If there was to be greater 'democracy', he argued, it would be better to grant it to non-party workers than to peasants.[77] Yet Bukharin was sceptical of the extension of 'democracy' to workers, fearing that it would threaten the regime.[78]

So, despite the attempts of Bukharin and others to present the NEP as a strategy that was based on the requirements of 'science' rather than the interests of particular classes, it was difficult to avoid the issue of class. As during the civil war period, the Politburo majority felt vulnerable to the left's arguments that it was not

[73] N. I. Bukharin, *Proletarskaia revoliutsiia i kul'tura*, 44–5.
[74] Bukharin was not alone in putting forward this analysis. For similar warnings of the danger of the 'gap' between communists and non-party masses, see *Trinadtsatyi s"ezd*, 233 (Stalin); *Chetyrnadtsataia konferentsiia*, 22 (Molotov).
[75] See, for instance, N. I. Bukharin, *O rabkore i sel'kore*, 58–62.
[76] Ibid., 26, 9.
[77] RGASPI, 17/2/109, 11.
[78] RGASPI, 17/2/109, 17.

doing enough to 'proletarianize' the party and the apparatus, but it also frequently found itself defending the NEP on the grounds that the proletariat could not yet be trusted and non-proletarian classes had to be protected and even favoured.[79] Generally, the NEP's more enthusiastic advocates accepted that non-proletarian classes had to be treated carefully and with suspicion.[80] Yet in the heat of debate with the left they were often rather more forthright in lauding the virtues of non-proletarian classes and deprecating workers. In 1924, Rykov went as far as to state that the intelligentsia (despite the continuing presence of 'bourgeois specialists') was entirely trustworthy, and had become a fully 'Soviet intelligentsia'.[81] Bukharin similarly tried to rehabilitate the peasantry. No longer, he insisted, should the peasantry be treated with the 'disgust and contempt' displayed by the left, but 'seriously' and 'with love'.[82] In the developing world outside the Soviet Union, also, the peasantry had a positive role: the colonized peasantry was the 'liberating force of our time' and the working class had to unite with it.[83] Nikolai Uglanov, the first secretary of the Moscow party organization, similarly accused the left of 'underestimating the peasantry' and its 'revolutionary energy', while 'idealizing' the working class.[84] Given this rhetoric, it is not surprising that the Politburo majority should have been charged with abandoning the cause of the proletariat.

'Equilibrium' and the philosophy of technicism

The NEP's advocates were also vulnerable on economic policy. The critics of the NEP argued, with some justification, that the new system could not deliver high rates of industrial growth. And the NEP's ideologists were indeed arguing for economic equilibrium: heavy industry, they insisted, could only develop as quickly as resources, largely extracted from the agricultural sector in the

---

[79] For the view that the working class was backward, see N. I. Bukharin, *Proletarskaia revoliutsiia i kul'tura*, 21–3.

[80] See, for instance, N. I. Bukharin, 'Put' k sotsializmu', 203.

[81] *I*, 4 December 1924.

[82] S. Cohen, *Bukharin*, 168.

[83] Ibid., 168. N. I. Bukharin, 'Put' k sostializmu', 226.

[84] *Chetyrnadtsatyi s"ezd VKP(b), 18–31 dekabria 1925 g. Stenograficheskii otchet* (Moscow–Leningrad, 1926), 196 (Uglanov).

course of trade between town and countryside, allowed. This was obviously an argument for slow industrial growth, as Bukharin himself admitted. For Bukharin, the alternative élitist revivalist economic policies defended by Trotsky during the civil war, when an activist state had used force and will-power to drive the economy forward while ignoring 'proportions' between different sectors of the economy, had proved to be damaging. Bukharin and the NEP's enthusiasts were increasingly sympathetic to planning after 1926, but they maintained a technicist framework: the plan was to maintain the economic equilibrium, a stable monetary system was to be used to regulate industry, and industry was to be developed gradually.[85] Both the liberal technicist and technicist elements in the NEP's economic policy shared a neo-classical view of economics, which emphasized balance and the primacy of objective economic conditions over politics and will.[86]

As will be seen, the left strongly criticized this approach, and in response Bukharin sought to defend his technicism by appealing to the authority of Marxist philosophy. In his *Historical Materialism* of late 1921, he presented a highly gradualist and anti-voluntaristic interpretation of dialectical materialism, which had much more in common with Lenin's *Materialism and Empiriocriticism* than with his *Philosophical Notebooks* or Engels's *Dialectics of Nature*. First, he developed a 'mechanistic' view of society: man and society were subject to natural laws; change occurred because society was in tension with its environment and was constantly trying to adapt to it.[87] The notion that change was the result of 'self-movement', in accordance with the unfolding of the dialectic in history, he denounced as teleology and idealism.[88] To explain change, one merely

---

[85] *Rasshirennyi plenum ispolkoma kommunisticheskogo internatsionala* (21 *marta—6 aprelia 1925 g.*). *Stenograficheskii otchet* (Moscow–Leningrad, 1925), 373–4. N. I. Bukharin, 'K voprosu o zakonomernostiiakh perekhodnogo perioda', *P*, 3 July 1926.

[86] For the 'neo-classical' economic thought of this period, see P. Sutela, *Socialism, Planning and Optimality* (Helsinki, 1984), 44.

[87] N. I. Bukharin, *Historical Materialism. A System of Sociology* (London, 1925), 239–41. For the debates between 'mechanists' and their opponents, see D. Joravsky, *Soviet Marxism and Natural Science, 1917–1932* (New York, 1961). P. Josephson, *Physics and Politics in Soviet Russia* (Berkeley, 1991), ch. 7; D. Bakhurst, *Consciousness and Revolution*, ch. 2; G. Wetter, *Der Dialektische Materializmus* (Freiburg, 1952), chs. 7–8.

[88] N. I. Bukharin, *Ataka. Sbornik teoreticheskikh statei* (Moscow, 1924), 116. In rejecting a dialectical approach to Marxist philosophy, Bukharin had much in common

needed to examine the effect of the forces of nature on societies and objects, as scientists did.[89] Naturally, these ideas could be used to denounce voluntaristic arguments that forces within society or individuals could overcome natural laws, as discovered by science.

Second, Bukharin argued that although, as the principles of dialectics stated, there were conflicts and contradictions in all social systems, and between society and nature, society tended to seek equilibrium, both internally and in its relations with nature. Bukharin was not denying that there were 'leaps' in nature as well as in politics.[90] He merely declared that they were things of the past. As he argued, capitalism had been a system of equilibrium, which had been disrupted by the revolutionary period, which in turn was to be superseded by a new equilibrium at a higher level—socialism. The Soviet Union had now undergone its revolutionary period and was now firmly in the post-revolutionary era; equilibrium therefore had to be restored. Once this had happened, a 'revolution in *tekhnika*' and an 'accelerated evolution of the productive forces' would take place, but this new phase would not be an extraordinary, revolutionary one. It would be a ' "normal", "organic" period in the evolution of the new social form', of socialism.[91] Human will, he insisted, could not transform the economy because it had to take account of economic constraints:

Every superstructural force, including also the concentrated authority of a class, its state authority, is a power; but this power is not unlimited. No force can transcend its own limits. The limits imposed upon the political power of a new class that has seized the power are inherent in the existing state of economic conditions and therefore of the productive forces. In other words: the alteration in the economic conditions that may be attained with the aid of the political lever is itself dependent on the previous state of the economic conditions.[92]

with Bogdanov. However, as Susiluoto has argued, Bukharin's system, unlike Bogdanov's, posited two 'passive' systems, nature and society, leaving little room for 'social activism or human creativity'. I. Susiluoto, *The Origins and Development of Systems Thinking*, 100.

[89] Bukharin insisted that he did not have a crudely scientific determinist view of historical change, and that he took due account of the impact of the superstructure on the base (*Historical Materialism*, 256; Cohen, *Bukharin*, 110–11). But ultimately he stressed the decisive role of the forces of nature in shaping society.

[90] N. I. Bukharin, *Historical Materialism*, 81.

[91] Ibid., 259–62.   [92] Ibid., 264.

Bukharin's own thinking on dialectics was not the subject of political controversy until the end of the 1920s. However, he shared an emphasis on the objective constraints on economic growth and science with a 'mechanist' school of philosophers, and with the so-called 'geneticists', an influential group of economists who were to become closely involved in the debates over political and economic strategy later in the decade.[93] As will be seen, the question of dialectics and its relationship with science became a central issue in conflicts over economic policy, and Bukharin's new interpretation of dialectics came under attack from voluntarists on the left.

The creation of the leftist coalition and the defence of proletarian values

The introduction of the NEP provoked considerable discontent within the party. P. S. Zaslavskii, a Moscow *raikom* secretary, reported rank-and-file communists' complaints to Molotov as early as July 1921: policy had changed too 'sharply'; enterprises had been given to former owners; and the 'plan for creating a base for heavy industry' had been 'ruined'.[94] Such criticisms were voiced not only by élitist revivalists, who objected to the regime's excessive faith in the market and who demanded a faster pace of industrial development, the most prominent of whom was Trotsky, but also by populist revivalists, who were hostile to the consolidation of the bourgeoisie's position and the abandonment of 'proletarian' policies. Both groups, hitherto divided, could unite on the basis of a joint commitment to a renewed 'advance' towards socialism. As the consequences of the NEP became more evident, a new alliance of élitist and populist revivalists against the increasingly liberal technicist leadership became very likely.

Even so, the alliance was more difficult to cement than it had been in 1917, in part because the experience of conflict during the civil war had exposed the differences between the two groups. By the winter of 1922–3 Trotsky had become one of the main spokesmen for heavy industrial development, dismayed at the effects of

---

[93] See A. A. Belykh, 'A. A. Bogdanov's Theory of Equilibrium and the Economic Discussions of the 1920s', *SS*, 42 (1990), 571–82.
[94] P. S. Zaslavskii to Molotov, 22 July 1921, *Bol'shevistskoe rukovodstvo*, 207.

Sokol'nikov's 'financial dictatorship' on growth.[95] But on social and political questions his views were more élitist than populist. He refused to use the rhetoric of class struggle and criticized the populist revivalist left for taking a narrow view of the working class's interests.[96] He also maintained his former position on party–state relations. The party, he insisted, had to support management and was to be prevented from interfering in economic affairs of which it was ignorant because it would only undermine 'specialization' and 'properly-organized work'.[97]

Towards the end of 1923, however, his rhetoric and that of his supporters began to change, and he began to use a more populist revivalist language, denouncing 'bureaucratism' within the party and calling for 'democratization'.[98] In large part, Trotsky's talk of party democracy was a response to attempts by the triumvirate of Stalin, Kamenev, and Zinoviev to deprive him of control of the war commissariat.[99] Yet Trotsky's statements were not just tactical. He spent some time analysing the nature and origins of bureaucratism in ways that were close to the thinking of the Democratic Centralists. 'Bureaucratism', he argued, had arisen because the party apparatus had become too closely associated with the state, and had become infected with its authoritarianism.[100] In contrast to his previous position, he now warned of the dangers of the party merging with the state.[101]

Even so, Trotsky remained wary of a full alliance with the remnants of the Democratic Centralists. Although many of his supporters signed the leftist 'Platform of the forty-six' of October 1923 together with leading Democratic Centralists, Trotsky did not.[102] In a series of articles calling for a 'New Course' in party affairs, he did accept many traditional populist revivalist ideas and solutions. Bureaucratism, he argued, had arisen in part because

[95] *T*, 773.

[96] *Dvenadtsatyi s"ezd*, 346.

[97] Ibid., 349–50. For Trotsky's insistence that the party support management, see Trotsky to Lenin, 10 March 1922, in R. Pipes, *The Unknown Lenin*, 148–9.

[98] 'The New Course', in L. D. Trotsky, *The Challenge of the Left Opposition, 1923–1925* (New York, 1975), 69, 84.

[99] R. Day, *Leon Trotsky*, 87.

[100] Trotsky, 'The New Course', 78.

[101] Ibid., 76–7.

[102] For Trotsky's attitudes towards the Platform of the forty-six, see I. Deutscher, *The Prophet Unarmed. Trotsky 1921–1929* (Oxford, 1970), 113–14.

proletarian party members had little influence, and this problem could be solved by 'means of substantial economic progress, a strong impulsion to industrial life, and a constant flow of manual workers into the party'.[103] Yet, despite Trotsky's support for the proletarianization of the party, his élitist pessimism about the abilities and cultural level of the working class is still evident. He accepted that the process of proletarianization was going to be very gradual and that, in the meantime, other classes would have to remain influential;[104] he also insisted that the proletariat would have to learn traditional *tekhnika* and science to overcome its cultural backwardness, and that it could only create a new culture on the foundations of bourgeois culture.[105] It is therefore not surprising that he said little about relations within the workplace, and he blamed 'bureaucratism' on party officials rather than factory management. Also, his 'New Course' articles placed more emphasis on generational divisions within the party than on class divisions. The older generation, he argued, dominated the apparatus and was cut off from more recent recruits and the youth, and therefore the problem of 'bureaucratism', he implied, could be solved by bringing in young people rather than workers into the party.[106]

Given the unwillingness of both Trotsky and the signatories of the 'Platform of the forty-six' to use a forthrightly 'proletarian' rhetoric, it is not surprising that the Left Opposition of this period seems to have elicited more support from students, the army, and members of the Moscow party organization than from workers.[107] By the

---

[103] Trotsky, 'The New Course', 73. See also 89–90.

[104] Ibid., 73–4, 90.

[105] L. D. Trotsky, 'Kul'tura i sotsializm' (1926), in *Sochineniia*, xxi. 438, 442; L. Trotsky, *Literatura i revoliutsiia* (Moscow, 1923), 167. Knei-Paz notes the contradiction between Trotsky's optimism about economic transformation and his pessimism about cultural transformation. See Knei-Paz, *The Social and Political Thought of Leon Trotsky*, 297.

[106] Trotsky, 'The New Course', 71.

[107] Larin, for one, noted the lack of working-class support. *Trinadtsataia konferentsiia RKP(b)* (Moscow, 1924), 67. For estimates of support for the left, see Darron Hincks, 'Support for the Left Opposition in Moscow: "New Course" Discussion, 1923–24', unpublished paper, CREES, University of Birmingham, 1990. For Trotsky's influence on the Moscow party, see Dzerzhinskii to Stalin and Ordzhonikidze, 5–6 October 1925, *Bol'shevistskoe rukovodstvo*, 311. Although Kevin Murphy has argued that working-class support for the left has been underestimated because the leadership deliberately obscured its influence. See K. Murphy, 'Opposition at the Local Level. A Case Study of the Hammer and Sickle Factory', *E–AS*, 53 (2001), 331–4.

mid-1920s, however, Kamenev and Zinoviev had taken the left in a more populist revivalist direction. Previously staunch defenders of the NEP, they were unlikely leaders of a revivalist left, and their political volte-face at the beginning of 1925 had much to do with personal political rivalries within the élite. Once Trotsky had been removed from the presidency of the Revolutionary Military Council in January 1925 and he was no longer a threat, the collective leadership, now without a common enemy, came under strain.[108] The most obvious way for Zinoviev and Kamenev to attack the dominant Stalin group was to criticize the NEP from a revivalist position, and it was easier to do this now that Trotsky had been defeated. However, there may have been other reasons why Kamenev and Zinoviev chose this course. Unlike Trotsky, Zinoviev gained more of his support from within the party, and in particular from the powerful Leningrad party organization, than from the industrial or military commissariats. He was therefore associated with groups more sympathetic to populist revivalist 'proletarian' rhetoric than the Trotskyist opposition of 1923–4.[109]

The Leningrad Opposition was therefore much more willing to use populist revivalist class language than was the Trotskyist opposition of 1923, and it was also more prepared to appeal directly to working-class material interests and to advocate egalitarianism in the workplace than Trotsky had been.[110] Indeed, Dzerzhinskii went so far as to describe it as a 'new Kronshtadt within our party'.[111] At the centre of the Zinovievites' critique of the Politburo majority lay the charge that it was guilty of a 'pro-kulak deviation' and that it was neglecting the working class.[112] In economic policy, they called for an advance to socialism on a number of fronts: they supported the expansion of industry to increase the numbers of workers and improve their living standards; and they insisted that the proletariat had now matured and the time was ripe for greater 'democracy'

---

[108] See I. Deutscher, *The Prophet Unarmed*, 241–6.

[109] C. Black argues that Zinoviev and the Leningrad party was representing the interests of a city and a proletariat that was suffering from the NEP. See his 'Party Crisis and the Party Shop Floor: Krasnyi Putilovets and the Leningrad Opposition', *E–AS*, 46 (1994), 107–26.

[110] For Zinoviev's defence of social egalitarianism, see his 'Filosofiia epokha', *P*, 19–20 September 1925.

[111] Dzerzhinskii to Stalin and Ordzhonikidze, 5–6 October 1925, *Bol'shevistskoe rukovodstvo*, 309–10.

[112] For the term 'pro-kulak deviation', see *Chetyrnadtsatyi s"ezd*, 168 (Petrovskii).

within the party.[113] Zinoviev claimed that the Politburo majority was motivated by a 'fear of the working class', and his ally, Lenin's widow, Krupskaia, accused Bukharin of a 'pessimistic' attitude to the abilities of the working class.[114]

In 1925 Trotsky refused to join the Leningrad Opposition because he was suspicious of Zinoviev's unlikely alliance with Commissar of Finance, Sokol'nikov, and because he took a middle course between the majority of the left and the leadership on questions of economic strategy.[115] He sympathized with Bukharin's desire to improve agriculture and he reacted against Zinoviev's virulent anti-kulak rhetoric and the proposals of leftist economists, like Preobrazhenskii, to exploit the peasantry.[116] Yet there were personal and ideological reasons for an alliance between the Trotskyists and the Leningraders. After the grain procurements crisis of 1925, Trotsky decided that Bukharin was too supportive of the kulaks, and by the beginning of the following year he accepted that the Politburo majority was favouring the kulak and the 'nepman' (or small businessman) at the expense of the proletariat.[117] He also objected to Bukharin's and Stalin's isolationist, autarkic approach to socialist development.[118] By July 1926 Trotsky, Kamenev, Zinoviev, and a number of Democratic Centralists had formed the United Opposition. Its programme was much more populist than Trotsky's earlier programme of 1923–4, and it unashamedly adopted the language of proletarian interests and endorsed populist revivalist notions of party 'democracy'.[119] At the centre of its proposals lay the 'all-round strengthening of all the social positions of the proletariat'.[120] While there was to be no 'direct attack' on

---

[113] *Chetyrnadtsatyi s"ezd*, 273 (Kamenev).

[114] *Chetyrnadtsatyi s"ezd*, 126, 164 (Zinoviev, Krupskaia).

[115] See Trotsky, 'Our differences', in Trotsky, *The Challenge of the Left Opposition, 1923–1925*, 300. For ideological differences between Zinoviev and Trotsky, see Trotsky's memorandum of 22 December 1925, T, 2975; R. Day, *Leon Trotsky*, 113–14; for personal differences, see E. H. Carr, *Foundations of a Planned Economy, 1926–1929* (London, 1971), ii. 3–4. See also I. Deutscher, *The Prophet Unarmed*, 255–6.

[116] *I*, 28 November 1925.

[117] T, 2975. See also Day, *Leon Trotsky*, 119. For similarities between Trotsky's and Zinoviev's position on the kulak at the beginning of 1926, see T, 2982, T, 2983.

[118] R. Day, *Leon Trotsky*, ch. 6.

[119] For Trotsky's concessions to Zinoviev on the issue of foreign concessions and anti-kulak rhetoric, see R. Day, *Leon Trotsky*, 159–61.

[120] 'The Platform of the Opposition', in L. Trotsky, *The Challenge of the Left Opposition 1926–27* (New York, 1980), 306.

bourgeois forces, the proletarian army always had to maintain its fighting spirit.[121] The party had to promote the 'advance of our country along the road to socialism' not only by raising productivity and increasing the weight of the socialist industrial sector but also by improving the 'material position of the working class'.[122] The United Opposition was therefore understandably described as 'super-industrial and super-proletarian' by the Politburo majority.[123] It combined groups which were primarily motivated by populist revivalist hostility to non-proletarians, allegedly profiteering at the workers' expense, with groups which were committed to a much more élitist model of economic and political development.

The United Opposition also defended a typically populist revivalist approach to authority relations. Only some form of participatory 'democracy', it claimed, would mobilize workers behind the regime and increase productivity. Trotsky himself moved towards this position, and in 1925 he explained that socialist society could not be established by 'administrative order' but only 'by way of the greatest initiative' and 'genuine revolutionary democracy'.[124] The Opposition criticized the Politburo majority for establishing 'bureaucratism', by which meant it tended to mean authoritarianism and alienation from workers, rather than merely 'red-tapism'.[125] Like the left of the civil war period, it analysed this problem in the context of class and class culture. The undemocratic spirit in institutions was blamed on the 'steady stream of non-proletarian influences' which flowed into the apparatus 'through the specialists and the upper strata of the office workers and intellectuals'.[126] 'Bureaucratism' was also seen as the result of the pursuit of petty-bourgeois policies injurious to the proletariat: because they were so unpopular among workers, the leadership had to use authoritarian measures to implement them.[127] Therefore, while the

---

[121] 'Proekt platformy bol'shevikov-lenintsev (oppozitsii) k XV s"ezdu VKP(b)' (1927), in Iu. Fel'shtinskii (ed.), *Arkhiv Trotskogo. Kommunisticheskaia oppozitsiia v SSSR, 1923–1927 gg.* (Moscow, 1990), iv. 114.

[122] Ibid., 117.

[123] *P* (editorial), 3 November 1926.

[124] *I*, 2 June 1925.

[125] 'The question of soviet bureaucratism is not only a question about red-tapism, about inflated staffs and so on. Fundamentally it is a question about the class role of the bureaucracy, about its social links and sympathies, about its strength and privileged position...', 'Proekt platformy', 139, 151.

[126] 'The Platform of the Opposition', 391, 360.

[127] 'Proekt platformy', 150.

oppositionists recognized the dangers from 'bureaucrats' of working-class origin, they still saw the solution as the 'proletarianization' of the party.[128] There was no attempt to undermine the authority of the apparatus fundamentally, or seriously to limit its powers, only to alter its composition and culture, to encourage 'discussion' and 'democratic' habits, and to change its political line.

This commitment to proletarianization and 'advance' also affected the left's approach to the peasantry. While it did not mount any fundamental challenge to the NEP order, it did demand greater assistance for poor peasant groups and the restriction of rich, 'capitalist' peasant influence.[129] As during the civil war period, its commitment to 'advance' required that 'backward' groups be forced to be more 'proletarian'; they were not to be the beneficiaries of 'democracy' until they had been 'proletarianized'. The left's approach to the other main 'backward' group, the non-Russian nationalities, however, was less forthright or coherent.[130] It therefore failed to appeal to the increasing hostility to the policy of 'indigenization' among Russian party members.[131]

By 1927, therefore, élitist and populist revivalist views had been reconciled, welded together by the language of class struggle. According to both, bourgeois influence was to blame for the poor state of the revolution, whether because it had destroyed 'democracy' or because it had exerted influence over the party élite, promoting a gradualist, anti-industrial, and anti-worker policy.[132] There were still serious tensions within the United Opposition over the issue of economic, class, and foreign policy. Trotsky did not share the narrowly pro-industrial attitudes of Preobrazhenskii and others on the left, and he was less willing to favour industry at the expense of agriculture.[133] He also came into conflict with populist revivalist leftists over the extent to which the interests of

[128] 'Proekt platformy', 148, 153.
[129] Ibid., 125–31.
[130] In its 1927 September programme, it abandoned Piatakov's position, and advocated intensified *korenizatsiia*. See 'Proekt platformy', 142–6.
[131] This relies on Martin's analysis. See T. Martin, *The Affirmative Action Empire*, 328–38.
[132] For this concept of bourgeois infection and its promotion of 'opportunist' and 'conciliationist' policies, see 'The Platform of the Opposition', 390.
[133] For these differences, see R. Day, *Trotsky*, 138–9, 147–8. For Preobrazhenskii's position, see D. Filtzer, 'Preobrazhensky and the Problem of the Soviet Transition', *Critique*, 9 (1978), 283–95.

workers were to be promoted. In early 1927 the Democratic Centralists departed from the United Opposition when Trotsky supported price reductions in industrial goods and yet again proved himself to be less willing to discriminate against the peasantry than his 'super-industrialist' colleagues.[134] Even so, there was an ideological logic behind the creation of the United Opposition, and it cannot be ascribed wholly to political opportunism. Given the tendency of Soviet political debate to be couched in terms of class, élitist and populist revivalists could unite in defence of workers and proletarian values against the bourgeoisie. They could also agree on the need for an advance towards socialism in the economic and political spheres. Although Stalin and Bukharin tried to present Trotsky and the United Opposition as 'pessimists' who did not believe in the possibility of socialism until the international revolution had been successful, this was a travesty of Trotsky's views.[135]

By the end of the 1920s, the revivalist commitment to the promotion of proletarian values and the assault on bourgeois values had enormous influence, not just among those who formally adhered to the left but more widely within Soviet society. The United Opposition was able to appeal to populist socialist opinion among Soviet workers, and while it is difficult to generalize about workers' responses, the evidence available suggests that they continued to find populist socialist rhetoric appealing.[136] As during the revolution, workers still frequently saw themselves as a virtuous, hard-working *nizy*, exploited and treated in an undignified way by the useless and parasitical *verkhi*. The main change since 1917, of course, was that the employers and tsarist police had now been replaced by communists, managers, or specialists. As one unemployed metal-worker declared: 'There are two classes today: the working class and communists who have replaced the nobles

---

[134] *T*, 3028; R. Day, *Leon Trotsky*, 173. See also R. Day, 'The Myth of the "Super-Industrializer": Trotsky's Economic Policies in the 1920s', in H. Ticktin and M. Cox (eds.), *The Ideas of Leon Trotsky* (London, 1990), 253–68.

[135] As Richard Day has argued, Trotsky opposed the slogan 'socialism in one country' because he believed that Russia had to become integrated into the world economy, not because he doubted the need to advance towards socialism. See R. Day, *Trotsky*, 171.

[136] This is not the place for a detailed analysis of working-class opinion. For analyses and sources, see L. Siegelbaum, *Soviet State and Society*, 100–13; V. Brovkin, *Russia after Lenin*, 183–9. For support for the left among the Moscow working class, see Kevin Murphy, 'Opposition at the Local Level', 334–50.

and dukes'.[137] As before 1917, there were frequent complaints that managers and specialists were 'rude' to workers. Party officials saw managers' and specialists' arrogance as one of the main reasons for working-class unrest.[138] 'Bourgeois' specialists were particularly unpopular and were thought to treat workers especially badly.[139]

Revivalism, the party and the 'proletarian' intelligentsia

Revivalist ideas also became widespread among a more influential group who were not necessarily associated with the political left: party activists and, in particular, the newly emerging Bolshevik intelligentsia. It became common at many levels of the party to worry about the corrupting influence of the bourgeoisie and the threats its attitudes posed to proletarian, ideological purity.[140] These concerns became particularly central during the 'proletarianization' and purge campaigns initiated by the leadership, which emphasized the party's role as an institution that was active in the creation of a new Soviet person, imbued with the proletarian spirit. The purge, during which the party member was supposed to confess ideological and moral sins, was a central part of this attempt to achieve moral and political revival.[141] The party also became more involved in the project of cultural transformation in universities and intellectual life more generally.[142] Similarly, from 1922 party intellectuals established 'proletarian' cultural groups in a number of areas of cultural activity to challenge the influence of the non-party, traditional intelligentsia and establish a committed, political

[137] GPU report to Stalin October 1926. Quoted in Brovkin, *Russia after Lenin*, 184.
[138] See, for instance, the meeting organized by the Central Committee apparatus on the reasons for conflicts in the textile industry, October 1928, RGASPI, 17/85/305, 21; protocol of a meeting of the secretariat of the Nizhegorod provincial committee, 23 or 24 March 1928, RGASPI, 77/1/235, 4.
[139] See, for instance, S. Kislitsyn, *Shakhtinskoe delo. Nachalo stalinskikh repressii protiv nauchno-tekhnicheskoi intelligentsii v SSSR* (Rostov on Don, 1993), 38.
[140] See E. Naiman, *Sex in Public*, 12–16 and *passim*.
[141] For the purge and the party's role in creating a new Soviet person, see M. David-Fox, *Revolution of the Mind*, ch. 2, 169–82; Kharkhordin, *The Collective and the Individual*, ch. 2; I. Halfin, *From Darkness to Light*, 264–82.
[142] For the party's increasing involvement in universities, and Agitprop's role in challenging the compromise with the non-party intelligentsia, see M. David-Fox, *Revolution of the Mind*, 64–75.

culture. Despite the leadership's refusal to undermine the 'bourgeois' intelligentsia, the 'proletarians' gained increasing influence over Soviet culture from 1924 to 1925.[143]

These Bolshevik intellectuals were interested in more than proletarianizing personnel and ensuring that the content of education and culture accorded with party policy. Sharing many of the ideals of the Proletkul't movement, they sought to establish a new, didactic, moralistic, and politicized education and culture, using agitational art and literature to transform and mobilize the population.[144] Within the theatre, artists staged plays designed to illustrate virtuous and negative behaviour, supposedly altering the viewers' worldview in the process. The most explicit form of this politicized, moralized, and melodramatic art was the mock trial, or 'agit-trial' (*agitsud*), in which particular sins, moral and ideological, were condemned. The characters who embodied these sins then confessed in a 'self-criticism' session. This type of political theatre obviously had a great deal in common with the political show trial and with rituals of 'self-criticism' in the party.[145]

Many Bolsheviks agreed that the party had to turn its attention to culture, and purges, self-criticism, and show trials were commonly employed as methods of cultural and ideological transformation throughout the NEP period. There was also a degree of consensus on the content of the ideal culture: all could accept that literacy, cleanliness, and discipline had to be brought to the population, and in particular to 'backward', non-proletarian groups.[146] However, there were divisions over how specifically Bolshevik and 'proletarian' the new culture was to be. As Michael David-Fox has argued in

---

[143] K. Clark, *Petersburg. Crucible of Cultural Revolution* (Cambridge, Mass., 1995), 184.

[144] For agitational literature, see R. Robin, *Socialist Realism. An Impossible Aesthetic*, trans. by C. Porter (Stanford, 1992), 229–33. For agitational theatre, see Lynn Mally, *Revolutionary Acts. Amateur Theatre and the Soviet State, 1917–1938* (Ithaca, 2000), 52–3. For the intellectual origins of these attitudes to art and literature, see Clark, *Petersburg*, 23–8; Boris Groys, 'The Birth of Socialist Realism from the Spirit of the Russian Avant-Garde', in J. E. Bowlt and O. Match (eds.), *Laboratory of Dreams. The Russian Avant-Garde and Cultural Experiment* (Stanford, 1996), 193–218; R. Robin, *Socialist Realism*, chs. 5–7.

[145] For comparisons between the *agitsud* and the show trial, see Julie Cassiday, *The Enemy on Trial. Early Soviet Courts on Stage and Screen* (DeKalb, 2001), 42–50, 110–33, 98. See also Lynn Mally, *Revolutionary Acts. Amateur Theatre and the Soviet State, 1917–1938* (Ithaca, 2000), 61–5.

[146] For this point, see M. David-Fox, 'What is Cultural Revolution?', 189, 191–2.

his study of higher education, tensions emerged between those who emphasized 'enlightenment' and those who stressed 'agitation'. The former interpreted 'culture' in a more technicist way, pressing for the achievement of basic goals such as literacy, and encouraging collaboration with non-party specialists; they clashed with those who favoured a more politicized education and stressed the importance of proletarianization.[147] A similar conflict can be discerned in debates over the ideal form of culture in the workplace between Platon Kerzhentsev and Aleksei Gastev, both previously associated with Proletkul't, although in this case the revivalist position had a more populist, 'democratic' colouring.[148] Kerzhentsev had been involved in the creation of a new politicized proletarian theatre, but in the 1920s he turned his attention to the creation of proletarian culture in the economic sphere. He established an organization, the League of Time, which aimed to improve the efficiency of workplaces, but which sought alternatives to Gastev's élitist methods.[149] He argued that the regime had to rely on the enthusiasm and spontaneous self-discipline of the working class rather than on the authority of an élite of specialist rationalizers.[150]

The writer Fedor Gladkov, another intellectual interested in the idea of proletarian culture, used literature to propagandize revivalist themes, and his novel *Cement* illustrated many of the ideas of the political left. It was one of the first novels to deal with the issue of economic construction and was designed to show how industrialization might be achieved if the ideal, heroic proletarian culture became dominant. Gladkov used his novel to illustrate the ideal qualities of the communist worker, while demonstrating where the source of evil influences lay.[151] *Cement* tells of the struggle of a civil

[147] The institutional affiliations of these groups within the Commissariat of the Enlightenment and Agitprop were complex. M. David-Fox, *Revolution of the Mind*, 64–75.

[148] For this conflict, see K. Bailes, 'Alexei Gastev', 389–91; S. Hanson, *Time and Revolution*, 123–5.

[149] R. Stites, *Revolutionary Dreams. Utopian Vision and Experimental Life in the Russian Revolution* (Oxford, 1989), 157.

[150] P. M. Kerzhentsev, *Printsipy organizatsii* (Moscow, 1968), 310; P. M. Kerzhentsev, 'N.O.T.', in A. N. Shcherban' (ed.), *Nauchnaia organizatsiia truda i upravlenie. Sbornik* (Moscow, 1965), 61–5. Although Kerzhentsev strongly criticized Bogdanov for his subjectivism and overemphasis on 'will'. See ibid., 62–3.

[151] For a comparison between the plot of *Cement* and other socialist realist plots, see K. Clark, *The Soviet Novel. History as Ritual* (Chicago, 1981), 255–60. For a different analysis of *Cement*, see R. Robin, *Socialist Realism*, 254–66.

war hero, Gleb Chumalov, to rebuild a cement factory which has fallen into ruin, in the face of opposition from 'bureaucrats' and specialists. The novel tries to steer a middle course between passive pragmatism and extreme revivalist demands for an assault on 'bureaucrats' and bourgeois sceptics, and at times it is suggested that the hero, Gleb, is guilty of excessively romantic revivalism.[152] But its message is generally clear: on one side stand energetic, virile, and impatient proletarian heroes, hostile to protocol and snobbery and desperate to apply the energy used in defeating the Whites to the industrial front; on the other are the embourgeoisified 'bureaucrats', who are both effeminate and technocratic—they have bourgeois manners, are obsessed with economizing, and describe all attempts to achieve rapid industrialization as utopian 'adventurism'. They concentrate on creating a perfect, efficient apparatus, but by placing power in the hands of 'alien' and 'hostile' specialists they allow corruption, maltreatment of workers, and other forms of 'economic counter-revolution' to take place.[153] Shramm, for instance, the Chairman of the Council of the People's Economy, is pictured as a figure with the 'soft face of a eunuch' and a monotonous 'mechanical' voice; he patronizingly regards Gleb as an irrational 'demagogue'.[154] Gleb responds, echoing the left's language, that while Shramm may be a communist, he does not have a 'workers' policy'.[155] Once Gleb is allowed to rebuild the factory, of course, he shows that a 'workers' policy' can reconstruct industry. Gleb himself is extraordinarily energetic, and is compared by one party official with a dynamo: if only the factory were harnessed to his energy, it would become extraordinarily productive.[156] But Gleb's power is not that of an individual, but is a component of the energy of the masses.[157] Using a combination of vitalist, organicist, and mechanistic metaphors, Gladkov described the masses as 'thousands of hands in thousands of strokes', combined together in the 'powerful movement of one body', a 'living human machine' that could transform nature and 'shook the stones to their depths'.[158] Gleb accepts that worker enthusiasm has to be united with science, and he works closely with the formerly hostile bourgeois specialist Engineer Kleist. But he rejects Kleist's description of worker

---

[152] See, for instance, Fedor Gladkov, 'Tsement', *KN*, 2 (1925), 104.
[153] Ibid., 108–9.   [154] Ibid., 104–6.   [155] Ibid., 104.
[156] Fedor Gladkov, 'Tsement', *KN*, 3 (1925), 53.
[157] Ibid., 70.   [158] Ibid., 70–1.

'enthusiasm' as a 'rain shower'—short-lived and 'harmful' because it prevented 'systematization' (*planomernost'*) and an 'organized division of labour'. As Gleb insisted, 'with enthusiasm we can break up mountains'; in the midst of economic ruin enthusiasm was absolutely necessary. Only when it had been used to build a strong economic foundation would it be possible 'to study the process of production systematically'.[159] Gladkov's hero was enunciating what was to become a typically revivalist approach to the use of labour, and to economic policy more generally: before the economy could be run in a 'systematic', planned way, it had to undergo a new revolution.

This language, of course, was highly reminiscent of that used by the *Vpered* Bolsheviks before the revolution. Gorky himself was to become critical of the proletarian cultural movement, but in 1927 he appealed to the romanticism of the *Vpered* period in an article on the tasks of the revolution on the occasion of its tenth anniversary:

At one time, in the period of dark reaction from 1907–1910, I called [the worker] a 'god-builder', placing in this word the notion that the person himself,... creates and embodies the ability to create miracles... of truth, of beauty... which the idealists attribute to a power that supposedly exists outside the person. By his own labour, the person becomes convinced that outside his reason and will there are no miraculous powers, except the elemental forces of nature, which he must master.[160]

The left, political will, and economic leaps forward

While Gladkov and other advocates of proletarian art and culture saw the motor of economic and social change in the energies of the masses, other Bolshevik intellectuals returned to another, less populist, tradition within revivalist Marxism: the attempt to show that revolutionary forces existed in nature and that dialectics could be applied to science. And although, echoing Bogdanov, they called their science 'proletarian', they tended to see it as the product of proletarian intellectuals with a privileged insight into the laws of nature given to them by Marxist theory, rather than the creation of an intelligentsia imbued with collectivist values.[161]

[159] Fedor Gladkov, 'Tsement', *KN*, 3 (1925), 71.
[160] M. Gorky, *Sochineniia*, xxiv. 292.
[161] They also disagreed with Bogdanov over dialectics.

Their efforts were helped by the publication, for the first time, of Engels's *Dialectics of Nature*, in 1925.[162]

As has been seen, in the early 1920s Bukharin tried to reconcile dialectics with ideas of equilibrium and a commitment to the supremacy of conventional science. But he and his views were challenged by a number of other theorists who called for a return to a more revolutionary interpretation of dialectics. As in the cultural sphere, much of this pressure for a particularly Marxist science was driven by the emergence of a Bolshevik intelligentsia with an interest in creating its own, non-bourgeois culture.[163] In the philosophical field, A. M. Deborin and his followers insisted that dialectics could raise conventional 'bourgeois' science to a higher level, and demanded that scientists reconsider their findings to take account of the revelations of dialectics. Dialectics, they argued, had shown scientists that special dialectical laws, such as the sudden transformation of quantity into quality, operated in nature.[164]

Mechanist philosophers, who shared many of Bukharin's assumptions, condemned the Deborinites for denying that the forces of nature, as discovered by science, could explain reality; they were, they claimed, guilty of 'vitalism', believers in special, supernatural, forces that scientists could not account for. They were also guilty of Bogdanovism in denying the primacy of the material.[165] Deborin replied to these charges by politicizing the conflict. He compared the mechanists with 'reformist' ultra-gradualist Marxist heretics who believed in 'evolution', denying the existence of the 'leaps' in nature and the 'revolutionary' 'emergence of the new'.[166]

Economics was affected by similar debates. A group of so-called 'teleologist' economists, like the Deborinites, insisted that 'bourgeois science' had to take account of dialectics, stressed the importance of sudden leaps in nature, and ascribed considerable

---

[162] D. Joravsky, *Soviet Marxism*, 215–17.

[163] For this process in the Communist Academy, see M. David-Fox, *Revolution of the Mind*, 215–19.

[164] D. Bakhurst, *Consciousness and Revolution*, 37–41; D. Joravsky, *Soviet Marxism*, 170–80; Josephson, *Physics and Politics*, 232–46; G. Wetter, *Der Dialektische Materialismus*, 184–91.

[165] L. Aksel'rod, 'Otvet na "nashi raznoglasiia" A. Deborina', *KN*, 5 (1926), 156–7. See also D. Bakhurst, *Consciousness and Society*, 39.

[166] A. Deborin, 'Nashi raznoglasiia', *LM*, 2 (1926), 16–17.

significance to human will-power.[167] They did not admit to being voluntarists, as they still believed that economic plans had to be feasible and drawn up in accordance with objective realities, but they also argued that an active and effective state could overcome what might appear to be objective scientific constraints on development.[168] For instance, Strumilin, an influential economist within Gosplan writing in 1927, criticized the so-called 'geneticist' economists who demanded that plans should be based 'only on a forecast of the objective and inevitable, independent of the will of economic subjects'. A plan, he insisted, had to be drawn up to 'concentrate the collective will of managers and workers of the whole country' on economic tasks.[169]

In debates over the first five-year plan in January 1928, Strumilin and the teleologists used explicitly dialectical arguments to support their view that high plan targets were feasible, in response to the mechanist views of geneticist planners. One of Strumilin's main opponents, Bazarov, had criticized the suggested plan targets, arguing that they ignored objective, scientifically established constraints; he compared the teleologists to the early 'utopian' socialists, and to medieval theologians who subordinated human reason to divine revelation.[170] But Strumilin defended the view that bourgeois science had to be adapted to reflect the findings of dialectics. While he accepted that economists had to base their arguments on an objective science that could not be falsified, science was not 'above classes'; 'science' was only a 'servant' of the 'purposive task established by our whole economic environment and our international and domestic class position'. He then quoted Engels to show that leaps from quantity to quality did occur in nature. It was therefore, he insisted, reasonable to believe that adherence to a 'socialist path' and socialist science could achieve higher tempos of development than those possible in the United States.[171] Such ideas were seized on

---

[167] D. Joravsky, Soviet Marxism, 178–9. For the use of a politicized, Marxist language in scientific debates of the period, see N. Krementsov, Stalinist Science (Princeton, 1997), 25–9.

[168] For the teleological school, see E. H. Carr and R. W. Davies, Foundations, i. pt ii. ch. 32; Sutela, Socialism, Planning and Optimality, 52.

[169] S. Strumilin, Ocherki sovetskoi ekonomiki. Resursy i perspektivy (Moscow–Leningrad, 1928), 479.

[170] O piatiletnem plane razvitiia narodnogo khoziaistva SSSR. Diskussiia v Kommunisticheskoi Akademii (Moscow–Leningrad, 1928), 78–9.

[171] S. Strumilin, Na planovom fronte, 1920–1930 gg. (Moscow, 1958), 395–405.

by political leaders. In 1926 Georgii Piatakov, an ally of Trotsky and now deputy chairman of Vesenkha, expressed his belief in the ability of the state to achieve extraordinary economic successes, breaking through the limits imposed by objective reality:[172]

we set ourselves a definite purpose and a task dictated by our will; we free ourselves to a considerable extent in the given circumstances from the clutches of what is given by history; we break the old bounds and gain considerably greater creative freedom.[173]

As this statement implies, Piatakov, like other supporters of Trotsky in the economic apparatus, might have formally adhered to the left's 'democratic' principles, but in reality they seem to have had little interest in them. Their voluntarism was an élitist one. For them, a small group of planners or experts, not the masses, would 'break the old bounds', and economic miracles could only be achieved by a highly centralized apparatus using harsh discipline. Piatakov applied this élitist approach to his work as deputy chairman of Vesenkha, and tried to implement his ambitious plans by imposing greater controls on Vesenkha's trusts to ensure that they used investments as fully as possible. He naturally encountered significant opposition, eventually clashing with his boss, Dzerzhinskii.[174]

The Stalin group, the apparatus, and the 'second period' of the New Economic Policy, 1925–7

By the second half of the 1920s, the liberal technicist strategy was on the defensive. The defection of Zinoviev and Kamenev to the left in 1925 was part of a more general disillusionment with market solutions within the élite, and a preference for greater state involvement in the economy. This change in atmosphere occurred for a number of reasons, but of central importance was the recognition of many within the leadership—and the Stalin group that increasingly dominated it—that industrialization had to be pursued more rapidly when the NEP appeared to have succeeded in restoring industry

---

[172] See A. Graziosi, ' "Building the First System of State Industry in History". Piatakov's Vesenkha and the Crisis of NEP', *CMRS*, 32 (1991), 539–80; Valentinov, *Novaia ekonomicheskaia politika*, ch. 6.
[173] Quoted in E. H. Carr and R. W. Davies, *Foundations*, ii. 791–2.
[174] A. Graziosi, 'Building', 550–1.

to its pre-war levels, and when the international situation was deteriorating.[175] From the middle of 1926, suspicion of the West had replaced the view, common within the élite throughout much of the 1920s, that some accommodation would be possible. Particularly worrying, for Stalin and other leaders, was the belief in 1926–7 that the British and French were planning to reorder Eastern Europe at the expense of Soviet interests and security. By September 1926 a full anti-imperialist campaign had been launched, and in January 1927 the élite was preparing for imminent war.[176] The liberal technicist strategy, which necessarily brought gradual economic growth, seemed to be increasingly inappropriate in these circumstances, and in this environment, supporters of more rapid industrialization had greater influence.[177] Within Gosplan, teleological planners became more dominant.[178] The leadership of Vesenkha also became more committed to rapid industrialization, following the appointment of Kuibyshev to replace Dzerzhinskii in 1926.[179] They were also joined by regional party bosses who became powerful lobbyists for more investment in their areas.[180]

Both Stalin and Bukharin accepted that industrialization had to be made a priority, but Stalin became the main advocate within the leadership for a change in policy. Bukharin did accept that industry required more investment, but his approach was still much more favourable to the peasantry and the market than Stalin's.[181] It was

[175] For an analysis of the industrialization debates, see A. Erlich, *The Soviet Industrialization Debate, 1924–1928* (Cambridge, Mass., 1960); L. Siegelbaum, *Soviet State and Society,* 165–180; E. H. Carr, *Socialism in One Country,* i. ch. 6. For the importance of the perception of the international situation, see R. Day, *Trotsky,* 91–7.

[176] For the 'war-scare' of 1926–7, see J. Sontag, 'The Soviet War-Scare of 1926–7', *RR,* 34 (1975), 66–77. Sontag argues that while the war-scare was manipulated by Stalin and others, there was a genuine fear of Western aggression. See also A. Di Biagio, 'Moscow, the Comintern and the War Scare, 1926–28', in S. Pons and A. Romano, *Russia in the Age of Wars,* 83–102.

[177] For these institutional interests, see L. Siegelbaum, *Soviet State and Society,* 165–80.

[178] For the views of Strumilin, see E. H. Carr and R. W. Davies, *Foundations of a Planned Economy, 1926–1929* (London, 1978), i. pt ii. ch. 34.

[179] D. Shearer, *Industry, State and Society,* 51. See also L. Siegelbaum, *Soviet State and Society,* 174–5.

[180] See J. Harris, *The Great Urals,* ch. 2.

[181] For the change in emphasis in Bukharin's pronouncements, see S. Cohen, *Bukharin,* 243 ff. For Bukharin's caution on investment in heavy industry, compare N. I. Bukharin, *V zashchitu proletarskoi diktatury. Sbornik* (Moscow–Leningrad, 1928), 225 with Stalin, *Sochineniia,* viii. 119–22.

Stalin who made the clearest statement that industry was to be the regime's priority at the fourteenth party congress in December 1925.[182] Now, he declared, the 'first period' of the NEP, which gave priority to agriculture, was over; the USSR had entered a 'second period' when attention had to be focused on industry; agriculture could not be improved now without the 'direct expansion of heavy industry'.[183]

Stalin's scepticism of the liberal technicist strategy was perhaps to be expected given his position before 1921. He seems to have retained a suspicion of the bourgeoisie and an emphasis on the role of class, culture, and ideas in politics throughout the 1920s.[184] Stalin's preference for the class pure and ideologically committed over the expert became an issue in party politics in January 1923, when Lenin decided to back Trotsky's criticisms of Rabkrin. In his final writings before his death, Lenin launched a devastating attack on Rabkrin for its complete failure to reform the state apparatus. He combined this with a denunciation of those who called for the development of 'proletarian culture'. The regime had to be satisfied with 'bourgeois culture', he insisted; 'bureaucratism' was the result of 'pre-bourgeois culture'. Rabkrin, he argued, therefore had to be given a new staff of experts who were 'not inferior to the best West European standards'.[185] They were to be workers and peasants by class origin, but were also to constitute a small, expert élite. Stalin had stepped down as head of Rabkrin in the previous year, but he was clearly one of Lenin's main targets. Even so, he remained unrepentant. In his speech as general secretary of the party at the twelfth party congress three months later, he presented an analysis of 'bureaucratism' that was very different to Lenin's. For Stalin, economic problems were caused by the fact that 'alien, bureaucratic, half-bourgeois' elements, people who distorted the political line and acted selfishly and corruptly, worked within the state apparatus. Economic policy would only be successful if the apparatus were made more efficient and staffed 'with people who are akin to the party in spirit'. Such reforms would not only improve the implementation of economic policy but would have a 'moral

[182] Stalin, *Sochineniia*, vii. 315.
[183] Ibid., viii. 119.
[184] R. Himmer, 'The Transition from War Communism to the New Economic Policy. An Analysis of Stalin's Views', *RR*, 53 (1994), 515–29.
[185] Lenin, *PSS*, xlv. 389–90.

aspect'; officials who considered themselves to be 'above the law' would have to be removed, and he called for the elimination of the 'traditions and habits of domineering bureaucrats'.[186] Unlike Lenin, Stalin wanted to purge the class alien and the arrogant, as well as the inefficient.

In the mid-1920s, Stalin expressed this harsh anti-bourgeois tone less frequently, possibly in part because his rival Trotsky himself had now moved to the left. Yet Stalin continued to stress the importance of socialist ideas in politics. In his *Foundations of Leninism* of 1924, Stalin devoted a section to 'style of work', in which he asserted the need to combine 'Russian revolutionary sweep' and 'American businesslike qualities [*delovitost'*]'. The former taken to extremes, he explained, could lead to ' "revolutionary" windbaggery' and a false faith in the ability of decrees to make fundamental transformations. American business-like qualities, on the other hand, without Russian revolutionary sweep, led to the disease of 'narrow and unprincipled *deliachestvo*' and 'empiricism', and caused Bolsheviks to 'degenerate' and abandon the revolution.[187] Stalin's discussion of this topic was rather different from Bukharin's analysis of the ideal Bolshevik 'psychological type' the year before. Bukharin also called for the combination of the Russian intelligentsia's 'breadth of scope' and 'theoretical analysis of events' with 'American practical grasp', but he used his disquisition to attack the absence of proper administrative specialization and to stress the importance of a proper technical education.[188]

Stalin had serious reservations about the cultural and intellectual left. He seems to have disapproved of the conflictual style and exclusiveness of proletarian cultural organizations, and preferred unity among all 'Soviet-inclined' cultural figures.[189] He also refused to accept the radical dialecticians' attempts to create a separate Marxist science, and generally argued that there was one universal

[186] Stalin, *Sochineniia*, v. 206–10. Lars Lih also argues that Stalin was particularly concerned with the issue of 'bureaucratism' in the 1920s. See L. Lih *et al.*, *Stalin's Letters to Molotov*, 10–17.

[187] Stalin, *Sochineniia*, vi. 187–8. See also Stalin's emphasis on the importance of ideas and working-class commitment to socialism in economic construction in 1927. Stalin, *Sochineniia*, x. 119.

[188] N. I. Bukharin, *Proletarskaia revoliutsiia i kul'tura*, 48–50.

[189] See, for instance, his involvement in the establishment of a 'society for the development of Russian culture' in 1922, and his criticism of Bogdanov and other 'proletarian ideologues'. *Istochnik*, 6 (1995), 131–8.

science that all communists had to master.[190] However, there is evidence that he shared some of the assumptions of the intellectual left. First, he accepted there was some relationship between class and science. 'New people', he explained, 'growing up in a country with its revolutionary habits and traditions', were better able to develop science than the 'old professors of the capitalist school', who were fettered by 'philistine [*meshchanskaia*] narrowness and routine'.[191] Second, he accepted that the regime should be building a 'proletarian culture', and his contacts with members of the 'proletarian' intelligentsia—some of whom Trotsky had alienated with his sharp rejection of the concept of proletarian culture—also suggest that Stalin continued to have an interest in their ideas.[192] He was one of Gladkov's sponsors and he supported the publication of *Cement* in a mass edition. He also had regular contacts with 'proletarian' writers and philosophers, and Sheila Fitzpatrick suggests that he may have been trying to build up his 'own 'group of young disciples'.[193] There is also evidence that he had regular lessons in Hegelian dialectics from the Deborinite philosopher Ian Sten between 1925 and 1928.[194]

From the middle of 1925 Stalin pushed for a departure from the gradualist, liberal technicist economic policies of the previous period.[195] There is some evidence that he was preparing for this move theoretically at the end of 1924, with his formulation of the principle 'socialism in one country'. With this clever slogan Stalin was able to call for an advance to socialism, while simultaneously denouncing the left. For Stalin, Trotsky's doctrine of 'permanent revolution' showed that he was 'pessimistically' denying the

[190] Stalin, *Sochineniia*, xi. 74–7; see also M. David-Fox, *Revolution of the Mind*, 218–19.

[191] Stalin, *Sochineniia*, vii. 88 (15 April 1925).

[192] For 'proletarian' writers' criticisms of Trotsky, see A. Kemp-Welch, *Stalin and the Literary Intelligentsia* (Basingstoke, 1991), 43–4.

[193] For this evidence, see A. Kemp-Welch, *Stalin and the Literary Intelligentsia*, 45; S. Fitzpatrick, 'Cultural Revolution Revisited', *RR*, 58 (1999), 204.

[194] Accounts come from E. P. Frolov, quoted in R. Medvedev, *Let History Judge. The Origins and Consequences of Stalinism* (London, 1972), 224–5, and from Dmitrii Volkogonov, *I. V. Stalin. Politicheskii Portret*, i. ch. 2 (Moscow, 1989), 126–7. According to both, Stalin was a poor pupil. Van Ree also sees little profound evidence of profound Hegelian, dialectical thinking in Stalin's writings. See E. Van Ree, 'Stalin as a Marxist Philosopher', 278–9, 302.

[195] See, for instance, his support for Dzerzhinskii's demands for more investment in the metallurgical industry. Stalin, *Sochineniia*, vii. 128–32.

possibility of building socialism in Russia until an international revolution had occurred. He was therefore contradicting Lenin's writings of 1917, which insisted that a socialist revolution could occur in economically backward countries. Thus Trotsky, according to Stalin, was really a 'Menshevik'.[196] Stalin was pursuing a tactic that he was to repeat in the future. He was presenting himself as the true proponent of the 'advance' to socialism, and claiming that the Trotskyist 'left' was, in reality, a 'rightist' force. Stalin was now arguing that because economic disruption had been overcome and industry restored, industrialization and the 'question of building socialism' had become of 'decisive importance'.[197]

Yet Stalin also used the slogan to justify an autarkic, isolationist state-building strategy, which he thought was vital given the external threats to the Soviet Union, and which contrasted with Trotsky's commitment to the USSR's integration into the international economy.[198] Of all Soviet leaders, Stalin seems to have been one of those most worried about the dangers posed by the capitalist world, and in January 1925 he supported an increase in the military budget on the ground that the 'danger of intervention' from the Western powers was again becoming 'real'.[199] If, as he explained later, the Soviet Union was to retain its independence and avoid becoming, like India or tsarist Russia, a colony or 'semi-colony' of the capitalist world, it had to produce heavy industrial goods.[200]

But Stalin's commitment to autarky and the interests of the Soviet state in the international arena were not incompatible with Marxist ideas, and he was not trying to replace socialism with nationalism. He consistently argued that the defence of the Soviet Union was important because it was an island of socialism in a hostile world, and he saw international relations as an ideological struggle rather than a competition between the interests of great powers. So, in 1925 he argued that Western powers would threaten the USSR because they were reacting to the increasing success of communism throughout the world.[201] He did believe that Russia was superior,

---

[196] Stalin, *Sochineniia*, vi. 362–80.

[197] Ibid., ix. 36.

[198] For the slogan 'socialism in one country', see 'K voprosam leninizma', Stalin, *Sochineniia*, viii. 75. For the debate and the position of Trotsky, see R. Day, *Leon Trotsky*, 97–104, 114–15, 145–8.

[199] Stalin, *Sochineniia*, vii. 11–14. See also R. Tucker, *Stalin in Power*, 45–50.

[200] Stalin, *Sochineniia*, viii. 121.   [201] Ibid., vii. 11–14.

but he avoided the nationalist view that this was based on Russia's culture or ethnicity and he opposed cultural Russification. It was Russia's socialism that made it superior, and its more advanced state and economy gave it pre-eminence over non-Russian states in the Soviet Union. As Stalin explained at the twelfth party congress, the Soviet Union represented the 'advanced detachment of the world revolution', and within it the Russian proletariat was 'the most cultured' element, compared with groups in the less industrially developed, backward nations, who were in the 'rear' of world imperialism.[202] The problem facing the regime was how best to establish unity between the Russian proletariat and the peasantry of the formerly oppressed nationalities, and the solution was the development of their economies, so that they would reach the level of the advanced Russian proletariat.[203] 'Great Russian chauvinism' and the imposition of Russian culture would only alienate them, as the Whites had found out during the civil war.[204] Stalin's view of the Russians as a revolutionary people was not unusual. As the conventional contrast drawn between 'Russian revolutionary sweep' and 'American *delovitost*' shows, the opposition between Russia and the West could be grafted onto the opposition between revolutionary spirit and capitalist pragmatism. Stalin was not alone in establishing a link between ideological purity and 'Russianness'. As Katerina Clark has argued, from 1924 to 1925, 'proletarian' cultural groups began to exhibit a hostility to Western influence.[205]

Stalin's support for rapid industrialization and autarky may also have had other sources. It is possible that he was also responding to the balance of forces within the apparatus, and in particular to pressure from regional party bosses, whose support was vital if the left was to be defeated in the Central Committee where their voting power lay. This group was a disparate and divided one. At times, regional organizations were clients of patrons at the centre, and these relationships determined their political position, as was the case when Zinoviev and Kamenev brought the whole of the Leningrad party organization behind the left after 1925.[206] But regional party bosses also had some independence from the centre, and

[202] Ibid., v. 236, 237, 240.   [203] Ibid., v. 240, 247–8.   [204] Ibid., v. 246.
[205] K. Clark, *Petersburg*, 188–9. For the diversity of views of the West in the Soviet press in the 1920s, see J. Brooks, 'Official Xenophobia and Popular Cosmopolitanism in Early Soviet Russia', *AHR*, 75 (1992), 1431–48.
[206] See G. Gill, *Origins*, 172–3.

during the conflict in the Politburo they had even more power, as factions in Moscow looked for allies in the Central Committee.[207] Regional party leaders, of course, did not operate as a coherent group, but they did share similar interests. During the civil war, as has been seen, even though some may have found the left's complaints about centralization and the power of state economic organizations appealing, they were too fearful of threats to their position from a potentially rebellious *nizy* to support the left. During the 1920s, however, the situation changed. Many party officials were extremely critical of the NEP: its liberal technicist elements reduced their control and appeared to be undermining the Dictatorship of the Proletariat by improving the position of the peasantry, traders, and minority nationalities.[208] Its technicist elements—the prizing of expertise, the subordination of party to state and of 'politics' to 'economics'—could also challenge their interests. Lenin's denunciation of 'bureaucratism' and 'communist conceit', and his appeals for 'scientific' expertise in the works he wrote just before his death, a theme taken up by Bukharin, were clearly aimed at local party bosses and activists.[209] Perhaps most importantly, regional party bosses shared with many industrial interests the desire for greater economic investment in their own regions. As James Harris has argued, there was a real danger that they might support the left. Yet the left's support for strong populist revivalist criticisms of the party élite and the vagueness of its economic proposals deterred them.[210] The left's and the Bukharin group's failure to appeal to these regional groups allowed Stalin to build up a powerful base of

---

[207] There is some controversy over the relationship between regional bosses and the centre. A traditional view argues that regional officials were dependent on patrons at the centre. See T. H. Rigby, 'Early Provincial Cliques and the Rise of Stalin', SS, 1 (1981), 3–28. Others see them as more independent of the centre and lobbying for their own interests, particularly at a time of turmoil at the top. In particular see J. Harris, *The Great Urals*, 43. Philip Roeder has presented this view of Soviet politics in a more abstract way: when the 'first tier' 'policy-makers' within the Politburo were divided, they sought the support of a 'second tier' 'selectorate'. During the 1920s regional party bosses were particularly important in the second tier. See P. Roeder, *Red Sunset*, esp. 51–62.

[208] For local party officials' resistance to the NEP, See R. Service, *Lenin*, iii. 214–18. For the opposition of local Russian party and soviet officials to 'indigenization', see R. Smith, *The Bolsheviks and the National Question*, 6.

[209] 'We need to learn to value science, to reject the "communist" conceit of the dilettantes and bureaucrats', Lenin, *PSS*, xlii. 344 (21 February 1921).

[210] For the views of regional party bosses, see J. Harris, *The Great Urals*, ch. 2.

support within the regional party apparatus by skilfully accommo-
dating their interests.[211]

Reminiscing in 1937 about his rise to power, Stalin himself
ascribed his success to his willingness to pay attention to the 'middle
cadres', people whom Trotsky ignored.[212] There was therefore
something in the left's allegation that the Stalin group represented
the 'stratum of "administrators"' in the party and state ('sloi
"upravlentsev"'), but they exaggerated the power of the regional
party officials and underestimated Stalin's own role.[213] The relationship between regional bosses and Stalin was a complex, reciprocal
one. There was plenty of room for tensions between them, but
Stalin's commitment to industrialization, his history of support for
'class struggle' and ambivalence about the NEP, and his hostility to
Trotsky and the left ensured that he was probably the most plausible
representative of regional party interests in the Politburo.

Stalin was, however, cautious, and it was some time before he
began to call for rapid industrialization. In 1925 his vision was
more technicist than revivalist. He argued that the state had to
embark on the establishment of socialism, but implied that it
would be a reasonably slow process: its 'economic basis' would
have to be built by 'means of welding agriculture and socialist
industry into one integral economy'. This would be achieved, presumably gradually, by creating an extensive network of consumer
and producer co-operatives and discriminating against private capital. Stalin was not talking about class struggle or a sudden leap
towards the abolition of classes. Only 'in the long term' would it be
possible to establish conditions of production and distribution that
would lead 'directly and immediately to the abolition of classes'.[214]

In the industrial, state sector, the Politburo majority's approach
can also be seen as technicist in inspiration. Resources for industrialization had to be extracted from industry as well as agriculture,
and therefore savings had to be made by disciplining labour. In April
1926 Stalin, on behalf of the Central Committee, launched the
'regime of economy', a campaign designed to cut administrative

---

[211] Although some local party bosses did support the Bukharinite right. For
Uglanov's support for Bukharin, see C. Merridale, *Moscow Politics*, 50–1.
[212] See Stalin's speech of 7 November 1937, reported by Georgi Dimitrov, in
G. Dimitrov, *Dnevnik. 9 mart 1933–6 fevruari 1949* (Sofia, 1997), 129.
[213] 'Proekt platformy oppozitsii', 151.
[214] Stalin, *Sochineniia*, ix. 22–4.

costs and increase labour productivity in order to achieve 'socialist accumulation'.[215] Stalin justified the campaign as part of a broader technicist strategy. At its centre was the creation of an efficient, strong, and hierarchical state machine that formulated a rational and balanced plan, taking account of the agricultural potential of the country; Stalin would have nothing to do with those who drew up 'fantastic plans' and created disappointment when they remained unfulfilled.[216]

Stalin did use revivalist language: he argued that cost-cutting, rationalization campaigns would be more effective if workers were 'drawn in' to them and became 'conscious participants' in building the economy; he also extolled the virtues of production conferences, established in 1923 to give workers, through the trade unions, the opportunity to discuss factory administration and to criticize management.[217] The leadership realized there was a real danger of serious worker discontent if workers did not feel involved in the campaign. Yet Stalin and his colleagues were eager to distance themselves from the left's position. Their views of production conferences were perfectly compatible with the instructions given to Rabkrin by its then head, Kuibyshev, in 1924: Rabkrin was to involve the masses in improving the apparatus, but it was not to mobilize them 'against the leaders of corresponding organs and enterprises'; strategies of 'opposition' and 'struggle' were inappropriate, and wherever possible Rabkrin was to act with the agreement of managers of enterprises.[218]

Indeed, the left's populist revivalist analysis of 'bureaucratism' as the 'gap' between apparatus and masses, caused by the influence of class alien groups, was explicitly challenged by officials. As D. Z. Lebed', a deputy commissar of Rabkrin wrote, Trotsky was wrong in alleging that the 'question of soviet bureaucratism' was an issue

---

[215] *Direktivy KPSS i sovetskogo pravitel'stva po khoziaistvennym voprosam 1917–1957 gody: sbornik dokumentov* (Moscow, 1957), i. 578–83. See also, S. N. Ikonnikov, *Sozdanie i deiatel'nost' ob"edinennykh organov TsKK-RKI v 1923–1934 gg.* (Moscow, 1971), 187 ff; E. A. Rees, *State Control in Soviet Russia, 1921–1934* (London, 1987),133–6; E. M. Khamovich, 'Iz istorii bor'by partii za rezhim ekonomii', *VI KPSS*, 12 (1984), 66–74.

[216] Stalin, *Sochineniia*, viii. 131–2.

[217] Ibid., viii. 140–1, 144–5. *Profsoiuzy SSSR. Dokumenty i materialy* (Moscow, 1963), ii. 338–9. For the role of production conferences, see W. J. Chase, *Workers, Society, and the Soviet State*, 264–82.

[218] *Trinadtsatyi s"ezd*, 278 (Kuibyshev).

of 'the class role of the bureaucracy, about its social links and sympathies, about its strength and privileged status'.[219] Rather, he suggested, 'bureaucratism' had to be defined as 'red-tape' and inefficiency, which in turn was caused by the 'lack of culture' and organizational ability in Russia.[220] The 'struggle against bureaucratism' therefore had to be directed 'in the first place against the organizational cumbersomeness and clumsiness of the apparatus'.[221]

The 'left turn' and the move to revivalism, 1927–8

By the end of 1927, however, there were signs that the Stalin group was not only abandoning its commitment to the liberal technicist elements of the NEP but also its technicism, and was moving towards the revivalism of the left. The failure of Soviet policy in China in April and the break with Britain in May seemed to bear out Stalin's predictions in 1925 that the capitalist world was preparing for intervention, and justified his conviction that rapid industrialization was absolutely essential.[222] Poor grain collections in 1927 forced a decision: between a 'retreat' to a more liberal policy that would encourage the peasantry to deliver grain by paying them a market price; and the continuation of the policy of rapid industrialization, which demanded that the state intervene and use compulsion.[223] From the autumn of 1927, the leadership began to abandon liberal technicism in agriculture and to call for a restriction on the private sector in the countryside. At the October 1927 Central Committee plenum Molotov called for 'new measures for the limitation of capitalism in the countryside', and for the development of 'state planning and the regulation of activity in agriculture'.[224] Even

---

[219] D. Z. Lebed', *Partiia v bor'be s biurokratizmom. Itogi XV s"ezda VKP(b)* (Moscow–Leningrad, 1928), 28.

[220] Lebed', *Partiia*, 31.

[221] D. Z. Lebed', *Sovety i bor'ba s biurokratizmom* (Moscow, 1927), 21.

[222] For foreign policy issues, see Reiman, *The Birth of Stalinism*, 11–18; Stalin, *Sochineniia*, ix. 329.

[223] For the reasons for changes in economic policy, see A. Nove, 'O sud'bakh NEPa', *VI*, 8 (1989), 172–6; R. W. Davies, *The Industrialisation of Soviet Russia 3: The Soviet Economy in Turmoil, 1929–1930* (London, 1989), 47–75; M. Reiman, *The Birth of Stalinism*, trans. by G. Saunders (Bloomington, 1987), ch. 4.

[224] RGASPI, 17/2/322, 9.

so, the leadership was still behaving cautiously—it was committed to an 'economic' struggle against the kulak, not a full class struggle involving the use of force.[225]

In the industrial sector, also, the Stalin group began to favour more revivalist strategies. Liberal technicist approaches came under attack, again because they obstructed growth and contradicted the interests of powerful industrial and regional party bureaucracies. The syndicates, which were successfully using market mechanisms to co-ordinate the industrial economy, were criticized, as was the NEP more generally, for imposing constraints on the expansion of production. They met particular hostility from Vesenkha's powerful regional trusts, which objected to the syndicates' attempts to impose market disciplines on them.[226] However, Stalin and his allies were not satisfied with a system dominated by the trusts and local enterprises. The trusts fought for a form of industrial organization that would give more power to operate in the way they saw fit, and free them, at least to some extent, from market disciplines.[227] They therefore undermined the NEP order, by demanding large investments in industry and calling for more state regulation of the economy. But they were defending a vision closer to technicism than to the highly centralized, militarized, and voluntaristic vision of Piatakov. They wanted high levels of investment but resisted attempts by the centre to control that investment. Power, they insisted, was to reside with the producers. With the appointment of the weak Kuibyshev as head of Vesenkha in 1926, they went some way towards achieving their ambitions.[228] The trusts were frequently able to prevent the centre from interfering in their affairs, often by forging alliances with local party bodies.[229]

In 1927–8 Stalin and sections of the leadership tried to challenge the wasteful and inefficient system defended by the trusts, by

---

[225] Stalin, *Sochineniia*, x. 311.

[226] This discussion of the role of the syndicates, and the conflicts over their position, is based on that in D. Shearer, *Industry, State and Society*, 53–66.

[227] Ibid., 69, 240.

[228] A. Graziosi, 'Building the First System of State Industry', 566–9.

[229] In 1926 Dzerzhinskii complained to Stalin that party secretaries and chairmen of soviet executive committees were putting pressure on economic organizations to give them subventions. The friendly relationship between party, soviet, and local economic officials led them to conspire together against the centre. Dzerzhinskii to Stalin, 28 March 1926, *Bol'shevsitskoe rukovodstvo*, 325–6. See also C. Merridale, *Moscow Politics*, 50–1.

pushing for a more élitist revivalist form of economic management. They exerted pressure on the industrial bureaucracy by establishing a strong centre, able to mobilize all resources in the face of resistance from recalcitrant officials. Until 1926 Piatakov hoped to establish Vesenkha as this control organization, but with his dismissal Rabkrin took over this role. Led by Stalin's energetic ally, Ordzhonikidze, and staffed by many officials with connections with Trotsky, Rabkrin enforced and raised plan targets, organizing highly disruptive inspections to show how managers could increase production.[230] Rabkrin accused managers of failing to use 'hidden reserves', and on the basis of their inspections Rabkrin pressed for enormous increases in the plan targets without greater investment. Rabkrin claimed that its suggestions were perfectly feasible and based on scientifically valid assumptions. But its use of quasi-military campaigns to squeeze industry was reminiscent of the voluntaristic, élitist revivalist Trotskyist tradition of the civil war period. As will be seen in the following chapter, this strategy became the foundation for Stalin's policies during the Great Break of 1928–30.

Yet Stalin also departed from this earlier Trotskyist tradition. Unlike Piatakov, Stalin, Ordzhonikidze, and Rabkrin combined élitist revivalism with a more populist revivalist strategy. Stalin seems to have been responding, in part, to increasing working-class unrest. The 'regime of economy' encouraged managers to cut costs, thus damaging workers' living standards, and industrial relations naturally became more tense.[231] Stalin, as general secretary of the party, was particularly aware of these problems, and he seems to have advocated concessions to workers. In August 1926, for instance, he urged that trade unions create an 'institute of trade union activists', half of whom were to be non-party workers;[232] in September, he accepted that the least well-paid workers had to receive something 'tangible'.[233] In February 1927, at a meeting to discuss

[230] For Rabkrin's procedures, see D. Shearer, *Industry, State and Society*, 85–92; E. A. Rees, *State Control*, 145–53.
[231] W. J. Chase, *Workers, Society, and the Soviet State*, 278–82; C. Ward, *Russia's Cotton Workers*, ch. 10; J. Hatch, 'The Politics of Industrial efficiency During NEP: The 1926 "*Rezhim ekonomii*" Campaign in Moscow', Paper presented at the IV World Congress for Soviet and East European Studies, Harrogate, 1990.
[232] Stalin to Molotov 30 August 1926, in L. Koshelova, V. Lel'chuk, V. Naumov, O. Naumov, L. Rogovaia, and O. Khlevniuk, *Pis'ma I.V. Stalina V.M. Molotovu, 1925–1936 gg. Sbornik dokumentov* (Moscow, 1995) (henceforth *Pis'ma*), 81.
[233] Stalin to Molotov, 23 September 1926, *Pis'ma*, 93.

strikes in the textile industry, he went even further. He refused to accept that industrial unrest could be blamed on working-class 'rowdies' (*buzotery*); rather, strikes were occurring because workers legitimately wanted a larger share of profits, because they were becoming more politically 'active' (*aktivnye*), and because economic, trade union, and party apparatuses were more 'bureaucratized' and insufficiently attentive to workers' demands. The only solution was to increase wages.[234] The reduction of the working day to seven hours in 1927 was in part designed to appeal to workers, as was the reduction in wage differentials between skilled and unskilled workers and between different branches of industry at the beginning of 1928.[235]

By the end of 1927 the Stalin group was expressing populist revivalist sentiments that were difficult to distinguish from those of the left, but, unlike the United Opposition, Stalin had managed to move to the left while maintaining the support of regional party bosses as a group. The tone of Ordzhonikidze's report on the work of Rabkrin at the fifteenth party congress in December 1927 differed markedly from Kuibyshev's report three years earlier and bore unmistakable signs of the leftist analysis of 'bureaucratism'. While he rejected the left's charge that the state apparatus was 'alien' to the working class, he was highly critical of officials, not merely for their inefficiency but also for their poor treatment of workers. Officials' 'treatment of people' had to change, he declared.[236] A cheap and efficient apparatus as existed in Germany was not enough: the apparatus had to be closely 'linked' with the masses and had to work together with workers and peasants rather than to 'command' them.[237] Ordzhonikidze now made it clear that the *nizy* had to participate in the struggle against 'bureaucratism'. The resolutions of the congress followed Ordzhonikidze's line and insisted that improvements in the *tekhnika* of state administration should not lead to the apparatus' 'isolation' and 'separation from the masses',

[234] RGASPI, 558/11/1110, 49–55 (25 February 1927).

[235] See *P*, 18 October 1927. For the success of this policy in discomforting the left, see E. H. Carr and R. W. Davies, *Foundations*, i. pt ii. 497. On wage differentials, see ibid., 500 ff. In practice both initiatives had consequences which were unpopular among workers.

[236] *Piatnadtsatyi s"ezd VKP(b). Dekabr' 1927 goda. Stenograficheskii otchet*, 2 vols. (Moscow, 1961), i. 440–1, 464.

[237] Ibid., 616. For similar views of 'bureaucratism', see Stalin's speech, ibid., 71, 77–9.

but had to be combined with mass participation in administration.[238] Those officials who behaved arrogantly to workers and peasants were, the congress declared, guilty of 'sabotage'.[239]

Stalin's speech at the congress also had a strongly revivalist flavour. While he generally praised the party, he condemned excessively close 'family' relations between party officials and economic organizations. At times, party officials who were working in economic and state organizations, instead of fighting against 'bureaucratism', had 'become infected with bureaucratism themselves and carry that infection into the party organizations'. This process was inevitable as long as the state existed, but it was possible to fight against it by reviving the party, 'raising the activism of the mass of the party membership', improving 'democracy' in the party, and preventing methods of 'persuasion' from being replaced with '*administrirovanie*'. However, some party leaders had not only suppressed 'democracy' and 'self-criticism' but they had also lost their revolutionary energy and their commitment to socialist ideology, a failing that was damaging because advance only took place 'in the process of struggle, in the process of the development of contradictions'. These bosses 'swim with the current (*po techeniiu*), smoothly and calmly, without perspective, without looking into the future'. They had become 'philistines', holding celebratory, sycophantic meetings at which there was plenty of applause but little sense of ideological direction.[240]

Stalin's criticism of 'bureaucratic' party officials and his rousing call for the revival of the party and its separation from the state was very close to the now defeated left's position, and it is not surprising that Nikolai Uglanov, the Moscow party boss who shared many of Bukharin's views and became closely associated with what came to be known as the 'Right Deviation', found it very difficult to respond to the speech. He claimed that he agreed with Stalin but, whether deliberately or not, he misinterpreted the sense of Stalin's comments, recasting them as a call for strong and efficient party leadership. He paraphrased Stalin's comments on ideological 'perspective' in leadership as a more élitist appeal for 'direction in leadership'. Stalin's criticisms of formalistic, celebratory meetings were interpreted

[238] *Dekabr'*, 621.
[239] Ibid., 618.
[240] Stalin, *Sochineniia*, x. 329–33.

as an attack on the absence of 'accuracy in everyday leadership' rather than of ideological direction and 'democracy'. Stalin's denunciations of 'family' relations between officials and the suppression of criticism were less easy to evade and distort. Here Uglanov in effect contradicted Stalin, arguing that such undemocratic practices were becoming rarer and that local party leadership had improved.[241] Uglanov's conception of the goals of the regime was clearly very different from that of Stalin, and it was not long before the tensions between them were to develop into open conflict.

[241] Stalin, *Sochineniia*, x. 144.

3

Mobilization and 'Class Struggle', 1928–1930

The issue of *Pravda* of 20 January 1929, on the eve of the fifth anniversary of Lenin's death, must have confused its readers. Its first page was dominated by Lenin's essay of January 1918, 'How to Organize Emulation', previously unpublished, which contained an aggressively populist revivalist message. It claimed that the revolution, by allowing workers to work for themselves rather than for capitalists, had created the conditions for 'workers' control', mass enthusiasm, and initiative. There were enormous 'untapped' reserves of organizational ability among workers and peasants which were waiting to be released. Centralized 'accounting and control' was the 'essence of socialist transformation', but it could be 'exercised only by the people'. The belief that only the bourgeoisie could run the economy was a 'disgusting prejudice', and indeed a 'war to the death' had to be waged against 'the rich and their hangers-on, the bourgeois intelligentsia'.[1] This article, however, was followed by two very different interpretations of Lenin's thought. The first, on pages 2 and 3, was entitled 'Lenin and the Tasks of Science in Socialist Construction' and written by Nikolai Bukharin. Bukharin said nothing about Lenin's belief in the efficacy of mass enthusiasm; Bukharin's Lenin was a technicist, a believer in rationalization and 'scientific leadership'.[2] The second, on page 4, was by Lenin's widow, Krupskaia, which presented an almost liberal technicist Lenin, committed to a gradual transition to socialism in the countryside.[3]

---

[1] *P*, 20 January 1929; see also *PSS*, xxxv. 195–205.
[2] N. I. Bukharin, 'Lenin i zadachi nauki v sotsialisticheskom stroitel'stve', *P*, 20 January 1929.
[3] N. Krupskaia, 'Il'ich o kolkhoznom stroitel'stve', *P*, 20 January 1929.

Pravda was reflecting the struggle over Lenin's ideological legacy within the Bolshevik party, and it was the Lenin of 1917–18 who ultimately prevailed. In launching the 'Great Break' of the late 1920s, Stalin established class struggle and mass mobilization as the teachings of the 'true' Lenin. Yet, Stalin was returning to the Leninism of the revolutionary period only in certain respects. It would be more accurate to see him as the heir of the revivalist United Opposition of 1926–7. Like the left, he combined the demand for mass participation and mobilization with a call for greater socialization of the economy (although he used methods the left would never have accepted, and went much further than they did in calling for centralization and economic leaps forward). In May 1929 he declared that mass enthusiasm was a 'lever' of socialist construction and quoted Lenin's article to justify 'socialist emulation' (*sotsialisticheskoe sorevnovanie*), a campaign designed to use industrial 'democracy' and moral incentives to enthuse workers to improve their productivity.[4]

Stalin's extraordinarily disruptive and often destructive policies during the 'Great Break' are therefore best understood if we appreciate this revivalist ideological context. The prevalence of 'utopian' populist egalitarian ideas among intellectuals during this period of 'cultural revolution' has been noted by many,[5] but several students of high politics have been reluctant to see populist revivalist Bolshevism, however diluted, as an integral part of Stalin's strategy. They have tended either to ignore it or to assume that Stalin was unsympathetic to it, but tolerated it because he thought that he could use them to gain support from 'below' and present himself as an ideological purist. So, for some liberal historians, Stalin was motivated by Marxist ideas, but this Marxism was highly élitist and technocratic, and was similar to the Bolshevism of the civil war period.[6] For conflictualist authors, the policies of this period had more to do with 'statism' than with Marxism, and should be contrasted with the more 'liberal' manifestations of Bolshevism during

---

[4] *P*, 22 May 1929.

[5] For the classic work on these themes, see S. Fitzpatrick (ed.), *Cultural Revolution in Russia, 1928–1931* (Bloomington, 1978).

[6] For Malia, the Bolshevism of the period consisted of a mixture of the technocracy and prometheanism of the Enlightenment *philosophes*, a 'Westernizing' hostility to the 'backward' peasantry, and a Marxist determination to destroy the market by means of class struggle. See Malia, *The Soviet Tragedy*, 186–8, 221–2.

the NEP.[7] According to one view, Stalin may have mouthed radical Marxist slogans in this period, but in reality he was a Russian 'national Bolshevik', whose real objective was the strengthening of a Russian state.[8]

The policies of this period were indeed intended to strengthen and centralize the state and the economy. But Stalin's commitment to centralization was of a peculiar type. Like his predecessors in the United Opposition, Stalin combined populist and élitist revivalist strategies, and élitist revivalist approaches were perhaps the most prevalent. Stalin insisted that a Bolshevik élite, armed with faith in socialism and breaking through the limits of bourgeois science, could push the economy and the polity towards a socialist system. The market was to be eliminated, the state and society were to be completely unified and integrated, all 'backwardness' was to be overcome, and extraordinary feats of production were to be achieved; the concessions made to 'backward' groups under the NEP, such as the peasantry, were no longer acceptable. There are, then, close parallels between Stalin's policies in the 1920s and the regime's behaviour during the civil war.[9] Yet Stalin's ideas in this period did not merely amount to the élitist revivalism of the civil war period, and he followed the United Opposition in combining it with populist revivalism. He adopted this approach to some extent in the countryside, promoting policies of class struggle reminiscent of the *kombedy* campaign of 1918, but it is more evident in the 'advanced' industrial, urban sector. He called for a 'cultural revolution' that would create a new 'proletarian' and 'democratic' spirit within the party and the working classes. Stalin also, in typical populist revivalist vein, tried to mobilize the party against the state apparatus. Echoing the United Opposition, he justified this mixture of élitism and populism as both a 'proletarian' policy of class struggle against bourgeois enemies, and as a strategy of rapid, revolutionary 'advance' along the road to socialism. His technicist and liberal technicist critics—Bukharin, Uglanov, Rykov, and the trade union leader Tomskii—he argued, were members of a 'Right Deviation'; they were calling for a cowardly 'retreat' and were therefore assisting the cause of the bourgeoisie, thus sabotaging

[7] See, for instance, R. Daniels, *Trotsky, Stalin and Socialism* (Boulder, 1991), 151.

[8] R. Tucker, *Stalin in Power*, 103–6.

[9] For comparisons with the 'militarization' of the civil war period, see S. Cohen, *Bukharin*, 314. See also D. Shearer, *Industry, State and Society*, ch. 4.

socialism. It was naturally difficult for him to explain this class struggle according to the traditional Marxist historical scheme, because the revolution and class struggle had already taken place in 1917. To solve this difficulty he argued that as humanity approached socialism the class struggle would intensify, because the stronger socialism became, the more viciously capitalist elements would fight it.[10]

We cannot know how far Stalin was motivated by the pragmatic desire to build up his own and central state power, or how far he believed that he was creating socialism; the available evidence suggests he saw no conflict between the two. But whatever the balance between various motivations, he pursued revivalism reasonably consistently, and his policies make best sense within the context of revivalist ideas. Yet while revivalist policies, in reconciling rapid industrialization, centralization, and a populist appeal to workers, had many practical advantages for Stalin, their unsustainability soon became clear. Voluntaristic economic policies caused chaos, as did the attempt to establish a highly centralized state-dominated economy at breakneck speed. Also the contradictions within the revivalist approach, between its élitist and its populist elements, became obvious: state-led rapid industrialization required a unified, disciplined effort, while class struggle and 'democratization' was divisive and undermined the ability of the centre to implement its will. Bukharin and others within the party pointed to these problems. But for Stalin and his revivalist allies, as for the United Opposition, there was no contradiction, as industrialization, class struggle, and 'democratization' were all 'proletarian' policies. It would be two years before Stalin was willing to accept elements of the right's technicist critique and begin to move away from revivalism.

Centralization, planning, and voluntarism

Stalin's economic strategy remained constant between 1928 and 1932: to pump as many resources from the countryside as possible into industry; and to strengthen the Soviet Union's defence against

---

[10] Stalin, *Sochineniia*, xii. 34. Lenin had already laid the ground for this idea. Lenin, *PSS*, xxxvi. 382.

foreign threats. As he wrote to Molotov in August 1930, 'we must *push* grain exports *furiously*'; if grain was not exported, 'we risk being left without our new iron and steel and machine-building factories...'.[11] Heavy industry was, for Stalin, vital now the international environment was unstable and the Soviet Union's security appeared to be under threat. As he explained in November 1928, the question of the 'fast rate of industrial development' faced the Soviet Union 'particularly acutely' because Russia was a backward country surrounded by hostile, capitalist powers; the 'environment at home and abroad' 'force a rapid rate of industrial growth on us'.[12] Yet for Stalin, as for the left before him, it was clear that industrialization had to be achieved in a particular way: it had to be accompanied by an 'advance' along all fronts towards socialism and a rejection of the concessions to the market made in 1921. He used Lenin's defence of the NEP in 1921 to justify the need for a sharp advance: 'we are now retreating...in order...afterwards to take a run and make a more powerful leap forward'.[13]

Economic circumstances at the end of 1927 and beginning of 1928 suggested to many that the time had come for this 'powerful leap forward'. By early 1928, the continuing grain shortages, caused by the peasants' refusal to deliver grain to the state for the low prices they were being offered, forced the leadership to make a choice between feeding workers and maintaining the ambitious industrialization targets on the one hand, and preserving the market relations of the NEP on the other. In early January, during a trip to Siberia to investigate the reasons for low grain procurements, Stalin made it clear that he had decided on the first option and was willing to undermine market relations and, therefore, the NEP. The market and material incentives, he argued, could no longer be relied on to motivate the peasantry to produce and deliver grain. The kulaks were refusing to give up their grain for a fair price, he claimed, and only force and class struggle would ensure that they delivered it.[14]

The scene was therefore set for an assault on all manifestations of 'backward' capitalism in the countryside. 'Class struggle' was

---

[11] Stalin to Molotov, 24 August 1930, in *Pis'ma*, 203–4. See also Stalin, *Sochineniia*, xii. 49–50.

[12] Stalin, *Sochineniia*, xi. 250–1, 247.

[13] Stalin, *Sochineniia*, xii. 118.

[14] Stalin, *Sochineniia*, xi. 4. For Stalin's position during this period, see J. Hughes, *Stalin, Siberia and the Crisis of the New Economic Policy* (Cambridge, 1991), ch. 5.

initiated against the 'kulak' (a term which was frequently applied to any peasant resisting collectivization), by mobilizing the poor peasantry against their rich neighbours and using state repression against them; this attempt to split villages was reminiscent of the *kombedy* system of the civil war period and was the basis of the 'Ural–Siberian method' of grain procurement.[15] Yet this approach was based on optimistic assumptions about the behaviour of the poor peasantry, and Stalin increasingly favoured another way of organizing the countryside that would transform the whole peasantry: the establishment of state and collective farms.[16] Collective farms would help the regime to force the countryside into the centralized, collectivist 'proletarian' model that theoretically obtained in the heavy industrial sector; they would 'rework, remake the peasantry, its psychology, its production in the spirit of moving closer to the psychology of the working class'.[17] The creation of a new, collectivized peasantry would, Stalin argued, provide a number of more practical benefits: it would facilitate procurement of grain by the regime, as kulaks who were 'sabotaging' procurement by 'withholding' grain, would be removed. Collectivization would also secure socialism and prevent the restoration of capitalism: because 'small-scale production' gave rise to 'capitalism and the bourgeoisie', the destruction of individual farming would allow the regime to 'destroy the possibility of restoring capitalism'.[18] It would also improve agricultural production by ensuring that peasants on larger farms could use new technology. Several of Stalin's statements, and those of other commentators in this period, suggest that they really believed that the time was ripe for socialist forms of economic organization and that they would be more productive than capitalism. In a private letter to Molotov of December 1929, he wrote enthusiastically of the allegedly huge increases in productivity achieved by peasants pooling their tools, even in unmechanized collective farms. According to Stalin 'the eyes of our rightists are popping out of their heads in surprise'.[19] At the same time, however,

---

[15] For the mobilization of the poor against the kulaks, see ibid., 159–62; S. Fitzpatrick, *Stalin's Peasants. Resistance and Survival in the Russian Village after Collectivization* (Oxford, 1994), 41–3.

[16] Stalin, *Sochineniia*, xi. 5.

[17] Ibid., xi. 163.

[18] Ibid., xi. 227–8.

[19] Stalin to Molotov, 5 December 1929, *Pis'ma*, 170.

Stalin recognized that it would take time to proletarianize the peasantry. As he explained the same month, it was mistaken to argue that 'members of collective farms have already been transformed into socialists': it was not easy to 'remake the peasant-collective farmer, to correct his individualist psychology'. Therefore, while the collective farm was essential for transforming peasant attitudes, class struggle would continue against kulak survivals within the collective farm.[20]

In the early stages of his campaign against the kulak, Stalin's waging of class struggle did not amount to a complete rejection of the market. In the summer of 1928 he still claimed that capitalist elements had to be overcome 'through the market, not avoiding the market'.[21] Yet by the beginning of 1929, Stalin was redefining the current period, which he still called the NEP, as one in which non-market relations between the state and the peasantry would become increasingly dominant.[22] Such statements encouraged those who believed that the Soviet Union was on the threshold of the full abolition of the market and of money.[23] In February 1930 Stalin tried to dampen this enthusiasm, arguing that the NEP, and the existence of some form of trade, would continue for some time. But he still argued that the Soviet Union was in a transition period that would ultimately lead to a 'socialist' society based on non-monetary product-exchange.[24]

The assault on 'backward' capitalism in the countryside was accompanied by moves to bring 'progress' to the other main area of 'backwardness': the non-Russian nations. For some on the left, this meant that the whole policy of *korenizatsiia* was to be abandoned and separate nations were to be merged into one socialist nation. Naturally such arguments appealed to local Russian party activists who resented the privileges given to non-Russian cultures and languages. Yet Stalin was unhappy with this radical solution and the 'Great Russian chauvinism' that it justified. In July 1930 he explicitly decoupled the question of nationalities from that of the

---

[20] Stalin, *Sochineniia*, xii. 164–5.

[21] Ibid., xi. 144–5.

[22] Ibid., xii. 43–9.

[23] For an example of this enthusiasm, see *ZI*, 9 February 1930. For a fuller account of these debates, see R. W. Davies, *The Soviet Economy in Turmoil, 1929–1930* (Basingstoke, 1989), 162–73.

[24] Stalin, *Sochineniia*, xii. 186–7.

peasantry, issues that had hitherto often been connected in the leadership's thinking. While capitalism was clearly giving way to socialism in agriculture and industry, national languages and cultures were flourishing, not merging into one. These two different trajectories could be explained, Stalin argued, by the fact that distinctions between nationalities could only be resolved by the achievement of socialism on an international scale, and not by the victory of socialism in one country.[25] The Great Break in nationality policy was therefore to consist of an acceleration of 'advance' through increased and more rapid *korenizatsiia*, combined with class struggle in the national minority areas.[26]

Stalin had the greatest confidence in the feasibility of the advance to socialism and the abolition of market relations in the industrial sphere. In January 1930, the leadership, under the influence of Piatakov, head of the State Bank (Gosbank), introduced a particularly ambitious reform of the credit system. Gosbank was to take control over short-term credit from the syndicates, credit was to be subject to the plan rather than commercial principles, and financial discipline was to be enforced by the state.[27] Stalin welcomed the reform as a move towards a fully planned, moneyless socialist economy; as he explained, 'firstly, Gosbank is being transformed into an all-state apparatus for accounting for the production and distribution of goods', and 'secondly, large masses of money are being freed from circulation'.[28]

Stalin therefore presented his ideal economy as a scientifically planned, co-ordinated machine. Yet, in practice, Stalin's planning was of a peculiar variety, and had much in common with élitist revivalist approaches to the economy. Plans were not just designed to co-ordinate the economy, setting targets based on available resources, as the technicist vision of economic equilibrium suggested. They became utopian documents, in which extraordinary targets were set with little reference to objective constraints. At the same time, the Stalinists did not only regard the state as a body of experts,

---

[25] Stalin, *Sochineniia*, xiii. 3–7. This was the first public statement of this position, but he had expressed it in an unpublished letter in March 1929. Ibid., xi. 333–55.

[26] For these policies, see Martin, *The Affirmative Action Empire*, 238–49; Y. Slezkine, *Arctic Mirrors*, ch. 7; Y. Slezkine, 'The Soviet Union as a Communal Apartment', 326–30.

[27] For this reform, see Davies, *The Soviet Economy in Turmoil*, 320–8.

[28] Stalin, *Sochineniia*, xii. 330–1.

presiding over a well-oiled mechanism and implementing their targets in an orderly and expeditious way; rather it was seen as a highly centralized, activist, intrusive body which used high-pressure techniques to force various elements of the economy to perform extraordinary tasks.

In large part, this form of command 'planning' was a response to the practical problems of running the Russian economy. Stalin insisted that the state would be much more effective than the market in integrating and regulating the economy, but the credit reform of 1930 showed how weak the state really was. For Stalin, the centralization of credit under the control of the state would lead 'to the establishment of good order in the whole credit system and to the strengthening of our rouble'.[29] Yet the state was not powerful or efficient enough to perform this role. Predictably, the reform led to administrative chaos, loosened controls over spending by industry, and fuelled inflation. The leadership's experience with the credit reform was replicated throughout the economy. The centre did not have a machinery sufficiently powerful and efficient to collect the information that would allow it to calculate what could be produced, and to make sure that its orders had been, in reality, fulfilled.

For Stalin, therefore, the state was not merely to co-ordinate the economy, calculating available resources and allocating them according to some rational scientific process. It had to take a more activist role, extracting 'hidden resources' from the economy and making sure that central orders were fulfilled. Stalin applied this approach to the agrarian sector, when he travelled to Siberia in early 1928 to investigate the reasons for the shortfall in grain procurements he blamed the problem on kulaks who were hiding resources from the state. He therefore demanded that the state increase its control over the alleged 'kulaks', who were witholding their grain until prices were higher. As he explained, 'as long as there are kulaks', he stated, 'there will be sabotage of the grain procurements'. Only the establishment of collective and state farms would establish control over the countryside, 'relegate the kulaks to the background', and deliver a marketable surplus.[30] The establishment of collective farms, however, did not end peasants' resistance to the state's extreme demands, and over the next two years Stalin constantly called for the mechanism of repression to be strengthened in

---

[29] Ibid., xii. 331.   [30] Ibid., xi. 1–9.

response to 'the desire of a whole number of collective farms to hide grain surpluses and sell grain on the side'.[31]

Stalin and the Politburo adopted a similar approach to the industrial economy, and endorsed the aggressive campaign methods favoured by Piatakov and other former Trotskyists in the 1920s. As he realized, to assume that the centre could co-ordinate the economy entirely according to scientific principles would play into the hands of industrial interests within Vesenkha, who naturally argued that objective circumstances prevented them from fulfilling 'taut' plans.[32] Stalin therefore continued to support Rabkrin in its attempts to find 'hidden reserves' within industry and its pressure for upward revisions to the plan.[33] He refused to accept that the constant increases in the plan were 'violating the principles of planning'. It was only once the plan was being implemented, and planners gained experience of the realities in the localities, that they could take into account 'all the possibilities latent in the depths of our system'.[34] Stalin's faith in Rabkrin is shown in his willingness to appoint Rabkrin officials to replace obstructive leaders of economic commissariats who were refusing to admit to these hidden resources. In 1930 he asked Molotov 'where else are we going to get outstanding people if not from Rabkrin?',[35] and in the same year Rabkrin officials effectively took over various commissariats: Ordzhonikidze became chairman of Vesenkha, Rozengol'ts was moved to the Commissariat of Trade, and Kalmanovich replaced Piatakov at Gosbank.[36]

Stalin and Rabkrin generally based their criticism of industrial officials on the claim that they were failing to do everything necessary to exploit existing resources; the centre therefore had to intervene to show how 'hidden reserves' might be mobilized.[37] Yet Stalin also justified extraordinary plan targets using rather more voluntaristic

---

[31] Stalin to Molotov, 10 August 1929, *Pis'ma*, 142.

[32] D. Shearer, *Industry, State and Society*, 70.

[33] For the Politburo's endorsement of Rabkrin's pressure for upward revisions in the plan, see R. W. Davies, *The Soviet Economy in Turmoil*, 187–94.

[34] Stalin, *Sochineniia*, xii. 347.

[35] Stalin to Molotov, 24 August 1930, *Pis'ma*, 204–5. Stalin was advocating the transfer of Rozengol'ts to the Commissariat of Trade.

[36] S. Fitzpatrick, 'Sergo Ordzhonikidze and the Takeover of VSNKh', *SS*, 36 (1985), 153–72.

[37] This is how Shearer defines the strategy of Rabkrin. See D. Shearer, *Industry, State and Society*, ch. 3.

arguments, derived from Marxist academics, such as the 'teleological' planners and the Deborinite philosophers.[38] The Deborinites' position was strengthened by the publication of Lenin's Hegelian *Philosophical Notebooks* of 1914 for the first time, in 1929.

Stalin probably followed the controversies in planning and economics, but it was not until December 1929 that Stalin publicly participated in these theoretical debates and denounced Bukharin, the 'geneticist' planners, V. Bazarov and V. Groman, and the theory of equilibrium. Stalin now demanded that particular attention be given to Marxist 'theory'; 'bourgeois theories', like the theory of equilibrium, were 'stuffing the heads of our practical workers with rubbish', and a 'relentless struggle' had to be waged against them.[39] At the same time, party officials favoured the Deborinites against the mechanists.[40]

Stalin seems to have sympathized with some of the voluntaristic sentiments of Marxist academics, uttering the famous voluntaristic slogan, 'there are no fortresses in the world the working people, the Bolsheviks, cannot capture'.[41] As in the past, he did not explicitly call for a new proletarian science and he denied that he was challenging objective scientific laws.[42] However, he still associated science with class, and gave succour to those distinguishing between a 'bourgeois' and a 'Marxist–Leninist' science.[43] He argued that 'practice' had to inform science, but insisted that this 'practice' had to be guided by 'theory', which in turn provided the 'power of orientation, clarity of perspective, confidence in work, faith in...our cause'.[44] His letters also suggest that he took the power of human will and belief in economic development seriously.[45] In August 1929, for instance, he expressed his concern to Molotov that the Cotton Committee and Gosplan did not 'believe in the

---

[38] Although by 1929 Strumilin expressed his scepticism of the high targets of the first five-year plan. See R. W. Davies, *The Soviet Economy in Turmoil* 191, 194. See also Sutela, *Socialism, Planning and Optimality*, 52–3.

[39] Stalin, *Sochineniia*, xii. 143–9, 171.

[40] D. Joravsky, *Marxism*, 226–9.

[41] Ibid., xi. 58.

[42] Stalin, *Sochineniia*, xii. 129.

[43] Ibid., xii. 142, 144. He was contrasting the 'bourgeois' 'theory of equilibrium' with the Marxist 'theory of reproduction'.

[44] Ibid., xii. 142.

[45] Lars Lih notes the importance of this theme in Stalin's letters. See L. Lih *et al.* (eds.), *Stalin's Letters to Molotov*, 50–2.

correctness' of targets set by the Politburo. 'Such an "idea" from the Cotton Committee members', Stalin continued, 'is the most vile form of wrecking and deserves the **harshest** punishment'.[46] He frequently expressed such complaints about officials' scepticism of high plan targets.[47] Indeed, lack of faith was, for Stalin, one of the greatest political sins, and at times he defined the Right Deviation simply as a group of people who lacked faith and refused to be mobilized. Speaking to worker and peasant journalists in December 1928, he denied that the rightists were necessarily traitors or enemies. Rather, they were people with a character defect: they were 'the sort of people who fear difficulties, who want life to go along at a peaceful tempo'; their minds were 'such that they do not have faith in all of this [i.e. rapid industrialization and collectivization]'; they had 'no compass' and 'no perspective, they see nothing ahead'.[48]

The importance of faith in politics and the dangers of 'demobilization' were discussed at length in Stalin's denunciation of the 'Right Deviation' at the April 1929 Central Committee plenum. Using one of the folksy anecdotes he favoured, he compared two types of fishermen on the banks of the Enisei in Siberia. One group, in the face of a storm, 'mobilizes all their energies, enthuses its fellows, and bravely guides the boat to meet the storm: "carry on, lads, hold the tiller more tightly, cut the waves, we'll win through!" '. The other group, however, could be compared to Bukharin and his allies. They 'lose heart, begin to whine and demoralize their own ranks'.[49]

'Self-criticism', the 'struggle against bureaucratism', and mobilization

It is unlikely that Piatakov and many of the former Trotskyists employed by Stalin in Rabkrin and elsewhere took 'democracy' very seriously. They saw Stalin as a leader who was allowing them

[46] Stalin to Molotov, 21 August 1929, Pis'ma, 148.
[47] See, for instance, Stalin to Molotov, 21 August 1929, Pis'ma, 148; Stalin to Molotov 24 August 1930, Pis'ma, 204.
[48] RGASPI, 558/11/1112, 3, 4, 6.
[49] Stalin, Sochineniia, xii. 17–18.

to implement the highly disciplinarian élitist revivalism which they had been advocating for so long.[50] Yet Stalin himself did not share their views, at least in the years 1928–9. Rather, he adopted the revivalist programme of the United Opposition in its entirety: policies designed to establish a centralized, co-ordinated, non-market system were not enough, especially in the more advanced, 'socialist' sphere. They had to be combined with proletarian 'democracy' and 'class struggle'. Workers were to be mobilized in a struggle against 'bureaucrats' within the apparatus.

There were strong practical reasons for Stalin to choose such a dangerous course. Planners within Gosplan and Vesenkha argued that enormously ambitious plans were feasible within existing financial constraints in part because, they claimed, enormous improvements in efficiency and labour productivity could be achieved; the optimum variant of the first five-year plan, adopted in 1929, assumed that labour productivity could rise by 110 per cent within five years.[51] Naturally, attempts to make workers pay for industrialization led to increasing discontent, and the leadership saw 'democratization' as a way of improving workers' mood. So, at a meeting of officials in the textile industry in October 1928, attended by Kaganovich, many participants agreed that attempts to increase labour productivity were responsible for the fact that the number of workers participating in strikes had risen from 11,000 in 1926 to 17,000 in 1928.[52] Kaganovich showed that he was willing to respond to pressure from below. He accepted that 'we have still not found the necessary tone in our approach to workers in relation to the difficulties of the current period', and he considered making concessions to workers, including a limited pay rise.[53] Similarly, V. P. Zatonskii of the Central Control Commission (TsKK), declared that communists 'must slightly slacken the taut reins, we must to some extent allow the masses the possibility of criticizing

[50] For this group; see D. Shearer, *Industry, State and Society*, 78–83; N. Valentinov, *Novaia ekonomicheskaia politika*, 79; See also *II plenum TsKK sozyva XV s"ezda VKP(b), 2–5 aprelia 1928 g.* (Moscow, 1928), 117–18 (Gol'tsman).

[51] R. W. Davies, *The Soviet Economy in Turmoil*, 68.

[52] See RGASPI, 17/85/305, 14 (October 1928), for political police (OGPU) figures. On strikes in this period more generally, see A. Pospielovsky, 'Strikes and Worker Militancy during NEP', CREES paper, University of Birmingham, March 1995, 6–8.

[53] RGASPI, 17/85/305, 75–6.

us'. It was better, Zatonskii declared, that workers criticize communists now, than that they attack them during a real crisis.[54]

The Stalin group was certainly aware of the power of populist socialist sentiment among workers. At a meeting with a 'delegation of workers' from Lugansk, Kaganovich expressed sympathy with workers' hostility to engineers and specialists and encouraged them to be 'brave' in criticizing them.[55] While the political police continued to suppress labour unrest, Stalin responded sympathetically to some instances of working-class discontent. His decision to press for the staging of a show trial of the engineers of the Shakhty mines in March 1928, thus encouraging a class struggle campaign against bourgeois specialists, can probably be explained, in part, as an attempt to conciliate working-class opinion and appeal to the populist socialism of workers.[56] This is suggested by a letter of 23 March from Ordzhonikidze on the affair:

I fully share the opinion of Comrade Menzhinsky [Chairman of the OGPU]...who judges the counter-revolutionary movement in the industrial areas to be extremely serious, demanding an urgent and energetic manner of action against this counter-revolution. It is extremely regrettable that the inactivity of local agencies has led to a considerable deterioration of the workers' mood. The monitoring of bourgeois co-workers [i.e. specialists] has become so loose that the latter interpret this apathetic behaviour as a sign of weakness on our part...The party's Central Committee and the Presidium of the Central Executive Committee hereby order the strictest surveillance over the bourgeois specialists at their work places as well as in their private lives.[57]

The 'self-criticism' and 'struggle against bureaucratism' campaigns had another function: they provided another 'lever' which the centre could use to control and check up on obstructive officials. Stalin made this objective clear, explaining that criticism from

---

[54] *II plenum TsKK*, 109–10.

[55] RGASPI, 81/3/73 (Kaganovich's meeting with a delegation of workers from Lugansk, 14 October 1929), 231, 250–1, 270–1.

[56] For a detailed discussion of the evidence, see S. Kislitsyn, *Shakhtinskoe delo*, 15–17.

[57] Letter from Ordzhonikidze, quoted in M. Reiman, *The Birth of Stalinism*, 150. This document, translated from the German, has been taken from secret reports held in the Political Archive of the German Foreign Ministry. For a similar judgement of working-class opinion in the Shakhty area expressed by Molotov in April, see RGASPI 17/2/354, 37–8.

above, from Rabkrin and the Central Committee was not enough: 'only by organizing a double press [*dvoinoi press*]—from above and from below—and only by transferring the principal emphasis to criticism from below, can we count on waging a successful struggle and rooting out bureaucratism'.[58] Following this strategy, Rabkrin mobilized reliable workers and party cells to participate in their investigations, and the Komsomol, using tactics similar to Kerzhentsev's League of Time in the 1920s, created 'light cavalry' brigades to involve rank-and-file members in controlling the apparatus's activities.[59] They were to make lightening 'raids' on shops, enterprises, and offices in order to expose bureaucrats and 'surprise the enemy in the place of his criminal activity'.[60]

Stalin's statements suggest, however, that he was not merely responding in a piecemeal way to threats from particular groups, pandering to discontented workers and using them to control obstructive officials. He was pursuing a well-established strategy, which he justified in traditional populist revivalist terms. For Stalin, the revolution had given the Bolsheviks a 'wealth of moral capital' in the 'hearts of workers', a 'legacy' that was being squandered by 'bad and useless heirs'.[61] The best way of improving labour productivity was therefore to employ that capital and enthuse workers, for 'only the labour enthusiasm and labour zeal of the vast masses can guarantee that progressive increase of labour productivity, without which the final victory of socialism over capitalism in our country is unthinkable'.[62] He portrayed these energies as 'colossal reserves latent in the depths of our system', 'deep down in the working classes and peasantry' which the Bolsheviks could release.[63] Like the Left Opposition of the 1920s, the Stalinists argued that the best way of unleashing these energies was to alter the relations between 'leaders' and the masses. Only 'self-criticism' (which normally meant criticism of leaders 'from below', by the

---

[58] Stalin, *Sochineniia*, xi. 73.

[59] For this account of the function of control organs, see *XVI konferentsiia VKP(b). Stenograficheskii otchet* (Moscow, 1929), 313; *II plenum TsKK*, 102 (Sol'ts).

[60] *III plenum TsKK sozyva XV s"ezda VKP(b), 25–29 avgusta 1928 g.* (Moscow, 1928), 26, (Lebed'); see also *Uchastie mass v rabote RKI. K XVI s"ezdu VKP(b)* (Moscow, 1930), 22–7.

[61] Stalin, *Sochineniia*, xi. 61.

[62] Ibid., xii. 120.

[63] Ibid., xii. 110.

'masses', in the period), Great Break and a more 'democratic' approach to leadership, would inspire them to use their potential. If workers, they argued, were allowed to show initiative and participate in discussion of decision-making, their enthusiasm for work and 'activism' (*aktivnost'*) would be increased. As the resolutions of the Central Committee plenum of November 1928 explained

> our mass organizations (trade unions etc.) frequently do not show the necessary sensitivity to the needs and demands of working men and women, in many cases lag behind the growth in the *aktivnost'* of the masses and therefore make completely insufficient use of the very great possibilities of mobilizing the strengths of the working class in...overcoming the difficulties of socialist construction.[64]

The connection between 'democracy' and *aktivnost'* was explained in psychological terms: Stalin argued that if workers participated in administration their 'feeling that they were masters' of the country (*chuvstvo khoziaina*) would be enhanced.[65]

Stalin also adopted populist revivalist views on the level of working-class consciousness to justify his new set of policies. Workers, he argued, could be trusted to participate in administration, and although they might not have achieved the ideal level of consciousness or 'culture' (*kul'turnost'*), 'democracy' was the most effective way of raising it. Self-criticism was, according to Stalin, 'one of the most important means of developing the cultural forces of the proletariat', and this 'cultural revolution' would transform the proletariat into the masters of the country.[66] Those who argued that workers were not culturally mature enough for 'democracy' were denounced as rightists, unwilling to trust the proletariat.[67]

The stress on the need to use 'democratic' methods to raise the 'cultural level' of the working class and bring out its special energies contrasted strongly with technicist attitudes that stressed the need for workers to become technically proficient and learn the best of bourgeois culture. Stalin did accept that proletarians had to learn

---

[64] *KPSS v rezoliutsiiakh*, iv. 143–4; See also *VIII vsesoiuznyi s"ezd professional'-nykh soiuzov. Stenograficheskii otchet* (Moscow, 1928), biulleten' no. 2, 25–6.
[65] Stalin, *Sochineniia*, xi. 37. See also *XVI konferentsiia VKP(b)*, 253 (Zatonskii).
[66] Stalin, *Sochineniia*, xi. 37–8.
[67] *P*, 25 August 1929. See also *PS*, 3–4 (February 1930), 59–60.

about 'trade' and 'science' from the bourgeoisie, and, if anything, official views of culture and education became even more utilitarian than before.[68] All knowledge was to contribute to the construction of socialism. But this was to be combined with the encouragement of the special qualities of the working class, its *aktivnost'*, 'revolutionary nature', and 'readiness for struggle' in the construction of socialism.[69]

The Stalinists did not only justify 'democracy' as the best way of inspiring workers to fulfil plans. They also saw it in terms of the Marxist historical scheme, as an element in the advance towards socialism. Although Stalin consistently refused to accept that the time was ripe for the withering away of the state, and he was always committed to the strengthening of the Dictatorship of the Proletariat, he did follow the moderate left of the civil war period in arguing that the 'gap' between leaders and the masses had to be narrowed.[70] Workers, he argued, had to become 'active participants in the leadership of the country', and a 'struggle against bureaucratism' had to be waged.[71] Like the populist revivalists of the civil war period, the Stalinists tended to define the term 'bureaucratism' as the separation of the apparatus from the masses and the absence of popular participation, rather than as 'inefficiency'. The Marxist legal theorist E. V. Pashukanis launched a particularly strong attack on the technicist notion that the 'struggle against bureaucratism' should be seen primarily as a rationalization campaign. A socialist regime had to transform authority relations, not just create an efficient administration.[72]

Stalin expressed similar views of 'bureaucratism' in this period. In June 1928 he wrote:

[68] Stalin, *Sochineniia*, xi. 76.

[69] Ibid., xi. 70.

[70] For Stalin's insistence that the state be strengthened, see ibid., xi. 250–1; ibid., xiii. 369–70. For warnings that the masses mistrusted leaders and that the *verkhi* had become arrogant, see RGASPI, 558/11/1111, 3 (10 April 1928).

[71] Stalin, *Sochineniia*, xi. 37.

[72] E. Pashukanis and S. Ignat, *Ocherednye zadachi bor'by s biurokratizmom. Doklady prochitannye v Institute Sovetskogo Stroitel'stva Kommunisticheskoi Akademii, 18 aprelia 1929 g.* (Moscow, 1929), 6. See also S. Ignat, 'Nashi zadachi v bor'be s biurokratizmom', *B*, 8 (1928), 58–9. For Pashukanis's thinking, see R. Sharlet, 'Pashukanis and the Withering Away of Law', in S. Fitzpatrick, *Cultural Revolution*, 169–88; E. Huskey, *Russian Lawyers and the Soviet State. The Origins and Development of the Soviet Bar, 1917–1939* (Princeton, 1986), 172.

It is impossible to regard bureaucratism in our organizations only as procrastination and red-tape [*volokita i kantseliarshchina*]. Bureaucratism is the manifestation of bourgeois influence on our organizations.[73]

These sentiments were echoed by Zatonskii at the sixteenth party conference, in April 1929. One of the most outspoken defenders of industrial managers, S. P. Birman, the director of the metallurgical trust Iugostal', had strongly opposed the introduction of 'democracy' and 'control from below' on the ground that they undermined labour discipline within factories.[74] While admitting some of Birman's charges, Zatonskii insisted that the creation of an efficient and disciplined administrative mechanism could not be pursued at the expense of 'democratization':

The situation is bad concerning the harassment and frequent transfers of officials... But to think that we can realize the great tasks which stand before us, with the strengths of the apparatus alone is absolute nonsense, however well-trained this apparatus is, as the roots of bureaucratism consist of the separation of our apparatus from the masses, whom it serves and whom it tries to govern.... We have things to learn from knowledgeable bureaucrats, from the Germans, Americans.... But the root of bureaucratism lies in... the fact that the apparatus acquires self-sufficiency. And this very bureaucratic apparatus speaks through the lips of some of our industrial managers, and, relying on rationalization, wishes to remain separated [from the masses] and thinks that things will be put in order only by means of rationalization operations without any investigations or the control of the masses.[75]

The Stalinists, more generally, saw their 'struggle against bureaucratism' as a turn towards the primacy of *politika*. An obsession with the purely 'economic' and 'technical', they argued, ignored the advantages that socialist 'politics' could bring. Both 'democratization' and ambitious planning were based on the voluntaristic assumption that the will, energy, and commitment of workers and officials to socialism could transform objective economic realities. Stalin argued that if Soviet officials were knowledgeable about, and fully committed to, Marxist ideological perspectives, they would be much more able to do their jobs properly. Those who

[73] Stalin, *Sochineniia*, xi. 131. See also D. Z. Lebed', *Partiia*, 28. For a more detailed an theoretical defence of this conception of 'bureaucratism', see E. Pashukanis, 'Ocherednye zadachi', 6.
[74] *XVI konferentsiia*, 235–9 (Birman).
[75] Ibid., 252–3 (Zatonskii).

adhered to conventional 'bourgeois' theory and science, he insisted, could not be effective leaders.[76] 'Democratization' and 'class struggle' could also transform the economy, according to the leadership. The state apparatus was therefore criticized for its *'deliachestvo'* (narrow-minded utilitarianism), as were Bukharin and the 'Right Deviation'.[77] As Kaganovich explained:

comrade Bukharin declares that the period of reconstruction is a phase of the technical revolution... accompanied by the smashing of old [social] relations. This is, incidentally, one of the roots of comrade Bukharin's errors, when he sees the current period not from a social-class point of view, but from a technical point of view... at a time when we are faced not simply with technical reconstruction, but with the radical destruction of all social-economic relations, accompanied by a technical revolution, and not the other way round.[78]

Socialist emulation and the democratic style of leadership

The Stalinist leadership, like the moderate left of the civil war period and the Left Opposition of the 1920s, had no intention of weakening central authority or introducing full mass participation in administration. Official statements consistently asserted that 'democracy' and 'self-criticism' were compatible with 'leadership' and executive authority; according to Stalin self-criticism was 'necessary not in order to weaken leadership, but to strengthen it, in order to transform it from paper leadership with little authority into living leadership which has real authority'.[79] In explaining how executive authority might be combined with participation, the Stalinists again followed the civil war left by placing responsibility on individual officials, urging them to alter their leadership 'style' and 'methods'. Officials were not to give up their powers to direct

[76] Stalin, *Sochineniia*, xii. 142–3.

[77] For criticisms of *deliachestvo*, see *BTsKK*, 2–3 (1928), 11 (Zatonskii).

[78] *B*, 23–4 (1929), 70 (Kaganovich). Tomskii also admitted in 1930 that he and his colleagues on the right had neglected the 'social significance' of policy and merely been concerned with 'the reconstruction of industry'. See *XVI s"ezd VKP(b). Stenograficheskii otchet* (Moscow–Leningrad, 1930), 143 (Tomskii).

[79] Stalin, *Sochineniia*, xi. 133. The leadership also denied that its commitment to 'one-man management' contradicted its democratic goals. For the decree, see *KPSS v rezoliutsiiakh*, iv. 311. Hiroaki Kuromiya argues that the *edinonachalie* decree was designed to combine effective authority with participation, in '*Edinonachalie* and the Soviet Industrial Manager, 1928–1937', *SS*, 36 (1984), 194.

the polity and the economy, but were to 'discuss' issues with subordinates and workers, and explain party policy to them. As one propagandist explained, 'democracy', far from undermining authority, should merely encourage officials to administer in a less authoritarian way:

Democracy does not at all presuppose the liquidation and elimination of leadership. The introduction of democracy only requires another method of leadership. Of course, administrative and command methods [*metod administrirovaniia i komandovaniia*] will not be compatible with democracy. Rather democracy is compatible with methods which include the explanation of the fundamental tasks[80]

Stalinist 'democratization' campaigns were therefore based on a conventional populist revivalist attempt to transform leadership style and behaviour, preventing leaders from 'putting on airs and considering themselves infallible' and thus 'improving the relations between the masses and the leaders'.[81] The Central Committee, in its *Address* on 'self-criticism' in June 1928, condemned party organizations for their undemocratic style of leadership, accusing them of 'command methods' (*komandovanie*), 'uncomradely methods' of argument with the party rank and file, and 'malicious inattention to the needs of the masses, conceited toadying and sycophancy to superiors';[82] 'mass work', and 'ideological-educative [*vospitatel'nyi*]' methods were much more suitable.[83] In industry, also, officials and managers were accused of 'rudeness' and arrogance towards workers.[84] In place of 'administrative methods' (*administrirovanie*), the leadership urged party organizations and state officials to adopt 'methods of leadership' which included 'explaining' the party's policies to workers in factories and the party rank and file and 'persuading' them, rather than merely instructing them, to obey orders.

The leadership's 'socialist emulation' campaigns, initiated in 1929, were also founded on this conception of 'democracy'. Based on Lenin's discussion of new forms of labour motivation in 'How to

---

[80] *Pk*, 19 (1928), 38–9.
[81] Stalin, *Sochineniia*, xi. 31.
[82] *P*, June 1928; see also *TPG*, 8 September 1928 (Rudzutak).
[83] *B*, 4 (1929), 66–7; *Pk*, 20–1 (1928), 4; *P*, 23 May 1928; *SADG*, 2 (1929), 38; *KR*, 3 (1929), 5; *Pk*, 8 (1928), 23–5.
[84] *P*, 11 March 1928 (Rykov); *II plenum TsKK*, 155 (Ordzhonikidze); *Rabota profsoiuzov sredi spetsialistov* (Khar'kov, 1929), 32.

Organize Emulation', the campaigns were designed to allow workers to show initiative, thus increasing their enthusiasm for work and encouraging them to fulfil extraordinarily high plan targets. Workers were 'voluntarily' to set themselves high work targets, 'emulating' other groups of vanguard workers in friendly competition, and they were also to have some role in deciding how these plans were to be fulfilled.[85] They were then to be allowed to criticize managers and make suggestions on questions of production, which, if reasonable, leaders had some obligation to act on.[86] 'Socialist emulation' was therefore to establish a new set of incentives, which avoided the need for the stick of coercion and the carrot of material incentives.[87]

Traditional material incentives were also challenged in the 'production collectives' and 'communes' of the period, which pooled wages collectively and paid workers equally irrespective of how much individuals produced.[88] These organizations seem to have been established by workers themselves, partly as a response to crisis and the inability of the factory authorities to organize wages and labour effectively, and they were partly based on traditional communal (or 'artel') forms of labour organization. As with the factory committees and soviets of the revolutionary period, they were welcomed by many Bolsheviks as almost 'communist' institutions, or 'cells of the future communist society', as one trade union official declared.[89] Other leaders were more sceptical, but collectivist forms of labour organization were tolerated until 1930.[90]

Stalinist 'democracy', therefore, like other populist revivalist ideas of democracy before it, did not endorse full and genuine

---

[85] On the 'democratic' implications of the socialist emulation movement, see L. Siegelbaum, 'Production Collectives and Communes and the "Imperatives" of Soviet Industrialization', SR, 45 (1986), 65–84; H. Kuromiya, Stalin's Industrial Revolution, esp. 115–35.

[86] Stalin, Sochineniia, xi. 132; E. Mikulina, Sorevnovanie mass (Moscow–Leningrad, 1929), 13 ff.

[87] For the role of socialist emulation in creating new socialist incentives, see P, 8 June 1930 (Kaganovich).

[88] See L. Siegelbaum, 'Production Collectives', 65–84; R. W. Davies, The Soviet Economy in Turmoil, 261–7; D. Filtzer, Soviet Workers and Stalinist Industrialization: The Formation of Modern Soviet Production Relations, 1928–1941 (London, 1986), 102–7.

[89] Pervyi vsesoiuznyi s"ezd udarnykh brigad (k tridtsatiletiiu s"ezda): sbornik dokumentov i materialov (Moscow, 1959), 71.

[90] L. Siegelbaum, 'Production Collectives', 79.

participation in administration, and certainly had nothing to do with liberalism or political pluralism.[91] Hence the power of the trade unions, which had played some role in defending workers in the NEP period, was destroyed. However, any form of mass participation in administration, even if it was just mass 'discussion', was very difficult to reconcile with effective executive action and the imposition of labour discipline. The right of the masses to 'discuss' administration may not have bound officials to follow their wishes, but it did imply that officials were under some duty to respond to mass opinion. It is therefore not surprising that these campaigns in industry did undermine the position and authority of many officials. As several studies of the period have shown, 'self-criticism' and the 'struggle against bureaucratism' had a highly disruptive effect on all levels of the apparatus and on industrial relations.[92] In his memoirs Viktor Kravchenko, who edited a factory newspaper at the time, remembered that as long as he remained 'within the limits of the party line', 'considerable freedom of speech' was possible; 'everyone was stimulated to "tell all" about defects, errors, methods for improving things', and 'attacks on the factory administration, trade-union functionaries and party officials, exposés of specific faults in production or management, were allowed'.[93] Studies of the party in the period also show that the call for 'inner-party democracy' by the leadership was instrumental in encouraging some insubordination in the lower ranks, even if higher party officials remained secure.[94] Stalin himself understood that the campaigns had had a serious effect on the standing of officials. Speaking in December 1928, he claimed that much had changed in the course of only one year. Before, workers had been afraid to criticize for fear of being accused of being enemies. Now, however, 'everybody abuses bureaucratism'.[95]

[91] For the leadership's refusal to allow criticism of the party line, see Stalin's attack on Sten and Shatskin, Stalin to Molotov, 29 July 1929, *Pis'ma*. See S. Cohen, *Bukharin*, 459–60.

[92] H. Kuromiya, *Stalin's Industrial Revolution. Politics and Workers, 1928–1932* (Cambridge, 1988), chs. 2, 3; V. Andrle, *Workers in Stalin's Russia: Industrialization and Social Change in a Planned Economy* (Hemel Hempstead, 1988), 18–21, 204 f.

[93] V. Kravchenko, *I Chose Freedom. The Personal and Political Life of a Soviet Official* (London, 1947), 52–3.

[94] C. Merridale, *Moscow Politics*, 211–13; P. Gooderham, 'Kirov's Party Organization: Developments in the Leningrad Party Organization, 1928–1934', unpublished discussion paper, CREES, University of Birmingham, 1983.

[95] RGASPI, 558/11/1112, 39 (8 December 1928).

The struggle against bourgeois culture

Like their revivalist predecessors on the left, the Stalinists defined their programme in the language of class and class culture. At the root of their populist and élitist revivalist approaches was the assumption that socialism could only be created if the psychology and behaviour of the population was transformed. Officials had to alter their attitude to the plan and their 'style' of leadership, while the masses had to become collectivist, disciplined, and enthusiastic. The Stalinists described this ideal culture and set of attitudes in typical revivalist terms, as 'proletarian'; scepticism of the plan and hostility to 'democracy' or 'bureaucratism' were the product of a 'bourgeois' culture. Predictably, political leaders generally supported the concept of 'proletarian culture', and 'proletarian' organizations in the cultural sphere such as the Russian Association of Proletarian Writers (RAPP) were given official encouragement.[96] A. I. Stetskii, the head of the Central Committee's new department of culture and propaganda (Kul'tprop), explicitly denounced Trotsky for denying that a separate proletarian culture existed, and he also criticized Bukharin for underestimating its potential.[97] Yet while Stalin declared that RAPP's general line was fundamentally correct, as before he was worried about its sectarianism and objected to the application of questions of class and class struggle to the literary sphere.[98]

For the Stalinists, therefore, socialism could only be constructed by struggling against these bourgeois attitudes, and in particular against their 'bearers' (*nositeli*) the 'bourgeoisie'. Like the United Opposition, the Stalinists identified three main class 'alien' groups as enemies: the kulaks, the nepmen, and the bureaucrats, an enemy *troika* who were, according to Kirov, the 'living human representatives of ... capitalist elements'.[99] If socialist agriculture could only

[96] For the literary sphere, see E. J. Brown, *The Proletarian Episode in Russian Literature, 1928–1932* (New York, 1953); Kemp-Welch, *Stalin and the Literary Intelligentsia*, ch. 3.

[97] For a discussion of Stetskii's draft resolution on literature of March 1930, see Kemp-Welch, *Stalin and the Literary Intelligentsia*, 71–2.

[98] See, for instance, Stalin, *Sochineniia*, xi. 326–7; Stalin to writers from RAPP, 28 February 1929, in A. Artisov and O. Naumov (eds.), *Vlast' i khudozhestvennaia intelligentsiia. Dokumenty TsK RKP(b)—VKP(b)—VChK—OGPU—NKVD o kul'turnoi politike, 1917–1953 gg.* (Moscow, 1999), 110.

[99] *Pk*, 21–2 (1928), 7–8. For a similar denunciation of this *troika*, see 'The Platform of the Opposition', 303.

be established by 'eliminating the kulaks as a class', so the 'struggle against bureaucratism' required a 'struggle' against the 'concrete bearers of the bureaucratic evil' (*konkretnye nositeli biurokraticheskogo zla*).[100]

It was generally accepted in this period that many of these 'bearers of bureaucratism' were officials of bourgeois class origin. The trial of the Shakhty engineers was particularly effective in establishing the bourgeois specialists as typical bureaucrats. The defendants were accused of using a 'bureaucratic', arrogant style of leadership;[101] they had allegedly 'scoffed at', 'beaten', and been 'rude' to workers.[102] Bourgeois specialists were also frequently accused of a more principled hostility or 'scepticism' towards the idea of worker participation in administration.[103] Their antagonism to 'democracy' was generally blamed on ingrained bourgeois habits and attitudes. As one report of 1929 claimed, specialists objected to worker participation because they had retained 'methods of leadership which were peculiar to the capitalist economy'.[104]

The Stalinist leadership also associated this bourgeois authoritarian psychology with moral 'degeneration' and corruption in everyday life. An article by a trio of writers, including the young party activist Nikolai Ezhov, explained the connection between bourgeois attitudes and moral lapses in their discussion of another set of scandals in the Astrakhan party organization:

The Astrakhan affair is a clear example where communists' philistinism (*meshchanstvo*) in personal life and corruption in morals and everyday life (*moral'no-bytovoe razlozhenie*) is closely intertwined with capitulation before capitalist elements and betrayal of the interests of the working class.[105]

---

[100] *XVI konferentsiia*, 307; for other uses of this phrase, see *Pk*, 23–4 (1928), 30–1; *Pk*, 9 (1928), 4.

[101] Report signed by Ordzhonikidze, published in Reiman, *The Birth of Stalinism*, 150–1; for the public announcement of this new view of specialists, see *P* (editorial), 10 March 1928.

[102] *P* (editorial), 10 March 1928.

[103] For complaints that specialists refused to participate in 'democratic' institutions, see *IT*, 6 (1929), 168–9; *Rabota profsoiuzov sredi spetsialistov* (Khar'kov, 1929), 32.

[104] *Rabota profsoiuzov sredi spetsialistov*, 35.

[105] N. Ezhov, L. Mekhlis, and P. Pospelov, 'Pravyi uklon v prakticheskoi rabote i partiinoe boloto', *B*, 16 (1929), 45. For similar statements, see Stalin, *Sochineniia*, xi. 71; RGASPI, 17/2/354/vyp. 2, 10 (Zhdanov, 9 April 1928); *KP* (editorial), 20 May 1928; *BTsKK*, 4–5 (1928), 1–5 (Iaroslavskii).

The other dangerous effect of bourgeois psychology, for official propagandists, was on attitudes towards the economy and the plan. For the Stalinists the bourgeois specialist was most likely to be sceptical about the plan and to have 'rightist' opinions, because he had a tendency to believe in conservative 'bourgeois' theory and science.[106] It was commonly argued that a large proportion of bourgeois specialists were consciously anti-socialist: according to Rykov in 1928, 10 per cent of bourgeois specialists were wreckers, and Molotov implied that an even larger proportion was hostile to socialism.[107] Even if they pretended to be loyal, bourgeois specialists were likely to be influenced by their anti-socialist background; as Molotov explained, 'their politics frequently exert pressure on their practical work' and their bourgeois attitudes distorted so-called 'figures' and 'facts'.[108] As a result, whether they were acting 'consciously or unconsciously', they were guilty of 'wrecking'.[109]

The 'bureaucrat' of Stalinist rhetoric was therefore bourgeois by class origin, an undemocratic bully, and a rightist figure who secretly did not believe in the advantages of the socialist system, consciously or unconsciously wrecking socialism. As one propagandist explained:

from an unwillingness to communicate with the working masses to connivance [with enemies], unsteadiness and shakiness—such is the path of the specialist who has not succeeded in renouncing his [tsarist] bureaucratic (*chinovnichii*) psychology, bourgeois habits, methods and customs.[110]

Bureaucrats were both anti-democratic and were 'unsteady' and 'shaky' about socialist economic policies because they did not understand *politika* and were not committed to socialist ideology: they believed in purely technical solutions to economic problems and had an overly 'pragmatic' or 'philistine' attitude to economic

---

[106] For the concept of 'bourgeois theory', see Stalin, *Sochineniia*, xii. 142.

[107] RGASPI, 17/2/354/vyp. 2, 4 (Rykov, 9 April 1928).

[108] V. M. Molotov, *Stroitel'stvo sotsializma—protivorechiia rosta. Doklad o rabote TsK VKP(b) na I Moskovskoi partiinoi konferentsii, 14 sentiabria 1929 g.* (Moscow, 1929), 103.

[109] *SGRP*, 5–6 (1929), 97; Molotov, *Stroitel'stvo sotsializma*, 103. See also Rozengol'ts's allegation that large numbers of old specialists were hostile to socialism and high plan targets, even after Shakhty. Rozengol'ts to Ordzhonikidze, later than 10 August 1929, in A. V. Kvashonkin, L. P. Kosheleva, L. A. Rogovaia, and O. V. Khlevniuk (eds.), *Sovetskoe rukovodstvo. Perepiska 1928–1941* (Moscow, 1999), 91.

[110] *SADG*, 12 (1929), 17.

development.[111] It was not to be assumed that because most specialists worked well, they were necessarily committed to *socialist* construction. The majority of specialists were ideologically neutral and were engaged in the struggle to master nature rather than a class struggle. For the Stalinists, only a truly socialist approach to the economy, involving appeals to the masses and the use of mass enthusiasm could deliver economic success.[112]

The Stalinists, like the old left oppositions, saw another solution to 'bureaucratism' in the purge of the state apparatus and the removal of bourgeois officials and specialists.[113] If, as Molotov asserted, 'bureaucratism' was 'one of the strongest manifestations of a class influence that is alien to the proletariat', the removal of bourgeois individuals was obviously an essential part of the 'struggle against bureaucratism'.[114] In November 1928 the Central Committee plenum called for a 'decisive purge of the party' and a 'radical purge' of the 'state apparatus' to rid it of its 'bureaucratic distortions'.[115] These purges were announced at the sixteenth party conference, in April 1929, and continued until May 1930.[116] They were justified using a mixture of biological and religious language. Iaroslavskii argued that purges were needed because bourgeois morals were threatening the 'cells of the party and soviet organism' with 'degeneration' (*pererozhdenie*).[117] Stalin, meanwhile, often described those accused of rightism as 'sinners'.[118]

---

[111] For the criticism that specialists believed in 'pure *tekhnika*' and neglected the class content of production, see *FNT*, 7–8 (1931), 6–7. For the use of the terms '*obyvatel'shchina*' and '*deliachestvo*' in this context, see the article by L. A. Shatskin, 'Doloi partiinuiu obyvatel'shchinu', *KP*, 18 June 1929.

[112] *Pk*, 10–11 (1928), 23–6.

[113] *XVI konferentsiia*, 308.

[114] V. M. Molotov, *V bor'be za sotsializm. Rech'i i stat'i* (Moscow, 1935), 60. Although for a more measured approach to 'bourgeois influence', see V. M. Molotov, *O podgotovke novykh spetsialistov* (Moscow–Leningrad, 1928), 57–8.

[115] *KPSS v rezoliutsiiakh*, iv. 148, 147.

[116] *XVI konferentsiia*, 309, 315–18. For a discussion of these purges, see Kuromiya, *Stalin's Industrial Revolution*, ch. 2; Merridale, *Moscow Politics*, 200–3.

[117] E. Iaroslavskii, 'Otkuda grozit opasnost' pererozhdeniia otdel'nykh kletochek partiinogo i sovetskogo organizma?', *BTsKK*, 4–5 (1928), 1–5. For the discourse of corruption, see Naiman, *Sex in Public*, 262–6.

[118] See, for instance, Stalin to Molotov, no earlier than 23 August 1930, *Pis'ma*, 198. Stalin, *Sochineniia*, xiii. 11.

The reverse side of the 'struggle against bureaucratism' was the mass promotion (*vydvizhenie*) of proletarians.[119] Well-trained proletarians, Stalin argued, would be much more committed to 'socialist' economic ideas and would be able to supervise the unreliable specialists.[120] The leadership also insisted that they would have a more 'democratic' psychology than bourgeois officials. Ordzhonikidze defended *vydvizhenie* in terms very similar to those employed by the Workers' Oppositionist Kutuzov in 1921:

If we have worker promotees... in our apparatus, then the apparatus will become much better and will become significantly closer to the masses. If an employee [i.e. official] who is the son of a worker comes to an enterprise, then the workers will talk to him more willingly and will speak about their needs more readily.[121]

Ordzhonikidze was therefore suggesting that promotees, with their proletarian psychology, would be able to employ a more 'democratic' style than their bourgeois predecessors.[122] For some, then, the objectives of *vydvizhenie* were closely connected with the anti-bureaucratism campaign, and one propagandist explicitly attacked those who failed to appreciate the 'democratic' objectives of the campaign:

It is necessary to repudiate decisively the view, to which some comrades are inclined, that *vydvizhenie* is simply a school to teach workers and peasants to administer. This is only one of the elements of *vydvizhenie*. *Vydvizhenie*, which is one of the channels by which the masses are involved in the administration of the state, has the direct objective of extending the links between state organs and the broad mass of working people, and of establishing numerous threads of worker and peasant influence over the state apparatus.[123]

---

[119] For the *vydvizhenie* campaign, see S. Fitzpatrick, *Education and Social Mobility in the Soviet Union, 1921-1934* (Cambridge, 1979), ch. 6.
[120] Stalin, *Sochineniia*, xi. 57-9; *KPSS v rezoliutsiiakh*, iv. 90-1.
[121] *II Plenum TsKK*, 158 (Ordzhonikidze).
[122] For other arguments that *vydvizhenie* was essential for the 'democratization' of the factory, see *Izv TsK*, 20-1 (279-80) (1929), 1; *Pk*, 14 (1928), 52.
[123] *SADG*, 14 (1929), 79; see also *KR*, 7 (1928), 41. For similar views, see E. Pashukanis and S. Ignat, *Ocherednye zadachi*, 6; *B*, 8 (1929), 64; A. Breitman, *O vydvizhenii rabochikh v sovapparat* (Leningrad, 1929), 4.

The ambiguities of class struggle

The class analysis of 'bureaucratism' was extremely powerful within Bolshevism. It had deep ideological roots within revivalist Bolshevik thinking, and there is a good deal of evidence that Stalin himself thought in these terms. It could also appeal both to workers and to party bosses of pure proletarian background, as it deflected blame for unpopular aspects of the regime onto class 'aliens'. And yet, as the left had found in the past, attacks on bourgeois 'bureaucrats' did not deal with the problem of 'bureaucratism'—or non-revivalist attitudes and behaviour—among party officials and managers of proletarian class origin. As Stalin put it, the 'communist-bureaucrats', who were the 'most dangerous type of bureaucrat', existed alongside the 'old bureaucrats (*chinovniki*)'.[124]

How, then, could the presence of 'bureaucratism' among proletarian officials be explained? Like their predecessors among the left, the Stalinists did not argue that these proletarian officials could become bureaucratic spontaneously, of their own accord; that might have raised worrying questions about the validity of Marxist class theory, implying that socialism itself was generating a new bourgeoisie of proletarian class origin. Rather, they suggested that they had been ideologically corrupted by the bourgeoisie, and in particular by bourgeois specialists. Stalin, for instance, explained that managers had failed to prevent the specialists from wrecking and treating workers badly in the Shakhty mines because they had 'merged with the bourgeois specialists in their way of life'.[125] Similarly, a Rabkrin official argued that managers suppressed self-criticism because they were 'influenced' by the specialists, repeating 'their thoughts and their words'.[126] Communist managers' scepticism of high plan targets was also blamed on the malign influence of the bourgeois specialists. One of the main messages promoted by the Shakhty trial was that bourgeois specialists could mislead communist officials.[127] As Stalin explained, the Shakhty affair showed

---

[124] Stalin, *Sochineniia*, xi. 71.

[125] Ibid., xi. 59.

[126] *III plenum TsKK*, 30 (Nazarov). See also Rozengol'ts to Ordzhonikidze, not later than 10 August 1929, A. V. Kvashonkin *et al.* (eds.), *Sovetskoe rukovodstvo*, 94; RGASPI 77/2/354/vyp. 2, 10 (Zhdanov, 9 April 1928).

[127] For the charge that managers 'mechanically' signed the plans of specialists, see *XVI s"ezd*, 79 (Kaganovich).

that the technically ignorant communist manager had become the 'blind follower (*khvostik*) of the bourgeois specialists'.[128]

Yet this diluted class analysis of bureaucratism retained a great deal of ambiguity. It complicated the leadership's attempts to control the 'struggle against bureaucratism' and the removal of 'bureaucrats', as it allowed both class origin and behaviour to be used as criteria for purging. As one TsIK official argued, the party had to

expel from it [the soviet apparatus] alien people who are hostile to us, not only according to their [class] origin, but mainly according to their work (the younger generation which began its work in the apparatus after 1917, after the October revolution, after the NEP, can also be alien, and can bring into our apparatus no less bureaucratism, no less red tape, no less rudeness and inattentive relations to visitors than our old [tsarist] bureaucratic (*chinovnichii*) apparatus)...[129]

The Stalinist leadership clearly wanted to use 'class struggle' and the 'struggle against bureaucratism' to enforce its revivalist policies and create an apparatus imbued with revivalist ideas. But, because it still associated 'bureaucratism' with alien class origin, anti-bureaucracy campaigns could be hijacked by proletarian officials who interpreted them in a neo-traditionalist way. In attempting to defend their proletarian 'caste', they could prevent purges from becoming attacks on officials with 'bourgeois', 'bureaucratic' attitudes by redefining the bourgeois danger, treating workers and peasants with dubious 'petty-bourgeois' backgrounds, or with some other black mark on their record as the real source of bourgeois contamination. Understandably, the central leadership strongly criticized this interpretation of the class struggle, and it condemned local party organizations for using repression against rank-and-file party members, who were insufficiently obedient to their bosses, or who were 'passive' (*passivnyi*), meaning that they did not attend party meetings or have a good knowledge of Marxism.[130] A. A. Zhdanov, first secretary of the Nizhnii Novgorod party organization, was particularly critical of the tendency to use the purges to expel 'passive' communists from the party as if they were 'useless ballast'. 'Educative' measures, he argued, were much more

---

[128] Stalin, *Sochineniia*, xi. 59.
[129] *XVI konferentsiia*, 270 (Fignater).
[130] D. Gurevich, *Za uluchshenie partiinoi raboty* (Moscow–Leningrad, 1929), 12–13.

appropriate for these cases; purges should only be directed at those who were 'alien and hostile' to the party.[131] In many ways, Zhdanov was echoing the sentiments of the leftist Miasnikov in 1921. Repression, he was suggesting, was perfectly legitimate, but it was not to be directed against virtuous workers. Kaganovich agreed: there was, he explained 'no contradiction between the growth of proletarian democracy on the one hand, and the growth of force and pressure on our class enemies on the other'.[132] It was made clear that the 'war' waged against unreliable groups within the working class was to be less repressive than that waged against the former 'exploiting classes'.[133]

Yet the language of class struggle could also be exploited by another group—the party rank and file and workers. The leadership's attack on communists who were behaving in a bourgeois way could be taken to mean that it was waging war against a new, communist bourgeoisie, and its rhetoric could encourage populist attacks on the apparatus from below. And such a broad definition of class had significant disadvantages for the leadership, because it could incite popular attacks on officials in the apparatus which, once unleashed, could not be easily controlled.

The international bourgeois conspiracy

Stalin's accusation that bourgeois specialists were standing in the way of the fulfilment of socialist plans was entirely in keeping with traditional revivalist discourse, and was reminiscent of the Workers' Opposition's charges that the bourgeoisie was sabotaging economic policy. But Stalin emphasized the connection between national security and the internal bourgeois threat. He also moved from rhetorical charges of conspiracy to the use of the judicial process against alleged 'wreckers'.

As has been seen, during the civil war Stalin was particularly worried about the presence of 'class aliens' both in the army and

---

[131] RGASPI, 77/1/290, 20 (Zhdanov, October 1930).

[132] SGRP, 1 (1930), 36; see also P, 16 June 1928.

[133] A. Abramov, O pravoi oppozitsii v partii (Moscow, 1929), 161, 179. See also Pk, 8 (1929), 33. For legislation enforcing this class distinction, see P. Solomon, 'Criminal Justice and the Industrial Front', in W. Rosenberg and L. Siegelbaum (eds.), Social Dimensions of Soviet Industrialization (Bloomington, 1993), 225.

in the 'rear' because they were unmotivated, they were likely to be disloyal, and they might conspire with foreign spies who were plotting to foment an internal counter-revolution. He expressed very similar views in July 1927, when responding to the deterioration of relations with the capitalist world, and in particular with Britain. The British, he alleged, were seeking to organize revolts in the Ukraine and the Caucasus, and were financing spies and wreckers. The proper response was not only to develop industry and defence but to 'strengthen our rear and cleanse it of scum', including the ' "illustrious" ' terrorists who set fire to our mills and factories', because the 'defence of our country is impossible in the absence of a strong revolutionary rear'.[134] The 'illustrious' terrorists referred to by Stalin were the twenty former tsarist officials shot in June in retaliation for terrorist acts allegedly committed by émigré organizations in Warsaw and Leningrad.[135]

Stalin presented the Shakhty case as a similar example of conspiracy between 'international capital', angry at the spread of international communism, and the bourgeoisie within the USSR. He told the Central Committee that the capitalist powers had turned from the 'political intervention' of the civil war period to 'economic intervention'. Foreign powers had used bourgeois specialists and former owners to wreck Soviet industry; it was foolish to believe that the specialists could organize the wrecking without foreign help.[136] Similarly, in 1931 he claimed that the specialists had engaged in wrecking because they had been told by foreigners, falsely, that they were about to organize an intervention.[137]

The Shakhty trial was followed by other show trials of bourgeois specialist 'wreckers' who had allegedly conspired with foreigners, infiltrated the apparatus, and corrupted communists: the Industrial party trial in November–December 1930, and the trial of the 'Union Bureau' of Mensheviks in the spring of 1931.[138] Most of the accused were non-party officials with important positions in the state apparatus, some of whom had a history of resisting high plan targets.

[134] Stalin, *Sochineniia*, ix. 329.

[135] For the circumstances surrounding these events, see Reiman, *The Birth of Stalinism*, 14–15.

[136] RGASPI, 558/11/1111, 5–8 (10 April 1928).

[137] RGASPI, 558/11/1115, 7 (13 May 1931).

[138] *Protsess 'prompartii' (25 noiabria—7 dekabria 1930 g.)* (Moscow, 1931); see also R. Tucker, *Stalin in Power*, 98–101.

According to the indictment at the Industrial party trial, a group of technical specialists high in the state apparatus, many of whom had formerly been Mensheviks, Socialist Revolutionaries, or liberals, including L. A. Ramzin, the director of the Institute of Thermal Technology and N. D. Kondrat'ev, an economist from the Commissariat of Finance, were guilty of drawing up economic plans designed to slow the growth of the economy. They had also organized a group of 2,000 engineers to sabotage various sectors of industry, paving the way for a *coup d'état*, supported by British and French intervention.[139] Those subsequently accused in the Menshevik trial were also technical specialists at the top of the state apparatus, and included V. G. Groman of Gosplan, the leading 'geneticist' economist.[140] The defendants admitted to conspiring with the 'Union Bureau of Mensheviks' abroad to wreck the credit system, cause shortages of consumer goods, and disorganize the economy by formulating false plan targets;[141] they were also accused of conspiring with the Industrial party and the 'Toiling Peasants' party', allegedly led by A. V. Chaianov, a leading agricultural economist who had questioned collectivization.

Stalin's intentions in pursuing these alleged conspirators are difficult to fathom. Some have seen him as entirely cynical, a politician who fabricated cases of conspiracy and sabotage for political purposes, whether to deflect criticism for economic problems onto unpopular scapegoats, to launch broader compaigns against groups which he believed were opposing him.[142] Others, however, have disagreed. Robert Tucker has argued that Stalin's psychology predisposed him to believe that many of his fellow-communists were 'two-faced' enemies.[143] Lars Lih, analysing the language of Stalin's letters to Molotov, has also suggested that he believed that his victims were guilty of sabotage. His view of Stalin's motivations, however, is different. Stalin, he argues, was a politician, prone to anger, who found it difficult to find out what was really happening in the economy. Deprived of unbiased information, he genuinely

[139] For the Industrial party trial, see K. Bailes, *Technology and Society*, ch. 4.

[140] V. A. Bazarov was also arrested in 1930, but was not put on trial.

[141] *Protsess kontrrevoliutsionnoi organizatsii men'shevikov (1 marta–9 marta 1931 g.)* (Moscow, 1931).

[142] For the argument that Stalin knew the charges were false, see O. V. Khlevniuk, *Politbiuro*, 37.

[143] R. Tucker, *Stalin in Power*, 475–8.

believed that difficulties were caused by wrecking and conspiracies.[144]

The language of Stalin's letters to his close associates is confusing, as it shows him both taking the charges of 'wrecking' seriously, and at the same time cynically directing interrogators to force the accused to admit to particular crimes so that their confessions could be used for broader political, propagandistic purposes.[145] So, for instance, Stalin wrote to Menzhinskii:

Ramzin's testimony is very interesting. I think the most interesting thing in his testimony is the question of the intervention in general, and the question of the timing of the intervention in particular. It appears that they aimed for an intervention in 1930, but postponed it to 1931 or even to 1932. This is quite likely and important.

But, having implied that he took the testimony seriously, he then proceeded to tell Menzhinskii in some detail precisely what the interrogation should establish, so that the testimony of Ramzin and others could be made available to the 'workers of the world', as part of an international campaign against foreign intervention.[146]

How, then, can we explain Stalin's apparent belief that his victims were guilty of conspiracy, and his simultaneous use of these charges instrumentally, for political purposes? What was the relationship, in his thinking, between the political and the straightforwardly criminal? Given the paucity of our evidence, and the difficulty of understanding a figure as complex as Stalin, any conclusions must be tentative. It is possible that he was deliberately manufacturing evidence of conspiracy to discredit people whom he wanted to destroy for other reasons, and the show trials clearly had broad political objectives. It is also possible that he genuinely believed that his victims were guilty of conspiracy and sabotage; the language of Stalin's letters certainly suggests that this was often the case. Yet we can account for this apparently contradictory evidence if we understand the revivalist context of Stalin's thinking, and the way in

---

[144] For Lih, Stalin's 'capacity for rational manipulation must have been severely limited by his own angry credulity'. See L. Lih *et al.*, *Stalin's Letters to Molotov*, 45–9, 57.

[145] For similar paradoxical evidence on Stalin's attitude to alleged conspirators in the 'doctors' plot' in the 1950s, see J. Brent and V. P. Naumov, *Stalin's Last Crime. The Doctors' Plot* (London, 2003), 216–17.

[146] *Kommunist*, 11 (1990), 99–100.

which it interacted with a number of other forces: his suspiciousness and predisposition to believe that foreigners were conspiring with the internal bourgeoisie; his ability to put pressure on subordinates to prove what he suspected; and his interest in the use of propaganda to transform the attitudes of the population.

For revivalists committed to mobilization, the success of socialism was dependent on people's commitment to socialist ideas. Lack of faith could, therefore, have real consequences: spreading 'rightist' ideas could undermine morale; and 'scepticism' in the plan could lead to economic failure, and could be seen as tantamount to 'sabotage'. Also, revivalists had long argued that people succumbed to non-socialist attitudes because they had been contaminated by their connections with bourgeois individuals.

Yet Stalin took these revivalist assumptions in particular directions. First, he regarded ideological threats in a geopolitical context, and was particularly worried about foreign ideological influence. And second, he was able to ensure that his suspicions were acted upon, because he had power over the political police. While Stalin sometimes implied that he saw no difference between intentional 'sabotage' and the unintentional 'sabotage' caused by scepticism and ideological heterodoxy, he frequently did distinguish between the two: he did not accuse everybody who displayed 'rightist' attitudes of actual sabotage. Rather, like revivalists before him, he seems to have believed that those who showed evidence of these ideological deviations might be guilty of sabotage and conspiracy, and when he encountered difficulties—whether as a result of industrial accidents or economic failure—he thought it likely that 'rightists', in league with the internal and external bourgeoisie, were in some way responsible. He then put pressure on the police to find what he believed might be true, and the police, through the use of torture and forced confessions, generally obliged. We certainly know of occasions when Stalin reacted to particular cases by instructing the police to look for evidence of conspiracy, even though they were initially sceptical of this explanation.[147] The

[147] For evidence of this, see Stalin's correspondence in 1934 with Kaganovich over the case of Nakhaev, a military official who had made open criticisms of the leadership. Stalin insisted that Nakhaev had to be a 'Polish-German' or Japanese agent, despite the view of Voroshilov that he was mentally unstable. Stalin to Kaganovich, 8 August 1934, O. V. Khlevniuk, R. W. Davies, L. P. Kosheleva, E. A. Rees, and L. A. Rogovaia (eds.), *Stalin i Kaganovich Perepiska. 1931–1936 gg.* (Moscow, 2001),

police's ability to 'prove' the existence of conspiracies in turn reinforced Stalin's belief in the threat from enemies.[148] And once a case had been established Stalin realized the advantages of using some of the cases for propagandistic purposes, staging show trials to demonstrate the connection between ideological heresy and real crimes, and rallying a broad public behind the revivalist view of the world.[149] Stalin made this broader, propagandistic goal clear in a letter to Molotov, in response to a query about what should be done with Kondrat'ev and his group:

> By the way, how about Messrs Defendants admitting their *mistakes* and disgracing themselves politically, while at the same time acknowledging the strength of the Soviet government and the correctness of the method of collectivization? It would not be a bad thing if they did.[150]

Stalin's assumption that at the root of many problems in the USSR lay the influence of 'rightist' attitudes, particularly in the state apparatus, that they could inspire people to commit real sabotage, and that they were generated by bourgeois conspirators in the pay of foreign powers who corrupted unwary communists, is evident in his treatment of the financial crisis of 1930. Piatakov's credit reform of January 1930 had exacerbated the already high levels of inflation brought about by the pursuit of rapid industrialization;[151] as a result people were hoarding silver coins and refusing to accept payment in paper money. Piatakov and the Commissar of Finance, N. P. Briukhanov, proposed a number of measures to solve the problem: they suggested that the money supply be increased by importing silver until a new nickel currency could be introduced; and that inflation

425; ibid., 411–12. The language of the letter suggests that Stalin was convinced that Nakhaev was a spy. See also Stalin's pressure on the police to investigate oppositionist 'enemies' following the Kirov murder, ch. 5, p. 329.

[148] For this argument, see E. Van Ree, *The Political Thought of Joseph Stalin*, 124–5.

[149] As has been seen, the show trial had precedents in the 'agit-trial' of the 1920s. But the show trial itself had precedents, most notably in the trial of the Socialist Revolutionaries of 1922, which used highly theatrical methods to communicate messages about the nature of revolutionary justice. See M. Jansen, *A Show Trial under Lenin. The Trial of the Socialist Revolutionaries, Moscow 1922* (The Hague, 1982); J. Cassiday, *The Enemy on Trial*, 42–50.

[150] Stalin to Molotov, 2 September 1930, *Pis'ma*, 211. Molotov had asked Stalin whether the case should be publicized, pointing out that news of the arrests was already known to other specialists and abroad. Molotov to Stalin, 30 August 1930, RGASPI, 558/11/769, 22 ob.-23 ob.

[151] For the credit reform and its objectives, see R. W. Davies, *The Soviet Economy in Turmoil* 320–8.

be controlled by increasing the production and import of consumer goods, by reducing exports, and reining in the costs of heavy industrial production.[152] Stalin and Molotov objected to these remedies, it seems, because they believed that spending resources on domestic consumption would undermine the fulfilment of the industrial plan; inflation had to be controlled without reducing plan targets.[153] The position of Piatakov and Briukhanov could therefore plausibly be seen as 'rightist' and 'bourgeois': by relying on market mechanisms they were drifting along with 'petty-bourgeois elemental forces', as Molotov put it. For Stalin and Molotov inflation had to be controlled by harsh, political methods; the proper way of solving the currency crisis was to mount a secret police campaign against coin hoarders and 'small-change speculators' who were sabotaging the economy.[154]

In his letter to Molotov, Stalin explained the 'rightist' policy errors of Piatakov and Briukhanov in typically revivalist terms. They had been corrupted by bourgeois specialists in the Commissariat of Finance, such as L. N. Iurovskii, and ultimately by Kondrat'ev and Groman, specialists who had already been accused of wrecking:

Both Piatakov and Briukhanov preached the need to import silver and pushed a corresponding resolution through the conference of the deputies (or the Labour Defence Council)—a resolution we **rejected** at *Monday's meeting* [of the Politburo], after branding them [unconscious] followers (*khvostiki*) of the financial wreckers. Now it's obvious even to the blind that Iurovskii (and not Briukhanov) directed the Commissariat of Finance's measures and that wrecker elements from the Gosbank bureaucracy (and not Piatakov) directed the Gosbank 'policy' as inspired by the 'government' of Kondrat'ev-Groman.[155]

---

[152] For Piatakov's proposals, see Piatakov to Stalin 19 July 1930, RGASPI, 85/27/397, 2–7, published in Kvashonkin *et al.* (eds.), *Sovetskoe rukovodstvo*, 117–29.

[153] Although ultimately Stalin and the leadership introduced this type of anti-inflationary policy, Stalin and Molotov clearly regarded Piatakov's suggestions as 'rightist' at the time. For Molotov's views, see Molotov to Ordzhonikidze, 29 August 1930, RGASPI, 85/27/113, 3–6, in O. V. Khlevniuk, A. V. Kvashonkin, L. P. Kosheleva, and L. A. Rogovaia (eds.), *Stalinskoe politbiuro v 1930-e gody* (Moscow, 1995), 118–19. For the conflict between Stalin and Piatakov, see Davies, *The Soviet Economy in Turmoil*, 431; *Pis'ma*, 178–80.

[154] Stalin to Menzhinskii 2 August 1930, RGASPI, 558/1/5275, 1. Quoted in *Kommunist*, 11 (1990), 96.

[155] Stalin to Molotov, no earlier than 6 August 1930, *Pis'ma*, 193–4.

Stalin described Piatakov as a 'genuine rightist Trotskyist (another Sokol'nikov)' who had to be 'watched closely'; he now represented 'the most harmful element in the Rykov–Piatakov bloc plus the Kondrat'ev-defeatist sentiments of the bureaucrats from the soviet apparatus'.[156] Stalin did not actually charge Piatakov with wrecking or conspiracy in the end, possibly because he did not receive any denunciations or other 'evidence', or possibly because he was wary of proceeding against such a high-ranking communist.

However, another case against a high-ranking communist— Bukharin—was pursued with rather more energy. In September 1929 the Politburo condemned Bukharin for struggling 'against the party's policy of an intensified offensive against the capitalist elements and their removal'. His views, the Politburo declared, 'reflected' the 'vacillations of petty-bourgeois segments [of the population]', and it followed that 'his actions can only nourish the illusions of capitalist elements about a retreat from the proletariat's offensive'.[157] But by August 1930 Stalin had gone further, and was suggesting that Bukharin and his friends were not only objectively helping the enemies of the regime but were involved in actual conspiracy. In a letter to Molotov he urged that all documents on the 'Kondrat'ev-Groman-Sadyrin' affair be sent to the Central Committee and TsKK, stating 'I don't doubt that a *direct* connection will be discovered (through Sokol'nikov and Teodorovich) between these gentlemen and the rightists (Bukharin, Rykov, Tomskii).'[158] Stalin's pressure may have elicited a denunciation of the military leader, Tukhachevskii, which alleged that he was planning a military coup together with the right. Stalin explained to Ordzhonikidze that it was possible that the 'Kondrat'ev–Sukhanov– Bukharin party' did plan to take power and abandon collectivization and high tempos.[159] He did not pursue the allegations, and subsequently declared in a letter to Molotov that he had discovered that Tukhachevskii was no threat.[160] However, the claim that Bukharin and the right were conspiring with foreigners and

---

[156] Stalin to Molotov, 13 September 1930, *Pis'ma*, 217.

[157] RGASPI, 17/3/753, 7–8.

[158] Stalin to Molotov, no earlier than 6 August 1930, *Pis'ma*, 194.

[159] Stalin to Ordzhonikidze, 24 October 1930, *Pis'ma*, 231–2. For this incident, see O. V. Khlevniuk, *Politbiuro*, 36–8; Kvashonkin *et al.* (eds.), *Sovetskoe rukovodstvo*, 146–7.

[160] Stalin to Molotov, 23 October 1930, *Pis'ma*, 231.

Tukhachevskii to reverse the achievements of socialism was to become the centre of the allegations against Bukharin in 1937–8.

Purifying and strengthening the party

Purges and show trials were one method of making sure that officialdom and the population responded to the revivalist strategy, but the Stalinists relied on more direct methods. Stalin needed to create institutional forces strong enough to compel managers within the enterprise to fulfil the plan and mobilize workers, and, like the left, he turned to the party. While he used Rabkrin and the OGPU to discipline managers and officials, he also urged that the party be revived and strengthened. The Stalinists, in typical populist revivalist terms, argued that the party was best able to force state officials to follow the General Line, and also to mobilize and inspire the masses, because it used methods of *vospitanie* and 'persuasion'. State officials, on the other hand, were more likely to 'lack faith' in the creative abilities of the working class and use harsh, '*administrativnye*' methods and orders.[161] The Stalinists therefore tried to strengthen the party, and promote the style of leadership that it represented, while weakening the state apparatus.

In significant respects, of course, the Stalinists' objectives were very different from those of the Democratic Centralists. While the Democratic Centralists were often local party officials, resisting excessive central interference in their affairs, the Stalinists wanted to strengthen the centre. Even so, both regarded the populist revivalist 'democratic' strategy as a way of promoting their interests. For both, a new 'democratic' style of leadership would unite the centre and localities in one energetic, mobilizational effort. Also, both saw the enemy as the overbearing state apparatus and the economic organizations that were suborning the party. The Stalinists particularly objected to the establishment of mutual protection arrangements, or 'family relations', between party and state officials, as they prevented the centre from controlling local officials.[162] Close collaboration between the 'corners' of the factory 'triangle',

---

[161] B, 8 (1928), 59; PS, 1 (1929), 14.

[162] For Stalin's concern with 'mutual protection' and '*artel*'-like' relations within party organizations, see Stalin to Molotov, 13 August 1930, Pis'ma, 202. See also RGASPI, 17/2/344, 19 (Rykov, 6 April 1928).

that is the party cell, the factory administration, and the trade union committee, was seen as particularly damaging.[163]

The Stalinists, like the earlier left oppositions, also argued that the merging of party and state allowed the state to corrupt the party by transmitting its 'bureaucratic' leadership style and its bourgeois attitudes. So, according to the resolutions of the sixteenth party conference, bureaucratism within the party apparatus was the result of

the intertwining of the party and soviet apparatuses, the diversion of a large number of party members into administrative work, the influence of elements of the bourgeois intelligentsia and bureaucracy on the party through communists who work in the state apparatus.[164]

The party, then, was becoming bureaucratic both because bourgeois influences within the state were contaminating it, and because party officials were taking the place of state officials. State organizations, it was implied, performed 'administrative work', which required anti-'democratic' methods; party officials who took on these tasks were therefore likely to become 'bureaucratic' themselves.[165]

The Stalinists proposed typically revivalist solutions to these perceived problems. The party had to disentangle itself from economic organizations and avoid the dangers of 'substituting' itself for them. The party could then return to its 'democratic' essence, pursuing 'party work', 'mass work', and 'political work'.[166] It then had to become the agent of 'democratization' in other institutions.[167] The party apparatus, and particularly the party cell in the factory, was therefore to be strengthened, mobilizing workers to check up on managers. Managers who tried to use the principle of

---

[163] For tensions within the factory 'triangle', see Kuromiya, *Stalin's Industrial Revolution*, ch. 7.

[164] *XVI konferentsiia*, 313.

[165] *XVI konferentsiia*, 314. For precisely the same terminology, see the Central Committee's 'Address' on self-criticism, *P*, 3 June 1928.

[166] For examples of appeals to the party to devote itself to 'democratic' 'party work', see V. M. Molotov, *O partiinykh zadachakh* (Moscow–Leningrad, 1927), 13, 24–5; *KR*, 23–4 (1928), 91, 94; *P*, 31 January 1928 (Lebed'); *Pk*, 15 (1928), 10; *Trud*, 25 May 1928 (Kaganovich); Molotov, *V bor'be za sotsializm*, 60. For criticisms of the party for engaging in 'economic work', see *Izv TsK*, 27 (243) (1928), 1.

[167] *PS* (editorial), 9 (11) (1930), 4; D. Z. Lebed', *Proletarskaia demokratiia i samokritika* (Moscow–Leningrad, 1928), 44–5; *Izv TsK*, 14 (235) (1928), 2.

'one-man management' to exclude party and trade union organizations from questions of production were condemned.[168]

It was understandable that revivalist solutions would appeal to many local party officials, despite the possibility that 'democracy' might threaten them. According to James Harris's study of the Urals, regional party organizations were split between enthusiastic supporters of rapid industrialization and those who had more sympathy with the specialists' scepticism, and they were probably similarly divided over the revivalist strategy of mobilization more generally.[169] 'Family' relations between party and state officials were commonplace, but in many places there were tensions between them. In one enterprise in Nizhnii Novgorod, for instance, the factory party secretary, Petrov, and the director, Erofeev, had been engaged in a long-running conflict. At issue were a number of concrete issues, such as who was to control appointments and bonuses. Yet Petrov fought this institutional battle using revivalist language, accusing Erofeev of being a 'bureaucrat', ignoring 'criticism', trusting specialists excessively while ignoring communists, and behaving in an 'arrogant' way.[170]

Narratives of class struggle

The Stalinists' emphasis on the role of the party was, therefore, part of a recognizably revivalist message, promulgated after 1928: the economic preconditions for progress towards socialism, they argued, were all in place; it was perfectly possible to engineer extraordinary economic leaps and for the apparatus and the masses to become one, as long as the culture and psychology of the population were transformed. Leaders had to believe in the plan and behave towards the masses in a 'democratic' way, while the masses had to work with enthusiasm and energy. Anybody with non-socialist, 'bourgeois' attitudes had to be re-educated or punished to prevent

---

[168] D. Z. Lebed', *Proletarskaia demokratiia*, 44–5. For other accounts of the party's role in 'democratizing' the state and economic organs, see *SADG*, 1 (1928), 53; *KR*, 5 (1929), 46–7. For criticisms of party organs which failed to 'democratize' state organs, see *III plenum TsKK*, 8 (Lebed'). For criticisms of managers for excluding the party, see *PS*, 19–20 (1930), 36–9.

[169] J. Harris, *The Great Urals*, 81–93.

[170] The conflict was arbitrated by A. A. Zhdanov, then the local party secretary. RGASPI, 77/1/235/1–16 (23 or 24 March 1928).

them from corrupting the healthy forces and sabotaging socialism; those institutions infected with these attitudes had to be supervised and purged by more reliable bodies.

This message was constantly put forward in political speeches, but in many ways the show trial was a better medium for its transmission to a larger audience. As the revivalist proponents of 'proletarian' culture had discovered, the trial was particularly appropriate for the communication of Bolshevik, and especially revivalist, rhetoric. The centrality of class and class virtue in Bolshevik political thought gave political concepts a peculiarly ethical character. Debates over economic policy focused not only on abstract, mechanistic arguments over the effects of various strategies on the economy but on their effects on classes and on whether they were 'proletarian' or 'bourgeois' in spirit; similarly the political system, its degree of 'socialism' and 'democracy', was judged not by the nature or strength of its institutions but in terms of relationships between individuals and the degree of virtue they displayed. The show trial was therefore a good medium through which to explain the elements of this political rhetoric, as it was a drama which featured real people, even if they were placed in semi-fictional circumstances. The trial allowed the leadership to define and present the beliefs, character, and behaviour of the internal enemy, whether it was the authoritarian 'bureaucratic' specialist of the Shakhty trial or the élite saboteur of the 1931 Industrial party trial, mobilizing the public against them and warning the potential bureaucrat to mend his ways. It was particularly good at demonstrating ideas of class infection, by describing and 'proving' the existence of the conspiracy.

If anything, though, the 'proletarian' production novel was an even more effective medium through which Bolshevik political ideas could be illustrated. As Régine Robin has defined it, the production novel was a 'novel of mastery', in which the hero sets out to fulfil a task, such as the building of a factory or the fulfilment of a plan, and seeks to manipulate or mobilize others to help him. Confronting him was the enemy, who tried to persuade others to help him to sabotage the task.[171] Like the trial, then, the production novel usually featured wrecking conspiracies, but it could show the virtuous as well the evil enemy. It could also deal with a wider range of

[171] R. Robin, *Socialist Realism*, 260–6.

issues than could the trial. It could show how officials were supposed to relate to those whom they were trying to influence or mobilize, and could define at length the proper and improper behaviour of officials and the correct and incorrect attitude of workers and officials towards their work. It could also demonstrate how the enemy operated, and the nature of 'hostile' ideas. More concretely, it could illustrate notions of class infection, by showing in an easily comprehensible form how particular individuals were corrupted by their class background or by contact with class aliens.

The leadership had not yet established effective control over literature and the period was a transitional one, in which Stalin and the political leadership intervened intermittently. However, as before, members of proletarian literary organizations were eager to politicize literature themselves, using their novels to elucidate the latest political line and to contribute to the ideological transformation of their readership.[172] A particularly good example of the political novel's ability to explain the leadership's position during the period is Vasilii Il'enkov's novel *Driving Axle*, published in 1931. The novel illustrates most of the themes of late-1920s revivalist Bolshevism and deals with a number of issues central to the leadership's thinking, including the relative roles of the proletariat and other classes in the building of socialism; the relationship between *politika* and *tekhnika*; 'democracy' and the relationship between workers and managers; the role of class origin in determining behaviour; the bourgeois specialists and wrecking; and party–state relations and the factory 'triangle'.[173]

The novel's structure was to become typical of the production novel, and owed a great deal to novels like *Cement*:[174] the hero returns to a factory or village, in this case a locomotive factory, to find that all is not well; he struggles against various obstacles and individuals who stand in his way and finally, with the help of the party official (although Il'enkov's party official, Vartanian, is not an entirely positive figure), he solves the problems and the plan is fulfilled. In this case the hero is Platov, a proletarian engineer and

---

[172] For the appeal of 'cultural revolution' themes to writers during the period, see K. Clark, *Petersburg*, ch. 12. For the close relationship between socialist realist novels and political rhetoric, see K. Clark, *The Soviet Novel*, 70–7.

[173] V. Il'enkov, *Vedushchaia os'* (Moscow–Leningrad, 1932).

[174] For the typical structure of the 'socialist realist' novel, see K. Clark, *The Soviet Novel*, 255–60.

beneficiary of *vydvizhenie*, who returns to his factory to find that the plan is not being fulfilled. The locomotive engines are of poor quality and relations between workers and specialists are tense. These problems have arisen because the management has failed to pursue a revivalist 'proletarian' policy. The communist manager of the plant, Korchenko, erroneously considers that pure *tekhnika*, and the bearers of that *tekhnika*, the technical specialists, are crucial, deprecating the role of *politika*, ideology, and the mobilization of the working class. As he explains to Vartanian:

'See here, Vartanian, I'm not accustomed to general discussions and I don't engage in abstract philosophy', said Korchenko stressing the final word contemptuously. 'For me the question is especially practical...Enthusiasm, of course, is not a dangerous thing. But all the same, engineers and foremen decide all matters...The strength is in them, Vartanian, and I have mastered this strength'.[175]

The consequence of this attitude is that the factory is run in a 'bourgeois' way. Instead of mobilizing the workers, Korchenko introduces a system of material incentives to reward the engineers;[176] more importantly, he is too trusting of the bourgeois specialists and gives them excessive power in the factory, accusing any workers who criticize them of 'specialist-baiting' (*spetseedstvo*). The specialists and their lackeys among the foremen display the typical behaviour of bourgeois individuals within revivalist Bolshevik thought. They are individualistic and corrupt: the engineer Kraiskii exploits the incentive system by bribing subordinates to pass defective products. They are snobbish and arrogant: the chief engineer Turchaninov wears a pince-nez, becomes overexcited about classical music and pianos, and uses elaborate language which workers cannot understand. They are rude and authoritarian: when Platov was a worker and refused to obey an order, Kraiskii had called him 'a lout' and was subsequently reprimanded for his rudeness. They refuse to accept that *politika* and ideology are of any importance in production, arguing that *tekhnika* is paramount and its 'bearers', the engineers, are supreme in the factory. As Akatuev, the bourgeois quality inspector, wrote in the Manual of Engine Construction he planned to publish:

---

[175] V. Il'enkov, *Vedushchaia os'*, 106–7.
[176] Ibid., 106. Vartanian implicitly criticizes material incentives, asking 'so you think that in our time the only stimulus is the ruble?'

'Respected comrades! Directors! Factory [party] committees! Regional [party] committees! [Party] cells! The norms of pressure! They're constant, both for capitalists and communists. You have to submit to *tekhnika*, to engineers, to the power of pressure!'... Submit to the pressure of science. He did not notice that he was writing these words down in the text of his book and was whispering in a voice that became hoarse and choked, thrusting his pen into the table. 'Submit!'[177]

The bourgeois specialists use their knowledge of science to explain away economic and technical failures as the consequence of object-ive scientific laws, and in this way they sabotage the plan. Turcha-ninov and Akatuev go even further and are discovered to have been conspiring with the members of a counter-revolutionary organiza-tion high up in Vesenkha to sabotage the economy. Motivated by pure hatred of socialism, they make sure that the driving axles are faulty and thus cause a train derailment in which several workers die.

The proper 'proletarian' way to run the factory is shown in the actions and words of Platov, Vartanian, and a number of workers, although these characters all have their faults: Platov is criticized for being too headstrong; and Vartanian is too sympathetic to the specialists and is too prone to vacillation. Even so, both Platov and Vartanian understand that *politika* is primary, not pure *tekh-nika*. Platov, who has studied dialectics as well as metallurgy, rec-ognizes that the purely technical explanation for the derailment, metal fatigue, is inadequate, as 'every accident has its reason and motive';[178] both he and Vartanian understand the 'political' reality that there are class enemies in the factory and vigilance must be increased, and Platov is able to expose the counter-revolutionary conspiracy. They also realize that pure *tekhnika* is useless without a greater role for the working class in administration. Vartanian explains very clearly the essence of the revivalist Bolshevik concept of *politika* and 'political work': officials are to trust the working class, employ 'democratic' methods of leadership, and communi-cate Marxist ideology to workers. A knowledge of the ideology will give workers an awareness of their broader place in history, of the 'process as a whole', and will therefore motivate them to work harder. As Vartanian resolves:

---

[177] V. Il'enkov, *Vedushchaia os'*, 206.
[178] Ibid., 283.

We must develop their [workers'] initiative. We must ensure that they know their detailed work and understand the process as a whole . . . We must trust them. Korchenko bothered and worried him. He remembered Korchenko's words about engineers: 'They're a power and I have mastered that power'. Is it really so? he thought . . . The main thing is to make sure that workers do not work [badly] as they did before.[179]

Vartanian is also shown learning how to perform his proper role within the factory 'triangle'. He generally refuses to 'merge' with the management, retaining a healthy scepticism towards managers' falsified claims of plan fulfilment. But this does not mean that he neglects the economic side of the plant's work. He realizes that to mobilize workers he must perform manual labour himself. He must know everything about the workers, about 'their feelings, their labour, so as to have the right to direct men who were constructing engines'.[180] This 'democratic' style of leadership is not only appropriate for the party secretary. Once the bourgeois wreckers have been arrested and Korchenko recognizes his errors, he also adopts this style, wearing workers' clothes and intervening in the details of production; he listens to the workers when they are dissatisfied with the orders of the management and is prepared to 'alter a great many things' in response to their views. Gradually the workers' 'cold expression of estrangement' is replaced 'by a gruff familiar attitude which indicated trust', and Korchenko found new support from the masses.[181]

Once the conspiracy has been exposed and proper leadership has been restored, workers' laziness, their persecution of specialists, and their 'petty-bourgeois egalitarian' complaints about the management and low pay gradually disappear. They display their class maturity and enthusiasm, overcoming the allegedly 'scientific' constraints which the bourgeois specialists appeal to. Ultimately they over-fulfil the plan and 'the force of enthusiasm and thought which filled the roused factory collective broke through the limitations of machinery'.[182]

Driving Axle, therefore, like many other production novels of the period, explains, by providing concrete examples, what the primacy of politika and a 'proletarian' policy meant in practice, and how revivalists thought that individuals' behaviour would have to

---

[179] V. Il'enkov, Vedushchaia os', 117.
[180] Ibid., 113.   [181] Ibid., 397.   [182] Ibid., 401.

change if socialism were to be built. It also expounded the revivalist view of the origins of political problems. Individuals of bourgeois class origin are at the root of the evil, either because they are politically hostile to Soviet power, like Akatuev, or because they have not shed bourgeois immorality and their old attitudes to labour, like Kraiskii, or both, like Turchaninov. Other engineers have less dangerous faults but are criticized in the novel. Strakhov, for instance, is honest and objects to the activities of the enemy specialists, but because he has not read Marx and Lenin and has a purely 'technical' approach to his work he cannot perceive the class struggle in the factory. In general, according to the novel, it is very difficult to rid one's self of the influences of one's bourgeois class background, as the romantic sub-plot shows. Akatuyev's daughter, Vera, falls for Platov, and she has to choose between proletarian and bourgeois values. She finally decides to betray her father, but it is too late, and she is rejected by Platov.

The real danger posed by the bourgeoisie, according to the novel, is its ability to influence good proletarian communists, blinding them with bourgeois 'science' and arguing for such bourgeois ideas as material incentives for specialists and 'scientific' explanations for accidents. Communists are taken in, both because they lack technical knowledge and because they have excessive respect for bourgeois values. Korchenko's lack of confidence in his own proletarian culture is one of the main reasons for his willingness to support the bourgeois specialists. He was unable to discuss music with Turchaninov and he 'felt contempt for himself and for his backwardness from current life and for his lack of culture'.[183] Yet *haut-bourgeois* class influences are not the only dangers in the socialist factory. Petty-bourgeois deviations among workers are also illustrated, although these, it is suggested, are easier to eliminate than bourgeois deviations, as long as the authorities adopt the right educative strategy. While Korchenko has a pessimistic view of the capabilities of the new workers from the countryside, Vartanian realizes that if the factory is regarded as a 'university for peasants' the problems of ignorance and poor discipline will be solved.[184] Vekshin, the son of a shoemaker, is treated sympathetically by the party and transformed into a true proletarian. He abandons his 'petty-bourgeois' commitment to the equalization of wages and

---

[183] V. Il'enkov, *Vedushchaia os'*, 194.   [184] Ibid., 58–9.

his belief that a bourgeoisie might form again unless everybody was paid equally.[185] Il'enkov, then, illustrated precisely how class infection was supposed to take place, what sort of people were likely to be victims of it, and what ideas and behaviour were signs of it; he also showed his readers what sort of behaviour was appropriate for workers, managers, and specialists.

The challenge to revivalism and the 'Right Deviation'

There was a great deal of opposition to the world-view presented in *Driving Axle*, although it was increasingly difficult to express it openly. 'Bourgeois specialists', such as Groman and Bazarov, objected to the high plan targets which upset the economic equilibrium. Their attitudes were shared by many factory managers and Vesenkha trust officials, who tried to resist Rabkrin's attempts to increase plan targets.[186] Vesenkha officials also objected to Rabkrin's and Gosbank's attempts to centralize industrial administration and credit.[187] Yet it was the populist revivalist elements of the Stalinists' programme that were particularly resented. Managers and Vesenkha officials frequently blamed the 'self-criticism', purge, and *vydvizhenie* campaigns of the period for a collapse in managerial authority and labour discipline.[188] A debate between Stepanov, the director of the Hammer and Sickle metalworks in Moscow, and Kobel'nikov, the president of the plant's production commission, published in Vesenkha's newspaper in March 1929, illustrates managerial hostility to 'democracy' particularly well. Kobel'nikov argued that workers should have the right to discuss plan targets and rationalization measures, but Stepanov disagreed, suggesting that the system of one-man management prevailing in the Red Army was a much more suitable model. Workers were too

---

[185] V. Il'enkov, *Vedushchaia os'*, 132–3, 142.

[186] For Vesenkha criticisms of Rabkrin, see S. Fitzpatrick, 'Ordzhonikidze's Take-over of Vesenkha', 158–60; E. Rees, *State Control*, 174–8. For Rabkrin's frustration with economic managers' resistance to high plan targets, see Rozengol'ts to Ordzhonikidze, not later than 10 August 1929, A. V. Kvashonkin *et al.* (eds.), *Sovetskoe rukovodstvo*, 92–4.

[187] D. Shearer, *Industry, State and Society*, 102–6.

[188] For criticisms of *vydvizhenie*, see *TPG*, 28 September 1928 (Kosior); *XVI konferentsiia*, 239 (Birman). For criticisms of 'self-criticism', see *TPG*, 31 July 1928 (Kuibyshev); *TPG*, 27 April 1929 (Birman).

ignorant to participate in management, he argued. Given the atmosphere of the times, it is not surprising that the newspaper took Kobel'nikov's side, and Stepanov was condemned for proposing a system of management even more dictatorial than capitalist factory organization.[189]

Economic officials were not in a position to bring these criticisms together into a coherent attack on the revivalism of the Stalinists, but the group surrounding Bukharin, Rykov, and Uglanov, the so-called 'Right Deviation', was. The 'Right Deviation' was a term coined by the Stalinists, and Bukharin and his group denied that they were members of any faction or opposition to the leadership. But their statements, in public and in private party discussions, show that they did mount a reasonably coherent technicist attack on the revivalism of the leadership.

Divisions between the Stalinist group and the right came into the open during January 1928, when Stalin first endorsed repression against the peasantry.[190] The right, and in particular Bukharin, soon expanded their criticism to a condemnation of the Stalinists' approach to planning and the eradication of the market. The peasantry, Bukharin argued, had to be manipulated using economic mechanisms, not force.[191] Plans had to be founded on scientific calculation and on existing resources; the economic equilibrium had to be maintained, and policy could not be based on the idea of economic leaps, or 'acrobatic *salto mortale*'; 'objective statistics' had to take priority over 'subjective will'.[192] Rykov, as head of Sovnarkom, applied this scepticism about high plan targets to economic policy, and resisted attempts by heavy-industrial interests to increase investment.[193]

In countering Stalinist voluntarism, Bukharin placed particular emphasis on the importance of science under the new regime. In an article entitled 'Science and the USSR' he argued that science should not be seen as a Western, capitalist phenomenon; 'the red banner of the October "great rebellion" ' was the banner not only of the

[189] *TPG*, 17 March 1929.

[190] For the right's opposition to the 'extraordinary measures', see S. Cohen, *Bukharin*, 278 ff.

[191] Bukharin to Stalin, 1928 (?), RGASPI 329/2/6, 58.

[192] N. I. Bukharin, 'Politicheskoe zaveshchanie Lenina', *P*, 24 January 1929.

[193] Rykov to Stalin, Molotov, and Bukharin, 7 March 1928, in A. V. Kvashonkin *et al.* (eds.), *Sovetskoe rukovodstvo*, 22–3.

emancipation of physical labour but also of the emancipation of science'.[194] While the party's task in 1917 had been to defeat the bourgeoisie, now it had to establish 'scientific leadership' and to direct the masses towards 'intensive constructive work'.[195] Bukharin's exaltation of science was, of course, hardly controversial. However, the right's 'science', unlike that of the Stalinists, was contrasted with *politika* and 'theory'.[196]

The right also took a technicist, and even liberal technicist view of class relations. It refused to idealize the proletariat or support the persecution of classes essential for high levels of production, whether the well-off peasantry or the expert, but hierarchical, bourgeois specialists. As before 1928, Bukharin insisted that the peasantry had to be nurtured and defended rather than condemned as unsocialist. In his speech to the eighth congress of the Komsomol, a bastion of revivalism, he criticized those who adopted an insular proletarian approach to other classes and behaved aggressively towards semi-proletarian and peasant groups. Komsomol members tended, he complained, to assume that only proletarians were truly 'socialist'. This attitude was wrong, and repression of the peasantry had to be replaced with educative methods.[197]

The right also criticized the Stalinists' 'proletarian' hostility to managers and specialists, and employed a more technicist rhetoric. Officials who had technical knowledge were to have power; they were to make decisions based on their scientific knowledge; disciplined workers were not to challenge these rational decrees. *Tekhnika* and 'science' were to be priorities and the 'bearers of science and *tekhnika*' had to be protected against Stalinist class struggle campaigns.[198] Rykov, for instance, protested to Menzhinskii in March 1928 that the arrest of the foreign Shakhty engineers was likely to 'sabotage' the construction of the economy:

Although at the moment it is of greatest importance to maintain party unity, which is most seriously endangered by the actions of oppositional

---

[194] N. I. Bukharin, *Nauka i SSSR* (Leningrad, 1928), 16.
[195] N. I. Bukharin, 'Lenin i zadachi nauki v sotsialisticheskom stroitel'stve', *P*, 20 January 1929.
[196] N. I. Bukharin, *Nauka i SSSR*, 7. Although Bukharin did urge members of the Komsomol to improve their mastery of theory. See N. I. Bukharin, *Tekushchie zadachi Komsomola. Doklad na VIII vsesoiuznoi s"ezde VLKSM 6 maia 1928 g.* (Moscow, 1928), 47.
[197] N. I. Bukharin, *Tekushchie zadachi komsomola*, 28–30.
[198] *P*, 13 April 1929 (Rykov).

and ultra-left elements ... the program of new construction remains one of our prime tasks. The Central Committee has declared that the reconstruction of the socialist economy is not possible without the help of foreign capital and foreign experts.

Our political position towards the bourgeoisie is not supposed to play a role here. I only remind you that Ilyich in his time already pointed to this necessity in the interest of our proletariat.[199]

Rykov was, then, arguing that the specialists, whatever their class origin and political position, had to be left alone because they were participating in a valuable economic task. But this reasoning rendered the right vulnerable to the charge that it was neglecting 'ideology' and *politika* completely. The right therefore tried to claim that the specialists, far from being politically unreliable, were now a virtuous semi-proletarian 'Soviet' group. At the Central Committee plenum of April 1928, Rykov gave a speech on the Shakhty specialists and accepted that serious wrecking had taken place, but he insisted that the majority of specialists had become more 'Soviet'. Their main fault was not disloyalty but refusal to take individual responsibility for their work.[200] The one figure on the right who did not share this sympathy for specialists is Mikhail Tomskii. At the April 1928 Central Committee plenum, he went further than Stalin in attacking the specialists, and even Stalin declared that he had 'over-criticized' them.[201] Yet Tomskii had his own reasons for joining the right. He was protecting the relative autonomy of the trade unions permitted under the NEP, and was resisting the Stalinist leadership's attempts to absorb them into the state.

The right did not only value the specialists for their technical expertise. They also generally approved of the hierarchical leadership style specialists introduced into the enterprise and were doubtful about the efficacy of proletarian labour heroism. As Shatunovskii, a figure associated with the right who worked in the economic apparatus, explained:

Of course, in all these heroic examples, labour and creativity are expended irrationally, wastefully. ... Labour heroism and workers' creativity are

---

[199] Rykov to Menzhinskii, 10 March 1928, quoted in M. Reiman, *The Birth of Stalinism*, 146.
[200] RGASPI, 17/2/354/vyp. 2, 8 (Rykov).
[201] RGASPI 17/2/354/vyp. 2, 54 (Tomskii).

necessary as long as labour is not very productive. In the conditions of productive, well-ordered labour there is no place for heroism[202]

Bukharin was rather more measured on the subject. He accepted that the 'energy of the masses' and 'science' were both 'levers' in mastering the forces of nature, but he mainly stressed the importance of 'science'.[203] The proletariat, he argued, was still not 'cultured' enough to run the economy efficiently. While it had expertise in the politics of class struggle, it could not understand administration.[204] Before the proletariat could participate in administration, it had to be imbued with 'a new labour culture'. A 'period of the cultural revolution' involving the 'mass alteration [peredelka] of people' was vital;[205] workers had to be transformed to fit in with the requirements of large-scale industry and industrialization had to be accompanied by a campaign to 'industrialize people' (industrializirovat' liudei).[206] Unlike the Stalinist revivalist approach to 'cultural revolution', Bukharin's approach largely ignored the issue of class. As Bukharin put it, the 'problem' of cultural revolution was to be treated as a 'problem of technical culture'.[207]

Given this attitude to class and the proletariat, it is understandable that the right was opposed to Stalinist 'democratization' campaigns. One of Bukharin's allies, A. Slepkov, for instance, argued that limitations should be placed on self-criticism.[208] Similarly, Uglanov warned that self-criticism was liable to 'brake' the development of the economy.[209] Bukharin did, at times, adopt the populist revivalist rhetoric of the leadership, but if his statements are

[202] Ia. Shatunovskii, Geroizm truda i rabochee tvorchestvo (Moscow–Leningrad, 1928), 60, 101. Shatunovskii worked in the planning department of the People's Commissariat of Transport and in Gosplan. For Shatunovskii and his association with the right, see H. Kuromiya, Stalin's Industrial Revolution, 185, n. 46; Stalin, Sochineniia, xi. 270, 281.
[203] N. I. Bukharin, 'Rekonstruktivnyi period i bor'ba s religiei', P, 12 June 1929.
[204] N. I. Bukharin, 'Na temy dnia' P, 27 May 1928, 2. See also N. I. Bukharin, Tekushchie zadachi komsomola, 22.
[205] N. I. Bukharin, 'Rekonstruktivnyi period'.
[206] N. I. Bukharin, Bor'ba dvukh mirov i zadachi nauki (Moscow–Leningrad, 1931), 19.
[207] N. I. Bukharin, O tekhnicheskoi propagande i ee organizatsii (Moscow–Leningrad, 1931), 17.
[208] B, 10 (1928), 3; P, 17 June 1928 (Slepkov). See also Stalin's criticism of Slepkov, Stalin, Sochineniia, xi. 98–100. For the debate over Slepkov's article, see E. H. Carr, Foundations of a Planned Economy, ii. 61–2.
[209] IV plenum MK VKP(b) sovmestno s plenumom MKK. Avgust 1929 g. (Moscow, 1929), 84 (Uglanov). For Uglanov's attempt to mobilize managerial support and

examined carefully it is clear that they were designed to obscure a technicist message. He did, as has often been pointed out, call for steps to be taken in the direction of the 'Leninist commune-state', but this did not amount to a call for popular participation in administration. Rather, he was criticizing the inefficiency caused by the 'hyper-centralism' of the apparatus, particularly in the economic sphere.[210] He did criticize the stifling of 'initiative' by officials and the regime but, as during the NEP period, he concentrated his fire on overzealous proletarian party officials rather than on bourgeois specialists.[211] Bukharin's 'bureaucrats', it seems, were party officials 'at the top', who implemented 'administrative acts' irrespective of the damaging effects which they were having on the working class and the poor and middle peasantry.[212] He made it clear that he preferred this non-revivalist definition of 'bureaucratism' in his speech to the Komsomol of May 1928:

In its well-known aspects [bureaucratism] can bear a directly class character; let's say for instance when the remnants of the governing classes from the old regime sit in our apparatus, and actively sabotage us or quietly and systematically 'go slow'...Bureaucratism also exists in the form of the germs of the notorious class degeneration of particular officials who originate from the working class...But it can be a manifestation of the incorrect system of work adopted by officials who originate from our class and who have not degenerated but have placed themselves in such conditions, in such relations, that they bring direct harm to our socialist construction and therefore objectively help our class enemy.[213]

Bukharin was, therefore, like some populist revivalists, criticizing the emerging neo-traditionalist order and implying that a 'new class' of proletarian bureaucrats had emerged. But he did not share the populist revivalists' objectives and analysis. He was trying to proffer a more structural, and potentially liberal, explanation for

his opposition to 'democracy', see F. M. Vaganov, *Pravyi uklon i ee razgrom, 1928–1930 gg.* (Moscow, 1970), 154–5; Merridale, *Moscow Politics*, 82–4.

[210] N. I. Bukharin, 'Zametki ekonomista', in N. Bukharin, *Put' k sotsializmu. Izbrannye proizvedeniia* (Novosibirsk, 1990), 365. For Cohen's view, see S. Cohen, *Bukharin*, 321.

[211] N. I. Bukharin, 'Tekushchii moment i zadachi nashei pechati', *P*, 2 December 1928.

[212] Ibid. Bukharin did accept that managers and state officials could be 'bureaucratic', but his main criticism was directed against party officials' attitudes towards the peasantry.

[213] N. I. Bukharin, *Tekushchie zadachi komsomola*, 18.

bureaucratism, suggesting that it was the consequence of administrative centralization, rather than the moral 'degeneration' of individual officials or the influence of bourgeois attitudes.

The crisis of revivalism

Although the right was defeated in 1929 and its leaders lost their influential positions (culminating in Rykov's removal from Sovnarkom in December 1930), the strength of many of the right's arguments became increasingly evident, as did the internal contradictions of revivalism and the utopianism of its assumptions. First, the tempos of the first five-year plan were wholly impractical. Unrealistically high investment and production targets led to shortages; enterprises in turn failed to fulfil plans and produced poor quality goods.[214] Second, the Stalinists' populist revivalist call for 'democracy' and 'class struggle' could undermine their own power. 'Self-criticism' could be used against Stalinists, as Stalin complained when *Pravda* used the slogan to attack his ally Sergei Kirov, the Leningrad party boss.[215] And third, the regime legitimized and unleashed populist socialist sentiments among the population, which inevitably undermined both managerial authority and labour productivity.[216]

Yet despite these difficulties, Stalin and the leadership continued their attempts to combine centralization and 'democracy'. Throughout the period, the leadership complained that labour discipline was poor, and tried to tighten controls. It seems that this had some effect on the shopfloor, as is suggested by the fact that the numbers of workers dismissed for indiscipline increased. However, the leadership always insisted that managerial control over workers was to be combined with participation and 'democracy'.[217] The September 1929 resolution establishing 'one-man management' (*edinonachalie*) in enterprises was a typical example of this approach.

---

[214] Davies, *The Soviet Economy in Turmoil*, 370–7.
[215] See Stalin's denunciation of *Pravda* in Stalin to Molotov, 13 September 1929, *Pis'ma*, 165.
[216] Davies, *The Soviet Economy in Turmoil*, 363.
[217] For attempts to increase controls over labour, while encouraging worker participation, see R. W. Davies, *The Soviet Economy in Turmoil*, 272–3, 278–83; H. Kuromiya, *Stalin's Industrial Revolution*, 98–9, ch. 7.

The decree was designed to give the manager power in the enterprise, yet at the same time it declared that factory and trade union committees had to have more involvement in formulating plans.[218]

Stalin was most willing to restrict 'democracy' when it undermined his political power and that of his allies. While criticism of high-level party leaders without the sanction of the leadership was rare, it did happen, most notably in the case of Pravda's criticism of Kirov in September 1929;[219] Stalin took action, removing Kovalev, the head of Pravda's party organization and an editor of the newspaper and criticizing the editorial board.[220] However, it does not seem that Stalin wanted this clamp-down on the press to signal the end of self-criticism, as he revealed in a letter to Gorky in January 1930. Gorky had retained his interest in mobilizing the energies of the working class, and hoped to do so by creating a literature with heroes which the masses could emulate. Yet his vision was now an élitist one, and he was dismayed at the populism of the leadership's message, alleging that it was giving rise to an anarchistic hostility towards the intelligentsia and that excessive criticism was undermining popular morale.[221] Stalin sympathized with him to some extent, and accepted that the press should pay more attention to the regime's achievements. But he rejected any suggestion that self-criticism be abandoned:

We cannot do without self-criticism. We cannot in any way, Aleksei Maksimovich. Without it, stagnation (*zastoi*), the decay of the apparatus, the growth of bureaucratism, the undermining of the creative initiative of the working class, are inevitable. Of course, self-criticism provides material for our enemies. But it also gives material (and a stimulus) for our movement forwards, for unleashing the constructive energies of the working people, for the development of emulation, for shock brigades etc. The negative side is balanced and *out*weighed by the positive side.[222]

Molotov also urged Stalin to annouce a clear reversal of the self-criticism policy following the Leningrad affair, and again he refused, although his reasoning was different:

---

[218] *KPSS v rezoliutsiiakh*, iv. 310–17.

[219] For another case in Moscow, see C. Merridale, *Moscow Politics*, 212.

[220] For details of this case, see *Pis'ma*, 173–4.

[221] Gorky to Stalin, 27 November 1929, *Izv TsK KPSS* 3 (1989), 184–5. Gorky alleged that 'self-criticism' was encouraging 'Makhaevism'. For Gorky's interest in positive heroes, see Gorky to Bukharin, 23 June 1925, ibid., 182.

[222] Stalin to Gorky, 17 January 1930, Stalin, *Sochineniia*, xii. 173.

... a special decree from the Central Committee plus a speech by Molotov *may be* understood (**will** be understood!) by party organizations *as a new course backward*, as an appeal: '*Rein in self-criticism*', which is of course not desirable and which will undoubtedly undermine the authority of the Central Committee (and Molotov) in the eyes of the best elements of the party *in favour of all and sundry bureaucrats*.[223]

Stalin seems to have been suggesting that a decisive change in policy would have serious disadvantages for two related reasons: first he was concerned about the ideological implications of such a change and its effects on his authority within the party; he had outmanoeuvred his rivals by defending a revivalist ideological position, and so to abandon any element of it would have been seen as a 'retreat'. And second, he was concerned about the institutional conflict with 'bureaucrats' in the apparatus, a struggle he had not yet won.

The leadership, therefore, continued to advocate 'democracy' and 'self-criticism', and relied on vague appeals that 'democracy' not be taken to extremes.[224] In industry, the leadership allowed shock workers and party officials to interfere in management, and managerial power remained weak throughout 1930.[225] Yet, as Stalin's statements show, he was well aware of the tensions between 'democratization' and the establishment of a unified, centralized planned system. It was only a matter of time before this synthesis, initially developed by the United Opposition in the 1920s, broke down. As will be seen in the following chapter, by the end of 1930 it had become clear to the leadership that it was unsustainable. Just as Lenin had been compelled to adopt a 'new course' in 1918, so Stalin was forced to accept, as he had described it in 1929, a 'new course backward', in the interests of economic order.

---

[223] Stalin to Molotov, 13 September 1929, *Pis'ma*, 164.

[224] See, for instance, Stalin, *Sochineniia*, xi. 132–7; RGASPI, 558/11/1112, 45.

[225] In Leningrad, for instance, over 60% of shock workers' brigade leaders were elected rather than appointed by managers. H. Kuromiya, *Stalin's Industrial Revolution*, ch. 7, esp. pp. 179–80.

4

The Search for Unity and Order, 1930–1935

In June 1931 Stalin gave a speech to a conference of industrial managers, commonly known as the 'six conditions' speech, which for the next few years was constantly quoted and cited as the main ideological pronouncement of the era. In the speech he declared an effective end to the 'class struggle' against the bourgeois specialists.[1] By 1934 repression had been moderated in the countryside as well, and in the same year members of the former oppositions were permitted to address the seventeenth party congress. It was now declared that the 'enemies of the party' had been defeated.[2] The pace of industrialization was no longer to be so hectic, and the second five-year plan of 1933–7 was much less ambitious than the first. Yet while the speech signalled a move away from repression of 'enemies', it also indicated a disillusion with 'democracy' and a turn to a strict form of 'one-man management' in factories. The future engineer Viktor Kravchenko, then a student in Dnepropetrovsk, appreciated the ambiguous message of the 'six conditions' speech. While he welcomed the new status accorded to specialists, he noted the leadership's restoration of hierarchy. For Kravchenko, 'with that strange Soviet genius for extremes, the evil of too many bosses was now replaced by the evil of a single and arbitrary boss, in which the last pretence of "workers' control" from below was thrown overboard'.[3] As will be seen, as managerial authority in industry was strengthened, so the party and state apparatuses

---

[1] *Sochineniia*, xiii. 51–80. For the original, unedited version, see RGASPI, 85/28/8, 172–208.
[2] *XVII s"ezd Vsesoiuznoi Kommunisticheskoi Partii (bol'shevikov), 26 ianvaria– 10 fevralia 1934 gg. Stenograficheskii otchet* (Moscow, 1934), 28 (Stalin).
[3] V. Kravchenko, *I Chose Freedom* (London, 1947), 77.

increased their power over many other areas of Soviet life. But this departure from revivalist politics is perhaps most evident in the cultural sphere, and in the ways the regime legitimized itself. The radical, 'proletarian' intellectuals were denounced in the early 1930s, and from 1933 to 1934 the principle of 'nationality' and Russian national culture and symbols began to dominate the regime's propaganda, as did what later became known as Stalin's leadership 'cult'.[4]

Commentators have noted the political changes of 1930–5, but they have differed over their meaning and significance. One of the most popular interpretations is most effectively captured in the title of Nicholas Timasheff's book, *The Great Retreat*. According to this view, the regime retreated from the 'communist experiment' and adopted a range of traditionalist policies, including the restoration of stability and social hierarchy.[5] Trotsky's analysis of Stalinism, expounded in *The Revolution Betrayed*, was similar, although he was much more critical of these developments than was Timasheff.[6] A more recent 'neo-traditionalist' literature has agreed with the notion that there was a turn away from radical approaches to politics in this period, but it has seen it less as a return to traditional Russian practices than as the unintended by-product of a highly statist form of modernization. In attempting to control society, the state inadvertently established a new set of status hierarchies.[7]

Some conflictualist historians have also emphasized the traditionalizing changes of the period, arguing that the social crisis of 1929–33

---

[4] For the emergence of Russian nationalist rhetoric in this period, see D. Brandenberger, *National Bolshevism. Stalinist Mass Culture and the Formation of Modern Russian National Identity, 1931–1956* (Cambridge, Mass., 2002), chs. 1, 3; D. Brandenberger and A. M. Dubrovsky, ' "The People Need a Tsar": The Emergence of National Bolshevism as Stalinist Ideology, 1931–1941', *E–AS*, 50 (1998), 873–92; Martin, *The Affirmative Action Empire*, 414–22; Tucker, *Stalin in Power*, 568–72. For the leadership 'cult', see S. Davies, *Popular Opinion in Stalin's Russia. Terror, Propaganda and Dissent, 1934–1941* (Cambridge, 1997), 147–52; G. Gill, 'The Soviet Leader Cult. Reflections on the Structure of Leadership in the Soviet Union', *BJPS*, 10 (1980), 167–86; B. Kiteme, 'The Cult of Stalin. National Power and the Soviet Party State', Ph.D. dissertation, Columbia University, 1989.

[5] N. S. Timasheff, *The Great Retreat. The Growth and Decline of Communism in Russia* (New York, 1946), 20–1; for the use of Timasheff's insight, see Fitzpatrick, *Education and Social Mobility*, 253–4.

[6] Trotsky, *The Revolution Betrayed*; for the 'Thermidorian' historiographical tradition, see G. Boffa, *The Stalin Phenomenon*, ch. 7.

[7] See S. Fitzpatrick, 'Ascribing Class'; T. Martin, 'Modernization or Neo-traditionalism?' Martin, however, argues for a more deliberate use of traditionalist discourse in 'An Affirmative Action Empire', 955–9.

allowed a traditional Russian political culture to triumph over the Bolsheviks' original modernizing goals.[8] Others have interpreted the period in the context of the 'state' versus 'society' paradigm, arguing that the period was one of 'moderation', or of a 'reconciliation' between the regime and the population.[9] They also used the evidence of the Menshevik émigré Boris Nicolaevsky to argue that 'moderation' was championed not by Stalin but by a party of 'moderates' in the leadership led by Sergei Kirov, who fought for influence with a group of 'hard-liners'.[10]

Many historians, however, have been much more sceptical of the notion of the 'retreat' of the early 1930s. As is to be expected, liberal commentators have been most forceful in arguing for continuity. So Malia, for instance, while noting the abandonment of leftist rhetoric, the use of national symbols, and the adoption of some 'compromises' in the economic sphere, insists that 'there never was a Soviet Thermidor'.[11] Stalin's goal, inherited from Marx, of creating 'non-capitalism', or a society without private property, remained the same throughout the 1930s. Stephen Kotkin also argues against the notion of a 'Great Retreat' under Stalin; for him a general commitment to 'progressive modernity'—to a welfare state, scientific planning and the central regulation of society—remained central to the thinking of the 'vast majority' of those who lived in the Soviet Union in the 1930s.[12]

Each of these interpretations touches on elements of Soviet society and politics in this period, although some have greater explanatory power than others. The beginning of the 1930s did witness significant changes in the political attitudes and behaviour of the leadership. There is considerable evidence that Stalin was deliberately forging a patriotic message to replace the language of class in

---

[8] See, for instance, M. Lewin, *The Making of the Soviet System*, 286–314. As S. Kotkin has argued, Lewin's views have something in common with those of Trotsky in *The Revolution Betrayed*. See S. Kotkin, *Magnetic Mountain*, 2–6.

[9] Stephen Cohen defended this view. See S. Cohen, *Bukharin*, 345. See also R. Tucker, *Stalin in Power*, 242–3; O. V. Khlevniuk, *Politbiuro. Mekhanizmy politicheskoi vlasti v 1930-e gody* (Moscow, 1996), 141.

[10] See B. Nicolaevsky, 'Letter of an Old Bolshevik', in B. Nicolaevsky, *Power and the Soviet Elite. 'The Letter of an Old Bolshevik' and Other Essays* (London, 1966), 30, 35. For accounts which rely on Nicolaevsky's analysis, see R. Conquest, *The Great Terror. A Reassessment* (1990), 24–5; R. Tucker, *Stalin in Power*, 238–47; S. Cohen, *Bukharin*, 341–7.

[11] M. Malia, *The Soviet Tragedy*, 204–7, 233–43.

[12] S. Kotkin, *Magnetic Mountain*, 618–21. See also D. Hoffmann, *Stalinist Values*.

the rhetoric of the regime.[13] He also, to a very limited extent, presided over some liberal technicist reforms. However, there is no evidence of a coherent 'liberal' group within the leadership, or of ideological conflict between 'moderates' and 'hard-liners;[14] nor is the period best characterized as one in which the state began to 'reconcile' itself with 'society'. While violent mass repressions against 'class enemies' became less frequent between 1933 and 1936, repression was redirected against other groups, and in some areas, such as industry, the regime adopted a more disciplinarian attitude towards workers than before. The neo-traditionalist approach is convincing in explaining how the abolition of the market and a policy of discipline increasingly, and often inadvertently, strengthened a powerful stratum of party bosses and the traditional, patron–client authority relationships they generated. The leadership's approach to a whole range of issues did, therefore, change at the beginning of the 1930s. Yet as critics of the retreat thesis have noted, there were also important continuities. The regime may have used new forms of legitimization, but it still believed that it was building socialism. It is clearly not possible to argue that Stalin was engineering a simple retreat from socialism to nationalism or conservatism.

The best way of capturing all of the various themes within the regime's worldview in the period is to see it as a rejection of the populist revivalist 'class struggle' of the Great Break period. Yet, while this change limited options to some extent, the leadership could still adopt several different strategies in its attempts to build a powerful and socialist state. It therefore found itself defending a number of versions of Bolshevism, sometimes simultaneously, and we need to appreciate the tensions within its thinking

Many of the leadership's policies in this period can be helpfully seen as a chaotic and incoherent retreat from ideological ambition to pragmatism under the pressure of economic realities. They can also be seen as a retreat according to the Marxist historical scheme, from the combination of élitist and populist revivalist Bolshevism of the late 1920s to a confused mixture of élitist revivalist, technicist,

---

[13] See D. Brandenberger, *National Bolshevism*, ch. 1.

[14] For criticisms of the Nicolaevsky analysis, see O. V. Khlevniuk, *Politbiuro*, 75 ff. and *passim*; J. T. Getty and O. V. Naumov, *The Road to Terror*, 575–6; J. A. Getty, 'The Politics of Repression Revisited', in J. A. Getty and R. T. Manning (eds.), *Stalinist Terror, New Perspectives* (Cambridge, 1993), 42–9.

liberal technicist, and neo-traditionalist Bolshevisms. Stalin's retreat therefore echoed Lenin's two-stage retreat in 1918 and 1921, and he was behaving after the 'revolution' of 1928–29 much as Lenin had after its predecessor of 1917. Initially, in 1930–1, Stalin decided he had to reject populist revivalism and to dilute his commitment to the use of moral incentives in mobilizing workers. 'Democracy' gave way to strict discipline and hierarchy, and, as in 1918, the specialists were rehabilitated. Yet the leadership was more reluctant to abandon high plan targets and 'class struggle' against the peasantry. Populist mobilization was replaced by an uneasy combination of élitist revivalist and technicist policies, which coexisted throughout this period and was particularly dominant during the years of economic crisis between 1930 and 1933. In these years Stalin seems to have hoped to use élitist, disciplinarian methods to attain extraordinary economic goals. Soon, however, the leadership had to accept that the state could not transform the economy and society rapidly by relying largely on shock methods and mobilization, and it increasingly moved towards a more technicist position. The technicist approach to economic policy, however, in turn required a further retreat to elements of the liberal model if material incentives were to work properly. By 1934–5 there were unmistakable signs of 'liberal' elements within official rhetoric; while the leadership was not returning to the early 1920s, it is not surprising that the period was to be dubbed a 'neo-NEP' by critical observers.

Stalin's justification and presentation of these changes of policy also had much in common with the arguments used by Lenin after 1918. Stalin sometimes admitted that he was 'retreating' from communism because the working class was not sufficiently mature. However, to a greater extent than Lenin, he generally tried to avoid the language of 'advance' and 'retreat', by claiming that in establishing an élitist socialism the Bolsheviks had almost achieved the ideal society promised by Marx and Engels. And he sometimes justified this élitist socialism in technicist terms, as a polity in which *politika* and class had ceased to be of importance, and where expert officials implemented scientifically rational decisions in a society without class or national differences. *Tekhnika* now had primacy; the policies of the Great Break period were at fault not because they were too 'advanced' or ambitious, but because they had failed to promote the business-like and disciplined culture necessary in a socialist society.

Yet technicist arguments and strategies had drawbacks. They entrenched the position of experts and the economic apparatus;

they were only compatible with moderate levels of growth; and they were ineffective in securing popular loyalty for the regime. It is therefore perhaps not surprising that Stalin was not satisfied with them, and he continued to favour strategies of mobilization, even though he was determined to avoid a repetition of the disorder of the Great Break period. One way in which he tried to combine unity and discipline with mobilization was by modifying the Bolshevism of the past, and developing a new form of élitist revivalism, based on a non-class 'national' or 'popular' (*narodnyi*) form of mobilization: the unified *narod*, now no longer divided by class, embodied socialism, and was to achieve heroic feats in the struggle against largely external enemies.

However, while this 'national' form of revivalist Bolshevism became more influential within the leadership's discourse, it was not easy to sustain, and it could be transformed into a neo-traditionalist ideology without any mobilizational potential. It was difficult to present the Soviet Union as a unified nation, and any use of the language of nationality was likely to draw attention to differences between the various nationalities of the Soviet Union, while suggesting that those differences were inherited and innate. And, at a time when the regime, for various reasons, continued to discriminate according to both ethnicity and class, this discourse contributed to the prevalence of a neo-traditionalist vision of society as a fixed hierarchy, in which Russians and proletarians had higher status than others. Stalin himself sometimes revealed neo-traditionalist thinking, but he was understandably unhappy that his revivalism had been distorted in this way. Neo-traditionalism placed loyal proletarian officials—and in particular the party apparatus—beyond criticism, and could be used to justify their attempts to resist mobilization and the centre's interventions in regional affairs. So, while endorsing technicism and sometimes betraying a neo-traditionalist set of assumptions, Stalin continued to use revivalist language: the 'class struggle' against 'bourgeois', 'bureaucratic', and 'rightist' attitudes was not over.

Economic ambitions and economic crisis

A number of forces precipitated the gradual move away from populist revivalism. First, Stalin's own political position was strengthened after the formal defeat and recantation of the right at the sixteenth party congress in June 1930. Just as the defeat of the left in December 1927 made it easier for Stalin to appropriate its ideas, so that of the right allowed him to move towards a more élitist position; he no longer had to fear so much that a retreat would give succour to 'bureaucrats' as he had before. The complete victory of the Stalinists also altered the balance of institutional forces. In November 1930 Ordzhonikidze finally won his struggle against Vesenkha and replaced Kuibyshev as its boss. The following month Sovnarkom also fell to the Stalinists, and Rykov was finally replaced by Molotov.[15] As powerful figures close to Stalin took over the running of the economy directly, they became more concerned with the practicalities of economic management and were less sympathetic to revivalist ideas. The change in Ordzhonikidze's views is particularly evident: as head of Vesenkha and then of the powerful People's Commissariat of Heavy Industry (Narkomtiazhprom) he increasingly became a defender of managerial and specialist authority, and his influence inevitably strengthened the new technicist direction of the leadership.[16] After his departure, Rabkrin was placed under more junior leaders and its influence waned.[17] Also, as will be seen, the party apparatus was increasingly remodelled so that it would become more amenable to the interests of state organizations.

Stalin himself seems to have initiated the retreat because economic crisis forced him to. By the summer of 1930 industry was in severe crisis. Ambitious capital investment had led to shortages of capital, labour and materials.[18] This was compounded by other difficulties, including food shortages caused by chaos in the countryside, purges and other disruptions in industry, and high plan targets.[19] Plans were far from being fulfilled, but Stalin for the time being firmly refused to compromise on the plan. The USSR, he insisted, had to catch up with the capitalist world if it were not to be threatened and humiliated by its enemies.[20] He was therefore insistent that plan targets continue to be very high: the

---

[15] D. Watson, *Molotov and the Soviet Government. Sovnarkom, 1930–41* (Basingstoke, 1996), 43–5.
[16] See S. Fitzpatrick, 'Ordzhonikidze's Takeover of Vesenkha', 153–72.
[17] Rees, *State Control in Soviet Russia*, 202 ff.
[18] R. W. Davies, *The Soviet Economy in Turmoil*, ch. 9; H. Kuromiya, *Stalin's Industrial Revolution*, 157–62.
[19] R. W. Davies, *The Soviet Economy in Turmoil*, 475–6.
[20] Stalin, *Sochineniia*, xiii. 38–40.

plan of 1931, based on the targets adopted at the sixteenth party congress, was a particularly extreme document, and was both un-realizable and incoherent. In the course of 1931 some plan targets were even increased.[21]

Stalin's strategy was to maintain high plan targets but husband resources, cutting costs and improving productivity.[22] He explained his thinking most clearly in his 'six conditions' speech. Unlike Germany, which had, according to Stalin, industrialized with the help of money it had extracted from France in the 1870s, and England, which had taken money from its colonies, the Soviet Union relied on its own sources of 'accumulation'. Its resources, however, were insufficient. This meant that either the government had to rely on printing money, which, if excessive, would lead to the unacceptable inflation of the past and could 'frustrate everything', or resources would have to be used more sparingly.[23]

The rejection of populist revivalism and 'proletarian' values

Labour was the one of the first targets of this new cost-cutting campaign, and Stalin and his colleagues mounted a sustained as-sault on the populist revivalist approach to labour that had been influential hitherto. The leadership increasingly abandoned its earl-ier faith in the effectiveness of 'democratic' mobilization and ap-peals to workers' consciousness, and began to stress the importance of the carrot and the stick. In the case of Stalin, this reassessment seems to have been accompanied by a more general reconsideration of the level of consciousness and virtues of the working class. Just as the turn to the left in 1928 was accompanied by a declaration of faith in the enthusiasm and activism of the proletariat and a hostility to 'class aliens', so the retreat of 1930–1, like Lenin's retreat of 1918, was marked by assertions that the proletariat, or at least certain sections of it, were unreliable and that the 'class struggle' against the bourgeoisie would have to be moderated.

The leadership had complained about poor labour discipline for some time, but in the autumn of 1930 Stalin called for a significant

[21] For this plan, see R. W. Davies, *Crisis and Progress*, 6–10.
[22] For the new direction in financial policy, see R. W. Davies, *The Soviet Economy in Turmoil*, 430 ff.
[23] RGASPI, 85/28/8, 193.

change in the regime's relationship with labour. Much more emphasis was now placed by the leadership on the shortcomings of workers and the impracticality of introducing moral incentives.[24] On 3 September 1930, the Central Committee's *Appeal* on the fulfilment of the targets of the third year of the five-year plan, while criticizing the conservatism and bureaucratism of specialists and managers and the continuing wrecking of class enemies, assigned particular blame for economic problems on labour indiscipline and turnover.[25] Stalin expressed his disillusionment with the proletariat even more clearly in a letter he wrote to Molotov on 28 September. He began by calling for the creation of a 'Commission of Fulfilment' under Sovnarkom, to check up on officials' fulfilment of directives. He then turned his attention to the problems caused by workers:

[establishing] the 'Commission of Fulfilment' embraces only *one* side of the matter, turning its edge against the bureaucratism of our apparatuses. In order to get our construction [of socialism] fully on track, we must embrace yet *another* side of the matter. I am speaking about the 'turnover' at enterprises, about 'flitters', about labour discipline, about the shrinking cadre of permanent workers, about socialist emulation and shock work, about the organization of supplies for workers. As the situation stands now, some of the workers work honestly according to the principle of [socialist] emulation; others (the majority) are negligent and transient, yet the latter are as well (*if not better*) provisioned, enjoy the *same* privileges of vacations, sanatoria, insurance etc., as the former. Surely this is an outrage? This can undermine any real foundation for socialist emulation and shock work![26]

If, as Stalin was alleging, the majority of the proletariat was not sufficiently virtuous or 'conscious', socialist, moral incentives would have to be diluted in favour of other incentives. Stalin reached this conclusion in his letter. He demanded that workers' rations be made much more strictly dependent on their productivity, and called for a new campaign against labour indiscipline and absenteeism.[27] But he clearly did not want to retreat too far. His frequent references to socialist emulation show that he was still

---

[24] See, for instance, *KPSS v rezoliutsiiakh*, iv. 169–75.
[25] *P*, 3 September 1930.
[26] Stalin to Molotov, 28 September 1930, *Pis'ma*, 224–5.
[27] Ibid., 225–6.

committed to mobilization and moral incentives.[28] He was also worried about possible opposition to any change in labour policy, as is implied in his letter:

This is, of course, a serious and complicated matter. We need to think about it thoroughly. Whether these measures can be applied *immediately* and in *all* branches of industry—this is also a problem. But this entire matter is extremely necessary and *unavoidable*. Think this matter over (and also the question of the 'Commission of Fulfilment') in a small circle of our closest friends and then inform me of their opinion.[29]

Yet, despite these concerns, measures to discipline the labour force were introduced in legislation in October and December 1930. As R. W. Davies has argued, they seriously undermined the 'relatively favoured position' which workers had enjoyed up until then.[30]

Stalin's new approach to incentives was also reflected in changes in wage policy. There had been some piecemeal criticism of 'wage egalitarianism' for some time, but the leadership's policy was ambiguous until early 1931 when Molotov and then Stalin, in the 'six conditions' speech, launched a campaign against the practice.[31] Stalin denounced wage egalitarianism on the grounds that it gave workers no incentive to improve their skills and exacerbated the problem of labour turnover.[32] Stalin then went on to make a more general defence of material incentives:

The worker understands socialism to mean that his material position will improve. If you shout about socialism in a hundred voices, but you do not improve his material position, he will spit on your socialism, and he will be correct, as socialism is the systematic improvement of the position of the working class.[33]

This passage was not published, but it suggests that Stalin was fundamentally questioning his earlier revivalist assumptions about the behaviour of the working class. Workers, he was implying, were primarily motivated by money, not by commitment to socialism.

---

[28] For the counter-plan movement, see R. W. Davies, *The Soviet Economy in Turmoil*, 427 ff.

[29] Stalin to Molotov, 28 September 1930, *Pis'ma*, 226 f.

[30] R. W. Davies, *The Soviet Economy in Turmoil*, 419. For the legislation, see ibid., 421–4.

[31] For the debate over the issue, see R. W. Davies, *The Soviet Economy in Turmoil*, 261–7; R. W. Davies, *Crisis and Progress*, 53–4.

[32] RGASPI, 85/28/8, 177.

[33] RGASPI, 85/28/8, 181.

Stalin's comments on *vydvizhenie* also show his pessimism about workers' ability to participate in administration, his view that workers' technical accomplishments were of primary importance, and his belief that only a minority of workers could be promoted to a higher position in society. He began by strongly criticizing the *vydvizhenie* campaign:

we are essentially tearing away from production (*vydvizhenie*!) all the workers who show some initiative and we hand them over to some office or other where they die of boredom in unfamiliar surroundings, devastating, in this way, the basic core of workers in production.

He then proposed that *vydvizhenie* was no longer to be pursued for political reasons—the involvement of workers in administration; the goals of production were to be primary:

Prohibit the *vydvizhenie* of workers **from the shop floor** to any and all apparatuses, encouraging their *vydvzihenie* **only** within **production** (or perhaps within the trade unions). Let workers from the shop floor (who know their trade) be promoted to assistant foremen, foremen, shop manager and so forth. **This** is the kind of *vydvizhenie* we need now like air, like water. Without this we will squander our entire core of industrial workers and will place our enterprises at the mercy of self-seekers.[34]

By March 1931 Stalin's sentiments had been embodied in legislation, and the leadership had banned the 'mobilization of workers from the shop floor for on-going campaigns'.[35]

In the sphere of labour relations, therefore, Stalin admitted that many of the policies of 1928–30 had been mistaken and overambitious, and at times placed his reassessment in the broader context of the Marxist historical scheme: the regime had 'advanced' too far along the road to communism and 'proletarian', egalitarian methods of administration were impractical given the current level of economic development. It was only in the higher stage of communism, Stalin argued, that wages could be equal; until then workers had to be paid 'according to work performed and not according to needs'.[36] Similarly, at the seventeenth party conference, in 1932, Molotov argued that economic equality and the withering away of the state would only be possible after a long period of

[34] Stalin to Molotov, 28 September 1930, *Pis'ma*, 225–6.
[35] *Spravochnik partiinogo rabotnika*, vyp. 8 (Moscow, 1934), 385–6.
[36] Stalin, *Sochineniia*, xiii. 57.

time.[37] He defended the decision of the Central Committee to drop the goal of 'eliminating the distinction between mental and manual labour' from its theses. It would take longer than a decade to achieve this transformation.[38] For Molotov, the final construction of socialism was now a distant goal: the Soviet Union had entered 'the first, lower phase of communist society (socialism)' but the achievement of socialism, which would happen when distinctions between workers and peasants had fully disappeared, would be 'far from completion' during the second five-year plan, that is the period 1933–7.[39]

Yet the leadership was naturally wary of the argument that it was having to retreat from the ambitious plans of 1928–9, and it was reluctant to admit that it had lost its faith in the working class. A different narrative, which underplayed the importance of class and avoided the notion of retreat, was therefore more popular. The Shakhty period, it was declared, had been one in which 'political tasks', such as class struggle and the reordering of social relations, had been a priority. Now, these problems had been solved, and technical tasks, which had little to do with class, were more important. As Stalin explained in his speech of February 1931:

It is time for Bolsheviks themselves to become experts. In the period of reconstruction, *tekhnika* decides everything... We have solved a number of the most difficult tasks. We have overthrown capitalism. We have taken power. We have constructed a huge socialist industry. We have turned the middle peasants onto the path of socialism... What remains to be done is not so much: to study *tekhnika*, to master science.[40]

As in the past, *tekhnika* meant more than 'technology'. As was traditionally the case in technicist rhetoric, it was associated with 'economics', and implied a hierarchical form of administration in which technically informed decisions were communicated efficiently

---

[37] *XVII konferentsiia VKP(b). Stenograficheskii otchet* (Moscow, 1932), 146 (Molotov).

[38] *XVII konferentsiia*, 148 (Molotov). See also P. P. Postyshev, *Za marksistko-leninskoe vospitanie* (Moscow, 1932), 73.

[39] *XVII konferentsiia*, 145 (Molotov). Kuibyshev was rather more optimistic (see ibid., 162), although in the draft of his speech he was even more so and stated that the goal of the second five-year plan would be 'the achievement of the first phase of communism—developed socialism'. He also argued, in contrast to Molotov, that in this period the foundations for the elimination of the distinction between mental and manual labour would be established. RGASPI, 79/1/561, 15–16.

[40] Stalin, *Sochineniia*, xiii. 41–2.

down a line of command. It was also contrasted with *politika* and a reliance on consciousness and ideology.[41] In his 'six conditions' speech Stalin listed the new qualities required of leaders: they were not to manage 'in general' or 'in the abstract', but 'concretely', 'in a strictly business-like [*delovoi*] way'. 'One-man management' had to replace the endless 'discussion' which the old style of leadership had generated.[42]

Given this change in direction, it is not surprising that the meaning of the 'struggle against bureaucratism' again changed. Now the evil of bureaucratism was equated with 'red-tapism'; 'democracy' and 'self-criticism' were given less emphasis. Stalin's 'six conditions' speech criticized managers for 'mismanagement', failing to exercise 'concrete' leadership, and providing 'paper leadership' without intervening in the technical details; he said nothing about their failure to listen to the voice of the masses.[43] Even Pashukanis, who had been one of the fiercest opponents of the technicist analysis of bureaucratism in 1928, wrote in 1932 that 'the main trouble with our apparatus and our officials...is the fact that they are not always sufficiently experienced, are not always able to comprehend complex situations, are not always sufficiently well trained'.[44] Speaking at a Central Committee meeting on the coal industry at about the same time, Ordzhonikidze did mention the need for 'Bolshevik self-criticism', but it is clear that he was trying to redefine the term to rid it of its populist revivalist implications. Ordzhonikidze implied that it was not to involve worker participation or criticism of management, but was to allow managers freedom to discuss technical matters; new methods in the running of the economy could not be developed without criticism. This criticism was to be published in the press, but 'campaign methods' were not to be used.[45]

Yet, while Stalin's reluctance to trust the consciousness of the working class is evident from the end of 1930, he was only moving away from his earlier populist revivalism. He continued to display voluntaristic, élitist revivalist views. As will be seen, he had not

[41] Stalin, *Sochineniia*, xiii. 37–8.
[42] Ibid., xiii. 78–9; RGASPI, 85/28/8, 202–3.
[43] Stalin, *Sochineniia*, xiii. 76–80.
[44] E. Pashukanis, *Proletarskoe gosudarstvo i postroenie besklassogo obshchestva* (Moscow, 1932), 37; see also *PS* (editorial), 11 (1931), 1.
[45] RGASPI, 17/165/18, 15 (May 1931).

abandoned his extreme, violent approach towards the peasantry, and continued to insist that if only officials believed in the plan, enormously high plan targets were feasible. The party, he explained in June 1931, had to arm 'our people' with a 'passionate faith in the possibility of fulfilling the plan'. Those who did not believe had to be punished: the party had to 'drive away all these wise men in quotation marks, so-called wise men, who talk to you about realistic plans and so forth'. 'Realism', for Stalin, was to be identified with the party's policy, not with some objective reality: 'realism means our plan... realism is you and us'.[46] The spring of 1931 saw the climax of the campaign against the 'bourgeois' specialists who had dared to question the voluntaristic assumptions of the plan, with the trial of Groman, Kondrat'ev, and other alleged members of the 'counter-revolutionary Menshevik organization'.[47]

The tempering of class struggle and the intelligentsia

At the same time, however, there were signs that the leadership was willing to protect the specialists as a group. In part, this was a reaction to the disruption caused by the Great Break. The authority of specialists had to be restored if labour discipline was to be re-established. Yet their rehabilitation also suggested that some within the leadership were pushing for a more technicist approach to the economy. Interests within Vesenkha, which objected to the revivalist stress on 'will' and hoped to defend science from political interference, now had a champion in the person of Ordzhonikidze.

The leadership as a whole accepted the rehabilitation of the specialists from the end of 1930. Although the trial of the 'Industrial party' was held in November 1930, the Politburo made it clear that it was not to be publicized as the Shakhty trial had been. While it did urge that propaganda expose the 'counter-revolutionary wrecking role of some elements from the élite of the old bourgeois engineers and property owners', party organizations were not 'to allow with this the defamation and indiscriminate accusations in respect of the

[46] RGASPI, 85/28/8, 207–8. For the published version see Stalin, *Sochineniia*, xiii. 79–80.
[47] *Protsess kontrrevoliutsionnoi organizatsii men'shevikov.*

mass of engineers in general'.[48] From the beginning of the following year party leaders, with Ordzhonikidze in the forefront, began to argue more explicitly that the campaign against the specialists had to be moderated. In February 1931 Ordzhonikidze called on the party to distinguish between hostile and loyal specialists and to establish good relations with the latter.[49]

However, the most explicit announcement that the bourgeois specialists were being rehabilitated was made at the conference of managers in June 1931 by Ordzhonikidze and by Stalin in his 'six conditions' speech. Interestingly, though, Stalin's and Ordzhonikidze's justifications for the new policy were slightly, but significantly, different. Both argued that the majority of the specialists now supported Soviet power, but Stalin implied that the change in class forces had been less fundamental than Ordzhonikidze suggested. Ordzhonikidze spoke first and denounced the unjust imprisonment of specialists and their treatment as second-class people, urging that they be treated as citizens with full rights. Echoing Rykov's sentiments of 1928, he argued that now a new group of young engineers had emerged who were 'our people, our intelligentsia'; it was unacceptable to continue to discriminate against engineers when they were sons of workers. A new intelligentsia was being created, as was essential because 'each ruling class has its own intelligentsia which it cares for and looks after'. It was no longer acceptable for non-experts, such as the secret police, to take over the role of specialists, and for the militiaman to become 'master of the enterprise'.[50]

Stalin took up many of the themes developed by Ordzhonikidze, but the emphasis of his speech was different. He agreed that the persecution of the specialists was unacceptable, but he stressed that it had been justified in the past. While he agreed with Ordzhonikidze that the proletariat, like every ruling class, had to have its own intelligentsia, he did not suggest that it had already emerged.[51] The attitude of the intelligentsia had changed, he implied, not because it

---

[48] RGASPI, 17/162/9, 81–2 (22 November 1930). Khlevniuk also notes that Stalin supported Ordzhonikidze in his defence of a Magnitogorsk engineer against the local party at the end of November. See O. V. Khlevniuk, *Politbiuro*, 71.

[49] G. K. Ordzhonikidze, *Stat'i i rechi, 1926–1937 gg.* (Moscow 1957), ii. 284–5, 287–9.

[50] RGASPI, 85/28/7, 135–6.

[51] RGASPI, 85/28/8, 198–9.

had yet been fundamentally transformed but because circumstances were different. In the years 1927–9 'half of the intelligentsia' had vacillated, and it was 'not surprising' that they should have done so when they thought that collective and state farms were failing, and when they believed that foreign intervention would expel the Bolsheviks. Now the situation had changed: the threat of foreign intervention had decreased and the agrarian situation had improved. This had led to a 'reorientation of the technical intelligentsia', and most of them had forsaken wrecking.[52] While Stalin declared that this change was 'not accidental' but was a 'significant turning point' (povorot), he still implied that the specialists were accepting necessity rather than turning to socialism with enthusiasm. He made this view even clearer in the published version of the speech, in which he declared that the old intelligentsia did not meet the defeat of capitalist classes with 'joy' and that 'very probably they still express sympathy with their defeated friends'.[53] He went on to insist that wreckers had not disappeared: 'wreckers exist and will continue to exist as long as we have classes and as long as capitalist encirclement exists'; while there were only few active wreckers, they would go deep underground 'for the time being'.[54]

Ordzhonikidze thus went further than Stalin in suggesting that the problem of the intelligentsia had been solved. He also implied that the 'technical' had to be separated from questions of class and politics. He condemned the use of 'intimidation' and judicial repression of engineers; in this unpleasant atmosphere 'healthy criticism, criticism of scientific thought is paralysed, technical thought does not develop'.[55] Managers had to be able to take 'risk' in production, without the threat of persecution, because people learned by their mistakes.[56]

On practical matters, however, Stalin and Ordzhonikidze were in broad agreement. The specialists were to be protected from persecution by the party and the OGPU, and accidents and mistakes were not to be treated, in general, as wrecking. The Politburo issued a directive on 10 July 1931 that was particularly forthright in its

[52] RGASPI, 85/28/8, 189–90. See also Stalin's speech at a meeting on the coal industry, 13 May 1931, RGASPI, 558/11/1115, 7.
[53] Stalin, Sochineniia, xiii. 70–1.
[54] Stalin, Sochineniia, xiii. 72. For a similar sentiment in the original speech, see RGASPI, 85/28/8, 188.
[55] RGASPI, 17/165/18, 11.   [56] RGASPI, 17/165/18, 16.

attempts to establish good conditions for specialists and discourage charges of wrecking. According to the resolution, the 'authority' of engineering and technical personnel was to be 'strengthened', some of them were to be appointed to managerial posts and their living conditions were to be improved. They were to be allowed to take risks in production, and their mistakes were to be treated as accidents rather than sabotage, and investigated by management rather than the OGPU. The OGPU was to be prevented from interfering in production and investigating accidents without permission of the management; its official representatives in enterprises were also expelled.[57]

As will be seen, Stalin continued to regard class origin and the political outlook of managers and specialists as an important criterion in judging their performance, and he never claimed that *tekhnika* could be separated from *politika*. Campaigns were intermittently launched against specialists and managers in industry: in 1933–4 officials in industry who produced defective goods were persecuted; and in the spring of 1933 two important trials of highly placed alleged saboteurs were staged.[58] However, even at the time of these show trials the leadership was reluctant to mount a more general campaign. The trial of British engineers working for Metro-Vickers and their Soviet associates in April was given a great deal of attention in the press, but in his speech as public prosecutor Vyshinskii made it clear that this was not to lead to a general attack on specialists. Indeed, he explicitly stated that 'it would be a great mistake ... to assume that the trial of these wreckers of power stations is evidence of the same thing that the Shakhty trial evidenced—that at the present time we have to deal with widespread wrecking among the technical intelligentsia.'[59]

The party turns its 'face to production'

The turn towards *tekhnika* naturally had implications for the organization that had been the main proponent of *politika* during the

---

[57] WKP, 162, 63. For decrees calling for the use of imprisoned specialists in economic work, see RGASPI, 17/162/10, 131 (5 August 1931); RGASPI, 17/162/11, 1 (15 September 1931).

[58] For these campaigns see Solomon, *Soviet Criminal Justice*, 145–6.

[59] *Wrecking Activities at Power Stations in the Soviet Union* (Moscow, 1933), 600.

Great Break: the party. As in the past, the technicist approach to politics demanded that the party involve itself in 'economic work' and move closer to the state; the party was now not to engage in the sort of mobilizations and political campaigning that might undermine state organizations.[60]

The first sign of significant changes in the party's role came with Kaganovich's reform of the party organization of January 1930. The party apparatus was reorganized into a number of more specialized departments, according to the so-called 'functional principle'.[61] Within the departments, even more specialized 'sectors' were created. Kaganovich justified these reforms as a way of transforming the party from an institution that was expert at mobilization for political and military campaigns, to one suited to the performance of 'economic tasks'.[62] The new departments would, he claimed, have more expertise in the selection and preparation of economic cadres in particular spheres of the economy, and this attention to specialist officials was vital in current circumstances. As Kaganovich explained, 'the appointment of . . . one director is much more important than the mobilization of 3–5 thousand people. We have to say this openly.'[63] Indeed, in this period all party organizations became increasingly involved in the details of economic management, and once the Stalinists had removed Rykov from Sovnarkom at the end of 1930, a great deal of decision-making on economic affairs was vested in the Politburo.[64] At the seventeenth party congress, in 1934, Kaganovich announced yet another reform of the

[60] For a discussion of these changes in Moscow, see C. Merridale, *Moscow Politics*, 114–16.

[61] RGASPI, 17/113/818, 6–7. For earlier drafts of the Central Committee decree, see RGASPI, 81/3/75, 12–59. For an analysis of this reform see L. A. Maleiko, 'Iz istorii razvitiia apparata partiinykh organov', *VI KPSS*, 2 (1976), 114–15.

[62] RGASPI, 81/3/54, 21–2 (18 January 1930); L. M. Kaganovich, *Ocherednye zadachi partraboty i reorganizatsiia partapparata* (Moscow–Leningrad, 1930), 45–7. A. A. Andreev, speaking in 1931 also declared that the Central Committee was intervening in 'economic work', see RGASPI, 17/2/466, 133.

[63] RGASPI, 81/3/54, 32 (18 January 1930).

[64] For the role of the Politburo in economic affairs, see Khlevniuk, *Politbiuro*, 63 ff. For the 'institution of party organizers', created in 1933 to allow the Central Committee to remodel management in particular sectors of the economy, see *Direktivy KPSS i sovetskogo pravitel'stva po khoziaistvennym voprosam: sbornik dokumentov* (Moscow 1957), ii. 378. See also *Istoriia Kommunisticheskoi Partii Sovetskogo Soiuza* (Moscow, 1971), Vol. iv. Part ii. 244–6; R. W. Davies, *Crisis and Progress*, 381–4. R. W. Davies, discussing these reforms, notes the significance of such close party involvement in industrial decision-making.

party apparatus to bring it even closer to industry and to encourage it to perform 'economic work'. 'Functional' departments were replaced by 'production-branch' departments, designed to shadow economic organizations. While these departments were to conduct agitation, propaganda, and other 'political' work, they were to do so only within a particular branch of industry, and this institutional arrangement inevitably strengthened the economic apparatus. Separate departments of culture and propaganda (Kul'tprop) were not to operate at lower levels of the party apparatus; in district and city party committees, departments were replaced by individual 'instructors' who were to be attached to a particular group of primary party organizations in factories, thus allowing the committees to come 'closer to production tasks'.[65]

Like technicist proposals for party reform in the past, the demand that the party become more involved in the economy was not supposed to breach 'one-man management' or undermine the power of managers;[66] it was expected that the opposite would happen. Party bodies were being urged to support economic management not to challenge it, a relationship between party and management that was strikingly similar to that previously denounced as 'collusion'. The Politburo and Central Committee therefore issued a series of instructions preventing party organizations from undermining management. On 10 July 1931, for instance, the Politburo sent a secret resolution to party organizations, forbidding them 'to cancel, correct or delay the operational instructions of managements of factories'.[67]

The re-establishment of the political departments suggests even more striking parallels with Lenin's technicist solution to party–state relations during the civil war period. Yet again, in particular areas where the economy was in crisis, the leadership decided to replace the party organization with a highly disciplinarian institution directly controlled from the centre. They were first introduced in the countryside to deal with the grain crisis: in December 1932

---

[65] XVII s"ezd VKP(b), 672, 561; L. M. Kaganovich, O vnutrennoi rabote i otdelakh rukovodiashchikh partiinykh organov. Rech' na soveshchanii zaveduiushchikh otdelami rukovodiashchikh partiinykh organov, 3 sent. 1934 g. (Moscow, 1934), 8; Maleiko, 'Iz istorii', 118–19; Spravochnik partiinogo rabotnika, vyp. 9 (Moscow, 1935), 113.

[66] See, for instance, RGASPI, 77/1/325, 21–2 (Zhdanov) (27 April 1931).

[67] WKP, 162, 63. See also M. Fainsod, Smolensk under Soviet Rule (London, 1989), 318–20; R. W. Davies, Crisis and Progress, 81–4.

it was announced that Machine-Tractor Stations were to be given political departments, and they were extended to the railways in March 1933.[68] As before, they were often highly unpopular with local party organizations.

This new role for the party naturally demanded that it change its style of work and abandon its previous emphasis on 'democratic' agitation and mobilization. Party committees were now to become more involved in the solution of practical problems of production. As Pavel Postyshev, a secretary of the Central Committee put it, the work of all party, trade union, co-operative, and other social organizations in the enterprise was to be subordinated to the 'task of fulfilling and over-fulfilling the plan'.[69] The rank-and-file communist was now expected to become a productive worker rather than a political agitator, and officials were told to become effective administrators.[70] Kaganovich summed up the leadership's technicist view of the party when discussing the 1934 reforms:

It is impossible to compare the party worker with that of the past. If previously the party worker was predominantly an agitator, now he knows production well, he has gone through the rich school of economic activity, his horizons have become wider, he has become a state official.[71]

Kaganovich was subordinating the party to the state and transforming the party into a hierarchical, disciplined, quasi-economic organization.

Narrative and the return to tekhnika

By the beginning of 1933, therefore, the leadership had adopted many of the central elements of the technicist approach to politics:

---

[68] R. W. Davies, *Crisis and Progress*, 244, 389–90; S. Fitzpatrick, *Stalin's Peasants*, 76–8. For political departments on the railways, and the unreliability of party organizations, see RGASPI, 81/3/45, 2. For Stalin's justification for the introduction of political departments in the countryside, see RGASPI, 558/11/1117, 32–5 (2 May 1933).

[69] *SADG*, 8–9 (1931), 3 (P. P. Postyshev). Postyshev's views were developed by propagandists. See *PS*, 22 (1930), 33.

[70] *P*, 21 January 1930. See also *PS*, 7 (1931), 5; D. Gurevich, *Za vedushchuiu rol' kommunista na proizvodstve* (Moscow–Samara, 1932). For the debate over whether the party member was to be a 'model producer' or a 'part-time administrator', see C. Merridale, *Moscow Politics*, 178–80.

[71] L. M. Kaganovich, *O vnutrennoi rabote*, 10.

attitudes to class, enemies, leadership style and behaviour, *tekhnika* and *politika*, the party's role, and planning had all changed. As has been seen, one of the most effective media through which the leadership could promote this message was the political novel, as novels could not only explain the changes in policy but present the form of behaviour and leadership style which was now acceptable. Valentin Kataev's work *Time, Forward!*, published in 1932, was particularly explicit in presenting the new ideas and can almost be seen as a fictionalized version of Stalin's 'six conditions' speech, to which the novel made direct reference.[72] The novel is the story of the struggle for the achievement of a world record in mixing concrete during the construction of the huge metallurgical combine of Magnitogorsk, and its hero is an engineer, Margulies. Yet while the subject-matter is very similar to that of *Driving Axle*, published only a year before, the portrayal of the stock characters and the nature of the ideas they were designed to represent was very different.[73] Unlike *Driving Axle*, which showed that plans would be fulfilled if *politika* was understood, Kataev presented a different balance between *tekhnika* and *politika*: his work was designed to show how *tekhnika* could be given primacy and, at the same time, high plan targets fulfilled and records achieved.

Margulies, like many socialist realist heroes, has the right instincts but is initially flawed, and has to go through a process of education before he achieves heroic status. However, unlike Platov, the hero of *Driving Axle*, his fault is excessive caution rather than excessive recklessness. Although there is a great deal of pressure, particularly from the manager of the sector, Korneev, for the brigade to beat the record recently set in Khar'kov, Margulies resists it because he is concerned with 'facts' and practicality rather than will. In response to Korneev's question 'You have no faith?', he replies: 'I am not sure, but that does not mean I have no faith... First I'll make sure, then I'll have faith.'[74] However, he realizes that he must at the same time avoid 'infection' with the disease of doubt in the plan: the very idea of opposition to setting records rouses an

---

[72] V. Kataev, 'Vremia, Vpered!', in Kataev, *Sobranie sochinenii* (Moscow, 1956), 205–6. For Kataev's use of the style of Stalin's speech, see R. Robin, *Socialist Realism*, 278–9. See S. Hanson, *Time and Revolution*, 155–62 for a different view of this novel.

[73] For a discussion of *Driving Axle*, see pp. 230–5.

[74] V. Kataev, 'Vremia, Vpered!', 252.

instinctive 'disgust' in him, even though 'in essence it was absolutely correct':

It demanded rejection, unmasking [*razoblachenie*]. There was a tiny bit of falsehood in it, the size of a pin-head or a malaria germ. It infected one subtly, penetrated into the brain, enfeebled one like an attack of malaria . . . Margulies detested it and feared it like the plague.[75]

He therefore tries to discover whether it is possible, scientifically, to break the record and consults the bourgeois specialist Professor Smolenskii, who lives in Moscow. Once he has been assured by the expert, and by an article in an industrial newspaper, that such a feat is practicable, Margulies reorganizes production to exploit the machinery more effectively. He also harnesses the enthusiasm of his workers, although not much is said about how he did this, and there is little emphasis on 'criticism' and 'democracy'. The record is finally achieved because the hero, while refusing to accept that existing scientific rules should not be questioned, ultimately adheres to the findings of science.

Unlike the bourgeois specialist criminals of *Driving Axle*, Margulies's enemies are party members. The main villain is the engineer Nalbandov, who criticizes any attempt to set a new record and has an 'academic' attitude towards scientific laws, believing in their 'sacredness and immutability'.[76] However, he is not a bourgeois specialist but a party member who is ready to be corrupted by the bourgeoisie. He has an 'abrupt, unceremonious' manner, but this is fake proletarianism, and in reality he has sympathy with a group of anti-Soviet foreign visitors, presenting himself to them as somebody with 'the remarkable, inspiring, though rather coarse, personality of a Bolshevik behind which was hidden a brilliant European education and refined culture'.[77] He also uses 'party' methods for careerist ends and plots to denounce Margulies, cynically weighing up whether it would be more effective to accuse him of rightist or of leftist opportunism.[78] It is not difficult to see in Nalbandov the 'Trotskyist' of Stalinist discourse, the party member who pretends to be a proletarian on the left, even though he actually has bourgeois attitudes. While the evil specialist is a proletarian, the bourgeois specialists in the novel are generally positive figures.

[75] Ibid., 254.   [76] Ibid., 414.   [77] Ibid., 338.
[78] V. Kataev, *Time Forward!*, trans. by C. Malamuth (New York, 1933), 314.

Professor Smolenskii, like Turchaninov in *Driving Axle*, likes classical music and the piano, but he is not condemned for his tastes.[79]

Margulies also has opponents on the 'left': the correspondent of
the regional newspaper, Semechkin, who embodies the empty agitational culture of the past, is presented as a particularly disagreeable
figure. He is a utopian who 'sought deeds of fame and of sweeping
dimensions'. He does not understand practical constraints and he
wishes 'to set everything in the world right', but the world 'did not
give in'. While he is 'clever', he is puritanical, 'poisonous, disap-
proving', and 'hostile to the world', and he criticizes Margulies
without any justification.[80] In contrast to Semechkin, who represents all that is bad in party-political work, the party secretary,
Filonov, is a model of correct leadership style. He is constantly
active and is approachable, and his office is always full of people.[81]
Most importantly, he is involved in the detail of factory life and in
'economic work', issuing orders on the supply of boots and canvas
baskets. Semechkin naturally regards this activity as trivial, and is
'profoundly disgusted and bored by all of this'. While Semechkin
criticizes the passivity of worker opinion and the suppression of
criticism in the press, Filonov tries to persuade him to adopt a more
practical approach. He tells him not to pursue the issue of the
record, but to publish 'factual material' on concrete subjects.[82] For
Filonov and Kataev, the practicalities of production were to be more
important than *politika*.

This also applied to the issue of 'enemies' and 'wrecking'. The
danger of sabotage is not central to the novel. There is an accident in
the novel, when the water to the concrete mixer is cut off and the
record is threatened, but this is blamed on a mistake made by
Semechkin, not on bourgeois wrecking.[83] Indeed, in one episode,
the foreman, Mosia, considers accusing Korneev of political deviation, but he realizes that accusations of political deviation are
inappropriate:

A little more and he would accuse Korneev of being a 'right opportunist in
practice'. But no! This manner of expression was not suitable for conversation

---

[79] V. Kataev, 'Vremia Vpered!', 296.

[80] Ibid., 300, 303.

[81] For similar views of the ideal party secretary in the 1920s, see D. P. Koenker,
'Factory Tales. Narratives of Industrial Relations in the Transition to NEP', *RR*, 55
(1996), 384–411.

[82] Ibid., 302–3.   [83] Ibid., 461–8.

between a good foreman and a good superintendent. It must be done some other way.[84]

Culture and tekhnika

The leadership's technicist attitude towards the technical intelligentsia was closely associated with its policy towards the cultural intelligentsia. Just as technical specialists were to be rehabilitated in the interests of economic construction, so the old cultural intelligentsia was to be protected from the 'proletarian' cultural movements and to be included in socialist society. These new policies were first announced in the literary sphere. In April 1932 the Politburo declared that the RAPP and other proletarian literary organizations were to be abolished and a new official 'Union of Soviet Writers' established. Similar measures were applied to other forms of culture.[85] *Pravda*'s criticism of the RAPP followed the message of Stalin's 'six conditions' speech. The RAPP, it declared, was guilty of ' "leftist" vulgarization', persecuting bourgeois fellow-travellers rather than winning them over.[86] Similarly, at a meeting between Stalin and writers in October 1932, Stalin explained that while the RAPP had had a role in the past, it had now outlived its usefulness because 'it was cut off from non-party writers', precisely the people who 'know life and are able to represent it'. 'Proletarian' policies had to be replaced by a serious attempt to attract non-party cultural figures to the regime.[87] Once established, the Writers' Union made every effort to incorporate previously disgraced 'fellow-travellers'; from August 1933, Maksim Gorky, who was committed to including some non-proletarian writers in the literary establishment, became president of its organizing committee.[88]

As with the rehabilitation of the technical intelligentsia, the change in policy was generally justified as part of a more general restoration of order after the chaos of the proletarian period in

---

[84] Ibid., 218.

[85] Published in *P*, 24 April 1932.

[86] *P*, 9 May 1932.

[87] RGASPI, 558/11/1116, 21 (speech to communist writers, 20 October 1932); RGASPI, 558/11/1116, 30 (speech to writers, 26 October 1932).

[88] Gorky could be outspoken on this subject, and Zhdanov criticized him for saying that 'communists have no authority among writers'. Zhdanov to Stalin, 28 August 1934, RGASPI, 77/3/112, 7–8.

culture. In 1932 Stalin strongly criticized the RAPP for promoting 'groupism' (*gruppirovshchina*), and for excessive 'intolerance' towards non-party writers.[89] The Stalinists' attempt to impose order and unity was to be applied to all other areas of cultural activity, as was made clear following the publication of Stalin's letter attacking the historical journal *Proletarian Revolution* in October 1931. The letter was a criticism of allegedly 'Trotskyist' interpretations of Bolshevik history and was subsequently applied to all areas of culture and theory, leading to several investigations into alleged Trotskyism in culture.[90] There was, of course, a risk that the letter would be interpreted as a signal for another period of politically inspired disruption and conflict, but the leadership insisted that this was not to be the case and Postyshev declared that the letter was not designed to lead to the use of 'administrative methods' against individuals.[91] Stalin evidently hoped that his letter, and the creation of party-controlled cultural unions, would enhance central control over cultural and ideological activity, while limiting the power of the proletarian intellectuals.

There are also signs that the leadership was moving towards a technicist position on its attitude towards class and culture more generally, and away from a commitment to a special 'proletarian' or socialist culture, although its views on this issue was more ambivalent. The slogan '*tekhnika* decides everything' was applied to culture as well as the economy, and it was implied by some that just as there was a single science which applied in both the bourgeois and the socialist world, so there were aspects of culture which Soviet intellectuals had to learn from the bourgeois past. If culture was to transform the population's mentality, it had to have artistic merit and be informed by artistic *tekhnika*, learned from the great masters of the past. Stalin now insisted that the 'proletarian' cultural movements, in their attempts to create a new, highly politicized culture, had neglected artistic quality and were producing a crude propagandistic art that had little popular appeal. He explained his instrumental attitude towards culture and his defence of traditional

---

[89] RGASPI, 558/11/1116, 21, 26.
[90] Stalin, *Sochineniia*, xiii. 100. For the offending article, see A. Slutskii, 'Bol'sheviki o germanskoi s.-d. v period ee predvoennogo krizisa', *PR*, 6 (1930), 37–73. See also J. Barber, 'Stalin's "Letter to the Editors of *Proletarskaia Revoliutsiia*" ', *SS*, 28 (1976), 21–41.
[91] P. P. Postyshev, *Za marksistko–leninskoe vospitanie*, 67.

methods of artistic expression in a speech to communist writers given in Gorky's house in October 1932. He told writers that they had to produce art for the people, and writers should therefore write plays, rather than books because that was what workers wanted to watch after a long day's work. And these plays had to be 'artistically done', whereas RAPP had promoted a 'vulgar' understanding of dialectics, and had refused to learn from the classics.[92] Stalin's emphasis on artistic quality became a central theme among the new literary establishment in this period, and its leader, Gorky, championed a partial return to a more traditional aesthetic that owed much to nineteenth-century realism.[93] Bukharin, in a particularly trenchant speech at the Congress of Writers, directly linked writers' need to master 'quality' with the 'mastery of *tekhnika*'.[94]

As will be seen, Stalin did not go so far as to argue that art or literature should be divorced from politics, or deny that it had anything to do with class. He demanded that literature transform the attitudes of the masses, and realism was to be combined with a 'revolutionary Romanticism' championed by Gorky. The doctrine of socialist realism, which declared that writers were to present 'reality in its revolutionary development', attempted to synthesize the mobilizational and transformative elements of proletarian literature with the aesthetic views and technical skills of the bourgeois 'fellow-traveller' writers.[95] But Stalin did make it clear that in the past an emphasis on arid ideology had undermined culture's effectiveness as propaganda. Replying to the question whether a poet needed to be a dialectician and incorporate the Marxist worldview into art, Stalin replied:

Of course he can. And it is good if he will be a dialectical materialist. But I want to say that he will then not want to write poetry (*General laughter*). I'm joking, of course, but, speaking seriously, you mustn't stuff an artist's head with abstract theses. He must know the theories of Marx and Lenin. But he must also know life. An artist must above all portray life truthfully.[96]

---

[92] RGASPI, 558/11/1116, 24, 20 (speech to communist writers, 20 October 1932).

[93] P, 28 January 1934 (Gorky); Pervyi vsesoiuznyi s"ezd sovetskikh pisatelei (Moscow, 1935), 13 (Gorky).

[94] Vsesoiuznyi s"ezd sovetskikh pisatelei, *Problems of Soviet Literature. Reports and Speeches at the First Writers' Congress* (London, 1935), 185–6 (Bukharin).

[95] For this view of socialist realism, see R. Robin, *Socialist Realism*, 214–15.

[96] RGASPI, 558/11/1116, 33 (speech to writers, 26 October 1932).

Some, however, did use the slogan of *tekhnika* to argue for a degree of depoliticization of science and culture, and Bukharin defended an almost liberal view of culture, as a sphere that not only had to be insulated from politics, but that would permit a limited diversity of views. Speaking on poetry at the Congress of Soviet Writers of 1934, he strongly criticized the RAPPists for merely translating the slogans of the day into rhyme. If writers were to contribute to the building of socialism they had to be allowed to discuss the diversity of Soviet reality:

The entire variety of life can and should serve as the material for poetic creation. Unity does not mean that we must all sing the same song at the same time—now about sugar beets, now about the 'living man' [a favourite theme of the RAPPists], now about the class struggle in the countryside, now about a Party membership card. Unity does not mean the presentation of the same ideal types and the same 'villains', nor the abolition—on paper—of all contradictions and evils. Unity consists in a single *aspect*—that of building socialism. All the richness of life, all tragedies and conflicts, vacillations and defeats, the conflict of tendencies—all this must be the material for poetic creation.[97]

Bukharin, of course, was not defending pluralism. His views of culture were similar to his ideas on politics and agriculture in the 1920s. He was arguing, optimistically, that if the party relaxed its controls over bourgeois groups, whether the intelligentsia or the peasantry, they would inevitably move towards socialism. A diverse, relaxed socialist culture would allow the human personality to 'grow' in a collectivist rather than an individualist direction.[98]

'Neo-NEP', markets, and the peasantry

The tension between liberalism and technicism is even more obvious in the area of economic policy. The leadership's new emphasis on the need to fulfil plans within the constraints of existing resources encouraged it to move away from a revivalist faith in mobilization towards a technicist emphasis on order and discipline. But it soon realized that money and market incentives had to supplement central decrees if the state was to impose discipline effectively, and there was increasing pressure for a more liberal technicist approach

---

[97] *Problems of Soviet Literature*, 246–7.   [98] Ibid., 254–5.

to economic policy. It was gradually accepted that only if costs were measured and mechanisms established to discipline the inefficient could productivity be raised. As Stetskii, one of the party Central Committee's leading propagandists, explained, 'cost accounting' (*khozraschet*) and money were a means of 'establishing strong socialist economic discipline and order'. Although he was apologetic about the use of money, he declared that it had to be tolerated because 'nobody has yet invented another instrument for calculating, for measuring what is called value...'.[99] Money and material incentives were also useful in disciplining and motivating workers, and from 1932 the leadership gradually replaced rationing with what it called 'Soviet trade', increasing the range of goods workers could buy.[100]

The leadership made significant attempts to introduce market principles in the area of finance at the beginning of 1931. Responding to the disasters caused by the 1930 credit reform, a new credit system was gradually introduced to allow the State Bank to limit the credit available to enterprises, and to establish 'cash plans', which would, it was hoped, rationalize production and cut costs.[101] Stalin endorsed these changes,[102] but Ordzhonikidze seems to have been a particularly strong supporter of financial incentives in this period, as R. W. Davies, the historian of these debates, has shown.[103] He evidently saw how useful market mechanisms could be in disciplining the enterprises under his control: those who were inefficient could be punished financially. In February 1931, he proposed that in addition to the system of centralized distribution of production, factories should establish contracts between each other; if the supplier of materials or goods failed to meet the contract it would not be paid.[104] Ordzhonikidze's plans came to nothing, and, more generally, attempts to impose financial discipline on enterprises failed, largely because the system remained one in which the fulfilment of the plan, not financial targets, were pre-eminent. There was also strong opposition to market-oriented reforms. In 1932 various

[99] *XVII konferentsiia*, 193.
[100] Ibid., 279.
[101] R. W. Davies, *Crisis and Progress*, 49–52.
[102] Stalin, *Sochineniia*, xiii. 75.
[103] R. W. Davies, 'The Socialist Market: A Debate in Soviet Industry, 1932–33', *SR*, 42 (1984), 201–23.
[104] Ordzhonikidze, *Stat'i i rechi*, ii. 257–83. For a full discussion of these proposals, see R. W. Davies, *Crisis and Progress*, 11–14; 49–52.

articles in *Za Industrializatsiiu*, the Narkomtiazhprom newspaper, argued that shortages and supply problems could only be solved if the central allocation of industrial goods to various branches of industry was replaced with a market in goods priced realistically.[105] Ordzhonikidze himself seems to have endorsed some of these ideas in an ill-prepared and unsuccessful experiment to replace central-ized allocation of iron and steel equipment with direct contracts between suppliers and consumers. However, these proposals were clearly going too far in a liberal direction for the Politburo. The journalists were condemned as 'rightist' and Ordzhonikidze was embarrassed.[106] Even so, in 1934–5 Narkomtiazhprom was yet again in the forefront of quasi-market reforms which gave greater powers over finance to the director of enterprises. In some factories they allowed the use of financial incentives to reward or punish individual brigades within the enterprise.[107]

The leadership sanctioned a particularly marked retreat towards the market in agriculture, initially, it seems, because it was worried about working-class discontent. High grain quotas and repression had caused chaos in the countryside and food shortages in towns. Workers had reacted by protesting and organizing strikes, most notably in the industrial town of Ivanovo-Voznesensk.[108] Possibly in response, the leadership decided to make concessions to the peasantry by increasing the use of economic incentives. In May and June 1932 quotas were reduced, and collective farmers and individual peasants were permitted to sell produce, above the quota delivered to the state, at high 'commercial' prices.[109] Party leaders were quick to reject allegations that these policies amounted to a 'neo-NEP'. But in giving peasants market incentives to produce grain the leadership was endorsing policies which had something in common with the NEP.[110]

---

[105] See, particularly, *ZI*, 23 June 1932.

[106] For these debates, see R. W. Davies, 'The Socialist Market', 201–23; R. W. Davies, *Crisis and Progress*, 225–8, 268–30, 343–7.

[107] See F. Benvenuti, 'A Stalinist Victim of Stalinism. "Sergo" Ordzhonikidze', in J. Cooper, M. Perrie, and E. A. Rees (eds.), *Soviet History, 1917–1953* (Basingstoke, 1995), 149–52. For the system of 'machine-brigade *khozraschet*' in the Makeevka metallurgical works, see O. Khlevniuk, 'Heavy Industry', in E. A. Rees (ed.), *Decision-Making in the Stalinist Command Economy, 1933–37* (Basingstoke, 1997), 111.

[108] For this unrest, see R. W. Davies, *Crisis and Progress*, 188–9; O. V. Khlevniuk, '30-e gody. Krizisy, reformy, nasilie', *Svobodnaia mysl'*, 17 (1991), 76–8.

[109] R. W. Davies, *Crisis and Progress*, 209–18.

[110] For denunciations of the concept of 'neo-NEP', see *P*, 6 August 1932 (Kaganovich).

Of course, the market reforms of 1932 were not as fundamental as those of the NEP. It remained illegal for private traders to act as intermediaries between collective farms and urban purchasers.[111] Also, there seems to have been some resistance within the leadership to a real retreat to the market.[112] Stalin seems to have been one of the more sceptical, and worried that 'speculators' would exploit the market;[113] he was reluctant to abandon the view that success in agriculture depended on the attitudes and political loyalty of the peasants, rather than on the effectiveness of material incentives. In June 1932, during the high point of agrarian liberalization, he accepted the principle of trade at commercial prices, but was concerned that freer prices would raise the cost of food in towns.[114] By the end of July, when it was clear that the state's grain procurements were not high enough and the reforms had not worked, Stalin seems to have altered his position and he criticized the market-oriented policies.[115] In a letter to Kaganovich and Molotov of 20 July, he used typically revivalist language, blaming agrarian problems on the evil actions of class enemies in the countryside rather than on an inadequate incentive structure. He alleged that former kulaks and other 'anti-social elements' were organizing the mass theft of 'co-operative and collective farm property', by which he meant grain and other foodstuffs, and called for stiffer punishments.[116] Stalin's deliberations resulted in the notorious decree on the 'strengthening of social (socialist) property', which imposed the death penalty for theft of collective farm property.[117] Stalin also criticized the recent legislation on the liberalization of collective farm trade. The decree, he claimed, 'to a significant degree' had 'revived kulak elements and speculators-resellers'. His solution was to bring in the secret police to oversee bazaars and markets.[118]

---

[111] For this distinction between NEP policies and current policies, see *P*, 3 June 1932 (Kalinin).
[112] For differences within the leadership, see R. W. Davies, *Crisis and Progress*, 213–17.
[113] See O. V. Khlevniuk, R. W. Davies, L. P. Kosheleva, E. A. Rees, and L. A. Rogovaia (eds.), *Stalin i Kaganovich. Perepiska 1931–1936 gg.* (Moscow, 2001), 131.
[114] Stalin to Kaganovich and Molotov, 26 June 1932, RGASPI, 81/3/99, 84–5.
[115] For the failure of 'neo-NEP' policies, see R. W. Davies, *Crisis and Progress*, 270–1.
[116] Stalin to Kaganovich and Molotov, 20 July 1932, RGASPI, 81/3/99, 107–9.
[117] RGASPI, 17/3/895, 14 (Politburo session of 8 August). For Stalin's thinking on the law, see Stalin to Kaganovich, 11 August 1932, RGASPI, 81/3/99, 144.
[118] Stalin to Kaganovich and Molotov, 20 July 1932, RGASPI, 81/3/99, 110–12.

Between the autumn of 1932 and the spring of 1933, the leadership launched one of the most savage repressions of the peasantry yet. Stalin and his allies justified the violence in crude class terms. They presented it as a way of protecting workers' interests against allegedly rapacious peasants, and more generally as a campaign against those who, influenced by kulaks, were sabotaging Soviet power by refusing to give up their grain. Kaganovich, for instance, declared that the leadership, in making concessions to the peasants during the summer of 1932, had 'insulted' the towns.[119] Similarly, in May 1933, in a letter to Mikhail Sholokhov, Stalin claimed that peasants had engaged in a 'go slow (sabotage!) and were willing to leave the workers and the Red Army without bread'; this amounted to a ' "silent" war against Soviet power', a 'war by starvation'.[120] Stalin developed this interpretation of peasant behaviour most fully at the January 1933 plenum. Although, he declared, collective farms were a socialist form of agriculture, they could include 'well-camouflaged anti-Soviet elements, organizing wrecking and sabotage there'.[121] Even so, Stalin's message was contradictory, and he did recognize the need for market incentives. He admitted that it was not only peasants' evil will that was responsible for shortages. Officials, he declared, had failed to use market mechanisms effectively and peasants were therefore withholding grain to sell on the market later, when prices were higher. Such behaviour was not sabotage but 'the most simple and most natural logic'.[122]

It was this latter, economic, interpretation of agrarian problems which was ultimately to win out, particularly as the repressive policy of the spring of 1933 led to famine and failed to solve the problems of food supply. In May the 'class struggle' against the kulaks was scaled down. In a decree of 8 May, Stalin and Molotov criticized local authorities and the OGPU for making groundless arrests and ordered that fewer peasants be imprisoned.[123] Moves were also made to rehabilitate many peasants condemned under the

[119] *ZI*, 12 October 1932.
[120] Stalin to Sholokhov, 6 May 1933, RGASPI, 558/1/3459, 4–5.
[121] Stalin, *Sochineniia*, xii. 228–9.
[122] Ibid., 218–20.
[123] RGASPI, 17/3/922, 50–5. For a discussion of the changes in policy in this period, see J. A. Getty, ' "Excesses are not permitted". Mass Terror and Stalinist Governance in the Late 1930s', *RR*, 61 (2002), 118–21.

harsh laws of 1929–33.[124] Repressions were not abandoned, and party leaders continued to allege that peasants were engaging in sabotage.[125] But there was no revival of violence in the countryside on the scale of 1932–3 until the period of the Terror. The leadership also increasingly sanctioned the use of market incentives within the collective farm, and Stalin launched a strong defence of them in February 1935. Contributing to a debate at the second congress of shock-worker-collective-farmers on the private plot within the collective farm, Stalin argued that concessions had to be made to the private interests of peasants if collective agriculture was to be productive.[126] Because the collective farms were not yet producing food in abundance, it had to be admitted 'frankly' and 'openly' that private agriculture within the collective had to be tolerated.[127] By 1935, then, Stalin was admitting that the peasant's desire to trade had to be accepted, albeit within the framework of collective agriculture. The peasant was not to be treated as an 'enemy' for displaying these 'bourgeois' attitudes. But Stalin's position was very different from many of the delegates, some of whom strongly objected to what they saw as a retreat from collectivist ideals.[128]

Attempts to introduce albeit limited market incentives may have benefited the peasantry to some extent, but it inevitably harmed poorer sections of the working class. From 1931 to 1932, the leadership began to move away from rationing to 'Soviet trade' in consumer goods, both in order to improve incentives and to reduce pressure on the state budget. By October 1934, the leadership had decided to abolish bread rationing, and other forms of rationing were abolished in the course of 1935.[129] Workers were now forced to pay higher prices. Although wages were raised to compensate the poorest, naturally many workers suffered.[130]

[124] See, for instance, the request of S. V. Kosior (the secretary of the Ukrainian party), subsequently acted on, that those working honestly in the collective farms be rehabilitated. S. V. Kosior to Stalin, 5 April 1934, in Sovetskoe rukovodstvo, 269.
[125] For 'hard-liners' within the Committee for Procurements during this period, see M. Lewin, The Making of the Soviet System, 162.
[126] For this debate see S. Fitzpatrick, Stalin's Peasants, 121–2.
[127] P, 13 March 1935.
[128] See S. Fitzpatrick, Stalin's Peasants, 120–2.
[129] KPSS v rezoiutsiiakh, vi. 182–6; Stalin to Kaganovich, 22 October 1934, RGASPI, 81/3/100, 84–5. See, in particular, O. V. Khlevniuk and R. W. Davies, 'The End of Rationing in the Soviet Union, 1934–1935', E–AS, 51 (1999), 557–609.
[130] For workers' responses, see S. Davies, 'Propaganda and Popular Opinion in Soviet Russia, 1934–1941', D.Phil. dissertation, University of Oxford, 1994, 169–77.

Stalin justified this acceptance of monetary incentives and the inequalities they produced theoretically, by arguing that money would only disappear under full communism. At the seventeenth party congress, he denounced those who engaged in 'leftist chattering' and called for the immediate transition to a moneyless economy and direct exchange. Only when the socialist stage of development had been completed would this be feasible.[131]

The leadership's increasing use of financial controls, combined with its realization that investment plans were overambitious, led to a less voluntaristic approach to planning. As Davies and Khlevniuk have shown, at times in 1931 and 1932 Stalin was prepared to accept less ambitious investment plans, but he still remained a reluctant moderate.[132] Meanwhile pressure for a more realistic approach came from Kuibyshev's Gosplan, while Ordzhonikidze, as was to be expected, fought for high allocations of investment while resisting high plan targets.[133] By the end of 1932, plans for 1933, for both investment and production, had been significantly reduced, and at the beginning of 1933 Stalin for the first time made a clear statement endorsing lower targets. He now effectively declared that the era of voluntaristic economic policy was over.[134] In answer to his rhetorical question 'can exactly the same policy of accelerating development to the utmost' as had been pursued during the first five-year plan be followed in the second?, he answered categorically 'no it cannot'. The regime had 'already achieved' the main objective of the first five-year plan, which was to place industry and agriculture on a 'new technical foundation' and to raise the defence capability to 'the proper level'. There was now no need 'to whip and spur on the country'. Lower rates of increase in industrial output were now justified. Whereas, according to Stalin, growth rates had reached 22 per cent annually under the first five-year plan, under the second five-year plan they were to be limited to 13–14 per cent.[135]

---

[131] Stalin, *Sochineniia*, xiii. 342–3.

[132] R. W. Davies and O. V. Khlevniuk, 'Gosplan', in E. A. Rees (ed.), *Decision-Making in the Stalinist Command Economy* (Basingstoke, 1997), 41.

[133] See R. W. Davies and O. V. Khelvniuk, 'Gosplan', 42 ff, 60.

[134] For the lower targets, see R. W. Davies, *Crisis and Progress*, 297–301.

[135] R. W. Davies and O. V. Khlevniuk, 'Gosplan', 45.

Technicism and the strengthening of the state

The leadership's new technicist approach towards economics, and the emergence of albeit underdeveloped liberal technicist policies, are also evident in the leadership's views of the role of the state. As has been seen, some revivalists had justified mass mobilization during the Great Break period by arguing that the time was ripe for the transition to the 'commune-state' and that the process of the ultimate withering away of the state and the abolition of law could begin. Stalin never endorsed this position, and indeed, he was hostile to it, but to some it seemed that it was compatible with his view of the 'struggle against bureaucratism'. With the new technicist emphasis on discipline and order, this rhetoric was outlawed and the leadership now declared that the state had to be strengthened.

Like all Bolshevik technicists, however, Stalin and his colleagues found it difficult to justify the strengthening of the state according to the Marxist historical scheme. The obvious way to do so was to present policy as a pragmatic 'retreat' from socialist promises and ideological ambition. Because class differences continued to exist and full equality was far off, it was argued, the state would have to continue to exist, regulating society by means of law. This was generally the position taken by the leadership at the seventeenth party conference, in January 1932. Molotov, speaking on the subject at some length, condemned those who argued that the state could be 'weakened'. During the first, lower phase of communism, which the Soviet Union had just embarked on, he explained, inequality would continue to exist, and 'bourgeois right', enforced by the state, would operate to maintain this inequality. Molotov added that the state would have to become stronger while bourgeois elements remained within the country, while a threat was posed from without and while the huge 'organizational-educational tasks' of 'restructuring' the masses remained.[136]

However, a less-defensive technicist rhetoric became much more prevalent among Stalin and his group. This implied that the strong state, rather than being the product of retreat, was to be a long-term, almost permanent, body, and could be celebrated. This state was no longer an instrument of oppression because it shared the

[136] *XVII konferentsiia*, 145–6.

interests of an increasing majority of the population.[137] Naturally, such rhetoric was more attractive to the leadership, as it allowed it to present its authoritarian policies as steps towards the strengthening of the socialist Dictatorship of the Proletariat rather than as a retreat towards bourgeois forms of hierarchy. According to this technicist vision, therefore, the state and society were beginning to merge; but, contrary to the populist revivalist view, the disciplinarian methods used by the state were to predominate, not the egalitarian values of the working class; unlike the élitist revivalist approach, the system would be managed by a stable system of carrots and sticks, which would apply to everybody, irrespective of their class origin or their level of political consciousness; and contrary to bourgeois liberalism, this incentive structure would be organized by the state, not left to the market. The power of 'political' institutions, like the police and the party, over the commissariats was to be reduced, and the economy was to be co-ordinated not by centralized campaigns but by a set of 'legal' rules and material incentives. Revivalist methods of administration, which relied on attempts to mobilize some parts of the population while persecuting others, judging people according to their political consciousness and class origin, were to be replaced with a more legalistic approach. Citizens were merely required to be loyal to Soviet power, obey rules, and perform their duties well.

The leadership first launched its campaign for the observance of 'law' at the expense of *politika* in response to developments in the countryside: it realized that coercive methods and 'class struggle' against the peasantry were damaging agriculture. In June 1932, in its decree on 'revolutionary legality', it moved to protect the peasantry from persecution by officials, extending the protection afforded to bourgeois specialists to the petty bourgeoisie.[138] When the leadership decided once again to conciliate the peasantry, after the repressions of 1932–3, Stalin and Molotov revived their campaign for 'legality' and extended it to the economy as a whole.[139] In

---

[137] For this Stalinist concept of the state and law, see E. Huskey, 'A Framework for the Analysis of Soviet Law', *RR*, 50 (1991), 57.

[138] *P*, 27 June 1932; RGASPI, 17/3/890, 11; Stalin described the decree as 'not bad'. Stalin to Molotov, before 25 June 1932, *Pis'ma*, 243.

[139] WKP, 178, 135–6. For the central role of Vyshinskii in the promotion of 'socialist legality', see Solomon, *Soviet Criminal Justice under Stalin*, 156–82; for Vyshinskii's views, see A. Ia. Vyshinskii, *Revoliutsionnaia zakonnost' na sovremennom etape* (Moscow, 1932).

July 1934 the secret police was reorganized and attached to the state apparatus, as part of the Commissariat of Internal Affairs (NKVD), and it lost many of its judicial functions to a strengthened court and procuratorial system. In July 1935 the leadership decreed that the NKVD could only make arrests with the agreement of the Procuracy and of the relevant economic or party organization.[140]

The technicist rationale behind 'revolutionary legality' was expressed particularly clearly at a meeting of Central Committee and Procuracy officials in August 1934 attended by, among others, Kaganovich and Molotov. In his speech to the meeting, Molotov declared that the decision to reorganize the secret police and to strengthen law was a 'decision that defines the work of all of our organizations' and had an 'enormous political significance'.[141] He went on to challenge a series of revivalist assumptions. People had to be judged according to whether they observed the law, rather than according to their political outlook or class position. The main failure of the secret police, according to Molotov, was its tendency to judge all cases according to 'political instinct, not on the basis of the law'. The objective 'facts of the investigation' were 'pushed into the background'; the secret police had been more interested in the subjective, that is in ensuring that 'the wrecker acknowledged his guilt'. Molotov accepted that there had been a time when this approach was valid, and in the secret police there had been several 'politically mature workers' who were able to judge cases according to political instinct. Now, however, it was inappropriate. The procurator now had to establish the facts and make the decision, at least in large part, according to the facts.[142]

The Stalinist conception of law was, then similar to Lenin's after 1918. Law would restore order and predictability into administration and ensure that the political line was carried out without the

[140] O. V. Khlevniuk, *Politbiuro*, 108; Solomon, *Soviet Criminal Justice under Stalin*, 166 f. *Slu*, 15 (1934), 18. For restrictions on the power of the secret police in the economic sphere, see O. V. Khlevniuk, *Stalin i Ordzhonikidze. Konflikty v Politbiuro v 30-e gody* (Moscow, 1993), 36; O. V. Khlevniuk, *1937-i: Stalin, NKVD i sovetskoe obshchestvo* (Moscow, 1992), 43; R. Thurston, *Life and Terror in Stalin's Russia, 1934–1941* (New Haven, 1996), 4–5. For the general strengthening of 'law' from the spring of 1934, see Solomon, *Soviet Criminal Justice under Stalin*, ch. 5; V. A. Viktorov, *Bez grifa sekretno. Zapiski voennogo prokurora* (Moscow, 1990), 202–4.

[141] RGASPI, 17/165/47, 153–5 (soveshchanie pri TsK VKP(b) rabotnikov prokuratury, 1 August 1934).

[142] RGASPI, 17/165/47, 161–2.

disruption caused by revivalist campaigns. It did not, as leaders were eager to point out, imply that repression was no longer to be used against 'class enemies'.[143] Even so, as during the NEP, the leadership hoped to use law and the Procuracy to protect certain elements of society, such as peasants, against certain parts of the state, such as over-zealous officials in party and secret police organizations. Hence, the leadership did use liberal technicist language to justify the legal reforms.[144] Kaganovich, for instance, declared:

We need to raise respect for the law [among officials], we need to raise respect for the citizen, so that he should know that he cannot arrest a citizen illegally, so that the citizen should know that there are laws which limit the power even of our officials (*rabotnikov*).[145]

The technicist thinking of the leadership and its use of liberal technicist language are particularly evident in the Stalin constitution of 1936.[146] The constitution was in large part designed to appeal to foreign observers at a time when the Soviet Union was eager to establish anti-fascist 'popular fronts' with non-communist socialist parties in the West.[147] Particularly important in this propaganda effort was the abolition of class discrimination, the introduction of secret and universal suffrage, and the granting of a large number of legally guaranteed 'rights' and freedoms, such as freedom of speech, of the press, and of assembly—although it was made clear that they

[143] RGASPI, 17/165/47, 2 (Kaganovich).
[144] For traces of liberal, or of what Huskey calls 'legalist', approaches to law in the Stalin period, see E. Huskey, 'Framework', 57.
[145] RGASPI, 17/165/47, 177.
[146] For Stalin's views, see RGASPI, 17/163/1052, 152. For Stalin's speech on the constitution at the eighth congress of soviets, see P, 26 November 1936. For discussions of the constitution, see J. A. Getty, 'State and Society under Stalin: Constitutions and Elections in the 1930s', SR, 50 (1991), 18–35; Ellen Wimberg, 'Socialism, Democratism and Criticism: The Soviet Press and the National Discussion of the 1936 Draft Constitution', SS, 44 (1992), 313–32.
[147] Stalin wrote that the introduction of a new electoral system was in part dictated 'by the interests of the international revolutionary movement, as such a reform must definitely play the role of an extremely powerful instrument to hit at international fascism' RGASPI, 17/163/1052, 153. The other reason cited by Stalin for the introduction of these reforms was that 'the situation and correlation of forces in our country at the present moment is such that we can only win politically in this matter.' Molotov justified the campaign for 'revolutionary legality' in a similar way, as a method of raising the authority of the party 'not only within, but also outside the boundaries of the Soviet Union'. RGASPI, 17/165/47, 164 (1 August 1934).

were only to operate 'in accordance with the interests of the working people, and in order to strengthen the socialist system'.[148]

Yet Stalin also used the constitution to explain and legitimize the technicist order he was trying to create. It declared that the strong Soviet state was legitimate and entirely compatible with the Marxist project. As Stalin explained in his speech on the draft constitution delivered in November 1936, the USSR was not merely a geographical expression as some alleged, but was a powerful state.[149] Also, it was a state that had 'in the main', created 'socialism'; it had 'brought about what Marxists in other words call the first, or lower, phase of communism'.[150] Capitalism and the exploitation of man by man had been abolished, and this had led to the disappearance of old class divisions and the 'distance between social groups'. The old exploited proletariat had become 'an entirely new class', 'the working class of the USSR'; the peasantry had become a new non-capitalist peasantry; the old unreliable intelligentsia had become 'an entirely new, working intelligentsia'. The Soviet Union therefore now contained two friendly, non-antagonistic classes, the workers and peasants, and one 'stratum', the workers' intelligentsia.[151] At the same time, it was a multi-national state in which all nations, with cultures 'national in form but socialist in content' lived together in 'friendship'.[152] All citizens now had 'equal rights'; 'neither property status (*imushchestvennoe polozhenie*), nor national origin, nor sex, nor office (*sluzhebnoe polozhenie*), but the personal abilities and personal labour of each citizen determines his position in society'.[153] This emphasis on the importance of individual achievement sounds almost liberal but, as Stalin pointed out, it was entirely in keeping with the principle of Marx's first phase of communism—'from each according to his abilities, to each according to his work'.[154] At some point, Stalin accepted, the principle of the higher stage of communism would be achieved—'from each according to his abilities, to each according to his needs'—but this was a matter for the party programme, not for the constitution which was designed to reflect what had already been achieved. In practice, Stalin was putting off any move towards a more egalitarian or democratic system to the distant future.

---

[148] For this point, see P. Solomon, *Soviet Criminal Justice*, 193.
[149] Stalin, *Sochineniia*, i. (xiv), 157–9.   [150] Ibid., i. (xiv), 149.
[151] Ibid., i. (xiv), 140–5.   [152] Ibid., i. (xiv), 147–8.
[153] Ibid., i. (xiv), 154.   [154] Ibid., i. (xiv), 150.

One of the most important provisions of the constitution was to enfranchize previously disenfranchised groups—the 'former people' (*byvshie*) or 'class aliens'—and in practice this rhetoric of class inclusiveness led to a series of laws and statements designed to prevent discrimination against class aliens and their families between 1934 and 1936. In 1935 the leadership ruled that kulaks and children of kulaks should be admitted to collective farms, although the issue remained a sensitive one, and the decision was not made public.[155] In December 1935 the Politburo ordered that exiled specialists be allowed to work in their speciality in their place of exile, and allowed their children to be educated;[156] in the same month, Stalin spoke against any discrimination against the children of class aliens, commenting famously that 'a son does not answer for his father'.[157]

Yet these attempts to rehabilitate class aliens did not mean the end of repression, and this period cannot be seen as one of general, principled relaxation or liberalism. The regime was turning its attention to other alleged enemies. The 'enemy' was not the person who lacked proletarian, socialist consciousness, but was the criminal, the disorderly, and the lazy—the person who challenged the cardinal principle of the period 'from each according to his ability, to each according to his work'. Between 1933, when a halt was called to the harsh assault on the peasantry, and 1936, arrests by the political police of people charged with all crimes, including political crimes, declined markedly.[158] At the same time, however, persecution was redirected against those accused of non-political crimes.[159] As David Shearer and Paul Hagenloh have argued, the regime targeted a broad group defined as 'socially harmful elements'—including petty criminals, those who were not engaged in 'socially useful labour', 'hooligans', and transients.[160] While, as will be seen,

[155] For this issue, see S. Fitzpatrick, *Stalin's Peasants*, 240–1.

[156] O. V. Khlevniuk, *Stalin i Ordzhonikidze*, 16–18.

[157] Although, as Fitzpatrick notes, there was little discussion of this comment in the press. See S. Fitzpatrick, *Stalin's Peasants*, 240.

[158] GARF (Gosudarstvennyi Arkhiv Rossiiskii Federatsii), 9401/1/4157, 201–5.

[159] See J. A. Getty, G. Rittersporn, and V. Zemskov, 'Victims of the Soviet Penal System', 1039; Thurston, *Life and Terror*, 11.

[160] D. Shearer, 'Crime and Social Disorder in Stalin's Russia. A Reassessment of the Great Retreat and the Origins of Mass Repression', CMR, 39 (1998), 119–48; and see D. Shearer, 'Social Disorder, Mass Repression and the NKVD during the 1930s,' CMR 42 (2001), 513–29; P. Hagenloh, 'Socially Harmful Elements and the Great Terror', in S. Fitzpatrick, *Stalinism*, 290–300. For the question of the children of

these groups were sometimes described in class terms, as petty-bourgeois elements, some in the judicial apparatus, such as Vyshinskii, suggested that class origin should no longer be emphasized by the law-enforcement agencies.[161] Similarly, in 1935, G. Iagoda, the head of the NKVD, implied that the class alien was no longer the main danger, posing the rhetorical question: 'in today's situation [when socialism had been constructed] a hooligan, a bandit, a robber—isn't this the most genuine counter-revolutionary?'.[162]

The persecution of 'socially harmful elements' was, therefore, entirely compatible with the stable, technicist image of society presented by the constitution, in which the party and the state presided over a contented, peaceful population, free of fundamental conflicts, motivated by the desire to better themselves and the state; the main groups threatening this paradise were the new counter-revolutionaries—the criminals and rootless. Yet this was not the only element of the thinking of Stalin and his allies, and there is considerable evidence that they were dissatisfied with the technicist view of politics. First, it justified the rule of the technically expert, the educated, and the hard-working rather than the party—the vanguard of the working class. Second, while the technicist claim that the regime's legitimacy was based on science and rationality may have appealed to elements of the Soviet élite and to Western Social Democrats, it did not generate popular feelings of loyalty; it was also difficult to reconcile with the strategy of mobilization which the Stalinist leadership, even after the crises of 1930–3, frequently believed was vital if the economy was to grow rapidly. And, as has been seen, Stalin had generally shown a much greater interest in *politika* and consciousness than the more scientistic Lenin. The Stalinists therefore tried to reconcile an emphasis on the role of ideas and mobilization in politics with the maintenance of order and the rule of the party apparatus. Molotov hinted at this thinking in 1934 when discussing how the Procuracy was to balance objective and subjective 'political' factors when judging Soviet officials. He was unhappy with the revivalist assumption that people

'class aliens', see L. Viola, 'Tear the Evil from the Root. The Children of the *Spetspereselentsy* of the North', in N. Baschmakoff and P. Fryer (eds.), *The Modernization of the Russian Provinces, Studia Slavica Finlandensia*, 17 (2000), 34–72.

[161] D. Shearer, 'Crime and Social Disorder', 137–9.

[162] Quoted in P. Hagenloh, 'Socially Harmful Elements', 299. For the campaign against 'hooliganism' in 1935 see also, *Slu*, 13 (1935), 9–10; *Slu*, 14 (1935), 6–8.

were to be assessed according to their commitment to Bolshevism, but he also clearly believed that the attitudes of the population mattered. It was therefore primarily loyalty to Soviet power, to the state, that was to determine the state's attitude towards the citizen, not just obedience to the law and knowledge of 'facts':

the procurator must understand how to decide the given matter both from the point of view of soviet laws and from the point of view of a Bolshevik. For this it is necessary to be not only a Bolshevik, he must be above all a Bolshevik, *or at least loyal to Soviet power*, he must know, secondly, soviet laws, and thirdly, he must know the facts.[163]

Bolshevik neo-traditionalism and the emergence of the Soviet 'estate' hierarchy

As Molotov's language suggests, in attempting to escape the revivalist emphasis on class struggle and forge a form of legitimation that was more effective than technicism, the leadership was moving towards an emphasis on loyalty to the state. If the population was to be mobilized, it was to be in the name of the state rather than potentially divisive proletarian values. But how could people be mobilized to defend the existing order? An obvious method, employed by non-socialist states, was to use a nationalist ideology. All citizens would be defined not as members of classes but as a united, all-inclusive *narod*, members of a nation. However, they would not just be the technicists' cogs in a machine. They would be heroes, sacrificing themselves to the nation.

Stalin moved towards this approach to some extent, and he increasingly did so during and after the war. In 1945, for instance, he defined socialism as a 'truly popular (*narodnyi*) system that grew from within the people'.[164] But he never embraced a conventional form of nationalism, and there was never any serious attempt to integrate the Soviet Union into a unified nation state. This was largely because Soviet identity was an ideological one, not a national one. As the Bolsheviks had long recognized, given the strength of existing national identities, any attempt to transform 'Sovietism' into a single national identity for the Soviet Union was

---

[163] RGASPI, 17/165/47, 161–2. Emphasis added.
[164] Stalin, *Sochineniia*, iii. (xvi), 6.

likely to be ineffective and unpopular. Hence, the leadership accepted that socialism was to co-exist with national cultures for the foreseeable future, and Soviet culture, according to the Stalinist formula, was to be 'national in form and socialist in content'. The Soviet Union was still to be defined primarily by ideology, not by a primordial national identity based on long history, deeply rooted culture, or ethnicity. As Stalin told the German writer Emil Ludwig in 1931, 'the task to which I have devoted my life…is not the strengthening of some kind of "national" state, but the strengthening of a socialist state, and that means an international state…'.[165]

Yet, as Stalin moved away from 'class struggle' as a legitimizing ideology, he increasingly tried to supplement the socialist ideological foundations of the Soviet Union with quasi-nationalist buttresses, and he did so by drawing on the power of Russian nationalism. While, of course, this brought dangers and could antagonize non-Russians, it was likely to be the most effective way of mobilizing the largest number of potential supporters in the population as a whole. It is probable that his approach to Russian nationalism was an instrumental one and that he saw it as an alternative form of mobilization to class struggle, as is suggested by his letter to the poet Dam'ian Bedny in December 1930. For Stalin, the workers of all countries applauded the 'Soviet working class' and 'first and foremost the Russian working class' for its revolutionary nature. The Russian working class and 'revolutionary Russia' had a long and noble history, which 'fills (cannot but fill) the hearts of the Russian workers with a feeling of revolutionary national pride that can move mountains and perform miracles'.[166]

As his representation of the Russian working class as a particularly revolutionary group suggests, Stalin was careful not to slip into primordial nationalism. His claims for Russia's superiority were still firmly based on its advanced, revolutionary qualities, not on its ancient culture. As has been seen, Stalin had expressed this view before, and it had long been common within the Marxist tradition to assume that some nations were more 'advanced' or 'progressive' than others.[167] But he was still trying to move away, gradually, from a class to a nationalist form of legitimation by locating advanced

---

[165] Ibid., i. (xiv), 105.
[166] Ibid., xiii. 24–5. For a discussion of this letter, see Martin, *The Affirmative Action Empire*, 271–2.
[167] See E. Van Ree, *The Political Thought of Joseph Stalin*, ch. 4.

socialist consciousness primarily in Russian workers, rather than in all workers. A similar attempt to maintain a balance between a nationalist and an internationalist class perspective can be seen in his famous speech of February 1931, when he told industrial managers that high economic tempos were vital if the USSR were not to suffer the fate of the old Russia, which had received 'continual beatings' at the hands of foreign enemies. It was, he argued, perfectly legitimate to promote national interests, even under socialism, for, while in the past the people had no possessed a fatherland, 'now we have overthrown capitalism and power is in our hands... we have a fatherland, and we will uphold its independence'. Even so, Stalin made it clear that he was subordinating nationalist to internationalist objectives: the 'obligations to the world proletariat' were 'more serious and more important' than 'our obligations to the workers and peasants of the USSR'.[168]

Yet by the mid-1930s, the Stalinist leadership, in its search for a more powerful nationalist form of legitimation, moved further away from the view that Russia's superiority was based entirely on its socialism, towards the more conventionally nationalistic view—that its status depended on its past glories.[169] As many have noted, the leadership placed a new emphasis on Russia's pre-socialist past, and deliberate attempts were made to promote these messages through education and propaganda.[170] The USSR was to be seen as both the creation of the proletariat and the successor to the Russian empire. The Bolsheviks were continuing the state-building project initiated by the tsars, but they were doing so in the interests of the 'people' rather than the aristocracy or bourgeoisie.[171]

Yet this use of a Russian nationalist message inevitably had implications for the regime's view of the relationship between Russians and non-Russian nationalities. Indeed, it strengthened the view that the USSR was to be seen as an ethnic hierarchy, in which Russians were superior to other peoples. This assumption was confirmed in some of the political pronouncements of the late

---

[168] Stalin, *Sochineniia*, xiii. 38–40.
[169] For the use of Russian nationalist messages in this period, see Brandenberger, *National Bolshevism*, chs. 1, 3.
[170] See, particularly, D. Brandenberger and A. M. Dubrovsky, ' "The People Need a Tsar" ', 873–92; D. Brandenberger, *National Bolshevism*, 47–54.
[171] See Stalin's speech of 7 November 1937, as quoted in Dimitrov, *Dnevnik*, 128.

1930s. In February 1936, for instance, *Pravda* declared that all Soviet peoples from the smallest to the largest were 'Soviet patriots with equal rights', but 'the Russian people, the Russian worker, the Russian toilers' were 'first among equals', because their role in the proletarian revolution had been 'exclusively great'.[172] This formula still ascribed Russians supremacy to their revolutionary qualities, and Stalin never endorsed a neo-traditionalist notion of ethnic hierarchies based on primordial national differences (although by the late 1940s he had moved further in this direction, claiming that Russia's status was based on its special cultural identity).[173] But however much Stalin insisted that hierarchies were to be based on socialist consciousness, and that consciousness could not be inherited, it is not surprising that the new emphasis on nationality should have reinforced an emphasis on inherited and essential characteristics, or that it should have been used by some to legitimize a neo-traditionalist order, in which Russian status could not be challenged.

The use of Russian nationalist language to legitimize the regime coincided and interacted with other political and social forces in the early to mid-1930s to strengthen the development of a neo-traditionalist conception of ethnic politics. The party's sense of instability as it faced internal disorder and external threats played a particularly important role in these changes. As the regime struggled to suppress internal disorder, the leadership found it useful to categorize the population, labelling ethnic groups as inherently socialist or anti-socialist. Rebellions against collectivization and grain requisitioning in the early 1930s were seen as proving the unreliability not only of kulaks but also of particular nationalities, such as the Ukrainians and peoples of the North Caucasus.[174] At the same time, foreign threats led to fears that hostile powers would use potentially disloyal diaspora ethnic groups against the Bolsheviks.[175] Neo-traditionalist ideas were therefore particularly useful in this context, as they could be employed to justify discrimination against allegedly disloyal nations. They also legitimized the power of the loyal—the

---

[172] *P* (editorial), 1 February 1936. For this hierarchy of nations, see T. Martin, *The Affirmative Action Empire*, 451–60; J. Brooks, *Thank You, Comrade Stalin!*, pp. 93–7.

[173] For this argument, see Van Ree, *The Political Thought of Joseph Stalin*, 197–9.

[174] See T. Martin, *The Affirmative Action Empire*, ch. 7; A. Weiner, *Making Sense of War*, 139–40.

[175] T. Martin, 'The Origins of Soviet Ethnic Cleansing', *JMH*, 70 (1998), 842–9.

Russians—affirming their innate superiority over other ethnic groups in the Union. As Terry Martin has argued, the leadership believed that in the interests of stability it had to appease the group it needed to maintain order—Russian party members. It therefore began to moderate the positive discrimination in favour of non-Russians that had occurred during the NEP and Great Break periods.[176]

A similar process of traditionalization can be seen in the leadership's attitudes towards class. As has been seen, from the early 1930s, Stalin insisted that class was of less importance, and he now argued that society was made up of a united Soviet 'people' (*narod*) or 'toiling people' (*trudiashchiesia*)—terms that did not have the class connotations of 'worker' (*rabochii*) or 'peasant' (*krest'ianin*); so article 3 of the constitution declared that 'all power belongs to the toiling people (*trudiashchiesia*) of the city and the countryside'.[177] But Stalin's message was a contradictory one, because he continued to insist that social background was relevant to an assessment of political consciousness. He thus presented society as a stable, non-conflictual class hierarchy in which workers were the first among equals:

the draft of the new constitution of the USSR proceeds from the fact that there are no longer any antagonistic classes in society; that society consists of two friendly classes, of workers (*rabochie*) and peasants; that it is these classes, the toiling classes (*trudiashchiesia klassy*), that are in power; that the leadership of society by the state (the dictatorship) is in the hands of the working class (*rabochii klass*), the most advanced class in society; that a constitution is needed in order to strengthen a social order welcome to and beneficial to the toilers.[178]

Understandably, given the regime's declarations that class harmony now existed in the Soviet Union, some participants in the discussion on the constitution thought the continuing class hierarchy was difficult to justify, and Stalin received criticisms on this score. But Stalin refused to replace the terms 'worker' (*rabochii*) and 'peasant' with the term 'toiler' (*truzhenik*). Only under communism, he argued, would workers and peasants become members of a fully

---

[176] T. Martin, *The Affirmative Action Empire*, 271–2.
[177] S. S. Studenikina (ed.), *Istoriia sovetskoi konstitutsii (v dokumentakh)*, *1917–1956* (Moscow, 1957), 729.
[178] Stalin, *Sochineniia*, i. (xiv), 152.

homogeneous society.[179] Stalin was, therefore, insisting that the class hierarchy was a temporary one, based on differences of consciousness rather than on essential characteristics. But it is not surprising that the leadership's insistence that there were differences between classes should have contributed to a neo-traditionalist view of social groups as status groups, each with their own privileges and occupying a fixed place in a hierarchy.

There were strong forces contributing to the traditionalization of class, and its treatment as a form of ascribed status and something that could not be escaped, rather than as a reflection of consciousness and something that could be achieved.[180] As has been seen, neo-traditionalist attitudes towards class were not new, and since the revolution there had been frequent complaints, particularly from revivalists on the left but also from technicists on the right, about the tendency of party officials to transform themselves into a new proletarian 'caste'. But as with the case of nationality policy, the chaos of the early 1930s contributed to the influence of a neo-traditionalist views, as officials sought to impose order by crudely categorizing sections of the population as loyal or disloyal. The internal passport system, established at the end of 1932 to prevent peasant migration to towns, was particularly important in solidifying this stratified social hierarchy. The passport system was designed to allow the police to keep information on citizens, including their occupation, social and ethnic background, and former criminal convictions. It therefore allowed the state to offer privileges to some groups, while denying them to others.[181] In particular, it allowed the police and local authorities to discriminate against 'unreliable' social groups, such as 'class aliens'—kulaks, priests and white guards—vagrants and criminals.[182]

This categorization encouraged all officials to think in essentialist, neo-traditionalist terms. But officials could have different views about the extent of discrimination, partly depending on their interests. The secret police, particularly under Iagoda, was eager to categorize the population into reliable and unreliable groups, assuming that they could maintain order by excluding the

---

[179] Ibid., 170–1.

[180] For an account of this process, see S. Fitzpatrick, 'Ascribing Class', 20–46.

[181] D. Shearer, 'Elements Near and Alien: Passportization, Policing, and Identity in the Stalinist State, 1932–52', *JMH* 76 (2004), 835–81.

[182] See P. Hagenloh, 'Socially Harmful Elements', 295–8.

unreliable—for instance by exiling them from cities and other 'socialist' areas. Local party officials could have divergent interests. At times they resisted discrimination because they needed labour, however politically suspect.[183] At other times they could encourage it. They had participated enthusiastically in the attack on 'class aliens' during the Great Break period; the Gulag system was partly expanded through their initiative in the early 1930s; and they encouraged the arrests of kulaks to populate the camps, sometimes in the face of criticism from the centre.[184]

The new hierarchy was not only conceived as a class or ethnic one but was also often seen as one of individuals. One way in which Stalin and the leadership tried to challenge the emphasis on class in the early 1930s was to stress the importance of the individual in history.[185] As Brandenberger argues, from 1934 officials and leaders consciously tried to create a 'pragmatic history', populated by individual heroes, often great historical figures, able to inspire people with patriotism. The history books of the past, with their abstract sociological categories, were to be rewritten in the interests of a usable past.[186]

Stalin's statements are full of appeals to people to emulate new socialist heroes. But he was not breaking fundamentally with his old revivalist approaches to politics. He was merely relocating the qualities of the old working class in the individual hero from the *narod*.[187] As Stalin explained in 1935, new heroes, the Stakhanovite workers, were emerging who, like the proletarians of the past, were 'simple, modest people', willing to break with conservative attitudes and old 'fetishes'. But now, he suggested, anybody could become a hero, whatever their class (and ethnic) origin: if the 'labouring

---

[183] D. Shearer, 'Elements Near and Alien', 859–64.

[184] James Harris argues that the Gulag system expanded as a result of regional authorities' need to resolve labour shortages in industrial areas, and their desire to repress disobedient peasants in agricultural areas. James Harris, in *The Great Urals*, ch. 5. For central criticisms of local officials' desire to use repression in the countryside in 1933, see Getty, ' "Excesses are not Permitted" ', 119.

[185] For Stalin's views on the importance of the individual's role in history, see his conversation with the German writer Emil Ludwig in December 1931. Stalin, *Sochineniia*, xiii. 105–6.

[186] D. Brandenberger and A. M. Dubrovsky, '"The People Need a Tsar"', 874–6. See also D. Brandenberger, *National Bolshevism*, 29–37.

[187] For the increasing emphasis on the individual in the later 1930s, see O. Kharkhordin, *The Collective and the Individual*, ch. 5.

person (*trudovoi chelovek*) works well and gives what he can to society, he is a hero of labour, he is covered in glory'.[188]

But despite Stalin's insistence that the élite was open, it is not surprising that the hierarchy of heroes, like those of ethnicity and class, should have often been seen as a fixed one. Stalin's leadership cult, which presented him as the supreme hero, was imbued with paternalistic imagery and language, which implied that authority was innate and could not be challenged by subordinates.[189] Regional party leaders also established their own cults, seeking a similar form of legitimacy.[190] Moscow was naturally hostile to this, and in 1937 accused party bosses of trying to secure authority by adopting a 'bourgeois' conception of heroism, based on the principles of 'class, national, race inequality'.[191] The fluid hierarchy of heroes defended by Stalin was becoming a Soviet 'family' in which fathers ruled over children.

There were, then, ideological preconditions for the development of neo-traditionalist attitudes among the Bolshevik élite: the desire to promote an ideology of national unity and stability, combined with the continuing insistence that ethnic and class groups had different levels of consciousness, was likely to contribute to a view of society as a fixed hierarchy. But this vision became particularly powerful in the mid-1930s because it was useful in legitimizing the regime's attempts to impose state control after a period of disorder, bolstering the status of reliable 'collaborator' groups and stigmatizing the unreliable.[192] In these circumstances, both revivalism and

[188] Stalin, *Sochineniia*, i. (xiv), 94–5, 88, 91.

[189] For the paternalistic themes in representations of leadership, see Brooks, *Thank You, Comrade Stalin!*, 83–9.

[190] For examples, see J. Baberowski, *Der Rote Terror. Die Geschichte des Stalinismus* (Munich, 2003), 163.

[191] *P* (editorial), 9 February 1937. See also *P* (editorial), 28 March 1937.

[192] The term 'collaboration', imported from the historiography of European imperialism, is perhaps useful here, as are comparisons with the experience of European empire. The British in India, for instance, found that their limited power forced them to rule through collaborator élites, and to 'retreat' from liberal political and economic policies which threatened those élites, and social stability more generally. Partly in response to the rebellion of 1857, the British increasingly moved away from a universalistic liberal ideology towards a neo-traditionalist one, which legitimized collaborator élites and stigmatized unreliable peoples by ordering society according to a supposedly 'traditional' fixed hierarchy of caste, religious, and ethnic groups, each with its own essential, inherited characteristics. As in the Soviet case, the hierarchy was both an ethnic and a social one, and the British used censuses to categorize the population. The case of British India is an extreme one, and

technicism were likely to be seen by some Bolsheviks as destabilizing, as they could justify challenges to the authority of the party
élite, whether on the grounds of its inadequate consciousness or its
lack of expertise.

Stalin, revivalism, and Romanticism

Yet, however widespread this paternalistic, hierarchical, and fundamentally conservative view of the world, it remained marginal
within the discourse of the leadership itself, and was often criticized.
Despite the gradual rejection of revivalist strategies, Stalin exhibited
a continuing tendency to see politics in revivalist terms: as a struggle
between proletarian and bourgeois attitudes, and between the
forces of rapid advance towards socialism and retreat to capitalism.
He also continued to insist that ideas and *politika* have primacy
over *tekhnika*.

Stalin's reluctance to abandon revivalism can be explained in
various ways. As has been seen, he had a history of using a revivalist
form of class analysis, stressing the power of ideas in politics. But he
also had strong political reasons for pursuing a revivalist course, as
both technicism and neo-traditionalism could weaken the party
leadership, and Stalin himself.

Stalin was particularly explicit in defending revivalism and the
primacy of ideas and *politika* over pure *tekhnika* and economics in
the speeches he gave to writers in October 1932. His famous description of writers as 'engineers of human souls' might appear to be a
defence of a highly technocratic, utilitarian approach to culture. But
his real message was that economic success was dependent on the
ideological transformation of the population, and he used typically
Romantic language to make his point, stressing the unity of the
spiritual and the material, and the priority of the spiritual. He told
his audience that there were two different types of production: the

---

neo-traditionalism was never so dominant in Soviet ideology or political culture,
but the Stalinist leadership was responding in a similar way to the disorder of
the early 1930s, and a comparable ideology legitimized particular reliable groups.
For British ideology in this period, see T. Metcalf, *The New Cambridge History
of India*, vol. 3 Pt. 4. *Ideologies of the Raj* (Cambridge, 1994), 43–52, chs. 3–4;
N. Dirks, *Castes of Mind. Colonialism and the Making of Modern India* (Princeton,
2001), esp. Ch. 10.

first involved in the manufacture of 'artillery, cars, engines'; and the second in the transformation of men's 'souls'. He then asked which type of production was more important and, while he accepted that 'sometimes tanks are more necessary', he then explained:

Your tanks will be worth nothing if the soul (*dusha*) in them is rotten. No, the 'production' of souls is more important than the production of tanks. The whole production of the country is linked with your [i.e. writers'] 'production'.[193]

Stalin also emphasized the importance of ideas and their role in transforming people into socialists in a strong defence of Romanticism in literature. Speaking slightly earlier in the month to an audience of communist writers, Stalin defined Romanticism as 'idealization, the exaggeration of reality'.While, he accepted, Romanticism could be unhealthy, as in the case of Schiller's 'bourgeois-gentry idealism', there was also a good Romanticism, represented by Shakespeare and Gorky: 'Gorky's idealization of man is the idealization of the new man of the future, the idealization of the new social system of the future . . .', he explained. 'We need the sort of Romanticism that would move us forward.'[194]

As Stalin made clear, his 'Romanticism' coincided with Gorky's. Gorky shared Stalin's worries about the ideological health of the population and his conviction that an understanding of the broader sweep of Bolshevik history would mobilize the masses. In 1929 he wrote to Stalin that a new programme of ideological education was needed to counter the dangerous 'pessimism' and 'philistinism' (*meshchanstvo*) among Soviet youth.[195] Similarly, in 1931 he suggested that a broader work on ideology and the history of the regime be published to coincide with the fifteenth anniversary of the revolution, to explain the nature of the Bolshevik project to a narrow-minded and sceptical youth.[196] He complained that 'blockheads' did not understand the huge scope of socialist construction; they were only interested in what happened within the limits of their own factory or collective farm. This was a particular problem among those who were of 'alien' background, whether peasants or *intelligenty*, but their 'scepticism' could also influence working-class

[193] RGASPI, 558/11/1116, 32 (26 October 1932).
[194] RGASPI, 558/11/1116, 27 (20 October 1932).
[195] Gorky to Stalin, 27 November 1929, *Izv TsK KPSS*, 3 (1989), 185.
[196] *Izv TsK KPSS*, 7 (1989), 216.

young people. The regime, Gorky insisted, had to fight against these tendencies if it was to achieve complete unity and effective mobilization; it was necessary 'that each unit that takes part in the creation of the new reality, should see as clearly as possible the whole mass of practical results of the embodiment of *workers' class* energy in the socialist cause'.[197] Gorky's solution was the publication of a three-part book that was rather similar in its mixture of ideology and history to Stalin's *Short Course* of party history published in 1938. It consisted of a history of Marxism and the party up until 1917, an account of the economic achievements of the period 1917–33, and a description of the future socialist society.[198] This project, of course, sounds like a rationalist one rather than a Romantic appeal to the emotions: young people, convinced by the success of Bolshevism, would become committed to the cause. But Gorky stated explicitly that the appeal was to be not just to 'reason' but also to 'imagination'.[199]

Revivalism, politics, and the economy

Stalin continued to bring his revivalist view of the world to his management of day-to-day politics, and particularly his treatment of the economic apparatus. As before, most tensions between Stalin and the commissariats were related to plan targets and investment. The commissariats tended to fight for low, fulfillable, plan targets, while demanding higher investment. Stalin, meanwhile, often supported Sovnarkom and Gosplan in their attempts to force Narkomtiazhprom and other commissariats to produce as much as possible for a low level of investment.[200] These tensions became particularly serious from 1932 when the central leadership tried to reduce investment and demanded that what had been built be

---

[197] This sentence was one of the several underlined by Stalin. Gorky to Stalin, 12 December 1931, in M. Gorky, *M. Gor'kii. Neizdannaia perepiska s Bogdanovym, Leninym, Stalinym, Zinov'evym, Kamenevym*, ed. by S. V. Zaika (Moscow, 1998), 285–6.

[198] Gorky, *Neizdannaia perepiska*, 286–7.

[199] Ibid., 287.

[200] O. V. Khlevniuk, *Politbiuro*, 89–92; O. V. Khlevniuk, 'Heavy Industry', 108–9. Stalin was particularly critical of the commissariats' demands that foreign currency be spent on imports. See Khlevniuk *et al.*, *Stalin i Kaganovich. Perepiska 1931–1936 gg.*, 31.

exploited as effectively and cheaply as possibly—the strategy of 'assimilation' (*osvoenie*) or 'mastery' (*ovladenie*) of production as the leadership called it.[201] Stalin presented the economic commissariats as one of the main forces obstructing economic growth, contrasting them with the party's 'Central Committee' which was defending the general interests of the USSR. So, for instance, in a letter to Ordzhonikidze of September 1931, Stalin argued that the 'economic apparatus', in trying to import expensive steel from abroad, was 'relying on the stupidity and muddle of the Central Committee'. He was, he said, faced with a choice: 'to put pressure on the state budget, while preserving the tranquillity of the economic apparatus, or to put pressure on the economic apparatus, while preserving the interests of the state'.[202] At about the same time, he criticized the Commissariat of Trade (Narkomvneshtorg) for opposing the interests of the state. He condemned the 'economic organs' for their 'criminal-scandalous attitude' to imports and demanded that those so-called 'communists' responsible be brought to court and punished.[203]

Stalin often blamed the behaviour of the economic commissariats on their excessive autonomy and their concern with departmental as opposed to general state interests. So, for instance, he argued that attempts by commissariats to overturn a decision of the Politburo restricting imports threatened to 'turn our Bolshevik party into a conglomeration of departmental gangs'.[204] Yet Stalin also used revivalist language to criticize the commissariats, condemning them as 'rightist' bureaucrats. There was, of course, no coherent ideological challenge to Stalin from the commissariats. Stalin was too powerful and none would disagree with him on a matter of principle. There was no division between coherent groups of revivalists and anti-revivalists within the leadership on ideological grounds.[205] Conflict was primarily personal and institutional.

---

[201] For the concept of *osvoenie*, see R. W. Davies, *Crisis and Progress*, 321.

[202] Stalin to Ordzhonikidze, 9 September 1931, RGASPI, 81/3/99, 27.

[203] Stalin to Kaganovich, 12 September 1931, RGASPI, 81/3/100, 112–13. For similar attacks on commissariats for wastefulness and failure to fulfil orders, see Stalin to Kaganovich, Molotov and Ordzhonikidze, 24 June 1932, RGASPI, 81/3/100, 71–4; Stalin to Ordzhonikidze, 29 June 1932, RGASPI, 558/11/779, 56–7; Stalin to Kaganovich, 4 October 1931, RGASPI, 81/3/99, 42.

[204] Stalin to Ordzhonikidze, 9 September 1931, RGASPI, 81/3/99, 27.

[205] For this point, see O. V. Khlevniuk, *Politbiuro*, 75 ff. and *passim*; J. A. Getty and O. V. Naumov, *The Road to Terror*, 575–6.

However, this should not lead us to assume that there was no ideological component to the institutional conflicts of the period.[206] It was in Stalin's interest to give these battles an ideological significance, just as it was in the interest of the commissariats and others in conflict with the party leadership to avoid the politicization of bureaucratic disputes. It was also plausible to accuse the commissariats of 'rightism', because they resisted high plan targets and objected to campaigns against conservative 'wreckers' among managers and specialists. The economic disasters of the early 1930s generated a wave of discontent within the party, on both the former right and the former left, and a number of senior party leaders were expelled from the party for criticizing Stalin's voluntaristic policies; from Syrtsov and Lominadze in 1930, to Riutin, Eismont, and Tolmachev in 1932.[207] At the seventeenth party congress, in January 1934, several members of the former left and right were allowed to speak, signalling an apparent relaxation in Stalin's attitude towards them. But he continued to be highly sensitive to signs of 'rightist' attitudes towards economics among his former rivals throughout the early 1930s. For instance, he supported Stetskii and others in their condemnation of an article, published in *Izvestiia* in May 1934, in which Bukharin allegedly criticized the first five-year plan's emphasis on heavy industry.[208] Stalin was still worried about the infectiveness of 'rightist' ideas and continued to interpret any sign of scepticism as 'right opportunism in practice'.

[206] According to Khlevniuk, these conflicts had a 'predominantly departmental, not political character'. O. V. Khlevniuk, *Politbiuro*, 94. However, O. V. Khlevniuk does state that Stalin elevated 'even relatively minor questions to the level of principle' and tried to justify himself 'theoretically'. See ibid., 97.

[207] For the charges against Syrtsov and Lominadze, see RGASPI, 82/2/53, 77–91 (Molotov, 4 December 1930). For the Syrtsov–Lominadze affair, see B. A. Starkov, 'Pravo-levye fraktsionery', in A. V. Afanas'ev, *Oni ne molchali* (Moscow, 1991), 125–44; R. W. Davies, *The Soviet Economy in Turmoil*, 411–15; for the Riutin affair, see B. A. Starkov, 'Delo Riutina', in Afanas'ev, *Oni ne molchali*, 145–78; R. W. Davies, *Crisis and Progress*, 247–53; M. N. Riutin, 'Stalin i krizis proletarskoi diktatury. Platforma "soiuza marksistov-lenintsev" ', in *Reabilitatsiia* 334–446.

[208] For the article, see 'Ekonomika sovetskoi strany', *I*, 12 May 1934. See the correspondence between Stetskii, Bukharin, Stalin, and others, published in A. V. Kvashonkin *et al.* (eds.), *Sovetskoe rukovodstvo*, 277–92. See also Stalin's condemnation of one of Bukharin's speeches of 1931 as 'unbolshevik', on the grounds that it implicitly criticized the leadership's neglect of consumer industry. Stalin to Kaganovich, 30 August 1931, RGASPI, 81/3/99, 14. Kaganovich condemned Bukharin's 'mechanistic philosophy'. Kaganovich to Stalin, 31 August 1931, in Khlevniuk *et al.* (eds.), *Stalin i Kaganovich*, 75.

As in previous years, Stalin did not accuse his colleagues in the commissariats of 'rightism' themselves, but did suggest that they were acting in a manner that was tantamount to rightism. So, for instance, he attacked M. L. Rukhimovich, the Commissar of Rail Transport (NKPS) for 'mocking the decrees of the Central Committee' and sowing 'demoralizing scepticism' 'in a Menshevik manner'.[209] As in the past, he also alleged that his allies had come under the influence of rightist bureaucrats in their apparatuses.[210] Ordzhonikidze received some of the most virulent criticism on this score. Stalin sought to discipline managers for producing defective goods, while Ordzhonikidze defended his subordinates, and on several occasions he tried to support them before the Politburo.[211] Sometimes he won and managed to reduce sentences on managers; on other occasions Stalin reacted harshly to Ordzhonkidze's attempts to defend his subordinates. As he wrote to Kaganovich in July 1932:

It is time to begin bringing managers of factories which are obliged to supply motor and tractor enterprises with steel to trial. If Ordzhonikidze begins to make a fuss he should be branded as a putrid slave to routine (*rutiner*) who supports the worst traditions of the right deviationists in Narkomtiazhprom.[212]

Stalin responded in a similarly aggressive way in August 1933 when Ordzhonikidze tried to defend his commissariat against charges that it was producing defective combine harvesters.[213] A number of managers of the Kommunar factory had been arrested for this alleged 'wrecking', and in his concluding speech in the trial, Vyshinskii argued that the case raised more 'general questions' about the work of economic organizations, and in particular Narkomtiazhprom and the Commissariat of Agriculture (Narkomzem). Vyshinskii was obviously implying that the commissariats would be subject to further attacks.[214] In Stalin's absence, Ordzhonikidze and Ia. Iakovlev of

[209] Stalin to Kaganovich, 19 September 1931, RGASPI, 81/3/99, 35.
[210] See, for instance, his warning that P. P. Postyshev was coming under the 'influence of grandee bureaucrats [*vel'mozh-biurokratov*]'. Stalin to Kaganovich, 4 September 1931, RGASPI, 81/3/99, 18.
[211] For these cases, see Khlevniuk, 'Heavy Industry', 113–16. Compare with Stalin's campaign of December 1933. See Solomon, *Soviet Criminal Justice*, 145 ff.
[212] Stalin to Kaganovich, 26 July 1932, RGASPI, 81/3/100, 6–7.
[213] For this case, see O. V. Khlevniuk, *Stalin i Ordzhonikidze*, 34–5; R. W. Davies, *Crisis and Progress*, 350–2.
[214] *P*, 23 August 1933.

Narkomzem succeeded in persuading the Politburo to condemn Vyshinskii's threatening statement. This clearly angered Stalin, and once he heard of the Politburo's decision he wrote to Molotov accusing Ordzhonikidze of 'hooliganism'.[215] The Politburo reversed its decision on the same day, but almost two weeks later Stalin wrote another letter to Molotov complaining about the behaviour of Ordzhonikidze and those Politburo colleagues who supported him:

The behaviour of Sergo (and Iakovlev) in the affair of the 'completeness of production' can only be called anti-party, as its objective aim is to defend the reactionary elements of the party *against* the Central Committee of the All-Union Communist Party (bolshevik). In fact the whole country is crying out against the incompleteness of production. The party has begun a campaign for completeness; an open press and punitive campaign; a sentence has already been passed on the enemies of the party who impudently (*naglo*) and maliciously (*zlobno*) violate the decisions of the party and government, but Sergo [Ordzhonikidze] (and Iakovlev), who is responsible for these violations, instead of repenting for his sins deals a blow against the procurator. Why? Not, of course, in order to rein in the reactionary violators of the party's decisions, but to support them morally, to justify them in the eyes of party opinion, and, in this way, to discredit the party's developing campaign, that is to discredit the practical line of the Central Committee. I wrote to Kaganovich that, contrary to my expectations, he turned out to be in the camp of the reactionary elements of the party in this matter.[216]

Although this letter does not mention class enemies, it still betrays much of the revivalist approach to politics and the economy. Those officials who do not fulfil plans and justify themselves, whatever their 'subjective' intentions are, have the 'objective aim' of attacking the Central Committee and are acting 'maliciously'. Not only that, but they are allying themselves with other enemies within the party, who are in a 'camp of reactionary elements'.

Stalin also continued to use revivalist language to press for improved economic performance, and he stressed the party's, and his own, function as mobilizer and motivator. In July 1932, for instance, he wrote to Kaganovich explaining why he now accepted that the grain procurement targets for the Ukraine had to be reduced, even though he had refused to consider such a concession the

---

[215] Stalin to Molotov, 1 September 1933, *Pis'ma*, 247.
[216] Stalin to Molotov, 12 September 1933, *Pis'ma*, 248–9.

previous month. There was nothing 'strange' about this apparent inconsistency, Stalin explained. At the end of June and beginning of July the harvest was being organized, and 'to speak *in this period about a reduction in the plan*...in the eyes of all and and in the presence of regional secretaries—means the final demoralization of (already demoralized) Ukrainians...'. It was another matter in August, when conditions were different and, among other changes, 'party and soviet forces' had 'already been mobilized' for the fulfilment of the plan.[217] Stalin was evidently thinking carefully about how best to mobilize and motivate party subordinates. He did not regard himself as somebody who merely issued orders to subordinates. He saw himself as a charismatic motivator, an expert analyst, and manipulator of the party's and the population's mood.

As in the past, Stalin regarded economic commissariats as particularly prone to 'scepticism' and lack of faith. In September 1931, for instance, he told Kaganovich that unless the 'gang' of sceptical bureaucrats operating in NKPS was replaced with 'new people who believe in our cause', the decisions of the Central Committee would be ignored.[218] However, from 1931 to 1932 regional party bosses were also criticized for their failures to ensure the fulfilment of plans and to 'assimilate' new plant, and they were held to be as responsible for poor results as economic officials were.[219] Relations with the centre were particularly damaged by their poor organization of the grain collections in 1932, and by actual resistance in some regions.[220] The party purge of 1933, announced in December 1932, was probably a response to this perceived recalcitrance.[221] It was justified using both a technicist language of 'discipline' and obedience to 'law', and a more revivalist rhetoric. It targeted a large number of groups, including ideologically suspect officials or, as the list of categories published in April 1933 described them, 'class alien and hostile elements', 'double-dealers' (*dvurushniki*) who pretended to be loyal to the party but were actually enemies, and careerist and 'bureaucratic' elements who were 'cut off from the masses'. Yet in practice the technicist language prevailed, and the focus of the purge

[217] Stalin to Kaganovich, 25 July 1932; RGASPI, 81/3/99, 115–17.
[218] Stalin to Kaganovich, 19 September 1931, RGASPI, 81/3/99, 35.
[219] J. Harris, *The Great Urals*, 137–45.
[220] See N. Shimotomai, 'A Note on the Kuban Affair. The Crisis of Kolkhoz Agriculture in the North Caucasus', *Acta Slavica Iaponica*, 1 (1983), 39–56.
[221] R. W. Davies, *Crisis and Progress*, 243–4.

was less on class aliens, or on ideologically suspect or undemocratic officials, undemocratic than on officials who had breached 'discipline' and rank-and-file party members. A central target of the purge were 'open and hidden violators of the iron discipline of the party and the state, people who do not fulfil the decisions of the party and the government' and who 'cast doubt on and discredit the decisions and plans of the party with chatter about their "lack of realism" and "unattainability" '.[222] Kaganovich, speaking to Moscow party members in May 1933, certainly gave most attention to this group, and the Purge Commission's reports on the conduct of the purge also emphasized the issue of plan fulfilment.[223] At the same time, the decree implicitly targeted poorly educated rank-and-file party members, or 'passives'. It did try to protect these party members from unjust expulsion and did not include them in its six categories of expellees, but by complaining about the indiscriminate admission of party members who were politically illiterate and ignorant of the rules and programme of the party, it allowed local party bosses to direct the purge against the party rank and file. The technicist language of order and discipline thus helped to ensure that the main victims of the purge were not party officials at higher levels but 'passives' and 'undisciplined' lower level district organizations, particularly in the countryside, where harsh procurement policies had not been enforced.[224] In Leningrad, for instance, a report of 1933 showed that, after appeals, 10 per cent of party members in the city were expelled, compared with 15.7 per cent in the countryside. Of the total, 31.8 per cent were charged with passivity, 21.3 per cent for breaches of party and state discipline, and 14.0 per cent were accused of being class alien elements or of hiding their social background.[225]

It is clear, however, that some in the party leadership were unhappy with local leaders' conduct of the purge and there was continuing pressure from within the leadership to check up on the political and ideological purity and loyalty of the party

[222] For drafts of the purge decree, see RGASPI, 81/3/95, 21–9; for the decree, see P, 29 April 1933.
[223] PRTs, 11 (1933), 1–11 (Kaganovich); RGASPI, 17/120/100, 91–2, 97, 99, 102, 107–8.
[224] For the devastation of rural party organizations, see S. Fitzpatrick, Stalin's Peasants, 76–8.
[225] RGASPI, 17/120/100, 106.

apparatus.[226] The Central Committee decided that it needed to rectify these failures by organizing an 'exchange of party documents' in those organizations which had completed the purge; as replacements were only to be issued after careful investigation this exercise was to be, in effect, another purge.[227]

Stalin made his dissatisfaction with party bosses particularly explicit in his report to the seventeenth party congress, in January 1934, and used the same combination of the language of 'discipline' and 'belief' to criticize them. He demanded 'real and concrete leadership' and an emphasis on 'fulfilment of decisions', and he condemned the waffling 'windbags' in the party who talked about mobilization but failed to achieve anything concrete.[228] But he also expressed more voluntaristic sentiments, and implicitly attacked the technicist view of politics. Now, he declared, 'everything, or almost everything', depended on the work of party and Soviet leaders; 'the role of so-called objective conditions' had been 'reduced to a minimum', and 'from now on nine-tenths of the responsibility for failures and defects in our work rest, not on "objective" conditions, but on ourselves, and on ourselves alone'.[229] Stalin then went on to argue for the continuing importance of Marxist ideas—the party, he claimed, had only achieved successes because it was guided by the teaching of Marx, Engels, and Lenin.[230] And, although he declared victory over class enemies, he refused to state that the ideological class struggle was over. Changes in consciousness lagged behind economic developments, and as long as the Soviet Union was encircled by capitalist powers, foreign enemies would 'revive and support the survivals of capitalism in the consciousness of people and the economy'.[231] He also insisted that only mobilization would be effective in building the economy, and the party alone could conduct it. There was a real danger, he argued, that after the end of the first five-year plan the party would 'demobilize its ranks'. Plans could

---

[226] Zhdanov, speaking in 1939, argued that the 'largest group' among those excluded in the 1933 purge were passives, and was highly critical of the purge for this reason. See RGASPI, 77/1/719, 29 (18 March 1939). For other criticisms of the conduct of the purge, see *XVII s"ezd VKP(b)*, 287 (Rudzutak). For these points, see J. A. Getty, *Origins*, 54 ff.

[227] J. A. Getty, *Origins*, 58.

[228] Stalin, *Sochineniia*, xiii. 370–2.

[229] Ibid., xiii. 366–7.

[230] Ibid., xiii. 377.

[231] Ibid., xiii. 349.

only be fulfilled 'in the course of struggle against difficulties', and that meant that 'we must develop vigilance in it [the party], not lull it to sleep'.[232]

Mobilization, of course, was perfectly compatible with the continuing authority of party bosses. But Stalin was implicitly threatening leaders: they only deserved this prestige if they had the right level of commitment to mobilization and Marxist—Leninist ideas. And Stalin made it clear that he was unhappy with their performance. He blamed the party's 'demobilization' on their complacency and unwarranted self-satisfaction,[233] and in an implicit denunciation of the neo-traditionalist justification for the high status of party bosses, he criticized 'grandees' who 'consider that party decisions and Soviet laws are not written for them but for fools'. They acted like this because they 'presume that the Soviet government will not decide to touch them because of their past services'. These people, Stalin declared, had to be demoted and publicly humiliated in the press.[234] Stalin also did something rather more practical to tighten up central control over local party organizations: he transformed Rabkrin and the TsKK into the Commission for Soviet Control (KSK) and the Commission for Party Control (KPK). The KPK was to have much more independence from local bosses than the TsKK.[235]

Stalin's statements in January 1934 illustrate the tensions within the leadership's attitude towards politics during the early 1930s. It wanted to see a system that worked like a machine, with officials and the masses obediently fulfilling orders from above, judged according to their efficiency. But it also wanted a high level of mobilization, in which officials and the masses, inspired by the ideas of Bolshevism, achieved miracles and struggled against 'class enemies'. Even so, it did not want this struggle to undermine authority and order, as had happened during the late 1920s. Stalin,

---

[232] Stalin, *Sochineniia*, xiii. 376.

[233] Ibid., xiii. 376.

[234] Ibid., xiii. 370.

[235] For this decision, see J. A. Getty, *Pragmatists and Puritans. The Rise and Fall of the Party Control Commission*, Carl Beck Papers, 1208 (1998), 1–5. For the strengthening of control over party bosses during this period, see O. V. Khlevniuk, 'The First Generation of Stalinist "Party Generals" ', 48–9; E. A. Rees, 'Republican and Regional Leaders at the XVII Congress in 1934', in E. Rees (ed.), *Centre–Local Relations*, 86–8.

having acquiesced in the restoration of order, began to believe that neither technicist nor neo-traditionalist solutions were entirely in his own interests or those of the economy. His speech at the seventeenth party congress was one of the first public airings of a theme that was to become increasingly important in the following two to three years.

5

Mobilization and Terror,
1934–1939

Evgenia Ginzburg, the wife of a regional party boss and one of many in the élite to suffer during the Terror, famously began her memoirs with the sentence: 'The year 1937 really began on the 1st of December 1934'.[1] By this, Ginzburg meant that the assassination of Kirov, and Stalin's use of the murder to launch a campaign against alleged enemies within the party, were the beginning of a process that led to the Terror of 1937–8. Stalin, she was suggesting, was adopting a fundamentally new terroristic approach to politics from 1934. While there is no evidence that Stalin planned the Terror of 1937–8 from the end of 1934, the murder of Kirov did lead to repressions over the next few months, and, more generally, contributed towards a new, more 'vigilant' approach to members of the former opposition over the next few years. Another event in December 1934 also suggests that the policies pursued since 1930–1 were being reconsidered. On 26 December, Stalin gave a speech to a group of officials in the metallurgical industry, at which he discussed the cardinal slogan he had adopted in 1931, '*tekhnika* in the period of reconstruction decides everything'. Stalin strongly criticized 'many' comrades who had 'wrongly understood' the slogan; they had applied it 'mechanically', valuing only 'naked *tekhnika*' and machines. Now emphasis had to be placed on 'the people who have mastered *tekhnika*'. 'People' had to be cherished and cultivated 'as tenderly and carefully as a gardener cultivates a favourite fruit tree'.[2] By May 1935 Stalin had explicitly abandoned

---

[1] E. Ginzburg, *Into the Whirlwind*, trans. by P. Stevenson and M. Harari (London 1989), 11.
[2] RGASPI, 558/11/1077, 13; published in I. V. Stalin, *Sochineniia*, ed. by R. McNeal (Stanford, 1967), i. (xiv), 49.

the slogan '*tekhnika* decides everything' and replaced it with the slogan 'cadres decide everything'.[3] Stalin was again arguing that 'ideas' and *politika*, or the motivation and consciousness of 'people', were central to the economic success and the welfare of the regime.

From the end of 1934 there are, therefore, signs that Stalin was adopting, albeit intermittently and inconsistently, a number of conventional revivalist policies, both élitist and populist. He was arguing that the 'demobilization' of the party, which he had identified in January 1934, had to be reversed, and he was attempting to force the pace of economic growth, revive the party, and organize disruptive 'democratic' anti-'bureaucratism' campaigns. He was challenging the technicist and neo-traditionalist approaches to politics which had emerged in the previous few years, and which to some extent he had endorsed, and he was arguing that if officials altered their 'methods' of work and mobilized the population, ambitious plans could be fulfilled and the country defended against foreign threats. He was also blaming 'bureaucrats', ideologically corrupted with 'rightist' ideas, for failures to fulfil economic plans. At the same time he seems to have suspected, as in the late 1920s, that at least some of these ideological heretics were conspiring, or might conspire, with foreign imperialists who were yet again threatening the Soviet Union, and he either instigated or approved of investigations which turned up 'evidence' that these plots were indeed taking place. Hence, an important element of the Terror consisted of two closely intertwined campaigns against officialdom, one directed at 'unbelievers', and the other at 'spies'. However, the Terror was a series of campaigns, and these attacks on the élite were followed by two other 'operations' which had little in common with the revivalist campaigns of the 1920s: first, 'national operations' directed at alleged conspirators among diaspora nationalities in the borderlands (such as Germans, Poles, and Koreans), which had been organized since the mid-1930s, but which intensified after mid-1937; and second, 'mass operations' against former kulaks and criminals throughout the Soviet Union, which began in the summer of 1937.

Much remains mysterious, and Stalin's thinking and decision-making is still difficult to comprehend, but an appreciation of the importance of revivalism in the politics of the period, this chapter will argue, contributes to a fuller explanation of the Terror than

[3] Stalin, *Sochineniia*, i. (xiv), 61–2.

some existing analyses, and helps us to incorporate the insights of both recent structuralist and intentionalist accounts. According to the 'moderate' structuralist approach of J. Arch Getty and Oleg Naumov, Stalin was reacting to regional party bosses' failure to obey central authority, and he also shared a peculiar Bolshevik mind-set, characterized by feelings of insecurity, obsession with party unity, and a tendency to see any disobedience as conspiracy.[4] In contrast, the 'moderate' intentionalist account of Oleg Khlevniuk and Arfon Rees denies that Stalin's power was seriously limited by local bosses, or that he was motivated by fear of resistance from the élite.[5] Rather, they argue, he was embarking on an aggressive, ruthless replacement of party bosses, whom he believed lacked practical ability, and he trumped up conspiracy charges to justify his purge.[6] He did feel insecure, but he was mainly worried about foreign enemies, who, he believed, would make use of an internal fifth column within the Soviet population as a whole; he therefore embarked on a pre-emptive persecution of all suspect groups within the Soviet Union.[7] However, if we appreciate the revivalist context of Stalin's thinking, it becomes easier to explain the relationship between the aggressive and planned aspects of the leadership's behaviour, stressed by intentionalists, and the reactive elements, emphasized by structuralists. Stalin seems to have assumed, as a revivalist mobilizer, that 'philistinism' and 'rightism' within the apparatus would undermine the system and sabotage the economy, and he was especially worried about these attitudes at a time of impending war. He also seems to have believed that these heretical views were likely (but not certain) to be connected with actual conspiracy and deliberate sabotage, and he therefore ordered the political police to begin investigations, putting them under pressure to find evidence to prove his suspicions. Hence, Stalin was aggressively and deliberately rooting out heretical attitudes and the 'conspirators' who 'bore' them, but he was also reacting to 'evidence' turned up by the police.

---

[4] J. A. Getty and O. V. Naumov, *The Road to Terror*, 12–14, 16, 22, 574. Khlevniuk also stresses the leadership's insecurity. O. V. Khlevniuk, *Politbiuro*, 194.

[5] E. Rees, 'The Great Terror: Suicide or Murder?', 448–9.

[6] O. V. Khlevniuk, 'The Stalinist "Party Generals" ', 59–60; E. Rees, 'The Great Purges', 195–6. For a similar view, see Tucker, *Stalin in Power*, 264–8.

[7] O. V. Khlevniuk, 'The Objectives of the Great Terror, 1937–38', 158–76; O. V. Khlevniuk, 'The Reasons for the "Great Terror" ', 159–70.

An understanding of this revivalist context also helps us to make use of both structuralist and intentionalist insights into the complex course of the Terror. Intentionalists emphasize its planned nature, at least from the middle of 1936; while structuralists interpret it as a much less coherent phenomenon, and emphasize contingency and reaction to events.[8] Yet, if we see the Terror as, at least in its early phases, a series of revivalist campaigns reminiscent of those of the late 1920s, it is easier to understand why it was such a protracted, diverse, and chaotic process, as the structuralists have shown, while presenting a picture that gives due weight to Stalin's calculating approach to politics and his (ultimately unsuccessful) attempts to keep all political developments under his own control.

First, as in the late 1920s, there were inevitable tensions between the desire to mobilize and the desire to maintain unity and order, and Stalin and his allies understood that the divisiveness of populist revivalism had the potential to undermine central power and the apparatus. They therefore acted cautiously and inconsistently, veering between populist and élitist strategies. And second, the pattern of the persecutions suggests that initially Stalin followed the typical revivalist view that the main danger to socialist construction came from economic officials in the state apparatus; they were certainly the main targets of the earlier campaigns against 'enemies' in 1936. While Stalin argued that the party apparatus had its share

---

[8] Getty and Naumov argue that from 1934 the centre began to mistrust the regional bosses, believing that they had too much power, but this institutional conflict had not yet become associated with the Bolsheviks' fearful world-view; Moscow was frustrated that the regions were failing to implement Moscow's demands, but there was no disagreement between the centre and the regions over the dangers from 'enemies' or the opposition. It was not until the autumn of 1936 that the Bolsheviks' fearfulness reinforced institutional conflicts, and that Stalin decided that some of those 'bureaucrats' who were resisting central policies were also conspiring against him, as the result of a complex interplay of fear of conspiracy and institutional interest. Nikolai Ezhov, then a Central Committee secretary with a particular interest in NKVD affairs, was trying to make a name for himself, and, using a mandate from Stalin, he pursued investigations into former oppositionists; the trail led to officials in the economic apparatus, many of whom happened to have Trotskyist pasts; once they were accused of being 'enemies' their associates in regional party organizations, whom Stalin believed had become too powerful, were also implicated. But it was only in the middle of 1937 that Stalin, faced with rumours of a military conspiracy, was really gripped with fear. Believing that the state was riddled with enemies, he instigated the arrest of the party bosses and lashed out at anybody who came under suspicion. At the same time, party bosses contributed to the escalation of the Terror, striking at 'enemies' in a way the centre considered excessive. J. A. Getty and O. V. Naumov, *The Road to Terror*, 247–9, 263–6, 442–90, 523–4.

of bureaucrats and enemies, he seems to have operated on the assumption that it could be purged and then mobilized to purge other institutions. It was only later that the higher echelons of the party were targeted, in part, at least, for protecting their colleagues in the economic apparatus. It is therefore not surprising that, as Stephen Kotkin has shown in his study of Magnitogorsk, party officials and the rank and file at a local level regarded the purges of the period as an attempt to resume the party's ideological mission and restore its revolutionary purity. The return to cultural and ideological puritanism within the party, seen during the Terror period, was also to be expected.[9]

Yet the campaigns of the late 1930s were not simply a reprise of those of the late 1920s. Developments since then had led Stalin to adapt his revivalism, and to behave, paradoxically, in both a more cautious and a more reckless way. It is likely that the disastrous experience of the early 1930s had shown the leadership the dangers of excessive radicalism, and that the dire international circumstances of the period impressed on Stalin the need to prevent revivalism from undermining unity and the stability of the state. First, while the leadership was, to some extent, returning to the voluntaristic themes of the earlier period, there were no serious attempts to challenge the material incentives and quasi-market mechanisms introduced in the early to mid-1930s. Second, the revivalist anti-bureaucratism campaigns of the late 1930s, while retaining elements of populism, were much more élitist than were their predecessors. Stalin was determined to ensure that the campaign against 'bureaucrats' and 'doubters' was kept within strict limits and did not threaten the party apparatus as a whole. Although the language of 'advance' towards participatory 'democracy', common during the Great Break period, did creep into the leadership's discourse, the leadership generally rejected the idea that the time was ripe for

---

[9] See Kotkin's analysis of how the party responded to the centre's purge campaigns, in *Magnetic Mountain*, ch. 7. See also the work of Jochen Hellbeck and Igor Halfin on the response of individual party members to the Terror, J. Hellbeck, 'Writing in the Age of Terror: Alexander Afinogenov's Diary of 1937', in L. Engelstein and S. Sandler (eds.), *Self and Story in Russian History* (Cornell, 2000), 69–93; I. Halfin, 'Looking into the Oppositionists' Souls: Inquisition Communist Style', *RR*, 60 (2001), 316–39. For cultural puritanism, see V. Volkov, 'The Concept of *Kul'turnost'*. Notes on the Stalinist Civilizing Process', in S. Fitzpatrick, *Stalinism. New Directions*, 226–7; for the argument that the years 1936–7 saw a turn towards puritanism in literature, see R. Robin, *Socialist Realism*, 294–5.

an advance towards a higher stage of socialism characterized by political and economic egalitarianism; the Soviet Union had reached socialism, it was claimed, and the present inegalitarian, statist system would remain for some time to come. And third, developments since the early 1930s—the increasing use of patriotic rhetoric, and threats from foreign enemies—encouraged leaders to think about the ideological threat as an ethnic problem as well as a class problem. The internal unbeliever was not just the 'bureaucrat' or 'class alien', but the fifth-columnist member of the diaspora nationality who might ally with a foreign invader.

However, changes in circumstances since the early 1930s also contributed to the radicalization of Stalin's purges, and it had become even more difficult than in the past to mobilize the 'masses' against specific officials while retaining the control Stalin desired. He was challenging regional party officials who had been given considerable powers during the industrialization and collectivization drives of the early 1930s, and who were in a position to deflect and distort his campaigns. And, because he was operating in a more threatening international environment, he was probably more worried about threats to security than he was before. He therefore initiated increasingly radical and populist campaigns to challenge entrenched officials, while at the same time fears, encouraged by these bosses, that his campaigns were undermining internal security, prompted him to organize neo-traditionalist attacks on allegedly unreliable groups within the population as a whole, defined by their class or ethnic background.

The return to revivalism, 1934–5

Stalin's reasons for moving away from the primacy of *tekhnika* and towards the politics of revivalism after the end of 1934 can only be speculated on, but it is likely that he was responding to a deteriorating international situation, and to tensions between the centre and the party and economic apparatuses over economic performance. It is also possible, though not certain, that he genuinely believed that the Kirov murder was organized by terrorists.[10] There is certainly

[10] It used to be commonly argued that Kirov and others in the Central Committee challenged Stalin in January 1934, and Stalin was responding to this political threat,

evidence that in the spring of 1935 Stalin viewed the domestic and international situation as he had seen it in 1927–8: foreign enemies were engaged in terrorism and were fomenting domestic opposition, and the proper response was to increase vigilance against the class enemy, to adopt higher production targets, and to mobilize the population, guaranteeing their loyalty and enthusiasm. All of these required a new primacy of *politika* over *tekhnika*.

The international situation had appeared threatening since Hitler came to power, but the Germans' announcement of conscription in the spring of 1935 seems to have been particularly worrying to the leadership. Marshal Tukhachevskii wrote an article for *Pravda*, published on 29 March, giving a frightening picture of German rearmament plans, and citing *Mein Kampf* and other evidence to stress the Nazis' aggressive intentions towards the Soviet Union. Stalin read and toned down the article before publication.[11] Two days earlier, Stalin had given a speech to the Orgburo in which he connected the increasing foreign threat with alleged oppositional activity in the cities. He argued that the latest internal and external threats were merely the most recent in a long history of subversion. In a brief 'survey of the history of class struggle since February 1917', he recounted how in the late 1920s foreign capitalists had counted on an 'internal revolution' by the peasantry. In 1933 and 1934, the position had improved as the collective farms had become stronger, but now a new danger came from the cities. Enemies had killed Kirov and tried to confuse ignorant students in the universities who, unlike older workers, did not know how much things had improved since 1917.[12] This threat had to be dealt with by increasing vigilance—by checking up on party documents and making sure that enemies did not hold party cards. But Stalin made clear

murdering him in December 1934 and then using violence to rid himself of all potential rivals. See, for instance, R. Conquest, *The Great Terror. A Reassessment*, ch. 2. In the absence of evidence, this view has become less common in recent years. For the argument that Stalin was probably not responsible for Kirov's murder, see Getty and Naumov, *The Road to Terror*, 141–7; A. Kirilina, *Rikoshet, ili skol'ko chelovek bylo ubito vystrelom v Smol'nom* (St Petersburg, 1993). For the Politburo commission of 1990 and its failure to discover evidence of Stalin's involvement in the murder, see D. Koenker and R. Bachman (eds.), *Revelations from the Soviet Archives. Documents in English Translation* (Washington, DC, 1997), 70–84. See also A. Knight, *Who Killed Kirov? The Kremlin's Greatest Mystery* (New York, 1999).

[11] *Izv TsK KPSS*, 1 (1990), 161–70. See also S. Pons, *Stalin and the Inevitable War*, 8.
[12] RGASPI, 558/11/1118, 94–5, 104 (27 March 1935).

that these security measures were all to be part of a more general attempt to improve 'propaganda work' which had been neglected as a result of the obsession with 'economic work'. As in the past, he demanded that the ideological commitment of the people be secured: 'How much moral capital has been accumulated, but we waste it recklessly. We are bad heirs—instead of accumulating new moral capital, we waste it.'[13]

For the Stalinists, the generation of 'moral capital' was not only needed if the regime was to survive, but was vital if they were to promote rapid economic development. Economically, the years 1934 and 1935 were relatively good ones, and plans were fulfilled more successfully than before, but from the beginning of 1935 investment plans, and particularly plans for defence, were increased.[14] Stalin pushed for higher investment and growth, overriding the caution of Gosplan, and the Politburo increased the plan for 1936 in the course of the year.[15] By October 1936 the investment plan for the year was 50 per cent above that of 1935 (although, as will be seen, this was moderated from the middle of 1936).[16] Yet even this level of investment was not enough for the leadership, and it tried to extract more from existing resources, and particularly labour.[17] The leadership was again moving towards ambitious planning, although it had learned from experience: there was never to be a return to the extreme voluntarism of the early 1930s.

As has been seen, Stalin was already dissatisfied with the inability of party bosses and economic officials to fulfil relatively low plans in 1933 and 1934. Stalin established the KPK and KSK in 1934 in order to control the apparatus, and in 1935 he took further measures to enhance central power. In February 1935 he promoted two figures who were to become scourges of officialdom. The first was Andrei Zhdanov, who replaced Kirov as secretary of the Leningrad party organization and became a Central Committee secretary; the second was Nikolai Ezhov, who had occupied various posts in the Central Committee, became head of the KPK, and was given responsibility for supervising the NKVD and its head, Genrikh

---

[13] RGASPI, 558/11/1118, 97–8, 101–2.
[14] See R. W. Davies and O. V. Khlevniuk, 'Stakhanovism and the Soviet Economy', *E–AS*, 54 (2002), 871–5.
[15] R. W. Davies and O. V. Khlevniuk, 'Gosplan', 54–5.
[16] Ibid., 55–7.
[17] For this point, see R. W. Davies and O. V. Khlevniuk, 'Stakhanovism', 877.

Iagoda.[18] Yet tensions between the centre on the one side, and local party bosses and economic commissariats on the other, were to become much greater as the centre became more demanding and as the Soviet economy encountered difficulties in 1936.[19]

In such circumstances, it is understandable that revivalist policies should have appealed to Stalin, and he signalled his new thinking in his speech at the Red Army Academy in May 1935. In this speech, which replaced the 1931 'six conditions' speech as the cardinal ideological statement for the next few years, he declared that the Soviet Union had entered a new period of its development which required a new set of objectives. Now that a powerful industry and agriculture had been created and people had 'mastered' *tekhnika*, the 'period of hunger in the area of *tekhnika*' was 'fundamentally' over. The 'old slogan, "*tekhnika* decides everything", which reflected the period which is already over, when we had insufficient *tekhnika*, must now be replaced by a new slogan, the slogan "cadres decide everything". This is the main thing now.'[20] The speech was in part concerned with a practical problem: the shortage of 'cadres', or officials, who had expertise and knew about technology.[21] But it was also a more general criticism of a technicist, mechanistic approach to the economy and society. As Stalin explained:

People have learned to value machinery and to make reports on how many machines we have in our plants and factories. But I do not know of one instance when a report was made with equal zest on the number of people we have raised in a given period, on how we have helped people to grow and become tempered in their work.[22]

Stalin used voluntaristic and Romantic language to press his point: '*tekhnika* is dead without cadres, but with cadres it has the opportunity to produce miracles...'.[23] He was urging that officials not

---

[18] Oleg Khlevniuk argues that this was part of a more general consolidation of Stalin's personal power within the Politburo. O. V. Khlevniuk, *Politbiuro*, 159–64.

[19] Roberta Manning argues that a serious industrial slowdown from the beginning of 1936 was followed soon after by an agricultural slowdown. She suggests that it was caused by a combination of shortages of foreign technology and of labour and the burdens of high defence expenditure. See 'The Soviet Economic Crisis', 116–41. For poor plan fulfilment in the Urals in 1936, see J. Harris, *The Great Urals*, 172–4.

[20] Stalin, *Sochineniia*, i. (xiv), 61–2. For examples of the impact of Stalin's speech, see *PRTs* (editorial), 12 (1935).

[21] See, for instance, the original version of the speech. RGASPI, 558/11/1077, 47.

[22] Stalin, *Sochineniia*, i. (xiv), 62.

[23] RGASPI, 558/11/1077, 48.

only be expert but that they be transformed into special socialist people, capable of using technology and science to perform extraordinary tasks. Technical education was not all that was required, but careful 'raising' and 'tempering'. Just as Lenin insisted that a powerful politician needed to undergo a fifteen-year process of 'forging', so it was necessary 'not only to breed, but also to forge' pilots.[24] As will be seen, this criticism of officials for exaggerating the importance of *tekhnika* and 'economic tasks', and thus neglecting *politika* and 'ideological principles' (*ideinost'*), became common over the next two years.

The slogan 'cadres decide everything' was, on the face of it, an explicitly élitist revivalist one. In contrast with the Great Break period, Stalin was expressing faith in the new 'stratum' of officials and educated people, not in the working class. Even so, the discourse surrounding the new slogan had strong populist revivalist overtones. It could be used to criticize officials, both for maltreating 'cadres' lower in the hierarchy—the term 'cadre' was often used to refer to lowly officials, and even to some workers-and for their scientific conservatism. If 'cadres decided everything', it was important that they be cadres of the right type, people who believed in socialism and who had also mastered *tekhnika*. So, in his speech to the Red Army Academy, Stalin argued that if industry had 'well-forged cadres, who have mastered *tekhnika*, we would have three times more production, even more, I assure you'.[25] Such statements coincided with criticisms of specialists who were allegedly inhibited by bourgeois conceptions of science. In early 1935, for instance, Kaganovich accused those who defended existing production norms, of being 'limiters', echoing the campaign against the 'bourgeois specialists' of 1928–31;[26] although the class origin of the limiter specialists was not an important issue in 1935, they were still alleged to have defended a 'bourgeois theory'.[27]

This mixture of populist and élitist revivalist messages became particularly evident in the rhetoric surrounding the Stakhanovite movement, launched in the autumn of 1935. The Stakhanovite move-

---

[24] This appears in the unpublished version of the speech. RGASPI, 558/11/1077, 49.

[25] RGASPI, 558/11/1077, 47.

[26] For this campaign, see E. A. Rees, *Stalinism and Soviet Rail Transport, 1928–1941* (Basingstoke, 1995), 114–17.

[27] *P*, 16 May 1935.

ment had much in common with the socialist emulation movements of the late 1920s. Workers were urged to emulate the miner Aleksei Stakhanov and other heroic workers, who had overfulfilled their production quotas.[28] As far as we know, it was Ordzhonikidze who first encouraged the use of Stakhanov's record for more general political purposes. He seems to have considered that the record could be used to put pressure on managers to increase production targets.[29] However, it is unlikely that he intended Stakhanovism to develop into the anti-managerial and voluntaristic campaign that it was to become. Rather it was Stalin who stressed its revivalist implications. In his speech to the first congress of Stakhanovites in November 1935, Stalin strongly criticized the 'vanity' of managers and specialists who 'cling to the banner of science' in rejecting attempts to raise labour norms or targets.[30] They did not realise that workers had become much more productive in the previous couple of years, and that worker heroes had emerged who were 'not afraid to break old norms'.[31] Therefore the more 'revolutionary people' among party and economic leaders had to help the backward to reform themselves.[32] The party had to 'smash the conservatism of some of our engineers and technicians' and 'give free range to the new forces of the working class'. Stalin denied that he was calling for the complete abolition of the technical norms set by specialists, or that he was challenging science *per se*. However, his message was implicitly voluntaristic, as he was suggesting that conventional science had to be changed to reflect the experience of heroic workers. 'Science', he claimed, could only be true science if it lent an 'attentive ear to the voice of experience, of practice' and of the Stakhanovites who embodied that experience.[33] Mikoian used similarly voluntaristic language, when he declared that the conditions were now ripe for a 'new, powerful leap' in economic development.[34]

---

[28] For the Stakhanovite movement, see L. Siegelbaum, *Stakhanovism and the Politics of Productivity in the USSR, 1935–1941* (Cambridge, 1988).

[29] *P* (editorial), 14 September 1935. For Ordzhonikidze's strong criticism of managers in the Donbass and his demand for a 'great shaking-up', see Ordzhonikdze to S. A. Sarkisov (first secretary of the Donetsk regional party committee), 6 September 1935, in *Sovetskoe rukovodstvo*, 310. For Ordzhonikidze's motives, see R. W. Davies and O. V. Khlevniuk, 'Stakhanovism', 877–8.

[30] RGASPI, 558/11/1078, 77.

[31] RGASPI, 558/11/1078, 76, 70–4.   [32] RGASPI, 558/11/1078, 84.

[33] Stalin, *Sochineniia*, i. (xiv), 92–101.   [34] *P*, 27 December 1935.

As Stalin's emphasis on the importance of the 'practical' experience of workers suggests, this discourse had very clear populist revivalist implications. Stalin was no longer dismissive about workers' class maturity, as he had been in 1930–1.[35] The Stakhanovite movement, he now argued, was significant because 'it contains in itself the first beginnings', however weak, of the 'cultural-technical rise of the working class' which would 'undermine the foundations of the contradiction between mental and manual labour' and thus prepare for the transition from socialism to communism.[36] This statement contrasted with Molotov's declaration in 1932 that the elimination of the division between mental and manual labour was a matter for the distant future.[37] Stalin was not signalling the beginning of the end of the division of labour. But he was challenging the authority of technical specialists by claiming that workers were reaching their level, and he was returning to the populist revivalist view that the time was ripe for an advance towards a more egalitarian form of socialism.[38]

In typically populist revivalist fashion, Stalin and his allies argued that if the masses could be trusted, and indeed were rivalling the intelligentsia in their technical ability and 'cultural level', it was possible to establish more 'democratic' relations between officials and masses, thus enabling leaders to mobilize the *nizy* and release their energies. Stalin gave his speech to the Red Army Academy a populist twist by criticizing poor treatment of those at the bottom of the apparatus:

The slogan 'cadres decide everything' demands that our leaders should have the most attentive attitude towards our workers (*rabotniki*), both 'little' and 'big', in whatever area they work, nurturing them carefully, helping them when they need support, encouraging them when they show their first successes, promoting them and so forth. Instead of this, in practice there are many cases of a heartless, bureaucratic and simply disgraceful attitude towards workers.[39]

By November Stalin was identifying the cadres who had to be cared for with the Stakhanovites. Stakhanovites were the new 'cadres of working [class] men and women (*rabochikh i rabotnits*)', and

---

[35] For this theme in his speeches, see Stalin, *Sochineniia*, i. (xiv), 56 (4 May 1935); 100 (17 November 1935); *VI*, 11–12 (1995), 19 (5 March 1937).
[36] Stalin, *Sochineniia*, i. (xiv), 83–4. [37] See Ch. 4, p. 255.
[38] RGASPI, 558/11/1078, 65. [39] Stalin, *Sochineniia*, i. (xiv), 62.

officials were therefore yet again being told to establish more 'democratic' relations with industrial workers.[40] Even so, the rhetoric associated with the Stakhanovite movement differed from that of the late 1920s in that heroic status was being granted to a particular élite group within the working class, rather than the working class as a whole.

The leadership also insisted that 'democracy' was to apply within the party to the party rank and file, and Stalin, with Zhdanov's help, launched the one of the first serious democracy campaigns within the party since the self-criticism campaigns of the Great Break period. Zhdanov was sent to the Saratov territorial committee to investigate complaints brought by the KPK, and in July 1935 he issued a well-publicized attack on the committee, which illustrated the distinction the leadership wished to draw between democratic and bureaucratic methods, and was designed to show all party leaders how to administer their organizations now that 'cadres decided everything'.[41] The Saratov committee, according to Zhdanov, had used 'repression' and 'administrative methods' against rank-and-file party members, rather than 'education' (vospitanie) and 'persuasion'.[42] There was no 'self-criticism', and the rank and file were too afraid to speak up.[43] All of these sins, according to Zhdanov, were a sign that the committee had not listened to Stalin's speech about the need to take care of cadres. Rather it had erroneously assumed that 'military discipline' could be applied to the party.[44]

In place of bureaucratic forms of leadership, Zhdanov argued, the party had to develop a form of agitation and propaganda, or 'party work', that allowed the masses to discuss policy.[45] As in previous

---

[40] RGASPI, 558/11/1078, 74.

[41] Zhdanov told the Saratov organization that he hoped that other organizations would learn from its mistakes. RGASPI, 77/1/478, 85 (7 June 1935). For the campaign against the Saratov organization, see J. A. Getty, Origins, 106–7; J. A. Getty, 'Pragmatists and Puritans', 19–20.

[42] P, 12 July 1935; RGASPI, 77/1/477, 2 (Zhdanov, 1 July 1935).

[43] RGASPI, 77/1/478, 56.

[44] RGASPI, 77/1/478, 53, 42. See also RGASPI, 17/120/187, 137. A military model of discipline was allegedly defended in an article in the local party press.

[45] The connection between agitprop and democracy was made by Kaganovich at the seventeenth party congress. See XVII s"ezd, 558. However, this link was particularly stressed by Zhdanov and became a central theme in his speeches. The resolution of Zhdanov's Leningrad party committee on 'party work' both condemned poor 'propaganda work' and 'ideological work' and criticized breaches of party

years, 'democracy' was not to allow any criticism of the party line, but it was still to have an effect on relations between the rank and file and local party leaders. Local organizations understandably feared the rank-and-file criticism that 'discussions' might bring, and tried to avoid implementing Zhdanov's reforms. The Saratov city party committee, for instance, subtly distorted the March 1935 Central Committee decree on the need to improve 'political–educational work', altering the requirement that party secretaries should give 'reports' to party meetings to the demand that they should merely provide 'information'.[46]

The Stalinist leadership justified its renewed emphasis on 'democracy' in typically populist revivalist terms. First, it argued that democracy would constitute an advance from the capitalist order towards socialist authority relations: Zhdanov, for instance, criticized party workers for treating men as if they were machines: this was a 'survival of the capitalist system which lessened the role of the person, which made the person an appendage of the machine'.[47] Second, as will be seen, democracy was seen as a way of preventing the creation of mutual protection networks among local party and economic officials.[48] And third, democracy was defended as a way of increasing the motivation of the rank and file and their loyalty and commitment to the party. Party leaders' failure to adhere to the party's democratic rules, according to Zhdanov, acted 'as a brake on the growth in the *aktivnost*' and independence of members of the party' and undermined 'the feeling of members of the party that they are masters (*chuvstvo khoziaina*)'.[49] Similarly, Stalin

'democracy'. See *PS*, 8 (1935), 7–8. For the renewed interest in 'propaganda work' in party organizations, see *Ocherki istorii Leningradskoi organizatsii KPSS* (Leningrad, 1968), 459–63; *Ocherki istorii Moskovskoi organizatsii KPSS* (Moscow, 1983), ii. 558–9.

[46] RGASPI, 77/1/478, 60. For the decree on the creation of departments of party cadres in city committees and the revival of party work see RGASPI, 17/114/580 (27 March 1935).

[47] RGASPI, 77/1/478, 53 (5 July 1935).

[48] For the condemnation of cronyism in Saratov in 1935, see RGASPI, 17/120/187, 52; similar criticisms of party leaders, such as Postyshev of Kiev, at the February–March 1937 Central Committee plenum, can be found in RGASPI, 17/2/612, vyp. 3, 50 (Kudriavtsev); *VI*, 11–12 (1995), 20 (Stalin); see RGASPI, 17/120/280, 11 (8 January 1937) for denunciations of Sheboldaev, secretary of the Azov–Black Sea territorial organization.

[49] A. A. Zhdanov, *Podgotovka partiinykh organizatsii k vyboram v verkhovnyi sovet SSSR po novoi izbiratel'noi sisteme i sootvetstvuiushchaia perestroika partiino-politicheskoi raboty* (Moscow, 1937), 24. See also *LP* (editorial), 18 March 1937.

explained the success of the Stakhanovites as, in part, the result of socialism's ability to treat labour well and value it. Only under socialism was labour valued, and labour heroism was only possible in the Soviet Union.[50] Yet Stalin did not insist that all material incentives be replaced with a new set of moral incentives. Stakhanovites were paid more than ordinary workers, and Stalin never reconsidered his rejection of 'egalitarianism' in 1931.

The revival of the party

The turn to from *tekhnika* to *politka*, however, did not only involve the 'democratization' of the party. It was part of a typically revivalist attempt to transform and purify the party and alter its relationship with the economic apparatus. The party, it was argued, had become too closely associated with the state and involved in economic work. It had therefore become 'bureaucratic', losing the ability to mobilize the masses, maintain control over the economic managers, and root out the ideologically suspect. The solution was for the party to separate itself from the state, purify itself, and concentrate on party-political work; then it would be fit to transform the state and society as a whole.

It appears that the leadership, and particularly Stalin, decided that the 'production-branch' structure of lower party organizations, adopted at the seventeenth congress, had to be reformed, on the grounds that it had led party organizations to stress 'economic work' at the expense of 'political work'. Only months after the congress, towards the end of 1934, 'functional' departments, dealing with agitation and other aspects of 'political work', were established in some city party committees, alongside production-branch departments.[51] But it was in March 1935, in response to fear of internal and foreign intervention, that Stalin pushed for a new emphasis on 'propaganda work' and 'party work' more generally, and condemned party organizations' obsession with 'economic work'.[52] As a result of his complaints, departments of party cadres were established in all city committees, organizations explicitly

---

[50] RGASPI, 558/11/1078, 73. Stalin, *Sochineniia* i. (xiv), 91.
[51] Maleiko, 'Iz istorii', 119; *Ocherki istorii Moskovskoi organizatsii KPSS*, ii. 480–1.
[52] RGASPI, 558/11/1118, 97–101.

designed to promote 'the revival of organizational and propaganda work among workers and working people in the cities'.[53] According to Zhdanov, Stalin saw the absence of departments in the city committees as one of the party's 'major shortcomings'.[54] A. A. Andreev, a secretary of the Central Committee, cast doubt on the 1934 reforms more directly at the February–March 1937 plenum. The production-branch organizations, he alleged, had neglected 'organizational-party work'.[55]

The demand that the party perform 'political work' rather than 'economic work' was more than an insistence that the party check up on officials' loyalty and hunt for enemies. It was also an attempt to prevent the party from becoming too close to economic organizations and using their methods of administration. Of course, party officials were subjected to a great deal of criticism in this period, but between 1935 and the middle of 1936, economic managers were seen by Stalinists as the group most hostile to *politika* and susceptible to 'pragmatism'.[56] In a draft of his speech to the February–March 1937 Central Committee plenum, Zhdanov complained that economic organizations had failed to attend to party-political work following the Kirov murder, unlike party organizations which had made real progress.[57] Molotov was even harsher in his criticisms of economic officials at the plenum. He responded angrily to a letter sent by Birman, now director of the Dnepropetrovsk metallurgical plant, to Ordzhonikidze, complaining that party officials were directing criticism at 'a particular category of workers'—the 'economic managers and the directors of large factories'. While Molotov accepted that party workers should not direct criticism 'in a one sided way' against economic managers, he accused Birman of putting all of the blame on the party and refusing to hold economic officials to account.[58]

---

[53] RGASPI,17/114/580, 1 (27 March 1935); *P*, 30 March 1935.

[54] RGASPI, 77/1/434, 5 (25 February 1935); 77/1/439, 5 (5 March 1935).

[55] *VI*, 8 (1995), 11–12.

[56] This view is particularly evident in the press in 1937. See, for instance, *ZI* (editorial), 12 February 1937; *P*, 12 April 1937. For the relative stability in relations between the centre and the regional party bosses between 1934 and 1936, see Khlevniuk, 'The First Generation of Stalinist "Party Generals" ', 46–52.

[57] RGASPI, 77/1/641, 105. Although this passage is only in a draft, not in the speech.

[58] RGASPI, 17/2/612, 15–16.

Given the potentially corrupting influence of economic organizations, the leadership argued, it was essential that party officials
should not collude with them, resist the centre's initiatives, or use
bureaucratic methods towards those below them.[59] The party, it
was claimed, was particularly likely to do this if it overempha-
sized 'economic work', and the conventional revivalist assumption
that 'economic work', in contrast to 'political work', involved
undemocratic behaviour was commonly expressed. Zhdanov, for
instance, argued that 'the root [of shortcomings in local party work]
consists in the fact that many abandon party-organizational and
mass work, substituting it for administrative methods [administrir-
ovanie] along economic lines'. He concluded that party committees
had to be 'freed' 'from the details of economic work'.[60] The allegation that party organizations had concentrated on 'economic work'
and, as a result, had failed to operate 'democratically' was an
extremely common one. Virtually all of the party organizations
criticized during this period, from the Saratov organization in
1935, to those denounced during the February–March 1937 plenum, were condemned for these sins.[61] Thus, it is not surprising that
first of the twelve measures proposed by Stalin at the plenum was
the following:

Above all it is necessary to turn the attention of our party comrades, who
are bogged own in 'current questions' in connection with some [state]
department or other, in the direction of the great international and internal
political questions.[62]

These 'political' questions included 'capitalist encirclement', wrecking by 'enemies', and party democracy.[63]

Revivalist demands for a new stress on 'party-political work'
were unwelcome to some party officials, but for others they were
more appealing, as they presented the economic apparatus as one of
the main sources of authoritarianism and 'apoliticism', and justified

---

[59] For criticisms of 'collusion', see P, 21 November 1936; P, 25 December 1936.
[60] RGASPI, 77/1/445, 23 (23 March 1935).
[61] For criticisms of the Saratov organization in 1935, see RGASPI, 17/120/187, 53;
for similar complaints about the activities of the political departments on the railways, see RGASPI, 17/120/158, 50 (11 January 1935); for attacks on Postyshev at the
February–March plenum on these grounds, see RGASPI, 17/2/612, vyp. 3, 50
(Kudriavtsev).
[62] VI, 4 (1995), 10.
[63] Ibid., 9.

attempts to undermine its influence.[64] So, for instance, the first secretary of the Donetsk regional party committee, S. A. Sarkisov, argued at the February–March 1937 plenum that the best way to ensure that 'party-political work' was performed by economic organizations was to alter their structure so that they could be properly controlled by the party. Sarkisov clearly wanted to exercise power over economic organizations and he complained that they operated 'without any supervision'. But it was difficult for his regional party apparatus to influence industrial administration, which was led from Khar'kov or even Moscow. Hence, he proposed that it be based in the regions, where it could be better supervised by the party.[65]

Party bosses at a factory level could also use revivalist rhetoric in their struggles against managers, as a dispute between the director and the party secretary of a Leningrad factory in the mid-1930s shows. The party secretary had alleged that the director ignored the party organization and made decisions unilaterally; he also possessed a bureaucratic style of leadership. Zhdanov, who was arbitrating the conflict, agreed with the charge: the director had a 'strict' and 'dry' personality, and always spoke as if he were giving an order. This was a sign of an 'incorrect relationship to his cadres': leaders were not just to give orders but to 'seek advice'. Yet Zhdanov went further than this, condemning the director for confusing a 'factory situation' with a 'military situation', and implying that he was establishing 'capitalist' social relations in the factory; he had to realize that

one-man management in our conditions sharply differs from the administration of enterprises by the capitalists, where there is no party organization, where often there are no trade unions, where there is no public opinion (*obshchestvennost'*) and where the director individually is in complete command.

Although Zhdanov did condemn the director, he also wished to calm the situation. He accused the party secretary of overreacting, and denied that the director was a 'definitively corrupted person' as

---

[64] For conflicts between local party and managerial organizations in Magnitogorsk, see S. Kotkin, *Magnetic Mountain*, 296–8.

[65] RGASPI, 17/2/612, vyp. 2, 39. This proposal, and the justification for it, foreshadowed Khrushchev's *sovnarkhoz* reforms of 1957.

some were suggesting; he was to be given time to 'break the bad sides of his character and alter his methods of leadership'.[66]

Zhdanov's criticism of managerial officials was echoed in the statements of the KPK and of its leader, Nikolai Ezhov. Ezhov was particularly unhappy about their excessive power and their ability to corrupt and suborn local party leaders. He noted bitterly that any 'powerful bureaucrat (*chinovnik*)', whether the manager of a trust or the director of a large factory, always managed to use their influence in regional party committees to have punishments imposed by party organizations lifted.[67]

A similar dissatisfaction with the close relationship between party and state explains the leadership's attacks on those party organizations that were particularly close to economic organizations. Ezhov told local party bosses in September 1935 that party organizations attached to economic departments were most guilty of resisting 'self-criticism'.[68] Also, predictably, the political departments were subjected to fierce criticism. The political departments were unpopular among party officials because they answered directly to the centre and were independent of regional party control. Yet they were also attacked, as during the civil war period, on the ground that they were too concerned with economic work. According to a Central Committee commission on the political departments on the railways, they took the place of economic officials, had little interest in 'mass work', and used harsh disciplinarian *administrirovanie* rather than *vospitanie*.[69] Ezhov also alleged that they had been much less effective in carrying out the purges than had conventional territorial organizations.[70] At the November 1934 plenum, the political departments of the Machine Tractor Stations were abolished, probably as a result of strong lobbying from regional party secretaries.[71] Subsequently, at the February–March 1937 plenum, Kaganovich extended this attack to the political departments on the railways, denouncing

---

[66] RGASPI, 77/1/541, 1–6. The speech is dated '1935–1937'.
[67] RGANI, 6/1/15, 123 (KPK plenum, 9 March 1936).
[68] RGASPI, 17/120/179 (25–6 September 1935).
[69] RGASPI, 17/120/158, 8, 16 and *passim* (11 January 1935); see also RGASPI, 17/2/612, vyp. 2, 34 (Kaganovich).
[70] RGASPI, 17/120/179, 14–15, 277–8 (25–6 September 1935).
[71] *KPSS v rezoliutsiiakh*, vi. 186–90. For criticisms of the political departments at the November Central Committee plenum, see 17/2/529, 120–1. For the relationship between party secretaries and the political departments, see O. V. Khlevniuk, 'The First Generation of Stalinist ' "Party Generals" ', 45–6, 48–9.

them for their obsession with 'economic work', their neglect of 'political work' and their 'separation' from the primary party organizations and territorial organizations.[72]

The leadership therefore hoped to prise the party away from the state, restoring its independence and returning it to its 'political' nature. However, like their revivalist predecessors, the Stalinists did not mean by this that the party should extricate itself from economy. Rather, the party, having abandoned undemocratic 'economic work', was to apply its 'political', mobilizing methods to the economic sphere and to transform economic organizations. As Zhdanov explained, the turn to 'party work' did not mean that 'we will not engage in economic questions'. Both party and economic officials had to be involved in economic affairs, but economic officials had to be concerned with 'things', such as technological processes, while the party had to deal with 'people', a much more difficult task. Party officials had to 'raise' people, encourage them to be active participants in socialist society, while liquidating the 'survivals of capitalism'. They were to intervene directly in the economy and ensure that all were working in a sufficiently socialist way.[73]

Zhdanov evidently believed that if the party employed this mobilizational strategy in the economy, it would secure both the loyalty of the population and the fulfilment of heroic production targets. He described the effects of 'party work' on the economy in enthusiastic terms:

at the time of the spring sowing campaign last year we [the party committee] promoted not hundreds, but thousands, tens of thousands of advanced workers... We went from the economy, we fought for twice, three times the norm, and as a result achieved a political [success]. Why? Because they [the peasants] were transformed into noble people and were transformed into political workers. They produced the cadres of our regional and city congresses; these cadres went into politics. This is a fact. Through the economy into politics.... we need to remember that we must hold questions about people (liudskie voprosy) firmly in our hands, know what the collective farmers' attitude is, whether they are mobilized or not, whether there is enthusiasm or not, whether there are Stakhanovites or not, how they feel. These are questions of party-political work.[74]

[72] RGASPI, 17/2/612, vyp. 2, 34–5. In April 1937 station and junction party committees were established. See E. Rees, *Stalinism and Soviet Rail Transport*, 176.
[73] RGASPI, 77/1/453, 10 ff. (20 April 1935).
[74] RGASPI, 77/1/645, 3–9 (21 March 1937).

This rhetoric and the relationship between party and state that it implied were the product of a typically revivalist analysis of the Soviet Union's problems. However, by the mid-1930s any revivalist challenge to the relationship between party and state had become very difficult. While relations between party and state were complex and varied, local party apparatuses were probably more closely enmeshed with state apparatuses than they had been before, and often shared similar interests. In large part, this was the result of the leadership's demand from 1930 that the party co-operate with economic officials and concentrate on 'economic work'. Tensions between local party bosses and economic officials still existed, but the interests of party and economic managers more often coincided, and as James Harris has argued, from the mid-1930s regional party bosses often allied with the economic apparatus to resist pressures from above.[75] Local party bosses even tried to give Moscow the impression that they were checking up on and criticizing managers by denouncing them in public, while privately assuring them of their support.[76] Attempts to challenge collusion and to mobilize the party against the state were therefore even less likely to be successful than they had been before.

Class struggle without the bourgeoisie

As during the Great Break period, the revivalist strategy of mobilization, 'democratization', and rapid economic advance was intimately connected with repression. If the establishment of socialism was dependent on the consciousness of the masses and the proper attitudes of officials, then it was as important to root out those who had a bourgeois and 'rightist' mentality. Efforts were therefore made to direct repression more accurately at officials with 'hostile' attitudes. This was not an entirely new development: as has been seen, the 1933 purge had been aimed at the 'bureaucratic' and 'hostile' within the apparatus. Even so, there is evidence that the leadership, particularly in its party purges, was trying to give repression a more revivalist focus; it also tried to move away from technicist repression—of the ill-disciplined *nizy*—and from neo-traditionalist repression, of stigmatized class aliens.

---

[75] J. Harris, *The Great Urals*, ch. 5.   [76] Ibid., 160.

Harsh anti-bureaucratic rhetoric is evident in the statements of several leaders of the period, but Zhdanov was particularly insistent on the need to unite democratization with persecution; as he declared in a speech in early 1935:

we have secured successes where we have developed self-criticism, where we have mercilessly driven out swindlers and the degenerated, where we have struggled against red-tapist-bureaucratic methods in work, where we have organized the *aktivnost'* of workers (*rabochikh*) and of all working people on the basis of *aktivnost'* and socialist emulation[77]

It was therefore the duty of party officials to combine the inculcation of communist ideas with the eradication of anti-socialist ideas, as he told Leningrad party officials three months later:

Comrade Stalin said that if an ordinary citizen of the USSR needs to have two eyes to see the class enemy, the party worker needs to have four eyes. You [party officials] meet survivals of capitalism in the economy and in the consciousness of people all the time and you need to be able to discern these survivals of capitalism.[78]

Yet while the notion that the apparatus was affected by the 'survivals of capitalism' echoed the rhetoric of the Great Break period, there were significant changes in the leadership's anti-bureaucratic rhetoric. The main one concerned class. As has been seen, revivalists had always found their traditional class explanation of 'bureaucratism' and anti-socialist attitudes an unsatisfactory one. Many of those accused of bureaucratism were Bolsheviks of proletarian class origin, but Stalinists still described their attitudes as bourgeois and tended to argue that the source of their attitudes was ideological contamination by individuals of bourgeois class origin. Yet by the mid-1930s the leadership seems to have considered that even this modified class explanation for the existence of bureaucratic attitudes placed too much stress on their origins among the old bourgeoisie. Now that the regime had formally declared that the old bourgeoisie had been defeated, it would have been difficult to revive a campaign against them as the source of bourgeois contamination. It is also likely that Stalin was wary of returning to the class struggle rhetoric that had been so disruptive in the late 1920s.

[77] RGASPI, 77/1/426, 10 (13 January 1935).
[78] RGASPI, 77/1/453, 19 (20 April 1935).

Moreover there is evidence that the leadership was unhappy with the class definition of bureaucratism for another reason: it was aware that campaigns against the old bourgeoisie were now even more likely than before to miss their real targets—the proletarian official with bureaucratic attitudes. By the mid-1930s, most proletarian officials in the party had few links with bourgeois specialists, and they were unlikely to find campaigns against the bourgeoisie threatening; indeed, they could participate in them enthusiastically, directing them away from officialdom towards uninfluential individuals of bourgeois class origin. Zhdanov criticized this tendency of local officials to distort campaigns in a meeting with officials from the Murmansk and Karelia party organizations in August 1935, and urged that political attitude and behaviour should be the primary determinants in the search for enemies, not class origin. There was to be no 'schematism in relation to former people (*byvshie liudi*) [i.e. class aliens and people with links to the former regime]':

Some of them we will shoot, if they are counter-revolutionaries, some of them we will reeducate, raise them into good people. In a word, it all depends on how this or that person behaves. But he [a Murmansk party official] tried to decide this question in relation to the former people by regarding all former people as enemies and to expel them from Murmansk.[79]

As will be seen, Stalin and his associates always objected to the neo-traditionalist view that class attitudes were inherited and could not be changed through education and personal transformation. Even so, leaders' attitudes towards class were still ambivalent, and they found it difficult to abandon the notion that those of bourgeois class origin were carriers of ideological infection. Immediately following the Kirov murder, large numbers of 'former people' were expelled from Leningrad, and the Leningrad NKVD was criticized for failing to recognize how dangerous those associated with the tsarist regime could be.[80] Similarly, Ezhov, speaking in April 1936, claimed that even though former tsarist bureaucrats, teachers, traders, and craftsmen and their children might have become workers by

---

[79] RGASPI, 77/1/489, 22 (14 August 1935).
[80] *P*, 20 February 1935; *Izv TsK KPSS*, 8 1989, 99–100; V. N. Khaustov, V. P. Naumov, and N. S. Plotnikov (eds.), *Lubianka. Stalin i VChK-GPU-OGPU-NKVD' ianvar' 1922–dekabr' 1936* (Moscow, 2003), 654–7.

occupation, they had 'brought the ideology of the petty bourgeoisie with them to a much greater extent than any other elements'.[81] At the same time, however, he strongly criticized those who continued to pursue a crude policy of class discrimination. So, for instance, he sacked a KPK official who had falsely accused a local party official of having a class alien background, and condemned his obsession with class origin.[82]

If, for Stalin and the leadership, class origin no longer provided a clear guide to political attitudes, the notion that former political oppositionists were the source of 'bourgeois' and 'rightist' views within the apparatus seemed to be more plausible. Several former members of the old oppositions held positions within the apparatus (and particularly within the economic apparatus), and officials had many more contacts with former oppositionists than with class aliens. This was particularly the case in the economic apparatus, where former élitist revivalist associates of Trotsky—people like Piatakov, now Ordzhonikidze's deputy at Narkomtiazhprom—had influential positions. Therefore the campaign against former oppositionists was much more compatible with an attempt to root out 'bureaucratism' and conservative attitudes in the apparatus than was a campaign against class aliens, and while Politburo leaders continued to see class aliens as a threat, they began to concentrate much more on the ideological danger from former 'Trotskyists' and 'rightists'. At the same time Stalin, as in the past, seems to have assumed that these ideological doubts were likely to manifest themselves in conspiracies to overthrow the regime.

The notion of the oppositionist conspiracy was not novel. As has been seen, Stalin had used the story of the oppositionist as the transmitter of bourgeois ideas from abroad, in embryo, in 1930 when he accused Bukharin and Rykov of conspiracy. Stalin had claimed that Bukharin, a 'preacher of terrorism', had conspired with rightist forces within the state apparatus and also with the Industrial party and its foreign backers. But by 1934 Zinoviev, Kamenev, and Trotsky had taken the place of the right as the originators of the conspiracy. The story had a basis in truth: there

[81] RGASPI, 17/120/179, 58–9.

[82] RGANI, 6/1/62, 106 (Protokol zasedanii biuro KPK, 11–22 April 1936). On another occasion Ezhov criticized those who limited the number of 'Soviet specialists' admitted into the party. RGASPI, 17/120/177, 74 (December 1935).

was a small underground Trotskyist organization within the Soviet Union, maintained from abroad by Trotsky's son Lev Sedov, although, of course, the charges of terrorism and conspiracy were fictitious.[83] More importantly, the story was plausible in ideological terms. While Trotsky had condemned the Stalinist regime on the revivalist grounds that it had become hierarchical and Thermidorian, he also criticized the excessively ambitious industrialization and collectivization policies.[84] The Zinovievites and Trotskyists could therefore be presented as a source of technicist ideas, especially in the economic apparatus. Indeed, it is possible that Stalin and Ezhov genuinely believed that the problems within the economy were caused, at least in part, by the influence of former Trotskyists in positions of responsibility.

Yet although the 'enemy' had now lost its class label, a language of class is evident beneath the language of oppositionism. In many ways, the campaign against the Trotskyists was very similar to that against the bourgeois wreckers during the Great Break era: in both cases 'hostile' individuals with 'rightist' ideas were alleged to be conspiring against the state and corrupting officials. The difference was that the originators of these opinions were now much closer to the party apparatus than they had been before. Stalin directly compared the 'class enemies' of the late 1920s with the 'oppositionists' of the 1930s in his speech to the Central Committee plenum in March 1937:

The Shakhty and Industrial party people were people openly alien to us. They were for the most part former factory owners, former managers for the old bosses, former partners in joint-stock companies, or simply old bourgeois specialists who were openly hostile to us politically... It is not possible to say the same about the present-day wreckers and saboteurs, about the Trotskyists. [They] ... are for the most part party people with a party card in their pockets, and as a result people who are *formally not alien*. If the old wreckers opposed our people, the new wreckers fawn on our people, praise them, suck up to them in order to worm their way into their confidence. The difference, as you see, is a substantial one.[85]

---

[83] See J. A. Getty, *Origins*, 119–21.

[84] Trotsky, *The Revolution Betrayed*, 40–2. For earlier criticisms of Stalin's 'adventurism' and 'ultra-leftism', see L. D. Trotsky, 'Ekonomicheskii avantiurizm i ee opasnost' ', *BO*, 9 (1930), 2, 7; Trotsky, 'Blok levykh i pravykh', *BO*, 17–18 (1930), 25.

[85] *VI*, 4 (1995), 8. Emphasis added.

But while Stalin stressed the differences between the two groups, at the same time he drew comparisons between them, and the new narrative laid the foundations for a quasi-class struggle against anti-revivalist individuals of spotlessly proletarian origin within the apparatus. This idea was obviously very dangerous for the regime, because it could be taken to mean that a 'new class'—the Soviet bureaucracy—had arisen under socialism, and that a new revolution had to be launched against it. While the leadership outlawed such an extreme interpretation of these ideas, by 1937 it was prepared to take the risk and use the old populist revivalist language of the Shakhty era in its assault against the apparatus.

The search for enemies within the élite, 1935: the case against Zinoviev, Kamenev, and Trotsky

The foundations of the story of the Trotskyist conspiracy were laid immediately after the murder of Kirov, and as in the late 1920s, the essence of the 'crimes' committed by the 'enemies' were ideological and political. It was the technicism or 'rightism' of the accused that was the core of the charges against them, although it is possible that Stalin and Ezhov also believed that they were guilty of conspiracy and sabotage.

If Stalin instigated the murder of Kirov, he used it cynically for propagandistic purposes, in order to wage a campaign against the former opposition; if he did not, he may well have believed that the former opposition was involved in some kind of conspiracy. But, whoever was behind Kirov's murder, Stalin was pursuing a revivalist agenda. In accordance with the old revivalist view that the real danger came from class aliens, a number of 'white-guardists' in Leningrad were executed immediately after the murder, but Stalin also seems to have wanted to use the murder to cast suspicion on former oppositionists;[86] according to Ezhov, it was Stalin who first issued the instruction: 'look for the murderers among the Zinovievites', despite the scepticism of Iagoda and the NKVD.[87] Stalin also seems to have been instrumental in identifying Kirov's murderers

---

[86] For reports of these, see *LP*, 6, 8, 11, 12, December 1934.

[87] Ezhov was speaking at the February–March 1937 plenum. A. N. Iakovlev (ed.), *Reabilitatsiia*, 153.

with a group of former supporters of Zinoviev in Leningrad, which he dubbed the criminal 'Leningrad Centre'.[88] This group had allegedly, in league with an unnamed foreign state, tried to make contact with Trotsky and white-guardist émigrés and planned terrorism, in order to implement the 'so-called Trotskyist–Zinovievite platform'.[89] Yet the secret police also seems to have wanted to make a bigger impression, by preparing a case against Kamenev and Zinoviev themselves.

While Stalin may have believed that Kamenev and Zinoviev were actually engaged in some form of conspiracy, the available evidence suggests that his views of conspiracy were similar to those he had expressed in 1928–30: it was the political and ideological aspect of these cases that was central. Kamenev and Zinoviev were seen as transmitters of 'rightist' ideas, and both could plausibly be depicted as representatives of rightists in the élite. In 1932 they had been accused of having read Riutin's anti-revivalist manifesto and of having failed to report it, a charge which Zinoviev subsequently admitted to.[90] They had also had close connections with Trotsky.

There were two elements to the charges against Zinoviev and Kamenev. The first was political, that they were leaders of a counter-revolutionary organization, the 'Moscow Centre'; the second was more straightforwardly criminal, that they had conspired with the Leningrad Centre to murder Kirov. But the statement signed by Zinoviev following his interrogation suggests that the logic of the case was primarily political.[91] Initially, he explained, he had considered the charges against him completely incomprehensible. 'Gradually', however, he understood 'the real meaning of these events'.[92] This 'meaning', presumably communicated to him by his interrogators, was that he was guilty because he had maintained his rightist attitudes. After 1930, he explained, he had told himself that Stalin's revivalist policies had been proved correct and deserved his support. But when new economic difficulties arose in 1932 he again became critical of Stalin. While 'subjectively' he had no desire 'to harm the party and the working class', objectively he became the

---

[88] See R. Tucker, *Stalin in Power*, 298–300.
[89] See A. N. Iakovlev (ed.), *Reabilitatsiia*, 123–47.
[90] Ibid., 150–1.
[91] For the full text of this statement, see ibid., 159–64.
[92] Ibid., 159.

'mouthpiece of those forces which wanted to stop the socialist assault, which wanted to break socialism in the USSR'. Although he and his associates claimed to support the general line, they hoped that they would be given influential posts and would be in a position to 'correct "mistakes"' and 'improve the regime'. He and his group did not consider that they were carrying out 'systematic anti-party fractional work', but 'in reality' they had organized a conspiratorial 'centre'.[93]

Zinoviev, then, was prepared to plead guilty to the political charges, but he refused to admit that he had ordered the assassination of Kirov or even that he knew of the existence of the Leningrad Centre. He would only accept that he had discussed his anti-party views with V. Levin, a member of the Leningrad Centre, in 1932, and that 'the boundary between this [action] and the animation of the anti-party organization of the former "Zinovievites" in Leningrad is, of course, very thin'.[94] So Zinoviev was willing to go along with the Stalinist logic to some extent: he admitted that he had continued to harbour rightist attitudes, that objectively this amounted to anti-party activity and that his ideas and those of the Moscow Centre had inspired the perpetrators of Kirov's murder. Kamenev, however, was even less willing to co-operate and flatly denied that he had participated in a Moscow Centre.[95] It was therefore difficult to claim that Kamenev and Zinoviev had participated in a genuine conspiracy. The report on the verdict of the trial, published in *Pravda* on 18 January, concluded that although no facts had been established proving that the Moscow Centre had incited the murder of Kirov, it had been shown that they knew about the 'terrorist sentiments' of the Leningrad group and stirred them up.[96]

Some, including Ezhov, seem to have been disappointed with the trial, and Ezhov continued to try to demonstrate that former oppositionists were involved directly in acts of terrorism, and were not just inspiring terrorism ideologically. Between 1935 and 1937 Ezhov wrote a number of versions of a work entitled 'From Fractionalism to Open Counter-revolution and Fascism', sent to Stalin for comments, which developed this theory.[97] He alleged

[93] Ibid., 160.   [94] Ibid., 162.
[95] Ibid., 166.   [96] *P*, 18 January 1935.
[97] For references to this work, see *Izv TsK KPSS*, 8 (1989), 82; B. Starkov, 'Narkom Ezhov', in J. A. Getty and R. Manning, *Stalinist Terror*, 24–5.

that there had been close links between the Zinovievites and the Trotskyists throughout the period.[98] He smeared the former Left Opposition with rightism, describing the Moscow and Leningrad Centres as 'Zinovievite–Kamenevite Mensheviks', and he claimed that the former oppositionists were planning to commit terrorist acts, including the assassination of Stalin himself.[99] Similar charges were made these charges at the June 1935 Central Committee plenum, when he accused A. S. Enukidze, the secretary of the Central Executive Committee of Soviets and responsible for the Kremlin's security, of failing to remove terrorists from the Kremlin's staff.[100] Yet, as Getty and Naumov have argued, Stalin does not seem to have wholeheartedly supported Ezhov's claim that Kamenev, Zinoviev, and Trotsky were themselves actually guilty of terrorism, and, as in 1930, he was reluctant to accuse prominent Bolsheviks of any more than ideological crimes.[101]

The search for enemies and the corrupted in the apparatus, 1935–6

Alongside attacks on ideological 'enemies' at the top of the party, the leadership launched campaigns against 'enemies' throughout the apparatus in party purges. The purges of 1935 and 1936, the so-called 'verification of party documents' and the 'exchange of party documents', were in effect purges of the party in the tradition of previous purges, and there was no direct link with the persecution of Kamenev and Zinoviev.[102] Even so, the leadership placed a strong emphasis on the need to root out those guilty of ideological crimes.

As in 1933, a range of categories of people, from corrupt and disobedient bureaucrats to 'enemies', were targeted. Initially, it appeared as if Moscow was trusting local party bosses with this purge, as it left them to organize the verification, in contrast with 1933 when the Central Purge Commission had been in charge.

---

[98] *Izv TsK KPSS*, 8 (1989), 82.
[99] A. N. Iakovlev (ed.), *Reabilitatsiia*, 170.
[100] RGASPI, 17/2/542, 55–82. Quoted in Getty and Naumov, *The Road to Terror*, 161–6.
[101] J. A. Getty and O. V. Naumov, *The Road to Terror*, 167.
[102] For the 'verification' and 'exchange', see J. A. Getty, *Origins*, ch. 3. The verification was announced before the murder of Kirov.

But Moscow was dissatisfied with the cursory way in which the purge was being conducted, and in the summer of 1935 it criticized local organizations, demanding a rerun of the verification.[103] The leadership was in part trying to ensure that the verification fulfilled its revivalist, anti-bureaucratic potential, and that it did not share the fate of the 1933 purge. As Ezhov explained, both the 1933 purge and the verification of party documents were designed to rid the party of 'filth' (skvernye), but only the 1933 purge was aimed at 'ballast' in the party, by which he meant the 'passives' who had ended up in the party 'by chance'.[104]

The verification and exchange of party documents were presented in a typically revivalist way. They were, according to Ezhov, designed to allow the party apparatus to know the attitudes of all communists, whether they were good socialists or had been corrupted by anti-socialist ideas. Checking up on party cards, for Ezhov, was not just a matter of administrative efficiency; it was designed to prevent 'hostile' individuals from hiding their political and class background by getting hold of stolen party cards.[105] As Ezhov put it at the December 1935 Central Committee plenum, the objective of the verification was to cleanse the party

of swindlers, impostors and elements who hang on to the party, to end the scandalous situation in the handing out and storage of party documents, to provide an exemplary register of communists and to know members and candidate members of the party well.[106]

Ezhov linked these campaigns with revivalist notions of party work and vospitanie. The purges were to expose hidden enemies who had party cards and would also allow officials to 'recognize many new Bolsheviks who were genuinely loyal to the party, whose presence in their organization they did not know about'.[107] Echoing Zhdanov's language, he declared that 'knowing people' was the 'fundamental of all fundamentals', as it would allow the 'raising of party life' and the improvement of 'party work'.[108] An article published in Pravda of August 1935 was even more explicit in associating the primacy of

---

[103] J. A. Getty, Origins, 60–78.
[104] RGASPI, 17/120/179, 272 (25–6 September 1935).
[105] RGASPI, 17/120/179, 29–30.
[106] RGASPI, 17/2/558, 6–7.
[107] RGASPI, 17/2/558, 9.
[108] RGASPI, 17/120/179, 63.

politika and ideology with the search for enemies in the apparatus. Party leaders who did not co-operate with the campaign for the checking of party documents demonstrated their 'apolitical practical attitude' (*praktitsizm*) and 'narrow utilitarianism' (*deliachestvo*), their lack of 'revolutionary vigilance' and 'class blindness', their neglect of 'revolutionary theory and ideological *vospitanie*', and their rejection of party-political work in favour of economic work. Such attitudes effectively demobilized the party; as the article put it, they 'lead to the *deliacheskii* degeneration of leadership and disarm communists in the face of increasing tasks and the class enemy who resists us furiously'.[109]

The definitions of the purges' targets varied over the period. Official statements on their identity were highly inconsistent, and party members were expelled for a number of reasons. A summary of the results of the various purges from the beginning of 1935 and February 1937 shows that the largest number of those expelled were 'whiteguards', 'kulaks', other 'class alien' and 'hostile' elements (27.5 per cent), closely followed by those who had been 'corrupted' (20.6 per cent), followed by 'others' (17.7 per cent), 'fraudsters (*aferisty*) and swindlers (*zhuliki*)' (8 per cent), those recruited in violation of the statutes (6.7 per cent), 'Trotskyists and Zinovievites' (5.5 per cent), and eight other smaller categories.[110] It is difficult to understand precisely what was meant by these categories, but informally the party leadership seems to have distinguished between 'dangerous' enemies—who had an oppositionist or class alien background, who were the carriers of alien ideologies, and who dissembled to the party about their real views—and a less dangerous group who were not serious ideological enemies. So, for instance, in December 1935 Ezhov grouped 'spies', 'whiteguards and kulaks', 'Trotskyists and Zinovievites', and 'fraudsters and swindlers' together, defining them as 'the most malicious and active enemies of the party'. Combined they made up over 30 per cent of those purged.[111] Similarly, Ugarov, second secretary of the Leningrad

---

[109] R. Khitarov, 'Ideinost' i deliachestvo v partiinoi rabote', *P*, 23 August 1935.

[110] RGASPI 17/120/278, 2 (Malenkov, 15 February 1937). The other categories were: on the register but having cut ties with the party—3.9%; passives, 3.4%; hid from the verification—2.4%; refused the verification—1.8%; spies, or those having links with spies—0.9%; expelled earlier but not given up party card—0.8%; did not go through the 1929 purge—0.8%, rightists—0%.

[111] RGASPI, 17/120/177, 20-1. An NKVD report of November 1935 on those arrested in connection with the verification confined its attention to similar

party organization, declared in December 1935 that 'more than half of all excluded from the party [in Leningrad] were class alien, hostile elements from among the white-guardists, kulaks, Zinovievites, Trotskyists, spies and others, against whom, above all, the sharp edge of the verification of party documents is directed'.[112]

These lists, therefore, suggest that the leadership, as in the late 1920s, wanted to expel and possibly arrest a limited group of ideological 'enemies' and alleged spies in the apparatus and then to purge a larger group of disobedient officials and party members who were guilty of various types of offence but were not enemies. However, it was easier to publish injunctions than to make sure that their logic was implemented. There were two ways in which the leadership's objectives could be frustrated. Firstly, it was possible that reformable communists corrupted by enemies could be described as enemies themselves; the purge would thus undermine the party apparatus as a whole, either by creating a dangerously alienated group of former communists, or by giving the rank and file and population as a whole the impression that the apparatus was riddled with enemies. This was more of a danger after 1935 than in 1928–30, because the 'Trotskyist' enemies, as proletarians, were much more closely connected with incumbent bosses than the old class aliens. The second problem was precisely the opposite: party bosses could protect themselves, distorting the categories in a way that deflected the purges downwards, towards the rank and file, just as they had done during the 1933 purge when they stressed the danger from 'passives'. Between 1935 and 1937 the leadership was constantly trying to steer a course between excessively forceful attacks on the apparatus and an acquiescence in party bosses' efforts to pervert revivalist objectives. But the difficulty of describing who was virtuous, who was irredeemably evil, and who was 'corrupted' but could be reformed, and the vague language used to describe each category, ensured that it was very likely to fail.

categories, implying that other categories were of less interest to the NKVD because they were less politically worrying. The categories mentioned were: spies, fraudsters, those who hid their social origin, former whiteguards and participants in counter-revolutionary rebellions, Trotskyists, and Zinovievites. RGASPI, 17/120/181, 163, 215 (figures for those arrested between 1 August 1935 and 27 October 1935).

[112] RGASPI, 17/2/561, 145.

In conducting the verification of party documents in 1935 and 1936, Ezhov was particularly concerned to make sure that the purge did not become an indiscriminate persecution of communists. He criticized some organizations for treating people expelled from the party as if they were all enemies, depriving them of their jobs and their apartments.[113] For Ezhov, even enemies could be taught to mend their ways, and if an enemy admitted the justice of his or her expulsion but asked for mercy, they were to be readmitted on appeal. Only if enemies had lied to the party about their past activities and attitudes were they to be cast out for ever, for the party could not trust them.[114]

In part, Ezhov was worried that the expulsion and maltreatment of large numbers of communists would create a large group of disaffected people who might then become genuine enemies of the regime.[115] But he was also concerned about the effect that a large-scale persecution of 'enemies' in the party might have on the stability of the regime itself. Speaking at a meeting with regional officials in September 1935 Ezhov spent some time discussing how the verification should be presented to the public. He argued that the regime could afford to reveal the party's 'weak spots' to workers and peasants, because workers trusted the regime and peasants were generally loyal. He therefore recommended that particular, individual 'double-dealers' (*dvurushniki*) and 'Trotskyists'—people who had claimed to adhere to the General Line while actually acting against it—should be 'exposed before the working masses'. But he was unwilling to go any further than this: it was, he said, inappropriate to 'raise all of the masses for the verification', or to organize an 'explanatory campaign', and he was unenthusiastic about the 'elucidation of the verification of party documents in the press, and particularly in *Pravda*'. A party official at the meeting agreed, reporting that many district committee officials thought that criticisms of the party had been taken to extremes. Ezhov accepted that the press had not struck the right 'note' in its coverage.[116] He evidently had no desire to destroy local party leaders. As he made clear, the Trotskyists had not tried to obtain 'commanding posts' in

---

[113] RGASPI, 17/120/240, 22 (Ezhov, January–March 1936); RGASPI, 17/2/568, 13 (Ezhov, 3 June 1936).
[114] RGASPI, 17/120/241, 8–11 (1 February 1936).
[115] RGASPI, 17/120/241, 9.
[116] RGASPI, 17/120/179, 270–4.

the party, but had become lowly accounting clerks with access to party documents.[117]

Yet the greatest difficulty facing Stalin and Ezhov was not the preservation of the apparatus but officials' ability to protect themselves from the centre. Regional party officials and their cliques, who were obviously threatened by purges which were directed at ideological enemies with an oppositionist background, successfully adopted strategies of passive resistance, largely by exploiting the ambiguities of the revivalist language of the 'enemy'. Their first tactic, as used in 1933, was to distort Moscow's demands that party members had to be virtuous, ideologically motivated, believers in socialism, into the requirement that party members should be knowledgeable about party dogma. So, rather than using the verification of party documents to investigate whether officials had attitudes which might be regarded by the centre as 'rightist' or alien, they targeted 'passives' among the rank and file. Ezhov's frustration with this practice is clear. He told party bosses that they had to be extremely careful when expelling 'passives', 'to measure ten times before cutting', and party organizations, he insisted, should not expel large numbers of innocent people, just because they were under pressure from the centre.[118] Stalin was particularly worried about the persecution of 'passives', and he even tried to stop the practice by altering the party statutes. The condition, laid down in the statutes, that each party member had to master the programme, statutes, and most important decisions of the party had to be removed, he argued, because the average party member could not be expected to be a 'finished Marxist'.[119]

The party bosses' second tactic was to exploit the leadership's ambiguous attitude to class and class origin, and to conduct neo-traditionalist purges which targeted people with a non-proletarian background, generally rank-and-file party members who had few connections with local cliques. Ezhov predictably condemned local party bosses for expelling party members for minor offences, such

---

[117] RGASPI, 17/120/179, 38.

[118] RGASPI, 17/120/240, 28; RGASPI, 17/120/241, 3–4. For Ezhov's and Zhdanov's criticisms of the large numbers of unjustified expulsions during the 1933 purge, see RGASPI, 17/120/179, 27–8; RGASPI, 77/1/719, 29 (Zhdanov, March 1939). Even so, Ezhov defended the verification in February 1936, arguing that the very small number of appeals against expulsion suggested that the party had carried out the verification correctly. RGASPI, 17/120/241, 44.

[119] RGASPI, 17/2/572, 73–4.

as the concealment of class origin, and then treating them as if they were dangerous enemies, depriving them of their jobs and expelling them from their apartments.[120] He also implied that he understood the motives behind regional bosses' persecution of class aliens: to protect the privileged party member of working-class origin. As he told a conference of regional party secretaries in September 1935, it was unacceptable that workers who had party cards should be 'inviolable'. This 'worship of the worker' was 'completely un-Bolshevik and un-Marxist'.[121]

In December 1935 Ezhov complained that local party bodies had not conducted the verification carefully enough, and a similar purge of the party, the exchange of party documents, was conducted in 1936. Even after this, however, the Central Committee continued to complain about local organizations' distortion of the campaign, and in some cases it had to intervene directly.[122] As Postyshev, now first secretary of the Kiev party organization, admitted, 'we felt the hand of comrade Ezhov, so to say, very firmly every day'.[123] Stalin seems to have taken an even more critical view of the regional secretaries than Ezhov, and implicitly criticized Ezhov at the June 1936 plenum for allowing the unjust persecution of passives.[124] Yet the expulsion of party members for passivity seems to have continued.[125] At the February–March 1937 plenum, Stalin again denounced those who did not 'care about members of the party and their fate', who regarded the expulsion of 10,000 members for 'passivity' as a 'trifle'.[126]

Some of the denunciations of party bosses in the press could be framed in very strong language. One article, published in August 1935, described party 'big-shots' (*shliapy*) who refused to conduct a proper verification of party documents as 'apolitical' people who were helping the enemy. While not accusing them of ideological opposition, it did compare them with those who lacked 'revolutionary perspective' in the struggle against the anti-Leninist oppositions and who were guilty of 'opportunism in practice'.[127]

---

[120] RGASPI, 17/2/572, 68–9.
[121] Quoted in J. A. Getty and O. V. Naumov, *The Road to Terror*, 201.
[122] RGASPI, 17/2/561, 128–9.
[123] RGASPI, 17/2/561, 163.
[124] RGASPI, 17/2/568, 135–6. This is argued convincingly in J. A. Getty and O. V. Naumov, *The Road to Terror*, 239–40.
[125] VI, 11–12 (1995), 20–1.
[126] VI, 11–12 (1995), 20–1.   [127] P, 23 August 1935.

Yet such strong language was much more common in the leadership's condemnation of the sins of economic officials. From the beginning of 1935 those who were sceptical of high plan targets on the railways were accused of being 'limiters', and authoritarian managers were denounced in the press for having bourgeois or capitalist attitudes, although the precise source of this bourgeois influence was generally not made clear.[128] By late 1935, however, leaders and the press were more forthright in charging 'bureaucratic', undemocratic officials, primarily within the economic apparatus, with explicitly hostile behaviour. Undoubtedly the tensions produced by the Stakhanovite Movement encouraged this populist revivalist response.[129] Managers and specialists who found it difficult to implement the voluntaristic economic policies of the leadership were berated for casting doubt on high plan targets and resisting working-class participation in administration. Ordzhonikidze was the first to raise the likelihood that 'backward leaders' in enterprises would show 'philistine scepticism' and 'sabotage' the movement, but he subsequently toned down his language and became more conciliatory to managers and engineers.[130] Other leaders, however, were more insistent that those managers who obstructed the Stakhanovite movement should be seen as saboteurs with capitalist attitudes. Zhdanov's statements were particularly aggressive, describing those who undermined Stakhanovism as 'enemies of the working class and of the party'.[131] Those who opposed Stakhanovism, he declared, were 'callous, conservative, bureaucratic' elements, 'survivals of capitalism', who still thought 'that the machine is the main thing, not the person'.[132]

Leaders' revivalist sentiments were soon translated into legislation.[133] In November 1935 the Russian Supreme Court decreed that administrative and technical staff accused of resisting the

[128] *P* (editorial), 15 June 1935.
[129] For this process, see L. Siegelbaum, *Stakhanovism*, ch. 3.
[130] *P* (editorial), 14 September 1935. For a different tone, see *P* (editorial), 18 November 1935. For the change in the tone of Ordzhonikidze's statements, see Siegelbaum, *Stakhanovism*, 81–2.
[131] *LP*, 22 October 1935.
[132] RGASPI, 77/1/505, 10 (21 October 1935).
[133] For revivalist statements, see *P*, 18 January 1936 (Zhdanov); RGASPI, 77/1/566, 13 (Zhdanov, 21 March 1936). In a speech of 16 November 1935, Zhdanov denounced saboteurs but he did accept that several directors were leading the movement effectively. RGASPI 77/1/517, 10, 13. For other, harsh, views of managers, see V. M. Molotov, *Stat'i i rechi, 1935–1936* (Moscow, 1937), 153, 158, 160.

Stakhanovite movement with 'counter-revolutionary aims' would be tried under article 58 of the criminal code, which dealt with political, counter-revolutionary crimes.[134] Although workers could be accused of sabotaging the movement, the campaign had a clear anti-bureaucratic character. A report of early 1936 to the KPK on the prosecution of saboteurs by the judicial apparatus reveals that 457 people had been convicted of sabotaging the Stakhanovite movement in 6 *krai*, most of whom were 'engineers, technicians, foremen, and chargehands'.[135]

By the beginning of 1936, therefore, most of the ideological and institutional elements of a revivalist campaign against 'enemies' and 'doubters' in the economic and party apparatuses were in place. Stalin and his colleagues were pressing for more ambitious economic growth and a strategy of mobilization, while many economic and regional party officials were unwilling or unable to comply. At the same time, as during previous revivalist campaigns, Stalin seems to have been cautious about pushing the campaign against the former opposition within the apparatus too far, for fear that he might weaken it fatally and undermine his own position.

The apparatus and resistance to revivalism

It was extremely difficult, if not impossible, for the party or economic apparatus openly to challenge the revivalist assumptions of the leadership, and therefore resistance was generally passive: officials would pretend to be enthusiastic about the centre's campaigns, while trying to limit their effects. Yet officials did try to defend themselves by attempting to manipulate language in their own interests, whether by propagating their own technicist and neo-traditionalist messages, or by distorting and blunting the leadership's revivalist language. Given the enormous importance of political language in explaining the proper relationship between officials and subordinates, and defining who the virtuous and who

---

[134] *Slu*, 36 (1935), 2.
[135] RGANI, 6/1/59, 184 (29 February–3 March 1936). For the persecution of managers and technicians for anti-Stakhanovite activity in this period, see R. W. Davies and O. V. Khlevniuk, 'Stakhanovism', 884–5; V. N. Khaustov, V. P. Naumov, and N. S. Plotnikov (eds.), *Lubianka*, 700–1.

the enemies were, it is understandable that they would risk the ire of the leadership. It is also not surprising that Stalin and his group would take these manipulations of political discourse seriously, and that the use of heterodox language would contribute to their view that there were ideological doubters in the apparatus, and particularly in the economic commissariats.

The economic commissars, and Ordzhonikidze in particular, were in an ambiguous position. On the one hand, Ordzhonikidze had responsibility for the fulfilment of the plan and was prepared to use revivalist arguments to put pressure on his subordinates. He was also a political leader rather than a technical specialist, and was used to employing revivalist language.[136] In general, however, he seems to have been uncomfortable with revivalist rhetoric and he tried, cautiously, to defend managers and technical specialists from criticism. He sometimes did this by arguing that managers were virtuous, wholly loyal people, who deserved a place within the hierarchical Soviet family, and not among the 'aliens'. So, Ordzhonikidze told a conference of engineers and technicians in November 1935 that young engineers had been 'raised by us' and were 'our children, our brothers'.[137] In May 1936, he was prepared to concede that many managers in the Donbass were conservative and ineffective, but he condemned those who shouted that 'all engineers, technicians, managers are saboteurs' and that the 'officers' of industry were people 'of an alien class'.[138] Similarly, his speech at the December 1935 plenum of the Central Committee referred to the 'conservatism and stubbornness' of some specialists, rather than their 'sabotage'.[139] Andreev may have been referring to his speech when he criticized some of the speakers at the plenum for evaluating 'the participation of technical personnel in the Stakhanovite movement too optimistically'.[140]

Ordzhonikidze and his fellow industrial commissars also deployed technicist arguments in their defence of their subordinates.[141]

---

[136] See, for instance, his criticisms of managers. RGASPI, 85/29/139, 115–19 (16 June 1936).

[137] 'Neopublikovannoe vystuplenie G. K. Ordzhonikidze', VI, 8 (1978), 94–7. See also RGASPI, 85/29/134, 57–8 (4 May 1936).

[138] RGASPI, 85/29/134, 57. Although Ordzhonikidze agreed with Sarkisov that the economic leadership in the Donbass was 'bad'. Ordzhonikidze to Sarkisov, RGASPI, 85/29/460, 2.

[139] RGASPI, 17/2/561, 6, 8.   [140] RGASPI, 17/2/561, 106–7.

[141] See, for instance, Ordzhonikidze's letters to Ezhov appealing on behalf of a number of managers and engineers in 1935 and the first half of 1936: RGASPI, 85/29/692, 85/29/700, 85/29/708, 85/29/746, 85/29/758.

This strategy is particularly evident in their discussions of the Stakh-anovite movement. Stakhanovism, they argued, was mainly useful as a spur to greater efficiency, discipline, and technical expertise. It was not primarily a revivalist campaign to promote new socialist author-ity relations in industry. Piatakov declared, for instance, that Stakh-anovism was not a 'mass demonstration' but the 'struggle for socialist labour productivity'. It was not enough to rely on 'propa-ganda and agitation' in organizing the movement; instead Stakhan-ovism had to be approached from a 'technical point of view'.[142] Ordzhonikidze, speaking at the December 1935 plenum, adopted a similar approach. Stakhanovism, he insisted, had to depend on 'elementary things', including the introduction of 'order into the enterprises', the proper organization of labour and the study of technological processes.[143]

The tone of other speeches at the plenum, however, was rather different. Kaganovich, Zhdanov, and Sarkisov, a strong critic of local managers, not only warned about sabotage but also stressed the ideological, 'political' importance of the Stakhanovite move-ment. Kaganovich, for instance, compared Stakhanovism with Lenin's *subbotniki*, describing it as a method of 're-educating people in the process of production and labour' and an attack on 'petty-bourgeois egoism'; Sarkisov, meanwhile, quoted Stalin's speech on cadres, stressing the role of 'people' rather than 'machines' or pure *tekhnika* in the movement.[144] Zhdanov, speaking after the plenum to a party meeting in Leningrad, launched a more explicit attack on the technicist interpretation of Stakhanovism. He criticized those people, both economic and party officials,

who consider that the Stakhanovite movement is necessary inasmuch as the {industrial and financial} plan is not fulfilled and the Stakhanovites help to fulfil it. It is true, of course, that the Stakhanovites have helped many of our economic, party and trade union officials to fulfil and overfulfil the plan...[145]

[142] *ZI*, 30 June 1936.
[143] RGASPI, 17/2/561, 8.
[144] RGASPI, 17/2/561, 37 (Kaganovich), 54–7 (Sarkisov). For Zhdanov's speech, see 123–5. For a discussion of Sarkisov's views and the politics of the Donbass, see F. Benvenuti, 'Industry and Purge in the Donbass, 1936–37', *E–AS*, 45 (1993), 57–78; Siegelbaum, *Stakhanovism*, 118–19.
[145] RGASPI, 77/1/537, 155–6 (30 December 1935). {} indicate passages deleted by Zhdanov in the draft.

Even so, he explained, this interpretation was an 'opportunist prag-matic'[146] one, because

the Stakhanovite movement carries within it, as comrade Stalin says, the seeds of the future communist society inasmuch as it represents the elements of the cultural and technical development of the working class of our country, on the basis of which the liquidation of the opposition between mental and physical labour [is possible]...[147]

Not only can differences of emphasis be discerned between the political and economic leaderships over the importance of political work in the economy. Tensions over plan targets also continued and, as in the early 1930s, Ordzhonikidze pressed for lower plan targets and came into conflict with Gosplan and the Politburo over the speed of industrialization at the end of 1935.[148] Yet there is also some evidence of tensions over the use of quasi-market mechanisms and monetary incentives. In preparation for the December 1935 Central Committee plenum, Ordzhonikidze's officials proposed that enterprise directors be allowed to keep part of their surplus so that directors could improve wage incentives for workers. How-ever, this suggestion was subsequently dropped; it is unclear on whose initiative this was done, but it may have been at the behest of Stalin and the political leadership.[149] Stalin never went back to the plans of the early 1930s to replace money with direct product-exchange, and he continued to argue that the regime had to use material incentives and promote the satisfaction of 'individual inter-ests'.[150] But some leaders may have been hostile to the continuing use of market mechanisms and material incentives. According to Molotov's reminiscences, he was unhappy about the continuing use of money–commodity relations and asked Stalin why they still persisted under socialism. Stalin replied that this development would be feasible only under communism, yet he himself was clearly concerned about the ideological, or at least the presenta-tional, implications of the excessive use of market mechanisms and

[146] This phrase was deleted by Zhdanov in the draft.
[147] Ibid.
[148] For this tension, see O. V. Khlevniuk, 'Heavy Industry', 121.
[149] RGASPI, 85/29/114, 8–9. Khlevniuk suggests that there were tensions between the political and economic leaderships over this issue. See O. V. Khlevniuk, 'Heavy Industry', 119.
[150] Sochineniia, i. (xiv), 17.

material incentives.[151] At the beginning of 1936 he wrote to members of the Politburo complaining that some newspapers, and particularly *Izvestiia* and the Narkomtiazhprom newspaper, *Za Industrializatsiiu*, were no longer using the word '*sorevnovanie*' ('emulation') and were replacing it with terms which had more capitalist connotations: '*konkurs*' or '*konkurentsiia*' ('competition'). Stalin blamed this practice on either the 'foolish' or the 'alien', and ordered that strict guidelines should be issued defining when the word *konkurs* could be employed.[152]

Regional party bosses expressed an even more ambiguous attitude towards the leadership's revivalist campaigns than did their counterparts in the economic apparatus. Some, like Sarkisov, embraced revivalist campaigns.[153] Others, like Postyshev, seem to have been more negative about them.[154] At times, Postyshev used the centre's call for more party-political work to criticize the commissariats. At the February–March plenum he and Kosior, who were themselves under attack by Stalin, were enthusiastic participants in the centre's assault on the economic apparatus.[155] Yet generally, his pronouncements in the period suggest that he was trying to deflect and distort the revivalist initiatives from the centre, often by reinterpreting them in a technicist, or at least élitist, way. So, for instance, Postyshev's contribution to the discussion on Stakhanovism at the December 1935 plenum concentrated, unusually, on the need to raise workers' labour norms and on criticisms of the trade unions' 'Menshevik' opposition to a necessary norm revision.[156] Postyshev's other statements on Stakhanovism also suggest that he was mainly interested in strengthening order and discipline, the better to fulfil plans, and he strongly objected to attacks on managers and specialists. In April 1936 he claimed that while some wreckers still existed, many enemies who had been active at the

---

[151] Molotov also recounts that Stalin, in 1936 or at some other time, accepted that Molotov was correct in theory, but insisted that 'life is one thing, theory another'. *Sto sorok besed s Molotovym. Iz dnevnika F. Chueva* (Moscow, 1991), 288.

[152] RGASPI, 558/11/1119, 1–2.

[153] See F. Benvenuti, 'Industry and Purge', 66–7.

[154] Molotov, interestingly, described Postyshev as somebody who had positive features, but who 'in his final period made mistakes, he was closer to the rightists'. *Sto sorok besed s Molotovym*, 409. Getty and Naumov argue that Postyshev was under attack in this period but was still supported by Stalin. J. A. Getty and O. V. Naumov, *The Road to Terror*, 513–14.

[155] RGASPI, 17/2/612, vyp. 2, 41–2.

[156] RGASPI, 17/2/556, 99–115.

beginning of the first five-year plan had become part of the 'Soviet people'. And at the end of May he delivered one of the strongest denunciation of the persecution of managers and specialists to be published in the press during this period. He was prepared to accept that managers and specialists had not organized the Stakhanovite movement adequately, he admitted that some saboteurs were operating in factories, and he approved of the campaign launched against sabotage by Sarkisov's Donetsk party organization 'as a whole'. But the main thrust of his criticism was directed at economic and party organizations in the Donbass, accusing them of failing to help managers to reform themselves and for 'permitting the indiscriminate and groundless categorization of several engineers and technicians as saboteurs and conservatives'.[157] He insisted that this 'political hooliganism' had to stop and that the status, authority, and even pay of engineers and technicians had to be raised if labour discipline and morale were not to deteriorate further:

In enterprises they do not raise engineers, technicians, leading foremen. We are communists, organizers! We must raise these workers to the same high position in the eyes of public opinion to which we raise the best Stakhanovite-workers.[158]

It may also be that Postyshev and his Kiev party organization were particularly resistant to Moscow's demand for a greater emphasis on 'party-political work' and 'democracy' in the party. Postyshev's organization was under investigation by the KPK for breaches of party democracy, in part, it seems, because a particular party member, who had been excluded from his and his wife's local patronage network, had friends in Moscow.[159] However, Postyshev was also prepared to defend his behaviour robustly. At the June 1936 Central Committee plenum, Ezhov criticized Postyshev's organization for quizzing party members on abstruse questions of economic theory, and then purging those who failed the tests for 'passivity'. Postyshev, however, was unrepentant, insisting that 'such discussion is important'.[160] As will be seen, his resistance to the centre's revivalist campaigns seems to have continued after the plenum.

[157] *P*, 2 June 1936.   [158] Ibid.
[159] This is argued in J. A. Getty and O. V. Naumov, *The Road to Terror*, 224–9.
[160] Quoted in J. A. Getty and O. V. Naumov, *The Road to Terror*, 238.

Regional party bosses also used less obvious methods to blunt revivalist campaigns of vigilance: by redefining the enemy as a figure outside the élite. So, R. I. Eikhe, the first secretary of the Siberian and West Siberian territorial committees, speaking at the December 1935 Central Committee plenum on the Stakhanovite movement, unlike many of his fellow speakers stressed dangers not from managers but from 'backward elements' among workers, who were greedily taking more from the state than they gave back.[161] Others tried to use the neo-traditionalist argument that class aliens posed a threat to the regime, particularly after 1935, when the leadership tried to rehabilitate them. The leadership's attempts to incorporate kulaks and their children into Soviet society met with opposition from collective farmers and party officials, and Stalin also indicated that there was resistance to his attempt to restore the rights of class aliens in his speech on the constitution in November 1936.[162] He strongly rejected the idea that former white-guards, kulaks, and priests would pose a threat to the regime if allowed to vote. It was, he explained, wrong to see all of them as hostile to Soviet power, and even if enemies were elected, party officials would be responsible because they had conducted their propaganda poorly. He aggressively denied the threat from class aliens with the terse injunction: 'If you are afraid of wolves, keep out of the woods.'[163]

Reopening the case against the Trotskyists, 1936

There is some evidence that in the spring and the summer of 1936 the defenders of the party and economic apparatuses were in a relatively strong position, and a number of statements were made, sanctioned from above, defending the managers against excessive revivalism.[164] Particular publicity was accorded to Postyshev's speech defending specialists against charges of sabotage. *Pravda* published it on 2 June, and five days later echoed its sentiments.

[161] RGASPI 17/2/561, 71.
[162] S. Fitzpatrick, *Stalin's Peasants*, 238–41.
[163] Stalin, *Sochineniia*, i. (xiv), 179.
[164] The change in official rhetoric in this period has been noted by a number of historians, including L. Siegelbaum, *Stakhanovism*, 119–35; O. V. Khlevniuk, *Stalin i Ordzhonikidze*, 60–4.

For *Pravda*, those articles in the Donetsk press and the 'many speeches at meetings' which accused the 'majority of engineering and technical personnel' of being 'saboteurs and conservatives' were 'nonsense'. There were, it insisted, many good specialists. The party had to help them, not persecute them.[165]

The new attitude of *Pravda* was not the only sign that the leadership's line had changed in a more cautious direction. At a meeting of the council of Narkomtiazhprom towards the end of June, managers and economic officials were given the opportunity to speak remarkably openly about the Stakhanovite movement and the attacks to which they had been subjected over the previous few months; furthermore their speeches were published in the industrial press. One of the most outspoken was A. I. Khachatur'iants, the director of the Stalinugol' coal-mining trust. He attacked the whole notion that managers and specialists who failed to develop Stakhanovism were guilty of sabotage.[166] In his speech, Ordzhonikidze agreed with Khachatur'iants, and ridiculed the idea that the new engineers educated and the old engineers re-educated in the nineteen years since the revolution should be saboteurs. They were 'good people', 'our sons, our brothers, our comrades, who are wholly and completely for Soviet power'.[167] The enthusiastic response of the central press to Ordzhonikidze's speech suggests that Stalin and the Politburo favoured, or had acquiesced in, this change of line.[168] Even Zhdanov declared that he agreed with Ordzhonikidze 'that it is not possible to declare that all engineers and technicians who do not lead the Stakhanovite movement are saboteurs'.[169] Attacks on the party apparatus were also scaled down, and in March 1936 KPK officials were told to support, not challenge, party secretaries.[170]

It is only possible to speculate on the reasons for these signs of official attempts to rein in revivalist campaigns. The persecutions of technicians and the damaging effects of the Stakhanovite movement on the efficient organization of the workplace may have strengthened the critics of revivalism.[171] Certainly, in July Sovnarkom and

[165] *P* (editorial), 7 June 1936.   [166] *ZI*, 28 June 1936.
[167] *P*, 5 July 1936.
[168] See, for instance, *P* (editorial), 10 July 1936; *P* (editorial), 30 August 1936.
[169] RGASPI, 77/1/600, 19 (16 July 1936).
[170] J. A. Getty, *Pragmatists and Puritans*, 21–6.
[171] O. V. Khlevniuk and R. W. Davies argue that investigations into the disruption of industry in Sverdlovsk, which blamed persecutions of managers and specialists, had an effect. See R. W. Davies and O. V. Khlevniuk, 'Stakhanovism', 186–9.

the Central Committee agreed that both investment and production targets for 1937 were to be substantially reduced.[172]

During the same period, however, Stalin made a number of decisions that were to be crucial in precipitating a renewed attack on the economic apparatus. Early in 1936, he had allowed or encouraged Ezhov to pursue the theory, enunciated in 1935, that Trotsky was at the head of a grand conspiracy, connected with Kamenev, Zinoviev, and former oppositionists within the apparatus, and involved in acts of terrorism. On 29 July he and Ezhov circulated party officials with a 'Secret Letter' revealing the results of the investigations, and in August, having secured the co-operation of Kamenev and Zinoviev, he staged a show trial of the alleged conspirators. It is not yet known why he made this decision, and historians have interpreted the archival evidence in very different ways. For Oleg Khlevniuk, Stalin's motives were primarily political: he wanted to stage a trial to undermine the party and state apparatuses and strengthen his power, and he used Ezhov to do his dirty work for him.[173] For others, he was responding to the international threat, demonstrated by the re-occupation of the Rhineland in March and the outbreak of the Spanish Civil War in July.[174] Getty and Naumov, however, while accepting that Stalin was trying to curb the powers of local officials, see Ezhov and the police investigation as primary.[175]

---

[172] R. W. Davies and O. V. Khlevniuk 'Gosplan', in E. Rees, *Decision-Making*, 56–7; R. Manning, 'The Soviet Economic Crisis of 1936–1940 and the Great Purges', in J. A. Getty and R. Manning, *Stalinist Terror*, 140.

[173] O. V. Khlevniuk, *Politbiuro*, 203–6.

[174] For this argument, see S. Pons, *Stalin and the Inevitable War*, 36, see also O. V. Khlevniuk, 'The Reasons for the Great Terror', 163–4.

[175] For Getty and Naumov, the NKVD discovered new 'evidence' of a Trotskyist conspiracy in early 1936, Stalin reopened the investigation into Kirov's murder and Ezhov, trying to further his career, used Stalin's mandate to implicate a large number of people, including Zinoviev and Kamenev, in the alleged conspiracy. Stalin subsequently staged a show trial of the former oppositionists in order to destroy personal and political enemies among the former opposition and create a climate in which future opposition was much less likely. The Secret Letter, informing party bosses of the case and the trial, was potentially threatening to the apparatus, but this was not its main objective. Rather, it led to a largely unplanned series of denunciations of economic officials who happened to be former Trotskyists. J. A. Getty and O. V. Naumov, *The Road to Terror*, ch. 7, 578. Harris also stresses the role of denunciations at a regional level in spreading violence in the summer of 1936, rather than central direction. See J. Harris, *The Great Urals*, 170–2.

It is unclear what was at the forefront of Stalin's thinking in the decision to open the case against the Trotskyists and to issue the Secret Letter: the NKVD's investigations or the desire to launch a revivalist campaign against unbelieving officials in the apparatus. Given Stalin's tendency to assume that rightist, sceptical attitudes and conspiracy often went together—either because hostile views were generated by contacts with enemies or because they predisposed their bearers to damage the economy and conspire with enemies—it is likely that both motivations were present. Yet, whatever his intentions, the language of the Secret Letter, with its charges that economic officials were guilty of sabotage, seemed to signal both a criminal investigation and a revivalist campaign against officials, and was interpreted in this way within the party as a whole.

The Secret Letter attempted to demonstrate the themes that Ezhov had tried and failed to prove in January 1935. The previous trial of Zinoviev and Kamenev, it claimed, had not revealed everything. New evidence, found by the NKVD in 1936, now demonstrated that 'Zinoviev and Kamenev were not only the inspirers of terroristic activity against the leaders of our party and government, but were also the authors of direct instructions' ordering both the murder of Kirov and the assassination of other party leaders, including Stalin. It had also been revealed that they had acted in a 'direct bloc with Trotsky and Trotskyists', and were members of an 'Anti-Soviet United Trotskyist–Zinovievite Centre'.[176] But, most worryingly for officials, the Secret Letter also alleged that enemies had wormed their way into positions of responsibility. First, it was alleged that they had infiltrated local party organizations, illustrating how poorly the verification of party documents had been conducted. Second, it was claimed that a group of 'secret Trotskyists and Zinovievites engaged in economic work' had helped the conspirators.[177] The letter went on to link the activities of former oppositionists and class aliens with sabotage by state officials. Now, it claimed, all distinctions between the 'spies, provocateurs, saboteurs, white-guardists, kulaks etc.' on the one side, and the Trotskyists and Zinovievites on the other, had been 'erased'.[178]

[176] *Izv TsK KPSS*, 8 (1989), 100–1.
[177] Ibid., 8 (1989), 111.
[178] Ibid., 8 (1989), 115.

As has been seen, the labels 'class alien', 'oppositionist', and 'saboteur' had been implicitly linked in official rhetoric before July 1936, but these connections had not been made so explicitly and strongly for some time; neither had Moscow called on party members to 'unmask' 'wrecker' enemies who had high positions within the apparatus. It seemed as if the leadership were about to stage another Shakhty or Industrial party trial. As before, there were enemies in the economic apparatus, and as before the main political lessons of the case were that the party had been insufficiently vigilant. The main difference between this scenario and the Shakhty case was that the enemies were communists and were acting 'under the cover of their communist rank'.[179] Given the language of the Secret Letter, it is not at all surprising that regional and local party organizations were very seriously affected—and in the case of urban organizations probably more seriously than at any time since the late 1920s. At party meetings in the localities convened to discuss the trial and the letter, party officials were sometimes unable to control the denunciations of alleged Trotskyists.[180]

The Secret Letter mentioned only briefly and vaguely the officials in the economic apparatus who were helping the members of 'Anti-Soviet United Trotskyist–Zinovievite Centre', but as the letter was being formulated and published Ezhov and the NKVD were pursuing officials with Trotskyist pasts within the apparatus. It is unclear how far denunciations drove these investigations and how far Stalin himself pushed them; Ezhov claimed that it was Stalin who was the most convinced that there were Trotskyist enemies in the apparatus and told him to overcome the resistance of Iagoda.[181] The first significant official to be arrested, on 26 July, was Sokol'nikov, former commissar of finance and associate of Trotsky's, and now first deputy commissar for the timber industry and candidate member of the Central Committee. On the night of 27–8 July an even

---

[179] A. N. Iakovlev (ed.), *Reabilitatsiia*, 210.

[180] Several researchers have found that the campaign against the Trotskyists only became significant in local party organizations after the publication of the Secret Letter. See, for instance, Kotkin, *Magnetic Mountain*, 312–14; see also D. Hoffman, 'The Great Terror at a Local Level: Purges in Moscow Factories, 1936–1938', in J. A. Getty and R. Manning, *Stalinist Terror*, 163–5.

[181] Both Ia. S. Agranov of the NKVD and Ezhov pointed to Stalin's role. See Iakovlev (ed.), *Reabilitatsiia*, 218; see also Ezhov's speech at the February–March 1937 plenum, in *VI*, 2 (1995), 18. For Iagoda's and Molchanov's resistance, see Iakovlev (ed.), *Reabilitatsiia*, 178.

more high-ranking economic official was implicated when Piata-kov's wife was arrested for her former connections with Trotskyism. Piatakov was then himself investigated, and was finally arrested on 12 September. Piatakov, Sokol'nikov, and others were all accused of being members of a 'Parallel Anti-Soviet Trotskyist Centre', and were tried in January 1937.[182]

The Secret Letter precipitated a flood of denunciations, and, as was to be expected given its emphasis on the dangers from economic officials in high positions, the economic apparatus seems to have suffered more than the party. As Harris has shown, regional party bosses in the Urals willingly followed the scenario established by the letter to deflect criticism from themselves, holding economic offi-cials in the central commissariats responsible for economic failures and accusing them of wrecking.[183]

However, it is also evident that the leadership knew how risky its strategy was, and it did not want to go too far, as is suggested by the mixed messages given by the leadership in the aftermath of the trial. These may, as has been argued by some, have been the result of tensions within the leadership over the conduct of the campaign against Trotskyists, and Ezhov and Iagoda certainly disagreed over the nature of the conspiracy and how extensive it was.[184] Yet it is more likely that Stalin was pursuing his attack on the apparatus aggressively, while simultaneously trying to keep it within strict limits. This is suggested by a decree, circulated, it seems, on Stalin's initiative, to all secretaries of city, territorial, and republican party organizations on 31 August. The order criticized local party organ-izations for expelling officials, and particularly enterprise directors, from the party without the 'advice and agreement' of the Central Committee, and demanded that all expulsions be approved at the highest level.[185] At the same time the leadership seems to have used the press to prevent the trial initiating a general campaign against managers and specialists. During the trial of Kamenev, Zinoviev, and their associates in August 1936, the defendants did mention

---

[182] A. N. Iakovlev (ed.), *Reabilitatsiia*, 218–19.

[183] J. Harris, *The Great Urals*, 178–9.

[184] For this argument, see Rittersporn, *Stalinist Simplifications*, ch. 2. For tensions between Ezhov and Stalin, and Iagoda, see O. V. Khlevniuk, *Politbiuro*, 203–7; A. N. Iakovlev (ed.), *Reabilitatsiia*, 178–9.

[185] Kaganovich and Ezhov to Stalin, 29 August 1936, RGASPI, 81/3/101, 97. See also O. V. Khlevniuk (ed.), *Stalin i Kaganovich*, 653–4.

their contacts with Trotskyists with positions in the apparatus, but little was made of this. Furthermore, the publicity surrounding the trial implied that there was no longer any danger from Trotskyists. *Pravda* declared that the opposition had been crushed and had no social base in the country; the number of Trotskyists was 'microscopic'.[186] At the same time, some party organizations were condemned for going to 'extremes', 'panicking', and 'groundlessly' categorizing party members and managerial officials as Trotskyists.[187]

The attack on the economic apparatus and the second Moscow trial, autumn 1936–spring 1937

In September, however, Stalin was more forthright in pursuing his revivalist campaign against the economic apparatus. It is likely that pressure from above and denunciations from below reinforced each other. The Secret Letter precipitated denunciations, which were then actively pursued by the NKVD with the active encouragement of Stalin. Ezhov was now in a stronger position to challenge Iagoda, who had already been subjected to criticism for his refusal to pursue the alleged links between Trotskyists and Zinovievites.[188] And Stalin, who may have been planning to remove Iagoda for some time, replaced Iagoda with Ezhov. Once Ezhov was in charge of the NKVD, he purged the organization and replaced regional NKVD bosses, who had links with regional cliques, with his own people.

The NKVD was searching for, and interrogating, people with Trotskyist pasts, but it was also following a revivalist script, pursuing economic officials accused of sabotage. It therefore investigated cases of corruption, plan underfulfilment, and poor treatment of workers, previously hidden by 'collusion' between local party and state officials. Given the limited availability of sources, it is difficult to follow individual cases, but as Harris has shown in his study of the Urals, the NKVD was interested in economic failures, and it was helped by officials who attempted to shift blame by denouncing others for sabotage and Trotskyism.[189]

---

[186] *P* (editorial), 4 September 1936.   [187] *P*, 5 September 1936.
[188] For Ezhov's moves against Iagoda, based on materials from the Ezhov archive, see O. V. Khlevniuk, *Politbiuro*, 204–5.
[189] J. Harris, *The Great Urals*, 182–5.

The leadership made it even clearer that the campaign against Trotskyism was to have a revivalist character when *Pravda* announced the opening of a trial in Novosibirsk in which several engineers were accused of causing explosions in the Kemerovo mines. They were also alleged to have been in league with German agents and Trotskyists, and, worryingly for the economic apparatus, with Piatakov, who was accused of helping Trotsky in his counter-revolutionary activity.[190] The case was taken further and expanded in the second Moscow show trial—the trial of the Anti-Soviet Trotskyist Centre of January 1937—which featured several high-level economic officials, including Piatakov. The message propagated by this trial was much more explicitly revivalist than the first Moscow trial of 1936; indeed, it could almost be described as a second Shakhty trial. As with the Shakhty case, the trial featured wreckers in the economic apparatus, who in turn were alleged to have been acting on behalf of a group of internal ideological enemies, who were themselves part of a plot by foreigners to dismember the Soviet Union.

The trial was a masterly confection designed to demonstrate all of the main themes of revivalist discourse. Several of the defendants were economic officials, but one exception was the former Trotskyist Karl Radek, who was presumably chosen as a 'theoretician' to demonstrate the link between Trotskyist ideas and wrecking. The main point of Radek's testimony was to show that there was little difference between Trotsky's ideas and those of the former Right Deviation. Indeed, it seems that Stalin considered the ideological lessons of the trial, and the explicit attack on rightism, as central. The Secret Letter had denied that the Trotskyists had any 'positive political programme acceptable for the toilers of our country' and had asserted that they were now merely 'unprincipled' terrorists, intent on overthrowing the system.[191] Yet by December 1936 Stalin wanted to stress the ideology of the Trotskyists. At the Central Committee plenum Stalin now explained that the Trotskyists did have a programme which was, in effect, the programme of the old Right Deviation: it included the 'restoration of private initiative in industry', the attraction of foreign capital, the restoration of capitalism in agriculture, and the strengthening of kulak interests.[192]

---

[190] *P*, 23 November 1936.   [191] A. N. Iakovlev (ed.), *Reabilitatsiia*, 208.
[192] Quoted in J. A. Getty and O. V. Naumov, *The Road to Terror*, 306. According to Sokolnikov, the Trotskyist programme was identical to the Riutin manifesto and the

In typical Stalinist style, however, the political issues were pre-sented in the lurid language of conspiracy. Initially, Radek stated, Trotsky had favoured an 'economic retreat within the framework of the Soviet state', but in 1934 he had decided that he could only come to power through the 'restoration of capitalism'.[193] In Radek's speech, Trotsky's criticisms of the implementation of collectiviza-tion became support for the complete removal of collective farms and the restoration of the kulaks; his earlier demand that the Soviet economy become more integrated into the world economy became support for foreign concessions and the alienation of the Ukraine to Germany; his willingness to recognize that economic inegalitarian-ism was inevitable for the time being became, in Radek's words, a demand for the revival of private capital in the cities and the drastic lowering of working-class living standards.[194]

The evidence given by the other defendants was designed to show how economic officials had put the Trotskyist programme into practice. It particularly emphasized the deliberate failure of eco-nomic officials to fulfil plans, and their conspiracy to harm workers by causing accidents.[195] The anti-worker nature of the Trotskyists' activities was a particularly important message of the trial. As one defendant claimed, the wreckers planned to 'sabotage the Stakhan-ovite movement and mistreat the workers', while, according to another, the Trotskyists deliberately sabotaged the building of hous-ing for engineers and workers.[196]

The trial, therefore, showed that 'Trotskyists' were, in essence, the same people as the 'bourgeois specialists' of the Shakhty period. The only difference was that their bourgeois attitudes were not the consequence of their class origin but were the result of 'opposition-ism' or political contamination from former oppositionists. Several defendants explicitly compared themselves with the Shakhty wreckers and one, at the instigation of Vyshinskii, even asserted that Trotsky had told them to forge an alliance with 'non-Trotskyist

---

'programme of the Rights', a statement which Vyshinskii quoted in his summing up. See *Report of Court Proceedings in the Case of the Anti-Soviet Trotskyite Centre. Verbatim Report* (Moscow, 1937), 158, 489.

[193] Ibid., 113–14.
[194] Ibid. See Trotsky, *The Revolution Betrayed*, 37–42, 289.
[195] For wrecking of the economy and the deliberate harming of workers, see Drobnis's testimony, ibid., 209–10.
[196] Ibid., 244–5, 210.

anti-Soviet people' such as the 'remnants of the Shakhty wreckers' among the 'old engineers'.[197]

Through the 1937 trial, therefore, Stalin stated publicly, for the first time since 1931, that the old bourgeois wreckers were active and that they were engaged in the same conspiracy as the Trotskyists, who had in turn earned the confidence of many party and state officials.[198] It was thus implied that workers were, in general, not to be condemned as wreckers. The trial also declared that the class enemy was not just engaged in wrecking the economy but also in restoring capitalism, reintroducing capitalist bureaucratic relations between officials and workers and capitalist forms of labour organization. And it suggested that enemies were guilty of the sins of the technicists, giving 'machines' priority over 'people'. As *Pravda* declared in an editorial entitled 'The Trotskyist Gang of Restorers of Capitalism':

The Trotskyists wanted the former capitalist system to be established in factories and plants again, as in the days of old. They wanted the worker, who now in the Soviet Union is the master in the factory with full rights, to become the slave of capitalism. [They wanted] the Soviet worker, who is now the master of the machine, to become its slave, an appendage of the machine.[199]

Zhdanov made these abstract formulations more concrete, speaking in June 1937:

Wreckers have not only inflicted material damage on us, destroying production... but they have also inflicted moral damage. You see, it is a fact, for instance, that at the Izhorsk factory the wrecker Sheptopakov, the former head engineer... beat up and antagonized technical cadres and tried to corrupt them... to corrupt Stakhanovites... The suppression of criticism and self-criticism... [and] dismissal [of subordinates] for criticism were all methods... widely used by wreckers.[200]

Once the trial had identified the Trotskyist enemy as the quasi-bourgeois, 'bureaucratic' economic official who had rightist attitudes towards the plan, it was likely that the official campaign against

---

[197] Shestov's testimony and Vyshinskii's interrogation, ibid., 159–61. See also Vyshinskii's speech, ibid., 465.

[198] For the Trotskyists' ability to earn the confidence of communists, see Drobnis's testimony, ibid., 207–8.

[199] *P* (editorial), 26 January 1937. See also *P*, 9 March 1937.

[200] RGASPI, 77/1/659, 104–5 (10 June 1937).

Trotskyism would become a much broader attack on managers, sometimes broader than the leadership intended, because long-running resentments of the 'bureaucratic' behaviour of managers and specialists could now be expressed as charges of Trotskyism.[201]

Ordzhonikidze, technicism, and the defence of the apparatus

Ordzhonikidze's response to the attacks on his commissariat was ambiguous. In a speech to his officials in February 1937, he told them to examine their consciences and ask why wrecking should have taken place. Much of his criticism echoed revivalist charges that officials were callous towards workers and cut off from the masses. 'Bureaucratic rust' had 'engulfed' the commissariat, and a 'shake up' was needed.[202] However, at the same time Ordzhonikidze tried to defend his subordinates from the end of 1936, and there is evidence that he expressed doubts about the revivalist campaign against his organization. In preparing for the February–March 1937 plenum, he sent emissaries to investigate plants where wrecking had allegedly taken place.[203] According to one of them, Professor Gal'-perin, who was charged with investigating the Kemerovo Chemical Combine, Ordzhonikidze explicitly told him to approach the matter as a 'tekhnik', and establish precisely what was due to wrecking and what was caused by other factors, such as involuntary mistakes. The commissions naturally found that there was no wrecking, and Ordzhonikidze allowed them to express their conclusions in their reports.[204]

Molotov, speaking at the February–March plenum, trenchantly condemned the reports, expressing astonishment that in a document of fifty-four pages 'the words "wrecker" and "wrecking" were completely absent'.[205] Stalin also implicitly criticized Ordzhonikidze in

---

[201] For the targeting of economic officials during 1937, see J. Getty and W. Chase, 'Patterns of Repression among the Soviet Elite', in J. A. Getty and R. Manning, *Stalinist Terror*, 225–46. For worker hostility to bosses during the period, see Sheila Fitzpatrick, 'Workers against Bosses: The Impact of the Great Purges on Labor–Management Relations', in L. Siegelbaum and R. G. Suny (eds.), *Making Workers Soviet*, 311–40.

[202] RGASPI, 85/29/156, 11–12.

[203] For a detailed discussion of these commissions, see Khlevniuk, *Stalin i Ordzhonikidze*, 100–2.

[204] *ZI*, 21 February 1937. See S. Z. Ginzburg, 'O gibeli Sergo Ordzhonikidze', *VI KPSS*, 3 (1991), 91–2.　　　　[205] *VI*, 8 (1994), 21.

his comments on Ordzhonikidze's draft resolution on industry, prepared for the February–March plenum. Stalin was clearly unhappy
that Ordzhonikidze had not dwelt on the problem of sabotage, and
wrote in the margins of the draft: 'Which branches [of industry] have
been affected by wrecking and how precisely ([state] facts)[?]'.[206]
Ordzhonikidze's death, probably as a result of suicide, prevented
him from delivering the speech, and his place was taken by Molotov,
but even after his death Stalin chastised him for his tendency to cover
up for enemies.[207] Ezhov expanded this criticism of Ordzhonikidze
into a more general attack on the commissariats for their pursuit of
departmental interests (vedomstvennost'), their tendency to defend
'their' departments however badly they worked, and their obstruc-
tion of the search for enemies.[208]

There were no fundamental ideological differences between Ordzhonikidze and Stalin or Ezhov. Ordzhonikidze never denied that
enemies existed; he was largely concerned to protect his people,
rather than to question the search for enemies more generally.
However, in his attempts to defend his commissariat from the
NKVD and the party, he used technicist language, which Stalin
recognized as such. In his draft resolutions for the plenum he
made a number of assertions that were unmistakably technicist in
tone, and his language suggests that his words were carefully
chosen. Indeed, they contained many of the main technicist themes:
the fundamental reliability of managers and technicians; the priority of discipline over mobilization; hostility to party organizations;
and a preference for tekhnika over politika. He accepted that Trotskyists had insinuated themselves into high posts in the economic
apparatus, and that they had been able to operate because managers
had been unwilling to believe that accidents were due to anything
but 'objective' circumstances, but he also criticized managers over
their neglect of order and discipline. The Trotskyists, Ordzhonikidze explained, 'used the absence ... of iron production order and
discipline, of a strictly worked-out regulation of the technical process ... ', and he quoted Lenin to the effect that any breach of 'Soviet
order' would be exploited by the enemy.[209]

[206] RGASPI, 85/29/158, 1.
[207] VI, 11–12 (1995), 17. For the most authoritative account of Ordzhonikidze's
last days, see Khlevniuk, Stalin i Ordzhonikidze, 111–29.
[208] RGASPI, 17/2/612, vyp. 2, 56–7. Stalin interjected, stating that the resolutions
on the subject were too mild.   [209] RGASPI, 85/29/158, 5.

Ordzhonikidze did point to weaknesses in 'political work' in industry, but he refused to blame the managers themselves for this problem. Party organizations, he claimed, were responsible. They considered economic officials to be purely 'managers', responsible for production, and refused to involve them in party affairs; they had forgotten that executives and engineers needed to be involved in the politics of the party and the working class. Stalin objected to this attempt to deflect blame from the commissariats; he wrote in the margin 'Ha ha. Perhaps the reverse?', 'the [economic] leaders themselves forgot'.[210]

Stalin was also unhappy with Ordzhonikidze's discussion of the relationship between *politika* and *tekhnika*. Ordzhonikidze wrote that managers, engineers, and technicians should not be 'apolitical' and merely concerned with *tekhnika*; while mastering *tekhnika*, they were 'to be well informed about everyday political life and be clearly aware of the friends and enemies of Soviet power' and party organizations were to 'help' them in their 'political *vospitanie*'.[211] This formulation was evidently far too mealy-mouthed for Stalin. It merely stated, vaguely, that economic cadres were to 'be informed about', rather than participate in, *politika*, and diluted the term 'political life' with the adjective 'everyday', implying a 'practical' rather than theoretical conception of *politika*. Stalin therefore edited the document, adding the phrase 'he [the manager] must also be a political worker himself'; he also told Ordzhonikidze that his point about political education should be stated 'more sharply' and made 'central', instructing him to include a discussion of 'the causes of idling (the apolitical, pragmatic selection of cadres, the absence of the political *vospitanie* of cadres)'.[212] Stalin seemingly wanted to make it clear that it was not primarily the absence of 'discipline' and 'order' that was responsible for poor economic results, but the 'apoliticism' of cadres. Stalin also expressed scepticism at Ordzhonikidze's proposals on industrial relations, taking a more anti-managerial line. He wrote that Ordzhonikidze's

[210] RGASPI, 85/29/158, 6.

[211] RGASPI, 85/29/158, 6–7. '... on [khoziastvennik, inzhener i tekhnik] dolzhen byt' v kurse povsednevnoi politicheskoi zhizni i otdavat' sebe iasnyi otchet o dru-z'iakh i vragakh sovetskoi vlasti [Stalin added: *on sam dolzhen byt' takzhe i politra-botnikom*], a partiinye organizatsii vsemerno dolzhny pomogat' politicheskomu [Stalin changed to: *bol'shevistskomu*] vospitaniiu khoziastvennykh i inzhenerno-tekhnicheskikh kadrov'.

[212] Ibid.

statements on the need to tighten up worker safety rules were too weak, and wrote a sceptical 'ha ha' alongside a statement on the need to reduce the incidence of industrial injuries.[213] He also queried a phrase which criticized production meetings 'of the old type'; Ordzhonikidze, he was implying, was wrong to cast doubt on the industrial democracy campaigns of the past.[214]

In his speech to the February–March 1937 plenum, Molotov also condemned officials for neglecting *politika*.[215] He explained that the regime had understood the slogan 'Bolsheviks must master *tekhnika*' in a 'one-sided way'. They had been obsessed with plan fulfilment, were guilty of 'narrow utilitarianism (*deliachestvo*)', and had 'politically gone backward rather than forward'. The ideal solution was 'the mastery of *tekhnika* in the full sense of the word together with the further strengthening of the Bolshevik [i.e. 'political'] qualities of our cadres'. However, he admitted that there was frequently a conflict between *tekhnika* and *politika* and stated: 'among us it has frequently happened that the mastery of *tekhnika* has been accompanied by the weakening of the Bolshevik qualities of the worker (*rabotnika*)'.[216]

Stalin was more direct in his criticisms of Ordzhonikidze and Narkomtiazhprom officials, and their tendency to resist revivalist Bolshevism, although he largely denounced their neo-traditionalist attitudes rather than their technicism. He accused many of them of believing that 'rank (*chin*) in itself gives a huge, almost exhaustive knowledge'. They had therefore refused to 'learn from the masses', and their failure to listen to the experience of workers, he alleged, had prevented them from running industry effectively.[217] He also blamed

[213] RGASPI, 85/29/158, 13. He wrote 'ha' (*kha*) and 'weak' (*slabo*) against the sentence '*Noting* that Soviet mines must be safe for workers, *to note* that the first and undoubted duty of all administrative-technical personnel, and in the first place the managers and chief engineers of mines and trusts, is *the fulfilment of existing rules of safety technology*' (underlining in Stalin's hand). The word 'note' was evidently too weak for Stalin.

[214] RGASPI, 85/29/158, 18. Stalin placed a question mark in the margin and underlined the following phrase: 'Organize in enterprises, instead of *the outdated and discredited production meetings* of the old type, regular (monthly) meetings of leaders of enterprises and Stakhanovites and leading shock-workers...'.

[215] Although Stalin was also unhappy with the draft of Molotov's speech. When Molotov referred to the need for *vospitanie* of cadres, Stalin added, 'it is not *vospitanie* in general that is needed, but political *vospitanie* of cadres'. RGASPI, 558/11/772, 39, 43.

[216] RGASPI, 17/2/612, vyp. 2, 11.

[217] VI, 10 (1995), 19.

Ordzhonikidze's tendency to protect enemies as a sign of neo-trad-itionalist, or feudal 'noble' (*dvorianskii*) and 'knightly' (*rytsarskii*) attitudes. The example he gave was his refusal to allow Stalin to show an 'anti-party' letter written by Lominadze, Ordzhonikidze's friend and client, to the Central Committee, in 1929 or 1930, because he had given his word to him that he would not. As a result of Ordzhonikidze's willingness to 'spare cadres', Stalin explained, Lomi-nadze's errors had not been corrected and he had gone on to become a confirmed enemy.[218] For Stalin, Ordzhonikidze was not an enemy, but was guilty of establishing neo-traditionalist patron–client relations with subordinates. He had also failed to use the correct revivalist leadership style—a style that Stalin had spoken about so much since the speech to the Red Army Academy in 1935—which was vital if the party was to know the inner thoughts of cadres, to mobilize them, and insulate them from ideological corruption. Ordzhonikidze had 'raised thousands of excellent economic and party people', but the Lomi-nadze case had shown that 'when you hide the mistakes of a comrade' and do not correct them, 'you spoil him, you spoil him for sure'.[219]

The attack on technicism and the right

Given Stalin's characterization of the Trotskyist conspiracy from December 1936 as one connected with an ideologically rightist challenge to the regime inspired by former oppositionists, it is not surprising that the former 'Right Deviation' should from an early stage have been implicated in the alleged conspiracy. Bukharin was an obvious figure for Stalin to involve, for, although he no longer had any real power, he was the best-known proponent of technicism and was almost as important an ideological rival as Trotsky. As has been seen, he had continued to express anti-revivalist sentiments as late as 1934 from his position as editor of *Izvestiia* and at fora such as the Writers' Congress.[220] Bukharin himself seems to have under-stood the political logic of the case against him when, in a letter written from prison in December 1937, he described the 'general purge (*chistka*)' as a 'great and bold' 'political idea' that 'could not

---

[218] For Ordzhonikidze's relationship with Lominadze, see O. V. Khlevniuk, *Stalin i Ordzhonikidze*, 21–9, 66–75.

[219] *VI*, 11–12 (1995), 17.

[220] See Ch. 4, p. 296.

have been managed without me'.[221] The first public mention of the former right's involvement in conspiracy was at the August 1936 trial, and the prosecutor, Vyshinskii, then revealed that he had initiated an investigation of Tomskii, Bukharin, Rykov, Uglanov, and others.[222] Yet the case against the right was unexpectedly dropped in September and Vyshinskii announced openly in *Pravda* that there was insufficient evidence to bring Bukharin and Rykov to trial.[223] In August 1936 Ezhov also stated that, while the right was guilty of knowing about the Trotskyists' activities, they did not want to join with them, and therefore only deserved the relatively mild punishment of exile.[224] This was the first of many delays in the prosecution of Bukharin, and Getty and Naumov argue that Stalin himself was at times reluctant to see Bukharin tried, possibly because he felt the evidence was not strong enough for a trial, or possibly because he was not yet convinced that Bukharin was guilty of conspiracy.[225] Yet while it might not have been a foregone conclusion that Bukharin would be tried or treated as harshly as the Trotskyists, his indictment accorded with the logic of the case against the Trotskyists: that there was an ideological link between right and left. As has been seen, at the December 1936 Central Committee plenum, Stalin declared that the Trotskyists' programme was very similar to that of the former Right Deviation,[226] and Ezhov worked to transform the ideological connection between right and left into a conspiratorial one by intimidating former oppositionists into testifying. Bukharin, however, continued to deny all charges and defended himself trenchantly at the Central Committee plena of December 1936 and February–March 1937.[227] It was not until June that Bukharin began to co-operate with the authorities, probably in response to threats to his family. The trial was finally held in March the following year, by which time a large

---

[221] Bukharin to Stalin, 10 December 1937, *Istochnik*, 0 (1993), 23.

[222] *Report of Court Proceedings in the Case of the Trotskyite–Zinovievite Terrorist Centre* (Moscow, 1936), 68; A. N. Iakovlev (ed.), *Reabilitatsiia*, 244; J. A. Getty and O. V. Naumov, *The Road to Terror*, 300–3.

[223] A. N. Iakovlev (ed.), *Reabilitatsiia*, 245.

[224] O. V. Khlevniuk, *Politbiuro*, 205–6.

[225] J. A. Getty and O. V. Naumov, *The Road to Terror*, 322–30, ch. 10. Getty and Naumov put forward a number of hypotheses as to why Stalin might have behaved inconsistently towards Bukharin.

[226] RGASPI, 17/2/575, 52–3.

[227] A. N. Iakovlev (ed.), *Reabilitatsiia*, 245–9.

number of other former party leaders had been forced to give evidence.[228] Yet even then Bukharin refused to admit that he played a direct role in conspiracy, only accepting ideological responsibility for the actions of the 'bloc of Rights and Trotskyists'.[229] In his final statement he declared:

I plead guilty to being one of the outstanding leaders of this 'bloc of Rights and Trotskyists'. Consequently, I plead guilty to what directly follows from this irrespective of whether or not I knew of, whether or not I took a direct part in, any particular act.[230]

Stalin may have believed that Bukharin was conspiring against him.[231] However, the logic of the case against him, like that against Kamenev and Zinoviev, was built on his ideological sins. At the February–March 1937 plenum a session was devoted to the 'right' which took the form of a closed, party trial. Molotov, one of the main speakers, stressed Bukharin's importance as rightist ideologue, claiming that while Rykov and Tomskii were mainly guilty of promoting their own cronies, Bukharin had propagated a non-Marxist ideology.[232] It was Bukharin's technicism, rather than his alleged conspiratorial actions, that interested most of the leaders at the February–March plenum of 1937 (with the exception of Ezhov). As Kaganovich made clear:

I maintain that Bukharin... cannot get away from the fact that ideologically, theoretically, politically, in the essence of its slogans, in its programme, the Riutin platform completely derives from your positions, beginning from 1928... Why did you not say a word about this? What do you think, that we are children? That we have assembled here to discuss who was where, on what street, which gate they went through, which car they used? *We are*

---

[228] B. A. Starkov, 'Narkom Ezhov', 35. See Bukharin's own account, *Report of Court Proceedings in the Case of the Anti-Soviet 'Bloc of Rights and Trotskyites' Heard Before the Military Collegium of the Supreme Court of the USSR, Moscow, March 2–13 1938* (Moscow, 1938), 777.

[229] *Report of Court Proceedings in the Case of the Anti-Soviet 'Bloc of Rights and Trotskyites'*, 770–2. For Bukharin's testimony at the trial, see S. Cohen, *Bukharin*, 376–81; R. Tucker, *Stalin in Power*, 497–500.

[230] *Report of Court Proceedings in the Case of the Anti-Soviet 'Bloc of Rights and Trotskyites'*, 370. Punctuated as in the original translation. For Bukharin's concluding speech and the alterations made to it by censors, see *Istochnik*, 4 (1996), 79 ff.

[231] Molotov, when asked about the accuracy of the charges in the 1970s, denied they had been fabricated, and explained that 'in political struggle everything is possible, if you support the other side'. *Sto sorok besed s Molotovym*, 196.

[232] *VI*, 8–9 (1992), 21.

interested in politics. Why do you not deal with the substance of these questions?[233]

Kaganovich had evidently been charged with an ideological demolition of Bukharin's position, and a batch of speeches and articles written in the early 1930s was sent to him.[234] The annotations on the speeches suggest that it was Bukharin's emphasis on the importance of *tekhnika* which was thought by Kaganovich or his advisers to be objectionable. Question marks and exclamation marks were placed against statements such as: 'The revolution (*revoliutsiia*) of the proletariat in our country has entered into its new phase: the phase of technical revolution (*perevorota*)', and 'the problem of *cultural revolution* is being turned round, into a problem of technical culture'.[235]

Kaganovich emphasized similar points in his speech on Bukharin's errors to the February–March 1937 plenum. Bukharin, he alleged, even after the defeat of the right, had made a number of statements on economic reconstruction 'without saying a word about classes, about kulaks, about politics... he characterized reconstruction only from the point of view of *tekhnika*'; he had 'departed from *politika* to such an extent that he spoke only from the point of view of *tekhnika*, he did not want to touch on *politika*'. He had also disagreed with the leadership on the central question of 'economic stimulus', or incentives.[236] Both Kaganovich and Molotov referred to articles Bukharin had published in *Izvestiia* in 1934 and 1935, and which Stalin had criticized at the time for their rightist content.[237] Osinskii, meanwhile, was brought on to denounce Bukharin's 'bourgeois-positivist', non-dialectical understanding of Marxist philosophy. According to Osinskii, he had denied that contradictions existed in nature, and heretically declared that he did not understand what Engels meant by the transformation of 'quantity' into 'quality', thereby implicitly casting doubt on the possibility of economic leaps forward.[238]

---

[233] *VI*, 10 (1992), 31. Emphasis added.   [234] RGASPI, 329/2/23.

[235] RGASPI, 329/2/23, 127, 140.   [236] *VI*, 10 (1992), 33.

[237] Kaganovich referred to Bukharin's article, 'Nekotorye itogi revoliutsionnogo goda i nashi vragi', *I*, 7 November 1935. *VI*, 10 (1992), 33–4. Molotov referred to Bukharin's 'Ekonomika sovetskoi strany', *I*, 12 May 1934. See *VI*, 8–9 (1992), 23–4, and above Ch. 4, p. 296.

[238] *VI*, 11–12 (1992), 5–6.

Bukharin himself may have understood that the essence of the case against him was political, but even so he was uncertain about Stalin's real motives. In his letter to Stalin of December 1937 he declared 'my heart boils over when I think that you might really *believe* that I am guilty of these crimes and that in your heart of hearts (*v glubine dushi*) you *yourself* think that I am really guilty of all these horrors.'[239] So consistent was Stalin in defining ideological heresy as conspiracy that even Bukharin, who knew Stalin well, was not sure whether he believed the charges or not.

Populist revivalism and the assault on the party, 1937

Until the middle of 1937 the powerful regional party bosses and their committees were not accused of being enemies despite the general hysteria about conspiracies and wreckers, and this has puzzled historians. For some, Stalin was merely waiting for the best time to destroy the party bosses whom he had already decided to arrest.[240] Other scholars tell another story, which stresses the role of unplanned denunciations from below in response to the Secret Letter, leading to heightened paranoia throughout the party and economic apparatuses.[241] There is, as yet, no evidence that Stalin planned to remove the party bosses as a group from 1936 and, given the current state of our knowledge, it is reasonable to see the period as a new stage in the revivalist campaign between late 1936 and early 1937 in which Stalin and his group tried to put even more pressure on the party and economic apparatuses, but without taking the dangerous step of removing the regional party bosses. Ezhov and the NKVD, having penetrated élite circles in the regions, discovered a great deal of collusion between highly placed party bosses and economic officials, some of whom had been accused of Trotskyism. The earlier revivalist assumption, that the party could easily be mobilized against 'enemies' within its own organizations and the state, was clearly flawed, and the leadership decided that it had to put even more pressure on the regional party apparatuses than before. It was implementing a strategy designed to break collusion

[239] Bukharin to Stalin, 10 December 1937, *Istochnik*, o (1993), 24.
[240] See R. Tucker, *Stalin in Power*, 272–6.
[241] J. A. Getty and O. V. Naumov, *The Road to Terror*, 261–5; J. Harris, *The Great Urals*, 182–90.

with economic officials and force the party to root out enemies and adopt a more revivalist, mobilizational style, but without undermining the party apparatus as a whole.

During the verification and exchange of party documents, it was largely officials at the lower levels of the party who suffered. It was only in the months between the conclusion of the exchange towards the end of 1936 and February 1937 that officials in the higher party committees (regional, territorial, and republican) were expelled in significant numbers; conversely, in this period a smaller proportion of those expelled came from lower party organizations (district and primary).[242] Towards the end of 1936 pressure was put on regional and territorial party committee secretaries, and the first to suffer were Sheboldaev, the secretary of the Azov–Black Sea territorial committee, and Postyshev. We can only speculate on the reasons for the choice of these two, but, as has been seen, Postyshev had already been criticized for resisting revivalist campaigns, and both of them seem to have been particularly resistant to the centre's attempts to find 'Trotskyists' within their organizations.[243]

The attack on Sheboldaev seems to have been connected with investigations of alleged Trotskyists, particularly in the economic apparatus, launched by the NKVD in the summer and autumn of 1936, and with the attempts by party bosses to protect them.[244] The NKVD tried to build a case against a number of important economic and city-level party officials, some of whom allegedly had Trotskyist pasts, but they encountered resistance from Sheboldaev's territorial party committee. In one case Liubarskii, secretary of the Shakhty city party committee, tried to protect managerial and

[242] See the figures of party officials expelled as enemies of the party, presented to the February–March 1937 plenum, from 29 regional, territorial and republican party organizations, RGASPI, 17/120/278, 15.

[243] For criticisms of the Azov–Black Sea organization, see RGASPI, 17/120/280, 3 (Andreev, January 1937). Figures compiled for the Central Committee in February suggest that there was some basis for the charge that the Azov–Black Sea and Kiev organizations were particularly resistant to the expulsion of enemies during the verification and exchange. Both had expelled a very low proportion of Trotskyists and Zinovievites from the party during the verification and exchange, and a high proportion after the exchange, i.e. towards the end of 1936 and beginning of 1937; Leningrad, Zhdanov's organization, and Moscow, in contrast, had expelled a high proportion during the verification and exchange. For these figures, see RGASPI, 17/120/278, 3.

[244] For a discussion of the Terror in the Donbass, see H. Kuromiya, 'Stalinist Terror in the Donbas', in J. A. Getty and R. Manning, *Stalinist Terror*, 215–22. See also F. Benvenuti, 'Industry and Purge in the Donbass', 57–78.

technical officials from the mine party organization and the NKVD, and he fought a running battle against them, while in turn protected by Sheboldaev.[245] He was finally removed for 'Trotskyism' under pressure from Moscow, and this, together with other cases of party 'collusion' with 'enemies', seems to have played a major role in Stalin's decision to remove Sheboldaev on 2 January 1937. Certainly Andreev, who visited the area to supervise Sheboldaev's removal, saw the affair in this light. In letters to Zhdanov and Stalin, he explained that 'shortsightedness' towards enemies of the party and inability to perform 'party work' were the main crimes of the Azov–Black Sea party leaders.[246]

Sheboldaev himself was not accused of Trotskyism; instead he was charged with neglecting politics and having been 'distracted' by economic work, of having 'degenerated from a political leader of the party into an economic leader (*khoziaistvennik*)'.[247] However, the leadership was associating other party officials with Trotskyism: candidate members of the bureau of the territorial party committee were accused of being enemies of the people and it was also alleged that the Azov–Black Sea territorial committee leadership knew about the activity of enemies and did nothing about it.[248] In addition, the party leadership was accused of suppressing worker criticism, something which the Trotskyists had also allegedly done.[249] As in 1928, Shakhty and the Donbass were at the centre of a revivalist campaign against rude, 'bureaucratic' managers and officials; now, though, these crimes were described as Trotskyist.

The attack on Postyshev began at much the same time as the assault on Sheboldaev, but as a candidate member of the Politburo and secretary of the Kiev party organization he was a more influential and important target. The case against Postyshev and his organization had much in common with that against Sheboldaev.

---

[245] For these cases, see the plenum of the Azov–Black Sea territorial committee, in RGASPI, 17/21/2196, 100–1; RGASPI, 17/120/280, 3–4. For a discussion of this case, see O. V. Khlevniuk, *1937-i*, 95–8. For documents on the fall of Sheboldaev, see J. A. Getty and O. V. Naumov, *The Road to Terror*, 333–52.

[246] Andreev to Zhdanov, 6 January 1937. RGASPI, 73/2/19, 1.

[247] Sheboldaev, quoting Stalin, in his speech to the plenum of the Azov–Black Sea territorial committee, 6 January 1937. Translated in J. A. Getty and O. V. Naumov, *The Road to Terror*, 343.

[248] RGASPI, 17/120/281, 11–13, 22.

[249] In their attempts to create dissatisfaction among the masses, the Trotskyists had allegedly prevented self-criticism and indulged in the 'humiliation of communist workers' RGASPI, 17/120/280, 3–6 (Andreev, January 1937).

Following the August 1936 show trial, former Trotskyists in the Kiev branches of the state apparatus were accused of wrecking, and Postyshev's party organization defended them. It was only at the end of 1936 that the Kiev party organization finally failed in its attempts to defend its people; on 13 January a decree of the Central Committee accused Postyshev of allowing enemies to penetrate the party and he was removed from his post.[250] Again, as in the Sheboldaev case, the charges against Postyshev did not just relate to his failure to remove 'enemies' and co-operate with the NKVD. He was also accused of breaches of democratic norms and neglecting party work.[251]

The definition of the Trotskyist as the opponent of democracy, combined with the charge that party leaders were suppressing criticism and protecting enemies, might suggest that Stalin was on the verge of condemning regional party first secretaries themselves as Trotskyists. Yet Postyshev and Sheboldaev were demoted but not arrested, and at the February–March 1937 Central Committee plenum regional party secretaries were not accused of hostile activity. Rather, they were condemned for faults typical of party 'philistines': their lack of ideological perspective and 'party-political work', it was alleged, had protected enemies. They were also guilty of establishing incorrect relationships between party and state. As Zhdanov explained, the 'so called triangle' between economic, party, and trade union officials

deprives the union and party organization of responsibility, disarms it in the struggle against the failings of economic leadership and, on the other side, disarms the manager himself... This is how the suppression of criticism occurs, and then it is already difficult for workers in such a factory to obtain justice. It seems to me that it is time to pose the question of the liquidation of triangles.[252]

---

[250] For an account of the origins of the Postyshev case, see O. V. Khlevniuk, *1937-i*, 99–101.

[251] *VI*, 11–12 (1995), 20. For Nikolaenko's speech criticizing Postyshev and his wife for their breaches of 'democracy', see *P*, 30 May 1937.

[252] *VI*, 5 (1993), 12. Stalin interrupted Zhdanov's speech, describing the 'triangle' as 'collusion' (*sgovor*) between officials rather than 'cronyism'. For similar denunciations of the 'triangle', see *P* (editorial), 19 March 1937; RGASPI, 88/1/1044, 34–8 (A. S. Shcherbakov, 27 March 1937). See also Malenkov's report on breaches of electoral rules in party organizations. RGASPI, 17/120/278, 30–3 (15 February 1937).

The demotion of party secretaries of the rank of Postyshev and Sheboldaev was an important step in the intensification of the centre's campaign against regional party bosses, but perhaps even more threatening was the leadership's decision to return to the populist revivalism of the late 1920s and launch a new 'democracy' campaign in the party. It was announced that for the first time multi-candidate elections were to be held by secret ballot and party bosses were to be subjected to the criticism of the rank and file. By this means the centre hoped to encourage the party rank and file to inform on their bosses, thus helping the investigations of 'enemies' and bureaucrats. The rank and file, Stalin insisted, were often able to discern the 'enemy' more effectively than party bosses.[253] As in 1928–30, Stalin was squeezing the middle-level apparatus in a 'double press': pressure from below was combined with pressure from above. Local NKVD officials were replaced, and the NKVD was separated from local party committees, removing them from the influence of local bosses and ensuring that they were answerable to the centre.[254]

Yet the new 'democracy' campaign had other purposes, and Stalin justified it at the February–March plenum in a more traditional, populist revivalist way. The masses, he declared, had special energies that Bolsheviks had to use in building socialism; only 'democratic', non-'bureaucratic' relations between officials and the masses could mobilize them. He employed a powerful image, derived from classical mythology, to express this populist revivalist idea of the importance of 'democracy'. Bolshevik leaders, he declared, could be compared with Antaeus, a figure from classical mythology who remained invincible as long as he maintained contact with and gained strength from the earth, his mother Gaia. He was only defeated when Hercules lifted him up and separated him from the earth. Bolshevik leaders, Stalin declared, had to have a similar relationship with the masses as Antaeus did with the earth. The strength of Bolshevik leaders consisted in the fact that

they do not want to break the links (sviazi), weaken the links with their mother, who gave birth to them and suckled them—with the masses, with the people [narod], with the working class, with the peasantry, with the little people. They are all Bolsheviks, sons of the people, and they will be invincible only in the event that they do not allow anybody to cut them off

---

[253] See Stalin's praise for the 'little person', comrade Nikolaenko, who was prepared to stand up to the Postyshev machine. VI, 10–12 (1995), 20.

[254] For this decree, see J. A. Getty and O. V. Naumov, The Road to Terror, 443–4.

(*otorvat*') from the earth and, as a result of this, lose the possibility, by touching the earth, their mother, the masses, of acquiring new powers (*novye sily*).[255]

Zhdanov announced the new 'democracy' campaign at the February–March plenum, and multi-candidate elections to party organizations were to be held before the end of April.[256] Some party bosses, including, Kosior, were clearly unhappy about the plan, and, although he could not question elections in principle, he insisted that they needed an extension of the election period. Stalin gave in to them, amending the election date to 20 May, but their worries about 'democracy' are unlikely to have been assuaged.[257]

The dangers of democracy

Stalin may have found the rhetoric of 'democracy' and the mobilization of the 'masses' against officials a useful weapon against a 'bureaucratic' apparatus, but he was well aware of their dangers, as he had been in 1928–30. As had been the case in the past, populist revivalist discourse, which set the virtuous *nizy* against the bureaucratic, semi-capitalist *verkhi*, had considerable resonance among some sections of the population.[258] Rank-and-file party members could again use the leadership's language of wrecking, vigilance, and class in ways which were more anti-authoritarian than the regime intended. 'Subversive' workers' opinions, as described by party and secret police organizations in 1936–7, certainly suggest that some were using this rhetoric to criticize the regime. So, for instance, according to the police, one Leningrad print worker, complaining in December 1936 about the forced state loan and rises in work norms, asserted that

We have exploitation just as before [under the Tsar], only before the bosses exploited for themselves, and now for society... We are in tears. You speak about vigilance. Vigilance, you should look for wreckers not amongst the non-party workers, but amongst the *verkhi*.[259]

[255] *VI*, 11–12 (1995), 20.   [256] *VI*, 5 (1993), 14 (Zhdanov).

[257] *VI*, 6 (1993), 12 (Kosior). *VI*, 11–12 (1995), 23 (Stalin).

[258] For a discussion of populist themes in popular discourse, see S. Davies, *Popular Opinion*, ch. 8. See also S. Kotkin, *Magnetic Mountain*, 341–4.

[259] Tsentral'nyi Gosudarstvennyi Arkhiv Istoriko-Politicheskikh Dokumentov Sankt Peterburga, 24/2v/1914, 5. Khazanova, 'Pechatnyi dvor', Leningrad. With thanks to Sarah Davies for this quotation.

Another Leningrad worker was even more explicit in associating enemies with a quasi-bourgeois bureaucracy: 'Look at the people [enemies] sitting there. They are employees[260] and employees create these things. Now if they sent old workers from the Karl Marx factory and a couple of young ones to tell Stalin to rebuild and change things...'.[261]

More ideologically orthodox party activists were probably even more able to use the leadership's 'democratic' purges to their own advantage, as they were better able to manipulate Bolshevik language. An incident from the diary of L. A. Potemkin, a student in a mining institute and enthusiastic supporter of the party, shows very clearly how individuals could relate the regime's language of class struggle and Bolshevik virtue to their own experience. Potemkin relates how he attended a purge meeting at the institute in January 1935, at which one of his professors, Grebenev, was expelled from the party for his previous connection with the ideologically heterodox and his failure to denounce Zinovievite enemies. He welcomed the verdict enthusiastically, endorsing the regime's message that the enemy was an official with a bureaucratic style, unable to elicit the *aktivnost'* of the masses:

He [Grebenev] did not interest me at all and I did not even like him. He spoke in a monotone and just gave all the facts in chronological order. There was no sense of party spirit or revolutionary clarity; he lacked motivation and zeal. He was cold and distant, he wasn't simple and direct like a real party man should be and he sounded stuck-up too. I remember how he cut me down at the Political Economy exam for pronouncing a word wrong. He crushed any desire I might have had to answer normally.[262]

Potemkin was expressing the typical revivalist view of the enemy which could be found in the press: he was the heterodox official with a dubious past, who behaved in a bourgeois, 'bureaucratic' way that betrayed his lack of enthusiasm and interest in ideology. But he also managed to exploit this language to his own advantage,

---

[260] *Sluzhashchie*, i.e. those who were not workers or peasants, including officials and intelligenty.

[261] Old worker, Karl Marx Factory, Leningrad, 1937, quoted in S. Davies, *Popular Opinion*, 132.

[262] 'Diary of L. A. Potyomkin', trans. in V. Garros, N. Kornevskaya, and T. Lahusen (eds.), *Intimacy and Terror. Soviet Diaries of the 1930s* (New York, 1995), 258.

blaming his own failures on the teacher's inability to mobilize his innate abilities.

During the election meetings of the spring of 1937 the leadership tried to exploit this popular resentment, but it could also go further than leaders intended, as they soon realized. The party election meeting at the Stalin automobile factory in Moscow was certainly seen by the leadership as an example of the dangers of 'democracy'. According to the *Pravda* correspondent, the meeting took twelve days because over 200 candidates stood for the presidium and 150 for the committee. The speakers from the floor were extremely outspoken. On one occasion officials were even compared by 'demagogues' to 'Goebbels' and described as 'barbarian-bureaucrats', an epithet which the journalist considered unacceptable. The dangers of 'democracy' became particularly obvious when candidates for the party committee gave their election speeches. According to the outraged reporter, as one candidate presented his biography an unidentified person in the hall shouted out, falsely, that the candidate's father had been a kulak; although this accusation was unfounded, others refused to present their candidatures for fear of similar treatment. As a result, only 16 of the original 150 candidates left their names on the list, most of whom were members of the old administration and party committee.[263] *Pravda* was implying that an excess of 'democracy' merely served to strengthen the old bureaucrats, allowing them to smear the rank and file as class aliens.

The Moscow meeting was compared unfavourably by *Pravda* with the election meeting at the Kirov factory in Leningrad.[264] *Pravda* made it clear that the meeting had been attended by Zhdanov, and its report was presumably intended to present the leadership's view of how elections were to be conducted. While there was justified criticism of candidates at the meeting, the article also noted the 'discipline' of the activists. The secretary of the committee was criticized, but the majority argued that his name should not be removed from the list of candidates, because he could be helped to 'reform' himself. Candidates were then questioned on whether they had 'mastered Bolshevism' and 'learnt from the masses', and finally a secret ballot was held. Of 43 candidates discussed, 17 were left on

[263] *P*, 22 April 1937. For other examples of the chaos created by the election campaign, see S. Fitzpatrick, *Everyday Stalinism. Ordinary Life in Extraordinary Times: Soviet Russia in the 1930s* (Oxford, 1999), 200–1.

[264] For the comparison, see *P*, 22 April 1937.

the ballot, of whom 5 were old members of the party committee, 6 were party workers at shop level, and 4 were communist workers from production; of these 11 were elected.[265]

The leadership therefore tried to control criticism but, as in 1928–30, the centre found it difficult to restrict 'democracy' while continuing to attack 'bureaucrats' within the apparatus. It merely appealed to the masses to combine 'democracy' with 'discipline'. As during the Great Break period, this had particularly damaging effects in industry, where workers used officially sanctioned 'self-criticism' to undermine managerial authority. A *Pravda* editorial reported a case in which a foreman on a Baku oil rig had refused to obey the directives of management, and allegedly told his superiors: 'you just try to punish me and I will criticize you severely for it'. Yet *Pravda*, while denouncing this behaviour, did not explain where the limits to democracy lay. It merely quoted the vague formula set out in Stalin's article 'Against the vulgarization of the slogan of self-criticism' of June 1928.[266] Zhdanov, similarly, could only encourage the rank and file not to go too far. Speaking in June 1937 he welcomed the fact that many regional party conferences had not removed their party committees, even though their work had been adjudged unsatisfactory. Such behaviour, he argued, showed the 'deep Bolshevik wisdom and growth [of the party masses], who understand the significance of a strong apparatus for our party, who do not link criticism with the destruction of the apparatus...'.[267]

The political atmosphere in 1937 was obviously very different from that in 1928–9. There was much less spontaneous activity by the rank and file in the late 1930s than there had been in the late 1920s, and in many cases the denunciations 'from below' in 1937 were directed from above, or were the result of pressure from above to find anybody who could plausibly be defined as an enemy.[268] There was, then, no real threat to the regime from below, but even so, as in the late 1920s 'democracy' campaigns escaped central

---

[265] *P*, 28 April 1937.

[266] *P* (editorial), 24 June 1937. Stalin's 1928 article was frequently cited in these months. See *B*, 16 (1937), 19–20; *B*, 17 (1937), 78; *P* (editorial), 7 March 1937.

[267] RGASPI, 77/1/659, 75 (10 June 1937). In the following year Zhdanov was more critical of 'enemies' who tried to 'discredit' inner-party democracy by failing to impose order on it. RGASPI, 77/3/14, 7 (22 August 1938).

[268] For comparisons between the two periods, see S. Fitzpatrick, *Everyday Stalinism*, 180–2, 199–201.

control, and by the middle of the summer it is likely that Stalin was more aware of the dangers of 'democracy'. Complaints about the collapse in labour discipline became more common, and in July 1937 the Politburo issued an order restricting the issue of sick-notes, which, as Donald Filtzer has pointed out, was the first significant piece of legislation designed to strengthen labour discipline to be issued since November 1932.[269] Changes in the rules for the Supreme Soviet elections also suggests that the leadership had decided to retreat from its 'democratic' promises. The election rules, published after the June 1937 Central Committee plenum, stipulated that there would be multi-candidate (although, of course, not multi-party) elections.[270] By the October plenum, however, the leadership seems to have abandoned these plans, presumably under pressure from regional party bosses.[271] The new rules now decreed that there would only be one candidate per seat, who would be a member of a 'bloc of party and non-party candidates'.[272]

The Terror intensifies, summer 1937

For some time, Stalin had been trying to restrict the arrests of 'enemies' to a limited number within the apparatus. At the February–March 1937 plenum, he both made sure that regional party bosses were not accused of hostile activity, and he tried to prevent the bosses from exaggerating the numbers of enemies within the party. He gave his audience a long disquisition on the number of former oppositionists remaining in the party, and after a complicated calculation based on figures from the 1920s, he came to the conclusion that there had only ever been about 30,000 of them— 18,000 had been arrested, and of the remaining 12,000 some had come over to the side of the leadership. Those party leaders who expelled tens and hundreds of thousands of party members were therefore not only disobeying the leadership, but helping the real

---

[269] For these complaints, see *P*, 27 May 1937; *P* (editorial), 24 June 1937; D. Filtzer, *Soviet Workers and Stalinist Industrialization*, 233.

[270] *PS*, 14 (1937), 20–28; RGASPI, 17/2/616, 8–9 (Iakovlev, 27 June 1937).

[271] For an account of the conflict over the elections, see J. A. Getty, 'State and Society under Stalin', 18–35.

[272] For a discussion of the way in which pre-election meetings were to work, see RGASPI, 77/1/665, 2–26 (Zhdanov, 22 October 1937).

enemies to escape.[273] In June 1937, Stalin again tried to explain who the enemies were and who they were not. He firstly criticized a neo-traditionalist obsession with class origin. Those who 'when they speak about enemy forces have in mind class (*klass*), estate (*soslovie*), stratum (*prosloiku*)' were guilty of a 'biological, not a Marxist approach'.[274] Yet he also denounced those who only concentrated on political background and judged everybody who had supported Trotsky at one time or another as an enemy. There were people who had never been Trotskyists who voted for the party in a 'formal' way but were of little use to the party; while some Trotskyists, who in the past had shown 'doubts' and voted against the party, were now reliable. Stalin insisted that people had to be judged by their deeds.[275] Soon after giving this speech, however, Stalin ordered that thousands of people be arrested and shot on the basis of their past, extending terror to the highest and the lowest in the land. He demanded the arrests of hundreds and thousands of 'enemies' in the population as a whole, and he also destroyed the regional party and economic leaderships.

Stalin's reasons for escalating the violence remain a mystery, and there is still disagreement over them. Getty and Naumov argue that Stalin believed recent information that military leaders were conspiring against him, and thought that party bosses were planning to join them. It was at this point that the Terror changed fundamentally, from a series of complex manœuvres between central and regional party leaders, into a fearful response to the belief that society as a whole was riddled with enemies.[276] Intentionalists, however, regard the period as one in which Stalin continued to escalate repression, rather than as a fundamentally new stage. Khlevniuk accepts that Stalin may have become more fearful in this period, but he sees his fear as a response to the deteriorating international situation, rather than a panicked reaction to evidence of conspiracy.[277] He was learning what he thought were the lessons of the Spanish Civil War: that an enemy fifth column behind the

---

[273] *VI*, 11–12 (1995), 21.

[274] *Istochnik*, 3 (1994), 73 (speech to the Commissariat of Defence, 2 June 1937).

[275] Ibid., 73–4.

[276] J. A. Getty and O. V. Naumov, *The Road to Terror*, 444–8, 583.

[277] Khlevniuk, 'The Reasons for the "Great Terror" ', 165–8. Rees is sceptical of the significance of the Tukhachevskii affair. See E. Rees, 'The Great Terror. Suicide or Murder?', 447–8.

lines would undermine the Soviets' ability to fight the Germans in a future war.[278] Stalin's thinking in this period remains obscure, but it is probable that he believed new evidence that the military leaders was conspiring against him, and he may have thought that party bosses, under pressure from Moscow, might join them. But we should not exaggerate the changes in the leadership's thinking in this period. Stalin was continuing to pursue his revivalist campaign both against officials whom he believed were conspiring against him, and against those who were not sufficiently committed, or who were resisting the search for 'enemies'. And he was still forced to deal with the dilemma of all revivalist campaigns: how to investigate and shake up the apparatus without destroying it. Stalin wanted to root out 'unreliable' party bosses, but at the same time he seems to have been worried that he was undermining the authority of the party and encouraging 'enemies' outside the élite to act against the regime. And learning the lessons of Spain, he feared that foreign interventionists could rely not only on traitors within the élite but also on 'fifth columnists' within society as a whole.

It is unclear what precipitated the fear of a conspiracy between party bosses and the military. Leaders had expressed suspicion of the army's leadership since the February–March 1937 plenum, and even before. And Stalin seems to have thought, as he had during the civil war, that many officers were not committed to socialism.[279] But at the same time Marshal Tukhachevskii, the deputy commissar for defence, was being denounced by arrested 'Trotskyists', and there had been rumours for some time, probably spread by the Germans, that he was conspiring with Berlin.[280] Stalin's speeches to party leaders during the period give every indication that he believed the allegations against Tukhachevskii, and it is also not surprising that Stalin should have worried about an alliance between regional party bosses and the army.[281] The army was organized territorially and there were close links between military leaders

---

[278] For Stalin's references to Spain, see RGASPI, 558/11/1120, 43–4. See also D. Shearer, 'Social Disorder', 530–1.

[279] See, for instance, RGASPI, 558/11/1120, 107–9 (Stalin, 1937).

[280] *Izv TsK KPSS*, 4 (1989), 42–80; for an account of the affair, see S. Pons, *Stalin and the Inevitable War*, 82–9. See also J. A. Getty and O. V. Naumov, *The Road to Terror*, 444–51.

[281] For his comments on the Tukhachevskii affair, see *Istochnik*, 3 (1994), 75–7 (2 June 1937); RGASPI, 558/11/1120, 103–4.

and the regional party apparatus.[282] At a time of extreme tension between the centre and regional party leaders, when Stalin thought he was meeting resistance to his attempts to purge regional apparatuses, it would have seemed very likely that the military might try to defend their colleagues.[283] This hypothesis is supported by the memoirs of Anna Larina, Bukharin's wife, which claim that NKVD interrogators accused her of expecting Tukhachevskii and the army to rescue her husband.[284] Also, it was only after the arrest of the military leaders, suddenly and secretly, that party bosses were accused of Trotskyism. Soon after the announcement of the military conspiracy a week later, however, most regional bosses were removed one by one in the course of a few months.

The leadership, then, may have believed that party leaders were plotting, or were about to plot against the regime, but as in the past it was not only concerned with actual evidence of conspiracy. It seems to have been as interested in finding evidence of 'rightist' attitudes and 'bureaucratic' behaviour, because it assumed that people with these attitudes were likely to collude with foreign enemies in the future, or undermine the internal unity and mobilization needed to resist the enemy. So, while Molotov's reminiscences generally insist that most of the charges of conspiracy were true, they sometimes suggest that the Terror was not so much aimed at those who were actually conspiring with foreign enemies, as at people who might conspire in the future, or who might compromise the war-readiness of the state because they were ideologically rightist or lacked 'faith' in socialism. So, Molotov rejected the argument that there would have been much less bloodshed had Bukharin won the political battles of the 1920s and 1930s. If the rightists had won and had Terror not been waged against them, he explained, 'a rancorous struggle would have raged throughout the country', and

---

[282] Roberta Manning suggests that I. P. Rumiantsev, leader of the Western Region party committee, was arrested because of his close connections with I. P. Uborevich, commander of the Belorussian military region (*okrug*), who had been implicated in the Tukhachevskii affair. Uborevich was a member of the regional party committee. See R. Manning, 'Massovaia operatsiia protiv "kulakov i prestupnykh elementov": apogei Velikoi Chistki na Smolenshchine', in E. V. Kodin, *Stalinizm v Rossiiskoi provintsii: smolenskie arkhivnye dokumenty v prochtenii zarubezhnykh i Rossiiskikh istorikov* (Smolensk, 1999), 231–3.

[283] Getty and Naumov argue this. See J. A. Getty and O. V. Naumov, *The Road to Terror*, 446.

[284] A. M. Larina, *Nezabyvaemoe* (Moscow, 1989), 27.

while 'we would not have submitted to Hitler', 'he would have gained much by this'.[285] Stalin took a similar view of the dangers posed by officials who lacked ideological commitment or who were guilty of rightism. In February 1938 a correspondence between Stalin and a lowly Komsomol propagandist, Ivan Ivanov, was published in *Pravda*. In the published text, Ivanov recounted how he had been accused by his superiors of Trotskyism because he had argued that the final victory of socialism would only be possible when international capitalism had been defeated. He therefore appealed to Stalin to judge the case. Stalin defended Ivanov and accused his bosses of exaggerating the strength of the regime. While accepting that the internal bourgeoisie was beaten, he declared that the Soviet Union had to defend itself because the international bourgeoisie was still threatening the Soviet Union. Ivanov's superiors were therefore not only guilty of ideological heterodoxy, but were themselves helping the enemy. 'Even if they are subjectively loyal to our cause', he explained, 'they are objectively dangerous for our cause, as by their boasting they, willingly or unwillingly (it makes no difference which!), lull our people to sleep, demobilize the workers and peasants and help our enemies to catch us off-guard in the event of international complications.'[286] In the current situation, it was 'necessary to keep our whole people in a state of mobilized readiness in the face of the danger of a military attack'.

Stalin therefore continued to persecute officials according to conventional revivalist criteria: whether they were enthusiastic believers in socialism; and whether they showed signs of rightism or technicism. In a speech to a group of military leaders on political conspiracies in the military in 1937, he strongly criticized those who believed that '*tekhnika* decides everything'; rather, he declared, 'the correct politics (*pravil'naia politika*) of the party decides everything'. The example of Napoleon, he explained, showed the truth of this slogan. He was successful militarily as long as he pursued policies which were in the interests of the people, such as the emancipation of peasants from feudal lords. He was defeated only when he no longer helped the people. Similarly the Bolsheviks had won the civil war because the people had supported the Red Army. Returning to some of the ideas he had defended during the debates

[285] *Sto sorok besed s Molotovym*, 408.
[286] Stalin, *Sochineniia*, i. (xiv), 266–73; *P*, 14 February 1938.

over 'military specialists' during the civil war, he insisted that even an 'average commander' could 'do much more than the most able bourgeois commander' if their politics were correct and it they had popular support. He advised military leaders not to 'waste the authority which you have obtained with the people' or they would be replaced by newly promoted commanders. Promotees might 'perhaps be less able' than existing officers, but they would be 'linked with the masses' and would bring many more advantages 'than you with your talents'.[287]

Stalin also continued to criticize regional party officials on conventional revivalist grounds, at the same time as they were being accused of conspiracy with foreigners. He sent trusted allies from Moscow to the regions to decide which party leaders were to be arrested, and it seems that emissaries had a role in investigating abuses of power, 'wrecking', protection of 'enemies' and poor treatment of subordinates, before recommending the right course of action to Stalin.[288] In some ways, therefore, these visits can be seen as the culmination of the centre's attempts to break 'collusion' in the localities and discover who was 'sabotaging' the centre's efforts to mobilize the party and improve the economy. The main difference with previous investigations was that party bosses were now arrested as 'enemies'.

At the same time, Stalin continued to use populist methods in his attack on local party bosses. His emissaries organized party plenums, at which party members were encouraged to denounce their 'enemy' bosses.[289] In August 1937 Stalin also ordered that a number of show trials of senior district officials be organized in the provinces. Defendants were accused of both sabotage and poor treatment of peasants, and many of the cases were based on genuine peasant complaints.[290] Most took place between September and December, but they were staged well into 1938.[291]

---

[287] RGASPI, 558/11/1120, 107–9 (Stalin, 1937).

[288] See, for instance, Zhdanov's evidence against the Orenburg party organization, RGASPI, 17/120/285, 147–301; see also his evidence against the Bashkir party organization RGASPI, 17/120/282, 283.

[289] See, for instance, Andreev's visit to Uzbekistan. Andreev to Stalin, 17 September 1937, RGASPI, 73/2/19, 34. Stalin and Molotov to Andreev, 21 September 1937. RGASPI, 73/2/19, 44.

[290] The order is published in J. A. Getty and O. V. Naumov, *The Road to Terror*, 457.

[291] For these trials, see S. Fitzpatrick, *Stalin's Peasants*, 297–312; R. Manning, 'Massovaia operatsiia', 242–6.

The Terror outside the party and the definition of the enemy

In the summer of 1937, therefore, Stalin, probably convinced by the threat of a widespread conspiracy within the highest reaches of the apparatus, decided to intensify his revivalist campaign against it. But he also directed the Terror outside the élite, and launched two mass terrors, the first against particular national diaspora minorities, and the second against those identified as common criminals, 'class aliens' and other 'former people' (including priests and those who had positions under the tsarist regime). People who fell into stigmatized social or ethnic categories were rounded up and deported, imprisoned, or executed. The persecutions of criminals followed in the tradition of earlier discipline campaigns, while the campaigns against national minorities and 'class aliens' depended on neo-traditionalist assumptions about politics. Victims were now being judged by their ethnic or class background, not primarily according to their ideological state.

Deportations and arrests of minority nationalities were not new, and were clearly connected with fears of foreign invasion. Since the mid-1930s, Moscow had deported diaspora national groups who lived on the borderlands and who were believed to be unreliable because they had links with foreign powers. These deportations had also been accompanied by arrests of members of diaspora nationalities throughout the Soviet Union on the ground that they were conspiring with foreigners.[292] But they were expanded and intensified from the summer of 1937, probably, in large part, because of increased fears of invasion.

Initially the regime's attention was directed towards diaspora nationalities, rather than 'indigenous' non-Russian nationalities of the Soviet Union. So, while the repression of diaspora groups was based on the assumption that ethnic groups had essential, immutable characteristics, they were directed at specific politically 'disloyal' nationalities. They do not seem to have been designed to

---

[292] See T. Martin, 'The Origins of Soviet Ethnic Cleansing', *JMH*, 70 (1998), 852–8. See also N. V. Petrov and A. B. Roginskii, ' "Pol'skaia operatsiia" NKVD 1937–1938 gg.', in A. E. Guranov (ed.), *Repressii protiv poliakov i pol'skikh grazhdan*, vyp. 1, (Moscow, 1997); I. L. Shcherbakov (ed.), *Repressii protiv rossiiskikh nemtsev v Sovetskom Soiuze v kontekste sovetskoi natsional'noi politiki* (Moscow, 1999); M. Gelb, ' "Karelian Fever": The Finnish Immigrant Community during Stalin's Purges', *E–AS*, 45 (1993), 1091–116; M. Gelb, 'An Early Soviet Ethnic Deportation: The Far Eastern Koreans', *RR*, 54 (1995), 389–412.

strengthen a neo-traditionalist hierarchy among the 'loyal' nations of the Soviet Union. Indeed, at the beginning of 1937 it even looked as if the leadership were returning to the policies of the Great Break, and Moscow criticized Postyshev for his neglect of *korenizatsiia* in the Ukraine, while calling for a renewed emphasis on indigenous culture. But from the autumn of 1937 this policy was reversed, and Moscow now targeted 'bourgeois nationalists' accused of hostility to Russians; the Terror now became associated with efforts to give pre-eminence to Russian language and culture. In March 1938 the leadership decreed that school students throughout the Soviet Union were to learn Russian, and the supremacy of Russia within the Soviet hierarchy was strengthened.[293]

These signs of ethnic neo-traditionalism were accompanied by a class neo-traditionalism, As one might except, fear of invasion convinced the regime as a whole of the need for a campaign of social as well as ethnic 'cleansing'. However, fear of war was reinforced by fear of the social disorder encouraged by the centre's 'democratization' campaigns. Both Moscow and regional bosses had reason to be worried that 'democracy' would encourage expressions of popular discontent. But regional leaders were particularly concerned, and in launching a revivalist attack on the apparatus, Stalin was giving party bosses greater incentives to protect themselves by clamping down on criticism and by deflecting terror towards lower levels of the party and non-party groups. As in the past, they used neo-traditionalist arguments, warning of the dangers from 'class aliens' and in particular former kulaks. As before, Stalin and his group had an ambiguous attitude towards the question of class aliens, typical of revivalist Bolshevism. They were also concerned that a mass repression of these groups would detract from on 'bureaucratism' within the apparatus, and they accused regional bosses of harbouring neo-traditionalist attitudes. But in the fearful atmosphere of mid-1937, they accepted that they had to remove potential threats within the population, and ordered mass terror.

There is a good deal of evidence that this campaign was encouraged by regional party bosses, who were responding to the centre's

---

[293] The narrative in this paragraph is based on T. Martin, 'Origins of Soviet Ethnic Cleansing', 852–8; T. Martin, *The Affirmative Action Empire*, 423–9. For the emphasis on Russian superiority, particularly from 1937 to 1938, see ibid., 451–60.

attempts to expand 'democracy' campaigns by demanding mass repressions against allegedly disloyal groups outside the party.[294] At the February–March 1937 plenum Zhdanov and the leadership decreed that the elections to the Supreme Soviet were to be held in accordance with the new constitution: secret ballots were to be used and 'class aliens', including former kulaks and priests, were to be allowed to vote for the first time. Regional bosses, however, were unhappy with these developments. They argued that before this type of election was held outside the party, the threat from 'class aliens' within the population had to be neutralized. The constitution seems genuinely to have worried local party bosses, party activists, and political policemen, as it convinced many ordinary people that the regime was changing its views of private property in the countryside and religion. NKVD sources reported that some peasants interpreted it as a sign that kulaks would return to the collective farm and that private plots would be expanded.[295] They also claimed that the constitution was encouraging religious groups, and that priests and religious organizations were particularly energetic during the electoral campaign, taking advantage of the provision that any legally registered organization was able to nominate candidates.[296]

Whether or not the new constitution and the Supreme Soviet elections really did present a serious challenge to communist authority, it is probable that regional party bosses were trying to redirect the Terror towards kulaks, priests, and other allegedly subversive groups, such as non-Russian 'bourgeois nationalists'. This may have been part of a deliberate strategy by the bosses to deflect the Terror away from themselves towards groups outside the apparatus; or they may have been eliciting the support of the centre against those whom they genuinely believed were threatening their authority in their regions. That they were using this strategy is evident during the frequently bad-tempered discussion of Zhdanov's report on the elections to the Supreme Soviet at the

---

[294] This is also argued Rittersporn, in *Stalinist Simplifications*, 158 ff., and by J. A. Getty, in ' "Excesses are not Permitted" ', 122–6.

[295] L. Siegelbaum and A. Sokolov (eds.), *Stalinism as a Way of Life*, ch. 3.

[296] For NKVD reports see *Neizvestnaia Rossiia XX veka. Pis'ma, memuary* (Moscow, 1992), 278. For party reports, see WKP, 111, 74. See also L. Siegelbaum and A. Sokolov, *Stalinism as a Way of Life*, 184–8; S. Davies, *Popular Opinion*, 107–8; S. Fitzpatrick, *Everyday Stalinism*, 282–3; J. A.Getty, 'State and Society', 18–36.

February–March plenum. Zhdanov presented the elections as part of a more general campaign of 'democratization', designed to improve relations between leaders and the masses and prevent 'bureaucratic' leaders from taking the 'trust of the people for granted'.[297] He accepted that some anti-Soviet groups, including priests, would become more active during the elections, and he did not rule out the repression of 'hostile' forces, but did not see this as a reason to delay or limit the scope of the elections. Indeed, he saw greater 'democracy' and closer links with the masses as the answer to any problems the party might encounter.[298] Several party leaders, however, were clearly unhappy with Zhdanov's line. Eikhe was particularly outspoken, demanding that he and more 'local' people be involved in the preparations for the elections, and complaining that he and his fellow regional bosses had not been given enough information about them.[299]

Most criticism of democracy at the plenum, however, was more implicit, and stressed the difficulty of organizing elections when there were so many aliens, and in particular kulaks and priests, among the population. Eikhe, secretary of a region which received a large number of class aliens exiled from other regions, was at the forefront of calls for presecution of this type of 'enemy'.[300] There were 93,000 people in his region, he claimed, who were potential enemies because they had been excluded from the party in various purges. Also youths and former kulaks were likely to engage in 'slander and provovation' during the elections.[301] Eikhe's 'enemies', unlike the leadership's 'Trotskyists', were clearly not party members or figures who held any position of influence, but were either people who had been previously expelled from the party, or those who had a class alien, and particularly a kulak, background. Kosior's 'enemies' were similar to Eikhe's: he stressed the need to keep watch over 'various passive, backward and at times also hostile people' in factories who could be 'the source of alien influences'.[302] Several other regional party bosses made similar speeches, pointing to the large number of kulak, religious, and nationalist enemies in their regions and the dangers they would present during the election

[297] VI, 5 (1993), 5–6.   [298] Ibid., 6.   [299] VI, 6 (1993), 6.
[300] In January 1936 Eikhe expressed concern about what was to be done with exiled kulaks. RGASPI, 17/120/240, 36–7.
[301] VI, 6 (1993), 5–6.
[302] Ibid., 7.

campaign.[303] Although they did not call for the cancellation of elections, they made their discontent clear.

An exchange between Molotov and Ia. A. Popok, the first secretary of the Turkmen republican party organization, suggests that the central leadership realized that local party bosses were trying to blunt the revivalist thrust of Zhdanov's proposals by demanding an assault on 'class aliens' and non-Russian nationalists. Popok listed the large number of nationalist, religious, and kulak enemies in the republic, and complained that kulaks were using the constitution as a justification for claiming the right to return to their former lands in collective farms.[304] All this, he claimed, amounted to 'a growth in the activism of hostile elements'. Molotov then interrupted him, clearly worried about the implications of his argument and trying to change the focus of the discussion to the campaign against 'bureaucrats' in the apparatus:

MOLOTOV. Not only hostile elements can express dissatisfaction with various of our shortcomings or our bad workers, but also Soviet people themselves. We need to take account of this.

POPOK. I will come to this. Together with this class-hostile activism we see the activization of nationalist elements, in particular in the soviet apparatus...

SHKIRIATOV. Comrade Molotov was not talking about this.

KOSIOR. Molotov was not talking about this.

POPOK. I understood that Viacheslav Mikhailovich [Molotov] spoke about this in particular, [and] I will speak about it.

VOICE: He spoke about honest Soviet people who can be dissatisfied.

MOLOTOV. Honest Soviet people can also be dissatisfied with bureaucrats. Such honest Soviet people can turn out to be against our candidates.

POPOK. I understood this, I will speak about this presently, comrade Molotov. Let me turn to this, but first I want to dwell yet more on one feature. We observe the activization of nationalist elements particularly in the soviet apparatus and in party cells in higher education institutes. Not long ago we were forced to liquidate some nationalist organizations of a semi-Trotskyist persuasion. They showed their activism largely after the promulgation of

---

[303] See, for instance, VI, 7 (1993), 10–11 (Evdokimov); VI, 6 (1993), 23–4 (Mirzoian); VI, 6 (1993), 25–6 (Popok).

[304] For Popok and the Turkmen party organization, see O. Khlevniuk, 'Les Mechanismes de la "Grande Terreur" des Années 1937–1938 au Turkmenistan', CMR, 39 (1998), 197–208.

the new constitution. The constitution is, for them, so to say, a legal form for this, in order to strengthen their activity.[305]

Having stubbornly refused to be distracted from his theme, Popok finally addressed Molotov's point and accepted that officials' 'bureaucratic work' could stimulate hostility to the regime, although he was much more willing to criticize the state apparatus than the party.[306] A similar tension between the central leadership and the regional secretaries over the subject matter of the discussion is evident later in the debate. E. G. Evdokimov, the new secretary of the Azov–Black Sea territorial committee, spoke about the need to democratize the party, but then launched into a lengthy disquisition on the threat from enemies and religious groups in his territory. Stalin interrupted, asking him to explain the absence of elections to party committees, while Mikoian told him that he was straying from the subject of the debate and Andreev tried to cut him off several times; when Andreev had finally succeeded in doing so, he complained that some speakers were saying very little about elections and democracy within the party, the subject that was supposed to be at the centre of the discussion.[307]

Regional party bosses continued to give warnings about dangers from kulaks and other enemies at the Central Committee plenum on 27 June 1937, when the draft electoral law was discussed, and at the plenum of 11 and 12 October.[308] The leadership did launch 'mass operations' against these groups, as will be seen, but it remained unhappy about officials' attempts to redefine the 'enemy' as the 'class alien' rather than the 'bureaucrat'. So, for instance, at the June 1937 plenum, Molotov strongly attacked the neo-traditionalist definition of virtue, arguing that present rather than past behaviour and loyalties were most important in judging suitability for office. For Molotov, 'the old evaluations of people' were 'now completely inadequate' and it was not enough for leaders to have joined the party before the revolution or fought for the Bolsheviks; rather the party needed leaders who had not been 'bureaucratized'.[309]

---

[305] *VI*, 6, (1993), 25–6.

[306] Ibid., 26.

[307] *VI*, 7 (1993), 7–11. Zhdanov made a similar criticism of the regional secretaries. Ibid., 18.

[308] See, for instance, RGASPI, 17/2/616, 154–5 (Isaev, 27 June 1937); RGASPI, 17/2/627, 10, 60 (Margolin, Volkov, 12 October 1937).

[309] RGASPI, 17/2/616, 187.

Similarly, speaking in the same month to officials at the Commissariat of Defence, Stalin ridiculed the notion that class origin should be used as a primary indicator of political reliability. Marx, Engels, and Lenin, he pointed out, had been from non-proletarian strata, and there were always non-proletarians who could serve the cause of the working class even better than 'pure, pure-blooded proletarians'.[310]

Regional party bosses did not only try to exploit the centre's ambiguous language of class; they also succeeded in distorting the meaning of the term 'Trotskyist'. While Stalin tended to see 'Trotskyists' as officials who were 'bureaucratic' or had 'rightist' attitudes but who were of proletarian class origin, the term was very likely to lend itself to rival interpretations which did not accord with revivalist intentions. It could be taken literally, to refer to anybody with a Trotskyist past, or it could be understood in the sense it was understood in the 1920s, as a leftist form of Bolshevism with support among workers. Stalin was eager to counter both interpretations in March 1937: it was wrong, he stressed, to condemn everybody who had a Trotskyist past or who had close relations with Trotskyists; indeed he noted that Dzerzhinskii had been a good leader even though he had been one of Trotsky's supporters.[311] It was also mistaken, Stalin argued, to view Trotskyism as a 'political tendency within the working class' as it had been seven or eight years earlier.[312] Yet, despite these warnings, Stalin found it difficult to control the definition of the term 'Trotskyist' and prevent it being used by local party and economic officials for their own purposes.

An interesting case of this phenomenon can be found in an article published in *Pravda* in June 1937. According to *Pravda*, the deputy director of a factory in the Crimea had imposed overly strict standards of hygiene on the workers who lived in the factory settlement; for the newspaper, this constituted a typical case of 'Trotskyist contempt for workers'. The workers refused to obey this 'provocative instruction' and complained to the factory party organization,

[310] *Istochnik*, 3 (1994), 74–5 (Stalin's speech to Commissariat of Defence, 2 June 1937).

[311] *VI*, 11–12 (1995), 12. The reference to Dzerzhinskii was omitted from the published version. For a similar point, see Stalin's speech to the Commissariat of Defence of 2 June 1937, *Istochnik*, 3 (1994), 74.

[312] *VI*, 4 (1995), 6.

which sided with the management, accusing the workers of 'Trotskyism' and threatening to take them to court. The district party committee had also supported the management, and although the deputy director was no longer at the enterprise, the workers had been fighting their case since March and the director was still in place. *Pravda* therefore called on the committee to take action against the 'Trotskyist' management.[313] As this story shows, the malleability of the term 'Trotskyist' allowed lower levels of the apparatus to use the Terror themselves in ways not intended by the leadership. Indeed Zhdanov, in his speech to the eighteenth party congress in 1939, listed a number of incidents when local party officials had unjustly accused their critics of Trotskyism.[314]

Yet, while Stalin may have thought that local party bosses were deliberately exaggerating the threat from 'enemies' outside the élite, he and the secret police seems to have agreed that class aliens and marginals within the population as a whole did pose a threat. So, for instance, he agreed with Stetskii's comments at the February–March plenum that there was a real danger that rural soviets would fall into 'alien hands' during the election campaign.[315] It was probably the same fear that led him to extend the Terror outside the apparatus.

The Politburo made one of the first attempts to direct terror against 'class aliens' among the population on 28 June 1937, and it is clear that regional bosses were heavily involved from the beginning.[316] The Politburo noted the 'uncovering in West Siberia of a counter-revolutionary insurrectionary organization amongst exiled kulaks', and ordered that a local *troika*, a tribunal consisting of the territorial party committee's first secretary, Eikhe, the head of the local NKVD, and the local procurator, be established to facilitate the investigation and execute summary justice.[317] It was

---

[313] *P*, 23 June 1937.
[314] RGASPI, 77/1/719, 162–82. Zhdanov was referring to KPK material.
[315] *VI*, 7 (1993), 5.
[316] On the 'mass operations', see M. Iunge and R. Binner, *Kak terror stal "bol' shim". Sekretnyi prikaz No. 00447 i tekhnologiia ego ispolneniia* (Moscow, 2003), which notes the 'zeal' of local bosses, but stresses the centre's role; M. Jansen and N. Petrov, *Stalin's Loyal Executioner. People's Commissar Nikolai Ezhov, 1895– 1940* (Stanford, 2002), 79–108; B. McLoughlin, 'Mass Operations of the NKVD, 1937–8: A Survey', in B. McLoughlin and K. McDermott, *Stalin's Terror. High Politics and Mass Repression in the Soviet Union* (Basingstoke, 2002), 118–52. For a different emphasis, see J. A. Getty, '"Excesses are not Permitted"', 113–38.
[317] See J. A. Getty and O. V. Naumov, *The Road to Terror*, 469; see also O. V. Khlevniuk, 'The Objectives of the Great Terror, 1937–1938', 161.

probably no accident that Eikhe was involved, a regional boss who had for some time been warning of the threat from class aliens. It was probably also significant that this decree was issued on the day after the discussion of the draft law on elections to the Supreme Soviet, and it is reasonable to speculate that Stalin was agreeing to local bosses' demands for a purge of the population before the elections took place.[318] The connection between the issue of internal democracy and the attack on class aliens is also suggested by the fact that the Politburo made the decision to extend this purge to the Soviet Union as a whole on 2 July, the day that *Pravda* published the rules for the Supreme Soviet elections.[319] The operation was intended to last from August until November, suggesting that it was designed to prepare for the elections to be held in December.[320] Regional party bosses were not only closely involved in the formulation of the mass operations but also in their implementation. They had power over death sentences and were asked to send the Centre details of the numbers they proposed should be shot or imprisoned.[321] As the regional bosses had been demanding, many of the victims of these 'mass operations' were former kulaks, although criminals, priests, and those accused of opposing the Bolshevik regime in the past also suffered in large numbers.[322]

Regional bosses were particularly enthusiastic about the mass operations. Some proposed target numbers of arrests which the centre thought too high: when drawing up Order No. 00447, which initiated the 'operation aimed at the repression of former kulaks, criminals and other anti-Soviet elements', Moscow established 'limits' (*limity*) which were sometimes lower than those requested by regional officials.[323] And once the limits were established, regional officials continued to press for higher targets, which Moscow sometimes refused. However, it frequently approved

---

[318] For the connection between the elections of 1937 and the mass operations, see J. A. Getty, ' "Excesses are not Permitted" ', 126. For an alternative view, see M. Iunge and R. Binner, *Kak terror stal "bol' shim"*, 212.

[319] For this point, see J. A. Getty ' "Excesses are not Permitted" ', 126.

[320] It was decreed that the 'mass operations' should last for four months from 5 August. Elections were held on 12 December. *T*, 4 June 1992.

[321] *T*, 4 June 1992. McLoughlin, 'Mass Operations of the NKVD', 124.

[322] J. A. Getty, ' "Excesses are not Permitted" ', 132. For the operation against kulaks, see D. Shearer, 'Crime and Social Disorder', 141–3; for the operation against criminals, see P. Hagenloh, 'Socially Harmful Elements', 300–2.

[323] J. A. Getty, ' "Excesses are not Permitted" ', 128–30.

them, and the evidence suggests that at times the centre encouraged officials to expand the blood-letting. According to his subordinates, Ezhov put a great deal of pressure on regional NKVD chiefs to make arrests, even if not all who were swept up in the campaigns were enemies; he insisted that it was better to purge too many than not enough, and that it was inevitable that innocent people would be killed.[324]

The end of the Terror, 1938

Yet while may of the leadership's statements on the mass operations implied that it was content for the police to use crude categories of class and political background in its persecutions of the non-party masses, it was less happy about these practices in the party purges, and it continued to criticize regional officials for targeting the wrong people. The most public indication of Stalin's dissatisfaction came at the January 1938 Central Committee plenum, when Stalin accused bosses of persecuting thousands of innocent communists while allowing the real enemies to go free. As the plenum's conclusions stated:

It is time to understand that Bolshevik vigilance consists in essence in the ability to unmask the enemy regardless of how clever and cunning he may be, irrespective of how he adorns himself, and not in indiscriminate or 'on the off-chance' expulsions [from the party], by the tens and hundreds, of everyone who comes within reach.[325]

The plenum denounced 'careerist communists', some of whom were 'enemies' and 'provocateurs' themselves, for trying to 'insure themselves against possible charges of insufficient vigilance through the indiscriminate repression of party members'.[326] These 'careerists' were clearly identified as local party bosses who either conspired in

---

[324] See M. Iunge and R. Binner, *Kak terror stal "bol'shim"*, 22, 46-9, 228–9. Getty, in contrast, stresses the centre's desire to limit repressions. See J. A. Getty, '"Excesses are not Permitted"', 128, 130. For Ezhov's statements, see M. Jansen and N. Petrov, *Stalin's Loyal Executioner*, 84, 89.

[325] *KPSS v rezoliutsiiakh*, v. 303–12.

[326] Ibid.

this 'false vigilance', or adopted a 'bureaucratic' and 'heartless' attitude towards the appeals of unjustly expelled party members. Their victims were often people falsely accused of hiding a class alien or oppositionist past.[327]

Yet regional party bosses were not always willing to take the blame for the distortion of terror, and even denied that terror had been indiscriminate. Kosior, under serious attack for excessive purging, tried to explain the excesses and justify the repressions of the previous few months. He admitted that he and his colleagues were at fault for failing to restrain others, but he blamed the expulsions on 'younger comrades and lower [party] organizations' and on the NKVD, which put pressure on his party organization.[328] He also tried to justify mass expulsions. The unjust expulsion of communists, he argued, was not a 'simple phenomenon'; the whole business was 'very complex' because 'we cannot disregard any statement [i.e. denunciation], whatever it is, we simply do not have the right, all the more since we have tens of cases when we dug out serious enemies on the basis of the most trifling statements'.[329] Stalin was not prepared to accept Kosior's self-justification, and he accused higher party organizations of demanding 'mild treatment' themselves while they persecuted the district party organizations below them. In response to Stalin's aggressive comments, Kosior again tried to defend himself and his fellow-secretaries, implying that many of those who had been successful in their appeals against expulsion from the party were actually enemies, or at least 'in general do not deserve [our] confidence'.[330]

However, while some statements at the plenum suggested that the leadership was again targeting the regional party bosses, this time for distorting the purges of the party in a neo- traditionalist direction, the main effect of its resolutions was to strengthen the party bosses, by restoring order and calling for the end of mass expulsions and the acceleration of appeals. Certainly, in the months after the

---

[327] Kosior, for instance, gave the case of an anonymous note that accused somebody of hiding the fact that his father was a trader as an example of unjust expulsion. RGASPI, 17/2/639, 18. For the reinstatement of people accused of having a dubious background and subsequently shown to have been unjustly charged, see the records of the Smolensk Komsomol, WKP, 416, *passim*.

[328] RGASPI, 17/2/639, 18, 19.

[329] RGASPI, 17/2/639, 18.

[330] RGASPI, 17/2/639, 19.

plenum purges of the party were moderated, although the persecution of élites did not cease completely.[331] The third Moscow trial of the 'Anti-Soviet "Bloc of Rights and Trotskyists" ' of March 1938 also seems to have been designed to signal that the search for 'enemies' in the party was over. Writing to Vyshinskii, Stalin told him that 'the verdict of the court should contribute to the restoration of normal conditions in the country', and in his summary of the case Vyshinskii did indeed imply that the conspiracy in the party had been dealt with.[332] Concerns about the effects of the repressions on the state's stability were an important factor in this change in policy, as is suggested by the fact that Zhdanov and Andreev criticized Ezhov for weakening the capabilities of the country by replacing competent with incompetent leaders.[333]

This restoration of the authority of the party apparatus and the moderation of attacks on the political élites were entirely compatible with the continuation of mass operations against non-élite groups, and a second phase of the operation against kulaks was announced in January 1938. While it was wound down in February–March 1938, the operations continued, now largely directed against ethnic minorities, and they were even bloodier than before. It was only in the autumn of 1938 that the leadership decided to halt them. The reasons for their end are unclear and the subject of controversy. It may be that Stalin became dissatisfied with the 'excesses' of the NKVD, or with its inefficiency; it may be that the mass operations were thought to have achieved their objectives; or it may be that Stalin and the party leadership believed that the NKVD had become too strong and needed to be cut down to size.[334] But whatever its thinking, the leadership presented the end of the operations as part of the restoration of order after a period of 'excesses'.[335] On 17 November the Politburo abolished the *troiki* and criticized the NKVD for carrying out arrests indiscriminately,

---

[331] For the ending of party purges, see also J. A. Getty and O. V. Naumov, *The Road to Terror*, 493–8; M. Jansen and N. Petrov, *Stalin's Loyal Executioner*, 128–9, 153.

[332] Stalin quoted in W. Hedeler, 'Ezhov's Scenario for the Great Terror and the Falsified Record of the Third Moscow Trial', in B. McLoughlin and K. McDermott, *Stalin's Terror*, 45; A. Vyshinskii, in *Report of Court Proceedings in the Case of the Anti-Soviet "Bloc of Rights and Trotskyites"*, 637.

[333] For these criticisms, see B. A. Starkov, 'Narkom Ezhov', 36.

[334] For differing explanations see M. Iunge and R. Binner, *Kak terror stal "bol'shim"*, 230–2; J. A. Getty and O. V. Naumov, *The Road to Terror*, 528–9.

[335] J. A. Getty and O. V. Naumov, *The Road to Terror*, 543–4.

while Ezhov was disgraced and accused among other things, of 'leftist overreaction' to the problem of enemies.[336]

This attempt to restore normality was also signalled by a number of statements and policies designed to promote a technicist message of discipline and order. In March, *Pravda* was redefining the concept of 'vigilance', to deprive it of its revivalist meaning: it now meant 'cultured work, literate leadership' and 'the struggle against lack of cleanliness'.[337] It also seems that the leadership wished to alter the balance between party and state, and between 'political' and 'economic work'. So, on 3 January 1938, the Central Committee condemned the Iaroslavl' city committee for exceeding its powers by appointing directors to factories. No city committee, it ruled, had these rights.[338] Commenting on the decree, *Pravda*'s editorial suggested that 'one-man management' was weak, and this situation had been caused by the absence of 'economic work and economic leadership' by the party; in the past, it claimed, party leaders in some organizations had subscribed to the enemy theory that economic officials were alien. Now new industrial executives had been promoted, who required 'energetic support and help from party organizations', not 'petty tutelage'. Only thus could one-man management and 'order' be restored in factories.[339]

The argument that insufficient 'economic work' by the party undermined the authority of managers and threatened the fulfilment of plans became a common theme in the press in the next few months.[340] However, one of the most outspoken and explicit criticisms of the earlier revivalist 'political' approach to leadership of the economy was delivered in an article entitled 'Party spirit (*partiinost'*) in the Manager's Work', written by A. Myshlenkov, the director of a carriage-building factory, and published on the second page of *Pravda* in July 1938. Myshlenkov implied that the leadership's previous emphasis on the party's 'political' role and mobilization had been mistaken:

---

[336] On the abolition of the *troiki*, see RGASPI 17/3/1003, 85–7. For various explanations for Ezhov's disgrace and fall, see B. A. Starkov, 'Narkom Ezhov', 36–8; M. Jansen and N. Petrov, *Stalin's Loyal Executioner*, 143–54; chs. 6–7; J. A. Getty and O. V. Naumov, *The Road to Terror*, 528–31.

[337] *P*, 27 March 1938.

[338] *P*, 4 January 1938.

[339] *P* (editorial), 4 January 1938.

[340] *PS*, 6 (1938) 55; *B*, 14 (1938) 9; *P*, 24 January 1938; *P*, 6 May 1938. See also *P*, 24 January 1938.

[The problem did not lie in the fact that] the primary party organization did not care at all about the political *vospitanie* of party and non-party Bolsheviks, or in the fact that it did not try to mobilize the masses. The trouble was that party work was extremely primitive and amounted to abstract 'political reports'...or showy, idle chatter, such as: 'We will not make a mess of things. We will be in the vanguard'.[341]

It was, according to Myshlenkov, very difficult for management to enlist the help of the party committee in its efforts to fulfil the plan and ensure that individual communist workers obeyed orders. He went on to claim not only that the party had neglected the economy, but that it had positively harmed production by challenging the authority of the director:

The violation of one-man management is not a [proper] tactic of the party. The situation became so bad that the director was always and in every case guilty in the eyes of the party committee, without differentiating between the responsibility of individuals. Party spirit in economic work means the strengthening of the principle of one-man management in all sections of the production apparatus... Party spirit in economic leadership is the striving for technical progress, the struggle against routine and lethargy.

This definition of 'party spirit in economic work' was very different from that provided in *Pravda* two years before, in May 1936. Then, *Pravda*'s commentator had asserted that 'the fundamental feature of party spirit in economic work is connections with the masses... Party spirit in economic work requires our managerial cadres, engineers and technicians to be able not only to teach workers but also to learn from them.'[342]

Closely connected with Myshlenkov's challenge to the revivalist view of the role of party organizations in the economy was his attack on the revivalist assumption that economic officials and directors should behave like party officials, adopting a 'democratic', mobilizatory style of leadership:

The false, ostentatious, 'familiar' democratism of the 'straight-forward chap', demagogy and the search for cheap popularity are alien to the Bolshevik leader. Mass work does not mean confusion. Attention to the masses in economic work involves business-like (*delovoi*) links with the masses... Before, in the factory it was considered that the main virtue of the director lay in the fact that he 'circulated' on the shop-floor. How did

---

[341] A. Myshlenkov, 'Partiinost' v rabote khoziastvennika', *P*, 7 July 1938.
[342] V. Tsifronovich, 'Partiinost' v khoziastvennoi rabote', *P*, 22 May 1936.

production benefit from this 'circulation among the people (*narod*)', what innovations followed from the director's absences? . . . The director. . . himself, was transformed from a production strategist into a senior foreman.[343]

The abandonment of populist class struggle, 1938–9

The end of the repressions therefore brought a swing in official propaganda against the excesses of populist revivalism, but Stalin does not seem to have whole heartedly adopted Myshlenkov's technicism, nor did he endorse neo-traditionalist strategies. Instead, he tried to formulate once and for all, in a clear and dogmatic form, an ideological position which he had been seeking for some time: one that retained a voluntaristic Bolshevism, able to create a cadre of Bolsheviks who could mobilize the population to achieve heroic feats, while ridding it of the destabilizing populism associated with internal 'class struggle' campaigns. He did not abandon the claim that the class struggle intensified as the Soviet Union progressed towards communism, but he moved towards a more élitist revivalism, a position rather similar to Trotsky's élitist revivalism of the civil war period, combining voluntarism and élitism. People were still to be motivated by moral incentives, and officials were to use 'political' methods to inspire those below them in the hierarchy; they were not to become an ossified caste, but were to be made up of enthusiasts and believers. However, Stalin had learned the lesson of 1936–8. There was to be no populist challenge to 'bureaucratized' officials and the internal 'class struggle' against a quasi-bourgeois officialdom was to be outlawed. Nor was there to be any talk of a rapid move towards the egalitarian commune-state.

Many of these themes had been outlined by Stalin at the seventeenth party congress, and he had been thinking about them for some time since the early 1930s. But it seems that the troubles of 1936–8 convinced him that he needed to codify a Marxism that was compatible with his state-building objectives, most notably in his *History of the All-Union Communist Party (Bolshevik): Short Course* published in September 1938, and in his report to the eighteenth party congress in 1939. Indeed, he said explicitly that officials had become enemies because they had neglected theory,

---

[343] Myshlenkov, 'Partiinost''.

and the *Short Course* would stop them lapsing again.[344] The work presented a highly ideologized version of party history, which explained the nature of orthodoxy and heresy in a way that could be easily understood by the average official.[345] It also included a section on Marxist philosophy.[346] Stalin insisted that the publication of the *Short Course* be accompanied by campaigns to promulgate the ideas contained within it, and he seems to have taken the project very seriously indeed. As Zhdanov declared, 'Comrade Stalin...said more than once that a good political text-book is worth more than several Magnitostrois [i.e. Magnitogorsk construction projects]'.[347]

One of the objectives of the *Short Course* and the propaganda campaign surrounding it was to present the existing order as verging on the ideal, and to postpone to a distant future the coming of any new, egalitarian form of socialism. It presented a picture of a harmonious society in which fundamental change was unnecessary, and at the eighteenth party congress in 1939 Stalin declared that there were no contradictions within socialism.[348] In particular, it justified the continuing existence of a strong state machine, and in a speech to a meeting of propagandists on the *Short Course* in October 1938, Stalin tried to explain how the state was compatible with the Marxist promise that the state would wither away under communism. In a rambling disquisition, he tried to rebut those who used Marxist theory to question the existence of the state. Some people, he explained, frequently asked why the state did not wither away:

Marx and Engels said that once proletarian power comes and socializes the means of production, the state must wither away. Why the hell does it not wither away?...20 years have gone by, the means of production have been socialized, but you do not want to wither away (*Laughter*).[349]

---

[344] RGASPI, 558/11/1122, 8 (27 September 1938).
[345] *History of the Communist Party.* For Stalin's insistence that the narrative clarify the nature of ideological struggle, see RGASPI, 558/11/1088 (13 April 1937).
[346] Stalin, *Sochineniia*, i. (xiv), 279–326; N. N. Maslov, 'Kratkii kurs istorii VKP(b)-entsiklopediia kul'ta lichnosti Stalina', in Iu. P. Senokosov (ed.), *Surovaia drama naroda: Uchenye i publitsisty o prirode stalinizma* (Moscow, 1989), 337–45; N. N. Maslov, 'Iz istorii rasprostraneniia stalinizma', *VI KPSS*, 7 (1990), 98–101; R. Tucker, *Stalin in Power*, 532–41.
[347] RGASPI, 77/1/707, 6–7 (December 1938).
[348] Stalin, *Sochineniia*, i. (xiv), 318–20, 366–7.
[349] RGASPI, 17/165/76, 162 (1 October 1938).

Stalin tried to deal with this problem by adapting Marxist theory in an unusually forthright, if unoriginal, way. He argued that Marx and Engels had developed their theory of the state by examining purely internal, class forces and had neglected the international context. If Marx and Engels had been asked whether the state would wither away in the circumstances of the 'capitalist encirclement', 'they would have said "no, it cannot wither away" '; unfortunately, nobody ever put this question to them.[350] Stalin also tried to explain away the populist revivalist model of the state presented in Lenin's *State and Revolution*. Lenin, he claimed, had only written *State and Revolution* to defend Marx's and Engels's doctrine of the state from the 'distortions' of 'opportunists', and he was planning to write a second volume in which he 'undoubtedly' planned 'to review and develop further the theory of the state, based on the experience gained during the existence of Soviet power in our country'. There was now, Stalin claimed, a need to 'further develop Marxist theory'.[351]

Stalin used a technicist argument to explain why the state had to be strengthened. Defence, he declared, could not be organized on the basis of a militia, as the army needed to be qualified, and *'tekhnika* decides everything' in the army. An army, in turn, had to be fed, and this required a state, run by 'experienced' rather than elected officials, to accumulate resources.[352] For Stalin, then, the state and a bureaucracy were not only required in the military sphere, but in the cultural and economic spheres as well; 'not one state', he argued, could 'administer a country without officials, without a command staff for the economy, for politics, for culture'.[353] At the eighteenth party congress he accepted that the state would wither away once the capitalist encirclement had ended, but he again stressed the state's economic and cultural role, and even implied that it would last into the communist stage.[354]

Stalin also challenged the populist revivalist ideas of class and class struggle that had been present in so much political discourse following 1935. At the eighteenth congress Stalin declared that

[350] RGASPI, 17/165/76, 168–72.
[351] *XVIII s"ezd Vsesoiuznoi Kommunisticheskoi Partii (b), 10–21 marta 1939 g., stenograficheskii otchet* (Moscow, 1939), 34.
[352] RGASPI, 17/165/76, 179–80.
[353] RGASPI, 17/165/70, 37–8.
[354] Stalin, *Sochineniia*, i. (xiv), 394–5.

Soviet society was now completely unified and that the whole population was now committed to socialism. He now implied that the internal ideological weaknesses which he had discerned during the period of the Terror had disappeared, and that 'in case of war, the rear and the front of our army, by reason of their homogeneity and internal unity, will be stronger than those of any other country...'.[355] This did not mean that the class struggle was over, but the class enemy was increasingly an external rather than an internal force.[356]

Stalin was particularly intent on defending the intelligentsia against a populist distortion of 'class struggle', and he stated, even more decisively than in the past, that traditional Bolshevik hostility to the intelligentsia was unacceptable.[357] At a speech in September 1938 to propagandists on the promulgation of the *Short Course*, Stalin was even more forthright in his defence of the intelligentsia, by which he meant all educated, white-collar workers, or 'employees' as they were often called.[358] In the past, he conceded, it had been reasonable to deride the intelligentsia, as 'it served not the earth, but heaven, not the people, but the exploiters'; now, however, the intelligentsia were former workers and peasants, and they had to be regarded as 'the salt of the earth'.[359]

Stalin, more generally, revealed a fundamentally élitist, anti-workerist view of society. The notion that old-style workers with 'calloused hands' were to be exalted, he argued, was unacceptable. The factory was 'now something like a laboratory... which is clean and where there are no calluses'; 'calluses are an evil of the past'.[360] There was, Stalin asserted, no point in propagandists trying to educate workers on the shopfloor; they should not forget that there were very few workers who had the free time to master theory, read books, or discuss politics.[361] Instead, they had to educate the intelligentsia, a group which propagandists had neglected in their obsession with workers. They had forgotten that members of the intelligentsia were loyal citizens, former workers and peasants.[362] Zhdanov followed Stalin in declaring that the intelligentsia had to

[355] Stalin, *Sochineniia*, i. (xiv), 346, 368.   [356] Ibid., i. (xiv), 271.
[357] *XVIII s"ezd.*, 37. See also *History of the Communist Party*, 344.
[358] RGASPI, 17/165/70, 35 (27 September 1938).
[359] RGASPI, 17/165/76, 199–200; RGASPI, 17/165/70, 39, 40.
[360] RGASPI, 17/165/70, 35.   [361] RGASPI, 17/165/76, 200.
[362] RGASPI, 17/165/70, 38.

be rehabilitated. At the eighteenth congress he announced that class discrimination, which had already been abandoned outside the party in 1936, would be renounced in the party as well, and class would no longer be taken into account when new members were admitted.[363] It had been reasonable, he argued, to raise a class 'barrier' to exclude the bourgeois at a time when the NEP was a 'corrupting influence'. But now that many *intelligenty* were of working-class origin it was wrong to discriminate against them.[364] Even so, Stalin clearly felt it was going too far to declare that the proletariat no longer had a privileged position and that all class distinctions had been overcome, and the regime still described the state as the 'Dictatorship of the Proletariat'[365]

Stalin's comment to propagandists that it was not worth educating workers might suggest that he was endorsing a neo-traditionalist vision of a rigid status hierarchy, with the intelligentsia at the top, and the workers and peasants at the bottom. Yet a few days before, speaking at the same conference, Stalin had put forward a very different view of the social order, arguing:

we want to transform the whole working class and the whole peasantry into the intelligentsia, to raise their level. Then we'll begin to have miracles in all areas of construction.[366]

Zhdanov also rejected the neo-traditionalist view of class, which some officials had expressed during the Terror. In a passage written for the nineteenth party congress which he subsequently omitted from his speech, Zhdanov criticized those who judged people purely according to their class origin:

The 'biological' approach to people is very widespread among us, when the existence of some not entirely 'convenient' relatives or other, frequently long dead, is made a criterion of the political loyalty of a worker. Such 'biologists', producing their distinctive theory of 'inheritance', try to look at living communists through a magnifying glass... These people forget that the recasting of consciousness, the recasting of people is a great process of

---

[363] *XVIII s"ezd*, 514–17, 668.
[364] RGASPI, 77/1/719, 10–13 (Draft of speech to the eighteenth congress, before 18 March 1939). The nationwide 'discussion' of Zhdanov's theses produced a number of criticisms of his proposals to relax class discrimination, one of which was published in the press. See O. V. Khlevniuk, *1937-i*, 251; RGASPI, 77/1/719, 100.
[365] *XVIII s"ezd*, 677.
[366] RGASPI, 17/165/70, 36.

vospitanie, that it is necessary to be able to see in people not only what links them to the past, but also what takes them forward.[367]

Stalin, like Zhdanov, continued to emphasize the importance of ideas and theory, and his language remained strongly revivalist.[368] Stalin may have favoured social mobility and the expansion of the intelligentsia, but his was not a hierarchy based solely on scientific expertise: it was one founded on ideological commitment, and he expected it to perform miracles. Speaking in October 1938 Stalin gave one of his most forthright defences of the importance of ideas and consciousness. For Stalin, 'the strength and importance of theory' was 'great and invaluable'; without it the party 'would have been forced to wander in the darkness of empiricism from one event to another'.[369] The party's success was largely, Stalin argued, the result of its mastery of ideology. Had the 'April Theses' not been written, the party would not have reorientated itself and the revolution would have been undermined.[370] Stalin then went on to defend the role of ideas more generally, criticizing the proponents of 'vulgar materialism':

they vulgarize when considering the role of social ideas in the development of society, they think that, well, that is to say, economic development is the fundamental base, but as for the superstructure in all this, what its role is, its trivial role, they vulgarize this and fall into the swamp of vulgarization... Lenin, who had developed social ideas, was the first Marxist who specifically worked out the question of the role of the key idea; Lenin organizes people, mobilizes them and leads them to the transformation of the old society into the new. New ideas arise on the base of economic trends and without them it is impossible to transform in the direction of implementation, of revolution.[371]

Knowledge of ideology, for both Stalin and Zhdanov, was particularly important for officials, because it would ensure their loyalty to the regime and prevent them from becoming corrupted by foreign

---

[367] RGASPI, 77/1/719, 45.
[368] For Zhdanov's continuing emphasis on 'party work', see RGASPI, 77/1/692, 37, 40, 110 (9 July 1938); RGASPI, 77/1/684, 32, 47 (28 May 1938); RGASPI, 77/1/690, 8 (8 June 1938). Molotov also seems to have stressed these themes. See V. M. Molotov, *2aia godovshchina oktiabr'skoi revoliutsii. Doklad na torzhestvennom zasedanii Moskovskogo soveta, 6 noiabria 1938* (Moscow–Leningrad, 1938), 21–2.
[369] RGASPI, 17/165/76, 144.
[370] RGASPI, 17/165/76, 142.
[371] RGASPI, 17/165/76, 152–4.

intelligence services, as had happened in the recent past.[372] More generally, however, ideological awareness would improve their motivation and leadership style. As Stalin explained at the eighteenth party congress, 'the higher the political level and Marxist–Leninist consciousness of workers in any branch of state and party work, the better and more fruitful will be the work itself...'.[373] Without a grasp of theory, the official would 'degenerate'—he would have no interest in 'the perspectives of our movement forward' and would merely become 'a narrow minded utilitarian without [a sense of] perspective (*besperspektivnyi deliaga*)', who 'blindly and mechanically' fulfilled orders from above.

Yet Stalin did not only locate the dynamism of the system in believing officials, and there are elements of populism in his statements in this period. He continued to claim that the enthusiasm of ordinary people drove the system forward, although, in contrast with the language of the late 1920s, heroism was located in individual heroes 'from the people', not on the working class as a collective body. So, for instance, in March 1938, Stalin praised moral incentives, which only operated in the Soviet Union, for their ability to produce popular heroes. In the West, only money was valued and heroes did not emerge from the people. In the Soviet Union, in contrast, people were not valued in rubles or dollars ('What is the dollar? A trifle!'), but for their heroic feats.[374]

Stalin expressed a similar belief that socialism would be driven forward by individuals from the 'people' who believed in socialism in his discussion of science. In a speech to educational officials in May 1938, he praised great 'men of science', like Lenin, but also 'simple people, practical people (*praktiki*)', like Stakhanov and the Arctic explorer Papanin. Following the example of Galileo and Darwin, they had challenged the old 'monopolists of science' and shown that traditional science was antiquated. Lenin, for instance, had not been afraid to challenge the eminent 'scientist' Plekhanov and argue for socialism in Russia, daring to go 'against the current (*protiv techeniia*)'. These were people who understood the 'power and significance' of scientific traditions but were not slaves to them, and had the 'courage (*smelost'*) and resoluteness (*reshimost'*) to

[372] RGASPI, 17/165/76, 200.
[373] *XVIII s"ezd*, 30–1.
[374] RGASPI, 558/11/1121, 27 (17 March 1938).

smash old traditions';[375] they thus 'moved science forward, despite old traditions, dispositions, customs, routine'.[376]

Traces of these voluntaristic sentiments are also evident in the philosophical sections of the *Short Course*. Stalin presented a materialist view of Marxism, declaring that the 'material world' was 'primary' and that the 'mind, thought' was 'secondary' and reflected matter, but he continued to insist on the importance of ideas.[377] While ideas had their origins in economic forces, and while they could only push history in a direction that was already determined by economic forces,[378] once they had emerged they could have a decisive role. Historical materialism, he explained, 'as regards the *significance* of social ideas, theories, views and political institutions', 'far from denying them, stresses the role and importance of these factors in the life of society, in its history'.[379] This analysis of the relationship between base and superstructure did not, in general, depart from Plekhanov's views.[380] Nor did it differ substantially from Stalin's earlier writings. As has been seen, he had frequently described the party in military and religious terms, as a military order, a 'command staff' that had to be imbued with an almost religious faith in a dogmatic set of principles.[381] However, Stalin's discussion of the role of ideas was striking, and he now declared that ideas were the crucial factor in historical development. Although the contradictions between classes and between productive forces and relations of production that drove history forward in the past no longer existed under socialism, development and progress had not stopped.[382] Now, as he explained at the

---

[375] *Sochineniia*, i. (xiv), 275–7.

[376] RGASPI, 558/11/1087, 18 (unpublished version).

[377] Stalin, *Sochineniia*, i. (xiv), 296.

[378] This is implied in RGASPI, 17/165/76, 152.

[379] Stalin, *Sochineniia*, i. (xiv), 298–9.

[380] Although Stalin did depart from Plekhanov to some extent: while Plekhanov had suggested that ideas only had a role in historical development when the ideological superstructure was lagging behind the economic base, Stalin was suggesting that even when both base and superstructure were in complete harmony, as in the Soviet era, ideas had a continuing role in driving history forward. See Van Ree, 'Stalin as a Marxist Philosopher', 285–6. Wetter argues for greater originality on Stalin's part. See G. Wetter, *Dialektische Materializmus*, 237–59.

[381] Compare with his telephone conversation as reported by P. P. Pospelov, a Central Committee secretary responsible for ideology, in which Stalin declared that 'Marxism is the religion of the class, its creed'. N. N. Maslov, 'Iz istorii rasprostraneiia Stalinizma', 100.

[382] For the end of contradictions under socialism, see Stalin, *Sochineniia*, i. (xiv), 318–20, 367.

eighteenth party congress, the 'driving forces (*dvizhushchie sily*)' were the 'moral–political unity of Soviet society, the friendship of the peoples of the USSR, Soviet patriotism'.[383]

Stalin's and Zhdanov's interest in ideology and politics also informed the institutional reforms of the period, which strengthened the party and gave it greater autonomy from the state. At the eighteenth party congress, the relationship between party and state was yet again reformed: the functional principle replaced the production-branch principle in all party committees, including the Central Committee. Production-branch departments were abolished (except in the areas of agriculture and school education) and functional departments were restored.[384] Zhdanov, defending these changes, argued that the old production-branch principle had led party organizations to spend all their time on 'economic work'. The party had also lost control over its personnel because the supervision of cadres had been divided between various production-branch departments.[385]

Stalin and Zhdanov, therefore, were attempting to transform revivalist Bolshevism so that they could better control it. By setting down the approved version of Marxism–Leninism in dogmatic form, a Marxism–Leninism that placed much less stress on class struggle and other potentially populist themes, Stalin hoped to enthuse officials, who would in turn mobilize the masses, while preventing them from 'distorting' Marxism in subversive directions. A similar attempt to retain the dynamic elements of Marxism–Leninism, while purging it of its more destabilizing elements, can be seen in Stalin's promulgation of the new definitive version of Marxist philosophy in the *Short Course*. It rejected Bukharin's theories of equilibrium and endorsed most of Engels's laws of dialectics, including the law of the transformation of quantity into quality.[386] But it also avoided the more Hegelian, Deborinite elements of dialectics in placing little stress on contradiction, thus refusing to justify conflict and sudden change.[387]

[383] Stalin, *Sochineniia*, i. (xiv), 367.

[384] *XVIII s"ezd*, 673–4; RGASPI, 17/114/653, 2; Maleiko, 'Iz istorii', 121.

[385] RGASPI, 77/1/719, 62, 65–6.

[386] Stalin, *Sochineniia*, i. (xiv), 283–6.

[387] The *Short Course*, for instance, omitted Engels's law of the 'negation of the negation'. For the contrast with Deborinism, see E. Van Ree, 'Stalin as a Marxist Philosopher', 282–3. Van Ree argues that this approach to dialectics can also be found in Stalin's earliest writings on philosophy.

The tension between élitist revivalism and technicism continued throughout the war and the late Stalinist period. With the need to reconstruct the economy, and possibly to compete with a Western science that had produced the bomb, *tekhnika* gained new prestige, as did its 'bearers', the technical intelligentsia.[388] In this environment, Stalin stressed to a greater degree than before that science was objective and should be free of class and political considerations.[389] Yet the Stalinist leadership, as before, was not satisfied with a technocratic order, and was not prepared to give up mobilization. Stalin never abandoned the theory of the sharpening of class struggle. The regime still claimed that it was promoting the radical transformation of society, and the party conducted campaigns to purify society of alien forces and influences.[390] Tensions between party and state also continued, as did calls for the party's revival.[391] But Stalin reconciled mobilization with stability by increasingly basing it on ethnic rather than class principles, avoiding the populist strategies of the 1930s.

It may be that Stalin considered initiating a new ethnicized revivalist mobilization campaign in 1952–3. As in the late 1930s, he insisted that a powerful enemy—now the United States—was seeking to subvert the Soviet system, though this time it was operating through Soviet Jews, who represented a new pro-American fifth column, rather than through class enemies or former oppositionists.[392] And as in the 1930s, he tried to demonstrate this message by fabricating a case against an allegedly conspiratorial group, in this case Jewish doctors. In large part, the purge was aimed at imposing greater control over the security apparatus. But it also had broader implications: Stalin was eager that the alleged conspirators be labelled 'right opportunists',[393] and the secret police even threatened

[388] For technocratic trends within post-war Soviet society, see J. Duskin, *Stalinist Reconstruction and the Confirmation of a New Elite, 1945–1953* (Basingstoke, 2001).

[389] For this change in Stalin's attitude to science, see E. Pollock, 'Stalin, Coryphaeus of Science', unpublished paper, January 2003, 18.

[390] For this argument, see Weiner, *Making Sense of War*, 16–21, 33–4, ch. 1. Weiner argues that ethnicity was a crucial issue in post-war campaigns of purification, even if it was not the only one; ibid., 114–22, 138–54.

[391] For these issues between 1939 and 1941, see J. Harriss, 'The Origins of the Conflict between Malenkov and Zhdanov', *SR*, 35 (1976), 287–303. For debates after the War, see Y. Gorlizki, 'Party Revivalism and the Death of Stalin', *SR*, 54 (1995), 1–22.

[392] For the language and themes of the Doctors' Plot campaign, see *P*, 13 January 1953.

[393] For this language, see Y. Gorlizki and O. Khlevniuk, *Cold Peace. Stalin and the Soviet Ruling Circle, 1945–1953* (Oxford, 2004), 158.

that it would be the beginning of a ' "country-wide purge" of gran-dees, idlers, degenerates'.[394] However, while Stalin was insistent that the campaign have wide publicity, it did not become a purge on the scale of the late 1930s, nor were show trials staged. This may have been because Stalin died before he could organize them, but it is more likely that he did not want to use the disruptive methods of the Terror again.[395]

There were populist elements to the campaigns against the Soviet Jews, and it seems that they were often interpreted as a renewed class struggle against the intelligentsia.[396] But it is unlikely that this was Stalin's intention, and populist revivalism was not influential within Bolshevik thinking after 1938. It was to re-emerge under Khrushchev, who introduced a new version of the revivalist strategy. Like the rest of the Strategy leadership, however, he had learned the lessons of the traumatic events of 1936–8. While he brought back some of the anti-bureaucratic elements of revivalist Bolshevism, 'class struggle' was never again to be seriously attempted in Soviet politics.

---

[394] S. A. Goglidze to L. P. Beria, March 26 1953, 5, quoted in J. Brent and V. P. Naumov, *Stalin's Last Crime*, 172.

[395] There is disagreement over Stalin's intentions. Some argue that he was planning a show trial and mass deportations of Jews, and only his death stopped him. See J. Brent and V. P. Naumov, *Stalin's Last Crime* 295, 309; Gorlizki and Khlevniuk, however, contend that he only ever wanted a limited purge. Y. Gorlizki and O. Khlevniuk, *Cold Peace*, 158–9.

[396] See, for instance, Y. Rapoport, *The Doctor's Plot of 1953*, trans. by N. A. Perova and R. S. Bobrova (Cambridge, Mass., 1991), 77–8.

CONCLUSION

Mobilization and 'Class Struggle' in Communist Politics

Party leaders did not speak at length about the Terror in the following years. The *Short Course* did discuss it, but in a rather peremptory way. The Terror was presented as a campaign against a group of 'white-guard pygmies' who had the strength of a 'gnat'. They were soon disposed of: the Soviet people 'approved the annihilation of the Bukharin–Trotsky gang and passed on to the next business'—the Supreme Soviet elections.[1] But we do have more helpful accounts and explanations left by those at the centre of power. Molotov, remembering the period decades later, described it as a measure designed to remove a potential 'fifth column' that threatened the party at a time of war, and Kaganovich's memoirs provide a similar justification.[2]

Yet other explanations for the Terror, present in the memoirs of Molotov and Kaganovich, and in the speeches of other party leaders at the time, have a rather different emphasis: the Terror was necessary not so much because enemies within the party might plot with foreigners but because they had ideological doubts, particularly of a rightist nature, which threatened to undermine the party's strategy of mobilization as war was approaching. So, Kaganovich presented the struggle against the 'enemies' as a broader ideological campaign against 'menshevizing Trotskyism' within the party.[3] Similarly, Molotov explained: '...we need to remember about Trotskyism

---

[1] *History of the Communist Party*, 346–8.
[2] *Sto sorok besed s Molotovym*, 390; L. M. Kaganovich, *Pamiatnye zapiski* (Moscow, 1996), 557–9.
[3] L. M. Kaganovich, *Pamiatnye zapiski*, 558.

and, especially, about the Right Deviation. The point is that in 1937 there was a considerable number of unstable, vacillating people.'[4] For Molotov, this lack of commitment prevented effective mobilization. He implied that complete ideological unity and devotion was required not just at time of war, but at all times, because 'socialism demands immense effort, including sacrifices'. Had the leadership not used terror there was a real danger that the leadership would have begun to 'shake', and 'disagreements' would have emerged in it 'like cracks and chinks'. If this had happened, the regime might not have survived the war.[5]

It is possible, then, to discern two justifications within official rhetoric for the campaigns against the apparatus during the late 1930s: a typically revivalist desire to put pressure on or remove those who were either insufficiently mobilized, or who were spreading rightist attitudes; and an obsession with security and loyalty, driven by the suspicion that cadres were conspiring, or might conspire, against the regime. Stalin sometimes distinguished between the two objectives, but as in the past he implied that security and ideological commitment were inextricably linked. Discussing the Terror at the end of 1938, for instance, Stalin declared that 'not all these wreckers were Trotskyist-Bukharinites' or 'spies'; their 'leaders' were spies, but the 'mass' of them were initially 'our people', who 'went off their heads' at a later stage because they were not 'real Marxists' and were 'theoretically weak'.[6] Spying and sabotage, therefore, could best be eliminated by campaigns of ideological remobilization. As Stalin explained at a meeting of propagandists in 1938, it was 'no accident' that foreign spies had 'spoilt' a part of the intelligentsia and cadres in the state apparatus: the party's failure to pay enough attention to their political education (*vospitanie*) had created the conditions for conspiracy.[7]

More than a year earlier, speaking at the February-March 1937 Central Committee plenum, Stalin explained the reasons for his decision to put pressure on officials in a similar way: his campaigns were a way of educating cadres and preventing their 'demoralization', in order to enable them to achieve the extraordinary feats

---

[4] *Sto sorok besed s Molotovym*, 392.
[5] Ibid., 393.
[6] RGASPI, 558/11/1122, 8–9 (speech to a meeting of propagandists, 27 September 1938).
[7] RGASPI, 17/165/76, 200 (1 October 1938).

necessary if socialism were to be built, and to prevent them from becoming spies. He denied that he was doing anything new, and insisted that he was following the traditions of earlier campaigns against officials. History, he argued, had taught the party that it had to go 'against the current' and criticize cadres if it was to 'educate' and strengthen them. Stalin cited a number of cases to prove his point. The first was the incident in 1930 when he had condemned officials for falsely claiming that they had collectivized large stretches of the countryside; the second was the Shakhty affair, when 'merciless criticism' had educated economic cadres in their mistakes and had therefore improved their quality, preventing their 'demoralization'; the third was the occasion when Ordzhonikidze's refusal to allow the party to investigate his friend Lominadze had 'spoiled' him. As this list of examples suggests, Stalin did not regard the 'rightist' failure to fulfil Moscow's demands as identical to conspiracy, but he implied that they were closely connected because one was likely to lead to the other. Lominadze had started off in the same position as the errant party cadres in the countryside, or the industrial officials of the Shakhty period; the solution in his case, as in the other two, was timely and harsh criticism.[8] Because he had not been condemned at an early stage, he had become a full enemy.

Zhdanov related ideological rightism to conspiracy even more explicitly when, in a speech to a meeting of the Leningrad regional party committee in June 1938, he explained the psychological process by which rightist scepticism led to disloyalty:

In conclusion I touch on [this]: well which of us did...betray, the petty members of the intelligentsia (*intelligentishki*), who had no faith in the people, the petty-bourgeois philistines from the working class (*meshchane iz rabochikh*), people who were seduced by the fact that many big shots took part in the conspiracy, and, they say, well let's jump on the bandwagon before it's too late, and they're all united in not having faith (*neverie*) in the power of the people, and above all in the strength and revolutionary potential of our peasantry. And so it was those confused little cowards, these petty-bourgeois philistines from the working class, like your Chudov,[9] existing from day to day, and then suddenly they're expected to fulfil some plan or other, and, they say, well wouldn't we be better off living in the old way, having the capitalist system back, as if we were under bourgeois rule?[10]

[8] *VI*, 11–12 (1995), 15–16.
[9] A Leningrad party official arrested for Trotskyism.
[10] RGASPI, 77/1/690, 16 (plan for speech to plenum of the Leningrad regional party committee, 8 June 1938).

Many revivalist themes are evident here, and they are expressed in Romantic and quasi-religious language: the 'enemies' are officials of working-class origin, who have petty-bourgeois attitudes. These amount to a 'lack of faith' in socialism, an undemocratic scepticism of the powers of the people and a 'philistine' desire to live 'from day to day' without achieving the extraordinary economic feats of which believers are capable. All of these sins are likely to lead to the desire to re-establish capitalism.

So although questions of security, spying and conspiracy were much more important in the leadership's thinking in the late 1930s than they had been in the late 1920s, and this can clearly be connected with the threatening international circumstances of the time, the Terror still needs to be seen in the context of the revivalism of the past. Stalin himself compared his campaigns against officialdom with those of the Shakhty period. Speaking at the February-March 1937 plenum, he brushed aside criticisms of his campaigns. He recalled that during the Shakhty affair some feared that to 'go against the current' involved offending people and 'making enemies' within the apparatus. But they had been proved wrong: the apparatus, he insisted, had only been strengthened by these campaigns.[11]

Yet Stalin clearly misjudged the effects of the Terror: the campaigns of the later 1930s, far from strengthening the Soviet regime, weakened it. Indeed, they led to even greater chaos than the campaigns of the Shakhty era. Why, then, did Stalin not only return to the risky strategies of the late 1920s, but pursue them in such an extreme way? I have argued that we can best answer this question if we place Stalin's response to the difficult environment of the late 1930s within the broader context of Bolshevik ideas and politics since 1917, and even before. Stalin's personality—his ruthlessness, his suspiciousness and his desire for personal power—were clearly crucial factors contributing to the Terror. Stalin also adapted and developed Bolshevik ideology, most notably by encouraging an explicit fusion of Marxist and nationalist ideas. But his objectives and the ways in which he tried to achieve them had much in common with those of his predecessors, because he was operating within a similar ideological context. He sought to transform the Soviet Union into an integrated, highly centralized, militarily

[11] *VI*, 11–12 (1995), 16.

powerful, extraordinarily productive society without private property, something he equated with Marx's first phase of 'communism',
or 'Socialism'.[12] and in trying to achieve his objectives he pursued
revivalist, technicist, and, at times, neo-traditionalist strategies,
each of which had advantages and disadvantages. Each could also
be justified by appealing to a Marxism that had been combined with
a number of other intellectual traditions—including Russian socialism and early twentieth-century Romantic anti-capitalism—and
that was also informed by fashionable ideas of military and industrial organization.

Of these, revivalist strategies—based on the assumption that the
party could build socialism by fostering a special revolutionary
'proletarian' set of attitudes in officials and the population—were
particularly attractive to many Bolsheviks, including Stalin, because
they promised to inject dynamism into the system, something technicism and neo-traditionalism were unable to do. However, they
were unsustainable, because it was very difficult to resolve one of
the central questions of Bolshevik politics: how could revivalist
mobilization be combined with the preservation of a unified state
on the one hand, and a well-ordered, planned economy on the
other—or, as the Bukharin group put it in 1921, how could the
'rallying of the party on the basis of the revival of party spirit' and
the 'establishment of the unity of the proletariat', be reconciled with
the 'strengthening of a firm administrative framework'.[13]

This study has shown how the Bolsheviks tried and failed to solve
this problem. They made successive efforts at domesticating revivalist mobilization, but, like the sorceror's apprentice, in releasing its
magic they were unable to keep its powers under control. Success
was very improbable. Not only did revivalist strategies challenge a
'scientific' approach to political and economic organization but, in
contrast to conventional nationalist forms of mobilization, they
were informed by a particular set of Marxist ideas and categories,
and were therefore inherently divisive. Even though Bolsheviks tried

---

[12] Like most Bolshevik leaders after 1921, he did not think seriously about how to
reach the stage of full 'communism', when all hierarchies had been eliminated. For his
unwillingness to speculate on the transition to communism in later years, see his
answer to questions at a meeting on the textbook on political economy in 1952.
Translated in E. Pollock, 'Conversations with Stalin on Questions of Political
Economy', Cold War International History Project, Working paper No. 33, July
2001, 53–4.

[13] For this quotation, see Ch. 1, p. 120.

to formulate élitist versions of revivalism that stressed class unity, it was very difficult to rid revivalism of the language of class, class struggle, and anti-bureaucratism—indeed, its effectiveness as a tool of mobilization depended precisely on this divisive spirit. And once these campaigns were unleashed, they were very disruptive to the regime's stability, both because they justified disruptive voluntaristic experiments and because they legitimized and encouraged a populist socialist hostility towards officials present within the party and society as a whole.

Before 1917, Lenin had made attempts to reconcile his scientism with his voluntarism and occasional populism, but the model he put forward in 1917 was deeply contradictory, and in the next few years the Bolsheviks fought bitterly over how to deal with the legacy of their revolutionary promises. One solution, initially adopted by Lenin but most identified with Trotsky, was to decouple mobilization from class struggle, and to formulate a highly élitist form of revivalism that embraced strict discipline and hierarchy. However, this strategy was understandably deeply unpopular within the party and among workers, as it expected enormous sacrifices while denying the need to advance towards the new egalitarian order promised in 1917. Lenin and the majority of the party soon moved towards a technicist position, accepting that mobilization would have to be moderated, or even sacrificed, in the interests of order and economic rationality. Sections of the party's left, however, did try to explain how populist revivalism could be rendered compatible with unity and stability, by demanding a transformation in the behaviour of officials. This moderate form of 'democracy', they argued, would bring officials closer to the masses, allowing them to mobilize workers while avoiding too much reliance on material incentives or 'bourgeois' discipline. Yet the strikes and rebellions of 1920–1, some of them in the name of populist socialist ideals, demonstrated that populist revivalism was likely to escape central control, and the left as a whole was discredited within the party. In the spring of 1921 the leadership announced both a 'retreat' to technicism and liberal technicism, and a ban on factions within the party aimed at the left.

Even so, by the second half of the 1920s, the revivalist left had transformed itself, and appeared to have combined populist mobilization with the demands of state-building and economic development in a much more convincing way, taking account of the practicalities of administration and economic management. The left was helped by the circumstances of the 1920s and the new importance of the debate on industrial development. Not only could leftists criticize the NEP on moral and ideological grounds, as a 'retreat' from Marx's socialism towards capitalism, but they could also condemn the leadership for its apparent failure to build a strong economy and state. The solutions proposed by revivalists differed in emphasis. Some relied on the civil war left's moderate populist revivalist claim that a proletarian bureaucracy, close to workers, could mobilize them and generate economic miracles. But others reconciled the dynamism of Bolshevik revivalism with stability and modernization in a different way, by developing a more élitist version, that appealed to Engels and dialectical materialism. The revolutionary, dialectical forces of nature, when understood and mastered by Marxist scientists, they argued, would propel society to wealth and socialism. However, they combined this élitist voluntaristic position with a rhetoric of class struggle: the Marxist science they were championing was contrasted with a conservative bourgeois science. While divisions between élitist and populist revivalists remained, the rhetoric of class struggle and the hostility to 'bureaucratism' and 'bourgeois' attitudes all facilitated an alliance between them. By the end of the 1920s, both strains of revivalism mounted a strong challenge to the politics of technicism.

It was this combination of populist and élitist revivalism that Stalin endorsed towards the end of the 1920s. Stalin's attitude towards the balance between the two, and how to reconcile working class mobilization with unity, changed over the course of his political career. At times, during the revolutionary period of 1905–7 and the civil war, he flirted with the Bolshevik left, and in the late 1920s he was clearly making efforts to appeal to populist socialist opinion. However, when faced with a clear contradiction between popular mobilization and unity, he generally decided in favour of the latter. His objective was, as he explained in 1937, to build a socialist state that was 'colossal, economically cohesive and tightly bound together politically'.[14] Indeed, his interest in geopolitics and international competition, evident during the civil war and

---

[14] In 1937, Stalin claimed that the Bolsheviks had inherited a 'conglomeration' from the tsars and transformed it into a cohesive state. RGASPI, 558/11/1122, 158 (7 November 1937).

throughout the 1920s, seems to have given him a particular obsession with the security of the state, and he frequently betrayed worries that internal fissures would be exploited by foreign enemies. Even so, he often followed the revivalist view that popular mobilization was essential for security, arguing that the best way to create a strong socialist state was to ensure that the regime had popular support and 'moral capital'. In a revealing statement in 1935, he implied that the main advantage of the socialist system lay in its ability to mobilize the people's energies. Comparing the Bolsheviks' one-party system with bourgeois multi-party systems, he asked rhetorically what the main advantage of the Soviet system was. His response was that it allowed 'the population, the people, the working class, to concentrate blows onto one point and conduct all operations according to a plan' in all areas of politics and economics; whether one was talking about 'the economic sphere, industry, agriculture, war, makes no difference'.[15]

As this formulation shows, Stalin did not only want to reconcile the tensions within revivalism, between popular mobilization and unity, but also the tensions between revivalism and technicism, or, as he put it, the 'concentration' of popular energies with the 'plan'. His views of the balance between *politika* and *tekhnika* were ambivalent and changed over time. He sometimes used technicist language, most famously at the victory parade in 1945, when he proposed a toast to the 'simple, ordinary, modest people', 'to the "little screws"' who ensured that 'our great state machine' worked efficiently.[16] He also rejected the extreme leftist view that culture and science were imbued with class values, and he denied that a new proletarian dialectical science would replace conventional science; throughout his life he clung to the Enlightenment notion that the Bolsheviks were leading the people along a path established by science, and that they were using reason to convince people of the correctness of the socialist project. He therefore never accepted the 'God-builders" view that socialism was an ethical system which Bolsheviks could use to inspire workers in a quasi-religious way, nor did he sympathize with the irrationalism of the Nazis.

However, Stalin was a less technicist Bolshevik than many, as his continuing admiration for the Romantic Bolshevik and former

---

[15] RGASPI, 558/11/1118, 113 (speech to military officials, June 1935).
[16] Stalin, *Sochineniia*, ii. (xv), 206.

God-builder Gorky suggests. He frequently placed 'ideas' and *politika* above *tekhnika*, and he stressed the importance of forces other than reason, such as 'faith' and 'energy', in the building of socialism. He also valued an ideologically inspired, quasi-military 'command staff' who could enthuse the population rather than the 'agronomists and engineers' Lenin regarded as the Bolsheviks' best teachers. Like the left before him, he often implied that it was not enough for society to be run as if it were a machine, operated by experts. It had to be mobilized and enthused: *tekhnika* and 'machines' were 'dead' unless they were infused with 'soul' and operated by cadres who believed. Sometimes he expressed populist revivalist sentiments, suggesting that true scientists had to listen to the 'practical people' (*praktiki*) among the working class; at other times his views were more élitist, implying that socialism would be built by officials who were committed to Marxism-Leninism, and who had abandoned bourgeois science in favour of a true, politically acceptable science. But throughout his life his language was full of Romantic themes: he frequently contrasted the narrow, 'pragmatic', 'utilitarian', petty-bourgeois or 'philistine' person with the visionary idealistic proletarian, or person from the 'people'; the follower of 'routine' with the fighter who goes 'against the current'; the 'dead', 'mechanical' approach to life, with the 'active' 'energetic' one. Stalin's emphasis on the centrality of socialist attitudes also led him to take a harsh approach to the bourgeoisie. From an early stage in his political life, Stalin had frequently expressed the view that the main threat to the mobilization he desired was the presence of 'alien' ideas, present within the former bourgeoisie and spread by foreigners who might plot with them to overthrow the regime.

Stalin also adopted a style of politics that accorded with these revivalist goals and assumptions. He saw himself as a mobilizer, a figure who 'knew' his cadres, carefully assessed their moods, 'raised' and 'nurtured' them by means of *vospitanie*, and made sure they were not prey to alien ideas. And he believed that this style of leadership at all levels of society would both increase his own power and solve many of the Soviet Union's problems. He also thought carefully about how to disseminate these ideas and approaches to leadership. For officials, he formulated slogans, made speeches and wrote or co-wrote textbooks; for the population as a whole, he edited films and plays and, most grotesquely, staged elaborate show trials. This style of politics also seems to have suited his personality, and his attitude towards politics and his psychology were connected in complex ways. His manipulative approach to people was useful for a leader who placed so much emphasis on propaganda; his suspiciousness of any potential dissent interacted with his belief that even the slightest lack of energy and commitment might undermine the system; and his ruthlessness suited somebody who saw himself as a quasi-military leader, a latter-day Napoleon mobilizing his people to sacrifice themselves for the greater good.

So, in 1927–8, as relations with the West deteriorated and the leadership was faced with the need to accelerate economic growth, it is not surprising that Stalin accepted many of the left's solutions to his economic quandaries, although, as was to be expected, he was more determined than the left had been that popular 'energies' should be confined within strict limits and should not undermine unity, security, and discipline. But he inevitably found this very difficult. The revivalist strategy of transforming the mentality of officialdom by targeting 'bourgeois' or 'rightist' individuals was extremely disruptive, and it was clear that there was no straightforward relationship between political attitude and class origin. Also, the use of the language of class struggle had some appeal to resentful workers, and could be used to challenge authority, particularly in the workplace. At the same time, voluntaristic experiments undermined specialists, and created disorder in the economy. By 1930–1 Stalin had led the Soviet Union into economic and social crisis.

Soon, like Lenin in 1918, Stalin was forced to abandon populist revivalism and adopt a much more élitist socialism. Hierarchy was restored, and was increasingly justified using technicist arguments. Yet Stalin, to a greater extent than Lenin, seems to have found technicism inadequate, and he continued to emphasize the importance of mobilization: it was not enough for people to obey orders handed down by experts; they had to be active and enthusiastic participants in the construction of socialism.

Even so, Stalin was not eager to return to the internally divisive mobilizations of the late 1920s, and from the mid-1930s he experimented with a new form of national, non-class mobilization. This strategy, however, faced a serious obstacle: there was no inclusive, Soviet identity that had any real popular emotional resonance, and for various reasons the leadership never declared that national and class differences had been overcome. Instead, it attempted to combine, uneasily, a vision of the Soviet Union as a wholly united and integrated state with the continuing assumption that there was a hierarchy of classes and peoples, with proletarians and Russians at the top. Understandably, this hierarchical view of the world, combined with a desire to enforce stability, reinforced the tendency to see society in neo-traditionalist terms, as a fixed hierarchy of status groups.

Neo-traditionalism, however, was even more effective than technicism in condemning the regime to stasis, and predictably Stalin was unhappy with this fundamentally conservative way conception of society. So when Stalin—fearful of German and Japanese aggression and suspicious of conspiracies—became convinced that the regime yet again faced serious internal and external threats, he again began to launch revivalist campaigns. The emerging technicist and neo-traditionalist order, he implied, was entrenching the position of a powerful group of officials, while demobilizing the political system and the economy at a time of impending war. It was also undermining unity, by failing to root out hostile attitudes that were either being spread by foreigners, or might be exploited by them in the future.

Yet Stalin seems to have learned lessons, and made greater efforts than in the late 1920s, to prevent mobilization from undermining unity and economic efficiency. He used the weapon of revivalism carefully, rooting out 'unbelievers' while trying to preserve the apparatus. Despite these efforts, however, the revivalist campaigns of the late 1930s were more disruptive and violent than those of a decade earlier. In large part this can be explained by the tense international situation, and by the regime's worries about internal stability after the disorder of the early 1930s. Stalin and the leadership were therefore more fearful of real or possible conspiracies than they had been before. But a crucial difference also lay in the groups Stalin was attacking. In challenging the cliques of loyal regional party bosses—a group that had been given considerable powers during the instability of the early 1930s—he was taking greater risks than he had in the late 1920s, when his main targets had been economic officials and a limited number of party leaders associated with the 'Right Deviation', and when he had successfully split local party organizations. Regional leaders were in a strong position to resist Moscow passively, and the conventional revivalist campaign, which used the language of anti-bourgeois 'class struggle' to target those with 'rightist' opinions, was likely to be either tooth-less or extremely dangerous, because it was now being used against officials of proletarian class origin. If class was interpreted in a neo-traditionalist way—as class origin—it was likely to let officials, who were mostly proletarian, off the hook; indeed officials could use 'class struggle' to consolidate their power. Yet if class was interpreted in a revivalist way—as class mentality and culture—the struggle against the 'bourgeoisie' could become a destabilizing attack on the bureaucracy and party as a whole, a second revolution against the 'new class'. Initially Stalin downplayed the issue of class, and tried to target 'rightist' officials by emphasizing the role of 'Trotsky-ism' as the main source of dangerous attitudes. However, the concept of Trotskyism became almost as difficult to control as that of class, and class itself remained an important theme in the leadership's rhetoric. And when officials obstructed the centre's campaigns, Moscow intensified the pressure by reverting to the old populist revivalist strategy, using a rhetoric of 'class struggle' to suggest that the bureaucracy had absorbed the undemocratic and inegalitarian attitudes of the old bourgeoisie. In response to this escalation, some party bosses distorted the revivalist language of class, using neo-traditionalist arguments to complain that the revivalist 'democracy' campaigns launched against them were inciting former kulaks, non-Russian nationalists, and other 'aliens' within the country to chal-lenge the regime. And at a time of imminent war, Stalin, also took these threats seriously. At the same time, he seems to have feared a counter-attack by party leaders in collaboration with the army. So in 1937, while using the police and the party rank-and-file in revivalist campaigns against the élite, he simultaneously sought to remove threats to the unity and stability of the Soviet Union, persecuting diaspora nationalities and other potentially disloyal groups, and organizing a neo-traditionalist terror against lowly 'class aliens' in order to protect the apparatus as a whole.

Stalin seems to have thought that the Terror was necessary and that, on balance, it had achieved its objectives, but as in the past he had failed to control revivalist campaigns and he was certainly not satisfied with the way in which they had been conducted. His attempt to go against the current had caused widespread chaos, and after 1938 the populist revivalist version of the class struggle was finally abandoned.

Mobilization and Marxist-Leninist politics: Stalinism and Maoism

Stalin was not the only European leader of the period to use a Romantic anti-capitalist language of 'will' and 'soul' to justify strategies of mobilization. His Nazi enemies also claimed that they could build a powerful state by combining popular commitment with the cause of technological and economic progress. Joseph Goebbels, for instance, analysing the reasons for Germany's defeat in the First World War, declared 'we did not lose the war because our cannons failed, but rather because our spiritual weapons didn't fire'.[17] And his solution to this deficiency was not to abandon technology, but to 'fill it inwardly with soul, to discipline it and place it in the service of our people and their cultural level'.[18] Yet while this language has similarities with Stalin's, the significant differences between Nazi and Soviet ideas and strategies suggest that the Marxist-Leninist context is crucial in understanding the peculiarities of Stalinist mobilization and its damaging effects. The voluntarism of the Nazi leaders may have damaged its military and economic performance, but, unlike Stalinist mobilization, the Nazis' mobilization was not based on divisive class struggle, nor did it undermine the regime by setting the population or rank-and-file activists against the intelligentsia and bureaucrats.[19]

The importance of Marxist-Leninist ideas and institutions, and the influence of a disruptive Marxist-Leninist form of mobilization, is also suggested by the similarities between mobilization campaigns in the Soviet Union and the People's Republic of China (PRC) in the 1950s and 1960s. Even though the personalities and attitudes of their leaders were very different, as were the political and cultural traditions and economic and international circumstances within which they operated, a similar ideology structured politics in both communist states, as did a comparable institutional framework, with an inbuilt tension between party and state and, within the party, between centre and regions.[20] Soviet and Chinese parties

[17] Joseph Goebbels, 1933, quoted in J. Herf, *Reactionary Modernism*, 195.
[18] Joseph Goebbels, 1939, quoted in ibid., 196.
[19] For the damaging effects of Nazi hostility to technical rationality, see ibid., ch. 8. For Hitler's voluntarism, see R. J. Overy, *War and Economy in the Third Reich* (Oxford 1994), 250–1, 253.
[20] For party-state tensions, see S. Zheng, *Party vs. State in Post-1949 China. The Institutional Dilemma* (Cambridge, 1997).

pursued policies chosen from a very similar range of strategies, and discussed them using similar political similar languages. And they both found themselves trying and failing to reconcile a revivalist form of mobilization with unity and order; indeed, the Chinese campaigns were more destabilizing than their Soviet counterparts. There are, of course, important differences, but a brief, if inevitably superficial, comparison helps to illustrate the difficulties facing communist leaderships as they applied Marxist-Leninist solutions to the problems of state-building and economic development.

The parallels between Chinese and Soviet experiences under communism have rarely been explored in any depth, possibly because it has often been assumed that the Chinese departed from a scientistic 'Soviet' Marxism-Leninism and developed a 'sinified' Marxism that stressed the role of ideas, morality and the subjective.[21] Mao Zedong himself had an interest in promoting this view after the Sino-Soviet split.[22] Yet Mao was criticizing a particular, broadly technicist version of Marxism-Leninism which he believed was dominant in the Soviet Union of the 1940s and 1950s, not the revivalism of the 1930s; while the Maoist statement 'the subjective creates the objective' went further than anything a Soviet leader would have said in the 1930s,[23] Mao would have agreed entirely with Zhdanov's declaration in 1939 that 'the role of the subjective factor, the role of cadres, the role of the mobilization of the masses... is exceptional'.[24] If we reconsider conventional views of

---

[21] For these distinctions between Leninism and Chinese Marxism see, for instance, M. Meisner, 'Leninism and Maoism: Some Populist Perspectives on Marxism-Leninism in China', in M. Meisner, *Marxism, Maoism and Utopianism* (Madison, 1982). For challenges to this view, see A. Walder, 'Cultural Revolution Radicalism: Variations on a Stalinist Theme', in A. Joseph, C. Wong, and D. Zweig, *New Perspectives on the Cultural Revolution* (Cambridge, Mass., 1991), 41–62; A. Walder, *Communist Neo-Traditionalism*, 113–22. There have been few sustained comparisons between the Soviet Union and China in the communist period. However, for a comparison an institutional focus, see Mark Lupher, *Power Restructuring in China and Russia* (Boulder, 1996). Deborah Kaple has examined the reception of Soviet ideas in the 1940s and early 1950s, and argues convincingly for the powerful influence of the Soviet model, but she is less interested in tensions within Stalinist thinking. See D. Kaple, *Dream of a Red Factory. The Legacy of High Stalinism* (Oxford, 1994).

[22] For Mao's criticism of the Soviet approach to Marxism in the late 1950s, see Mao Tse-tung, *A Critique of Soviet Economics*, trans. by Moss Roberts (New York, 1977),106–10. He was commenting on *Political Economy: A Textbook* and Stalin's *Economic Problems of Socialism in the USSR*.

[23] Quoted in S. Schram, *The Thought of Mao Tse-Tung* (Cambridge, 1989), 132.

[24] RGASPI, 77/1/714, 10 (25 February 1939).

Bolshevik ideology in the 1930s, it becomes clear that the leadership of the Chinese Communist party after 1949 thought about solutions to the problems facing it in ways reminiscent of the thinking of their Soviet counterparts in the 1930s. Like the Bolsheviks in the 1920s and 1930s, China's leadership under Mao was committed to eliminating 'backwardness' and moving towards the goal of communism which, among other things, involved the creation of a strong, modern state and a non-market economy. Clearly, non-communist Chinese thought and culture had a important effect on Chinese Marxism-Leninism, as did the Chinese party's experiences in leading a peasant guerilla army before it came to power—experiences very different from those of its Soviet counterpart before 1917. Yet the Chinese party shared important aspects of the Soviets' ideological and political-cultural inheritance, and it had been subject to a great deal of Soviet influence, both before and after the establishment of the PRC in 1949.[25]

As in the Soviet Union, Marxism-Leninism offered the Chinese leadership a number of ideas about the proper administration of the state and strategies for reaching communism, which had much in common with the revivalist and technicist approaches I have identified. Questions of equality and incentives, 'politics' and 'economics' or 'technique', class and class culture and the speed of advance towards communism, were central to political debate, and, like Stalin, Mao led the Chinese Communist party along a zigzag path, to and from revivalism. Mao also, like Stalin, launched two enormously disruptive revivalist campaigns: the first intended to achieve a rapid economic 'leap forward'; and the second, following a period of either 'rational' consolidation or 'retreat' (depending on one's point of view), designed to transform a party apparatus that Mao believed had become 'rightist' and 'bureaucratic'.

When the Chinese communists came to power, they used mass mobilization and purges (or 'rectification' campaigns) for a number

---

[25] For the relationship between Soviet Bolshevism and Chinese communism before 1949, see A. Dirlik, *The Origins of Chinese Communism* (Oxford, 1989); H. Van de Ven, *From Friend to Comrade. The Founding of the Chinese Communist Party, 1920–1927* (Berkeley, 1991); M. Luk, *The Origins of Chinese Bolshevism. An Ideology in the Making, 1920–1928* (Hong Kong, 1990). These works generally emphasize the indigenous origins of Chinese Communism. For a work that stresses the influence of Soviet thinking and the Comintern, see S. Smith, *A Road is Made. Communism in Shanghai, 1920–1927* (Honolulu, 2000). For studies of the relationship between Bolshevism and Chinese communism after 1949, see above, n. 20.

of purposes: to promote land reform, increase production, and persecute alleged counter-revolutionaries.[26] However, by 1952 the leadership had decided that this approach to politics was counter-productive. Between 1952 and 1955 the Chinese Communist party consciously adopted technicist solutions, imitating the socialism that prevailed in the USSR after 1945. The regime stressed the need for planning by experts, hierarchy, discipline, one-man management, and 'revolutionary legality', rather than the 'democratic' mass mobilization of the revolutionary period. A graduated wage system replaced more egalitarian systems of reward, in the hope that material incentives would encourage officials to improve their expertise.[27] While political virtue was still demanded of party officials, particular emphasis was placed on their technical skills.[28] The party also changed its relationship with the state as mobilization became less fashionable, and economic departments enabled it to intervene more effectively in the economy and shadow the state.[29]

However, Mao became increasingly unhappy with this technicist strategy, which he came to describe as 'Soviet', and he challenged it intermittently from 1955, initiating a series of campaigns that culminated in the 'Great Leap Forward' of 1958.[30] In part, he was dissatisfied with the social and political consequences of technicism: it seemed to have produced an officialdom obsessed with status and lacking revolutionary spirit. But he was also discontented with its emphasis on 'scientific' planning and its inability to deliver rapid economic development; he was particularly disenchanted with the more liberal technicist approach of the economist Chen Yun, who advocated a greater use of market mechanisms and material incentives in industry and agriculture.

[26] For these campaigns, see H. Harding, *Organizing China. The Problem of Bureaucracy* (Stanford, 1981), 42–64; J. Strauss, 'Paternalist Terror: The Campaign to Suppress Counterrevolutionaries in the People's Republic of China, 1950–1953', *Comparative Studies in Society and History*, 44 (2002), 80–105.

[27] For 'regularization' of the administration, see H. Harding, *Organizing China. The Problem of Bureaucracy* (Stanford, 1981), 70–2; for the emphasis on 'revolutionary legality', see S. Zheng, *Party vs State*, 58–62.

[28] For an appeal to party officials to emphasize 'practice' and to gain 'professional proficiency at new jobs' in order that they be able to exercise leadership over the state, see *Selected Works of Liu Shaoqi*, ii. 253–5 (April 1956).

[29] H. Harding, *Organizing China*, 82–3.

[30] For the 1955 campaigns, see *Selected Works of Mao Tsetung*, v. 184–283; Frederick C. Teiwes, 'The Establishment of the New Regime', in R. MacFarquhar, *The Politics of China. Second Edition. The Eras of Mao and Deng* (Cambridge, 1997), 61–86.

It was in Mao's own personal interest, as it was in Stalin's, to place 'politics' (*zhengzhi*) rather than 'technique' (*jishu*) 'in command', as he was a party leader, not a technocratic state administrator.[31] But a reversal of the technicist strategy did not only benefit Mao: like Stalin in the late 1920s, he had the support of coalition of industrial and regional party interests which were pressing for more investment.[32]

The 'Great Leap Forward' of 1958 was a variation on the typical revivalist Marxist-Leninist campaign, and while it had peculiarly Chinese features it had much in common with Stalin's first five-year plan. Huge resources were pumped into heavy industry at the expense of consumer industry, agriculture, and living standards.[33] Mao, like Stalin, claimed that if party officials had the proper commitment to socialist ideas they could mobilize the masses and economic miracles would ensue.[34] Also, like the revivalist Bolsheviks, he found a model for this form of government in his military experience.[35] Extraordinary economic targets were set, and the status of the technically knowledgeable was challenged; indeed Mao insisted that party officials could easily become as expert as scientists, and science and culture were subjected to extreme politicization and 'proletarianization'.[36] These ideas were

---

[31] For Mao's thinking, see K. Leiberthal, 'The Great Leap Forward and the Split in the Yan'an Leadership, 1958–65', in R. MacFarquhar, *The Politics of China*, 92–8.

[32] Bachman argues that the Great Leap was largely formulated by heavy industrial and planning interests. See D. Bachman, *Bureaucracy, Economy and Leadership in China. The Institutional Origins of the Great Leap Forward* (Cambridge, 1991), ch. 5. Teiwes, Sun, and Chan, however, argue for the central role of Mao throughout the period. See F. Teiwes and W. Sun, *China's Road to Disaster. Mao, Central Politicians and Provincial Leaders in the Unfolding of the Great Leap Forward, 1955–1959* (New York, 1999); Alfred L. Chan, *Mao's Crusade. Politics and Policy Implementation in China's Great Leap Forward* (Oxford, 2001). For demands by provincial party bosses in China for greater investment before the Great Leap Forward, see Bachman, *Bureaucracy, Economy and Leadership*, 144; R. MacFarquhar, *The Origins of the Cultural Revolution*, Vol. 1: *Contradictions among the People, 1956–7* (Oxford, 1974), 133; S. Zheng, *Party vs. State*, 95–8.

[33] R. MacFarquhar, *The Origins of the Cultural Revolution*, Vol. 2: *The Great Leap Forward, 1958–1960* (Oxford, 1983), 326–30.

[34] Mao Tse-tung, 'Talks at the Beidahe Conference', August 1958, in *The Secret Speeches of Mao. From the Hundred Flowers to the Great Leap Forward*, ed. by R. MacFarquhar, T. Cheek, and E. Wu (Cambridge, Mass., 1989), 434–6.

[35] Ibid., 428, 434–5, 437–8.

[36] H. Harding, *Organizing China*, 174–5; for literary policy during the Great Leap Forward, see D. W. Fokkema, *Literary Doctrine in China and Soviet Influence, 1956–1960* (The Hague, 1965), ch. 6.

combined with more populist revivalist policies, and Mao sanctioned a 'democratization' of leadership style and a significant decentralization of economic power, in order to bring decision-making closer to the masses and thus encourage the masses' creativity.[37] These reforms, combined with the use of non-material incentives in the Chinese version of socialist emulation campaigns (competition and assessment (*pingbi*)), would, it was claimed, allow workers to achieve extraordinary results.[38] Non-material incentives were particularly dominant in the countryside, where Mao went much further than Stalin ever did in endorsing egalitarianism and collectivism in the new rural communes.[39] Yet Mao's ideological justification for these policies still had much in common with Stalin's in the late 1920s: they were all elements in an advance along the path from capitalism towards communism and an ideological class struggle against bourgeois attitudes. He alleged that party officials, particularly in the countryside, had come under the 'bad influence' of the bourgeoisie and were prey to 'rightist' views. The party therefore had to be 'rectified', or purified of 'the rightist mentality', so that the party would better be able to eradicate these dangerous attitudes in the population as a whole.[40] Mao, like Stalin, saw his attempt to propel society towards socialism or communism as another revolution, designed to mobilize the population and prevent complacency: as he explained, 'our revolutions are like battles. After a victory, we must at once put forward a new task. In this way, cadres and the masses will forever be filled with revolutionary fervour instead of conceit.'[41] As in the Soviet Union in the late 1920s, revivalism strengthened the position of the supreme leader and of the party apparatus: Mao and the senior Vice Chairman of the party, Liu Shaoqi, came into conflict with state officials, and regional party bosses were given more power over the state apparatus.[42]

[37] C. Riskin, *China's Political Economy. The Quest for Development since 1949* (Oxford, 1987), 119–20. See also Xiaobo Lu, *Cadres and Corruption. The Organizational Involution of the Chinese Communist Party* (Stanford, 2000), 106–7.

[38] X. Lu, *Cadres and Corruption*, 83–6.

[39] For the communes, see R. MacFarquhar, *The Great Leap Forward*, ch. 5.

[40] H. Harding, *Organizing China*, 158–9.

[41] Quoted ibid., 166.

[42] Although MacFarquhar argues that tensions between Mao and Liu are evident as early as this period: Mao emphasized the role of the masses, while Liu took a more élitist line, and stressed the role of the party hierarchy in mobilizing the masses; Mao

The Great Leap predictably led to chaos. Its populist decentral-izing elements undermined the authority of planners and managers, while its voluntaristic elements—the arbitrary raising of plan tar-gets and the new incentive system—led to economic crisis. Attempts to proletarianize and industrialize the countryside by developing industry there also contributed to enormous waste. These radical experiments contributed to famine and the deaths of an estimated 30 million people.[43] Like Stalin in 1930–1, Mao was forced to change course, and to lead what could be seen as a retreat. The leadership again adopted technicist policies on all fronts: from the early 1960s it was declared that 'objective laws' limited 'man's subjective ability to mould nature', and plan targets were substan-tially reduced;[44] excessive egalitarianism was criticized and mater-ial incentives were reintroduced throughout the economy; in agriculture collectivism was diluted and private plots increased;[45] and in industry worker participation was restricted, management was strengthened, and the party was told not to undermine its prerogatives but to assist the state apparatus in promoting eco-nomic growth.[46] Specialists were again given more authority, and politics was no longer to have such a degree of primacy over expertise. It was claimed that intellectuals were not the 'bourgeois rightists' of the past; the leadership declared that they were to play a full part in economic construction, and that they would be most effective if they were able to use their skills without excessive political interference.[47] No longer did the party insist that science had a class character, and literary figures were told to emphasize quality and use traditional artistic forms.[48] All of these changes were part of the leadership's attempts to impose order in response to the chaos and economic decline following the Great Leap.

---

was also less hostile to those at the top of the state hierarchy than Liu, although both were critical of lower-level state officials. See R. MacFarquhar, *The Great Leap Forward*, 51–63. See also S. Zheng, *Party vs. State*, 91–8.

[43] For the debate over the numbers of victims, see J. Becker, *Hungry Ghosts. China's Secret Famine* (London, 1996), ch. 18.

[44] H. Harding, *Organizing China*, 184; R. MacFarquhar, *The Origins of the Chinese Cultural Revolution*, Vol. 3: *The Coming of the Cataclysm, 1961–1966* (Oxford, 1997), ch. 4.

[45] Ibid., chs. 1–3.

[46] Ibid., 86–9.

[47] Ibid., 90–1.

[48] Ibid., 90–1, 118.

Power was centralized and the apparatus as a whole tightened its control over 'unreliable' elements in the population.[49] As Lynn White has argued, in this period party officials were particularly assiduous in discriminating on the basis of class labels: those who were of proletarian class origin or who had proved themselves politically in the past were privileged; while those with 'bad' class or political labels often faced persecution.[50] As in the Soviet Union in the mid-1930s, the restoration of order was accompanied by the strengthening of a neo-traditionalist status hierarchy, in part based on class orgin.

Mao, however, retained a populist revivalist approach to politics, and became increasingly dissatisfied with these developments. This led to tensions within the leadership, much greater than those within the 1930s Soviet leadership, and Mao became particularly frustrated with a group of party leaders that included Liu Shaoqi and Deng Xiaoping, the general secretary of the Communist party.[51] While he seems to have accepted that there could be no return to the Great Leap Forward and the use of mass mobilization for rapid economic development, he was still discontented with the technicist and neo-traditionalist order that he believed was emerging as a result of the new course. He also believed that the use of material incentives, the emphasis on expertise rather than ideological commitment, and the retreat from egalitarianism and mobilization were undermining the socialist nature of the system. Like Stalin, he placed a great deal of blame on officials: he considered that 'corruption' and 'bureaucratism' in the apparatus—the pursuit of private or clannish goals rather than the state's objectives, the development of a quasi-caste hierarchy within the party, and the

---

[49] For centralization, see H. Harding, *Organizing China*, 184–7, 199–200; K. Leiberthal, 'The Great Leap Forward', 113–17.

[50] Lynn T. White, *Policies of Chaos. The Organizational Causes of Violence in China's Cultural Revolution* (Princeton, 1989), chs. 8–9, esp. pp. 194–7, 218–20.

[51] The nature of high politics in this period is still obscure, but it seems that while there were tensions from 1962, it was only in 1964–5 that Mao's disenchantment with his colleagues became serious. For varying approaches to party politics, see F. Teiwes, *Politics and Purges in China. Rectification and the Decline of Party Norms, 1950–1965* (New York, 1979), ch. 11; Leiberthal, 'The Great Leap Forward', 113–47; MacFarquhar, *The Coming of the Cataclysm*, Pts. 2–3. For Liu's view of China as a meritocratic 'corporate hierarchy', see L. Dittmer, *Liu Shao-ch'i and the Chinese Cultural Revolution. The Politics of Mass Criticism* (Berkeley, 1974), 190–3.

separation of the apparatus from the masses—all had their roots in officials' contamination by rightist, bourgeois, and revisionist ideas. He also claimed that political rivals had exaggerated the importance of technique at the expense of class struggle.[52] He insisted that these problems could best be challenged by the inculcation of greater ideological commitment to socialism.[53]

In the early 1960s, therefore, the broad commonality of view between the supreme leader and the higher reaches of the party apparatus, which had existed during the Great Leap Forward, began to come apart, just as it had in the Soviet Union from the mid-1930s. In 1962 Mao launched a 'Socialist Education Movement' to purge or re-educate officials who were accused of corruption or anti-socialist attitudes, so that they would better be able to root out bourgeois attitudes among the population.[54] However, these rectification campaigns, like the Soviet party purges of 1933–6, could be interpreted in revivalist or non-revivalist ways. Mao favoured mobilization and criticism from below, and increasingly saw the main targets of the rectification as those, particularly at higher levels of the local party apparatuses, who were guilty of ideological sins. Liu Shaoqi, who conducted the campaigns, however, failed to organize the criticism of higher officials from below. He preferred to rely on centrally organized work teams rather than mass mobilization and, using a neo-traditionalist argument reminiscent of that employed by Soviet regional party bosses in 1936–7, he claimed that the poor and lower-middle peasants whom Mao wanted to mobilize could not be depended on because they had turned out not to be of pure proletarian class origin. He also interpreted the campaigns as an attack on corrupt officials lower in the apparatus rather than on ideologically revisionist officials at higher levels.[55] In practice, it seems that the Socialist Education Movement was used by local party bosses to strengthen their cliques

---

[52] Compare, for instance, the charges leveled against Liu Shaoqi in 1968 with those leveled against Bukharin in the late 1920s and 1930s. Liu was accused of having neglected the importance of 'classes and class struggle in a socialist society' and of having argued that 'by doing good work in "technical innovation and technical reform" ', communism could be achieved. *Renmin ribao*, 3 November 1968.

[53] S. Schram, *The Thought of Mao Tse-Tung*, 162–3; X. Lu, *Cadres and Corruption*, 116–17.

[54] R. MacFarquhar, *The Coming of the Cataclysm*, 334–43.

[55] For the tensions over the Socialist Education Movement, see R. MacFarquhar, *The Coming of the Cataclysm*, 419–27; H. Harding, *Organizing China*, 201–16.

and 'good', 'proletarian' elements while rooting out those with class alien backgrounds:[56] a populist revivalist campaign was being transformed into a neo-traditionalist one. In 1964 and 1965, therefore, Mao criticized the rectification campaigns and sought to reform them along populist revivalist lines. He managed to restrain the punishment of lower ranking officials for corruption, and he tried to redirect the rectification against higher officials. But again he failed, and attempts to subject county-level officials to criticism 'from below' had little effect.[57] Like Stalin, Mao found it extremely difficult to prevent the distortion of purges aimed at élites into discipline campaigns aimed at lower levels of society. He also eventually lost faith in the ability of the party apparatus to reform itself and mobilize the population, and increasingly relied on the army, just as Stalin had relied on the NKVD.[58]

By May 1966 Mao, frustrated with high-level resistance to his revivalist campaigns, had decided that rightist attitudes had infected members of the Central Committee, and he launched the Great Proletarian Cultural Revolution against those who wanted to take the 'capitalist road', the 'representatives of the bourgeoisie who have sneaked into the Party, the Government, the army and various cultural circles'. However, Mao encountered the same problems that faced Stalin in 1936–8. Like Stalin, he wanted to shake up the party and remove those with 'rightist' attitudes, without destroying the apparatus as a whole. He was also working within a typically revivalist conceptual framework, and saw the dangerous attitudes as, in essence, 'bourgeois'. Furthermore, he shared Stalin's understanding of the drawbacks of using revivalist 'class struggle' against an apparatus that was largely proletarian by class origin: officials could either escape the campaigns by interpreting class in a neo-traditionalist way; or, if the leadership succeeded in enforcing a revivalist interpretation of class, it could unleash popular resentment against the 'new bourgeoisie' and lose control.

---

[56] L. White, *Policies of Chaos*, 194–7.

[57] H. Harding, *Organizing China*, 212, 214–16.

[58] On the role of the army, see K. Leiberthal, 'The Great Leap Forward', 126–30; H. Harding, 'The Chinese State in Crisis, 1966–1969', in R. MacFarquhar, *The Politics of China*, 155–7. Mao also relied on Kang Sheng, who had security expertise and had allegedly been trained by the NKVD in Moscow between 1933 and 1937. For Mao and Kang, see R. MacFarquhar, *The Coming of the Cataclysm*, 291–2.

Mao was less sympathetic to neo-traditionalist attitudes than Stalin. He made this clear when, asked in 1964 how the main struggle within society should be defined, he replied, 'we need not concern ourselves with class or stratum but with power-holders...'. Another participant in the discussion expressed Mao's objections to neo-traditionalist interpretations of class struggle even more explicitly:

We must not talk about strata. Otherwise, if you emphasize the bourgeois engineering and technical personnel, or the petty thieves and pickpockets, or students who come from uninfluential capitalist families, the cadres would be very enthusiastic. The consequence is that cadres might slip away easily, and it will be impossible to strike at them.[59]

Mao's revivalist class struggle against the apparatus was also more radical and consistent than Stalin's. His slogan 'to rebel is justified' went much further than anything Stalin would have said, and his declaration: 'don't be afraid of making trouble. The bigger the trouble we make, the better', was more extreme than Stalin's appeal to the party to go 'against the current'. Also, in his desire to mobilize the 'masses' against the apparatus, he was prepared to imply that the bureaucracy had become a 'new class', declaring that 'in socialist society new bourgeois elements may still be produced'.[60]

Even so, despite this radicalism, Mao did not develop a coherent theory of the bureaucracy as a new bourgeois class, nor did he call for its complete destruction. Instead, he maintained an ambiguous position: he declared both that class enemies were new proletarian 'bureaucrats' and that they were members of the 'old classes';[61] and while at times he implied that the new bourgeoisie he had identified were isolated corrupted individuals, at other times he suggested that all officials were likely to become bourgeois because of the position and status they held.[62]

As in the Soviet Union, this ambiguity over the identity of the 'enemy', combined with the typical revivalist use of 'democracy' campaigns against 'bureaucrats', played a large part in transforming

---

[59] Quoted in R. Kraus, *Class Conflict in Chinese Socialism* (New York, 1981), 86–7.

[60] S. Schram (ed.), *Mao Unrehearsed. Talks and Letters, 1956–71* (Harmondsworth, 1974), 168.

[61] R. Kraus, *Class Conflict*, 119; S. Schram, *The Political Thought of Mao Tse-tung*, 165–6, 178; H. Harding, *Organizing China*, 263–5.

[62] Ibid., 164.

the party leadership's attack on élites into political convulsions that affected the whole of society. However, the Chinese campaigns had even more disruptive effects than their Soviet counterparts. In response to Mao's aggressive and radical stance, local officials tried to deflect the 'class struggle' from themselves, using neo-traditionalist arguments to justify the persecutions of class aliens. Rather like the 'biologists' condemned by Zhdanov in 1939, they defended themselves using 'class pedigree theory', according to which political reliability depended entirely on class origin and was inherited. Those of proletarian class origin and their children, they claimed, were virtuous, while those of bourgeois class origin were enemies.[63]

Mao, like Stalin, soon lost control of the language of class and enemies,[64] and, more generally, of his campaigns, although he created much greater chaos than Stalin did. The Cultural Revolution, unlike Stalin's Terror, led to serious social conflict, as local party bosses established Red Guards recruited from those of 'proletarians' or 'good' class background, while they were challenged by Maoist 'rebel' groups, often made up of individuals of 'bad' or 'bourgeois' class background, and others who felt themselves discriminated against by party officialdom.[65] Although the Cultural Revolution did not involve organized mass killings along the lines of Stalin's mass operations, it certainly led to a great deal of violence:

[63] G. White, *The Politics of Class and Class Origin: The Case of the Cultural Revolution*, Contemporary China Papers 9 (Australian National University, 1976), 28 ff.

[64] As one revealing circular from the centre of December 1968 declared: 'The names you use to refer to the enemy should conform to those explicitly provided in the documents of the centre and the Cultural Revolution Small Group, e.g. traitor; spy; arch-unrepentant capitalist roader; unreformed landlord... You should not use ambiguous and vague terminology that is likely to result in...the widening of the scope of the attack. Among those who have committed capitalist-roader errors, the arch-unrepentant are only a minority, while those who are capable of accepting education and of correcting their errors are a majority.' Quoted in M. Schoenhals, *Doing Things with Words in Chinese Politics. Five Studies*, Chinese Research Monograph, No. 41 (Center for Chinese Studies, Berkeley, 1992), 38.

[65] There is some disagreement on the basis of conflict within society during the Cultural Revolution. For interpretations which stress class labels and socio-economic background, see H. Y. Lee, *The Politics of the Chinese Cultural Revolution. A Case Study* (Berkeley, 1978); R. Kraus, *Class Conflict*. For the view that workers were mobilized on the basis of political networks, see A. Walder, 'Beijing Red Guard Factionalism. The Social Interpretation Reconsidered', *Journal of Asian Studies*, 61 (2002), 437–71. For a synthetic approach, see E. J. Perry and Li Xun, *Proletarian Power. Shanghai in the Cultural Revolution* (Boulder, 1997), chs. 2 and 3.

it has been estimated that half a million died, and many more suffered in other ways.[66]

As many differences as similarities are evident from this brief comparison of Stalin's and Mao's attitudes and behaviour during the Terror and the Cultural Revolution. First, the balance between the concern with national security and the desire to mobilize society on the basis of socialist values differed in each case. It is probable that Mao, like Stalin, was worried about threats to the survival of socialism, but he saw these threats as primarily internal and ideological: he seems to have feared that on his death China would reject his legacy and become as 'revisionist' as the Soviet Union.[67] Mao did accuse his victims of conspiring with foreigners, and the Cultural Revolution did take place at a time of international tension over Vietnam, but Mao was much less concerned with the question of foreign invasion and spies than was Stalin.[68] Second, Mao's views of Marxism differed from Stalin's in a number of ways. Most obviously, Mao's anti-urbanism contrasts sharply with Bolshevik prejudice against the peasantry, but his revivalism was also much more populist than Stalin's. Unlike Stalin he seems to have thought seriously about the transition to full communism,[69] and he was much more reckless in his willingness to challenge the apparatus and initiate disorder. Indeed, Mao criticized Stalin for his élitism: neither the slogan 'technique decides everything' nor the slogan 'cadres decide everything', he argued, took sufficient account of the masses.[70]

These divergences between the attitudes of Soviet and Chinese leaderships help to explain some of the many differences between Stalin's Terror and Mao's Cultural Revolution. First the Terror—and especially the mass operations against ethnic and class aliens—acquired a much more neo-traditionalist character than the Cultural Revolution; second, it had a more economic focus than the Cultural Revolution, and Stalin was more concerned than Mao with rooting out economic officials who were failing to prepare the country for

---

[66] For estimates of deaths, see H. Harding, 'The Chinese State in Crisis, 1966–9', 243–4. For violence in the Cultural Revolution, see A. Thurston, *Enemies of the People* (New York, 1987).

[67] This is argued by Harding in 'The Chinese State in Crisis', 233–4.

[68] R. MacFarquhar, *The Coming of the Cataclysm*, 375–7.

[69] See, for instance, Mao Tse-tung, *The Secret Speeches*, 484.

[70] Quoted in S. Schram, *The Thought of Mao Tse-tung*, 131.

war; third, it was a more élitist set of campaigns, involving organized operations conducted by the secret police rather than popular mobilizations, and there was much less spontaneous popular action 'from below'; and fourth, there was much less emphasis on re-educating 'enemies' and a greater willingness to 'cleanse' and kill.[71] Yet, the differences between the conduct of Terror and the Cultural Revolution should not be exaggerated. In many cases the attack on revisionist 'capitalist roaders' was carried out in public by mobilized Red Guards, but many officials—about 2 million in all—were interrogated and criticized in secret by the blandly named Central Case Examination Group (CCEG). Like the NKVD, the CCEG set itself the task of discovering 'hidden enemies' and unmasking the 'inner thoughts' of its captives through the use of torture.[72]

Mao, of course, was strongly influenced by Stalin's thought, but the similarities between their behaviour are not the result of simple copying—indeed Mao explicitly criticized Stalin's Terror as a 'leftist' error.[73] Rather, both leaders were operating within a similar ideological framework. For various reasons, which probably differed in the case of each leader, they were trying to reinvigorate a system that they believed had become demobilized and lost its revolutionary spirit during the 'retreat' from the economic leap forward. They blamed 'bourgeois', 'rightist' attitudes, largely among officials, for these 'capitalist' or 'feudal' phenomena, and they launched highly destabilizing campaigns of 'class struggle' to root them out.

In his novel *Chevengur*, completed in 1928, the writer Andrei Platonov told of a group of poorly educated but idealistic Bolsheviks who decide to establish communism in a town on the steppe. They disagree over how to go about it: Prokofii Dvanov, the secretary of Chevengur's local state organization, favours going slowly and cites Marx to prove the necessity of the 'long calm of Soviet power'.[74] But Chepurnyi, the chairman of the party's

---

[71] For Mao's views on the need for re-education and his criticisms of Stalin's Terror, see R. MacFarquhar, *The Coming of the Cataclysm*, 473.

[72] M. Schoenhals, 'The Central Case Examination Group, 1966–79', CQ, 145 (1996), 87–111.

[73] For Mao's criticism of Stalin's 'leftist' deviation in 'exterminating counter-revolutionaries', see S. Schram, *The Thought of Mao Tse-tung*, 151.

[74] Andrei Platonov, *Chevengur. Roman* (Moscow, 1988), 256.

Revolutionary Committee, is more impatient: 'the bourgeoisie was alive, there was no communism' and the local authorities counselled only gradual progress, a policy 'in which Chepurnyi intuitively suspected the deception of the masses'.[75] Under Chepurnyi's influence the Bolsheviks decide to kill Chevengur's bourgeoisie. But, despite the massacre, communism still does not arrive, and Chepurnyi yet again becomes anxious that the revolution is losing its way and that the Bolsheviks are becoming demoralized:[76] 'Will we ourselves not become exhausted from the long march of the revolutionary spirit?', he asks Prokofi. 'I may be the first to become besmirched and exhausted as a result of maintaining power. It's impossible to be better than everybody else for ever!'[77] The reason for the failure to achieve communism, Chepurnyi persuades his comrades, is the continuing existence of the 'half-bourgeoisie' which 'indirectly oppresses us'.[78] The Bolsheviks therefore expel the half-bourgeosie from Chevengur as well. But even then they worry that they might return, and Chevengur remains a vigilant, armed camp.[79]

Platonov's treatment of Bolshevik language and ideas was exaggerated and often surreal, and Stalin, of course, was no Chepurnyi—he was far from being a utopian intent on propelling society towards full communism.[80] But Platonov did capture an important element of revivalist Bolshevik thinking. Like Chevengur's communists, revivalist Bolsheviks, including at times Stalin, believed that the 'long calm of Soviet power' would only lead to *stasis,* demoralization, and the 'spoiling' of cadres, and that the remnants of the bourgeoisie (or at least of bourgeois attitudes) were responsible for the failure to progress towards the ideal society, whatever that might be. Their conviction that the revolutionary spirit, essential if the state were to be powerful, could only be sustained by continuing the revolution against the bourgeoisie—and those influenced by the bourgeoisie—explains why even leaders as shrewd as Stalin initiated such seemingly irrational policies.

The Marxist idea of revolution had always been Janus-faced: it justified the violent persecution of 'class enemies', while simultaneously

[75] Ibid., 233.   [76] Ibid., 255.   [77] Ibid., 257.
[78] Ibid., 250.   [79] Ibid., 263.
[80] Gorky, justifying official censorship of *Chevengur* in 1929, described Platonov's characters as 'idiots and nut-cases' rather than true revolutionaries. See R. Robin, *Socialist Realism,* 226.

encouraging enormous idealism and self-sacrifice among the class 'pure'. Yet, when yoked to state-building projects by ruthless leaders at a time of vicious international competition or war, it had horrific consequences for large sections of society, including the revolutionaries themselves. It also damaged the reputation of Soviet socialism, and of the entire Marxist-Leninist project. Although Stalin may have believed that he was reinvigorating the spirit of the revolution, he probably contributed more than anybody else to its demise.

Bibliography

Newspapers and journals (abbreviations in parentheses)

Acta Slavica Iaponica
American Historical Review (AHR)
Biulleten' oppozitsii (Paris) *(BO)*
Biulleten' TsKK VKP(b) i NK RKI SSSR i RSFSR (BTsKK)
Bol'shevik (B)
British Journal of Political Science (BJPS)
Cahiers du Monde Russe (CMR)
Cahiers du Monde Russe et Sovietique (CMRS)
China Quarterly (CQ)
Comparative Studies in Society and History
Europe–Asia Studies (E–AS)
Front nauki i tekhniki (FNT)
History of European Ideas
International Review of Social History
Inzhenernyi trud (IT)
Istochnik
Istoriia SSR
Istoricheskii arkhiv
Izvestiia (I)
Izvestiia TsK VKP(b) (Izv TsK)
Izvestiia TsK KPSS (Izv TsK KPSS)
Jahrbücher für Geschichte Osteuropas (JGO)
Journal of Asian Studies
Journal of Modern History (JMH)
Kommunist
Kommunisticheskaia revoliutsiia (KR)
Komsomol'skaia pravda (KP)
Krasnaia nov' (KN)
Kritika. Explorations in Russian and Eurasian History
Leningradskaia pravda (LP)
Letopisi marksizma (LM)
Literaturnaia gazeta (LG)
Moskovskie novosti (MN)

Otechestvennye arkhivy
Partiinaia rabota v tseke (PRTs)
Partiinoe stroitel'stvo (PS)
Partrabotnik (Pk)
Past and Present
Pod znamenem marksizma (PZM)
Political Theory
Pravda (P)
Predpriiatie
Proletarskaia kul'tura (PK)
Proletarskaia revoliutsiia (PR)
Radical Science Journal
Renmin ribao (People's Daily) (Beijing)
Revolutionary Russia
Russian History/Histoire Russe (RH/HR)
The Russian Review (RR)
Slavic Review (SR)
Slavonic and East European Review (SEER)
Sotsialisticheskii vestnik (Paris) (SV)
Sovetskaia iustitsiia (SIu)
Sovetskoe gosudarstvo i revoliutsiia prava (SGRP)
Soviet Studies (SS)
Sputnik agitatora dlia goroda (SADG)
Sputnik kommunista (SK)
Stakhanovets (S)
Studies in East European Thought
Torgovo-promyshlennaia gazeta (TPG)
Trud (T)
Vestnik Kommunisticheskoi Akademii (VKA)
Voprosy istorii (VI)
Voprosy istorii KPSS (VI KPSS)
Voprosy profdvizheniia (VP)
Za industrializatsiiu (ZI)

Archival

Rossiiskii gosudarstvennyi arkhiv noveishei istorii (RGANI)
    fond 6, Komissiia Partiinogo Kontrolia pri TsK VKP(b)
Rossiiskii gosudarstvennyi arkhiv sotsialo-politicheskoi istorii (RGASPI)
    fond 17, Tsentral'nyi komitet
    fond 71, Institut Marksizma–Leninizma pri TsK KPSS
    fond 73, Lichnyi fond A. A. Andreeva

fond 77, Lichnyi fond A. A. Zhdanova
fond 79, Lichnyi fond V. V. Kuibysheva
fond 81, Lichnyi fond L. M. Kaganovicha
fond 82, Lichnyi fond V. M. Molotova
fond 88, Lichnyi fond A. S. Shcherbakova
fond 85, Lichnyi fond G. K. Ordzhonikidze
fond 329, Lichnyi fond N. I. Bukharina
fond 558, Lichnyi fond I. V. Stalina
Smolensk Archive (WKP)
Trotsky archive (T)

Congresses, conferences, and trials

Chetyrnadtsataia konferentsiia VKP(b). Stenograficheskii otchet (Moscow–Leningrad 1925).

IV plenum MK VKP(b) sovmestno s plenumom MKK. Avgust 1929 g. (Moscow, 1929).

Chetyrnadtsatyi s"ezd VKP(b), 18–31 dekabria 1925 g. Stenograficheskii otchet (Moscow–Leningrad, 1926).

Desiatyi s"ezd RKP(b), mart 1921 goda. Stenograficheskii otchet (Moscow, 1963).

Deviataia konferentsiia RKP(b), sentiabr' 1920 goda. Protokoly (Moscow 1972).

Deviatyi s"ezd RKP(b), mart–aprel' 1920 g. Protokoly (Moscow, 1960).

Dvenadtsatyi s"ezd, 17–25 aprelia 1923 goda. Stenograficheskii otchet (Moscow, 1968).

Odinadtsatyi s"ezd RKP(b). Stenograficheskii otchet (Moscow, 1961).

O piatiletnem plane razvitiia narodnogo khoziaistva SSSR. Diskussiia v Kommunisticheskoi Akademii (Moscow–Leningrad 1928).

Pervaia Moskovskaia oblastnaia konferentsiia VKP(b). Stenograficheskii otchet. Vyp. I, sentiabr' 1929 g. (Moscow, 1929).

Pervyi vserossiiskii s"ezd sovetov narodnogo khoziaistva, 1918 (Trudy) (Moscow, 1918).

Pervyi vsesoiuznyi s"ezd sovetskikh pisatelei (Moscow, 1935).

Pervyi vsesoiuznyi s"ezd udarnykh brigad (k tridtsatiletiiu s"ezda): sbornik dokumentov i materialov (Moscow, 1959).

Piatnadtsataia konferentsiia VKP(b), 26 oktiabria–3 noiabria 1926 g. Stenograficheskii otchet (Moscow–Leningrad, 1927).

Piatnadtsatyi s"ezd VKP(b). Dekabr' 1927 goda. Stenograficheskii otchet, 2 vols. (Moscow, 1961).

Protsess kontrrevoliutsionnoi organizatsii men'shevikov (1 marta–9 marta 1931 g.) (Moscow, 1931).

Protsess 'prompartii' (25 noiabria–7 dekabria 1930 g.) (Moscow, 1931).

Rasshirennyi plenum ispolkoma kommunisticheskogo internatsionala (21 marta–6 aprelia 1925 g.). Stenograficheskii otchet (Moscow–Leningrad, 1925).

Report of Court Proceedings in the Case of the Anti-Soviet 'Bloc of Rights and Trotskyites' Heard Before the Military Collegium of the Supreme Court of the USSR, Moscow, March 2–13 1938 (Moscow, 1938).

Report of Court Proceedings in the Case of the Anti-Soviet Trotskyite Centre. Verbatim Report (Moscow, 1937).

Report of Court Proceedings in the Case of the Trotskyite-Zinovievite Terrorist Centre (Moscow, 1936).

XVI konferentsiia VKP(b). Stenograficheskii otchet (Moscow, 1929).

XVI s"ezd VKP(b). Stenograficheskii otchet (Moscow–Leningrad, 1930).

XVII konferentsiia VKP(b). Stenograficheskii otchet (Moscow, 1932).

XVII s"ezd Vsesoiuznoi Kommunisticheskoi Partii (bol'shevikov). 26 ianvaria - 10 fevralia 1934 g. Stenograficheskii otchet (Moscow, 1934).

Soveshchanie po voprosam sovetskogo stroitel'stva. Ianvar' 1925 g. (Moscow, 1925).

III plenum TsKK sozyva XV s"ezda VKP(b), 25-29 avgusta 1928 g. (Moscow, 1928).

Trinadtsatyi s"ezd RKP(b), mai 1924 goda. Stenograficheskii otchet (Moscow, 1963).

XVIII s"ezd Vsesoiuznoi Kommunisticheskoi Partii (b), 10–21 marta 1939 g. Stenograficheskii otchet (Moscow, 1939).

Vos'moi s"ezd RKP(b), mart 1919 goda. Protokoly (Moscow, 1959).

VIII vsesoiuznyi s"ezd professional'nykh soiuzov, Stenograficheskii otchet (Moscow, 1928).

Vsesoiuznyi s"ezd sovetskikh pisatelei, *Problems of Soviet Literature. Reports and Speeches at the First Writers' Congress* (London, 1935).

II plenum TsKK sozyva XV s"ezda VKP(b), 2–5 aprelia 1928 g. (Moscow, 1928).

Wrecking Activities at Power Stations in the Soviet Union (Moscow, 1933).

Document collections

Akhapkin, I. (ed.), *First Decrees of Soviet Power* (London, 1970).

Artisov, A., and Naumov, O. (eds.), *Vlast' i khudozhestvennaia intelligentsiia. Dokumenty TsK RKP(b) – VKP(b) – VChK – OGPU – NKVD o kul'turnoi politike, 1917–1953 gg.* (Moscow, 1999).

Bazanov, V. G. (ed.), *Agitatsionnaia literatura russkikh revoliutsionnykh narodnikov: potaennye proizvedeniia 1873–1875 gg.* (Leningrad, 1970).

Brovkin, V. (ed.), *Dear Comrades. Menshevik Reports on the Bolshevik Revolution and the Civil War* (Stanford, 1991).

Bunyan, J. (ed.), *The Origins of Forced Labor in the Soviet State, 1917–1921: Documents and Materials* (Baltimore, 1967).

Dekrety sovetskoi vlasti, Vol. 1 (Moscow, 1957).

Direktivy KPSS i sovetskogo pravitel'stva po khoziaistvennym voprosam 1917–1957 gody: sbornik dokumentov (Moscow, 1957).

Fel'shtinskii, Iu. (ed.), *Arkhiv Trotskogo. Kommunisticheskaia oppozitsiia v SSSR, 1923–1927* (Moscow, 1990).

Garros, V., Kornevskaya, N., and Lahusen, T. (eds.), *Intimacy and Terror. Soviet Diaries of the 1930s* (New York, 1995).

Goliakov, I. (ed.), *Sbornik dokumentov po istorii ugolovnogo zakonodatel'stva SSSR i RSFSR za 1917–1928 gg.* (Moscow, 1953).

Iakovlev, A. N. (ed.), *Reabilitatsiia. Politicheskie protsessy 30–50-kh godov* (Moscow, 1991).

Karataev, N. K. (ed.), *Narodnicheskaia ekonomicheskaia literatura* (Moscow, 1958).

Khaustov, V. N., Naumov, V. P., Plotnikov, N. S. (eds.), *Lubianka. Stalin i VchK–GPU–OGPU–NKVD ianvar' 1922–dekabr' 1936* (Moscow, 2003).

Khlevniuk, O. V., Davies, R. W., Kosheleva, L. P., Rees, E. A., and Rogovaia, L. A. (eds.), *Stalin i Kaganovich. Perepiska 1931–1936 gg.* (Moscow, 2001).

Khlevniuk, O. V., Kvashonikin, A. V., Kosheleva, L. P., and Rogovaia L. A. (eds.), *Stalinskoe politbiuro v 1930-e gody* (Moscow, 1995).

Koenker, D., and Bachman, R. (eds.), *Revelations from the Soviet Archives. Documents in English Translation* (Washington, DC, 1997).

Kokurin, A. I., and Petrov, N. V. (eds.), *GULAG (Glavnoe upravlenie lagerei), 1917–1960* (Moscow, 2000).

Kommunisticheskaia Partiia Sovetskogo Soiuza v rezoliutsiiakh i resheniiakh s"ezdov, konferentsii i plenumov TsK, 8th edn. (Moscow, 1970).

Kosheleva, L. P., Lel'chuk, V., Naumov, V., Naumov, O. V., Rogovaia, L. A., and Khlevniuk, O. V. (eds.), *Pis'ma I.V. Stalina V.M. Molotovu, 1925–1936 gg. Sbornik dokumentov* (Moscow, 1995).

Kvashonkin, A. V., Kosheleva, L. P., Rogovaia, L. A., and Khlevniuk, O. V. (eds.), *Sovetskoe rukovodstvo. Perepiska, 1928–1941* (Moscow, 1999).

Kvashonkin, A. V., Livshin, A. Ia., and Khlevniuk, O. V. (eds.), *Bol'shevistskoe rukovodstvo. Perepiska, 1912–1927. Sbornik dokumentov* (Moscow, 1996).

Neizvestnaia Rossiia XX veka. Pis'ma, memuary (Moscow, 1992).

Pipes. R. (ed.), *The Unknown Lenin. From the Secret Archive* (New Haven, 1998).

Profsoiuzy SSSR. Dokumenty i materialy (Moscow, 1963).

Sbornik dekretov i postanovlenii po narodnomu khoziaistvu, 2 vols. (Moscow, 1918–1921).

Studenikina, S. S. (ed.), *Istoriia sovetskoi konstitutsii (v dokumentakh), 1917–1956 gg.* (Moscow, 1957).

Primary

Abramov, A., *O pravoi oppozitsii v partii* (Moscow, 1929).

Bogdanov, A. A., *Elementy proletarskoi kul'tury v razvitii rabochego klassa* (Moscow, 1920).

—— *Empiriomonizm. Stat'i po filosofii* (Moscow, 1905).

—— *O proletarskoi kul'ture.1904–1924* (Moscow, 1924).

—— *Vera i nauka* (Moscow, 1910).

—— *Zadachi rabochikh v revoliutsii* (Moscow, 1917).

Breitman, A., *O vydvizhenii rabochikh v sovapparat* (Leningrad, 1929).

Bukharin, N. I., *Proletarskaia revoliutsiia i kul'tura* (Petrograd, 1923).

—— *Ataka. Sbornik teoreticheskikh statei* (Moscow 1924).

—— *Historical Materialism. A System of Sociology* (London, 1925).

—— *Tekushchii moment i osnovy nashei politiki* (Moscow, 1925).

—— *Bor'ba za kadry. Rech'i i stat'i* (Moscow–Leningrad, 1926).

—— *O rabkore i sel'kore. Stat'i i rechi* (Moscow, 1926).

—— *Nauka i SSSR* (Leningrad, 1928).

—— *Tekushchie zadachi Komsomola. Doklad na VIII vsesoiuznoi s"ezde VLKSM 6 maia 1928 g.* (Moscow, 1928).

—— *V zashchitu proletarskoi diktatury. Sbornik* (Moscow–Leningrad 1928).

—— *Bor'ba dvukh mirov i zadachi nauki* (Moscow–Leningrad, 1931).

—— *O tekhnicheskoi propagande i ee organizatsii* (Moscow–Leningrad, 1931)

—— and Preobrazhensky, E., *The ABC of Communism. A Popular Explanation of the Program of the Communist Party of Russia*, trans. by E. Paul and C. Paul (Ann Arbor, 1966).

—— *Proletariat i voprosy khudozhestvennoi politiki. Stenogramma rechi, proiznesennoi na literaturnom soveshchanii pri TsK v fevrale 1925 g.* (Letchworth, 1979).

—— *Izbrannye proizvedeniia* (Moscow, 1988).

—— *Put' k sotsializmu. Izbrannye proizvedeniia* (Novosibirsk, 1990).

Chernyshevskii, N. G., *Polnoe sobranie sochinenii* (Moscow, 1939–51).

Dimitrov, G., *Dnevnik. 9 mart 1933–6 fevruari 1949* (Sofia, 1997).

Engels, F., *Dialectics of Nature*, trans. by Charles Dutt (London, 1940).

—— *Anti-Dühring. Herr Eugen Dühring's Revolution in Science* (Moscow, 1959).

Furmanov, D., *Izbrannoe* (Moscow, 1946).

Gastev, A., *Kak nado rabotat'* (Moscow, 1972).

Ginzburg, E., *Into the Whirlwind*, trans. by Paul Stevenson and Manya Harari (London, 1989).

Ginzburg, S. Z., 'O gibeli Sergo Ordzhonikidze', *VI KPSS*, 3 (1991).

Gol'tsman, A. Z., *Dorogu initsiative rabochikh. Doklad proizvodstvennykh soveshchanii na sobranii fabrichno-zavodskogo aktiva M K, 21/III/29 g.* (Moscow–Leningrad, 1929).

Gorky, M., *Meshchane* (Moscow, 1950).

—— *Sobranie sochinenii v tridtsati tomakh* (Moscow, 1953).

—— *M. Gor'kii. Neizdannaia perepiska s Bogdanovym, Leninym, Stalinym, Zinov'evym, Kamenevym*, ed. by S. V. Zaika (Moscow, 1998).

Gurevich, D., *Za uluchshenie partiinoi raboty* (Moscow–Leningrad, 1929).

—— *Za vedushchuiu rol' kommunista na proizvodstve* (Moscow–Samara, 1932).

Heitman, S. (ed.), *Put' k sotsializmu v Rossii. Izbrannye proizvedeniia N. I. Bukharina* (New York, 1967).

History of the Communist Party of the Soviet Union (Bolsheviks) (Moscow, 1945).

Il'enkov, V., *Vedushchaia os'* (Moscow–Leningrad, 1932).

Kaganovich, L. M., *Ocherednye zadachi partraboty i reorganizatsiia partapparata* (Moscow–Leningrad, 1930).

—— *Ocherednye zadachi partraboty posle XIV konferentsii* (Moscow, 1925).

—— *O vnutrennoi rabote i otdelakh rukovodiashchikh partiinykh organov. Rech' na soveshchanii zaveduiushchikh otdelami rukovodiashchikh partiinykh organov, 3 sent. 1934 g.* (Moscow, 1934).

—— *Pamiatnye zapiski* (Moscow, 1996).

Kataev, V., *Sobranie sochinenii* (Moscow, 1956).

—— *Time Forward!*, trans. by C. Malamuth (New York, 1933).

Kerzhenstev, P. M., 'N.O.T.', in A. N. Shcherban' (ed.), *Nauchnaia organizatsiia truda i upravlenie. Sbornik* (Moscow, 1965).

—— *Printsipy organizatsii* (Moscow, 1968).

Kollontai, A. M., *The Workers' Opposition* (London, n.d.).

Kravchenko, V., *I Chose Freedom. The Personal and Political Life of a Soviet Official* (London, 1947).

Larin, Iu., *Gosudarstvennyi kapitalizm voennogo vremeni v Germanii (1914–1918 gg.)* (Moscow, 1928).

Larina, A. M., *Nezabyvaemoe* (Moscow, 1989).

Lebed', D. Z., *Sovety i bor'ba s biurokratizmom* (Moscow, 1927).

—— *Partiia v bor'be s biurokratizmom. Itogi XV s"ezda VKP(b)* (Moscow–Leningrad, 1928).

Lenin, V. I., *Polnoe sobranie sochinenii*, 5th edn. (Moscow, 1958–65).

Liu Shaoqi, *Selected Works of Liu Shaoqi* (Beijing, 1984–91).

Lunacharskii, A., *Religiia i sotsializm* (St Petersburg, 1908).

Mao Tse-tung, *Selected Works* (Beijing, 1969–77).

—— *A Critique of Soviet Economics* trans. by Moss Roberts (New York and London, 1977).

—— *Mao Unrehearsed. Talks and Letters, 1956–71*, ed. by Stuart Schram (Harmondsworth, 1974).

—— *The Secret Speeches of Mao. From the Hundred Flowers to the Great Leap Forward*, ed. by R. MacFarquhar, T. Cheek, and E. Wu (Cambridge, Mass., 1989).

Marx, K., *Capital* (New York, 1967).

—— *The Critique of the Gotha Programme* (Beijing, 1976).

—— *Preface and Introduction to a Contribution to the Critique of Political Economy* (Beijing, 1976).

Marx, K., and Engels, F., *Selected Works*, 2 vols. (Moscow, 1961).

—— *Karl Marx Frederick Engels Collected Works*, 47 vols. (London, 1975–93).

—— *The Manifesto of the Communist Party* (Beijing, 1988).

Mikhailovskii, N. K., *Polnoe sobranie sochinenii*, 5th edn. (St Petersburg, 1911).

Mikulina, E., *Sorevnovanie mass* (Moscow–Leningrad, 1929).

Molotov, V. M., *O partiinykh zadachakh* (Moscow–Leningrad, 1927).

—— *O podgotovke novykh spetsialistov* (Moscow–Leningrad, 1928).

—— *Stroitel'stvo sotsializma i protivorechiia rosta. Doklad o rabote TsK VKP(b) na I Moskovskoi partiinoi konferentsii, 14 sentiabria 1929 g.* (Moscow, 1929).

—— *Stat'i i rechi, 1935–1936* (Moscow, 1937).

—— *2aia godovshchina oktiabr'skoi revoliutsii. Doklad na torzhestvennom zasedanii Moskovskogo soveta, 6 noiabria 1938 g.* (Moscow–Leningrad, 1938).

Nicolaevsky, B., 'Letter of an Old Bolshevik', in B. Nikolaevsky, *Power and the Soviet Elite 'The Letter of an Old Bolshevik' and Other Essays* (London, 1966).

Ordzhonikidze, G. K., *Stat'i i rechi, 1926–1937 gg.*, 2 vols. (Moscow, 1957).

—— 'Neopublikovannoe vystuplenie G. K. Ordzhonikidze', *VI*, 8 (1978), 94–7.

Osinskii, N., *Stroitel'stvo sotsializma – obshchie zadachi organizatsiia proizvodstva* (Moscow, 1918).

Owen, R., *A New View of Society and Other Writings*, ed. by G. Claeys (Harmondsworth, 1991).

Pashukanis, E., *Proletarskoe gosudarstvo i postroenie besklassogo obshchestva* (Moscow, 1932).

Pashukanis, E., and Ignat, S., *Ocherednye zadachi bor'by s biurokratiz-mom. Doklady prochitannye v Institute Sovetskogo Stroitel'stva Kommunisticheskoi Akademii, 18 aprelia 1929 g.* (Moscow, 1929).

Platonov, A., *Chevengur. Roman* (Moscow, 1988).

Plekhanov, G. V., *Sochineniia*, ed. by D. Riazanov (Moscow, 1923–7).

Postyshev, P. P., *Za marksistko–leninskoe vospitanie* (Moscow, 1932).

Rabota profsoiuzov sredi spetsialistov (Khar'kov, 1929).

Reiss, H. (ed.), *The Political Thought of the German Romantics, 1793–1815* (Oxford, 1955).

Henri, Comte de Saint Simon, *Selected Writings* (Oxford, 1952).

—— *Selected Writings on Science, Industry and Social Organization*, ed. by K. Taylor (London, 1975).

Shatunovskii, Ia., *Geroizm truda i rabochee tvorchestvo* (Moscow–Leningrad, 1928).

Slovar' sovremennogo russkogo literaturnogo iazyka (Moscow–Leningrad, 1954).

Spravochnik partiinogo rabotnika, 8 vyp. (Moscow, 1934).

Stalin, I. V., *Sochineniia*, 13 vols. (Moscow, 1946–51).

—— *Sochineniia*, ed. by Robert McNeal (Stanford, 1967), i(xiv)–iii(xvi).

—— *The Essential Stalin*, ed. and with intro. by Bruce Franklin (London, 1973).

Sto sorok besed s Molotvym. Iz dnevnika F. Chueva (Moscow, 1991).

Strumilin, S., *Na planovom fronte, 1920–1930 gg.* (Moscow, 1958).

—— *Ocherki sovetskoi ekonomiki. Resursy i perspektivy* (Moscow–Leningrad, 1928).

Trotsky, L. D., *Literatura i revoliutsiia* (Moscow, 1923).

—— *Sochineniia* (Moscow, 1927).

—— *The Revolution Betrayed. What is the Soviet Union Doing and Where is it Going?* (New York, 1960).

—— *Terrorism and Communism* (Ann Arbor, Mich., 1971).

—— *The Class Nature of the Soviet State* (London, Mich., 1973).

—— *The Writings of Leon Trotsky (1930–1931)*, ed. by G. Breitman and S. Lovell (New York, 1973).

—— *The Challenge of the Left Opposition, 1923–1925* (New York, 1975).

—— *My Life. An Attempt at Autobiography* (Harmondsworth, 1975).

—— *The Challenge of the Left Opposition, 1926–27* (New York, 1980).

Uchastie mass v rabote RKI. K XVI s"ezdu VKP(b) (Moscow, 1930).

Vyshinskii, A. Ia., *Revoliutsionnaia zakonnost' na sovremennom etape* (Moscow, 1932).

Zhdanov, A. A., *Podgotovka partiinykh organizatsii k vyboram v verkhovnyi sovet SSSR po novoi izbiratel'noi sisteme i sootvetstvuiushchaia perestroika partiino-politicheskoi raboty* (Moscow, 1937).

Zinoviev, G., *Partiia i soiuzy (k diskussii o roli i zadachakh profsoiuzov)* (Petrograd, 1921).

Secondary

Abrams, M., *Natural Supernaturalism. Tradition and Revolution in Romantic Literature* (New York, 1973).

Acton, E., *Rethinking the Russian Revolution* (London, 1990).

Afanas'ev, A. V. (ed.), *Oni ne molchali* (Moscow, 1991).

Agursky, M., 'The Nietzschean Roots of Stalinist Culture', in B. Rosenthal (ed.), *Nietzsche in Soviet Culture. Ally or Adversary?* (Cambridge, 1994).

Ahn, Byung-joon, *Chinese Politics and the Cultural Revolution: Dynamics of Policy Processes* (Seattle, 1976).

Andrle, V., *Workers in Stalin's Russia: Industrialisation and Social Change in a Planned Economy* (Hemel Hempstead, 1988).

Apter, D., 'The Mobilization System as a Modernization Prototype', in Apter, *The Politics of Modernization* (Chicago, 1967), 357–90.

Avineri, S., *The Social and Political Thought of Karl Marx* (Cambridge, 1968).

Avrich, P., *Kronshtadt, 1917* (Princeton, 1970).

—— 'Bolshevik Opposition to Lenin: G. I. Miasnikov and the Workers' Group', *RR*, 43 (1984), 1–29.

Bachman, D., *Bureaucracy, Economy and Leadership in China. The Institutional Origins of the Great Leap Forward* (Cambridge, 1991).

Bailes, K., 'Alexei Gastev and the Soviet Controversy over Taylorism, 1918–1924', *SS*, 29 (1977), 373–94.

—— *Technology and Society under Lenin and Stalin: Origins of the Soviet Technical Intelligentsia, 1917–1941* (Princeton, 1978).

Baker, K., *Inventing the French Revolution. Essays on French Political Culture in the Eighteenth Century* (Cambridge, 1990).

—— 'A Foucauldian French Revolution', in J. Goldstein (ed.), *Foucault and the Writing of History* (Oxford, 1994), 187–205.

Bakhurst, D., *Consciousness and Revolution in Soviet Philosophy. From the Bolsheviks to Evald Ilyenkov* (Cambridge, 1991).

Becker, J., *Hungry Ghosts. China's Secret Famine* (London, 1996).

Beecher, J., *Charles Fourier. The Visionary and his World* (Berkeley, 1986).

Beiser, F., *Enlightenment, Revolution and Romanticism. The Genesis of Modern German Political Thought, 1790–1800* (Cambridge, Mass., 1992).

Belykh, A. A., 'A. A. Bogdanov's Theory of Equilibrium and the Economic Discussion of the 1920s', *SS*, 42 (1990), 571–82.

Benvenuti, F., *The Bolsheviks and the Red Army, 1918–1922* (Cambridge, 1988).

—— 'Industry and Purge in the Donbass', *E–AS*, 45 (1993), 57–78.

—— 'A Stalinist Victim of Stalinism. "Sergo" Ordzhonikidze', in J. Cooper, M. Perrie, and E. A. Rees (eds.), *Soviet History, 1917–1953* (Basingstoke, 1995), 134–57.

Berki, R. N., *Socialism* (Letchworth, 1975).

Biggart, J., 'Bukharin and the Origins of the "Proletarian Culture" Debate', *SS*, 39 (1987), 229–46.

—— 'Bukharin's Theory of Cultural Revolution', in A. Kemp-Welch (ed.), *The Ideas of Nikolai Bukharin* (Oxford, 1992), 131–48.

Black, C., 'Party Crisis and the Party Shop Floor: Krasnyi Putilovets and the Leningrad Opposition', *E–AS*, 46 (1994), 107–26.

Boffa, G., *The Stalin Phenomenon*, trans. by N. Fersen (Ithaca, NY, 1992).

Brandenberger, D., *National Bolshevism. Stalinist Mass Culture and the Formation of Modern Russian National Identity, 1931–1956* (Cambridge, Mass., 2002).

—— and Dubrovsky, A. M., ' 'The People Need a Tsar': The Emergence of National Bolshevism as Stalinist Ideology, 1931–1941', *E–AS*, 50 (1998), 873–92.

Brent, J., and Naumov, V. P., *Stalin's Last Crime. The Doctors' Plot* (London, 2003).

Brinton, M., *The Bolsheviks and Workers' Control* (London, 1970).

Brooks, J., 'Official Xenophobia and Popular Cosmopolitanism in Early Soviet Russia', *AHR*, 97 (1992), 1431–48.

—— *Thank You, Comrade Stalin! Soviet Public Culture from Revolution to Cold War* (Princeton, 2000).

Brovkin, V., *The Mensheviks after October. Socialist Opposition and the Rise of Dictatorship* (Ithaca, NY, 1987).

—— *Behind the Front Lines in the Russian Civil War. Political Parties and Social Movements in Russia, 1918–1922* (Princeton, 1994).

—— *Russia after Lenin. Politics, Culture and Society, 1921–1929* (London, 1998).

Brown, E. J., *The Proletarian Episode in Russian Literature, 1928–1932* (New York, 1953).

Calhoun, C., *The Question of Class Struggle. Social Foundations of Popular Radicalism during the Industrial Revolution* (Oxford, 1982).

Campbell, J., *Joy in Work, German Work* (Princeton, 1989).

Caplan, J., *Government without Administration. State and Civil Service in Weimar and Nazi Germany* (Oxford, 1988).

Carr, E. H., *The Bolshevik Revolution, 1917–1923*, 3 vols. (London, 1966–71).

—— *Socialism in One Country, 1924–1926*, 3 vols. (London, 1978).

—— and Davies, R. W., *Foundations of a Planned Economy, 1926–1929*, 2 vols. (London, 1971).

Cassiday, J., *The Enemy on Trial. Early Soviet Courts on Stage and Screen* (DeKalb, 2001).

Chan, A. L. *Mao's Crusade. Politics and Policy Implementation in China's Great Leap Forward* (Oxford, 2001).

Chang, P., *Power and Policy in China* (University Park, 1975).

Chase, W. J., *Workers, Society and the Soviet State. Labor and Life in Moscow, 1918–1929* (Urbana and Chicago, 1990).

Churchich, N., *Marxism and Morality. A Critical Examination of Marxist Ethics* (Cambridge, 1994).

Clark, K., *The Soviet Novel. History as Ritual* (Chicago, 1981).

—— 'The "Quiet Revolution" in Russian Intellectual Life', in S. Fitzpatrick, A. Rabinowitch, and Richard Stites (eds.), *Russia in the Era of NEP* (Bloomington, 1991), 210–30.

—— *Petersburg. Crucible of Cultural Revolution* (Cambridge, Mass., 1995).

Claudin Urondo, C., *Lenin and the Cultural Revolution*, trans. by Brian Dean (Sussex, 1977).

Clements, B. E., *Bolshevik Feminist. The Life of Aleksandra Kollontai* (Bloomington, 1979).

Clowes, E., 'Gorky, Nietzsche and God-Building', in N. Luker (ed.), *Fifty Years On. Gorky and his Time* (Nottingham, 1987), 127–44.

Cohen, G., 'Bourgeois and Proletarian', in S. Avineri (ed.), *Marx's Socialism* (New York, 1973), 101–25.

Cohen, S. 'Bolshevism and Stalinism', in R. Tucker (ed.), *Stalinism. Essays in Historical Interpretation* (New York, 1977), 3–30.

—— *Bukharin and the Bolshevik Revolution* (Oxford, 1980).

—— *Rethinking the Soviet Experience. Politics and History since 1917* (Oxford, 1985).

Conquest, R., *The Great Terror. A Reassessment* (London, 1990).

Courtois, S., Werth, N., Panne, J.-L., Paczowski, A., Bartosek, K., and Margolin, J.-L., *The Black Book of Communism. Crimes, Terror, Repression*, trans. by J. Murphy and M. Kramer (Cambridge, Mass., 1999).

Daniels, R., *The Nature of Communism* (New York, 1962).

—— *The Conscience of the Revolution. Communist Opposition in Soviet Russia* (New York, 1969).

—— *Trotsky, Stalin and Socialism* (Boulder, 1991).

Danilov, V. P., *Rural Russia under the New Regime*, trans. by O. Figes (Bloomington, 1988).

David-Fox, M., *Revolution of the Mind. Higher Learning among the Bolsheviks, 1918–1929* (Ithaca, NY, 1997).

—— 'What is Cultural Revolution?', *RR*, 58 (1999), 181–201.

Davies, R. W., *The Socialist Offensive. The Collectivisation of Soviet Agriculture 1929–1930* (London, 1980).

—— *The Soviet Collective Farm, 1929–1930* (London, 1980).

—— 'The Socialist Market: A Debate in Soviet Industry, 1932–33', *SR*, 42 (1984), 201–23.

—— *The Soviet Economy in Turmoil, 1929–1930* (Basingstoke, 1989).

Davies, R. W., and Khlevniuk, O. V., 'Gosplan', in E. A. Rees (ed.), *Decision-Making in the Stalinist Command Economy, 1932–37* (Basingstoke, 1997), 32–56.

—— 'Stakhanovism and the Soviet Economy', *E–AS*, 54 (2002), 867–903.

Davies, S., 'Propaganda and Popular Opinion in Soviet Russia, 1934–1941', D.Phil. dissertation, University of Oxford, 1994.

—— *Popular Opinion in Stalin's Russia. Terror, Propaganda and Dissent, 1934–1941* (Cambridge, 1997).

Day, R., *Leon Trotsky and the Politics of Economic Isolation* (Cambridge, 1973).

—— 'The Myth of the "Super-Industrialiser": Trotsky's Economic Policies in the 1920s', in H. Ticktin and M. Cox (eds.), *The Ideas of Leon Trotsky* (London, 1990).

Deutscher, I., *The Prophet Armed* (New York, 1965).

—— *The Prophet Unarmed. Trotsky 1921–1929* (Oxford, 1970).

Di Biagio, A., 'Moscow, the Comintern and the War Scare, 1926–28', in S. Pons and A. Romano (eds.), *Russia in the Age of Wars, 1914–1945* (Milan, 2000), 83–102.

Dirks, N., *Castes of Mind. Colonialism and the Making of Modern India* (Princeton, 2001).

Dirlik, A., *The Origins of Chinese Communism* (Oxford, 1989).

Dittmer, L., *Liu Shao-ch'i and the Chinese Cultural Revolution. The Politics of Mass Criticism* (Berkeley, 1974).

Djilas, M., *The New Class* (New York, 1957).

Donald, M., *Marxism and Revolution. Karl Kautsky and the Russian Marxists, 1900–1924* (New Haven, 1993).

Draper, H., *Karl Marx's Theory of Revolution.* Vol. 2: *The Politics of Social Classes* (New York, 1978).

Duskin, J., *Stalinist Reconstruction and the Confirmation of a New Elite, 1945–1953* (Basingstoke, 2001).

Eley, G., 'History With the Politics Left Out – Again?', *RR*, 45 (1986).

Eliaeson, S., 'Weber's Politics in their German Context', in S. Turner (ed.), *The Cambridge Companion to Weber* (Cambridge, 2000), 131–48.

Engelstein, L., 'Culture, Culture Everywhere: Interpretations of Modern Russia Across the 1991 Divide', *Kritika*, 2 (2001), 363–93.

Erlich, A., *The Soviet Industrialization Debate, 1924–1928* (Cambridge, Mass., 1960).

Farber, S., *Before Stalinism. The Rise and Fall of Soviet Democracy* (Oxford, 1990).

Fainsod, M., *How Russia is Ruled* (Cambridge, Mass., 1953).

—— *Smolensk under Soviet Rule* (London, 1989).

Ferdinand, P., 'Bukharin and the New Economic Policy', in A. Kemp-Welch (ed.), *The Ideas of Nikolai Bukharin* (Oxford, 1992), 40–68.

Ferro, M., *October 1917. A Social History of the Russian Revolution*, trans. by N. Stone (London, 1980).

Figes, O., *Peasant Russia, Civil War. The Volga Countryside in Revolution, 1917–1921* (Oxford, 1990).

—— and Kolonitskii, B., *Interpreting the Russian Revolution. The Language and Symbols of 1917* (New Haven, 1999).

Filtzer, D., *Soviet Workers and Stalinist Industrialization: The Formation of Modern Soviet Production Relations, 1928–1941* (London, 1986).

Fitzpatrick S., 'The "Soft" Line on Culture and its Enemies: Soviet Cultural Policy 1922–1927', *SR*, 33 (1974), 267–87.

—— (ed.), *Cultural Revolution in Russia, 1928–1931* (Bloomington, 1978).

—— *Education and Social Mobility in the Soviet Union, 1921–1934* (Cambridge, 1979).

—— 'Ordzhonikidze's Takeover of Vesenkha: a Case-study in Soviet Bureaucratic Politics', *SS*, 37 (1985), 153–72.

—— 'Workers against Bosses: The Impact of the Great Purges on Labor–Management relations', in L. Siegelbaum and R. Suny (eds.) *Making Workers Soviet. Power, Class and Identity* (Ithaca, NY, 1994), 311–40.

—— *Stalin's Peasants. Resistance and Survival in the Russian Village after Collectivization* (Oxford, 1994).

—— *Everyday Stalinism. Ordinary Life in Extraordinary Times: Soviet Russia in the 1930s* (Oxford, 1999).

—— (ed.), *Stalinism. New Directions* (London, 2000).

—— 'Ascribing Class: The Construction of Social Identity in Soviet Russia', in Fitzpatrick, *Stalinism, New Directions* (London, 2000), 20–46.

Fitzpatrick S., and Gellately R. (eds.), *Accusatory Practices. Denunciation in Modern European History, 1789–1989* (Chicago, 1996).

Fleischer, H., *Marxism and History*, trans. by E. Mosbacher (London, 1973).

Freeden, M., *Ideologies and Political Theory. A Conceptual Approach* (Oxford, 1996).

—— *Ideology. A Very Short Introduction* (Oxford, 2003).

Freeze, G., 'The Soslovie (Estate) Paradigm and Russian Social History', *AHR*, 91 (1986), 11–36.

Geary, D., *Karl Kautsky* (Manchester, 1987).

Gelb, M., ' "Karelian Fever": The Finnish Immigrant Community during Stalin's Purges', *E–AS*, 45 (1993), 1091–116.

—— 'An Early Soviet Ethnic Deportation: The Far Eastern Koreans', *RR*, 54 (1995), 389–412.

Getty, J. A., *The Origins of the Great Purges. The Soviet Communist Party Reconsidered, 1933–1938* (Cambridge, 1985).

—— 'State and Society under Stalin: Constitutions and Elections in the 1930s', *SR*, 50 (1991), 18–35.

—— 'The Politics of Repression Revisited', in J. A. Getty and R. Manning (eds.), *Stalinist Terror, New Perspectives* (Cambridge, 1993).

—— ' "Excesses are not Permitted": Mass Terror and Stalinist Governance in the Late 1930s', *RR*, 61 (2002), 113–38.

—— *Pragmatists and Puritans. The Rise and Fall of the Party Control Commission*, Carl Beck Papers (1998), 1208.

—— and Chase, W. J., 'Patterns of Repression among the Soviet Elite', in J. A. Getty and R. Manning (eds.), *Stalinist Terror. New Perspectives* (Cambridge, 1993), 225–46.

—— and Naumov, O. V., *The Road to Terror. Stalin and the Self-Destruction of the Bolsheviks, 1932–1939* (New Haven, 1999).

—— Rittersporn, G., and Zemskov, V., 'Victims of the Soviet Penal System in the Prewar Years: A First approach on the Basis of Archival Evidence', *AHR*, 98 (1993), 1017–49.

Getzler, I., *Kronstadt, 1917–1921* (Cambridge, 1983).

Gilbert, A., *Marx's Politics. Communists and Citizens* (Oxford, 1981).

Gill, G., 'The Soviet Leader Cult. Reflections on the Structure of Leadership in the Soviet Union', *BJPS*, 10 (1980), 167–86.

—— *The Origins of the Stalinist Political System* (Cambridge, 1990).

Gispen, K., *Poems in Steel. National Socialism and the Politics of Inventing from meimar to Bonn* (New York, 2002).

Gooderham, P., 'Kirov's Party Organisation: Developments in the Leningrad Party Organization, 1928–1934', unpublished Discussion Paper, CREES, University of Birmingham, 1983.

Gorlizki, Y., 'Party Revivalism and the Death of Stalin', *SR*, 54 (1995), 1–22.

Gouldner, A., *For Sociology* (London, 1973).

—— *The Two Marxisms. Contradictions and Anomalies in the Development of Theory* (London, 1980).

Granick, D., *Management of the Industrial Firm in the USSR* (New York, 1954).

Graziosi, A., ' "Building the First System of State Industry in History". Piatakov's Vesenkha and the Crisis of NEP', *CMRS*, 32 (1991), 539–80.

—— 'At the Roots of Soviet Industrial Relations and Practices. Piatakov's Donbass in 1921', *CMR*, 36 (1995), 95–138.

Greenfeld, L., *Nationalism. Five Roads to Modernity* (Cambridge, Mass., 1992).

—— *The Spirit of Capitalism. Nationalism and Economic Growth* (Cambridge, Mass., 2001).

Groys, B., 'The Birth of Socialist Realism from the Spirit of the Russian Avant-Garde', in J. Bowlt and O. Match (eds.), *Laboratory of Dreams. The Russian Avant-Garde and Cultural Experiment* (Stanford, 1996).

Guranov, A. E. (ed.), *Repressii protiv poliakov i pol'skikh grazhdan*, vyp. 1 (Moscow, 1997).

Hagenloh, P., 'Socially Harmful Elements and the Great Terror', in S. Fitzpatrick (ed.), *Stalinism. New Directions* (London, 2000), 286–308.

Haimson, L., *The Russian Marxists and the Origins of Bolshevism* (Boston, 1955).

Halfin, I., *From Darkness to Light. Class, Consciousness and Salvation in Soviet Russia* (Pittsburgh, 2000).

—— 'Looking into the Oppositionists' Souls: Inquisition Communist Style', *RR*, 60 (2001), 316–39.

—— 'Between Instinct and Mind: The Bolshevik View of the Proletarian Self', *SR*, 62 (2003), 34–40.

—— 'The Demonization of the Opposition. Stalinist Memory and the "Communist Archive" at Leningrad Communist University', *Kritika*, 2 (2003), 45–80.

Halfin, I., and Hellbeck, J., 'Rethinking the Stalinist Subject: Stephen Kotkin's "Magnetic Mountain" and the State of Soviet Historical Studies', *JGO*, 44 (1996), 456–63.

Hanson, S., *Time and Revolution. Marxism and the Design of Soviet Institutions* (Chapel Hill, 1997).

Harding, H., *Organizing China. The Problem of Bureaucracy* (Stanford, 1981).

—— 'The Chinese State in Crisis, 1966–1969', in R. MacFarquhar, *The Politics of China. The Eras of Mao and Deng*, 2nd edn. (Cambridge, 1997), 148–247.

Harding, N., *Lenin's Political Thought. Theory and Practice in the Democratic and Socialist Revolutions* (London, 1983).

—— 'Socialism, Society and the Organic Labour State', in N. Harding (ed.), *The State in Socialist Society* (Basingstoke, 1984), 1–50.

—— 'Bukharin and the State', in A. Kemp-Welch, *The Ideas of Nikolai Bukharin* (Oxford, 1992), 85–112.

—— *Leninism* (Basingstoke, 1996).

Harrington, A., *Reenchanted Science. Holism in German Culture from Wilhelm II to Hitler* (Princeton, 1996).

Harris, J., *The Great Urals. Regionalism and the Evolution of the Soviet System* (Ithaca, NY, 1999).

Harriss, J., 'The Origins of the Conflict between Malenkov and Zhdanov, 1939–1941', *SR*, 35 (1976), 287–303.

Haslam, J., *The Soviet Union and the Struggle for Collective Security in Europe, 1933–39* (London, 1984).

Hatch, J. 'The Politics of Industrial efficiency During NEP: The 1926 "*Rezhim ekonomii*" Campaign in Moscow', Paper presented at the IV World Congress for Soviet and East European Studies, Harrogate, 1990.

Hedeler, W., 'Ezhov's Scenario for the Great Terror and the Falsified Record of the Third Moscow Show Trial', in B. McLoughlin and K. McDermott, *Stalin's Terror. High Politics and Mass Repression in the Soviet Union* (Basingstoke, 2002), 34–55.

Hellbeck, J., 'Writing in the Age of Terror: Alexander Afinogenov's Diary of 1937', in L. Engelstein and S. Sandler (eds.), *Self and Story in Russian History* (Ithaca, NY, 2000), 69–93.

Herf, J., *Reactionary Modernism. Technology, Culture and Politics in the Third Reich* (Cambridge, 1984).

Himmer, R., 'On the Origin and Significance of the Name "Stalin" ', *RR*, 45 (1986), 269–86.

—— 'The Transition from War Communism to the New Economic Policy. An Analysis of Stalin's Views', *RR*, 53 (1994), 515–29.

Hoffmann, D., 'The Great Terror at a Local Level: Purges in Moscow Factories, 1936–1938', in S. Fitzpatrick, *Stalinism. New Directions* (London, 2000), 163–7.

—— 'European Modernity and Soviet Socialism', in D. Hoffmann and Y. Kotsonis (eds.), *Russian Modernity: Politics, Knowledge, Practices* (Basingstoke, 1999), 245–60.

Holmes, L., *For the Revolution Redeemed. The Workers' Opposition in the Bolshevik Party, 1919–1921*, The Carl Beck Papers in Russian and East European Studies (1990).

Holquist, P., 'To Count, to Extract, and to Exterminate. Population Statistics and Population Politics in Late Imperial and Soviet Russia', in R. G. Suny and T. Martin (eds.), *A State of Nations. Empire and Nation-Making in the Age of Lenin and Stalin* (New York and Oxford, 2001), 111–44.

—— *Making War, Forging Revolution. Russia's Continuum of Crisis, 1914–1921* (Cambridge, Mass., 2002).

Horne, J., 'Mobilizing for Total War', in Horne. (ed.), *State, Society and Mobilization in Europe during the First World War* (Cambridge, 1997), 1–17.

Hough J., and Fainsod, M., *How the Soviet Union is Governed* (Cambridge, Mass., 1979).

Hughes, J., *Stalin, Siberia and the Crisis of the New Economic Policy* (Cambridge, 1991).

Huskey, E., *Russian Lawyers and the Soviet State. The Origins and Development of the Soviet Bar, 1917–1939* (Princeton, 1986).

—— 'A Framework for the Analysis of Soviet Law', *RR*, 50 (1991), 153–70.

Ikonnikov, S. N., *Sozdanie i deiatel'nost' ob"edinennykh organov TsKK-RKI v 1923–1934 gg.* (Moscow, 1971).

Ingerflom, C., *Le citoyen impossible. Les racines russes du Leninisme* (Paris, 1988).

Istoriia Kommunisticheskoi Partii Sovetskogo Soiuza, 6 vols. (Moscow, 1964–1980).

Janos, A., *Politics and Paradigms. Changing Theories of Change in Social Science* (Stanford, 1986).

Jansen, M., *A Show Trial Under Lenin. The Trial of the Socialist Revolutionaries. Moscow, 1923* (The Hague, 1982).

Johansson, K., *Aleksej Gastev. Proletarian Bard of the Machine Age* (Stockholm, 1993).

Joravsky, D., *Soviet Marxism and Natural Science, 1917–1932* (New York, 1961).

Josephson, P., *Physics and Politics in Soviet Russia* (Berkeley, 1991).

Jowitt, K., *New World Disorder: The Leninist Extinction* (Berkeley, 1992).

Kaplan, F., *Bolshevik Ideology and the Ethics of Soviet Labor, 1917–1920. The Formative Years* (London, 1969).

Kaple, D., *Dream of a Red Factory. The Legacy of High Stalinism* (Oxford, 1994).

Kemp-Welch, A., *Stalin and the Literary Intelligentsia* (Basingstoke, 1991).

—— (ed.), *The Ideas of Nikolai Bukharin* (Oxford, 1992).

Kershaw, I., *The Nazi Dictatorship. Problems and Perspectives of Interpretation*, 3rd edn. (London 1997).

Khamovich, E. M., 'Iz istorii bor'by partii za rezhim ekonomii', *VI KPSS*, 12 (1984), 66–74.

Kharkhordin, O., *The Collective and the Individual in Russia. A Study of Practices*, (Berkeley, 1999).

Khlevniuk, O. V., *1937–i: Stalin, NKVD i sovetskoe obshchestvo* (Moscow, 1992).

—— *Stalin i Ordzhonikidze. Konflikty v Politbiuro v 30–e gody* (Moscow, 1993).

—— 'The Objectives of the Great Terror, 1937–1938', in E. A. Rees, J. Cooper, and M. Perrie, *Soviet History, 1917–53 : Essays in Honour of R. W. Davies* (Basingstoke, 1995), 158–76.

—— *Politbiuro. Mekhanizmy politicheskoi vlasti v 1930–e gody* (Moscow, 1996).

—— 'The People's Commissariat of Heavy Industry', in E. A. Rees (ed.), *Decision- Making in the Stalinist Command Economy, 1933–37* (Basingstoke, 1997), 94–123.

Khlevniuk, O. V., 'Les Méchanismes de la "Grande Terreur" des années 1937–1938 au Turkmenistan', *CMR*, 39 (1998), 197–208.

—— 'The First Generation of Stalinist "Party Generals" ', in E. A. Rees (ed.), *Centre–Local Relations in the Stalinist State, 1928–1941* (Basingstoke, 2002), 37–54.

—— 'The Reasons for the "Great Terror": The Foreign Political Aspect', in S. Pons and A. Romano (eds.), *Russia in the Age of Wars, 1914–1945* (Milan, 2000), 159–70.

—— and Davies, R. W., 'The End of Rationing in the Soviet Union, 1934–5, *E–AS*, 51 (1999), 557–610.

Kingston-Mann, E., *In Search of the True West. Culture, Economics, and Problems of Economic Development* (Princeton, 1999).

Kirilina, A., *Rikoshet, ili skol'ko chelovek bylo ubito vystrelom v Smol'nom* (St Petersburg, 1993).

Kislitsyn, S., *Shakhtinskoe delo. Nachalo stalinskikh repressii protiv nauchno-tekhnicheskoi intelligentsii v SSSR* (Rostov on Don, 1993).

Kiteme, B., 'The Cult of Stalin. National Power and the Soviet Party-State', Ph.D. dissertation, Columbia University, 1989.

Knei-Paz, B., *The Social and Political Thought of Leon Trotsky* (Oxford, 1975).

Knight, A., *Who Killed Kirov? The Kremlin's Greatest Mystery* (New York, 1999).

Kodin, E. V., *Stalinizm v rossiiskoi provintsii: smolenskie arhivnye dokumenty v prochtenii zarubezhnykh i rossiiskikh istorikov* (Smolensk, 1999).

Kolakowski, L., 'Marxist Roots of Stalinism', in R. Tucker (ed.), *Stalinism. Essays in Historical Interpretation* (New York, 1977), 283–98.

—— *Main Currents of Marxism*, 3 vols., trans. by P. S. Falla (Oxford, 1978).

Kolonitskii, B., 'Antibourgeois propaganda and anti-"burzhui" consciousness in 1917', *RR*, 53 (1997), 183–96.

Konecny, P., 'Chaos on Campus. The 1924 Student *Proverka* in Leningrad', *E–AS*, 46 (1994), 617–35.

Kotkin, S., *Magnetic Mountain. Stalinism as a Civilization* (Berkeley, 1995).

—— '1991 and the Russian Revolution: Sources, Conceptual Categories, Analytical Frameworks', *JMH*, 70 (1998), 384–425.

—— 'Modern Times. The Soviet Union and the Inter-war Conjuncture', *Kritika*, 2 (2001), 111–64.

Kowalski, R., *The Bolshevik Party in Conflict. The Left Communist Opposition of 1918* (Basingstoke, 1991).

Kraus, R., *Class Conflict in Chinese Socialism* (New York, 1981).

Krementsov, N., *Stalinist Science* (Princeton, 1997).

Krylova, A., 'Beyond the Spontaneity–Consciousness Paradigm: "Class Instinct" as a Promising Category of Political Analysis', *SR*, 62 (2003), 1–23.

Kuleshov, S. V, Volobuev, O. V., Pivovar, E. I., et al. (eds.), *Nashe ote-chestvo. Opyt politicheskoi istorii* (Moscow, 1991).

Kuromiya, H., '*Edinonachalie* and the Soviet Industrial Manager, 1928–1937', *SS*, 36 (1984), 185–204.

—— *Stalin's Industrial Revolution: Politics and Workers, 1928–1932* (Cambridge, 1988).

Lee, H. Y., *The Politics of the Chinese Cultural Revolution. A Case Study* (Berkeley, 1978).

Leggett, G., *The Cheka. Lenin's Political Police* (Oxford, 1986).

Lewin, M., *Russian Peasants and Soviet Power. A Study of Collectivization* (New York, 1968).

—— *Political Undercurrents in Soviet Economic Debates* (London, 1975).

—— *Lenin's Last Struggle* (London, 1975).

—— *The Making of the Soviet System. Essays in the Social History of Inter-War Russia* (Oxford, 1985).

Leiberthal, K., 'The Great Leap Forward and the Split in the Yan'an Leadership, 1958–65', in R. MacFarquhar, *The Politics of China. The Eras of Mao and Deng*, 2nd edn. (Cambridge, 1997), 87–147.

Lih, L., 'The Bolshevik Sowing Committees of 1920, Apotheosis of War Communism?', Carl Beck Papers in Russian and East European Studies, 803, (1990).

—— *Bread and Authority in Russia, 1917–1921* (Berkeley, 1990).

—— 'The Political Testament of Lenin and Bukharin and the Meaning of NEP', *SR*, 50 (1991), 241–52.

—— 'The Mystery of the *ABC*', *SR*, 56 (1997), 50–72.

—— 'How a Founding Document was Found; or, One Hundred Years of Lenin's *What is to be Done?*', *Kritika*, 4 (2003), 5–49.

Lih, L., Naumov, O. V., and Khlevniuk, O. V. (eds.), *Stalin's Letters to Molotov* (New Haven, 1995).

Lovell, D., *From Marx to Lenin. An Evaluation of Marx's Responsibility for Soviet Authoritarianism* (Cambridge, 1984).

—— *Marx's Proletariat. The Making of a Myth* (London, 1988).

Lu, Xiaobo, *Cadres and Corruption. The Organizational Involution of the Chinese Communist Party* (Stanford, 2000).

Luk, M., *The Origins of Chinese Bolshevism. An Ideology in the Making, 1920–1928* (Hong Kong, 1990).

Lukes, S., *Marxism and Morality* (Oxford 1985).

Lupher, M., *Power Restructuring in China and Russia* (Boulder, 1996).

McAuley, M., *Bread and Justice. State and Society in Petrograd, 1917–1922* (Oxford, 1991).

McCagg, W. O., *Stalin Embattled, 1943–8* (Detroit, 1976).

McClelland, J. C., 'Utopianism Versus Revolutionary Heroism in Bolshevik Policy: The Proletarian Culture Debate', *SR*, 30 (1971).

McDaniel, T., *Autocracy, Capitalism and Revolution in Russia* (Berkeley, 1988).

MacFarquhar, R., *The Origins of the Cultural Revolution*, vol. 1: *Contradictions among the People, 1956–7* (New York, 1974).

—— *The Origins of the Cultural Revolution*, vol. 2: *The Great Leap Forward, 1958–1960* (Oxford, 1983).

—— *The Origins of the Chinese Cultural Revolution*, vol. 3: *The Coming of the Cataclysm, 1961–1966* (Oxford, 1997).

—— (ed.), *The Politics of China. The Eras of Mao and Deng*, 2nd edn. (Cambridge, 1997).

McLellan, D., *Marxism after Marx. An Introduction* (London, 1979).

McLoughlin, B., 'Mass Operations of the NKVD, 1937–8: A Survey', in B. McLoughlin and K. McDermott, *Stalin's Terror. High Politics and Mass Repression in the Soviet Union* (Basingstoke, 2002).

Macrae, D., 'Populism as an Ideology', in G. Ionescu and E. Gellner (eds.), *Populism. Its Meanings and National Characteristics* (London, 1969).

Maleiko, L. A., 'Iz istorii razvitiia apparata partiinykh organov', *VI KPSS*, 2 (1976), 111–22.

Malia, M., *The Soviet Tragedy* (New York, 1994).

Malle, S., *The Economic Organization of War Communism, 1918–1921* (Cambridge, 1985).

Mally, L., *Revolutionary Acts. Amateur Theatre and the Soviet State, 1917–1938* (Ithaca, 2000).

Mandel, D., *The Petrograd Workers and the Soviet Seizure of Power. From the July Days to July 1918* (London, 1984).

Manning, R., 'Massovaia operatsiia protiv "kulakov i prestupnykh elementov": apogei Velikoi Chistki na Smolenshchine', in E. V. Kodin (ed.), *Stalinizm v rossiiskoi provintsii: smolenskie arhivnye dokumenty v prochtenii zarubezhnykh i rossiiskikh istorikov* (Smolensk, 1999), 230–54.

—— 'The Soviet Economic Crisis of 1936–1940 and the Great Purges', in J. A. Getty and R. Manning (eds.), *Stalinist Terror. New Perspectives* (Cambridge, 1993).

Marot, J. E., 'Alexander Bogdanov, Vpered and the Role of the Intellectual in the Workers' Movement', *RR*, 49 (1990), 241–64.

Martin, T., 'An Affirmative Action Empire: Ethnicity and the Soviet State, 1923–1938', Ph.D. dissertation, University of Chicago, 1996.

—— 'The Origins of Soviet Ethnic Cleansing', *JMH*, 70 (1998), 813–61.

—— 'Modernization or Neo-traditionalism? Ascribed Nationality and Soviet Primordialism', in S. Fitzpatrick (ed.), *Stalinism. New Directions* (Cambridge, 2000), 348–67.

—— *The Affirmative Action Empire. Nations and Nationalism in the Soviet Union, 1923–1939* (Ithaca, 2001).

Maslov, N. N., 'Kratkii kurs istorii VKP(b)-entsiklopediia kul'ta lichnosti Stalina', in Iu.P. Senokosov (ed.), *Surovaia drama naroda: Uchenye i publitsisty o prirode stalinizma* (Moscow, 1989).

—— 'Iz istorii rasprostraneniia stalinizma', *VI KPSS*, 7 (1990), 98–101.

Mayer, A. J., *The Furies. Violence and Terror in the French and Russian Revolutions* (Princeton, 2000).

Mayer, R., 'The Status of a Classic Text: Lenin's *What is to be Done?* after 1902', *History of European Ideas*, 22 (1996), 307–20.

Medvedev, R., *Let History Judge. The Origins and Consequences of Stalinism* (London, 1972).

Megill, A., *Karl Marx and the Burden of Reason. (Why Marx Rejected Politics and the Market)* (Oxford, 2002).

Meisner, M., 'Leninism and Maoism: Some Populist Perspectives on Marxism–Leninism in China', in M. Meisner, *Marxism, Maoism and Utopianism* (Madison, 1982).

Mendel, A., *Dilemmas of Progress in Tsarist Russia. Legal Marxism and Legal Populism* (Cambridge, Mass., 1961).

Merridale, C., *Moscow Politics and the Rise of Stalin. The Communist Party in the Capital, 1925–1932* (Basingstoke, 1990).

Metcalf, T., *The New Cambridge History of India*, Vol. 3, Pt. 4. *Ideologies of the Raj* (Cambridge, 1994).

Murphy, K., 'Opposition at the Local Level. A Case study of the Hammer and Sickle Factory', *E–AS*, 53 (2001), 329–50.

Naiman, E., *Sex in Public. The Incarnation of Early Soviet Ideology* (Princeton, 1997).

Nove, A., *An Economic History of the USSR* (London, 1969).

—— 'O sud'bakh NEPa', *VI*, 8 (1989), 172–6.

Ocherki istorii Leningradskoi organizatsii KPSS (Leningrad, 1968).

Ocherki istorii Moskovskoi organizatsii KPSS (Moscow, 1983).

Overy, R. J., *War and Economy in the Third Reich* (Oxford, 1996).

Patenaude, B., 'Peasants into Russians: The Utopian Essence of War Communism', *RR*, 54 (1995), 552–70.

Pavliuchenkov, S., *Voennyi kommunizm v Rossii. Vlast' i massy* (Moscow, 1997).

Perry, E., and Li Xun, *Proletarian Power. Shanghai in the Cultural Revolution* (Boulder, 1997).

Petrov N. V., and Roginskii A. B., ' "Pol'skaia operatsiia" NKVD 1937–1938 gg.', in A. E. Guranov (ed.), *Repressii protiv poliakov i pol'skikh grazhdan*, vyp. 1 (Moscow, 1997).

Polan, A., *Lenin and the End of Politics* (London, 1984).

Pollock, E., 'Conversations with Stalin on Questions of Political Economy', *Cold War International History Project*, Working Paper No. 33, July 2001.

—— 'Stalin, Coryphaeus of Science', unpublished paper, January 2003.

Pons, S., *Stalin and the Inevitable War, 1936–1941* (London, 2002).

—— and Romano, A. (eds.), *Russia in the Age of Wars, 1914–1945* (Milan, 2000).

Popov, V. P., 'Gosudarstvennyi terror v sovetskoi Rossii, 1923–1953 gg. (istochniki i ikh interpretatsiia)', *Otechestvennyi arkhivy*, 2 (1992), 20–32.

Pospielovsky, A., 'Strikes and Worker Militancy during NEP', CREES paper, University of Birmingham, March 1995.

Priestland, D., 'Bolshevik Ideology and the Debate over Party–State Relations, 1918–1921', *Revolutionary Russia*, 10 (1997), 37–61.

Rapoport, Y., *The Doctors' Plot of 1953* trans. by N. A. Perova and R. S. Bobrova (Cambridge, Mass., 1991).

Rattansi, A., *Marx and the Division of Labour* (London, 1982).

Rees, E. A., *State Control in Soviet Russia, 1921–1934* (London, 1987).

—— *Stalinism and Soviet Rail Transport, 1928–1941* (Basingstoke, 1995).

—— (ed.), *Decision-Making in the Stalinist Command Economy, 1932–37* (Basingstoke, 1997).

—— 'The Great Terror: Suicide or Murder?', *RR*, 59 (2000), 446–50.

—— *Centre–Local Relations in the Stalinist State, 1928–1941* (Basingstoke, 2002).

—— 'The Great Purges and the XVIII Party Congress of 1939', in Rees, *Centre–Local Relations in the Stalinist State, 1928–1941* (Basingstoke, 2002), 191–211.

Reiman, M., *The Birth of Stalinism*, trans. by G. Saunders (Bloomington, 1987).

Remington, T., *Building Socialism in Bolshevik Russia. Ideology and Industrial Organization, 1917–1921* (Pittsburgh, 1984).

Riasanovsky, N. V., *The Teaching of Charles Fourier* (Berkeley, 1969).

Rigby, S., *Engels and the Formation of Marxism. History, Dialectic and Revolution* (Manchester, 1992).

—— 'Engels after Marx: History', in M. B. Steger and T. Carver (eds.), *Engels after Marx* (Manchester, 1999).

Rigby, T. H., *Lenin's Government: Sovnarkom 1917–1922* (Cambridge, 1979).

—— 'Early Provincial Cliques and the Rise of Stalin', *SS*, 1 (1981), 3–28.

Rittersporn, G., *Simplifications Staliniennes et complications Sovietiques. Tensions sociales et conflits politiques en URSS, 1933–1953* (Paris, 1988).

—— *Stalinist Simplifications and Soviet Complications. Social Tensions and Political Conflicts in the USSR, 1933–1953* (Chur, 1991).

Roberts, P., ' "War Communism": A Reexamination', *SR*, 29 (1970), 238–61.

Robin, R., *Socialist Realism. An Impossible Aesthetic*, trans. by C. Porter (Stanford, 1992).

Roeder, P., *Red Sunset. The Failure of Soviet Politics* (Princeton, 1993).

Rosefielde, S., 'Stalinism in Post-Communist Perspective. New Evidence on Killings, Forced Labour and Economic Growth in the 1930s', *E–AS*, 46 (1996), 959–87.

Rosenberg, W., 'The Social Background to Tsektran', in D. Koenker, W. Rosenberg, and R. Suny (eds.), *Party, State and Ideology in the Russian Civil War* (Bloomington 1989), 349–73.

Rosenthal, B., *New Myth, New World from Nietzsche to Stalinism* (University Park, 2002), ch. 3.

Rowney, D., *The Transition to Technocracy. The Structural Origins of the Soviet Administrative State* (London, 1989).

Sakwa, R., 'The Commune State in Moscow, 1918', *SR*, 46 (1987), 429–49.

—— *Soviet Communists in Power. A Study of Moscow during the Civil War, 1918–1921* (London, 1988).

Sanborn, J., *Drafting the Russian Nation. Military Conscription, Total War and Mass Politics, 1905–1925* (DeKalb, 2003), ch. 3.

Schapiro, L., *The Communist Party of the Soviet Union* (London, 1970).

—— *The Origins of the Communist Autocracy: Political Opposition in the Soviet State. First Phase, 1917–1922* (London, 1977).

Schoenhals, M., 'The Central Case Examination Group, 1966–79', *CQ*, 145 (1996), 87–111.

—— *Doing Things with Words in Chinese Politics. Five Studies*, Center for Chinese Studies, Berkeley, Chinese Research Monograph, No. 41.

Schram, S., *The Thought of Mao Tse-Tung* (Cambridge, 1989).

Schull, J., 'Ideology and the Politics of Soviet Literature under NEP and Perestroika', D.Phil. dissertation, University of Oxford, 1991.

Service, R., *The Bolshevik Party in Revolution, 1917–1923. A Study in Organizational Change* (London, 1979).

—— 'From Polyarchy to Hegemony: The Party's Role in the Construction of the Central Institutions of the Soviet State, 1917–1919', *Sbornik*, 10 (1984), 77–90.

—— *Lenin, A Political Life*, 3 vols. (Basingstoke, 1991–5).

—— 'Joseph Stalin: The Making of a Stalinist', in J. Channon (ed.), *Politics, Society and Stalinism in the USSR* (London, 1998).

Sewell, W., 'Ideologies and Social Revolutions. Reflections on the French Case', *JMH*, 57 (1985), 57–62.

Sharlet, R., 'Pashukanis and the Withering away of Law', in S. Fitzpatrick (ed.), *Cultural Revolution in Russia, 1928–1931* (Bloomington, 1978), 169–88.

Shcherbakov, I. L. (ed.), *Repressii protiv rossiiskikh nemtsev v Sovetskom Soiuze v kontekste sovetskoi natsional'noi politiki* (Moscow, 1999).

Shearer, D., *Industry, State and Society in Stalin's Russia, 1926–1934* (Ithaca, 1996).

—— 'Crime and Social Disorder in Stalin's Russia. A Reassessment of the Great Retreat and the Origins of Mass Repression', *CMR*, 39 (1998), 119–48.

—— 'Social Disorder and Mass Repression and the NKVD during the 1930s', *CMR*, 42 (2001), 504–34.

Shimotomai, N., 'A Note on the Kuban Affair. The Crisis of Kolkhoz Agriculture in the North Caucasus', *Acta Slavica Iaponica*, 1 (1983), 39–56.

Shirk, S., 'The Decline of Virtuocracy in China', in J. L. Watson (ed.), *Class and Social Stratification in Post-Revolution China* (Cambridge, 1984).

Siegelbaum, L., 'Soviet Norm Determination in Theory and Practice, 1917–1941', *SS*, 36 (1984), 45–68.

—— 'Production Collectives and Communes and the "Imperatives" of Soviet Industrialisation', *SR*, 45 (1986), 65–84.

—— *Stakhanovism and the Politics of Productivity in the USSR, 1935–1941* (Cambridge, 1988).

—— *Soviet State and Society Between Revolutions, 1918–1929* (Cambridge, 1992).

—— ' "Dear Comrade, You Ask What we Need". Socialist Paternalism and Soviet Rural "Notables" in the mid-1930s', in S. Fitzpatrick (ed.), *Stalinism. New Directions* (London, 2000), 231–55.

Siegelbaum, L., Sokolov, A., Kosheleva, L., and Zhuravlev, S., *Stalinism as a Way of Life. A Narrative in Documents* (New Haven, 2000).

Siegelbaum, L., and Suny, R. G. (eds.), *Making Workers Soviet. Power, Class and Identity* (Ithaca, NY, 1994), 311–40.

Skinner, Q., 'Some Problems in the Analysis of Political Thought and Action', *Political Theory*, 23 (1974), 277–303.

Skocpol, T., 'Cultural Idioms and Political Ideologies in the Revolutionary Reconstruction of State Power: A Rejoinder to Sewell', *JMH*, 57 (1985), 86–96.

Slezkine, Y., *Arctic Mirrors. Russia and the Small Peoples of the North* (Ithaca, NY, 1994).

—— 'The USSR as a Communal Apartment; or, How a Socialist State Promoted Ethnic Particularism', in S. Fitzpatrick (ed.), *Stalinism. New Directions* (London, 2000), 313–47.

Smith, J., *The Bolsheviks and the National Question, 1917–1923* (Basingstoke, 1999).

Smith, S., *Red Petrograd. Revolution in the Factories, 1917–18* (Cambridge, 1983).

—— 'Taylorism Rules OK?', *Radical Science Journal*, 13 (1983), 3–27.

—— 'Workers and Civil Rights in Tsarist Russia, 1899–1917', in O. Crisp and L. Edmondson (eds.), *Civil Rights in Imperial Russia* (Oxford, 1989).

—— 'Workers and Supervisors: St Petersburg, 1905–1917 and Shanghai, 1895–1927', *Past and Present*, 39 (1993), 131–77.

—— 'Workers against Foremen', in L. Siegelbaum and R. G. Suny (eds.), *Making Workers Soviet. Power, Class and Identity* (Ithaca, NY, 1994), 113–37.

—— *A Road is Made. Communism in Shanghai, 1920–1927* (Honolulu, 2000).

Sochor, Z., 'Soviet Taylorism Revisited', *SS*, 33 (1981), 246–64.

—— *Revolution and Culture. The Bogdanov–Lenin Controversy* (Ithaca, NY, 1988).

—— 'On Intellectuals and the New Class', *RR*, 49 (1990), 283–92.

Solomon, P., 'Criminal Justice and the Industrial Front', in W. Rosenberg and L. Siegelbaum, *Social Dimensions of Soviet Industrialization* (Bloomington, 1993), 223–47.

—— *Soviet Criminal Justice under Stalin* (Cambridge, 1996).

Sontag, J., 'The Soviet War-Scare of 1926–7', *RR*, 34 (1975), 66–77.

Sorenson, J., *The Life and Death of Soviet Trade Unionism, 1917–1928* (New York, 1968).

Starkov, B. A., 'Delo Riutina', in A. V. Afanas'ev (ed.), *Oni ne molchali* (Moscow, 1991), 145–78.

—— 'Pravo-levye fraktsionery', in A. V. Afanas'ev (ed.), *Oni ne molchali* (Moscow, 1991), 125–44.

Steger, M., and Carver, T. (eds.), *Engels after Marx* (Manchester, 1999).

Steenson, G., *Karl Kautsky, 1854–1938. Marxism in the Classical Years* (Pittsburgh, 1978).

—— *After Marx, before Lenin. Marxism and Socialist Working-Class Parties in Europe, 1884–1914* (Pittsburgh, 1991).

Steinberg, M., *Moral Communities. The Culture of Class Relations in the Russian Printing Industry, 1867–1907* (Berkeley, 1992).

—— *Voices of Revolution 1917* (New Haven, 2001).

Stites, R., *Revolutionary Dreams. Utopian Vision and Experimental Life in the Russian Revolution* (Oxford, 1989).

Strauss, J., 'Paternalist Terror: The Campaign to Suppress Counterrevolutionaries in the People's Republic of China, 1950–1953', *Comparative Studies in History and Society*, 44 (2002), 80–105.

Suny, R. G., and Martin, T., *A State of Nations. Empire and Nation-Making in the Age of Lenin and Stalin* (New York and Oxford, 2001).

Susiluoto, I., *The Origins and Development of Systems Thinking in the Soviet Union. Political and Philosophical Controversies from Bogdanov to Bukharin and Present-day Re-evaluations* (Helsinki, 1982).

Sutela, P., *Socialism, Planning and Optimality* (Helsinki, 1984).

Tait, A., 'Lunacharsky – A Nietzschean Marxist?', in B. Rosenthal (ed.), *Nietzsche in Russia* (Princeton, 1986).

Talmon, J., *The Origins of Totalitarian Democracy* (Harmondsworth, 1986).

Taylor, C., 'Socialism and Weltanschauung', in L. Kolakowski and S. Hampshire (eds.), *The Socialist Idea* (London, 1974), 45–58.

Teiwes, F., *Politics and Purges in China. Rectification and the Decline of Party Norms, 1950–1965* (New York, 1993).

—— 'The Establishment of the New Regime', in R. MacFarquhar (ed.), *The Politics of China. The Eras of Mao and Deng*, 2nd edn. (Cambridge, 1997), 61–86.

Teiwes F., and Sun, W., *China's Road to Disaster. Mao, Central Politicians and Provincial Leaders in the Unfolding of the Great Leap Forward, 1955–1959* (New York, 1999).

Thurston, A., *Enemies of the People* (New York, 1987).

Thurston, R., *Life and Terror in Stalin's Russia, 1934–1941* (New Haven, 1996).

Tucker, R., *Stalin as Revolutionary, 1879–1929. A Study in History and Personality* (London, 1974).

—— 'Stalinism as Revolution from Above', in Tucker, *Stalinism. Essays in Historical Interpretation* (New Brunswick, 1999), 77–108.

—— *Stalin in Power. The Revolution from Above, 1928–1941* (New York, 1990).

Vaganov, F. M., *Pravyi uklon i ee razgrom, 1928–1930 gg.* (Moscow, 1970).

Valentinov, N., *Novaia ekonomicheskaia politika i krizis partii posle smerti Lenina. Gody raboty v VSNKh vo vremia NEPa* (Moscow, 1991).

Van de Ven, H., *From Friend to Comrade. The Founding of the Chinese Communist Party, 1920–1927* (Berkeley, 1991).

Van Ree, E., 'Stalin's Organic Theory of the Party', *RR*, 52 (1993), 43–57.

—— 'Stalin's Bolshevism, the First Decade', *International Review of Social History*, 39 (1994), 361–81.

—— 'Stalin and the National Question', *Revolutionary Russia*, 7 (1994), 214–38.

—— 'Stalin as a Marxist Philosopher', *Studies in East European Thought*, 52 (2000), 259–308.

—— *The Political Thought of Joseph Stalin. A Study in Twentieth-Century Revolutionary Patriotism* (London, 2002).

Venturi, F., *Roots of Revolution. A History of the Populist and Socialist Movements in Nineteenth Century Russia* (New York, 1966).

Viola, L., 'Tear the Evil from the Root. The Children of the *Spetspereselentsy* of the North', in N. Baschmakoff and P. Fryer (eds.), *The Modernization of the Russian Provinces, Studia Slavica Finlandensia*, 17 (2000), 34–72.

Vogel, E., 'From Revolutionary to Semi-Bureaucrat: The 'Regularisation' of Cadres', *CQ*, 29 (1967), 36–60.

Volkogonov, D., *I. V. Stalin. Politicheskii portret* (Moscow, 1989).

Volkov, V., 'The Concept of *Kul'turnost'*. Notes on the Stalinist Civilizing Process', in Fitzpatrick (ed.), *Stalinism. New Directions* (London, 2000), 210–30.

Von Laue, T., *Why Lenin, Why Stalin?* (Philadelphia, 1964).

Vucinich, A., *Social Thought in Tsarist Russia. The Quest for a General Science of Society, 1861–1917* (Chicago, 1976).

Walder, A., *Communist Neo-Traditionalism. Work and Authority in Chinese Industry* (Berkeley, 1986).

—— 'Cultural Revolution Radicalism: Variations on a Stalinist Theme', in A. Joseph, C. Wong, and D. Zweig (eds.), *New Perspectives on the Cultural Revolution* (Cambridge, Mass., 1991), 41–62.

—— 'Beijing Red Guard Factionalism. The Social Interpretation Reconsidered', *Journal of Asian Studies*, 61 (2002), 437–71.

Walicki, A., *The Controversy over Capitalism. Studies in the Social Philosophy of the Russian Populists* (Oxford, 1969).

—— *Marxism and the Leap to the Kingdom of Freedom* (Stanford, 1995).

Walker, R., 'Soviet Marxism–Leninism and the Question of Ideology. A Critical Analysis', PhD thesis., University of Essex, 1987.

Ward, C., *Russia's Cotton Workers and the New Economic Policy. Shopfloor Culture and State Policy 1921–1929* (Cambridge, 1990).

—— *Stalin's Russia*, 2nd edn. (London, 1999).

Watson, D., *Molotov and Soviet Government: Sovnarkom, 1930–41* (London, 1996).

Weber, M., *Economy and Society*, ed. by G. Roth and C. Wittich (Berkeley, 1978).

Weiner, A., *Making Sense of War. The Second World War and the Fate of the Bolshevik Revolution* (Princeton, 2001).

Wetter, G., *Der Dialektische Materializmus* (Freiburg, 1952).

White, J., *Karl Marx and the Intellectual Origins of Dialectical Materialism* (Basingstoke, 1996).

White, J., *Lenin. The Practice and Theory of Revolution* (Basingstoke, 2001).

White, L., *Policies of Chaos. The Organizational Causes of Violence in China's Cultural Revolution* (Princeton, 1989).

Wilde, L., 'Engels and the Contradictions of Revolutionary Strategy', in M. Steger and T. Carver (eds.), *Engels after Marx* (Manchester, 1999), 197–214.

Williams, R. C., ' "Collective Immortality". The Syndicalist Origins of Proletarian Culture, 1905–1910', *SR*, 39 (1980), 389–402.

—— *The Other Bolsheviks. Lenin and his Critics, 1904–1914* (Bloomington, 1986).

Wimberg, E., 'Socialism, Democratism and Criticism. The Soviet Press and the National Discussion of the 1936 Draft Constitution', *SS*, 44 (1992), 313–32.

Wittke, C., *The Utopian Communist. A Biography of Wilhelm Weitling, Nineteenth-Century Reformer* (Baton Rouge, La., 1950).

Woehrlin, W., *Chernyshevsky, Man and Journalist* (Cambridge, Mass., 1971).

Wolfe, B., *Three Who Made a Revolution. A Biographical History* (New York, 1964).

Yack, B., *The Longing for Total Revolution. Philosophic Sources of Social Discontent from Rousseau to Marx and Nietzsche* (Berkeley, 1992).

Yedlin, T., *Maxim Gorky. A Political Biography* (Westport, Conn., 1999).

Zelnik, R., *Labor and Society in Tsarist Russia: The Factory Workers of St Petersburg, 1855–1870* (Stanford, 1971).

Zheng, S., *Party vs. State in Post-1949 China. The Institutional Dilemma* (Cambridge, 1997).

Zhuravlev, V. V., Volobuev, O. V., Gorshkov, M. K., Kuleshov, S. V., Sorokin, A. K., and Shelokhaev, V. V. (eds.), *Vlast' i oppozitsiia. Rossiiskii politicheskii protsess xx stoletiia* (Moscow, 1995).

Index